THE PAPERS OF

James Madison

SPONSORED BY
THE UNIVERSITY OF VIRGINIA

THE PAPERS OF

James Madison

PRESIDENTIAL SERIES

VOLUME 2

1 OCTOBER 1809–2 NOVEMBER 1810

EDITED BY

J. C. A. STAGG

JEANNE KERR CROSS · SUSAN HOLBROOK PERDUE

UNIVERSITY PRESS OF VIRGINIA

CHARLOTTESVILLE AND LONDON

The Papers of James Madison have been edited with financial aid from the Ford, Mellon, and Rockefeller Foundations, the National Historical Publications and Records Commission, and the Commonwealth of Virginia. From 1956 to 1970 the editorial staff was maintained jointly by the University of Chicago and the University of Virginia. The University of Chicago Press published volumes 1 through 10 of the first series (1962–77).

THE UNIVERSITY PRESS OF VIRGINIA
Copyright © 1992 by the Rector and Visitors
of the University of Virginia

First published 1992

Library of Congress Cataloging-in-Publication Data
(Revised for Volume 2)

Madison, James, 1751–1836.
  The papers of James Madison.

  Vol. 2 edited by J. C. A. Stagg, Jeanne Kerr Cross,
and Susan Holbrook Perdue.
  Includes bibliographical references and index.
  Contents: v. 1. 1 March–30 September 1809—v. 2.
1 October 1809–2 November 1810.
  1. United States—Politics and government—1809–
1817—Sources. 2. United States—Foreign relations—
1809–1817—Sources. 3. United States—History—War of
1812—Sources. 4. Madison, James, 1751–1836.
I. Rutland, Robert Allen, 1922– . II. Stagg, J. C. A.
(John Charles Anderson), 1945– . III. Cross, Jeanne Kerr.
IV. Perdue, Susan Holbrook. V. Title.
E302.M19 1984   973.5′1′092   83-6953
ISBN 0-8139-1345-4 (v. 2)

Printed in the United States of America

THE PAPERS OF

James Madison

PRESIDENTIAL SERIES

VOLUME 2

1 OCTOBER 1809–2 NOVEMBER 1810

EDITED BY

J. C. A. STAGG

JEANNE KERR CROSS   SUSAN HOLBROOK PERDUE

UNIVERSITY PRESS OF VIRGINIA

CHARLOTTESVILLE AND LONDON

The Papers of James Madison have been edited with financial aid from the Ford, Mellon, and Rockefeller Foundations, the National Historical Publications and Records Commission, and the Commonwealth of Virginia. From 1956 to 1970 the editorial staff was maintained jointly by the University of Chicago and the University of Virginia. The University of Chicago Press published volumes 1 through 10 of the first series (1962–77).

THE UNIVERSITY PRESS OF VIRGINIA

First published 1992

Library of Congress Cataloging-in-Publication Data
(Revised for Volume 2)

Madison, James, 1751–1836.
 The papers of James Madison.

 Vol. 2 edited by J. C. A. Stagg, Jeanne Kerr Cross,
and Susan Holbrook Perdue.
 Includes bibliographical references and index.
 Contents: v. 1. 1 March–30 September 1809—v. 2.
1 October 1809–2 November 1810.
 1. United States—Politics and government—1809–
1817—Sources. 2. United States—Foreign relations—
1809–1817—Sources. 3. United States—History—War of
1812—Sources. 4. Madison, James, 1751–1836.
I. Rutland, Robert Allen, 1922– . II. Stagg, J. C. A.
(John Charles Anderson), 1945– . III. Cross, Jeanne Kerr.
IV. Perdue, Susan Holbrook. V. Title.
E302.M19 1984   973.5'1'092   83-6953
ISBN 0-8139-1345-4 (v. 2)

To
Sara Dunlap Jackson

Contents

1809

CONTENTS

CONTENTS

1810

CONTENTS

CONTENTS

CONTENTS

CONTENTS

CONTENTS

CONTENTS

CONTENTS

CONTENTS

CONTENTS

CONTENTS

Preface

The documents in this volume cover James Madison's tenure in the presidency between 1 October 1809 and 2 November 1810. This thirteen-month period was dominated by foreign policy issues, particularly the problems arising from the relations of the United States with the belligerent powers of France and Great Britain. The difficulties of preserving American neutrality in the age of the Napoleonic Wars have frequently been narrated by historians, and Madison has not always appeared to advantage in their accounts. Yet the difficulties the president had to contend with can scarcely be exaggerated. Over the summer of 1809 the settlement of Anglo-American differences negotiated by Madison and his colleagues with British minister David Montague Erskine in April had collapsed after its repudiation by the government in London. In response, Madison had reimposed the restrictions of the Nonintercourse Act against Great Britain in August; but after his return to Washington in October he had to try either to negotiate a new agreement with Erskine's successor, Francis James Jackson, or to devise new and more effective ways of restricting American trade than those permitted by the terms of the law of 1 March 1809.

The attempt to negotiate with Jackson was brief and futile. Madison quickly discerned that the minister had neither the authority nor the disposition to settle any of the Anglo-American disputes, and in the first week in November he broke off the discussions in protest against Jackson's insulting and overbearing manner. Thereafter, the task of trying to restore harmony between Great Britain and the United States was entrusted to William Pinkney in London, whose official letters to and from the State Department were supplemented by a lengthy personal correspondence with the president which is included in this volume.

Madison's dismissal of Jackson, however, provided no solution to other long-standing difficulties with Great Britain. The Nonintercourse Act of March 1809 had never been intended to apply significant pressure to the economy of the British Empire, and the measure was, moreover, due to expire at the end of the second session of the Eleventh Congress. Personally, Madison had never liked the Nonintercourse Act; it had, in his opinion, allowed Great Britain to benefit too much, even if only indirectly, from the resumption of American trade after the repeal of the Embargo. His misgivings here were reinforced by Albert Gallatin, who desired new trade policies to furnish the government with more customs revenue. If this revenue was not provided, the treasury secretary warned, he would have no alternative but to raise loans in order to balance the federal budget. This policy would be unpopular, however, since it would amount to abandoning the commitment of successive Republican administrations after 1801 to retire the national debt.

The second session of the Eleventh Congress that gathered in Washington at the end of November 1809 was therefore dominated by efforts to balance these conflicting requirements. The most important piece of legislation sought by the administration was a navigation act, subsequently known as Macon's Bill No. 1. Its logic was simple. The bill removed all restrictions on American commerce, while excluding at the same time armed and unarmed vessels of the European belligerents from American ports. The effect would be to confine exports to and imports from the territories of the European belligerents to American vessels. In the event of the belligerents' retaliating against the measure by excluding American vessels from their ports, the bill also contained a clause prohibiting the importation of belligerent goods and produce into the United States unless carried from their place of origin in American vessels. Since Great Britain enjoyed a far greater share of American trade than did France, the operation of Macon's Bill No. 1 would have brought hardship to that nation in one of two ways: if the British government acquiesced in its terms, British shippers would be excluded from American ports and from trading in American products; or, if the British government chose to retaliate, British goods would be excluded from American markets. Either outcome was intended to provide strong motives for Great Britain to repeal its orders in council. The United States, however, would gain more customs revenue and also be spared the problem of enforcing domestic trade restrictions against its own citizens.

The passage of Macon's Bill No. 1 would not have precluded the administration from adopting further measures to improve the nation's defenses against belligerent violations of its neutral rights. Madison indicated as much to Congress in his message of 3 January 1810 calling for militia reform, the enlistment of volunteer forces, and the placing of the army and navy establishments in a state of readiness. The legislature failed to follow these initiatives. The preparedness proposals were debated at length but never adopted by the House of Representatives; and although that body approved Macon's Bill No. 1 on 29 January 1810, the Senate repeatedly amended it in ways the House would not accept. As the Pennsylvania senator Andrew Gregg observed, there was a "prodigious reluctance" in Congress to depart from the status quo until further news had been received from Europe. The resulting policy of "procrastination," he added, "suspended the passage of Macon's bill . . . & on this ground it will be lost if it is pressed" (Gregg to William Jones, 14 Mar. 1810 [PHi: William Jones Papers]).

In an effort to fill the policy vacuum about to result from the impending demise of the Nonintercourse Act, Madison, in the first week of April, suggested that Congress consider continuing the measure but modifying it to the extent that its reenactment be postponed to some specified future time. Should one of the belligerents repeal its measures restricting American commerce in the interval, the president could then reimpose nonintercourse against the other. This proposal, however, fared no better than the administration's earlier recommendations. Unable to resolve the disagreements between the House and the Senate and relying on reports suggesting that William Pinkney in London had satisfactorily negotiated the nation's differences with Great Britain, Congress, as it adjourned on 1 May, passed a measure known as Macon's Bill No. 2. Under its terms, American commerce was freed from all restraint, while the president was authorized to return to the policy of nonintercourse only if one of the belligerents should first repeal its antineutral measures and the other then fail to do likewise within a period of three months. For a variety of reasons, some of Madison's contemporaries were inclined to blame him personally for this outcome, which they attributed to a failure of leadership on his part. This view has been echoed by subsequent generations of historians, but it is in some respects too harsh. It ignores the extent to which the administration did make its policy preferences known to legislators, while at the same time it exaggerates the ability of the president to obtain the passage of favorable legislation in the face of any serious obstacles to his wishes in Congress.

For his part, though, Madison never had any doubts about the "feeble" aspects of Macon's Bill No. 2, and he unequivocally condemned the "unhinged" state of the congressional coalitions that had made its passage possible. But the president did anticipate that the measure might have its uses in dealing with his difficulties with France. Franco-American relations had deteriorated steadily after the passage of the Nonintercourse Act, and Napoleon had made his displeasure with the United States evident by his increasingly arbitrary seizures of American vessels and their cargoes in the ports of his empire. His imperial whims were finally embodied as a fixed policy in the Decree of Rambouillet in March 1810, and although Madison was angered by the development, he was at first uncertain how to respond, other than by renewed and predictably ineffectual diplomatic protests. He calculated, though, that the resumption of unrestricted American trade after 1 May 1810 would so favor British shipping interests that Napoleon might come to see the logic of repealing his own decrees against neutral commerce in order to provide the president with an incentive to restore nonintercourse against Great Britain (JM to Jefferson, 23 Apr. 1810; JM to William Pinkney, 23 May 1810).

Madison's expectations on this score were borne out, to some extent, in the duc de Cadore's letter to American minister John Armstrong on 5 August 1810. Napoleon offered to repeal the Berlin and Milan decrees on 1 November, "it being understood" that the United States in the interim had compelled Great Britain to respect American rights by repealing the orders in council. The hypothetical conditionality of this offer was problematic insofar as it demanded that Madison make a response by 1 November while still leaving Napoleon some freedom to judge the extent of his own concessions thereafter. Nevertheless, the news of the Cadore letter, as it was slowly transmitted to the United States in the fall of 1810, was still regarded in many quarters as a fair triumph for American diplomacy; and Madison was immediately under pressure to respond. The president certainly had his doubts, but by the third week in October he had decided in principle, nonetheless, that he should restore nonintercourse against Great Britain, and he eventually issued a proclamation doing so on 2 November.

Subsequent events were to prove that the step was not without its disadvantages, but it should not be forgotten that the alternative of ignoring the Cadore letter would not have given the president an easier way out of his dilemma. Great Britain would have persevered with the orders in council, while Napoleon, who would have certainly taken offense if Madison had disregarded the Cadore letter, would have been free to extend his seizures of American shipping. Such an outcome would have then placed Madison in a situation not unlike that experienced by President John Adams during the Quasi-War of the late 1790s, and it is hardly surprising that he opted to avoid it. From the president's perspective, it was better to assume that the Berlin and Milan decrees had been repealed and for him to press Great Britain again to revise its own policies on the grounds that these could no longer be justified as fair retaliation against French maritime policy. In this context, the weapon of nonintercourse would have its uses, and as Madison's letters to Armstrong and Pinkney on 29 and 30 October 1810 show, he had hopes that Great Britain could be persuaded to modify the orders in council on that basis.

Relations with France and Great Britain, however, were by no means the only major foreign policy problem to claim Madison's attention in 1809–10. Of equal importance was the dissolution of the Spanish-American Empire, a development which had been precipitated by Napoleon's invasion of the Iberian Peninsula in 1808. By 1810 several of the larger, more populous Spanish-American colonies had embarked on their quest for greater autonomy from Madrid, and the prospect of similar developments occurring in East and West Florida compelled Madison to respond. As many of the documents in this volume reveal, Madison was especially preoccupied by the problem of West Florida, and he eventually issued a proclamation annexing the region to the United States on 27 October 1810. The considerations leading him to do so have been discussed in an editorial note, but the contents of that note itself raise the more fundamental question of how far Madison's executive decisions can be adequately traced through an edition of his personal correspondence.

While the case of West Florida may be an extreme one, its very complexity does highlight the fact that in many instances after 1809 the best sources of information about Madison's presidential decisions are to be found not in his own correspondence but in records that fall outside the criteria established for the inclusion of documents in this edition. An examination of the enclosures identified by the editors in Madison's communications with his cabinet colleagues and the executive department clerks during his summer residence at Montpelier after mid-July 1810, for example, will sufficiently demonstrate the point; but the same situation also prevailed while the president was in Washington where neither he nor his cabinet members kept systematic records relating to the papers they exchanged among themselves. Consequently, it has often been necessary for the editors to cast a very broad evidentiary net in order to come to an understanding of the considerations that governed some of Madison's presidential decisions. And as the annotation to some of the documents in this volume suggests, that net must include a great variety of personal papers and memoirs, newspapers, and the dispatches and other correspondence of foreign diplomats serving in the United States.

It is, of course, impossible for an edition of Madison's personal papers to provide a comprehensive guide to all the records relating to his administrations, but the editors, in any instances where it has been possible to do so, have sought to present his correspondence in a manner that indicates the existence of other historical sources where significant evidence about the president's conduct may be found. While it might seem frustrating at first sight that Madison's personal letters do not always provide very much information about some of his most important decisions, the magnitude of the problem can furnish interesting insights into the fourth president's style of management. And to the extent that historians will eventually be able to compare Madison's conduct in the executive branch with that of his predecessors and in far greater detail than has hitherto been the case, they will be able to generate fresh perspectives on the development of the presidential office. They may find in some respects that Madison's executive management did not depart very greatly from the precedents established by Washington and Jefferson, but as they do so they will also discover that President Madison was often far better informed about, and much more involved in, the daily swirl of events than any of his biographers have previously suspected.

For these reasons, therefore, the editing of Madison's papers after 1809 requires almost as much attention to the people who came into contact with the president as it does to Madison himself. Unfortunately, with the exception of Albert Gallatin, the surviving personal papers of Madison's cabinet colleagues and their departmental clerks are neither extensive nor very informative for the 1809–10 period. In no case is this more true than for Secretary of State Robert Smith, with whom Madison had to shape and execute all of his foreign policy decisions. The problems posed by the paucity of the documentary record with respect to Robert Smith are compounded, moreover, by the need to interpret the surviving evidence in the context of a host of rumors about his increasingly strained dealings with Madison. The resentments provoked by the manner of Smith's appointment to the State Department in March 1809 grew steadily worse, so much so that by January 1810 Joel Barlow could report that if the matter were not remedied, it would "injure Mr. Madison very gravely & the nation still more." The root of the problem, as Barlow reminded Thomas Jefferson, was that "Gallatin & Smith cannot agree," and he feared that the outcome would be the departure of the former from the cabinet. This, Barlow predicted, would "infallibly divide the republicans," the "great majority" of whom, including "all Mr. Madison's best friends," were revolted by Smith's "projects," which he described as being aimed "at nothing less than the presidency at the next election" (Barlow to Jefferson, 15 Jan. 1810 [DLC: Jefferson Papers]).

Barlow assumed that Madison was at least aware of the situation, but the president seems to have been more immediately concerned with a problem of a rather different order, namely how to obtain from Robert Smith a satisfactory performance of his State Department duties. On this score he clearly failed to get what he wanted, and it is evident that for much of the period covered by this volume Madison was to some extent involved in the secretarial task of drafting diplomatic correspondence. How far the president actually wrote the letters that went out under the signature of Robert Smith, however, can probably never be accurately determined. The reader, nonetheless, can gain some insights into the dimensions of the problem in the correspondence between Madison, Robert Smith, and British minister Francis James Jackson in October and November 1809.

In order to illuminate aspects of Madison's relationship with Robert Smith, the editors have included in this volume summaries of some of the attacks made on the president in the form of open letters addressed to him through the columns of the nation's newspapers. Among them are the rambling and often incoherent diatribes written by John Randolph of Roanoke under the pseudonym of "Mucius"; but of greater importance are the letters of "Tammany" published by Baptist Irvine in the Baltimore *Whig*, a journal generally understood to reflect the thinking of Robert Smith and his brother Samuel. The "Tammany" letters summarized in this volume, however, are but a pale reflection of Irvine's more extreme editorial tactics, some of which went to truly outrageous lengths in order to make the point that it was not Robert Smith but Gallatin and Madison who were responsible for the nation's diplomatic difficulties.

Throughout the early months of 1810, Irvine, writing under the pseudonym of "Ariel," reported on politics from the national capital. As he did so, he gave extensive currency to the charge that presidential negligence was the root cause of every problem in American foreign policy. His many discourses on this theme culminated on 24 March in the allegation that Madison's "weakness" had allowed Gallatin to subvert the nation's foreign policy by permitting Nathaniel Macon of North Carolina to offer bribes of $20,000 to secure passage of the "submissive" legislation introduced into the House of Representatives in the member's name. Other Republican newspapers, notably William Duane's Philadelphia *Aurora General Advertiser*, took up variations on this theme, and Madison, as he later admitted to Robert Smith, was by no means indifferent to the gross misrepresentations emanating from such sources. Whether the president ever discussed the matter with Robert Smith in the period covered by this volume is unclear, though Irvine occasionally mentioned that he received hints from Washington that his editorials were unfair and unjustified. His attacks, nevertheless, continued, and they did nothing to improve the relationship between the president and his secretary of state. Eventually, Madison was driven to dismiss Robert Smith from the cabinet in April 1811, but his decision to do so can hardly be understood without reference to the newspaper material included in this volume (Baltimore *Whig*, 24 Mar. 1810).

Most of the remaining documents in this volume do not deal with foreign affairs or national politics, but they are, nonetheless, indicative of the wide range of public and private papers that daily crossed the president's desk. Madison had to find time to supervise the construction of public buildings in Washington, conduct diplomacy with Indian tribes, deputize for cabinet members who were occasionally absent, answer addresses sent to him by public meetings deploring the behavior of Francis James Jackson, act as agent for the marquis de Lafayette in the matter of his Louisiana lands, and deal with a constant flow of applications for office. On this last subject, the editors have decided to include a larger number of these letters of application than was the case in the first volume of the presidential series of this edition. Among their reasons for doing so is the wish to give readers some more information about how far the president might have been influenced by this correspondence and, more particularly, to reveal something of the outlines of the extensive lobbying campaign waged by Postmaster General Gideon Granger and others to fill the seat on the United States Supreme Court held by Associate Justice

William Cushing. That campaign began long before Cushing's death in September 1810, and it was to continue well into 1811 before Madison was able to end it by securing the appointment of Joseph Story.

To do justice to this heterogeneous body of material the editors, as is explained in the Editorial Method, have chosen to be selective and, in the case of lengthy documents that are already easily accessible in published sources elsewhere, to resort to summaries as a device to save space. Documents relating to the host of routine matters that came before the president, such as the initiation of prosecutions for violations of the law or the granting of pardons for minor offenses, have also generally been omitted. Readers of the volume should always be aware, though, that much more of the president's time was taken up with minor administrative matters than its contents can ever indicate.

Yet even the most considered editorial policies of selection and summarization can hardly conceal the impression that there survive in Madison's personal papers for 1809–10 a large number of documents that are interesting in their own right but often relatively inconsequential in nature. This matter deserves some further comment. Much of this material appears to be the residue of the way Madison handled the paperwork of his presidencies. Here it is important to recall that Madison, unlike Jefferson, never used a letterpress or a polygraph to help him with his correspondence during his Washington years. Consequently, throughout these "most busy periods of his life," as he later told Jared Sparks, he "often wrote in haste, and seldom kept copies" (Herbert B. Adams, *The Life and Writings of Jared Sparks* [2 vols.; Boston, 1893], 2:36). And since much of the correspondence received and written by the president at this time was usually transmitted elsewhere in order to implement policy decisions, the final consequence was that large bodies of material came to be separated from Madison's personal papers, while these, in turn, tended to become a repository for documents that were less essential to the business of government. It would, moreover, have been virtually impossible for Madison to have recovered substantial and important executive correspondence during his retirement as he was able to do with personal letters relating to earlier periods of his life, particularly those he had written to close friends such as Jefferson and Monroe. The result has been to leave some apparent gaps in Madison's personal papers for his presidential years that can only be filled by diligent research in other historical sources.

It is worth remembering in this context, too, that President Madison inherited from his predecessor not only a political legacy but also much of his cabinet and even his private secretary. Isaac Coles, the last of Jefferson's personal secretaries, served Madison in the same capacity for the first nine months of his administration until he was replaced by his brother, Edward, in January 1810. It is more than likely, therefore, that

Madison also continued the methods that the third president had already established for dealing with administrative correspondence. These had been laid down by Jefferson in a circular letter to his department heads on 6 November 1801, and no evidence survives to suggest that Madison ever reconsidered these matters, at least not before he reprimanded his secretary of war, John Armstrong, in the summer of 1814 for failing to convey correspondence to him in the very ways that had been provided for by Jefferson in 1801 (Ford, *Writings of Jefferson*, 8:99–101; JM to Armstrong, 13 Aug. 1814 [DLC, series 3]).

Assuming, therefore, that Madison perpetuated Jefferson's administrative practices, it would have meant that the president himself dealt in the first instance with *all* the correspondence addressed to him personally—no matter how trivial its contents—and only thereafter referred it to a cabinet member, either for action or inaction. That Madison did, in fact, follow such a practice can be confirmed by a close study of the dating of the dockets on many of the letters addressed to the president that are now located in the records of government departments. And following Jefferson's method with respect to other correspondence, Madison would also have seen much, if not all, of the material addressed to his cabinet colleagues, both for the purposes of information and, if necessary, for some discussion about the nature of the response. Occasionally, direct evidence of Madison's role in shaping these responses can be found in brief notes and on dockets, but, with the notable exception of the correspondence of Robert Smith, these matters in most instances were probably dealt with in conversations of which no record has survived. Otherwise, Madison may simply have been content to approve the decisions made by his colleagues.

By these means Madison would have tried to be, as Jefferson had wished to be before him, "always in accurate possession of all facts and proceedings in every part of the Union, and to whatsoever department they related." As he did so, he almost certainly did much of his own secretarial work, for there is little evidence that the duties of his personal secretary in this regard were particularly onerous. There survive only a few presidential letters in the hand of Edward Coles, whose tasks seem to have been more those of a general aide than a strictly clerical assistant. That this was so is confirmed by Edward Coles himself after he had settled into his duties in February 1810. "The President," he reported, "has given me very little employment for the last 8 or ten days, but he has just been in, with a hankerchief full of papers in each hand, for me to arrange for him." It is, however, now quite impossible for any editor to reconstitute, much less publish, the contents of these presidential handkerchiefs (Ford, *Writings of Jefferson*, 8:100; Edward Coles to John Coles, 3 Feb. 1810 [PHi: Coles Collection]).

For all these reasons, then, Madison's presidential papers are the most difficult segment of his surviving correspondence to edit in consistently satisfying ways. It will always be a matter for regret that Madison, unlike Washington or Jefferson, bequeathed no executive diaries, no systematic personal records, no inventories of correspondence, and not even any lists of dinner invitations to assist historians with the detailed reconstruction of his years in the presidency. He left, instead, a great many obstacles to be overcome if a properly researched assessment of his personal imprint on the government of the early republic between 1809 and 1817 is ever to be attempted. These obstacles, however, are not always insuperable, and the efforts made to remove them will result in a greatly improved understanding of the life and times of the fourth president.

Acknowledgments

The editors are grateful to Robert A. Rutland, former editor in chief of *The Papers of James Madison*, for the preliminary research and editing he devoted to this volume before his retirement in 1986. Thomas A. Mason, former associate and acting editor, also made important contributions. Donald L. Singer, archivist at the National Historical Publications and Records Commission, has responded with invariable care and promptness to our increasing demands on his time. The following persons provided helpful advice and assistance: John Catanzariti and Eugene R. Sheridan of *The Papers of Thomas Jefferson*; Mary A. Giunta, Sara Dunlap Jackson, and Timothy D. W. Connelly of the National Historical Publications and Records Commission; Charles M. Harris of *The Papers of William Thornton*; Michael Hendry of the University of Virginia Classics Department; Louise T. Jones of the Historical Society of Pennsylvania; Kathrine Maus of the University of Virginia English Department; Ann Miller of Montpelier; Lucia C. Stanton of the Thomas Jefferson Memorial Foundation; Jane F. Wells of the English Department, Marshall University; the staff of the University of Virginia Library; and our neighbors at *The Papers of George Washington*.

Editorial Method

The guidelines used in editing *The Papers of James Madison* were explained in volumes 1 and 8 of the first series (1:xxxiii–xxxix and 8:xxiii) and also in the first volume of the secretary of state series (1:xxiii–xxvii). These guidelines have been followed in the presidential series. Considerable effort has been made to render the printed texts as literal, faithful copies of the original manuscripts, but some exceptions must be noted. Missing or illegible characters and words in a damaged or torn manuscript are restored by conjecture within angle brackets. Words consistently spelled incorrectly, as well as variant or antiquated spellings, are left as written; however, misspelled words that may appear to be printer's errors are corrected through additions in brackets or followed by the device [*sic*]. The brackets used by Madison and other correspondents have been rendered as parentheses. Slips of the pen have been silently corrected, but substantial errors or discrepancies have been noted. Most addresses and postmarks, as well as most notations or dockets made by various clerks, editors, and collectors through the years, have not been recognized in the provenance unless germane to an understanding of the document. Routine endorsements Madison made on documents late in his lifetime have not been noted. When the enclosures mentioned are newspapers or other ephemeral publications that would have been immediately separated from the document, the absence of such items has not been noted in the provenance.

As has already been noted in the preface to this volume, the amount of material surviving from Madison's two presidential administrations has required the editors to adopt a policy of increased selectivity. The primary criterion in the editors' decision to print, abstract, or omit a document is a judgment on the extent to which it illuminates James Madison's thoughts or his personal or official life. The degree of involvement he had with the document, either as recipient or sender, is of paramount concern. Other considerations, though not decisive in themselves, have been whether the document was of a routine nature (such as a letter of transmittal, application, or recommendation) or was of intrinsic interest in adding a new dimension to our understanding of the man or, in the case of a lengthy document, whether it had been previously published in an easily accessible source such as *American State Papers* or *The Territorial Papers of the United States*. A large number of bureaucratic documents bearing his signature were generated as a result of the broad responsibilities of Madison's office; those that produce little useful information and do not warrant abstracting are silently omitted (such as letters of appointment and ship's papers). Occasionally, omitted documents are referred to in the notes.

In preparing abstracts the editors have tried to summarize the contents of manuscripts, avoiding unnecessary detail while providing readers with a guide to the most important issues raised and the writer's approach. Editorial additions to these abstracts (except for purposes of identification) appear in brackets or in footnotes. Place-name spellings in abstracts have been modernized and variant spellings of personal names standardized.

Depository Symbols

In the provenance section following each document the first entry tells where the source of the text is located. If the document was in private hands when copied for this edition, the owner and date of possession are indicated. If the document was in a private or public depository in the United States, the symbol listed in the Library of Congress's *Symbols of American Libraries* (13th ed.; Washington, 1985) is used. When standing alone the symbol DLC is used to cite the Madison Papers in the Library of Congress. Documents in the National Archives, Washington, are designated DNA with the record group and in most cases a second symbol corresponding to the official classification. In the case of foreign depositories, PRO indicates holdings in the Public Record Office, London, while those in European archives cited by the symbols AAE and AHN are explained below. The location symbols for depositories used in this volume are:

AAE	Archives du Ministère des Affaires Etrangères, Paris
AHN	Archivo Histórico Nacional, Madrid
CSmH	Henry E. Huntington Library, San Marino, California
CtLHi	Litchfield Historical Society, Litchfield, Connecticut
DeGE	Eleutherian Mills Historical Library, Greenville, Delaware
DLC	Library of Congress, Washington, D.C.
DNA	National Archives, Washington, D.C.

	CD	Consular Despatches
	DD	Diplomatic Despatches
	DL	Domestic Letters
	IC	Instructions to Consuls
	IM	Instructions to Ministers
	LAR	Letters of Application and Recommendation

	LRHR	Legislative Records of the House of Representatives
	LRRS	Letters Received by the Secretary of War, Registered Series
	LRUS	Letters Received by the Secretary of War, Unregistered Series
	LSIA	Letters Sent by the Secretary of War Relating to Indian Affairs
	LSMA	Letters Sent by the Secretary of War Relating to Military Affairs
	LSP	Letters Sent to the President
	ML	Miscellaneous Letters
	NFL	Notes from Foreign Legations
	TP	Territorial Papers
GU		University of Georgia, Athens
ICHi		Chicago Historical Society, Illinois
InU		Indiana University, Bloomington
MdBS		Saint Mary's Seminary and University, Baltimore
MdHi		Maryland Historical Society, Baltimore
MeHi		Maine Historical Society, Portland
MHi		Massachusetts Historical Society, Boston
MiD		Detroit Public Library, Michigan
Ms-Ar		Mississippi Department of Archives and History, Jackson
MWiCA		Sterling and Francine Clark Art Institute, Williamstown, Massachusetts
NEh		East Hampton Free Library, New York
NHi		New-York Historical Society, New York City
NHyF		Franklin D. Roosevelt Library, Hyde Park, New York
NIC		Cornell University, Ithaca, New York
NjGbS		New Jersey State Teachers College, Glassboro, New Jersey
NjMoHP		Morristown National Historical Park, Morristown, New Jersey
NjP		Princeton University, Princeton, New Jersey
NN		New York Public Library, New York City
NWM		U.S. Military Academy, West Point, New York
OClWHi		Western Reserve Historical Society, Cleveland, Ohio
PHi		Historical Society of Pennsylvania, Philadelphia
PPAmP		American Philosophical Society, Philadelphia
PPRF		Rosenbach Foundation, Philadelphia
PRO		Public Record Office, London
PSC		Swarthmore College, Swarthmore, Pennsylvania
ViU		University of Virginia, Charlottesville

Abbreviations

FC   File copy. Any version of a letter or other document retained by the sender for his own files and differing little if at all from the completed version. A draft, on the other hand, is a preliminary sketch, often incomplete and varying frequently in expression from the finished version. Unless otherwise noted, both are in the sender's hand. A letterbook copy is a retained duplicate, often bound in a chronological file, and usually in a clerk's hand.

JM   James Madison.

Ms   Manuscript. A catchall term describing numerous reports and other papers written by JM, as well as items sent to him which were not letters.

RC   Recipient's copy. The copy of a letter intended to be read by the addressee. If the handwriting is not that of the sender, this fact is noted in the provenance.

Tr   Transcript. A copy of a manuscript, or a copy of a copy, customarily handwritten and ordinarily not by its author or by the person to whom the original was addressed.

Abstracts and Missing Letters. In most cases a document is presented only in abstract form because of its trivial nature, its great length, or a combination of both. Abstracted letters are noted by the symbol §.

The symbol ¶ indicates a "letter not found" entry, with the name of the writer or intended recipient, the date, and such other information as can be surmised from the surviving evidence. If nothing other than the date of the missing item is known, however, it is mentioned only in the notes to a related document.

Short Titles for Books and Other Frequently Cited Materials

In addition to these short titles, bibliographical entries are abbreviated if a work has been cited in a previous volume of the series.

Annals of Congress.   *Debates and Proceedings in the Congress of the United States* . . . (42 vols.; Washington, 1834–56).

ASP.   *American State Papers: Documents, Legislative and Executive, of the Congress of the United States* . . . (38 vols.; Washington, 1832–61).

Brant, *Madison.*   Irving Brant, *James Madison* (6 vols.; Indianapolis and New York, 1941–61).

CVSP. William P. Palmer et al., eds., *Calendar of Virginia State Papers and Other Manuscripts* (11 vols.; Richmond, 1875–93).

Callahan, *List of Officers of the Navy.* Edward W. Callahan, *List of Officers of the Navy of the United States and of the Marine Corps from 1775 to 1900* (New York, 1900).

Carter, *Territorial Papers.* Clarence Carter et al., eds., *The Territorial Papers of the United States* (28 vols.; Washington, 1934–75).

Chinard, *Letters of Lafayette and Jefferson.* Gilbert Chinard, ed., *The Letters of Lafayette and Jefferson* (Baltimore, 1929).

Evans. Charles Evans, ed., *American Bibliography . . . 1639 . . . 1820* (12 vols.; Chicago, 1903–34).

Heitman, *Historical Register.* Francis B. Heitman, *Historical Register and Dictionary of the United States Army, from Its Organization, September 29, 1789, to March 2, 1903* (2 vols.; Washington, 1903).

Jackson, *The Bath Archives.* Lady Jackson, ed., *The Bath Archives: A Further Selection from the Diaries and Letters of Sir George Jackson from 1809 to 1816* (2 vols.; London, 1873).

Lipscomb and Bergh, *Writings of Jefferson.* Andrew A. Lipscomb and Albert Ellery Bergh, eds., *The Writings of Thomas Jefferson* (20 vols.; Washington, 1903–4).

Madison, *Letters* (Cong. ed.). [William C. Rives and Philip R. Fendall, eds.], *Letters and Other Writings of James Madison* (published by order of Congress; 4 vols.; Philadelphia, 1865).

Madison, *Writings* (Hunt ed.). Gaillard Hunt, ed., *The Writings of James Madison* (9 vols.; New York, 1900–1910).

Malone, *Jefferson and His Time.* Dumas Malone, *Jefferson and His Time* (6 vols.; Boston, 1948–81).

Mayo, *Instructions to British Ministers.* Bernard Mayo, ed., *Instructions to British Ministers to the United States, 1791–1812,* Annual Report of the American Historical Association of the Year 1936, vol. 3 (Washington, 1941).

OED. *Oxford English Dictionary.*

PJM. William T. Hutchinson et al., eds., *The Papers of James Madison* (1st ser., vols. 1–10, Chicago, 1962–77, vols. 11–17, Charlottesville, Va., 1977–91).

PJM-PS. Robert A. Rutland et al., eds., *The Papers of James Madison: Presidential Series* (2 vols. to date; Charlottesville, Va., 1984—).

PJM-SS. Robert J. Brugger et al., eds., *The Papers of James Madison: Secretary of State Series* (1 vol. to date; Charlottesville, Va., 1986—).

Senate Exec. Proceedings. *Journal of the Executive Proceedings of the Senate of the United States of America* (3 vols.; Washington, 1828).

Shaw and Shoemaker. R. R. Shaw and R. H. Shoemaker, comps.,

American Bibliography: A Preliminary Checklist for 1801–1819 (22 vols. to date; New York, 1958—).

Swem and Williams, *Register.*   Earl G. Swem and John W. Williams, eds., *A Register of the General Assembly of Virginia, 1776–1918, and of the Constitutional Conventions* (Richmond, 1918).

U.S. Statutes at Large.   *The Public Statutes at Large of the United States of America* . . . (17 vols.; Boston, 1848–73).

VMHB.   *Virginia Magazine of History and Biography.*

WMQ.   *William and Mary Quarterly.*

Madison Chronology

1809

1 October	JM arrives in Washington from Montpelier.
8 November	Informs British minister Francis James Jackson that no further communications will be received from him.
27 November– 1 May 1810	Second session of the Eleventh Congress.
29 November	JM delivers annual message to Congress.

1810

1 May	Signs Macon's Bill No. 2 into law.
9 July	Leaves Washington for Montpelier.
11 July	Arrives at Montpelier.
13–14 August	Thomas Jefferson visits JM at Montpelier.
ca. 21 August	George W. Erving visits JM at Montpelier.
ca. 14 September	JM visits Jefferson at Monticello.
3 October	Leaves Montpelier for Washington.
6 October	Arrives in Washington.
27 October	Draws up proclamation annexing portions of Spanish West Florida to the U.S.
2 November	Issues proclamation announcing the imposition of nonintercourse against Great Britain three months hence unless that nation ceases to violate the neutral rights of the U.S.

Significant Federal Officers

1809

President Madison's Cabinet

Secretary of State	Robert Smith
Secretary of War	William Eustis
Secretary of the Treasury	Albert Gallatin
Secretary of the Navy	Paul Hamilton
Attorney General	Caesar A. Rodney

Supreme Court

Chief Justice	John Marshall
Associate Justices	Samuel Chase
	William Cushing
	William Johnson
	Henry Brockholst Livingston
	Thomas Todd
	Bushrod Washington

Other Ranking Positions

Vice President	George Clinton
Speaker of the House of Representatives	Joseph B. Varnum
U.S. Minister to Great Britain	William Pinkney
U.S. Minister to France	John Armstrong
Postmaster General	Gideon Granger
Chief Clerk, State Department	John Graham

THE PAPERS OF
James Madison

From George Bernard and Others

Your petitioners George Bernard, William Langhorne, Henry D. Ende, and William M. Allen beg leave to shew that the great inconveniencies experienced by the people of our Western Country in going to market, with the benefits & advantages that would result from improvement of roads & countries through which they pass, have led us to contemplate the establishment of a turnpike and Stage road on the way from the State of Tennessee to New Orleans; and to be informed thereon we have been to take a view of the Countries through which such road must pass, with the difficulties to be encountered in the attempt.

We find that a road crossing the Tennessee River about the Muscle Shoals and running the streightest course for Orleans would shorten the distance from Nashville in Tennessee to New Orleans to nearly two hundred miles less than the present road makes in its rout by Natchez, and are induced to think it may be cut on ground as good if not better than the present road to Natchez. We find the Indians approve the idea of improvements on the present road, but are cautious of giving further advantages out of their hands; they say travellers prefer calling on white men who occupy stands they have granted to the United States, and they will grant no more.

Many influential characters amongst them have settlements on the present road and are interested in its improvement, they are averse to granting another—yet we think it probable we might induce them to grant what is desired. We would offer them Instructors in Mechanisms and Literature of characters that might be relied on to answer the useful purposes required of them and meet the approbation of the Indians, or whatever we could find would answer their purposes and be interesting to the United States to encourage amongst them. We should wish to present them liberal advantages, for we are apprized that a great part of the works of such a ro[a]d being of a kind that might be easily damaged or destroyed, should such a plan ever be executed on terms dissatisfactory to them, they would avail themselves of such opportunity to incommode us. We should also endeavour to engage them to be watchful of and prompt to inform against and bring to justice offenders who might commit depredations on the works or against travellers, for we learn in their Countries that murders and robberies are committed and go unpunished. The Labour and expense of such a work must be great, and should be on the nearest road that can be had.

With such objects in view we humbly sollicit you to grant us authority to negociate with other authorities to whom we must have referrence, and to obtain of them what be necessary to our plan, and also for such encouragement as the objects merit[1]

GEORGE BERNARD
WILLIAM LANGHORNE
HENRY D. ENDE
WILLIAM M. ALLEN

RC (DNA: RG 107, LRRS, G-13:5). Enclosed in David S. Garland to Eustis, 25 Jan. 1810 (ibid.). Undated but probably written and sent to Washington sometime before the meeting of the second session of the Eleventh Congress on 27 Nov. 1809.

1. The petition was taken up by Representative David S. Garland of Virginia who wrote to the War Department that he understood Bernard had left with either the secretary of war or the president "the nessesary papers in support of his application." In February 1810 Eustis responded that the president wished for further details about the proposed road before deciding on whether to incur the expense of acquiring the land from the Indian tribes concerned (Garland to Eustis, 22 and 25 Jan. 1810 [DNA: RG 107, LRRS]; Garland to Eustis, 9 Feb. 1810 [DNA: RG 107, LRUS]; Eustis to Garland, 10 Feb. 1810 [DNA: RG 107, LSMA]).

¶ From Albert Gallatin. Letter not found. *Ca. 2 October 1809*. Offered for sale in Parke-Bernet Catalogue No. 1516 (1954), item 274, which describes the letter as a ten-line note regarding the "claim of Govr. Harrison for an annual compensation . . . respectfully submitted to the President," docketed at the top "Vincennes, August 30th, 1809," and endorsed by JM, "Approved." Also mentioned in Gallatin to William Henry Harrison, 27 Sept. 1809, where Gallatin acknowledged Harrison's letter of 30 Aug. 1809 [not found] requesting payment for his management of the Wabash saline and an inquiry into that management; Gallatin promised to lay the letter before JM "on his return to the Seat of Government" (Carter, *Territorial Papers, Indiana*, 7:672).

From William Ray

FLORIDA, NEAR AMSTERDAM POST OFFICE,

SIR,   MONTGOMERY COUNTY, (N. Y.) October 4th. 1809.

Early last Spring I lodged a Book entitled "Horrors of Slavery" in the post Office,[1] to be sent to you at Washington, together with a poetical epistle; and having some doubts respecting its safe arrival, on account of my not receiving any a[n]swer, I have taken the liberty to request you to let me know, as speedily as convenient, whether you *have*, or *have not* received it. The latter of which I am most inclined to believe; for I am not willing to suspect that even the *Chief Magistrate* of a free people, who owes his political existance to the suffrage of men of all ranks, would treat with silent contempt the honest effusions or the well-meant offering of one who has greatly suffered in the cause of that Government over which he presides. I am, Sir, with high Consideration, Your most obedient Humle. Servant.

WM. RAY.

RC (DLC).

1. Ray sent his book, *Horrors of Slavery; or, The American Tars in Tripoli*, to JM on 22 Mar. 1809. The work was based on Ray's personal experiences as a captured American seaman (*PJM-PS*, 1:73 n. 1).

To Albert Gallatin

DR SIR   Thursday Morning. [5 October 1809][1]
Mr. Smith has had an official conversation with Mr. Jackson, and is to see him again today at One OC. He is to be with me in the mean time at ½ after 10, when I wish you to join the consultation.

J. M.

RC (NHi: Gallatin Papers). Docketed by Gallatin. For conjectural date, see n. 1.

1. The only Thursday falling between 3 Oct., when British minister Francis James Jackson presented his credentials to JM, and 9 Oct., when conversations with him were summarily ended, was 5 Oct. (Brant, *Madison*, 5:88; *ASP, Foreign Relations*, 3:308).

From Hubbard Taylor

DEAR SIR   WINCHESTER CLARKE CY. Octr. 5th. 1809
I have just met with Major Morrison[1] on his Way to the City of Washington, and I cannot omit droping you a line. I wrote you since the return of Major J. Taylor,[2] wherein I informed you of your Land business &C. and also took the liberty to say some thing on the subject of Leasing the Saline Salt Works,[3] & probably I may have exceeded the limits of an individual. If so hope you will excuse it, as I realy have no view, but the publics good, & not acquainted how far much information of a private nature is proper to go to you direct, or even thro any of the departments, but having felt a great Anxiety in the Article of Salt, was the strong inducement. And I am pleased to hear that that Article is geting in great plenty on the Great Kanawwa, by the abundance of Salt-Water found there. The prices of that Article is in the interior of our County hereabouts from $1.75 to $2—a price not to be complain off.

3

I saw the old Comm'drore[4] lately he has not recoverd the effects of his fall from his Horse, and his Lady I fear will live but a short time if she is not already Dead. All the rest of our relations are well as far as I hear lately excerpt [sic] a Son in Law of Mine, who was il[l] about 2 week's past since which I have not hred [sic].

We are all anxiety to hear what may be the real object of Mr Jackson, but expect little at the hands of the British, where circumstances do not force them to what they ought to do. The Citizens of this State I believe feel all that just indignity aga[i]nst both Britain & France, for their agressions and will I am sure support the General Government in such Measures as they may adopt as most proper to be pursued. You will be pleased to present my sincere respects to Mrs. Madison and believe me to be with the most respectfull regar[d] yr obdt. Hble sert

H: TAYLOR

RC (DLC). Docketed by JM.

1. James Morrison (1755–1823), a veteran of the Revolution, moved to Lexington, Kentucky, in 1792 and became active in state politics. He was also a contractor for the U.S. Army and had recently supplied the troops under the command of Brig. Gen. James Wilkinson in the camp at Terre aux Boeufs. He was introduced to JM by Wilson Cary Nicholas and later served as deputy quartermaster general for the Northwest Army in the War of 1812 (*The Biographical Encyclopedia of Kentucky* . . . [1878; Easley, S.C., 1980 reprint], p. 108; James Ripley Jacobs, *Tarnished Warrior: Major-General James Wilkinson* [New York, 1938], pp. 255–56; Nicholas to JM, 19 Oct. 1809).

2. Letter not found.

3. See Hubbard Taylor to JM, 16 June 1809 (*PJM-PS*, 1:256–57).

4. Richard Taylor (1749–1825), a first cousin of James Madison, Sr., married Catharine Davis circa 1771. He commanded schooners of the Virginia state navy during the Revolution and rose to the rank of commodore. For his Revolutionary services he was granted lands in what is now Oldham County, Kentucky, where he moved in 1794 (William Kyle Anderson, *Donald Robertson and His Wife, Rachel Rogers;* . . . also, *A Brief Account of the Ancestry of Commodore Richard Taylor of Orange County, Virginia, and His Naval History during the War of the American Revolution* [Detroit, 1900], pp. 234, 236, 245–55).

§ From George Joy. *5 October 1809, Gothenburg, Sweden.* Transmits copy of his letter to JM of 9 Sept. Awaits in Gothenburg the arrival of "the Documents necessary to support my Pretensions," which have been delayed by irregular mail and wartime interruptions. If he does not receive papers within forty-eight hours, proposes proceeding to Copenhagen without them. The wind and weather make it possible that the American ship that will carry his letter "going North about should arrive before many that were ready to leave England a Month Ago."

RC (DLC). 3 pp. Postmarked Boston, 21 Dec. Filed with duplicate of Joy to JM, 9 Sept. 1809 (*PJM-PS*, 1:369). Joy wrote that he was also transmitting a triplicate of his 3 Aug. letter to JM (*PJM-PS*, 1:318).

To Thomas Jefferson

DEAR SIR   WASHINGTON Ocr. 6. 1809

I inclose for perusal a letter from Mr. Dupont D. N. What does he mean by his desire "to contribute" to the Execution of his project of Education?[1] You will observe that he has sent for you a copy of the Works of Turgot,[2] as far as Edited. Be so good as to point out the mode in which you wish them to be transmitted. I expect a Waggon here next month which can take them to Orange,[3] if you prefer that conveyance to a water one to Richmond.

The late news from Europe will be found in the Newspapers. Jackson has been presented, and is on the threshold of business. He is not deficient in the diplomatic professions, but nothing appears, to contradict the presumption that he is so in the requisite instructions.

We left Montpellier on friday last and reached Washington on monday about 3 OC. The heat was very oppressive on the road & has so continued since our arrival; notwithstanding a fine shower of rain the evening before the last. Be assured always of my affectionate & high respects

JAMES MADISON

RC (DLC). Docketed by Jefferson, "recd Oct. 8." Enclosed Pierre Samuel DuPont de Nemours to JM, 11 July 1809 (*PJM-PS*, 1:285–86).

1. DuPont had written a treatise embodying a national plan for education in the U.S. and told JM he was eager to implement the scheme (*PJM-PS*, 1:285–86 and n. 1).

2. DuPont sent JM seven volumes of his edition of Turgot's *Works* and asked the president to convey other sets to Jefferson, the American Philosophical Society, and his children then living in Delaware. DuPont's edition was published in nine volumes in Paris, 1808–11 (ibid.; E. Millicent Sowerby, comp., *Catalogue of the Library of Thomas Jefferson* [5 vols.; Washington, 1952–59], 3:51–53).

3. JM forwarded the volumes to Jefferson by stagecoach on 17 Nov. (Sowerby, *Catalogue of Jefferson's Library*, 3:52).

From Benjamin Rush

DEAR SIR,   PHILADELPHIA October 6th: 1809.

My Son Richard Rush has requested me to beg the favor of you to accept of the enclosed pamphlet upon the Administration of Justice in Pennsylvania.[1] At the same time, receive Dear Sir a copy of three lectures upon Animal life extracted from a new edition of my medical inquiries now in the press,[2] a Mark of the great regard, of your sincere & Affectionate Old friend

BENJN: RUSH

RC (DLC). Docketed by JM.

1. [Richard Rush], *Reflections upon the Administration of Justice in Pennsylvania. By a Citizen* (Philadelphia, 1809; Shaw and Shoemaker 18483).

2. Rush's *Three Lectures upon Animal Life, Delivered in the University of Pennsylvania* was first published as a pamphlet in Philadelphia in 1799. A revised edition appeared as "An Inquiry into the Cause of Animal Life" in Rush's *Medical Inquiries and Observations* (3d ed.; 4 vols.; Philadelphia, 1809; Shaw and Shoemaker 18548), 1:1–99. The preface to this edition bears the date 31 Oct. 1809. Rush apparently sent to JM either the 1799 pamphlet or an offprint from the 1809 edition.

From James Riddle and Others

SIR   [ca. 8 October 1809]

A representation has been forwarded to the Sec'y at war, praying that Lieutenant Small[1] who Commands the Garrison in this Place may be bro't to a court martial for his barbarous and inhuman Conduct towards his Soldiers and his abuse of the Inhabitants of the town.[2] Reposing Unlimeted Confidence in you, Sir, as the Supreme Executive of the Nation and as Commander in Chief, of the Military We in behalf of the Citizens, pray your Attention to the Memorial to the Sec'y of war And hope immediate Steps will be taken to bring Mr. Small to the Punishment his Villianous Conduct Merits. We are Sir, with the most cordial approbation of your Conduct as P. U. S. Your obt. fellow citizens

Sign'd &ca.   JAMES RIDDLE
[and seven others]

RC (DNA: RG 107, LRRS, R-256:4). Undated. Postmarked Pittsburgh, 8 Oct.

1. Francis Walsh Small of Louisiana was commissioned an ensign in 1806, was promoted to second lieutenant in 1807, and resigned from the army in 1810 (Heitman, *Historical Register*, 1:892).

2. A memorial from the inhabitants of Pittsburgh to Eustis, dated 4 Oct. 1809, complained of Small's mistreatment of his men and was accompanied by eighty-seven signatures (DNA: RG 107, LRRS, C-633:4).

To the Republican Meeting of Washington County, New York

WASHINGTON Ocr. 9. 1809.

I have recd. fellow Citizens; your Address of the 14th. Sepr.[1] with a just sense of the favorable manner, in which it reviews and approves the course pursued by the Administration first in relation to the arrangement made in April last with the M. P: of H. B. M. and next in consequence of the disavowal of that arrangement.

Whatever may be the sequel of this abortive result to a transaction so reasonable in its terms, & so auspicious in its tendencies, it is a consoling reflection that the U. S. will have given the most incontestible evidence of that conciliatory disposition, by which they have been constantly guided; and that it may the more confidently be expected that all true friends to their Country, sacrificing the spirit of party to its honor & its welfare, will unite in whatever measures the maintenance of these may call for.

I thank you for the friendly regards which you have been pleased to manifest towards me, & I sincerely join in extending to my illustrious Predecessor, in his retirement the veneration & grateful remembrance, due to his exalted endowments and his arduous services.

J. M

Draft (DLC). Addressee determined from internal evidence.

1. *PJM-PS*, 1:376–77.

From Thomas Jefferson

DEAR SIR   MONTICELLO Oct. 9. 09.

I recieved last night yours of the 6th. & now return mr. Dupont's letter. At a time when I had a hope that Virginia would establish an University I asked of mr. Dupont & Dr. Priestly to give me their ideas on the best division of the useful sciences into Professorships. The latter did it concisely; but Dupont wrote an elaborate treatise on education which I still possess. After I saw that establishment to be desperate, & with it, gave up the view of making it the legatary of my library, I conceived the hope, & so mentioned to Dupont, that Congress might establish one at Washington. I think it possible that the willingness he expresses to contribute to the execution of his *plan*, may be by becoming President, or a professor. But this is conjecture only. The copy of Turgot's works he has sent me will come best by the mail stage, if put into the care of any passenger of your acquaintance who may be coming as far as Fredericksburg, and will there get Benson to transfer the packet to the Milton stage. Jackson's mountain will, I think produce but a mouse. The affairs of Walcheren & Spain may perhaps give him a little courage.[1] The crop of corn turns out worse than was expected. There certainly will not be half a common crop. It's scarcity and price will produce infinite distress. I set out in three days for Richmond,[2] where I am summoned to be on the 20th. ⟨With my best respects to mrs. Madison I am ever affectionately yours

Th: Jefferson⟩

RC (DLC); FC (DLC: Jefferson Papers). Complimentary close and signature clipped from RC; supplied from FC.

1. News had just reached the U.S. that a British expedition had occupied the island of Walcheren in late July preparatory to an advance on Flushing and Antwerp, while in Spain at the same time Sir Arthur Wellesley defeated French forces at the Battle of Talavera (*National Intelligencer*, 4 and 6 Oct. 1809).

2. This was Jefferson's last trip to Richmond. His visit evoked a spontaneous celebration and several public dinners (ibid., 30 Oct. 1809; Malone, *Jefferson and His Time*, 6:14).

Madison, Francis James Jackson, and Robert Smith
9 October–11 November 1809

EDITORIAL NOTE

The role played by JM in shaping Robert Smith's correspondence with Francis James Jackson poses editorial problems of unusual difficulty. These problems do not require the removal of obstacles to an understanding of JM's views about the conduct of the British minister during his short and unfortunate mission; they raise, instead, ultimately unanswerable questions about the extent to which JM actually wrote the diplomatic notes sent to Jackson under the signature of Robert Smith. It seems reasonable to suppose JM would have assumed in the first instance that all the correspondence arising from Jackson's mission would be carried on by the secretary of state, with the president and his other cabinet colleagues contributing to it in the form of advice and suggestions offered during the course of their consultations. But after the first two meetings between the British minister and the secretary of state—held on 4 and 5 October 1809—it became evident to JM that the normal diplomatic convention of discussions followed by the exchange of notes would not yield useful results, at least for the United States. The president decided, therefore, shortly before Smith was due to meet with Jackson for the third time on 6 October, that all further transactions between the two parties should be conducted in writing only and that their verbal communications accordingly would be reduced to a minimum. Smith conveyed this decision to Jackson in his note of 9 October, the contents of which also attempted to define a clearer basis for future negotiations with the British minister.

JM was driven to this step for a number of reasons. Doubtless he wished to prevent a repetition of the sort of conversations that had taken place earlier in the year with Jackson's predecessor, David Montague Erskine. The misunderstandings that had arisen on those occasions, as they were disclosed over the summer of 1809, had obviously been instrumental in the decision of the British government to disavow the agreement Erskine had concluded with JM on 17 April 1809; and they were now, moreover, a central point of contention between Smith and Jackson as they began their discussions. The secretary of state, suspecting (as did JM) bad faith on the part of the British government, demanded an explanation for the disavowal of the Erskine agreement. Jackson evaded the request, insinuating as he did so that the administration had, at best, misunderstood the nature of Erskine's instructions or, worse, perhaps even deliberately misrepresented them.

Furthermore, the conversations held between 4 and 6 October made it plain that it would be difficult, if not impossible, to prevent the issues under discussion—namely, reparations for the *Chesapeake* affair, the disavowal of Erskine's agreement, the repeal of the orders in council, and the lifting of the Nonintercourse Act—from becoming so entangled and conflated as to preclude the prospect for a settlement of any one, let alone all, of them. It is also possible that by now JM had come to entertain doubts about the ability of the affable but somewhat inept Smith to hold his own in an exchange with the abrasive and redoubtable Jackson, and if this were so, the president could hardly have been unmindful of the fact that in due course much, if not all, of the correspondence of the two diplomatists would have to be made public as Great Britain and the United States attempted to justify their respective stands. Furthermore, there were some advantages for the president in the delays that would result from reducing the negotiations to written form, for although JM had few illusions by the time he returned to Washington in October that Jackson had the authority to settle very much, he was prepared to wait and see if events in Europe, notably Napoleon's recent victories over Austria and the prospect of similar French success in Spain and the Netherlands, might not lead to a more accommodating stance in Great Britain (JM to Jefferson, 6 Oct. and 6 Nov. 1809).

For all these reasons, then, JM seems to have taken on much of the burden of writing the American notes to Jackson after 9 October 1809. It is also likely that Smith continued to submit draft proposals to JM for these notes during this period, though there are signs that the secretary of state rapidly tired of the disputatious nature of the exchanges and urged the president to break off the correspondence "as unworthy of the attention of the govt." (Smith to JM, 29 Oct. 1809). Unfortunately, it is now impossible to ascertain exactly how far the final notes received by Jackson embodied the contributions of the president as distinct from those of the secretary of state. Only one draft in the hand of Robert Smith survives from this period—that for an instruction eventually sent to William Pinkney on 11 November 1809—but a comparison of this draft with the final version strongly reinforces the impression that during these weeks JM must have either rejected or substantially reworked a good deal of what his colleague had proposed. A closer examination of Smith's rejected draft for the 11 November instruction, moreover, permits the reader to surmise some of the reasons why JM would have been dissatisfied with Smith's work at this time.

The instruction to Pinkney arose from the need to explain JM's decision on 8 November to terminate the correspondence with Jackson, and the arguments to be employed for that purpose would have to fulfill the requirement of persuading both the British government and the American public as to the justice of the president's action. After Smith had stated in his draft, however, that JM ended the correspondence with Jackson "on account of his personal Misconduct and under the persuasion that so reprehensible a proceeding was not within the views of his Sovereign," he failed to develop the case and proceeded instead to indict the British government rather than its minister for the breakdown of the negotiations. As an attempt to put Jackson in the wrong, therefore, Smith's draft was clearly unsatisfactory, and it was probably for this reason that JM replaced it with a shorter communication to Pinkney on 11 November which was forwarded to London at the earliest opportunity. Lengthier and more detailed statements of the administration's complaints against both Jackson and the British ministry were then left for later occasions, notably the instructions sent to Pinkney on 23 November and the "Exposition of the Conduct of the Honorable Francis James Jackson, in His Correspondence with Robert Smith Esq.," which appeared under the signature of "Publius" in the *National Intelligencer* on 4 and 6 December 1809. These two documents, the latter particularly, are important statements of the administration's grievances against Great Britain, and it is by no means unlikely, even though there is no conclusive evidence on the matter, that JM had a hand in their composition (Draft of Smith to Pinkney, ca. 9 Nov. 1809; Smith to Pinkney, 11 and 23 Nov. 1809 [DNA: RG 59, IM]).

The Smith-Jackson correspondence, however, is not the only instance in this volume where there is evidence that JM was so unhappy with the draftsmanship of the secretary of state that he intervened in order to remedy its deficiencies. There also survive in various forms early versions of the instructions to John Armstrong under the dates of 5 June and 5 July 1810; and it would seem that JM completely rejected Smith's draft in the first case, while in the second he simply wrote out the whole draft himself. That JM felt it necessary from time to time to perform some of the more essential departmental functions of one of his colleagues undoubtedly contributed to his increasing dissatisfaction with Smith. That dissatisfaction was to culminate in Smith's dismissal from the cabinet in April 1811, and on that occasion JM reminded Smith that the business of his department "had not been conducted in the systematic and punctual manner, which was necessary, particularly in the foreign correspondence." The president further complained of the "crude & inadequate" nature of Smith's work, which, he said, he was "in the more important cases generally obliged to write . . . anew, under the disadvantage sometimes of retaining, thro' delicacy some mixture of his draft." In this context,

JM especially recalled to Smith's attention that the 1809 correspondence with Jackson "had in a manner, fallen entirely on my hands." Many subsequent readers of the Smith-Jackson letters, moreover, did not hesitate to affirm, as did the former secretary of the navy Benjamin Stoddert, that JM was "the Scribe in this Correspondence" (Draft of Robert Smith to John Armstrong, 5 June 1810; Madison's Draft of Robert Smith to John Armstrong, 5 July 1810; "Memorandum as to R. Smith," Apr. 1811 [DLC]; Stoddert to Jackson, 6 Dec. 1809, enclosed in Jackson to Canning, 13 Dec. 1810 [PRO: Foreign Office, ser. 5, vol. 64]).

Given, then, the extent to which JM clearly performed some of the more important departmental functions of Robert Smith, there might seem to be a case in favor of publishing the entire Smith-Jackson correspondence, if not even more of the outgoing letters of the State Department, as part of JM's papers. There are, however, a number of reasons against adopting so broadly conceived an editorial policy in these volumes. These involve the ultimate impossibility of determining JM's precise contribution to the correspondence of his secretary of state as well as the purely practical difficulties of attempting to publish such a large number of documents in a letterpress edition. Even the Smith-Jackson correspondence considered by itself is quite a sizable body of material, and it has, moreover, long been easily accessible in *American State Papers* (*ASP, Foreign Relations*, 3:308–23). For these reasons, therefore, the editors have settled for a compromise measure: summaries of Robert Smith's letters to Jackson will be published at the appropriate places among JM's other papers to enable readers to follow the development of the controversy with the British minister and thus assess JM's response to it. To understand the story in all its complexity, however, readers will have to supplement this edition of JM's papers with a number of other sources, which can only be mentioned briefly in this volume. The most important of these, in addition to *ASP, Foreign Relations*, are the relevant series in the records of the Department of State (DNA: RG 59), the official and personal papers of Francis James Jackson deposited in the British Public Record Office (PRO: Foreign Office, ser. 5 and 358), and those of Jackson's personal letters that have been published in the volumes of the *Bath Archives*.

§ Robert Smith to Francis James Jackson. *9 October 1809, Department of State.* Expresses regret that British government has disavowed the agreement signed with David Erskine and then sent by the new British minister no explanation of this disappointing act. States terms understood to be the price Great Britain would exact prior to an official revocation of the orders in council now hampering American commerce. If there is any misconception of the facts, then a correct statement should be laid before the president. To prevent future misunderstanding, asks that oral communications cease and any further discussions "be in the written form."

Tr, two copies (DNA: RG 233, President's Messages; and DNA: RG 46, Legislative Proceedings, 11A-E3). 6 pp. Enclosed in JM's 29 Nov. annual message to Congress. Printed in *ASP, Foreign Relations*, 3:308.

From the Inhabitants of the Louisiana Territory

[ca. 10 October 1809]

THE REMONSTRANCE of the undersigned inhabitants of the Territory of Louisiana,

MOST RESPECTFULLY SHEWETH,

That the term of service of John B. C. Lucas,[1] judge of the General Court, and Commissioner of Land Titles in this Territory, is by law almost expired, and his re-appointment to the first, and continuance in the last office, is deemed by them as a great public calamity.

The undersigned feel sensibly the precarious tenure of their rights, when passion takes the place of reason on the Bench, when the *Judge* turns *Advocate*, when the individual who is not an obsequious flatterer of the Judge is sure to experience the rancorous enmity of a revengeful disposition clothed in the sacred ermine of his office, and when the names of the parties alone determines the measure of justice to be allotted. They cannot, and they will not, under these circumstances respect such a Judge, they must abhor a tribunal where they are insulted in the prosecution of their rights.[2]

Without these reasons, they conceive that a Commissioner ought not to be a Judge of the General Court, his decisions as *Commissioner* unfit him to sit on the same cases as *Judge*. Evils such as these, in their opinion ought to find a remedy in the *wisdom* and *Justice* of the *President* and *Senate*.

Wherefore they pray for the reasons aforesaid, that the said John B. C. Lucas, *may not be re-appointed as Judge*, and may be *removed as Commissioner of Land Titles* as aforesaid.

BERND PRATTE
[and thirteen others]

Printed broadside (DNA: RG 233, Various Select Committee Reports, HR 11A-F10.4). Addressed "TO HIS EXCELLENCY *The President of the United States*, AND THE *Honorable the Senate thereof*." Conjectural date assigned by comparison with another petition prepared at St. Louis on 10 Oct. 1809 and an advertisement of 26 Oct. 1809 concerning this petition (Carter, *Territorial Papers, Louisiana-Missouri*, 14:323–27, 338).

1. John Baptiste Charles Lucas, a native of France, was a Republican congressman from Pennsylvania, 1803–5. He served as land commissioner, 1805–12, and judge, 1805–20, for the northern district of Louisiana (later the Missouri Territory) at St. Louis.

2. Lucas knew of this petition and suspected that it had been sent to JM. He declared to the secretary of war that it "contains no specifick Charges, it is a mere piece of slanderous declamation" (Lucas to William Eustis, Dec. 1809, Carter, *Territorial Papers, Louisiana-Missouri*, 14:355; see also Lucas to JM, 22 Mar. 1810, and nn.).

From Stephen Cathalan

SIR   MARSEILLES 12th. Octob 1809.

Copy of mine of the 3d. June last[1] is herewith. I have had since the pleasure to make the personal & worthy acquaintance of Mr. R. C. Nicholas Nephew of Robt. Smith Esqre. Secretary of State, he is on the eve of leaving this place for Tunis. He was bearer of a passeport with strong recommendation from you, I shewed him all the civilities & attentions in my power & was glad that he used of the offer of my best services.

Any Citizens of the U. States you will recommend, or introduce to me, I will render them any Service & their Stay here as agreable & usefull as they may wish, or expect from me.

S. C.

RC and duplicate (DLC). RC filed with Cathalan to JM, 3 June 1809.

1. *PJM-PS*, 1:221–22.

From John G. Jackson

MY DEAR SIR.   MONTE ALTO CLARKSBURG P O Octr 12th 1809

Have the goodness to enclose the within Packet to Mrs. Washington.[1] We hear very little now of the movements of the British Cabinet towards us, & still less of Jackson's course—the public expectation has so long been abused that a state of Apathy and indifference has in some degree succeeded the excitement produced by British perfidy. They do not now contemplate the evils inflicted by G B with more concern than the subjugation of Austria & the contests in Spain—that is to say not as immediately affecting us but probably doing so in their consequences. I would now as soon attempt to move the rocky top of the Allegany to battle as make war with G B for existing differences without some new crisis to aid me. We must therefore play ⟨a⟩ cautious game if we avoid yielding some important right. The Elections have recently been favorable & rather confirm than shake my position: the people were drawn astray by popular tumult, they are returning to a state of quiet & acquiescence, & if they are maintained in it, earth & Hell cannot shake them. But go to War—or lay embargoes—Taxes &c & my life on it we kick the beam.[2] Excuse these reflections. I wanted to say something & they obtruded on me. With love to my dear Sister M & yourself yours sincerely

J G JACKSON

13

RC (DLC). Docketed by JM.

1. Lucy Payne Washington (1777–1848) was the widow of George Steptoe Washington (ca. 1773–1808) and the sister of Mary Payne Jackson (John G. Jackson's deceased wife) and Dolley Payne Madison. During JM's presidency she and her three children frequently stayed at the executive mansion (*PJM*, 15:358 nn. 6, 7; Moore, *The Madisons*, p. 227).

2. Kick the beam: "(of one scale of a balance) to be so lightly loaded that it flies up and strikes the beam; to be greatly outweighed" (*OED*).

From Charles Peale Polk

SIR,   CITY OF WASHINGTON October 12th. 1809.

My feelings are deeply excited by the Step which I now take in addressing a letter to you, not knowing in what light it may be viewed. But of this I am conscious that I do it with the most respectful motive. I take the liberty of enclosing several letters for Your perusal, and among them One which I had the honor of receiving from you in April 1801,[1] in which you were pleased to say "I shall not fail to make known your pretensions in every quarter where it may be requisite, and that it will afford me real pleasure, if in any, an opportunity of providing for the public service should be embraced with an accomplishment of your wishes & advantage."

My Object in addressing you is to obtain your permission to use that letter on an Occasion of great importance to me at this time. It has long been the source of grief to my mind to know how grossly I was calumniated to you soon after the reception of that letter. I hope however that a probation for seven years of correct conduct in this City, has done away the unfavorable impression made upon your mind by the misrepresentation of my Character. For the highest ambition of my life is to stand well with the wise and good among my countrymen.

Before I close this letter, I deem it proper to state that an opportunity will *shortly* offer of serving the interest of a growing family by an increase of my Salary.[2] The enclosed letters will explain that object, and believing that your letter to me will be highly important, I ask your consent to use it, which has never been done heretofore by me. I have the honor to be with very great respect, Sir, Your obedient Servant.

CHARLES PEALE POLK
Penn[s]ylvania Avenue near the
Seven Buildings[3]

RC (DLC). Enclosures not found.

1. Letter not found (calendared in *PJM-SS*, 1:105).

2. Charles Peale Polk (1767–1822) was Charles Willson Peale's nephew and foster son. He painted portraits of the Isaac Hite family and of JM's parents. Since 1806 he had served as a Treasury Department auditor's clerk (*PJM-SS*, 1:66 n. 3; Lillian B. Miller, ed., *The Collected Papers of Charles Willson Peale and His Family: A Guide and Index to the Microfiche Edition* [Millwood, N.Y., 1980], p. 65; Hunt-Jones, *Dolley and the "Great Little Madison,"* p. 2).

3. The Seven Buildings were financed by Robert Morris and built by James Greenleaf circa 1796 at the intersection of Pennsylvania Avenue and Nineteenth Street N.W. Some of them served as premises for the State Department, 1800–1801, and JM's residence, 1815–17 (Constance McLaughlin Green, *Washington: A History of the Capital, 1800–1950* [2 vols. in 1; Princeton, N.J., 1976], 1:xv, 4, 78; Allen C. Clark, *Greenleaf and Law in the Federal City* [Washington, 1901], p. 143).

From Francis W. Small

SIR, PITTSBURGH Octr. 12. 1809

Permit me respectfully to solicit a suspension of your Excellencys opinion, respe[c]ting a Memorial addressed to you from a party in this Town, until next Mail, wch. Memorial is calculated to injure me in your estimation, and that of the Public, and in the mean time with due deference, I beseech your perusal of a candid statement of the facts, which I have transmitted to the Honle. the Sec. of War, John Smith Esqr. Chief Clerk, and the Acting Adjt. and Inspr. of the Army Lt. Colo. Whiting.[1]

I do assure you Sir, most sacredly on my honor, that I am done the greatest injustice to, and that I never drew my dirk in the Streets, until most violently attacked, and then after forbearance was exhausted and in my own defence, (which Major Denny,[2] and Capt. Graham,[3] the relation of the Chief Clerk of the Dept. of State can testify). I shall however rejoice at a Court of Enquirey being ordered, Knowing that it must terminate honourably to me, and to the shame, and confusion of my persecutors. I have the honor to be with the highest sentiments of respect & Esteem, Your Excellencys, Most Obedt. humble Sert

FRS. W. SMALL, Lieut.
2d. Regt. US. Infy.

RC (DNA: RG 107, LRRS, S-699:4). Docketed by a War Department clerk as received 24 Oct. 1809.

1. Lieut. Col. John Whiting of the Fourth Infantry was acting adjutant and inspector of the army from 17 July to 17 Aug. 1809 (Heitman, *Historical Register*, 1:1030).

2. Ebenezer Denny was a contractor for the army in Pittsburgh.

3. Henry Richard Graham was a captain in the First Rifle Regiment (ibid., 1:467–68).

¶ To Thomas Jefferson. Letter not found. *13 October 1809*. Acknowledged in Jefferson to JM, 25 Oct. 1809. Listed in Jefferson's Epistolary Record (DLC: Jefferson Papers) as received in Richmond on 20 Oct. Encloses a check on the Bank of Norfolk.

§ From the Inhabitants of the Michigan Territory. *Ca. 15 October 1809.* Petitioners seek removal of Gov. William Hull on the grounds that he has dealt unfairly with Canadian owners of fugitive slaves, consorted with a Chippewa Indian who murdered a tribesman, issued illegal orders to the militia, allowed the territorial defenses to deteriorate, implemented an illegal arrangement with an Indian interpreter regarding a trading license, wasted public money, and fostered a "system of favouritism" that included the pardon of a wrongdoer who violated the "rights of the Judiciary." Concludes that Hull ignores court proceedings, hinders the work of the court, and issues "defamatory Proclamations upon the Judges."

Printed broadside (DNA: RG 107, LRUS, H-1810). 1 p. Undated. Unsigned. Reprinted in Carter, *Territorial Papers, Michigan,* 10:296–99. Hull sent the broadside to the secretary of war with his letter of 24 Nov. 1809. He denounced Judge Augustus B. Woodward as the instigator of the petition: "Fifty Copies of it have been published more than a Month, and . . . only five or six persons have been found to sign it." Hull also professed, "Whether this petition will ever reach the Presidt or not, is a subject about which I have no concern" (ibid., 10:295).

§ From an Unidentified Correspondent. *15 October 1809, Urbana.* Demands that JM implement the principles of the report on public credit that he signed with Alexander Hamilton and Oliver Ellsworth on 18 Sept. 1783.[1]

RC (NN). 3 pp. Unsigned.

1. JM's correspondent was referring to the "Address to the States by the United States in Congress Assembled" of 26 Apr. 1783 (see *PJM,* 6:487–94).

§ From Richard Purdy. *16 October 1809, Orange Court House.* Encloses draft on JM from Gideon Gooch for $47.59. Expects JM knows the circumstances and hopes it will be convenient to remit the amount promptly.

RC and enclosure (DLC). RC 1 p. Enclosed draft (1 p.), dated 8 Oct., is for £14 5s. 7d.

To the Secretary of the Republican Meeting of Columbia, South Carolina

SIR   Ocr. 17. 1809

I have recd. the Resolns. unanimously entered into by the Citizens of Columbia, & covered by your letter of the 20th. of Sepr.[1]

The very unexpected & inauspicious turn given to our relations with

G. B. by the disavowal of the friendly Arrangt. concluded by her accredited Minister, cd. not fail to excite a lively sensibility among a people conscious of their own just purposes, and satisfied of the reasonable views & good faith, which have been evinced by their own Govt.

In such a posture of our Affairs, it is a happy consideration, that a disposition, more & more prevails, to review the course which has been pursued in our foreign relations with a due attention to the causes which have produced & prolonged the embarrts. which have distinguished them; and to unite in support of the public Authorities in the measures which may be best adapted to the peculiarity of the crisis.

Such a Union alone can be wanted to command respect from foreign nations to our rights, or to vindicate them with success.

I tender to my fellow Citizens of Columbia my respects & friendly wishes.

J. M.

Draft (DLC). Addressed to "John M. Creyon Esqr."

1. See Republican Meeting of Columbia, South Carolina, to JM, 4 Sept. 1809 (*PJM-PS*, 1:352). Creyon's letter to JM (misdated 30 Sept.) is printed in the *National Intelligencer*, 8 Dec. 1809, along with JM's reply.

From Caesar A. Rodney

MY DEAR SIR,   WILMINGTON October 17th. 1809

Mr. Poydras[1] declined the printing of Mr. Lisley's able & argumentative work,[2] which had been translated at the Secretary of States office, & which only required to be corrected previously to publication. The enclosed pamphlet was transmitted to me, by Mr. Poydras (& which I had not seen before) as the work he desired to have correctly translated & printed.[3] Not being conversant with the French language myself, I have had recourse to a young gentleman well acquainted with it for his aid, & I find the work so declamatory & in some respects so personal, that I do not consider it sufficiently temperate & dignified, for a publication which the goverment or any officer of it, has sanctioned. The "*Suaviter in modo,*" is never inconsistent with the "*Fortiter in re.*" However desirous of seeing the sound & luminous arguments of Mr. Lisly, an accomplished Civilian, published in answer to the numerous pamphlets on the other side, I must confess I do not think the work enclosed will be likely to produce any benificial effects. Let Mr. Livingston appeal to the passions or excite the feelings if he pleases; The United States ought not to follow the example. It is the honest & sincere wish of the Goverment, that right & justice may be done in the case agreeably to the facts & the law. A temperate discussion is the surest method of obtaining this result. Should your ideas correspond with mine I shall inform Mr. Poydras that I do not consider the pamphlet calculated to attain the object he wishes.

I presume Mr. Jackson has begun to unfold his veiws & wishes. I hope his mission may terminate favorably. But I do not anticipate such a result. Let the issue be what it may, the administration will be placed on higher ground. In this State I am well convinced a radical change of sentiment is taking place among the people. Even the Federal leaders have experienced an alteration in their opinions, & appear disposed at such a crisis, to support the Goverment. I trust their future conduct will evince their sincerity. The Spanish Ambassador will not I apprehend, create much difficulty.

Remember me particularly to Mrs. Madison & Mrs. Cutts & beleive me Dear Sir, Yours Very Sincerely

C. A. RODNEY

RC (DLC).

1. Julien Poydras de Lalande was the Orleans Territory delegate in the House of Representatives, 1809–11.

2. On 2 Jan. 1809 Orleans territorial governor William C. C. Claiborne had forwarded to JM Louis Moreau de Lislet's "Mémoire au soutien des droits des Etats-unis à la Batture du Faubourg Ste. Marie" (136 pp.; dated at New Orleans, 31 Dec. 1808 [DNA: RG 59, Records Relating to the Livingston Claim to the *Batture* in New Orleans]). The manuscript was never published, and the translation made in the Department of State has not been found. In May 1810 Jefferson requested JM to send him Moreau's "Mémoire" for use in preparing his defense against Edward Livingston's suit over the batture. Neither the original manuscript nor the translation could be located in Washington, however, and it was not until October 1810 that Rodney was finally able to provide Jefferson with "the original papers of Mr. Lisle on the subject of the batture." Jefferson then used the manuscript extensively in revising his own memorial on the batture for publication in 1812 (Jefferson to JM, 30 May 1810; JM to Jefferson, 4 June 1810; John Graham to Jefferson, 11 June 1810, and Rodney to Jefferson, 18 Oct. 1810 [DLC: Jefferson Papers]; see also Jefferson's "The Batture at New Orleans. The Proceedings of the Government of the United States in Maintaining the Public Right to the Beach of the Mississippi, Adjacent to New Orleans, against the Intrusion of Edward Livingston," Lipscomb and Bergh, *Writings of Jefferson*, 18:56 n. 2).

3. In his reply to Rodney on 22 Oct. JM acknowledged receipt of "the pamphlet of T. on the Batture." Rodney possibly enclosed one of two pamphlets written by J. B. S. Thierry. The contents of both Thierry's *Examen des droits des Etats-Unis et prétensions de Mr. Eduoard Livingston sur la Batture* (New Orleans, 1808; Shaw and Shoemaker 16306) and his *Réponse à Mr. Du Ponceau* (New Orleans, 1809; Shaw and Shoemaker 18748) conform to Rodney's description that the work he sent to JM was "so declamatory & in some respects so personal" as to be not "sufficiently temperate & dignified" to receive the sanction of the administration. Both works, however, had already been translated into English in New Orleans (Shaw and Shoemaker 16307 and 18749), though Rodney may not have been aware of this fact.

From Francis W. Small

SIR,   FORT FAYETTE, PITTSBURGH, October 17th. 1809.

I had hoped, to have been enabled to forward to you, pr. this Mail, my vindication from the vile charges, that have been exhibited against me, in the "Common Wealth," but I cannot possibly do so, until next Mail, then however, they shall positively be forwarded,[1] *and until then*, I respectfully hope, and humbly crave, a suspension of your opinion, feeling perfectly confident, and convinced, that I shall there, exhibit to you; incontrovertible *proofs* undeniable *proofs*, that my conduct, has been strictly correct *prudent* and cautious, as well as strictly honorable, and such; as I am bold to say, will secure to me your entire approbation, and esteem, whilst it will shew to your entire satisfaction, that the petitions, and statements, gone forth against me, are not only totally *destitute of truth*, but are absolutely fraught with the vilest, and most rancorous *falsehoods*.

Yesterday Judge Roberts in Court discharged me from my bail, before whom, I proved that Cunningham,[2] had done acts in the Garrison, for which, He went unpunished; that would have caused Him, to have been Sentenced to death, before a Military tribunal.

The same party that have attacked me, now threaten the Judge, with a petition to the State Government; to have Him removed; because He done justice. With the highest consideration & respect, I have the honor to be Your Excellency's Most Obedient humble Servt.

                                        FR. W. SMALL, Lieut. Comg.

RC and enclosure (DNA: RG 107, LRRS, S-700:4). RC docketed by a War Department clerk as received 24 Oct. 1809. Enclosure (1 p.) is an affidavit from Capt. Henry Richard Graham testifying that he considered Small to be a gentleman.

1. Copies of Small's printed vindication can be found enclosed in Small to Eustis, 19 Oct. 1809 (DNA: RG 107, LRRS, S-705:4), and Ephraim Pentland to Eustis, 19 Oct. 1809 (ibid., P-361:4).
2. Christopher Cunningham was an enlisted soldier in the garrison at Pittsburgh who had filed an affidavit complaining of having been violently assaulted by Small (see James Riddle and others to JM, ca. 8 Oct. 1809, and n. 2).

§ From Nicholas Boilvin. *17 October 1809, Prairie du Chien.* Wrote president earlier[1] but received no answer, so he makes another effort to acquaint JM with the Indian situation on the Mississippi. Tribes living on frontier would have attacked settlements in destructive fashion but are afraid of the Sioux, Falsovoin, Fox, and "a large Party of Puants, all of whom are in favor of the United States." These Indians have told him that English traders have encouraged hostile tribes to ravage American settlements, but he discounts their reports. Many promises have been made to the Indians but not fulfilled; result is that peace is maintained with difficulty. Has carried on John Campbell's business since he died. In return for his exertions Dearborn promised him equal footing with other agents. His situation is remote, and he is constantly harassed by Indians—these facts should be considered in determining his compensation. Governor Lewis and General Clark can testify as to his character and fitness.

RC (DNA: RG 107, LRRS, B-622:4). 4 pp. Franked at St. Louis on 23 Nov. Boilvin sent an almost identical letter to the secretary of war on this same day, which is printed in Carter, *Territorial Papers, Louisiana-Missouri*, 14:330–32.

1. *PJM-PS*, 1:208.

From David Bailie Warden

SIR,   PARIS, 18 october, 1809

I am almost ashamed to address you again on the subject of my continuance here as Consul and agent of Prize Causes, but my anxiety prompts me to it. With General Armstrongs' advice, I had proposed to embark for Washington, on board the vessel which carries this, charged with his dispatches and communications, but the arrival of the *Wasp* has destroyed my project, and prevented me from having the honor of being personally known to you. I still flatter myself, that you will be pleased to nominate, and recommend me to the Senate as Consul for Paris. I shall labor to be as useful as possible to you, and to the Government. All other pursuits shall yield to my duties in this respect. General Armstrong promises to write to you in my behalf.[1] I am now much occupied with the business of Prize-Causes, being charged with the defense of several Vessels and their Cargoes. The intention of the Emperor with regard to those that have not infringed the laws of blockade, is yet unknown. Much will depend on the success, or failure of the projects he has formed. It is suspected that all those vessels, whose destination was for England, or that have been visited by her vessels of war, will be condemned by the Council of Prizes, if that Court is permitted to decide upon them. This, however, depends on the Emperors' Will.[2] His arrival in Paris is daily expected.[3] I am, Sir, with great respect, your very obedient, and humble Servant,

DAVID BAILIE WARDEN

RC and duplicate (DLC); letterbook copy (MdHi: Warden Papers). Duplicate and letterbook copy dated 17 Oct. Minor variations between the copies have not been noted.

1. For Armstrong's ambivalent recommendation of Warden to Jefferson, see *PJM-PS*, 1:155 n. 2.

2. Napoleon's response to the news of the failure of the Erskine agreement, the British orders in council of April 1809, and the terms of the Nonintercourse Act of 1809 was embodied in a decree, apparently drafted in Vienna on or about 4 Aug. 1809. Although never officially promulgated, the decree stated in effect that every American ship which entered the ports of France, Spain, or Italy would be seized and confiscated as long as the Nonintercourse Act continued to be executed against French vessels in the harbors of the U.S. Napoleon publicly indicated that these assumptions would govern his policy toward the U.S. in a letter sent from Altenburg by Champagny to Armstrong on 22 Aug. 1809 and published in the Paris *Moniteur* on 6 Oct. 1809 ("Minute de Décret Impérial," art. 3 [AAE: Political Correspondence, U.S., 62:263]; Champagny to Armstrong, 22 Aug. 1809, in Henri Plon and J. Dumaine, eds., *Correspondance de Napoléon Ier* [32 vols.; Paris, 1858–70], 19:374–76 [translation in *ASP, Foreign Relations*, 3:325–26]).

3. This sentence is not on the duplicate or letterbook copy.

§ From the Merchants and Underwriters of Philadelphia. *Ca. 19 October 1809.* After the Embargo law expired, the memorialists outfitted and dispatched several ships with valuable cargoes to European ports. Neutral character of ships was established by adequate documentary evidence, but "in every instance in which they have been met with by Danish cruizers, they have been captured . . . and with their cargos have been condemned (with very few exceptions)." Fearing that the papers carried may have been destroyed or otherwise tampered with and realizing that similar circumstances have affected other American ships now in Danish ports, the memorialists ask that the U.S. government dispatch "a publick vessel and a person to represent the case to The Danish government or such other measures as the wisdom of The President may deem proper."

RC (DNA: RG 233, President's Messages). 2 pp. Bears sixty-nine signatures. Undated. Sent to secretary of state with the merchants' resolutions of 19 Oct. 1809 authorizing preparation of the memorial; submitted with JM's message to the House of Representatives, 12 Jan. 1810 (*Annals of Congress*, 11th Cong., 2d sess., 1200–1201). Printed, with the resolutions, in *ASP, Foreign Relations*, 3:332–33.

§ From Wilson Cary Nicholas. *19 October 1809, Warren.* Introduces Maj. James Morrison of Kentucky, "one of the most respectable of the revolutionary Officers, and one of the most amiable men I am acquainted with."

RC (DLC). 1 p. Nicholas was nearing the end of his service as a Virginia congressman (he resigned on 27 Nov.).

§ From Jonathan Robinson and Samuel Shaw. *19 October 1809, Montpelier, Vermont.* Recommends Cornelius P. Vann Ness for the office of U.S. attorney in Vermont.[1]

RC (DNA: RG 59, LAR, 1809–17, filed under "Vann Ness"). 1 p. Jonathan Robinson and Samuel Shaw were, respectively, a Republican senator and a Republican representative from Vermont during the Eleventh Congress.

1. On 19 Dec. 1809 JM nominated Vann Ness to be U.S. attorney for Vermont, and the Senate confirmed the appointment the next day (*Senate Exec. Proceedings*, 2:130–31).

§ Robert Smith to Francis James Jackson. *19 October 1809, Department of State.* Answers Jackson's letter of 11 Oct. by explaining the purpose for requesting that communications be in written form. Jackson's interpretation of the request has "converted an intimation of the expediency [of written exchanges] into a general prohibition of all verbal communications whatever." The point was to avoid misunderstandings. Requests Jackson to demonstrate that his government had "*strong and solid reasons*" for disavowing the Erskine agreement. Sets forth the American view of that agreement and explains the hopes entertained in Washington of a clarification—"a proper explanation"—of the British king's negative reaction. If Canning's letter to Erskine of 23 Jan. 1809 contained the only conditions acceptable to Great Britain and that point had been made clear to the Americans at the time, no agreement would have been reached. Now Great Britain insists that any future pact must limit American trade with the colonies of Britain's enemies and allow the Royal Navy to enforce the acts of Congress. The latter condition touches "one of those vital principles of sovereignty, which no nation ought to have been expected to impair." Discusses reparations in the *Chesapeake* affair, the British orders in council, and the interdicted trade with Holland. Concludes that "you are not authorised to tender explanations for the disavowal, or to propose any new arrangement, nor to conclude any agreement, but solely to receive and discuss propositions [for resuming trade with U.S., while bound to hold out for the two unacceptable conditions], both inadmissible, one, altogether irrelevant to the subject; and the other requiring nothing less than a surrender of an inalienable function of the national sovereignty."

Tr, two copies (DNA: RG 233, President's Messages; and DNA: RG 46, Legislative Proceedings, 11A-E3). 29 pp. Enclosed in JM's 29 Nov. annual message to Congress. Printed in *ASP, Foreign Relations*, 3:311–14.

To Nelly Conway Madison

MY DEAR MOTHER   WASHINGTON Oct. 20. 1809

Dolly wrote to you by the last mail. I have the satisfaction of sayg that we continue well. I pray that you may also enjoy the same blessing. As I think you ought to enlarge your purchase of corn, & lose no time in doing it, the crop being every where alarmingly short, & the price likely of course to get very high, I inclose you one hundred dollars, and if desired, will send you another. Whatever surplus you may buy, I will gladly take off your hands. Let Sister Rose[1] notify the rect. of the money. Yr affece. son

JAMES MADISON

RC (ViU). This is one of three known letters JM wrote to his mother. His letter of 8 Aug. 1814 is in the Library of Congress, and the third, dated 25 Feb. 1816, was owned by James F. Ruddy of Rancho Mirage, California, in 1988.

1. Frances Taylor Madison Rose (1774–1823), wife of Dr. Robert H. Rose, was JM's youngest sister.

To William Raynolds

SIR   WASHINGTON Ocr. 20. 1809

I have recd. your letter of the 30th. Ult:[1] pledging the support of the officers of the 4 Brigade, in the 3d. Division of Ohio Militia, to such measures as may be adopted by the Govt. at the present conjuncture.

With every allowance for the extraordinary course of events in Europe, the violent & unprovoked conduct of the principal Belligerents towards the U. S. justifies the feelings which it has excited in all good Citizens.

Among the occurrences least to have been anticipated, is the refusal of the B. Govt. to carry into effect the arrangt. made by its Pub: Minister here. It forms a prominent point in our foreign relations. And whilst that and so many other differences, involved in them, remain unsettled, the readiness to maintain the honor & essential interests of the Nation, of which you have communicated an example, is as seasonable as it is laudable. I offer to yourself, and your associates, my respects & good wishes.

J. M

Draft (DLC).

1. Muskingum County, Ohio, Militia to JM, 30 Sept. 1809 (*PJM-PS*, 1:392–93).

To the Secretary of the Republican Meeting of Nashville, Tennessee

SIR   WASHINGTON Ocr. 20. 1809

I have received, under cover of your letter of Sepr. 11. the resolutions of sundry Citizens of Nashville.[1]

Their determination to maintain the honor and rights of the Nation is a proof of the patriotic spirit which animates them. And it accords with the same spirit, to pledge their support, in the present conjuncture, to the constituted Authorities in such measures as may be found best adapted to it.

The approbation expressed of the measure taken by the Executive, in consequence of the disavowal of the arrangement which had renewed our commerce with the British dominions, contributes to strengthen the conviction of its propriety. I wish my fellow Citizens of Nashville to be assured of the satisfaction I derive from that consn.[2] as well as of my respects & friendly wishes

Draft (DLC). Addressed to William Dickson.

1. *PJM-PS*, 1:372–73. JM had given Dickson a recess appointment as register of the land office in Madison County, Mississippi Territory. The Senate confirmed his appointment on 17 June 1809 (*Senate Exec. Proceedings*, 2:122, 124).
   2. Someone, possibly JM at a later time, interlined "consideration" here.

From John Strode

WORTHY SIR   CULPEPER 20 Oct '09
Nothing but the dread of unseasonably intruding Offensively on Your inestimable time has prevented me long Since from Approaching Your hand with Solicitations to favour me Some longer with that kind benevolent indulgence which I have as Yet experienced from Your goodness, I can & will when ever You Say the Word give You Ample Security for the debt I owe You, and ever remain bound under a due Sence of all the feelings which gratitude respect & esteem can produce on the Sensibillity of the human Heart.

Pray condescend to Write me half a line, I'll wait on You at the City or Any thing else You will be pleased to direct.

Among the many Weighty and important Matters which You[r] elevated Station must of Course bring into consideration perhaps none is more productive of trouble than that of Selecting proper persons to fill the places of trust in the different departments under Government, in order to come at the Merit of individual Characters must I presume in most cases be derived from the Testimonials produced by the Applicants, in that point of View as a Citizen of the United States, I have ever considered it not Only a priviledge but also an indispensible duty to give my Testimony, however little it may Weigh, in favour of those I may consider eminently Qualified.

I am informed that the Office of Post master at New Orleans is become Vacant by the resignation of Mr Cenas,[1] and that Mr. Robert Chew now of the City of N. York, is one among the Candidates for that place, I am indubitably informd that Mr Chew is well qualified to discharge the duties of that department, having resided Several Years in the City of N. Orleans as a clerk in the Mercantile House of Messrs. Chew & Relf, where He did Actually perform the duties of the Post office during the time it was held by His Brother Mr. Beverley Chew under the Appointment of Governor

Claiborne and is well acquainted with the Language & manners of the inhabitants of that place, And I have many reasons to confidently believe He Merits and will if appointed fill the place with great propriety and unremitting attention to its important duties. With every Sentiment of esteem & respect & Gr⟨a⟩titude I am Worthy Sir Yr. most Obliged hble Serv

JOHN STRODE[2]

RC (DNA: RG 59, LAR, 1809–17, filed under "Chew").

1. Blaize Cenas was appointed postmaster at New Orleans in 1804 and apparently held the position until his death in 1812 (Carter, *Territorial Papers, Orleans*, 9:267; Rowland, *Claiborne Letter Books*, 6:106).

2. John Strode had served as manager of the ironworks near Fredericksburg, Virginia, during the Revolution and as a justice of the peace of Culpeper County from 1784. JM and Jefferson often stayed at his house, Fleetwood, during journeys to and from Philadelphia and Washington. He acted as an inspector of arms manufactured for the Virginia militia, 1801–2, and represented his county in the House of Delegates, 1810–12 (*PJM*, 12:248 n. 1, 14:337; *CVSP*, 6:315–16, 9:197, 283–84).

From James Taylor

DEAR SIR   BELLE VUE Octo 20h. 1809

I hope this will find yourself & my amiable friend Mrs. Madison in good health, also her son.

My family is in good health except my self. I have been much indisposed for about two Months, but have been able to go about principal part of the time.

I am in hopes I shall gain strength as the weather is geting cooler.

We have had a fine crop of grapes this Season for the age of my Vines. We often thought of you & Mrs. M & wished we could have thrown you a few bunches as a Specimen. I think we shall be able in a few years to make our own wine. Indeed I expect to make some next Season. Judge Todd[1] intends to bring you a bottle or two as a sample in Feby next. I think I can boast of a greater variety of choice fruits than any one in this state or indeed any one whom I Know. I have some of the same Kind of pears that are at my fathers & I think you have of them, and a great variety of other Kinds beginning to bear.

Our friends in this Country are generally well—my brother Hubbard was well very lately.

We are all anxiety to Know what propositions Mr Jackson has to make to our Goverment. Our Citizens throughout this state are very indignant at the Conduct of the British Govt. and approve highly, that of our own.

Be so good as to accept with my friend Mrs. M the best Wishes of myself & Mrs. T and am Dr. Sir Your friend & Sert.

                                                            JAMES TAYLOR

RC (DLC). Docketed by JM.

1. Thomas Todd (1765–1826), a native of King and Queen County, Virginia, migrated to Kentucky as a young man and rose to the state's highest judicial post before Jefferson appointed him in 1807 to the U.S. Supreme Court. In 1812 he married Lucy Payne Washington, Dolley Madison's sister.

§ From the Indiana Territorial Legislature. *21 October 1809, Vincennes.* Forwards resolution urging the reappointment of William Henry Harrison as territorial governor.[1]

Printed copy (*National Intelligencer*, 8 Dec. 1809). Signed by Gen. Washington Johnston, Speaker of the House, and Thomas Downs, president of the council.

1. JM reappointed Harrison for a second term of three years on 19 Dec. 1809 (*Senate Exec. Proceedings*, 2:130).

To Caesar A. Rodney

DEAR SIR   WASHINGTON Ocr. 22. 1809

I have duly recd. yours accompanied by the pamphlet of T.[1] on the Batture. You are right I think in your ideas on the subject, and wd. do well in writing to Poydras as you suggest.

Onis could not as you anticipated, be recd.[2] Whatever noise may be made on the occasion, the thing can not admit of doubt with men who consult their judgments, not their sympathies with Spain, nor their enmities towards the administration. Is Ferdinand or the Junta, in actual possession of the Govt.? This is the sole question for us, a question of fact, which all the most recent & authentic information decides in the negative.

Jackson & Mr. S. have been breaking a lance. When shall we have the pleasure of your aid in our deliberations? Accept my affectionate respects.

                                                            JAMES MADISON

RC (NjP).

1. Probably J. B. S. Thierry (see Rodney to JM, 17 Oct. 1809, and n. 3).

2. Luis de Onís had arrived in Washington on 19 Oct. as the minister of the Supreme Junta of Spain to the U.S. JM's reluctance to recognize him grew out of the accession of Joseph Bonaparte to the Spanish throne, which led to rival groups' claiming to be the de facto government in Spain. Since the British backed the Supreme Junta, ruling in the name

of Ferdinand VII, Onís sought aid from Francis James Jackson, whose younger brother, George Jackson, was secretary of the British legation to the Junta. On 24 Oct. Onís and Jackson chanced upon the president at the Georgetown races, where the British minister introduced Onís to JM. As Francis James Jackson reported: "I have done what I could for Onis, but Madison refuses to receive him. This resolution was taken, it appears, some time before his arrival." Onís became persona non grata because of his indiscretions, but JM finally recognized him as Spanish minister late in 1815 (Samuel Flagg Bemis, ed., *American Secretaries of State and Their Diplomacy* [10 vols.; New York, 1927–29], 3:260–61, 275; Brant, *Madison*, 5:98–99, 494 n. 19; Jackson, *The Bath Archives*, 1:29; *ASP, Foreign Relations*, 3:404).

§ From John P. Van Ness. *22 October 1809, Washington*. Writes in support of David Bailie Warden's candidacy for the position of U.S. consul at Paris.

RC (DNA: RG 59, LAR, 1809–17, filed under "Warden"). 1 p.

To William Pinkney

DEAR SIR   WASHINGTON Ocr. 23. 1809

My last[1] was inclosed in the dispatches which, in consequence of a failure in reaching the British Ship of war at Norfolk, were committed to Mr. A. Lee. I conclude therefore that altho' out of season, it finally got safe to hand.

You will see in the communications from the Dept. of State, what has passed with Mr. Jackson. No reply to Mr. S.s answer has yet been made.[2] It appears that the B. Govt. continues to be equally ignorant of our character, & of what it owes to its own. From the conversation of Mr. C. on the 2d. & 3d. conditions in the printed instructions to Mr. E. it was justly inferred that they wd. have been erased from the Ultimatum. And it could hardly be supposed that to the occlusion of our Trade to Holland, the only apparent difficulty remaining, every consideration of Justice, dignity, and even consistency would be so readily sacrificed. For it is impossible not to see that the avowed object is no longer, to retaliate on an enemy, but to prevent our legitimate commerce from interfering with the London Smuglers of Sugar & Coffee. How can a nation expect to retain the respect of Mankind whose Govt. descends to so ignoble a career?

What will be the future course of Mr. Jackson, or that of his Govt. or of Congs. I do not undertake to anticipate, farther than that Congs. will in some form or other keep up a counteraction to the misconduct of both Belligerents. As to Mr. J. it cannot be supposed that he has any effective authority to overcome the difficulties before him. Altho' we continue sincerely anxious to facilitate his doing so, yet no[t] a little indignation is felt, at the mean & insolent attempt to defraud the U. S. of the exculpatory explanation dictated by the respect due to them; and particularly at the insinuation in Jackson's answer that this Govt. colluded with Mr. E. in violating his instructions.[3]

You will observe by the Gazettes that Mr. Onis, appointed by the Spanish Junta, is just arrived here as a Minister Plenipo: of Ferdinand; and that efforts are made to turn the question of his being received, to party purposes. The principle of neutrality on one hand, and on the other, the limited authority of the Executive which does not extend beyond the point of fact, could never permit the reception of Mr. Onis in the actual state of things in Spain. The wonder is that the Junta shd. have exposed themselves to such an experiment; more especially, at the moment chosen for it. But it is not wonderful, that the measure should be ascribed, as it universally is here, to instigations, of the B. Govt. calculating that a reception of Onis, if that sd. unexpectedly happen, would lead to a reupture [*sic*] with France; & that a rejection might throw some advantage into the hands of the party opposed to the administration, and by displeasing old Spain, & perhaps the Cols. favor the monopolizing views of G. B. If such was their policy it may be hoped, that they will be disappointed. It is a remark in every mouth, that it was a mockery of the Junta, to press on it such an experiment at the very moment, the British army, was abandoning the cause of Ferdinand as desperate.[4]

The public opinion or rather that of the discontented party has already undergone, a considerable change in favor of the system pursued in our foreign relations, and the change is still going on. In Maryld. & Vermont, the fact is shewn by the late elections.[5] And all accts. from the Eastward prognosticate that the next elections in Massts. N. H. & R. Island, will reverse those which took place during the fever which the Embargo was made to produce. Reflection alone would probably have brought about such a change. But it has been hastened by the disappointment of all parties, as to the Conduct of G. B. on the subject of Mr. Erskine's Arrangement; and by the severe experience, that a trade limited to the B. dominions, is but a mouthfull, and not as the people were told it wd. be a bellyfull. The shipments to the W. Inds. have been ruinous. In the Mediterranean the losses, owing to captures, recaptures & markets glutted from Engd. will not be less than 25 or 30 perCt. In the Baltic, & the N. of Europe, the speculations are still more entirely blasted. The lumber merchts. who struck at the great demand in England, have been successful; and the others have been saved from loss, by the expected consequence of the Disavowal of Mr. Erskine.

The most remarkable feature in our internal prospects, is the astonishing progress of manufactures, more especially in the Household way. Throughout the middle, S. & W. countries, they have taken a lasting root; it being found, that with the aid of the machineries accomodated to the family scale & of habit, cloathing & many other articles can be provided both cheaper & better than as heretofore. Passion is spur also to interest in the case. Nor is necessity without its influence; for in truth, the planters & farmers being deprived of the customary markets & prices for their produce, can no longer pay for their customary supplies from Abroad.

Our Season has been every where remarkably cold & with some local exceptions, so destitute of rain, that the crops of Indn. Corn is the shortest known for many years. The case is the same with Tobo. & some other articles. Our Wheat Crop was of good quality, but short in quantity; and the dryness of the fall is unfavorable to the next Crop. If Mr. Joy shd. be in Engd. be so good as to tell him, that [I] shd. have written to him by this oppy; but from the inference, that he wd not be there. Accept assurances of my esteem & regard.

JAMES MADISON

RC (NjP: Pinkney Papers). Docketed by Pinkney.

1. JM to Pinkney, 21 Apr. 1809 (*PJM-PS*, 1:128–29).

2. Robert Smith had forwarded to Pinkney copies of his letters of 9 and 19 Oct. 1809 to Francis James Jackson. At the time JM wrote this letter, Jackson's reply of 23 Oct. apparently had not reached the presidential desk (Smith to Pinkney, 11 and 23 Oct. 1809 [DNA: RG 59, IM]).

3. Writing to Robert Smith on 11 Oct., Jackson claimed that Erskine had revealed the three conditions stipulated by Great Britain for the repeal of the orders in council and then alluded to the "reasons which induced you to think that others might be substituted in lieu of them. It may have been concluded between you," Jackson continued, "that these latter were an equivalent for the original conditions; but the very act of substitution evidently shows that those original conditions were, in fact, very explicitly communicated to you, and by you, of course, laid before the President for his consideration. I need hardly add, that the difference between these conditions and those contained in [Erskine's] arrangement of the 18th and 19th of April, is sufficiently obvious to require no elucidation" (*ASP, Foreign Relations*, 3:309).

4. On the same day JM wrote this letter, the *National Intelligencer* printed a report that Sir Arthur Wellesley was withdrawing his army from Spain to Portugal to reembark it on a British fleet sent there for that purpose.

5. The election results JM mentioned were printed in the *National Intelligencer* on various dates between 4 and 25 Oct. In Maryland the Republicans obtained a majority of eight seats in the House of Delegates, while in Vermont the legislature elected a Republican governor and council.

To Benjamin Rush

DEAR SIR   WASHINGTON Oct. 23. 1809

I duly recd. the two pamphlets which you were so obliging as to inclose me;[1] and had hoped ere this to have had the pleasure of reading them.

From a glance at a few pages of the one on the Judiciary subject, I perceive that is very handsomely written at least. The subject of the other I have no doubt is handled in the elegant and philosophical manner so familiar to the pen of the Author. It is a subject which I have never sufficiently examined to justify any opinion on its merits. My superficial reflections on it, have I confess led me to suppose that some indistinctness of terms has mixed itself with the question. A susceptibility of life under circumstances altogether natural, seems not to be essensially different from what might be called a vital principle.[2] On this point I shall doubtless be a better judge after having received the instruction which awaits me, in your developement. Be assured always of my affecte. esteem

JAMES MADISON

RC (DLC: Benjamin Rush Papers). JM's franked cover (docketed by Rush) became separated from the RC and in 1987 was in the undated Rush Papers.

1. See Rush to JM, 6 Oct. 1809.
2. In "An Inquiry into the Cause of Animal Life," Rush asserted, "Life is the *effect* of certain stimuli acting upon the sensibility and excitability which are extended, in different degrees, over every external and internal part of the body" (Rush, *Medical Inquiries and Observations* [1809 ed.], 1 : 10).

From Samuel Stanhope Smith

DR SIR,   CAPITOL HILL Octr. 23d. [1809]

Permit me to represent to you that at the first organization of the New Orleans territory, my son, at the particular invitation of two Judges, left the city of New York for that territory, under the assurance of being appointed clerk of the supreme court; those gentlemen believing it part of their powers to make the appointment. The governour after a considerable time, perceiving the office to be lucrative, desired it for one of his relations, & required my son to deliver the papers of the office to the new clerk. He refused, & brought the case before the court, who, at two solemn hearings at considerable intervals, confirmed him in an appointment for which he had left his first residence, & his friends, believing it would be permanent during his good behaviour. Young Mr Claibourne despairing of the office, left the territory. But the governour now considering it as a dispute of power between himself & the court, waited an appointment of a new judge, when renewing his attempt in favour of another person, he obtained the voice of a majority of the court, determining the power to be vested in the governour.

I have thought it proper to put you in possession of these circumstances, not with any view to remonstrate against any exercise of the governour's power, in whatever way he has exercised it, but as introductory to a farther representation which I request permission to make.

The confidence of my son in the perman[en]ce of his office, the profits of which satisfied his desires, induced him, in a great degree, to relinquish that attention, which I could have wished he had still paid to the practice of his profession. He is now therefore to commence it anew; & consequently, under some disadvantages in the beginning. That he may not be obliged to depart too far from that stile of living, not extravagant, I believe, but such as his situation at that time seemed to justify, if not to require, it would be peculiarly gratifying to me, since he has removed so far from my assistance, & protection, if he could, without injury to others, receive some appointment in that country, not interfering with his professional duties, which would promote his interests there.

I shall do myself the honor of calling to take my leave of you & Mrs. Madison, but do not solicit any answer personally to this application.[1] I have simply made this short statement, & suggested the request founded upon it, & desire to leave it entirely to your own convenience, to the particular views of government, & the occurrence of events, when, & how far, you may think it proper to comply with it. And I am ever, with the greatest regard, & the most sincere respect, Yr. Mo. obdt. & Mo. hble. servt

SAML S SMITH.

RC (DNA: RG 59, LAR, 1809–17, filed under "Smith, Samuel B.").

1. Smith had written JM earlier regarding the dismissal of his son, John Witherspoon Smith, and apparently tried to keep the matter alive in a letter to Dolley Madison in late December (*PJM-PS*, 1:115–16; Dolley Madison to Smith, 10 Jan. 1810 [NjP: Crane Collection]).

From Thomas Jefferson

DEAR SIR   EPPINGTON[1] Oct. 25. 09

I recieved at Richmond your favor covering a check on the bank of Norfolk for 743. Doll. 15. cents the balance in full of our accounts. I have learnt from P. Carr[2] that under an idea that Rodney was about to resign, & on a desire expressed by mr. R. Smith to him or some other person that Wirt should be sounded, it had been found that he would accept.[3] I do not know whether it was communicated to me in expectation that I should write it to you, or whether it may have communicated to you more directly.

Altho' I repel all applications generally to recommend candidates for office yet there may be occasions where information of my own knolege of them may be useful & acceptable, & others where particular delicacies of situation may constrain me to say something. Of the latter description is the application of John Monroe (cousin of the Colonel) who in expectation that the Governor of Illinois means to resign, has sollicited my saying to you he would accept that office.[4] I had formerly appointed him Atty. of the West district of Virginia. He resided at Staunton & there lost the respect of many by some irregularities which his subsequent marriage has probably put an end to. His talents I believe are respectable, without being prominent: but I really believe you know as much of him as I do, having seen him my self once or twice only, & then for short intervals. Particular circumstances oblige me to mention him, without feeling a single wish on the subject, other than that it should be given to the fittest subject, which you will do of your own motion. Ever affectionately yours

TH: JEFFERSON

RC (DLC); FC (DLC: Jefferson Papers).

1. Eppington was the Chesterfield County home of Congressman John Wayles Eppes, Jefferson's nephew and son-in-law (Betts, *Jefferson's Garden Book*, p. 60).

2. Peter Carr (1770–1815) was Jefferson's nephew. JM supervised his education while Jefferson served as U.S. minister to France. Carr attended the College of William and Mary and in 1789 visited JM in New York. He practiced law from 1793 and represented Albemarle County in the Virginia House of Delegates, 1801–4 and 1807–8 (Elizabeth Dabney Coleman, "Peter Carr of Carr's-Brook . . . ," *Papers of the Albemarle County Historical Society*, 4 [1943–44]: 5–23).

3. Rodney continued to serve as attorney general until 5 Dec. 1811.

4. John Monroe, a judge of the superior court of Kentucky, had requested Jefferson's support in seeking the territorial governorship of Indiana (John Monroe to Jefferson, 1 Aug. 1809 [DLC: Jefferson Papers]).

From Robert R. Livingston

DEAR SIR   CLERMONT 25th Octr 1809

Tho I know that your time is occupied by more important concerns, yet the interest you take in the introduction of merino sheep induces me to hope that you will find leasure (at least when you return to your farm) to run over the little treatize which accompanies this letter.[1] It was written with a view to remove the prejudices of common farmers, who are suspicious of every thing new, & to instruct them as to the mode of forming & managing a flock. For four years past I have been persuing this object, in the course of which, I have written several little essays which have had more affect than I had hoped. I compute that there will next spring be at least 35000 descendants from my flock within this State & Masachusetts. Tho many of these will only be quarter Merino, yet even that degree of blood makes a very considerable difference both in the Quantity & quality of the wool, as well as in the beauty of form.

I was extreamly disappointed that your friendly intentions were frustrated by Genl Armstrongs not having interest to procure a permit for sheep to be sent by the Mentor,[2] & the rather, as he had written to Coll Livingston[3] when at Bordeaux, that it would meet with no difficulty, & that a permit should be sent when wanted. Had not Coll Livingston relyed upon this, he might himself have obtained one at Paris, or when at Bayone from the Emperor, who as well as the Empress shewed many civilities to him & my daughter & made many inquiries relative to my pursuits in America or from Mr De Champaigne who made them many polite offers & expressed a wish to serve them. Fortunatly however, I have reared a fine flock from those I have imported. I am satisfyed that in the course of ten or twelve years wool will be as important a staple of the northern as cotton now is of the southern states. You can hardly conceive the ardour we now very generally manifest for the improvment of our flocks in this & the eastern States.[4] No price is thought too great for a tup, & mine are all bespoke two years in advance. Many of us have increased our flocks ten fold, I shall myself winter this year 600. These flocks are all composed of picked sheep, selected with a view to their being crossed with merino rams. So that I trust you will not find my hope so extravagant as it may appear at first view. Let us keep peace & sacrafice nothing for a precarious commerce, and we shall find resources within ourselves to supply all our wants.

Permit me now Sir, to touch upon a painfull subject which delicacy to Mr Jefferson has hitherto kept me, & my connections from saying any thing upon, but which has now become a matter of so much notoriety, & excited such alarm among men of all parties in this, & the nieghbouring states where the rights of property seem to be more an object of attention than in some others, that further silence might be construed in to an approbation of the measure, or a disregard for the interests of one that we essteem & Love. You will easily see sir that I allude to the eviction of my brother from a property dearly earned by exile from his friends & family, & which is essential to the settlement of his affairs with his public & private creditors.[5] I am satisfied that Mr Jefferson must have been grosly imposed upon by the misstatment of some malicious person, or he never could have been led to wound by such an act of severity, the interest of a man who certainly had rendered him essential services at the time of his election, or the feelings of a family to whom he has owed his principal support within this state. I enter no further into the merits of the case, than to say, tho my education & habbits have led me much into the company of eminent lawyers, I have never yet met with one that had a doubt either as to the merrits of his title, or of the unconstitutionality of the means used to divest my brother of his esstate. Reflecting men of all parties, & among them the warmest of Mr Jeffersons friends, acknowledge, that if under the shadow of a law which would be unconstitutional if it realy applyed to the case, an individual can be deprived of his esstate without the forms of law, if the inferior officers of the executive can trample on the process of the courts with impunity, that we have ceased to live under a free Government. Forgive me Sir, if I add, that as this wrong was done by the executive, a reference to the legislature can not dispence with the claim he has upon the executive to [see] him righted. I flatter myself Sir, that however free these remarks may appear, your candour will admit that they are not less dictated by my personal esteem for you, & my conviction that the constitution & the law will be your constant guide than by my affection for my brother. I have the honor to [be] with the highest essteem & most respectful attatchment Dear Sir Your most Obt hum Servant

ROBT R LIVINGSTON

P. S. I have taken the liberty to place a book for Mr Jefferson & one for Mr Custis[6] under your cover.

RC (DLC); draft (NHi: Livingston Papers). Postscript not included in draft. Stylistic differences between RC and draft have not been noted.

1. Robert R. Livingston, *Essay on Sheep; Their Varieties—Account of the Merinoes of Spain, France, &c.* . . . (New York, 1809; Shaw and Shoemaker 17926).

2. French officials refused an export license for the sheep after JM had offered cargo space on a public vessel (*PJM-PS*, 1:38, 230–31).

3. Robert L. Livingston married Robert R. Livingston's daughter Margaret Maria in 1798. He served as his father-in-law's secretary in France, 1801–4, and remained in that country for several years thereafter (George Dangerfield, *Chancellor Robert R. Livingston of New York, 1746–1813* [New York, 1960], pp. 281–82, 309, 380–81, 386, 409–10).

4. In the draft the remainder of this paragraph reads: "I have refused from two different gent 1000 ℔ for a favorite ram of my own breeding, & I am told by Docr Bard that his must has been refused for another in Dutches County who makes this year 600 ℔ by tuping the ewes of farmers in that neighbourhood. Many of us have already extended our flocks to five & six hundred when we usualy only kept about 40 or fifty & one gent in Genessee has now 1500. These flocks are always composed of picked sheep selected with a view to crossing them by Merino rams. So that I trust you will not think my hope so extravagant as it appears at first view. Let us keep peace, & sacrafice nothing for a precarious commerce, & we shall find resources within our selves to supply all our wants."

5. Livingston referred to the Batture controversy involving his brother Edward's claims to alluvial riverfront land in New Orleans. Those claims, which Jefferson had challenged in 1808 by taking the position that the land in question belonged to the U.S., led to a long and complex legal battle when Livingston brought a suit against the retired president in 1810 in order to recover his title. The dispute has been extensively discussed by the biographers of

both Jefferson and Livingston and by several legal historians (see Malone, *Jefferson and His Time*, 6:55–73; William B. Hatcher, *Edward Livingston: Jeffersonian Republican and Jacksonian Democrat* [University City, La., 1940], pp. 139–89; Dargo, *Jefferson's Louisiana*, pp. 74–101; and Edward Dumbauld, *Thomas Jefferson and the Law* [Norman, Okla., 1978], pp. 36–74). Many of the public documents on the matter are printed in *ASP, Public Lands*, 2:5–9, 12–102.

6. George Washington Parke Custis (1781–1857) lived at Arlington, in Fairfax County, Virginia, where he pursued an interest in farming and wool production.

§ From the Indian Inhabitants of New Stockbridge, New York. *25 October 1809*. The inhabitants, who are "part of the Moheconnuk Tribe of Indians," express gratitude for the $350 annual grant but ask that instead of receiving only cash a part of the annuity be paid "in certain articles of Clothing and Impliments of Husbandry." Lists hoes, plows, "Cotton-Shirting," blankets, and other goods, which are sought for distribution "under the Inspection & direction of Mr. Parish the Superintendant of Indian affairs in this Department."

RC and enclosures (DNA: RG 107, LRUS, M-1809). RC 1 p. Addressed to the president and signed by David Zuns and three others. Cover addressed to secretary of war. Docketed by a War Department clerk as received 29 Dec. 1809. Enclosures are a power of attorney to William Holmes and Cornelius Konkapot (1 p.) and a list of sixty-seven inhabitants of the village (1 p.).

Madison and Lafayette's Louisiana Lands
26 October 1809

EDITORIAL NOTE

A full account of the American efforts to recompense the marquis de Lafayette for his Revolutionary War services has yet to appear. The business was a long and complicated one, as was JM's involvement in it. This commenced in 1802 while JM was secretary of state and continued into his second presidential term. Not even retirement from the presidency in 1817, however, would entirely relieve JM from his entanglement in Lafayette's concerns, and as late as 1829 he was still receiving correspondence arising from his participation in events that had begun more than a quarter of a century earlier. In this respect, the story of Lafayette and his Louisiana lands was a difficult, but by no means a wholly unusual, episode in the annals of European land speculation in the New World.

JM had known Lafayette since 1784, and it is clear that he did not respond warmly to the Frenchman's optimistic and enthusiastic personality. He regarded the marquis as shallow and vain, although he never let this opinion blind him to the importance of Lafayette's sincere commitment to the cause of American liberty. When Congress voted a cash payment of $24,424 in 1794 to assist Lafayette's family during the hard times that befell them in France after 1791, JM very probably supported the measure, and in one of his final acts before leaving Congress in 1797 he had also approved of the American efforts then being made to secure Lafayette's release from his Austrian captivity at Olmutz. By the beginning of the nineteenth century Lafayette had been restored to his estates and to his family, but he was often in indifferent health and also in considerable financial distress (see *PJM*, 8:120–21 and nn., 16:498–99).

News of Lafayette's plight was transmitted to the United States by American visitors to Paris, including James Monroe and John Dawson, who had succeeded to JM's seat in the House of Representatives in 1797. Even Lafayette himself, when he took the initiative in reopening his correspondence with JM in December 1802, did not trouble to conceal that he was financially embarrassed, and he hinted he would be happy to accept any gift that well-disposed American friends might offer him. Evidently Dawson had raised the possibility during his visit in 1801 that Lafayette might receive some of the land warrants that had been set aside for officers of the Continental army, and it was Dawson again, in 1803, who attached a rider to a military lands bill to award the marquis an 11,520-acre tract in the lands reserved for Virginian veterans in the region north of the Kentucky and Ohio rivers. It is unlikely that Dawson took this step without the knowledge of both Jefferson and JM, and the former, to increase the value of the grant, subsequently sought and obtained congressional consent in 1804 to relocate Lafayette's lands in the recently acquired Orleans Territory. Lafayette was quick to respond. On learning of the congressional grants of 1803–4, he forwarded JM several powers of attorney to act on his behalf, and JM thus became Lafayette's American agent, a position he held for more than a decade (Lafayette to JM, 1 Dec. 1802 [NIC]; Lafayette to JM, 7 July 1803 and 5 Oct. 1804 [PHi]).

From 1804 onward Lafayette sent JM many profuse and lengthy letters, which JM seldom bothered to acknowledge, much less reciprocate in kind. Generally, JM preferred to discharge his agency to Lafayette by communicating instructions and suggestions to others better placed to execute them. These included, principally, treasury secretary Gallatin, Orleans territorial governor William C. C. Claiborne, and Armand Duplantier, a former French army officer who had settled in Louisiana and whom JM chose in 1805 for the tasks of selecting and surveying the best lots of land to be comprised in Lafayette's tract. At all times JM was careful to try to give effect to his client's wishes, but the reality of his situation on many occasions was that he had little enough solid news to announce. Consequently, he tended to leave it to others, notably to Jefferson, to American diplomatic agents abroad, or to Duplantier himself, to report back to the eager and anxious Lafayette in France. Throughout this correspondence the marquis constantly expressed his deep sense of gratitude for any actions taken on his behalf, but he also protested on more than one occasion against what he felt to be an element of coldness and reserve in JM's handling of his affairs (JM to Armand Duplantier, 2 June 1805 [DLC]; Lafayette to JM, 16 Oct. 1805, 10 June 1807, and 26 Sept. 1807 [PHi]; JM to Lafayette, 21 Feb. 1806 [DLC]; JM to Lafayette, 1 May 1809, *PJM-PS*, 1:150–51).

Of necessity Lafayette had little choice other than to entrust the managing of his business to JM, but he had nonetheless a fairly clear notion of how his Louisiana lands should repair his fortunes. His first priority was to realize a portion of his new asset in cash to permit him to discharge by 1807 a large debt, owed mainly to Alexander Baring and Daniel Parker, who had advanced him funds during the years immediately after his release from Olmutz. With his debt cleared, Lafayette then wanted to draw a permanent revenue from long-term leases on his remaining lands while at the same time building up an investment to bequeath to his heirs. To help raise the cash, Jefferson had suggested that some of Lafayette's grant be located in urban property with a potentially high commercial value, and in April 1806 Duplantier accordingly filed a warrant for 1,000 acres adjacent to the downtown area of New Orleans (Lafayette to JM, 10 Oct. 1804 and 22 Apr. 1805 [PHi]).

The city area, however, was subject to a multitude of competing titles, including some in the name of Jean Gravier, whose legacy in the form of Edward Livingston's claim to the New Orleans batture was to return to haunt both Jefferson and JM during the summer of 1810. The City Corporation also contested Duplantier's actions, and in response Jefferson had to secure further congressional action in 1807, both to adjust the City Corporation's claims and to allow Lafayette to receive warrants for lots containing as little as 500 acres of land. On that basis, Duplantier then filed another warrant for 503 acres of New Orleans land in November 1807, but the business of resolving the remaining competing claims in order to give Lafayette clear title dragged on for years. Ultimately, the marquis did not receive the patents for this New Orleans land until his visit to the United States in 1824–25, but long before then he had been compelled to make other arrangements for discharging his debt, and these effectively nullified his plans for drawing long-term financial benefit from his gift (Lafayette to JM, 15 Nov. 1806 [PHi]; Jefferson to Lafayette, Jan. 1804, 14 Feb. 1806, and 26 May 1807, in Chinard, *Letters of Lafayette and Jefferson*, pp. 226, 242, 257).

The location and disposal of the remaining 11,000 acres of Lafayette's grant was almost as difficult and complicated as the New Orleans transactions. In October 1805 Lafayette, whose needs and expectations were considerable and always growing, had expressed an interest in some rich Mississippi bottom cotton lands, and JM, after consulting with territorial governor Claiborne, suggested in 1806 that Duplantier file some claims in the parish of Pointe Coupee. But here too there were delays, arising as before from conflicting titles, the inaccuracies of earlier surveys, and the seemingly interminable processes of the law. More than one settler in the Pointe Coupee region appealed to JM to mediate with Lafayette in the matter of conflicting titles, and some of these disputes were not resolved until the 1850s. By the spring of 1810, however, much of the business regarding the lands at Pointe Coupee had been completed, and in May of that year JM was finally able to entrust nine patents for 9,000 acres of land to David Parish for conveyance to Lafayette in France (Lafayette to JM, 16 Oct. 1805 [PHi]; JM to Lafayette, 21 Feb. 1806 [DLC]; JM to Lafayette, 18 and 19 May 1810; George de Passau to JM, 10 Oct. 1810; Ebenezer Cooley to JM, 5 Jan. 1811 [DNA: RG 59, ML]).

Unfortunately, by this time Lafayette's financial situation had deteriorated still further, since he had neither received cash from his New Orleans land nor been able to discharge the debt that had fallen due in 1807. Consequently, as soon as he received the first lot of his Pointe Coupee patents late in 1810, Lafayette had little option but to try to sell them in order to clear his debt. He found that the value of American land on the European market was considerably less than he had anticipated. Nevertheless, over the next two years Lafayette sold all of his Pointe Coupee land and also some of his New Orleans property. His purchasers were three Englishmen—Alexander Baring, Sir John Coghill, and Henry Seymour. Baring took 5,000 acres at Pointe Coupee, while Coghill purchased the other 4,000 acres and paid for an interest in the tract at New Orleans as well. At this time, too, Lafayette sold his remaining 2,000 acres of Pointe Coupee land to Henry Seymour, even though he did not receive the patents for them until 1814 (Lafayette to JM, 12 Mar. 1811, 12, 13, 22 Apr., 6 Oct. 1812, and 18 Aug. 1814 [PHi]).

As a result of these transactions, Lafayette was finally able to proclaim in late 1814 that he was "perfectly Clear of debts and pecuniary Embarrassments," and he thereafter pressed JM to expedite the details concerning the title to his grant in New Orleans. Progress here, however, was no more rapid than it had been earlier. As has already been mentioned, the marquis eventually received title to 503 acres of city land after his visit to New Orleans in 1825. Much of this property was still encumbered with conflicting claims and many of them were subsequently found to be valid. The matter was finally settled in 1835, but by then both the marquis and his English purchaser were dead (Lafayette to Jefferson, 14 Aug. 1814, Chinard, *Letters of Lafayette and Jefferson*, p. 346).

These problems with the Louisiana lands notwithstanding, the grant had clearly eased some of Lafayette's difficulties, even if he did not obtain as much financial benefit as he had anticipated or would have liked. Possibly, he might have been better off in this respect had he and Jefferson decided to leave the grant in its original location northwest of the Kentucky and Ohio rivers, but in any event Congress redressed the matter in 1824 by making another gift of $200,000 in cash along with a further allotment of 23,040 acres of public land. For JM, though, the business proved to be an unremitting and seemingly never-ending task, and one might surmise that when he joined Lafayette and Jefferson in November 1824 for their final meeting, the matter of Louisiana land was never mentioned (*U.S. Statutes at Large*, 6:320).

(Secondary sources used for this note: Kathryn T. Abbey, "The Land Ventures of General Lafayette in the Territory of Orleans and State of Louisiana," *La. Historical Quarterly*, 16 [1933]: 359–73; and Paul V. Lutz, "Lafayette's Louisiana Estate: The Unusual Dealings between the Marquis and Three Wealthy Englishmen," *La. Studies*, 6 [1967]: 333–60.)

From Lafayette

MY DEAR SIR   PARIS 26h October 1809

I Wish Gnl. Armstrong May before the departure of the Vessel Know Something More of the Late Austrian peace than the principal Ministers of the Emperor Knew of it Last Evening. They Have Been informed With the public that a treaty Has Been Signed. They are to day Summoned to fontainebleau. The Rest is Mere Conjecture which Cannot fail to be Soon Ascertained. Yet the General form of the Business Has Appeared to Gnl.

Armstrong to Contain Sufficient information, With Respect to the Main Concerns of the U. S., for an immediate dispatch to You.[1] I Will not let it Go, Before I Return to La Grange, Without Letting You Hear of a friend Whose Affection and Good Wishes Accompagny Every public and personal Concern of Your life. I Have not this Very Long While Heard from You. Nothing Has Reached me from M. duplantier Since the Letter Where He Considered the Remisness of the City in not Availing themselves of the Grant of Congress for their Boundaries as a Circumstance Which Might Become Very Advantageous to me. But He Has Sent Neither titles or documents for the Remaining part of the Lot Near the town, nor for the other Locations. Had they Been forwarded to, and of Course Signed By You, they Would Have Come With the Last Vessels. The Want of them Has Hitherto defeated Every Arrangement tried in Europe for a General Clearance of My fortune, and the temporary Means to prevent An Unretrievable Ruin Have, in the Course of Several Years, Greatly increased the Load and the danger, So that it Becomes more difficult and Extremely Urging to Come to a Conclusion. If it Were once done, I Would Be Very Easy in the Moderate Life I Lead With My family of children and Grand children, 13 in all, on the farm which, Under My Agricultural pursuits thrives Very Well, and a Small Addition of Revenue, as Explained in My former letters, Would Have Been Amply Sufficient. But the important, and to fulfill Your kind Views in My Behalf, the Necessary point is to Be Enabled, By the proper titles, to Be Countenanced in the Arrangements which Should at once Relieve me from the increasing Weight of My debts in Europe. To Be Under Such an obligation to the Exertions of my friends, and the Benevolence of the people in the United States is a Circumstance of which I feel Equally proud and Happy. While I Enjoy the great Share You Have in it, My dear Madison, I Regret the trouble it gives You, and the ⟨wants⟩ there Have Been for Such an Extent of Magnificent Kindness. I Beg You to present My Grateful aknowledgements to Mr. Gallatin And with Affectionate Apologies for the importunate Repetition of private pecuniary Concerns, I shall only, this day, offer You the Expression of My old friendship and Highest Regard

LAFAYETTE

RC (PHi). Docketed by JM.

1. Armstrong, anxious to notify the Madison administration of the terms of the Treaty of Vienna, contracted to hire the ship *Happy Return* to carry diplomatic dispatches to New York and to take as passengers some released American seamen who had been captured and imprisoned by a French cruiser. On the day Lafayette wrote, Armstrong informed Robert Smith that while he was "still in the dark as to the details of the treaty," he had learned that one provision surrendered to France "all the Country South of the river Sava. . . . [Thus] France gets all the ports of the Adriatic" (DNA: RG 59, DD, France). The result extended Napoleon's Continental System from northern Germany to the fringes of the Ottoman Em-

pire (Georges Lefebvre, *Napoleon: From Tilsit to Waterloo, 1807–1815*, trans. J. E. Anderson [New York, 1969], pp. 65–69).

From Thomas B. Robertson

SIR   NEW ORLEANS 26 Oct 09

The Office of Navy Agent has become vacant in consequence of the unfortunate death of Mr Spence. I recommend with much pleasure Mr Samuel Hambleton as a gentleman in all respects qualified to discharge the duties of that Office.[1] I have the honor to be Very respectfuly yo ob St

TH B ROBERTSON[2]

RC (DNA: RG 45, Misc. Letters Received). Cover marked "Received under envelope to, and forwarded by Paul Hamilton."

1. JM later nominated John K. Smith for the vacancy (see Paul Hamilton to JM, 4 Dec. 1809, and n. 1).
2. Thomas B. Robertson was secretary for the territory of Orleans from 1807 to 1811.

§ From Jared Mansfield. *26 October 1809, Chambersburg, Pennsylvania.* Requests JM to continue David Phipps, presently a retired sailing master on half pay, in actual service so that he might "receive the full emoluments of that place." Describes Phipps's career as a naval officer during the Revolution and as a lieutenant in the U.S. Navy during the Adams administration. Mentions that Phipps is a man of "republican principles" whose "property & the best of his life, have been exhausted at the call of his country, & he has received little or no compensation."[1]

RC (DNA: RG 45, Misc. Letters Received). 3 pp.

1. JM referred this letter to the secretary of the navy, who informed Mansfield that "early attention will be paid to the Subject, and that there exists a strong disposition with me, to respect in any instance the claims of meritorious veterans." Phipps evidently served as sailing master until his death in 1825 (Paul Hamilton to Mansfield, 22 Nov. 1809 [DNA: RG 45, Misc. Letters Sent]; *ASP, Naval Affairs*, 1:1089; Callahan, *List of Officers of the Navy*, p. 435).

¶ To John Strode. Letter not found. *26 October 1809.* Acknowledged in Strode to JM, 7 Feb. 1810. Proposes an arrangement for repayment of debt owed by Strode. The Montpelier plantation manager, Gideon Gooch, will act on JM's behalf.

To William Bentley

Sir   WASHINGTON Ocr. 28. 1809

SIR   WASHINGTON Ocr. 28. 1809

I received in due time your friendly letter of August 12. last.[1]

My respect for your sentiments as well as justice to my own, require that I should say, in explanation of my not complying with your considerate hint, that I was restrained by an apprehensiveness, that an expression, at that period, of the gratitude and admiration which I feel in a degree exceeded by no Citizen, for the venerable Hero of 77. & inflexible Patriot of 1809, might be ascribed less to the real motive, than to the approaching event in Vermont. I will confess also, that without some incident particularly susceptible of, if not inviting the step suggested, its apparent abruptness & awkwardness must always expose it in some degree to a misconstruction, very likely to impair the benevolent effect. I shall not however lose sight of the idea; nor neglect the present occasion of assuring you, that the feelings which led to it, have not failed to enhance the esteem, which I have long known to be due to your eminent talents, & the virtues which adorn them.

JAMES MADISON

RC (NjP: Crane Collection).

1. Bentley had asked JM to send Maj. Gen. John Stark a congratulatory letter noting the anniversary of the Battle of Bennington (*PJM-PS*, 1:328–29). JM hesitated to respond from fear that such a letter might be misused in the 5 Sept. Vermont state election, in which Republicans made substantial gains (Bennington, Vt., *Green-Mountain Farmer*, 25 Sept. and 2 Oct. 1809).

To the Chairman of the Republican Meeting of McIntosh County, Georgia

SIR   WASHINGTON October 28. 1809

I have just recd. under your cover of Sepr. 25.[1] the unanimous Resolutions of a Meeting of the Inhabitants of McIntosh County.

In the present unsettled State of our external affairs, and particularly in that produced by the refusal of the British Government to fulfill an engagement, characterized as was that of its Minister Plenipotentiary; faithful Citizens of every Section of their Country, can not but be warmly alive to the multiplied wrongs which it has suffered; and to the important duty of supporting the Constituted Authorities, in the discharge of theirs.

The Resolns. which you have transmitted, are a proof that the Citizens of the County of McIntosh, are animated by such feelings. As far as these may be seconded by a confidence in the principles & views which guide the Ex. Dept. it becomes me to express the sensibility which is due to it; to which I add my respects & friendly wishes for those at whose Meeting you presided.

Draft (DLC). Addressed to "Col. John McIntosh."

1. McIntosh's covering letter was dated 6 Oct. 1809 (see *PJM-PS*, 1:390–91 and n.).

To Eleuthère Irénée DuPont

S<small>IR</small>   W<small>ASHINGTON</small> Ocr. 28. 1809
    I recd. lately from your father a Copy of the Works of Mr. Turgot, for you, accompanying one which he was so good as to forward for myself.[1] Having thus long waited in vain for an opportunity to Wilmington, other than the Mail, for which the Packet, Consisting of seven Vol: 8°., would be too large, I think it best to enable you, by this information, to co-operate in seeking a proper conveyance. The Books will be delivered or disposed of, as you may please to intimate. Accept my friendly respects
                                                        J<small>AMES</small> M<small>ADISON</small>

RC (DeGE).

1. On Pierre Samuel DuPont de Nemours's edition of Turgot's *Works*, see JM to Jefferson, 6 Oct. 1809, and n. 2. DuPont de Nemours's son, Eleuthère Irénée, had previously written JM concerning his gunpowder factory (E. I. DuPont to JM, ca. Oct. 1804 [DeGE]).

From Albert Gallatin

S<small>IR</small>.   T<small>REASURY</small> D<small>EPARTMENT</small> Octer. 28th 1809
    I have the honor to enclose two letters from the district attorney of Georgia, respecting the misbehaviour of Benjamin Wall Marshal for that district.[1] The business of the Savannah custom house had been transacted in so improper manner for a great length of time by the successive collectors, that unable to arrange & understand their respective accounts, I was obliged to send there last winter an intelligent clerk of this Department, for the purpose of making a thorough investigation of former transactions, and of giving such directions as might prevent a recurrence of similar irregularities.[2] He staid there several months and returned last summer,

when it was discovered that the Marshal was accountable for more than two hundred thousand dollars, being the amount of executions which he had either omitted to enforce, or which having collected he had not paid over. The district attorney was instructed to adopt every possible means to make him account; and as it was extremely desireable to ascertain what amount had been collected & what was still due by the persons against whom the executions had been issued, it was thought eligible (with the advice of the district attorney) that he should be permitted to hold the office some time longer. It will, however, be perceived by the enclosed letters, as well as by the memorandum marked *A*, that he will, on the 14th of next month, either have accounted, or be committed for contempt. As the object for which he was continued will therefore, by that time, be either accomplished or unattainable; and as it is important to put it immediately out of his power to encrease the amount of his delinquency by collecting more money as Marshal; I beg leave respectfully to submit the propriety and necessity of his removal. I think that perfect confidence may be placed in the fidelity and judgment of the district judge and district attorney, and that their joint recommendation in favor of John Eppinger as a proper person to succeed Mr Wall, may be fully relied on.

RC (DLC). Signature clipped. Enclosed memorandum not found.

1. Gallatin probably enclosed William Bellinger Bullock's letters to Gabriel Duvall dated 30 Sept. 1809 (2 pp.) and 13 Oct. 1809 (2 pp.) (DNA: RG 217, Letters Received from Marshals, District Attorneys, and Others). In his 30 Sept. letter Bullock, the district attorney for Georgia, enclosed extracts from the district court minutes of 20, 26, and 29 Sept., which granted successive extensions in the case against U.S. marshal Benjamin Wall. On 13 Oct. Bullock reported that "the Marshal has recd. upwards of twelve thousand Dollars, which he has not paid over to the collector or myself," and he enclosed extracts from the district court minutes of 5 and 12 Oct., the latter of which "peremptorily ordered that . . . Benjamin Wall . . . make due return" by 14 Nov. 1809.

2. Gallatin had sent William Parker, a clerk in the auditor's office, to investigate and report on arrangements at the Savannah customhouse and to introduce accounting procedures that had been recommended but neglected. Parker reported irregularities in execution of bonds by Benjamin Wall, and Gallatin directed Bullock to try "to obtain a true account and to recover the money." He asked Bullock to recommend a suitable successor for Wall, "Yet an immediate removal might encrease the difficulties." JM nominated John Eppinger as Wall's replacement on 18 Dec., and the Senate confirmed his appointment a week later (Gallatin to Bullock, 12 July 1809, Gallatin to Wall, 12 July 1809, reproduced in Carl E. Prince and Helene H. Fineman, eds., *The Papers of Albert Gallatin* [microfilm ed.; 46 reels; Philadelphia, 1969], reel 19; *Senate Exec. Proceedings*, 2:130, 133).

§ From Lewis Lowrey. *28 October 1809, Halifax Court House, Virginia.* Encloses certificates received for Revolutionary War service and asks JM to see that they are exchanged for a land office warrant. Requests this favor "as I am so Crazy & infirm that I am not able to wait on you myself."

RC (DNA: RG 107, LRUS, L-1809). 1 p. Enclosures not found. Docketed by a clerk, "Ackgd. 4h. Novr. 1809." JM referred the request to the secretary of war, who sought from Lowrey evidence of his enlistment and his service until the end of the Revolutionary War (Eustis to Lowrey, 6 Nov. 1809 [DNA: RG 107, LSMA]).

§ From Carré de Sainte-Gemme. *28 October 1809, Saintes, Charente Inférieure, France.* Offers JM felicitations as "a man who lived some years in the happy land of United States and was honoured with your acquaintance."

RC (DLC). 1 p.

From James Dinsmore

SIR   MONTPELEIR Octr 29th 1809

I intended before you went from here to mention to you whether you would not think it adviseable to put two windows in the end of the library room? but it escaped My Memory; I have been Reflecting on it Since and beleive it will as without them the wall will have a very Dead appearance, and there will be no direct Veiw towards the temple Should you ever build one. My reason for omitting them in the Drawing was that the Space might be occupyd for Book Shelves but I beleive there will be sufficiency of room without as the peirs between the windows will be large and the whole of the other end except the breadth of the door may be occupyd for that purpose: Should you approve of putting them you will please to let me know by return of post. It will also be Necessary to add 24 lights of 12 by 18 inch glass to the Memod.[1] You will also please to Mention when we May expect the Sheet Iron & whether it will be of the breadth Specifyed; also whether Mrs Madison wishes a boiler fixed in the kitchen & what will be the Size of it. Mr Chisholme has done Makeing Bricks and has got the foundation for the addition dug out. You will please to Mention whether you wish a Cornice put up in the Passage, I have no doubt but it would be a considerable addition to the look of it. I Shall Send a Memdm by Mr Gooch of Some nails & other things that we Shall want by the waggon in addition to that already furnished. Inclosed I Send you the Size of the egg & Dart Moulding for the Bedmould of the Cornice to be put up in the Dineing room; it will add greatly to the Beauty of the Cornice & I Suppose May Cost about 0/9d per foot. Should you approve of it, would wish it to be sent on by the waggon. Mr Andrews will Make it on Short notice. Mr Chisholme requests me to mention that he will thank you to Send him one Hundred Dollars as Soon as Convenient. I am Sir with respect your Humble Servt

JAS. DINSMORE

RC and enclosure (DLC). Enclosure is a drawing of a section of "100 feet egg & dart moulding of this Size."

1. Dinsmore's memorandums requesting construction supplies at Montpelier have not been found, but his surviving carpentry accounts, dating from September 1809 to December 1812, provide a detailed record of material used (ViU: John Hartwell Cocke Papers). For an example of these accounts, see Hunt-Jones, *Dolley and the "Great Little Madison,"* p. 68.

From Albert Gallatin

SIR: TREASURY DEPARTMENT 29th. Octr 1809

It having been understood last autumn that a number of intruders had settled on the public lands in Madison County (Bend of Tennessee) Mississippi Territory Mr Thomas Freeman was instructed by direction of the President to notify those persons that unless they signed declarations that they had no claim to the land & obtained permissions to remain as tenants at will, they would be removed by force.[1] A very general compliance took place, the heads of three to four hundred families having signed the requisite declaration, and a Mr Michael Harrison who appeared to be the only Yazoo claimant on the land having promised to remove. But after the lands had been advertised for sale he published an advertisement herein enclosed[2] dated from Madison County giving notice of his claim &c.

This induced me to write to Mr Dickson the Register whose answer I have now the honor to enclose.[3] The threats & notices have not effected the sales: for about 24 000 acres have been sold in three weeks for a sum exceeding Sixty thousand dollars. But the Sheriff has stated that there are more than three hundred families of intruders who he thinks will keep forcible possession. Under these circumstances it is submitted whether Michael Harrison should be immediately removed by force,[4] or whether it would be desirable that Congress should in the first place extend the time for granting permissions to remain on the land as tenants at will and afterwards to carry rigourously the law into effect on those who shall not have complied with its terms or will refuse to give possession to the purchaser. I have the honor to be respectfully Sir Your Most Obedt Servt

ALBERT GALLATIN

Tr (DNA: RG 56, Letters Relating to Public Lands). For enclosures, see nn. 2 and 3.

1. Acting on behalf of the president in 1808, Gallatin had authorized Freeman, the deputy surveyor in the Mississippi Territory, to serve notice on settlers in the designated area that they could apply for permission "to remain on the land as tenants at will." Any settlers who acted under Yazoo Company titles either "forcibly to occupy the lands, or to extort money from ignorant Settlers" were, however, to be removed (Gallatin to Freeman, 25 Oct. 1808, Carter, *Territorial Papers, Mississippi*, 5:659–60). For the background, see

Thomas P. Abernethy, *The South in the New Nation, 1789–1819* (Baton Rouge, La., 1961), pp. 164–66.

2. The advertisement is on a newspaper clipping attached to an extract of a letter from William Dickson, 22 July 1809 (reproduced in *Papers of Gallatin* [microfilm ed.], reel 19).

3. William Dickson to Gallatin, 28 Sept. 1809 (Carter, *Territorial Papers, Mississippi*, 6:20–21).

4. Michael Harrison held land and sold claims under a title from one of the fraudulent Yazoo land companies. Since the Supreme Court decision in *Fletcher* v. *Peck* strengthened his position, Harrison remained a source of trouble for Gallatin (Gallatin to secretary of war, 5 July 1810, *ASP, Public Lands*, 2:251).

From John G. Jackson

SIR,   CLARKSBURG, Oct. 29th, 1809.

I have the honor to transmit to you the enclosed resolutions, in compliance with the wishes of the officers and privates of the 119th regiment of Virginia militia.[1]

I derive peculiar satisfaction from assuring you, that notwithstanding many of the persons who united in the resolutions have been inimical to the last and to the present administration, their hostility is particularly offered up upon the altar of their country's safety; whereby they evince, that when it becomes a question—not which of two rival parties shall fill the great offices of state, but whether the rights, the honor, and liberties we enjoy, shall be invaded with impunity, or maintained in the same spirit with which they were established—all the petty feuds and minor dissentions amongst them, will be disregarded, and but one voice be heard for UNION and OUR COUNTRY. They indeed show, that theirs is an honest difference of opinion, subordinate to the great duties of patriotism; to the paramount interests of the nation; and afford a pleasing presage of what the government may justly expect from all ranks of citizens whose feelings and interests are truly American, when necessity shall drive it to the last resort of nations.

For myself, sir, and in the name of the regiment, I solicit, that if the services of the militia be wanted, our tender may be accepted. I have the honor to be, Your most obedient,

J. G. JACKSON

[Enclosure]

At a regimental muster of the 119th regiment of Virginia militia, held at William Martin's, in the county of Harrison, on the 28th of October, 1809—John G. Jackson, Lieut. Col. Commandant, was appointed Chairman, and Major Isaac Coplin, Secretary.

The Chairman addressed the regiment upon the critical situation of our affairs, proceeding from the injustice of foreign nations—adverted to the reliance which the government and people place upon the militia as the natural, best defence of the state, and firmest bulwark of its liberties; enjoined upon them the strictest attention to discipline and to the measures of the government; so that if the legions of the United States were called into service, knowing their duty, the justice of their cause and the necessity of the appeal to arms; they may strike terror into the mercenary ranks of their enemies, and by a prompt, decisive blow stop the ravages of a protracted war.

The Chairman then submitted the following resolutions, and the question being put upon them severally, they were UNANIMOUSLY adopted.

RESOLVED, That we will, at all hazards, maintain the rights and liberties of our country, transmitted to us by the fathers of the revolution, against the unjust aggressions of all nations.

RESOLVED, That the freedom we enjoy can be preserved alone by vigilantly attending to the faithful administration of our national concerns.

RESOLVED, That we have been mindful of our duty in examining those concerns, and the result is a conviction, that our government has asked nothing which can be HONORABLY abandoned, or JUSTLY refused.

RESOLVED, That the injustice of foreign nations has convinced us of the necessity of relying upon our energies alone, for the maintenance of our rights, and if they persist in their attacks upon us, we will rally around our government and exert those energies for the chastisement of the aggressors in the most effectual manner which God and nature shall enable us.

RESOLVED, That we place a firm re[li]ance upon the wisdom and discretion of the President, and Congress of the United States, to assert our rights in the manner our honor requires;—and we hereby tender our services to our country, if they shall determine to resort to war, for maintaining those rights.

RESOLVED, That the Chairman be requested, on behalf of the officers and privates of the regiment, to forward a copy of these resolutions to the President of the United States.

(Signed) J. G. JACKSON,
     Chairman.

(Signed) ISAAC COPLIN,
     Secretary.

Printed copy (Baltimore *American, and Commercial Daily Advertiser*, 15 Jan. 1810). Covering letter misdated 19 Oct. 1809; date corrected on the basis of enclosure and JM to Jackson, 3 Dec. 1809.

1. Jackson had been appointed commandant of the regiment on 23 May (Stephen W. Brown, *Voice of the New West: John G. Jackson, His Life and Times* [Macon, Ga., 1985], p. 110).

From Robert Smith

SIR,   Sunday Morning [29 October 1809]

I have not yet sufficiently regained my health to give the necessary attention to Mr Jackson's last letter.[1] But it appears to me that we can't consider it a satisfactory explanation, especially after having so solemnly declared that to be satisfactory it must shew not merely a violation of instructions but must moreover shew reasons strong & solid. What then are the reasons which we can admit or can consider strong & solid? We cannot accept this without in my Opinion abandoning the ground taken in the preceding notes. I am disposed, at present, to think it best to discontinue the correspondence with Jackson as unworthy of the attention of the govt. and to say to Pinkney whatever we wish to be laid before Congress. I will be fully able to attend at any hour tomorrow a consultation upon the question whether Mr Jackson ought to be answered or upon any other subject. With great Regard &c &c &c

                                                              R SMITH

RC (DLC: Rives Collection, Madison Papers). Undated. Date here assigned on the basis of internal evidence and circumstances described in n. 1.

1. On 1 Nov. Smith wrote to Francis James Jackson, mentioning an illness that "for several days" rendered him "utterly unfit for business." Smith evidently had before him Jackson's letter of 23 Oct., which, in turn, was Jackson's response to Smith's letter of 19 Oct. where the secretary of state had stipulated that the British minister should show "*strong and solid reasons*" to explain the disavowal of the agreement Erskine had made with the U.S. (*ASP, Foreign Relations*, 3:311–14, 317).

To Thomas Jefferson

DEAR SIR   WASHINGTON Ocr. 30. 1809

In the operation of removing from my former quarters, the Digest of the City Code & business, which you had been so good as to furnish me, has, by some unaccountable accident, been either lost, or possibly so thrown out of place, as not to be found.[1] I have written to Capt: Coles,[2] to take Monticello in his way, and ask the favor of you to permit him to take another copy, from your Original. As that letter however may not reach him, I must beg you to signify my wishes to him, in case he should call on you as he probably will.

The Works of Turgot, remain on hand for want of some person to take charge of them to Fredg. They fill a Box abt. 15 inchs. by 12. & 8 inchs deep; too large therefore for the Mail. I shall avail myself of the 1st. oppy.

for sending it on by the Stage. I was in hope, that the Race-field would have furnished some known person, returning by way of Fredg: but I was disappointed;[3] there being very few Virginians there, & none from the Southern districts.

We just learn the melancholy fate of Govr. Lewis which possibly may not have travelled so quickly into your neighbourhood.[4] He had, it seems betrayed latterly repeated symtoms of a disordered mind; and had set out under the care of a friend on a visit to Washington. His first intention was, to make the trip by water; but changing it, at the Chickasaw Bluffs, he struck across towards Nashville. As soon as he had passed the Tennessee, he took advantage of the neglect of his Companion, who had not secured his arms, to put an end to himself. He first fired a pistol, at his head, the ball of which glancing, was ineffectual. With the 2d. he passed a Ball thro' his body, wch. being also without immediate effect, he had recourse to his Dirk with wch he mangled himself considerably. After all he lived till the next morning, with the utmost impatience for death.

I inclose the latest accts. from Europe. Onis has returned to Philada. The reality or degree of his disappt. is not easily ascertained. His last conversation with Mr. Smith, did not manifest ill humour. How could he expect a different result, in the actual State of things? And what motive Can Spain or the Colonies have, in any State of things, to make enemies of the U. S? I see nothing to change the view of Jackson, which I formerly hinted to you.

RC (DLC: Rives Collection, Madison Papers). Complimentary close and signature clipped. Docketed by Jefferson, "recd. Nov. 5."

1. In his reply of 6 Nov. 1809, Jefferson mentioned that he had given copies of the document sought by JM to Thomas Munroe and Robert Brent in order that the officials of Washington, D.C., "might understand what I considered as the limits separating our rights & duties." Possibly Jefferson was referring here to some notes he had drafted between 12 and 18 Oct. 1803 (DLC: Jefferson Papers). In addition to listing the legislation relating to the national capital, these notes also defined the powers of the president to implement the plan for the city of Washington after Congress had assumed jurisdiction over the District of Columbia and established a corporation for its government.

2. Letter not found.

3. JM had attended the Georgetown races on 24 Oct. (Brant, *Madison*, 5:99, 494 n. 19).

4. For the circumstances of Meriwether Lewis's death at Grinder's Stand in central Tennessee on 11 Oct., see Howard I. Kushner, "The Suicide of Meriwether Lewis: A Psychoanalytical Inquiry," *WMQ*, 3d ser., 38 (1981): 464–81.

From Robert Taylor

DEAR SIR   Oct 30th. 1809.

Yours inclosing a fifty dollar bill[1] was duly received and according to direction $47.59 were paid to Mr. Purdy a receipt for which is now inclosed to you—the residue shall be paid to your brother upon the first opportunity. Yrs afftely

ROBERT TAYLOR[2]

RC (DLC). Enclosure not found.

1. Letter not found.
2. Robert Taylor (1763–1845) was an Orange County resident and JM's second cousin. He corresponded with JM occasionally throughout his life (*PJM*, 15:52 n. 3).

From an Unidentified Correspondent

SIR   PHILADELPHIA, [ca. 30] October [1809]

Although I have not the honour of being known to you, I take the liberty of addressing You on a subject of great importance to the Nation and to our party. It is reported here that the Spanish Minister lately arrived at New-York will not be received by the Government, which I hope is a federal fabrication as nothing can justify the refusal of a Minester under such circumstances.[1] I will not presume to point out to you the line of conduct which our Government ought to persue on this occassion. But I consider it my duty to state to you a piece of information I have lately received which will enable you to appreciate the motives by which certain persons are actuated with respect to Spain. A friend in whom I have confidence, has informed me that a Spaniard now in this City of the name of Sarmiento[2] is in possessions [*sic*] of General Smiths Bonds for a debt due to the Spanish Government of upwards of $300,000 £112,000 for dutys on certain Cargos sent from Baltimore to Vera-Cruz. It is said that the payment Of those Bonds have been evaded for upwards of two years under various pretences, and it will probably be a strong motive for the Secretary of State to oppose the reception of the Spanish Minister.

You will readily see that the family of Mr Smith are deeply interested in the overthrow of the Old Spanish Government. I am sorry to find that the present Secretary of State is by no means a good character, and generally considered remarkably cunning. I wish you had not been compelled to appoint him in place of Mr Gallateen. If you have any doubts about the debt due by General Smith to the Spanish government, our friend Dallas can procure you the necessary information as he appears to be intimate with the gentleman that holds the Bonds. Our friends in this City are much dissatisfied with General Smith and his Brother respecting the Leghorn Bills.[3] These transactions injure our cause. I have the pleasure to inform you that even the federalists do not appear dissatisfied with you or Mr Gallateens. I am most respectfully

RC (NN). Unsigned. Date assigned on the basis of the circumstances described in n. 1.

1. On 27 Oct. 1809 the Philadelphia *Aurora General Advertiser* had printed a report described as a Federalist trick that Luis de Onís, who had arrived in New York on 3 Oct., would not be received by the administration.

2. Francisco C. Sarmiento of Philadelphia was an agent for a Spanish treasury official, Don Manuel Sixto Espinosa, and also the brother-in-law of the Philadelphia merchant John Craig. In September 1805 Sarmiento had obtained from Espinosa a permit for Craig to ship flour to Veracruz, and Craig, shortly thereafter, entered into partnerships with both David Parish and Robert Oliver of Baltimore for that purpose. In 1807, however, Sarmiento also sold similar permits to Smith and Buchanan of Baltimore, thus enabling that firm to trade with Veracruz in opposition to the partnerships formed by Craig, Oliver, and Parish (Stuart W. Bruchey, *Robert Oliver, Merchant of Baltimore, 1783–1819* [Baltimore, 1956], pp. 265–67, 288, 299 and n. 197, 312).

3. See *PJM-PS*, 1:68–69 n. 1.

§ From William Cocke.[1] *30 October 1809, Rutledge, Tennessee.* Laments the death of Governor Lewis and offers to serve as his replacement if JM wishes.

RC (DNA: RG 59, LAR, 1809–17, filed under "Cocke"). 2 pp.

1. Cocke had served as a U.S. senator from Tennessee, 1796–97 and 1799–1805, and had recently lost the governor's race to Willie Blount.

§ From François Vigo. *30 October 1809, Vincennes.* Encloses resolutions passed on 28 Oct. 1809 by the officers of the militia that he commands.

Printed copy of RC (Carter, *Territorial Papers, Indiana*, 7:678); printed copy of enclosure (*National Intelligencer*, 8 Dec. 1809; reprinted in Esarey, *Messages and Letters of William Henry Harrison*, Indiana Historical Collections, 1:385–87). Enclosed resolutions of the militia of Knox County, Indiana Territory, urged JM to reappoint William Henry Harrison to the territorial governorship.

§ From the Citizens of Clark County, Indiana Territory. *Ca. 1 November 1809.* Signatories express their disapproval of the petitions circulating in favor of the reappointment of William Henry Harrison as territorial governor. Harrison's principles are "repugnant to the Spirit of *Republicanism*," and the petitioners "mention his sanctioning of a law for the Introduction of *Negroes*." Petitioners pray for a governor "whose Sentiments are more Congenial with those of the People, and with those principles of Liberty which are the greatest Security of our rights."

Printed copy (Carter, *Territorial Papers, Indiana*, 7:705–7). Addressed "To the Honorable the President and Senate of the United States of America." Signed by William Ferguson and 173 others. Undated. Date here assigned by comparison with François Vigo to JM, 30 Oct. 1809.

§ From William Duane. *1 November 1809, Philadelphia*. Introduces Christopher Fitzsimmons of Charleston, South Carolina, and Hugh Colhoun of Philadelphia, both of them admirers of JM's "principles and measures, and those of your predecessor."

RC (DLC). 2 pp. Docketed by JM.

§ Robert Smith to Francis James Jackson. *1 November 1809, Department of State*. Jackson's letter of 23 Oct. discloses that Erskine knew he lacked full authority to negotiate. "It necessarily follows, that the only credentials, yet presented by you, being the same with those presented by him, give you no authority" to make a binding agreement. In such circumstances, negotiations carried on by the U.S. "would not only be a departure from the principle of equality . . . but would moreover be a disregard of the precautions and of the self respect enjoined on the attention of the United States." As to Jackson's intimation that Smith realized Erskine was violating his instructions, asserts "this government had no such knowledge," for if it had, "no such arrangement would have been entered into." Warns that "it [is] my duty to apprize you, that such insinuations are inadmissible in the intercourse of a foreign minister with a government that understands what it owes to itself."

Tr, two copies (DNA: RG 233, President's Messages; and DNA: RG 46, Legislative Proceedings, 11A-E3). 5 pp. Enclosed in JM's 29 Nov. annual message to Congress. Printed in *ASP, Foreign Relations*, 3:317.

From Eleuthère Irénée DuPont

SIR,   ELEUTHERIAN MILLS, November 3d 1809.

I have received the letter with which you have been pleased to honour me. From its contents I find that you have received from france two copies of the works of Mr. Turgot, one of which is intended for me. Give me leave, Sir, to apologise for the liberty taken by my father in making use of your name for sending me the said books; the interruption of trade between france and this country will I hope be considered by you as an excuse.

My partner Mr. Peter Bauduy,[1] who is now at washington for our business, will do himself the honor of waiting upon you and will take charge of the books.

Please to accept of the assurance of my gratefulness and of the hight respect with which I have the honor to be Sir of your Excellency the most obedient and humble Servant,

E. I. duPont.

RC (DLC); FC (DeGE).

1. Peter Bauduy was a wealthy Santo Domingan refugee who settled near Brandywine Creek. He invested heavily in the DuPont powder mill "and used his credit to prod Delaware banks into lending Irénée cash" (Marc Duke, *The Du Ponts: Portrait of a Dynasty* [New York, 1976], pp. 74–75).

§ From John Carroll. *3 November 1809, Baltimore*. Introduces Julius de Menou, a young man who wishes "an opportunity of expressing his respectful veneration for your worth and character, his love and attachment to the government and manners of this country, in which he has been educated from his infancy." Adds his own expression of high esteem.

RC (DLC). 2 pp. Docketed by JM. Carroll was the archbishop of Baltimore. JM received three other letters on de Menou's behalf—from Robert Goodloe Harper, dated 2 Nov. 1809, William DuBourg, 3 Nov. 1809, and Edward Lloyd, 6 Nov. 1809 (DNA: RG 59, LAR, 1809–17, filed under "De Menon" [*sic*]).

§ From John Leonard.[1] *3 November 1809, Barcelona*. Complains of Israel Thorndike's efforts to discredit him in the eyes of the administration.

RC (DNA: RG 59, CD, Barcelona). 2 pp. Addressed to JM as secretary of state and marked "triplicate." Docketed by a clerk as received 19 May 1810.

1. John Leonard of New Jersey had been appointed consul at Barcelona in 1803 (*Senate Exec. Proceedings*, 1:459–60).

To Hobohoilthle

[6 November 1809]

The President of the United States who sits in the place of General Washington, the head of that Government, and your Father, talks to you this day. He receives by Colo. Hawkins your Talk on the 29th. of September.[1] That Talk was at Chattuckfoule. It was from Cowitah and Cussituh, the head towns of Muscogee. It has come strait as if from your mouth to his ear. He answers you. You are the Father and King of your Nation.[2] He believes you are a good Father, because you love your Land and your own Children. He listens well to your talk, because you are a true man. He believes you speak truth.

Your land you say is small, and you have a great many Warriors, and cannot spare any more of it. The line was drawn by us both. Your Land is your own. Nobody can make it smaller without your consent. The Trees and the Game and everything which your land produces is also your own. Nobody can touch them without your leave. The President will not allow them to do it. But you know there are some bad man every where. Some of these men have gone onto your land, and turned out their Cattle & Horses, and hunted, and cut down some of your Trees. The President forbids it. Colonel Hawkins will prevent it in future as much as he can. Particularly on the side of Ocmulgee.[3] Colo. Hawkins has sent Captain Freeman out to make enquiry and put a stop to it.

Our line is on the water's edge. The Islands belong to you. The White People must fish from their own land. They have no right to fish from your land without your leave. If they go ashore on your Side, they must not cut down your Trees. Colo. Hawkins will be told not to suffer it.

You say you are poor; look at your Father, the President when he talks to you concerning this. Turn your ear to him, and believe what he says.

Fence in your Lands, plow as much land as you can, raise corn & Hogs & Cattle. Learn your young Women to card & spin, & let those who are older learn to weave. You will then have food and cloathing and live comfortably. The President advises you to do this. He knows that his red Children can live well if they will follow his advice. Colo. Hawkins will give you Cards and Spinning-wheels and Looms to weave in. Some of your white brothers are also poor, but their fathers put them to such work as is fit for them and they live very well.

Your Powder-Horns you say are empty & you have no bullets. Colo. Hawkins will give you Bullets & fill your Powder-Horns. You can shoot Turkies and kill some Deer; but it is better for you to spin & weave cloathing, and to plow the Land and raise Corn & Cattle.

The President looks at you with the eye of a Father. He hears your Talk as the Talk of a Friend whom he esteems. He keeps Colo. Hawkins, who is a good man, among you to hear your complaints, and to advise and assist you. If the White People trespass again upon your lands talk first to him. If you have any other complaints to make, make them known first to him. Afterwards & when you chuse, talk to the President. His Ear is always open to you. He is your Friend. He holds out his hand to you.

FC (DNA: RG 75, LSIA). Enclosed in William Eustis to Benjamin Hawkins, 6 Nov. 1809 (ibid.).

1. Hobohoilthle to JM, 29 Sept. 1809 (DNA: RG 107, LRRS, H-498:4), forwarded in Hawkins to Eustis, 10 Oct. 1809 (ibid., printed in C. L. Grant, ed., *Letters, Journals, and Writings of Benjamin Hawkins* [2 vols.; Savannah, 1980], 2:556–57). In his address, Hobohoilthle complained to JM that the Muskogee land had "become small and we hope there

will be no more encroachments on us, as we are a poor people." He asked JM to prevent further encroachments by settlers and livestock.

2. Hobohoilthle (whose name was spelled in a variety of ways) was an Indian spokesman who resided in the villages of the Upper Creek people. In the 1780s and 1790s he had often favored good relations with Americans, who usually referred to him as the Tame King of Tallassee. In his later years, however, Hobohoilthle became critical of American encroachment on traditional Creek hunting grounds, and in 1809 he appears to have acted as the principal speaker for the national council of the Creek Confederation (Angie Debo, *The Road to Disappearance* [Norman, Okla., 1967], p. 75; James F. Doster, *The Creek Indians and Their Florida Lands, 1740–1823* [2 vols.; New York, 1974], 2:12–18).

3. The Creek tract lay between the Oconee and Ocmulgee rivers in central Georgia (Debo, *The Road to Disappearance*, p. 378).

To Thomas Jefferson

DEAR SIR   WASHINGTON Novr. 6. 1809

I recd. your letter from Eppington. I had not heard that either the Attorney Genl. or the Govr. of Illinois meant to resign.

Inclosed are several letters for you recd. from France by the return of the Wasp. You will see the propriety of my adding one to myself from Mr. Short;[1] to be returned after perusal. Our information from Paris, of the 19th. of Sepr. gives no countenance to the rumoured renewal of hostilities in Austria. The delay of peace in form, alone keeps alive such rumours. But why should such an event flatter the hopes of G. B? According to all the lessons of experience, it would quickly be followed by a more compleat prostration of her Ally. Armstrong had forwarded to the French Court the measure taken here in consequence of the disavowal of Erskine's arrangement, but there had not been time for an answer. The answer to the previous communication, had been, let England annul her illegal blockade of France, & the Berlin decree will be revoked; let her then revoke her Orders of Novr. & the Milan decree falls of course.[2] This State of the question between the two Powers, would promise some good; if it were ascertained that by the Blockade of F. previous to the Berlin decree was meant that of May, extending from the Elb to Brest, or any other specific Act. It is to be feared, that there is an intentional obscurity, or that an *express* & general renunciation of the British practice is made the condition. From G. B. we have only Newspaper intelligence. The change in the Ministry seems likely to make bad worse; unless we are to look for some favorable change, in the extremity to which things must rapidly proceed under the quackeries & corruptions of an administration headed by such a Being as Percival.[3] Jackson is proving himself a worthy instrument of his Patron Canning. We shall proceed with a circumspect attention to all the circumstances mingled in our affairs; but with a confidence at the same time, in a just sensibility of the Nation, to the respect due to it.

RC (DLC: Rives Collection, Madison Papers). Complimentary close and signature clipped. Docketed by Jefferson, "recd Nov. 24."

1. Short to JM, 15 Sept. 1809 (*PJM-PS*, 1:379–80).

2. JM was quoting here from the concluding paragraph of Champagny's 22 Aug. 1809 letter to Armstrong (see *ASP, Foreign Relations*, 3:326).

3. The British foreign secretary, George Canning, fought a duel with the secretary for war and the colonies, Lord Castlereagh, on 21 Sept., after which both ministers resigned from the cabinet. Ill and incapacitated by a stroke since late August, Prime Minister Portland resigned in October. His successor, Spencer Perceval, was unable to complete his cabinet appointments until December.

From Thomas Jefferson

DEAR SIR   MONTICELLO Nov. 6. 09.

Yours of Oct. 30. came to hand last night. Capt Coles passed this place on the 31st. to Washington. I gave a copy of the paper you desire to Thomas Monroe[1] for his government; and, through him, another to Mayor Brent, that the city magistracy might understand what I considered as the limits separating our rights & duties. Capt Coles can borrow either of these probably for copying. Should they be lost, on my return from Bedford, for which place I set out tomorrow, I will send you mine to be copied.

On the 3d. & 4th. we had a fall of 3. I. rain, more than had fallen in the 3. months following the 14th. of July. This morning the thermometer is at 33½°. A few spiculae of white frost are visible here; but I expect it is severe in the neighborhood, & that there is ice. I recieved a note from the Chevalr. de Onis which I answered.[2] Perhaps he may make this the occasion of expressing his mind inofficially to me. Affectionately yours

TH: JEFFERSON

RC (DLC); FC (DLC: Jefferson Papers).

1. Thomas Munroe (see *PJM-PS*, 1:187 n. 1).

2. Luis de Onís to Jefferson, 17 Oct. 1809, and Jefferson to Onís, 4 Nov. 1809 (DLC: Jefferson Papers).

§ From Joseph Crockett. *6 November 1809, Lexington, Kentucky*. Seeks reappointment as U.S. marshal for Kentucky after his term expires on 26 Jan.

RC (DNA: RG 59, LAR, 1809–17, filed under "Crockett"). 1 p. JM also received a letter from Harry Innes, dated 27 Nov. 1809, endorsing Crockett's reappointment (ibid.). JM nominated Crockett for a further four-year term on 19 Dec. 1809 (*Senate Exec. Proceedings*, 2:130).

From John Armstrong

private

DEAR SIR,   [ca. 7 November 1809]

I send by M. Auriol the post-[s]cript, of which I spoke in my last.[1] It will reach it's destination, but without any hope of it's working the necessary conversion. Indeed I now consider this as impossible, for to public Error, is now added the whole wieght of private interest. So long as the *rule* lasts, a single *exception* to it, makes the fortunes of two or three new men, who are about starting into notice, and who must otherwise take something from the public coffers. Accordingly these exceptions, under the name of pass-ports, are as really, though not quite so publicly at market, as turnips or potatoes, and their price, about 50 per Cent, on the value of the article here. From everything I hear of your cotton-spinning & other establishments I hope that the evil of the times is beginning to work it's correspondent good, and that what we may loose by commerce, will be eventually made up by a full & vigorous employment of the capital of the country on its own materials. I am Sir, with the truest attachment & respect Your most faithful & obedient humble servant

J ARMSTRONG

RC (DLC). Addressee not indicated. Later docketed by JM, "Aug: 1810." Conjectural date here assigned on the basis of internal evidence (see n. 1).

1. The postscript mentioned by Armstrong has not been found. Possibly it was the postscript Armstrong mentioned that he intended to add to an "informal note" sent to the comte d'Hauterive sometime in October 1809 to protest against aspects of the French commercial system. The bearer of the document, M. Auriol, was mentioned by Armstrong on 18 Nov. as being on the point of leaving Paris for the U.S. (Armstrong to Robert Smith, 18–26 Oct., 18 Nov. 1809 [DNA: RG 59, DD, France]).

From Henry Dearborn

DEAR SIR,   BOSTON Novr. 7th. 1809

I take the liberty of observing to you that Col Jona Russell[1] of Providence is now here and about sailing for Toninggen, and if no Consul has been appointed for that place Col Russel would be pleased with the appointment, and as his Character is well known to you I presume you will with pleasure confer the appointment desired. If you should think proper to make the appointment, and will please to direct the Commission to my care I shall have an early opportunity of sending it to him. Yours with respectful esteem

H. DEARBORN

RC (DLC).

1. Jonathan Russell (1771–1832) of Rhode Island achieved prominence as a New England Republican leader on the basis of his widely reprinted Fourth of July oration of 1800, after which Jefferson appointed him to the customs collectorship in Bristol. In the course of his European travels after 1809, Russell was to serve briefly as chargé d'affaires in Paris and London, and in 1813 JM named him to be minister to Sweden, a nomination that the Senate declared to be "inexpedient." JM renominated him to the court of Sweden in 1814 and at the same time added him to the diplomatic team headed by Albert Gallatin and John Quincy Adams that was to negotiate the Treaty of Ghent ending the War of 1812 (*Senate Exec. Proceedings*, 1:401, 2:347, 384, 454).

From Charles W. Goldsborough

SIR,   NAVY DEPARTMENT 7 Novr. 1809

The secretary of the Navy having been unexpectedly detained in South Carolina by the extreme illness of two of his family, & it being probable that he will not be here for some days to come, it appears to me to be my duty to submit, for your consideration, the accompanying papers.

No 1. which affords a view of the Navy appropriations to the ⟨4⟩th ins inclusively[1]

A   statement of the Warrants drawn upon the sum of $75 000, transferred from the appropriation for "Provisions" to that of "Repairs"

B   statement of the Warrants drawn upon the sum of $25 000 transferred to the Contingent Fund.

By these papers it appears that of the appropriations made for the support of the Navy for the year 1809 there was on the 4th ins unexpended the sum of $935,757:31

that of the 75m.$ transferred to the appropriation for "repairs" there remains unexpended the sum of $1,499:12

that of the 25m.$ transferred to the appropriation for "Contingent Account" there remains unexpended the sum of $10,296:73.

All the other appropriations excepting that for "Clothing of the Marine Corps" will it is hoped be found abundant.

The appropriations for Repairs of vessels & for Clothing of the Marine

Corps, both require the aid of additional sums to be transferred from other appropriations—& there are other appropriations which can abundantly spare as much as can be so required.

On account of repairs there are now requisitions upon the Department from agents at different places to an amount exceeding $20,000, which without a transfer of Funds can not be remitted. The Constitution while at sea lost several spars—the Wasp lately returned requires to be over-hawled in her rigging & sails—& the John Adams, in the service upon which she is about to proceed, at a very inclement season, ought to be provided with a number of extra Stores. If, with this information, I might be permitted to suggest the sum necessary to effect these objects & to meet current demands during the present year, I should not estimate it at less than 50,000 dollars—the appropriation for "Provisions" could well spare 75 000$.

The enclosed letter from col: Wharton[2] explains the cause of the deficit in the appropriation for "Clothing of the Marine Corps"—the deficit is estimated at 2 500$—& the appropriation for the "Quarter master's Dept. of the Marine Corps," could well spare that sum.[3] I have the honor to be, sir, with the highest respect, yr. mo: obt. servt

CH: W: GOLDSBOROUGH
for
Paul Hamilton

RC (DLC); letterbook copy (DNA: RG 45, LSP). RC docketed by JM. Enclosures not found, but see n. 2.

1. Goldsborough was concerned because Congress was scheduled to convene on 27 Nov., and by the 1809 act regulating the treasury, war, and navy departments the secretary's annual report on expenses would soon be due. The law gave the president discretionary power to shift money from one account to another "during the recess of Congress," provided a report was "laid before Congress during the first week of their next ensuing session" (Goldsborough to JM, 19 Aug. 1809, *PJM-PS*, 1:332–33; *U.S. Statutes at Large*, 2:535–37). The Navy Department appropriation for 1809 was $1,014,000 (*ASP, Finance*, 2:308).

2. Goldsborough probably enclosed Franklin Wharton's letter to him of 8 Sept. 1809 (copy, DNA: RG 127, Letterbook, 1807–10, Commandant's Office, U.S. Marine Corps), mentioning that the "Advanced Prices" of many articles of clothing purchased by the agent at Philadelphia had "caused a deficiency in the Amount, necessary to compleat the Number of Suits, which will be wanted." Wharton therefore suggested that as there were unexpended moneys in the quarter and barracks masters departments and the contingent account, "the deficit as above stated, may be taken therefrom." Navy captain Franklin Wharton had been serving as lieutenant colonel commandant of the Marine Corps in Philadelphia since 1800.

3. On 9 Nov. 1809 JM directed that the transfer recommended by Goldsborough be made (*ASP, Naval Affairs*, 1:295).

¶ From Philip E. Thomas. Letter not found. *7 November 1809, Baltimore*. Listed in Registers of Letters Received by the Secretary of War (DNA: RG 107), which indicates that Thomas wrote for the Committee of Friends on Indian Concerns about the education of three Indian boys brought in by Captain Hendricks. A letter from Messrs. Mott of New York proposing to undertake the business was enclosed.

From Andrew Ellicott

DEAR SIR,   LANCASTER November 8th. 1809.

In the year 1801, I left Gauld's survey of the dry Tortuga's, and the Florida reef and keys[1] in the Navy department: It is on a large scale, and consists, if my recollection serves me, of four, or five large sheets: it is of immense value to our country since the acquisition of Louisiana, on account of the coasting trade round Florida point, into the gulf of Mexico. You will find some account of this survey in my printed Journal pages 254, and 255.[2] As this work of Mr. Gauld's was suppressed, or at least confined to the pilots, and privateers of the Bahama islands after the British lost the Floridas during our revolutionary war, it may be considered as out of print to the United States.

This survey does merit, if in my opinion any survey ever did merit, a new impression, which I should have pressed long before this time, had not the drudgery of a little office, from which I was never absent one day, for more than six years, occupied my whole attention.[3] The analysis to the survey is wanting, which I am certain I can supply from Mr. Gauld's notes, together with those of Captn. Roman,[4] and my own: it would probably be comprized in less than 100 pages.

Being now at leisure, I am ready to undertake that business, or any other in the geographical way, particularly the determination of three, or four points, with the soundings on our coast, and east Florida; which merit particular attention, and which ever since my return from our southern boundary, I have been desirous of examining. These are the frying-pan shoals, Cape Hattaras, Cape Carnaveral, and the entrance on the Florida reef at key Biscanio. Accurate charts, on a large scale of all those points, especially the two latter, with the correct latitudes, and longitudes are wanted: because, it frequently happens, that dangerous places when critically examined, are found to contain good harbours, and become places of safety, rather than of danger to vessels. The dry Tortugas, were avoided for two centuries, but since the survey made by Mr. Gauld, they are frequented for safety.

Having the best apparatus in this country for executing such work, I feel somewhat mortified, that both myself, and instruments should be rendered useless for want of employ, while any thing remains to be done, in which both the safety of our citizens, and the interest of our coasting trade are involved. I have the honour to be, with sincere esteem, and respect, your old acquaintance, friend and hbe. servt.

ANDW. ELLICOTT

RC (DLC); FC (DLC: Ellicott Papers).

1. George Gauld, *Observations on the Florida Kays, Reef and Gulf . . . Also, a Description, with Sailing Instructions, of the Coast of West Florida, . . . to Accompany His Charts of Those Coasts* (London, 1796).

2. Ellicott, *The Journal of Andrew Ellicott, Late Commissioner . . . for Determining the Boundary between the United States and the Possessions of His Catholic Majesty* (Philadelphia, 1803; Shaw and Shoemaker 4147). Ellicott wrote that Gauld's treatise, "made by the direction of the Board of Admiralty of Great Britain, may justly be considered as one of the most valuable works of the kind extant, but unfortunately it is little known" (ibid., p. 254).

3. Ellicott was removed from his post in the Pennsylvania Land Office in 1808 after Simon Snyder was elected governor (Catharine Van Cortlandt Mathews, *Andrew Ellicott: His Life and Letters* [New York, 1908], p. 214).

4. Bernard Romans, *A Concise Natural History of East and West Florida* (New York, 1775; Evans 14440).

From Almon Ruggles

SIR   RIVER HURON OHIO Novr. 8th 1809

Being informed that you are wishing to procure the Maps & surveys *generally* of the State of Ohio I take the liberty to transmit you a Map of the FireLand so called[1] or of the half Million acres of Land, granted by the Legislature of the State of Connecticut, to certain persons who Suffered by fire during ⟨the late⟩ Revolutionary War with Great Brittain Which you will be pleased to accept from your Obedt Servt.

ALMON RUGGLES

RC (OClWHi). Enclosure not found.

1. In 1807–8 Ruggles had surveyed and mapped for the Sufferers' Land Company the Western Reserve tract granted in 1792 by the Connecticut General Assembly to the victims of the British raids on Connecticut in 1779 and 1781 (Helen M. Carpenter, "The Origin and Location of the Firelands of the Western Reserve," *Ohio State Archaeological and Historical Society Quarterly*, 44 [1935]: 163–203).

§ **Robert Smith to Francis James Jackson.** *8 November 1809, Department of State.* Jackson's letter of 4 Nov. not only repeats the assertion that American negotiators with Erskine knew the British minister was exceeding his instructions but aggravates "the same gross insinuation." Thus, to preclude future opportunities for such abuse, informs Jackson "that no further communications will be received from you" and the British government will be so notified. In the meantime, any communications "affecting the interests of the two nations" will have to be carried on through another channel.

Tr, two copies (DNA: RG 233, President's Messages; and DNA: RG 46, Legislative Proceedings, 11A-E3). 2 pp. Enclosed in JM's 29 Nov. annual message to Congress. Printed in *ASP, Foreign Relations*, 3:318–19).

From Charles W. Goldsborough

SIR,   NAVY DEPARTMENT 9 Novr 1809

The most prompt attention shall be paid to your instructions;[1] but permit me, sir, respectfully to observe, that it will take many days to prepare the statements required: those which can be furnished, by the Executive branch of the Department, shall be ready, by the time the Secretary of the Navy shall return—those which the Accountant alone can furnish may not be prepared at so early a day. But still, I confidently hope, that the whole will be prepared before the meeting of Congress; & that the Secretary of the Navy will have the honor of laying them, with the most satisfactory explanations, before you.

In the mean time, as there are some very urgent demands upon the Department, I shall not, I trust, be considered as presumptuous, in stating it as my opinion, that the public service would be promoted by an immediate transfer of funds; & I found this opinion upon the subjoined Estimate,

Monies required to pay drafts at this time actually made upon the Department on account of Repairs of vessels

Draft of Jas. Morrison—for yarns		6 344:50
has been due for some days		
Do. of Keith Spence. repairs of G. Boats		2 500.
Do. Do. Do. do.		2 514.30
Do. Do. Do do		750.
all these drafts are now due		
Requisition of Jno. Bullus		8 000.
see paper marked A		
Requisition of T. Armistead. norfolk		<u>3 000</u>
all these are now due		$23 108:80
Probable wants		
Replaceing the topmasts of the Constitution &c.	X	4 500.

New rigging & Sails for the Wasp	X	7 000
Extra Stores for the Jno. Adams	X	4 000
Navy yards—Washn.—New York & Norfolk		11 000
for other demands, from a distance which can not be foreseen	X	20 000
	total	69 608.80

The items marked thus X are wholly conjectural—we have no precise information of the wants of either of the vessels—all the information we have is, that the Constitution had several spars carried away, which have since been replaced, & for the expence of which we are daily expecting a requisition from the agent at Norfolk: that the Wasp requires overhawling in her sails & rigging; & with respect to the John Adams We know that, on such a voyage, extra stores, such as running rigging, canvas, spare spars &c are indispensible—& we have but a small portion of such stores on hand. It may not be improper for me here to state that the John Adams can proceed on the projected service, with as little extra expence as any other suitable vessel.

With respect to the appropriation for clothing of the Marine Corps, the deficit has arisen from the advanced price of cloths, woollens, & blankets—at the time the estimate for the year 1809 was made, it was supposed they could be purchased at the price then estimated—these articles however experienced a sudden rise. The whole wanted for this year has not been purchased; but the commandant has applied for permission to purchase them, & assured me that the men would suffer exceedingly if he should not be authorized to provide them.

In the hope, Sir, that these statements, altho' hastily made & extremely incomplete, will satisfy you that I have not erred in the suggestion that the public service would be promoted by your making a transfer of funds immediately, I avail myself of the intimation which you have been pleased to give, in conclusion of your instructions, & transmit herewith the requisite form for your signature.[2] I have the honor to be with the highest respect, Sir, Yr obt. servt.

CH W GOLDSBOROUGH
for
Paul Hamilton

[Enclosure]

A

Extract of a letter from John Bullus navy agent New York—dated Novr. 1st. 1809.

"I have found it necessary to draw for money under the head of 'Repairs' to pay for supplies purchased previous to receiving your Circular letter of the 8th. August last, as well as to make purchase of Such articles as were immediately required for the different Vessels before they could go to Sea."

RC and enclosure (DLC); letterbook copy and copy of enclosure (DNA: RG 45, LSP). RC docketed by JM.

1. Letter not found, but see Goldsborough to JM, 7 Nov. 1809, n. 3.
2. Someone, possibly JM, wrote here in pencil: "☞ filled up with 75,000 drs. according to the sum pencilled in the Blank."

From Charles W. Goldsborough

SIR,   NAVY DEPARTMENT 9 Novr 1809

I almost fear that I may be considered troublesome; but I beg that you will attribute my frequent applications to you, to an anxious desire to leave no duty unfulfilled—to anticipate what the Secretary, if present, would have performed.

To enable the Department to comply with the enclosed requisition, to prepare the Navy Estimates for the year 1810, it is essential that we should know whether any addition to, or reduction of, the number of vessels, now in commission, is intended to be made; & allow me to state, that it will take six or eight day's close application to prepare all the details of an Estimate.

If you will be pleased to instruct me upon this point, I shall lose no time in preparing the Estimates required: so that by the time the Secretary will probably arrive, he will have it in his power to lay them before you without delay. I have the honor to be Sir, with the most perfect respect, Yr obt hble St.

CH: W: GOLDSBOROUGH
for
Paul Hamilton

RC (DLC); letterbook copy (DNA: RG 45, LSP). RC docketed by JM. Enclosure not found.

Draft of Robert Smith to William Pinkney

MR PINKNEY   [ca. 9 November 1809]

By the frigate L'Africaine I transmitted to you copies of my letters to Mr Jackson bearing date the 9 & 19 of October and also a Copy of his letter to me bearing date the 11h. October.

You will by this Conveyance receive duplicates of those letters and also the sequel of the Correspondence consisting of three letters from him of 23 & 27 Oct & of the 4 Nov and of two letters from me of the 1st & 8 Nov.

This correspondence will afford you a view of what has taken place between Mr Jackson & this Govt and of the painful necessity of my last letter.[1] You will thence perceive our distressing dilemma between our disposition to make another experiment in Negotiation and our regard for the honor and character of this Govt. Offended and traduced in the letters of this Gentleman. We, however, took the step we did with respect to Mr Jackson altogether on account of his personal misconduct and under the persuasion that so reprehensible a proceeding was not within the views of his Sovereign. Of this you will not fail to give to the British Govt. the most explicit assurance and in a manner the most likely to ensure it a favorable Consideration. And it is confidently believed that this determination of the American Govt cannot be regarded but as the result of an unavoidable necessity. Had this Course not been taken, our only alternative would have been, either an implied acquiescence, by our silence, in an insinuation, which, we knew, to be utterly groundless, or a submission on the part of this Govt to the task of discussing with a foreign minister so gross an accusation. To such humiliation, it cannot be expected that this Govt. could stoop.

If our discussions with Mr Jackson had not been thus interrupted, it is evident, they would not have terminated in an adjustment of the existing differences, either as to the affair of the Chesapeake or as to the revocation of the orders in Council.

As to the affair of the Chesapeake nothing has been tendered by him but a cold proposition to restore the seamen taken out of the frigate and to make a provision for the families of such men as were killed. And this has been tendered as a satisfaction for the insulted honor of the U. States and as a reparation for the expensive injuries to the frigate, for the mortifying frustration of her intended cruise, for the numerous inconveniences incident to that disappointment, for the men killed and wounded and for the wanton invasion of the State of Virginia.

In the Offer to restore the men there is a reservation of a right in his B. Majesty to claim the discharge of such of them as shall be proved to be *deserters* from his Majestys service. It will recur to your recollection that the three seamen claimed by us are Citizens of the U. States that they had been taken out of Merchant Vessels and impressed into the British service and when the ship, in which they were had come into the waters of the U. States, that they *deserted* from her. Under this reservation then the Govt. is asked to recognise a right in his Britannick Majesty to exercise a Control over these three men after they shall have been restored to the bosom of their Country and to the priveledges of American Citizens, merely because they had been deserters from the British service into which they had been forced in violation of every principle of Natural & Political Law.

In the arrangement made with Mr Erskine, it was among other things, formally stated by that Minister that his Britannick Majesty was desirous of making an honorable reparation for the aggression Committed on the frigate the Chesapeake, that in addition to his prompt disavowal of the act, his Majesty, as a Mark of his displeasure, did immediately recal the offending Officer from an highly important & honorable Command and that he was willing, if acceptable to the American Govt to make a suitable provision for the *wounded*. Reasonable & equitable as these terms obviously are, nothing of the kind is to be found in the proposition made by his successor.

His Britannick Majesty has in this case disavowed the aggression, and yet has rewarded the aggressor by promoting him to a distinguished Command. He has disclaimed the act of taking the men from our frigate, and yet has claimed the right of withholding them from us. And the ungracious Offer now made to restore them is ascribed to the alledged Circumstance of the President's Proclamation of the 7th July 1807 having been annulled, as if the U. States had been the aggressor and had accordingly made the first advance towards conciliation.[2]

As to the orders in Council it is evident that Mr Jackson had not been authorised to make to this Govt. any propositions with respect to their revocation, nor to accede to any made to him but upon the terms specified in the letter of instruction to Mr Erskine of the 23d Jany. Upon this subject he was in my several Conferences with him very distinct and unreserved. But in his letter of the 11h Oct instead of the frank exposition requested in my letter of the 9h. in case I had in any instance misapprehended his meaning, he has exhibited an elaborate argument to shew that he could not have made such a statement "with that view" which my representation had presented. But with whatever view the statement may have been made by him, the objection to it on the part of the U. States, cannot but remain in principle precisely the same. In his last letter of the 4h. Inst., instead of a plain precise denial of the admissions ascribed to him, he has deemed it expedient to refer us to his two *preceding letters*, as shewing that he had in no way given room to suppose that he had ever made any such statement. And when we recur to these letters we perceive that they Contain, as I have just stated, not an absolute but a more qualified objection to the statement in my letter of the 9 Oct. And it will not escape your notice, that the qualification annexed to the Objection does not make any essential change in the Original representation.

Draft (DLC: Rives Collection, Madison Papers). Written in pencil in Smith's hand.

1. The instruction sent to Pinkney on 11 Nov. included Smith's draft up to this point. The remainder of the draft was replaced by a shorter note stressing the insulting nature of Jackson's behavior and instructing Pinkney to request his recall. Pinkney was also directed to inform the British ministry that Jackson's recall should not become an obstacle to "communications, which may lead to a friendly accommodation." The administration was still willing to receive a minister, "who, with a different character, may bring all the authorities and instructions requisite for the complete success of his mission" (Smith to Pinkney, 11 Nov. 1809 [DNA: RG 59, IM]).

2. Smith wrote the preceding paragraph on a separate page and marked it for insertion here.

§ From Solomon Myer. *9 November 1809, Washington.* Sends by his son the manuscript of a political treatise and seeks JM's opinion of tract as a guide to whether to devote "further labour and expence" to the effort. Contemplates publishing the work anonymously, in the tradition of *Common Sense.* Knows JM will not reveal his secret and asks JM to return his only copy of the manuscript to the son "in a day or two."

RC (DLC). 1 p.

§ From James Taylor. *9 November? 1809, Newport.* Capt. Jervis Cutler has solicited Taylor's intervention on his behalf. Cutler has been dismissed from the service, probably owing to an allegation that he had interfered in the election of a congressman in Ohio. Cutler denies charge. Taylor praises Cutler's abilities as a recruiter.

RC (DLC). 3 pp. Dated "9th. 1809." Docketed by JM. Address on cover indicates Cutler carried the letter from Kentucky. Cutler was never reinstated, but in 1810 the secretary of war reported favorably on his claim for additional pay, which Congress authorized in 1814 (*ASP, Claims*, p. 407; *U.S. Statutes at Large*, 6:143).

§ Presidential Proclamation. *10 November 1809, Washington.* By the terms of article 6[1] of the treaty concluded at Detroit, 7 Nov. 1807, between the U.S. and the Ottawa, Chippewa, Wyandot, and Potawatomi nations, the said nations were entitled to reserve six sections, each containing one mile square, within the cession then made to the U.S., subject to the approval of the president of the U.S. The said nations having indicated to Gov. William Hull of the Michigan Territory "their election to locate one or two of the said sections on the River St. Clair," the president approves of the location.

FC (DNA: RG 75, LSIA). 1 p. Enclosed in William Eustis to William Hull, 14 Nov. 1809 (ibid.).

1. See *ASP, Indian Affairs*, 1:747.

To Henry Dearborn

DEAR SIR   WASHINGTON NOVr. 13. 1809

I have recd. your favor of the 7th. Tonningen being included in the Consulate of Mr. Forbes who resides at Hamburg,[1] and being now the real commercial port of that Consulate, it would not consist with what is due to him, to comply with the wishes of Col. Russel. Mr. F. has acquitted himself as one of the most intelligent and active of the Consular Corps; and when not at Tonningen himself, is understood to have an Agent there.

The Intelligencer of this Morning will tell you that the insults to this Govt. interwoven by Mr Jackson in his correspondence with the Secy. of State, have required that the door should be shut agst. a farther repetition of them. It appears to have been a favorite object with him to create a footing for the impudent charge agst. the administration, of entering into a collusive arrangt. with his Predecessor.[2] The use to have been made of the insinuation if not at once blasted is obvious. Present me respectfully to M⟨rs. Dearborn,⟩[3] and be assured of my sincere & constant esteem.

JAMES MADISON

RC (MeHi: Fogg Collection). Addressee not indicated; determined by comparison with Dearborn to JM, 7 Nov. 1809.

1. John Murray Forbes took up his duties at Hamburg in the summer of 1802 (Forbes to JM, 20 Aug. 1802 [DNA: RG 59, CD, Hamburg]).
2. The *National Intelligencer*, 13 Nov. 1809, reported Jackson's charge that Erskine had divulged Canning's 23 Jan. instructions to Smith and JM, adding that "in Mr. Jackson's next letter the same gross insinuation having been reiterated, and even aggravated, it only remained . . . to inform Mr. Jackson . . . that no further communications would be received from him."
3. Faintly legible, this name appears to have been erased.

From the Vermont General Assembly

SIR—   [15 November 1809][1]

On your being invited to the highest office in the gift of a great and happy nation, by a large majority of the unbiassed suffrages of a free and independent people, the general assembly of the state of Vermont avail themselves of the earliest opportunity, to express their high satisfaction at your elevation, which results from a full confidence in your long tried wisdom and integrity, as well as for that uniform zeal and attachment, which you have invariably manifested to promote the best interests of your country.

With peculiar gratification we reflect, that a person is advanced to the presidential chair, who has long been associated with the illustrious Jefferson and his copatriots, and whose useful labors have tended to advance the honor, maintain the rights, and secure the peace and happiness of our common country. The wise, prudent and impartial measures of your predecessor, aided by your faithful co-operation, have, under the blessing of Divine Providence, long preserved this highly favored nation from all those fatal evils which have for so many years spread misery, devastation and death throughout devoted Europe.

It is a truth, however melancholy the reflection, that a disgraceful spirit of opposition and insubordination to the laws of the general government, has been excited and fomented in some parts of the Union, and by those who have long claimed the exclusive confidence of the people; but it is equally true that notwithstanding the inflammatory addresses, protests, and resolutions, presented to the public, together with the combined influence of foreign intrigue and domestic treachery, a spirit of returning patriotism and of union has lately dawned upon us, from which we anticipate the most happy effects, both at home and abroad.

The embarrassed state of our foreign relations, has been and still is productive of the most serious evils to the commercial and agricultural interests of this country. The belligerent powers of Europe, under a color of retaliating upon one another, have issued and enforced orders and decrees, aimed at the entire destruction of our lawful commerce, the insulting pretensions and injurious effects of which too plainly shews that lawless plunder, stimulated by unprincipled avarice and a thirst for universal dominion, are the governing objects.

The visionary blockade of almost a whole continent, the order forbidding neutrals to trade from one port to another of an enemy, the destruction of our vessels on the high seas by fire, and the total interdiction of our lawful commerce, except on the conditions of tribute and submission to the mandates of a foreign power, are hostile to the spirit, and opposed to every ingenuous and patriotic feeling which inspires a nation of freemen. Yet these are not all, nor even the greatest injuries we have received. Orders have been issued apparently designed to excite our citizens to insurrection, and acts of disobedience to the government and laws of this country. Our seamen, not only on the common highway of nations, but also in sight of our own shores, after long and dangerous voyages, and in momentary expectation of treading their native soil among their families and friends, have been impressed, torn from every thing they held dear, and forced into an ignominious servitude on board of foreign ships of war.

Our territorial jurisdiction has been violated, the hospitality of our ports and harbors abused, our citizens murdered whilst in the peaceable pursuit of domestic concerns, our national flag insulted, the blood of our seamen wantonly shed, and the perpetrators of these horrible acts have been secured and protected from punishment by mock trials, or in some instances by an exemption from trial; and as a further reward for such deeds, have enjoyed the smiles and received the promotions from that very government, under whose authority they acted, while it hypocritically pretended to disavow the deed: nor has any reparation been yet tendered, except on terms more humiliating than the outrages themselves. And while they adhere to the tenor of their proclamation of the 16th day of October, 1807,[2] little hopes are entertained that they will be disposed to enter into suitable arrangements to redress such aggravated evils.

These accumulated injuries and unprovoked aggressions upon national rights are not however without their beneficial effects; for they have at last awakened the great majority of the American people to a just sense of their true interests, and excited a laudable spirit of ambition throughout the Union to promote the establishment of domestic manufactures, and other internal improvements, which under the fostering care and guardianship of an enlightened government, will in the end render us in a great measure independent of the old world.

The people of Vermont, though almost wholly devoted to agricultural pursuits, have, during our late and present commercial embarrassments, felt a common interest with her sister states, and have long and anxiously waited in the hope, that the strict and impartial neutrality, maintained by the general government towards all nations, the just and reasonable offers of accommodation it has repeatedly made, would have before this brought the offending nations to a sense of justice, and created a disposition to restore to us the peaceable enjoyment of our national rights; but in this they have been disappointed, and with extreme concern behold the most friendly, just and pacific overtures treated with silent contempt by one nation, and by another met with what (if possible) is still worse, faithless, delusive propositions and arrangements, calculated solely to weaken the hands of government, and to defeat those wise precautionary measures, adopted to obtain a redress of wrongs.

Surely there is a point among nations as well as individuals, beyond which longer forbearance would become criminal, and honorable and manly resistance our indispensable duty: And we view the freedom of commerce upon the ocean, when pursued conformable to the established law of nations, the restoration of our impressed seamen, exemption and security against further impressment, among those rights which ought not to be surrendered but with our national existence.

While impressed with these weighty considerations, we can discover no just cause for despondency or alarm, and we are strengthened in this opinion from this pleasing reflection, that the path of our present political pilot is lighted by the most illustrious examples of virtue and patriotism, which have gone before him, and that the same principles which inspired the sages and heroes of the revolution will continue to guide the policy of our present administration; and if honorable adjustments cannot be made, however reluctant we may be to hazard our fortunes upon the warring elements; yet rather than relinquish any of our sacred rights, or should justice be longer unreasonably denied us, we confidently assure you, that we will rally round the standard of government, cheerfully obey the first call of our country, and unite with them in the last solemn appeal to nations, relying and trusting in that Almighty Being who directs and controls the destinies of the world, to guide us to a favorable issue.

Printed copy (*Journals of the General Assembly of the State of Vermont, at Their Session Begun . . . October, A.D. 1809* [Randolph, Vt., 1810; Shaw and Shoemaker 21898], pp. 68–70); also printed in *National Intelligencer*, 8 Dec. 1809). Minor variations between the two copies have not been noted.

1. On 19 Oct. 1809 James Fisk introduced a motion in the Vermont General Assembly for a committee to address resolutions to the president of the U.S., and a committee of three was appointed. The address was read to the assembly on 26 Oct. and approved on 31 Oct. by a vote of 118 to 71. There is, however, no evidence that the address was either considered or approved by the governor and council of Vermont before they adjourned on 8 Nov., and the Speaker of the House seems to have forwarded it to JM a week later. No covering letter has been found (*Journals of the General Assembly of . . . Vermont*, pp. 39–40, 70, 96; JM to the Vermont General Assembly, 26 Dec. 1809).

2. In the proclamation referred to, George III ordered his "natural born subjects" serving in foreign vessels to return to their native country. The proclamation, which was based on the doctrine of indefeasible allegiance, by refusing to recognize the right of the U.S. to naturalize British subjects served to justify the practice of impressment (*ASP, Foreign Relations*, 3:25–26).

From John Dawson

DEAR SIR   FREDERICKSBURG Nov: 16. 1809

The unfortunate death of Go: Lewis leaves that office vacant. I have some thoughts of accepting the appointment shoud I be calld to it, altho I shoud wish to see you before it is made.

No person knows better than yourself how far I am capable of discharging the duties and what my claims on the public are. With sincere regard Your friend

J DAWSON[1]

RC (DNA: RG 59, LAR, 1809–17, filed under "Dawson").

1. John Dawson (1762–1814), a Harvard graduate, began corresponding with JM in 1785. He represented Spotsylvania County in the Virginia House of Delegates, 1786–89, and in the 1788 ratifying convention, where he was an Antifederalist. A delegate to the Continental Congress, 1788–89, he was elected as a Republican to the seat in the House of Representatives that JM vacated in 1797, and he served until his death (*PJM*, 7:199 n. 17).

From William McKinley

DEAR SIR,   WEST LIBERTY 16 Novr. 1809

Had I Known on the 13th of Septr last when I wrote in favour of Thos. Keneday of Pittsburgh[1] that he was an Aliean, my name would not have been on the list, and now begg leave to withdraw it.

By accident a few days Since I fill in company with Said Keneday, he Says that he was a Scot, in the British Servise, and on account of his attachment to the republican System, resigned and came to these United States about two years Since.

Permit me to say that it is a wast of Public money to continue, Pittsburgh, Charles town, Marietta, Cencinatti, Lewisville, and Sumdrie other places on the ohio, Ports of Entrie, there is no Kind of use for them that I can see.

Enclosed is a Copy of my answer to C Hamond & Co. Accept my best Respects

WILLM. MCKINLEY

RC (DLC). Enclosure not found.

1. McKinley had recommended Kennedy for an army commission (*PJM-PS*, 1:375–76; see also ibid., 1:153 n. 2).

From David Bailie Warden

SIR,   PARIS, 17 November, 1809.

I have the honor of sending you some newspapers and two memoirs relating to Prize Causes, and am, Sir, with great respect, Your very obedt and very humble Sert

DAVID BAILIE WARDEN

RC (DLC). Docketed by JM. Enclosures not found.

§ From Gabriel Richard. *17 November 1809, Detroit.* As director of the Spring Hill Indian school, Richard reports on progress made in equipping the facility; however, no new buildings have been erected. Encloses accounts and certificate from Governor Hull attesting to Richard's activities on behalf of "about twelve Indian Children." Alludes to Jefferson's plan for Indian education and believes JM also will "chearfully patronise the Civilisation of our Indian neighbours." President Jefferson suggested the school might be turned into a privately owned one, under Richard's direction, and Gallatin proposed selling it at public auction. Richard then offered to buy the school privately for $2,100—the price paid for it by the government in 1808. Should that plan be adopted, Richard is still willing to buy the school, provided he would have four or five years to pay off the debt. Hopes the school can be maintained as a private institution, for that would be more economical and, in the long run, more efficient. Has stated the situation and now asks that a decision be made. If Spring Hill is to remain a public property a considerable sum should be spent on improvements and for feeding, clothing, and instructing the Indians.

RC and enclosures (DNA: RG 107, LRRS, R-267:4). RC 5 pp. Docketed by a War Department clerk as received 22 Dec. Surviving enclosures are Richard's "References to the Enclosed Account" (2 pp.) and Hull's 9 Nov. certification (2 pp.). RC and enclosures printed in Carter, *Territorial Papers, Michigan*, 10:287–92. For more on the Indian school, see the Memorandum from Jefferson, Mar. 1809 (*PJM-PS*, 1:1, 2 n. 4); Jefferson to JM, 7 Dec. 1809, and nn.

From Charles Pinckney

DEAR SIR,   November 18. 1809 IN CHARLESTON

I had the honour, of writing you lately, which, I hope you have received.[1] At the request, of a number, Of our Respectable Citizens, who have not the pleasure, of a Personal Acquaintance with you, I take the liberty, of, transmitting you Some intelligence, which it is believed, important you Should Possess. I do so, because at, this time, it is almost impossible, for our Members of, Congress, to know of it—all of them except one, live very, distant, from the Sea-Coast, & Seldom, or ever come to, Charleston. Mr. Marion has never, I understand, returned to this State since June, & has been extremely, ill, in the upper Parts of Virginia—he therefore can, know nothing of it.[2] It is, that immense quantities, of British goods, are pouring daily, into Amelia, in Florida, from whence they are Smuggled, into Georgia, &, this State, in a manner, & *to a value*, to exceed, Credibility. The innumerable Creeks, & inlets, in, both States, & the facilities, which they, & the boundaries, Of, Florida, & Georgia, furnish, are Such as to make it, impossible, under our existing regulations, to prevent it. Twenty Cutters, it is Said, would not do it, particularly, in the Winter Season, on a Coast So dangerous as this is.

The Evil is increasing every moment, in a most, rapid manner, by which means, all the effects, intended by the Non intercourse act, are in this Section, Of the Union, entirely Prevented. So far from, injuring Great-Britain, the existing State of things, in this quarter, is become precisely I should, Suppose, what She wishes. She pours in her, Manufactures on us in any quantities, She pleases, *free, of duty, or impost here*. She receives all the, Cotton, & Rice, & Other Produce, She wants, at her own prices, & carries it from Amelia *in her own Ships*, throwing all the charges, of the double Shipment, insurance, &ca—in, Short, all that are, incident, to the, circuitous route, on the, American Planter, for She will regulate her Prices, by the European, Markets. Our real American Merchants, & friends of the, Country, view with great concern, the manner, in which the intentions, of our general government, are thus frustrated, for certainly, if, the same Smuggling, of British Goods, & defrauding Of the Revenue, exists in any degree, in the Northern States, the present Situation, of our Commerce, as it respects Great, Britain, must be more, Advantageous to her, than She could ever even have hoped.[3] I do, not know if the Northern States furnish the Same facilities, for, Smuggling, as the Southern Coast, & Particularly with the help, of, Amelia does, but if they do, & they have begun, you must probably, have heard of it. If they do not, enough, can be easily, Smuggled, through the Southern States, to supply them. The thing speaks already, openly, for itself, for British Goods, are becoming, as cheap, or cheaper, than ever known[4] *& in greater Quantities*.

It is not for me to say what is best to be done. We know Our political Vessel is in the hands of as able a Pilot as any that could be found & are sure her courses will be right & such measures alone pursued as are consistent with the honour & true interests of our country.

DEAR SIR

Since writing the above, Our intelligence on this subject increases, & particularly as to the arrival of British Vessels at Amelia full of their manufactures—some passed our Bar yesterday & the day before in sight, & numbers go the same way out of sight of our Bar. It is said many which arrive are reported empty, or in Ballast, merely to prevent suspicion, but are at the same time full of Goods to be smuggled. Our informants transmit this information confidentially, as they do not wish by being known to expose themselves to the resentments & Oppression of the British Party & Merchants in Charleston, which in Money affairs is very powerful here. While Goods are cheap, our Cotton & Produce are low being entirely now at their mercy. I am dear sir With great regard & Esteem always Yours Truly

CHARLES PINCKNEY

I should have paid my respects to yourself & Mr Jefferson in person before, but the long & uncommon & dangerous illness of my eldest Child has prevented & still detains me.

RC (DLC). Partly in a clerk's hand (see n. 4). Marked by Pinckney "(Duplicate in part)."

1. Pinckney to JM, 5 Sept. 1809 (*PJM-PS*, 1:353–54).

2. Robert Marion of South Carolina served in the House of Representatives, 1805–10.

3. Although the Nonintercourse Act prohibited commerce with both belligerent powers, British naval domination of the transatlantic sea-lanes prevented French ships from entering U.S. ports and allowed British vessels easy access to harbors and inlets where American laws could be evaded. For discussions of the significance of this illegal trade at Amelia Island and in various Canadian ports, see François Crouzet, *L'Economie Britannique et le Blocus Continental, 1806–1813* (2 vols. in 1; Paris, 1958), 2:472, 474, 485, 520, 702–4; and Eli F. Heckscher, *The Continental System: An Economic Interpretation* (Oxford, 1922), pp. 137–38.

4. Remainder of letter, dateline, and address in Pinckney's hand.

From James Taylor

DEAR SIR   LEXINGTON KY. Novr. 19h. 1809

I have this moment reached this am informed that The Honble John Coburn has been recommended by many of the respectable Citizens of St. Louis as the successor of Governor Lewis.

Having heretofore expressed to you my high Opinion of Mr. Coburns Capacity & disposition to serve his Count[r]y[1] it would appear superfluous to say much in this letter.

I shall only say that I am clearly of Opinion that no man could be appointed who would meet the approbation of the people of the Western country more generally than Mr. Coburn.

I have just seen an address to the Senators of our state from this place signed by all the influential Citizens of the place requesting these gentlemen to use their influence to procure the appointment for the Judge.[2] The

Judge has just returned from attending his Court and I am flattered with a hope that Mrs. Coburn will consent to remove to that Teritory.

Should any vacancy happen and you can from information believe that James W. Moss[3] would fill an appointment that might present its self, you would confer a singular Obligation on me by giving him such a one as you think he is qualified to fill. He is a man of about 30 years of age with strong mind good clasical education and well acquainted with business of all Kinds. In my opinion he would make a good Secretary, Indian agent, Commissioner &c. Mr. John Grayham & The Honble B. Howard are will acquainted with him & I flatter my self will support what I have here said.

I have it in contemplation to visit the City in Course of the Winter. I have a long and large account to settle and I think it will be prudent to come on & attend to it in person, particularly as under the late laws & regulations of the Offices it will be a difficult matter to forward my a/cs in that way that may insure their correct settlement.

I suppose it will [be] about the latter end of January that I shall reach your City. Be so good as to present my best respects of your good Lady and assure your self of my esteem & good wishes. In haste

JAMES TAYLOR

RC (DNA: RG 59, LAR, 1809–17, filed under "Coburn").

1. See Taylor to JM, 29 Apr. 1809 (*PJM-PS*, 1:143–44 and n. 1).
2. Taylor was referring to one of two letters addressed to Buckner Thruston and John Pope and dated 18 Nov. 1809, one signed by Elisha Warfield and thirty-eight others and the other by Thomas January and forty others. JM received both of these letters from Thruston and Pope on 16 Dec. 1809 (DNA: RG 59, LAR, 1809–17).
3. James W. Moss was surveyor at the port of Limestone, Kentucky (*Senate Exec. Proceedings*, 2:57, 63).

§ From William C. C. Claiborne. *19 November 1809, New Orleans*. His official letters to Gallatin will give details of the rascality of William Brown, the local customs collector who has absconded with a large sum of public money. The office thus vacated is lucrative, and the collector can reside a mile from the city during the summer so that "he may calculate on enjoying health." Sounded out Benjamin Morgan to see if he would accept an appointment, but he refused. Knows of no others whom he would willingly recommend. The position is one of great influence, so that the designated person "should unite to sterling Integrity, pure Republicanism." Takes the liberty of writing JM so candidly because of his desire to see "the Government of the United States respected and beloved by the People of this Territory."

RC (DNA: RG 59, LAR, 1809–17, filed under "Brown"). 3 pp. Printed in Carter, *Territorial Papers, Orleans*, 9:858.

From David Gelston

DEAR SIR,   NEW YORK November 20th. 1809

I received a letter some time ago from my correspondent in London, informing me, that a vessel from Bordeaux, bound to New York, had been taken and carried into Falmouth, in which he observed was a pipe of brandy marked **WL** consigned to me, and for which he had interposed a claim—the pipe of brandy I have since received via Boston, it is now in Store—no account has been received from any quarter giving any information who was the owner.

It has occurred to me as probable the pipe may belong to you or Mr. Jefferson as it was (I suppose) shipped originally by Mr Lee;[1] if it belongs to you, your order respecting it will be immediately attended to. Very sincerely your's

DAVID GELSTON

RC (DLC).

1. William Lee of Massachusetts (1772–1840) served as U.S. commercial agent at Bordeaux, 1801–16 (Mary Lee Mann, ed., *A Yankee Jeffersonian: Selections from the Diary and Letters of William Lee of Massachusetts* [Cambridge, Mass., 1958], pp. 299–300).

§ From John Brown.[1] *20 November 1809, Frankfort, Kentucky.* Recommends John Coburn for the vacant governorship of Louisiana Territory.

RC (DNA: RG 59, LAR, 1809–17, filed under "Coburn"). 1 p. Printed in Carter, *Territorial Papers, Louisiana-Missouri*, 14:339.

1. John Brown (1757–1837), a longtime acquaintance of JM's, was one of the first U.S. senators from Kentucky, 1792–1805.

From James Dinsmore

SIR   MONTPELEIR Nov 21st 1809

Your favour of the 3d & one enclosed from Mr Latrobe of the 9th. have been received;[1] the principal point on which I wished to be informed respecting the Sheet Iron is ommitted, Viz the breadth of it, for on that depends the arrangement of the Joist—with respect to Main gutters to receive the water from the Minor ones they would certainly be a great advantage & without them the water from the eve's will be always running into the Passage but to adopt them it will be necessary to have Copper or lead as we have not room to give Sufficient fall for Sheet Iron gutters. It will take Seventy two feet in length by eighteen inches wide; that much of the Sheet iron may be omitted.

As you intend makeing a drawing room of the centre room I would propose that the door into the Passage at the head of the Cellar Stair Should be dispenced with as a door there would take from the uniformity of the room & the wind[o]ws Serveing as doors out to the Colonade will nearly answer every purpose that one there Could, besides it Can be added at any future time Should it be found necessary. I Should like to have 150 Small patrins[2] for the Surbase of the Drawing room; Sent by the waggon. Inclosed is a Memo of additional articles wanted by it. The width of the Colonade has been long Since determined on & Cannot now be altered as the flooring is all prepared 11½ feet is as wide as we Can make it and I beleive that it is full as wide as it would be proper to Make it; I will thank you to Send me one Hundred Dollars when it Suits your Conveniency. I am Sir with respect your Very Humble Servant

JAS. DINSMORE

RC (DLC). Docketed by JM. Enclosure not found.

1. Letters not found.
2. Dinsmore may have meant patten-nails.

§ From the Mississippi Territorial Legislature. *22 November 1809*. Asks JM to take the necessary measures to extinguish Indian land title to the "rich and beautifull country on the Yazou which seperates our settlements from each other." Assures JM the purchase "is of the first importance to the prosperity of our Territory."

RC, two copies (DNA: RG 59, TP, Mississippi; and DNA: RG 107, LRUS, A-1810). 1 p. Signed by Speaker Ferdinand L. Claiborne and council president Alexander Montgomery; signed and dated by clerks of both chambers. Enclosed in David Holmes to Robert Smith, 29 Nov. 1809 (DNA: RG 107, LRRS, H-543:4). Printed in Carter, *Territorial Papers, Mississippi*, 6:31–32.

Memorandum from Albert Gallatin

[ca. 23 November 1809]

President's message

3d Paragraph. If in any instance &a.—The generality of the expression may encourage the idea that the renewal of the non-intercourse may not have been legal, or suggest that the want of strict legal authority was felt in other & more important points than that which alone we had considered as doubtful. I would therefore prefer to say—"If in permitting British vessels to depart without giving bonds, not to proceed to their own ports it should appear that the tenor of legal authority has not been strictly pursued, this must be ascribed to the anxious desire which was felt that no individuals should be injured by &a[1]—and I rely on the regard of Congress for the equitable interests of our own citizens to adopt whatever further provisions may be found requisite for the absolute[2] remission of penalties involuntarily incurred."[3]

I perceive nothing else which requires alteration, unless it be the phraseology of two or three Sentences

---

"a spirit *honorable* to the councils of a Nation . . . . . .[4] careful of its *honor*["]

"contending *Nations* (in endeavouring &a) *have* abridged the means of procuring from *itself*["]

---

last sentence of the message—The transcriber must have omitted some words in the three last lines—["]It becomes us to pray that (under &a) *it* may prove the Almighty Guardian &a." To what does *it* refer. I do not understand the idea intended to be conveyed.

In order not to keep the message from any of the other gentlemen who may not have seen it, I return it this day, but cannot furnish the financial paragraph till to morrow.

A. G.

Ms (DLC: Rives Collection, Madison Papers). In Gallatin's hand. Docketed by JM, "As to Message to Congs." Conjectural date assigned by comparison with the president's annual message of 29 Nov., a draft of which (not found) JM apparently submitted to various cabinet members.

1. Someone, possibly JM, interlined here in pencil: "so unforeseen an occurrence."
2. Someone, possibly JM, crossed through "the absolute" and interlined "a general" in pencil.
3. JM incorporated the sentence suggested by Gallatin into his annual message of 29 Nov. 1809.
4. Gallatin's ellipsis points.

From Benjamin Henry Latrobe

Sir,   CAPITOL, WASHINGTON, Novr. 23d. 1809
I have the honor to submit to you the following sketch of expenditures on the furniture of the President's house. The detail of the *principal* articles

comprised in the first item, has been submitted to You, & I do not therefore occupy your time by repeating the same.[1]

Amount of payments on accts. fully settled,	8.575.59
Monies placed in the hands of Mr Deblois[2] & expended for minor articles of domestic use, not yet fully disbursed or accounted for,	500.—
Monies paid on account of the furniture of the drawing room, in Philadelphia & Baltimore, not yet fully settled & paid for	1.550.—
	10.625.59
Commission at 2 ℔ Cent.	212.51
	10.838.10

NB. The furniture of the Drawing room will amount to about *3.800$*.
The accounts are not yet entirely ascertained; but the amount will not
exceed that sum materially. I expect daily from Philadelphia the Lamps
necessary to light the drawing room to pay for which the sum in hand—to
wit: 161$. 90 cts.—will probably be enough to liquidate the account.
There are also outstanding some accounts in this city for Sheeting, china,
&c, not yet sent in.

On account of the furniture of the drawing room, it is my wish to pay
to Mr. Rae[3] who is now here, the sum of 1.000$ this day; & also to be
enabled to liquidated [*sic*] all accounts & balances outstanding as soon as
possible, so as to account immediately to the Treasury for the sum of
11.000$ received, by Vouchers for accounts fully settled, the only vouch-
ers which are admissible. To do this I request a warrant for 1.500$ on
account. This will leave a balance of 1.500$ of the appropriation—a sum
of which 1000$ will I expect, remain applicable to the current demands of
the next 3¼ Years, as it is evident, that no important articles of new furniture can be purchased, nor are there I presume, any of essential importance deficient.

In the expenditure stated above, as provided for, I have calculated the
difference of value between a new carpet for the drawing room, and that
now upon the floor. This difference is estimated by Mr Rae at 100$. The
present carpet being of the pattern of that of the house of Representatives,
and being rather faded than worn, will be as useful at the Capitol as a new
one, & in fact, the pattern not being now to be procured, will be essential
to make those parts of the carpet at the Capitol which are not injured
useful. I am with high respect Yours faithful hble Servt

B H Latrobe

P.S. My son waits upon you with this letter the urgency of the business at the Capitol preventing my leaving it. I also beg to apologize for the marks of haste, in transcribing this letter.

RC (DLC). Docketed by JM.

1. See Latrobe to JM, 29 May and 7 July 1809 (*PJM-PS*, 1:212–13, 278).
2. Louis Deblois was an Alexandria merchant who served as a director of the Washington branch of the Bank of the United States between 1806 and 1811. He was also an agent and consul for Portugal in both Alexandria and Washington between 1808 and 1819 (John C. Van Horne and Lee W. Formwalt, eds., *The Correspondence and Miscellaneous Papers of Benjamin Henry Latrobe* [3 vols.; New Haven, 1984–88], 1:436 n. 1).
3. John Rae, an upholsterer in Philadelphia, provided Latrobe with interior decorations for the public buildings in Washington between 1807 and 1811 (ibid., 2:506 n. 5).

§ From Frederick Bates.[1] *23 November 1809, Secretary's Office, St. Louis.* Encloses an address requesting the appointment of John Coburn as territorial governor.

RC and enclosure (DNA: RG 59, LAR, 1809–17, filed under "Coburn"). RC 1 p. Enclosure (8 pp.) is an address dated 3 Nov. 1810 and signed in three sections. The first section is signed by Clement B. Penrose and thirty-eight others, the second by Macky Wherry and fifteen others, and the third by James Baldridge and thirty-eight others. Printed in Carter, *Territorial Papers, Louisiana-Missouri*, 14:339–42.

1. Frederick Bates (1777–1825) had been appointed secretary of Louisiana Territory in 1807. He served as acting governor, 1809–10, during the period between Meriwether Lewis's death and the arrival of his successor, Benjamin Howard (Thomas M. Marshall, *The Life and Papers of Frederick Bates* [1926; 2 vols.; New York, 1975 reprint], 1:3–41).

To David Gelston

DEAR SIR   WASHINGTON Novr. 24. 1809

I have recd. your favor of the 20th. I cannot doubt the pipe of Brandy to which it relates belongs to me. I have long known that one sent by Mr. Lee, was carried into England, where I understood that the neutral part of the Cargo was acquitted; the Vessel being condemned. Mr. Jos. Forrest now in N. Y. with a vessel coming round hither, has been requested to take charge of the Article. You will oblige me therefore by making use of the oppy: taking into consideration whether a Case over the Pipe be necessary to secure the Brandy agst. adulteration. Be pleased also to drop me notice of whatever expences are to be repd. you; and to accept my friendly respects

JAMES MADISON

RC (owned by Marshall B. Coyne, Washington, D.C., 1991).

Memorandum from William Eustis

[ca. 24 November 1809]

The fortifications which had been commenced on the seaboard, as will appear by a statement from the war department, are in many parts compleated, furnished with cannon and capable of affording a respectable defence. But another season will be required to finish the works in the harbour of New York, those at N. Orleans and in some other places where they have been delayed by unavoidable causes.

By the enlargement of the works and the employment of an additional number of workmen at the public armories, the supply of small arms is annually increasing and they are at the same time improving in quality. From this source & from those made on private contract it is expected a number sufficient for the public exigencies & without having recourse to importation.

No material alteration in the state of the army[1] has taken place, excepting that its effective force is in some degree diminished by sickness & other casualties, and by the resignation of a number of valuable officers in consequence of the favorable change which was manifested in our foreign relations.

Ms (DLC). In Eustis's hand. Misdated 1812 in the *Index to the James Madison Papers*. Date assigned by comparing the contents with the paragraph on the War Department in JM's annual message to Congress of 29 Nov. 1809.

1. JM omitted any reference to the state of the U.S. Army in his annual message to Congress.

Memorandum from Albert Gallatin

[ca. 24 November 1809]

The sums which had been previously accumulated in the Treasury, together with the receipts during the year ending on the 30th day of Septr. last (& amounting to more than nine millions of dollars) have enabled us to fulfill all our engagements and to defray the current expences of Government without recurring to any loan. But the insecurity[1] of our commerce and the consequent diminution of the public revenue will probably produce a deficiency in the receipts of the ensuing year, for which as well as for other details I refer you to the statements which will be transmitted from the Treasury.

Ms (DLC: Rives Collection, Madison Papers). In Gallatin's hand. Conjectural date assigned by comparison with Gallatin's closing sentence in his memorandum to JM, ca. 23 Nov. 1809, and JM's annual message of 29 Nov. 1809.

1. The remainder of the paragraph is written on an attached scrap of paper. JM inserted the entire paragraph into his annual message.

From Alfred Madison

DEAR UNCLE   WILLIAMSBURG Novr. 24th. 1809
By this you will find that I am at present in Wmsburg. I have at length commenced my course in Wm & Mary College—which has been so long famed for its dissipation & intemperance. I have been here about three weeks—& consequently have had some opportunity of forming an estimate of the advantages to be derived from attending the lectures delivered in this College. The Bishop[1] is certainly a very amiable & good man & he appears to have compiled & improved his lectures on Natural Philosophy with a great deal of labour & much Judgement. We are now reading Vattel on the law of nations[2]—from the principles laid down in this Author, & from a paragraph in Rutherforth[3] the Bishop, is decidedly of opinion that, agreeable to the law of nations the British government was bound to ratify the treaty made by Mr. Erskine, with the American government—but the law of nations can afford but a feeble barrier against the encroachment of a power which has long since manifested such a disregard ⟨for⟩ those principles, which have been heretofore held sacred. If Justice were the object, & reason the guide of all nations, it would be pleasing to reflect what a powerful & insurmountable bulwark the law of Nations, would form, to our rights & National prosperity—but under existing circumstances it would be but an idle speculation. We have heard of Mr. Jackson's dismissal. Thos⟨e⟩ with whom I have conversed on the subject, seem to have heard of his disrespectful conduct with the utmost indignation, and, of his consequent dismissal with the greatest satisfaction. At the present important crisis of our affairs, few can be uninterested. Although I have heretofore been but little concerned about local Politics, I should like very much, at present to read some of the News Papers. I will therefore be much obliged to you, if you will occasionally inclose me such, as will be useless to you & may probably afford me much satisfaction, & some improvement at the same time. With my best love to my Aunt, I remain yours affectionately

ALFRED MADISON[4]

RC (NN).

1. The Right Reverend James Madison, president of the College of William and Mary.

2. Emmerich de Vattel, *The Law of Nations*, was first published in French in 1758.

3. Thomas Rutherforth, *Institutes of Natural Law: Being the Substance of a Course of Lectures on Grotius de Jure Belli et Pacis* (2 vols.; Cambridge, 1754–56).

4. Alfred Madison (ca. 1790–1811) was JM's nephew, the son of William Madison. He became ill while still a college student and was sent to Philadelphia, at JM's bidding, for treatment by doctors Rush and Physick. He died there of "a settled pulmonary affection" (Rush to JM, 7 Dec. 1810 [DLC: Rives Collection, Madison Papers], and 30 Jan. 1811 [DLC]; Richmond *Enquirer*, 12 Feb. 1811).

From Thomas Jefferson

DEAR SIR   MONTICELLO Nov. 26. 09.

Your letter of the 6th. was recieved from our post office on the 24th. after my return from Bedford. I now re-inclose the letters of Mr. Short & Romanzoff, and with them a letter from Armstrong for your perusal, as there may be some matters in it not otherwise communicated.[1] The infatuation of the British government & nation is beyond every thing immaginable. A thousand circumstances announce that they are on the point of being blown up, & they still proceed with the same madness & increased wickedness. With respect to Jackson I hear of but one sentiment, except that some think he should have been sent off. The more moderate step was certainly more advisable. There seems to be a perfect acquiescence in the opinion of the Government respecting Onis. The public interest certainly made his rejection expedient; and as that is a motive which it is not pleasant always to avow, I think it fortunate that the contending claims of Charles & Ferdinand furnished such plausible embarrasment to the question of right: for, on our principles, I presume, the right of the Junta to send a minister could not be denied. La Fayette, in a letter to me expresses great anxiety to recieve his formal titles to the lands in Louisiana.[2] Indeed I know not why the proper officers have not sooner sent on the papers on which the grants might issue. It will be in your power to forward the grants or copies of them by some safe conveyance, as La Fayette says that no negociation can be effected without them.

I inclose you a letter from Majr. Neely,[3] Chickasaw agent, stating that he is in possession of 2. trunks of the unfortunate Governor Lewis, containing public vouchers, the manuscripts of his Western journey, & probably some private papers. As he desired they should be sent *to the president*, as the public vouchers render it interesting to the public that they should be safely recieved, and they would probably come most safely if addressed to you, would it not be advisable that Major Neely should recieve an order on your part to forward them to Washington addressed to you, by the stage, & if possible under the care of some person coming on? When at Washington, I presume, the papers may be opened & distributed, that is to say, the Vouchers to the proper offices where they are cognisable; the Manuscript voyage Etc to Genl. Clarke who is interested in it, and is believed to be now on his way to Washington; and his private papers if any to his administrator, who is John Marks, his half brother.[4] It is impossible you should have time to examine & distribute them; but if mr. Coles could find time to do it the family would have entire confidence in his distribution.[5] The other two trunks which are in the care of Capt Russel at the Chickasaw bluffs, & which Pernier[6] (Govr. Lewis's servt.) says contain his private property, I write to Capt Russel, at the request of mr. Marks, to forward to mr. Brown[7] at N. Orleans to be sent on to Richmond under my address. Pernier says that Governor Lewis owes him 240. D. for his wages. He has reci[e]ved money from Neely to bring him on here, & I furnish him to Washington, where he will arrive pennyless, and will ask for some money to be placed to the Governor's account. He rides a horse of the Governor's, which with the approbation of the Administrator I tell him to dispose of & give credit for the amount in his account against the Governor. He is the bearer of this letter and of my assurances of constant & affectionate esteem & respect

TH: JEFFERSON

RC (DLC); FC (DLC: Jefferson Papers).

1. Jefferson probably enclosed John Armstrong's letter of 19 Sept. 1809 (DLC: Jefferson Papers; listed in Jefferson's Epistolary Record [ibid.] as received 24 Nov.), in which the American minister reported that an observer "counted in the Downs [on the English Channel coast], upwards of twenty of our ships which had been brought in by British cruisers. . . . In what does this differ from a state of war, except in the patient submission with which we bear it?" Believing that the U.S. had been too forbearing, Armstrong advocated war against both Great Britain and France.

2. Lafayette to Jefferson, 16 Sept. 1809 (ibid.).

3. James Neelly to Jefferson, 18 Oct. 1809 (ibid.).

4. John H. Marks of Albemarle County.

5. Capt. Gilbert C. Russell, the commanding officer at Chickasaw Bluffs (Fort Pickering), recalled that Lewis left the fort for his eastern destination "with his papers well secured and packed on horses" (Donald Jackson, ed., *Letters of the Lewis and Clark Expedition, with Related Documents, 1783–1854* [2 vols.; Urbana, Ill., 1962], 2:573). Isaac A. Coles reported to Jefferson that the papers had reached Washington and "they were opened by Genl. Clarke and my self, when every thing of a public nature was given to the Dept. to which it properly belonged, every thing relating to the expedition to Genl. Clarke, & all that remained is contained in the five little bundles now directed to you." Coles asked Jefferson to hold Lewis's private papers "at Monticello, until called for by Mr. Wm. Meriwether, for whom they are intended" (Coles to Jefferson, 5 Jan. 1810, ibid., 2:486–87).

6. John Pernier (or Pernia), a free mulatto (ibid., 2:468 n. 1).

7. William Brown, the collector at New Orleans who had recently absconded (see Claiborne to JM, 19 Nov. 1809).

To Thomas Jefferson

DEAR SIR   WASHINGTON NOVr. 27. 1809

A gentleman of intelligence & good standing in Kentuckey lately signified to a friend here,[1] that he was much in conversation with Col. Monroe during his trip to that country, and that Sentiments which were repeatedly dropped by him, left no doubt, that altho' he de[c]lined a more important Station at N. O. he would not object to the vacancy produced by the death of Govr. Lewis, which would place him in a more eligible Climate. I can not bring myself to believe, that the Gentn. has not drawn a conclusion entirely erroneous, and that any step taken on a contrary supposition, would not be otherwise than offensive. Still it may be my duty in a way that can not have such an effect, to acquire certainty on the subject. Will you permit me, with that view to ask of you to give a turn to conversation, with Col. M, which may feel the disposition of his mind, without indicating any particular object. I need not suggest, that it will be desireable that the first opportunity occurring should be made use of.

I understand there is likely to be a Quorum in both Houses today notwithstanding the late bad weather.

It seems that Turreau has dispatches by a French sloop of War which left Bayonne Early in Ocr. He is but just arrived from Baltimore, & there has not yet been any communication with him. From the date of the opportunity, it is not probable that any thing is recd. as to our Affairs either more recent or important than the information from Genl. A. by the Wasp, which will be laid before Congs.[2] Yrs. always with affecte. respects

JAMES MADISON

RC (DLC). Docketed by Jefferson, "recd. Nov. 29."

1. The Kentucky gentleman was James Morrison, and his friend was the State Department clerk John Graham (John Monroe to James Monroe, 10 Feb. 1810 [NN: Monroe Papers]; James Monroe to John Taylor, 9 May 1810, *Proceedings of the Massachusetts Historical Society*, 3d ser., 42 [1908–9]: 328).

2. See JM's annual message to Congress, 29 Nov. 1809, n. 3.

From George W. Erving

Private—No 43

DEAR SIR   SEVILLE NOVr. 28 1809

The last letter which I took the liberty of addressing to you was dated Cadiz June 10t.[1] I do not now propose to trouble you with any political reflexions in addition to what are contained in the official dispatch of this

date to the department of state, inclosed herewith;[2] but write for the purpose of earnestly solliciting your attention to the request which I made for
leave of absence in my dispatch to the department No 47 of Augt. 11.
1808, in my unofficial letter to you of the same date, & subsequently in
one of May 5t 1809:[3] As is intimated in this last, I presume that you may
have judged a formal permission to be unnecessary, calculating upon a
state of things in this country which if it did not absolutely compel me to
depart, woud at least fully authorize my departure; or that you may have
supposed that the silence of governt on the subject woud be construed by
me into an acquiescence with my proposal: but I have not felt sufficiently
confident on this last point; & as to the first, the state of things adverted
to has not occurred, nor in spite of present appearances, do I forsee that
it will occurr so shortly as is generally calculated on; but on the contrary
it seems to me that the ballance may be kept nearly in its present position
for a very long period: by the late report laid before the french Senate, it
woud appear that the emperor does not intend to move any of his force
from Germany into Spain, but calculates upon a depot of abt. 35.000
recruits being sufficient for filling up the ranks here; by that report his
actual force here is much exaggerated, & the calculations of the report, if
not intended to mislead the judgemen⟨t,⟩ are as I beleive very erroneous,
& founded upon very false information as to the actual state & means of
this country: but supposing even that the emperor shoud send 80.000 additional troops, (& I do think that any number short of that will eventually
be only so many men sacrificed) & that these advance, the supreme Junta
(or the Cortes if in session) will have to change its residence, but Whilst
there is one district of Spain free, that district will be the rallying point;
it seems to be imagined that if the french shoud be in sufficient force to
occupy Seville, that the Junta have no resource but to fly to Cadiz & there
embark, but this is by no means its present intention; besides the Emperor
cannot expect to occupy these southern provinces, till he has done something in Portugal; tho the English will not assist in defending spain, they
will fight hard for Portugal, a sort of derelict which they hope to be able
to appropriate to their own exclusive use; and as to Cadiz they expect also
(with the same view) to make a stand there, a part of their army will retreat
thither under pretext of embarking, in pursuance of this plan they will
order a great number of transports thither, & a fleet sufficiently powerful
to command the whole of the spanish now assembled there.

I beg leave to suggest to you also the consideration whether in point of
policy it may not be better that I shoud go upon leave of absence, than
that I shoud wait till the last moment. I forbear to dilate on similar reflexions, because every thing under this head will be present to you, & because your determination will be regulated by a more complete & exact
view of the subject than I am able to take. I dare not act only on my own

discretion having been so very long a time without receiving any communication whatever from the department to afford me the least light or direction in this so extraordinary an epoch.

As to what relates to my personal views, I have before taken the liberty to State to you that my anxiety to go has encreased, & in effect my private affairs have sufferred & are suffering very essentially, not from bad faith in the agents whom I have entrusted with the management of my property, but because many things to be done relating to it, can only be done by myself, & many of my most important private papers are in London.[4]

I therefore again submit the matter to you in this view persuaded that it will meet with your attention, & with as much friendship & favor as publick considerations will enable you to give it. Dear Sir with the sincerest respect & attachment always your very faithful & most obliged St

GEORGE W ERVING

PS. Having seen in a Baltimore paper an extract from one of my dispatches said to have been received by a gentleman there "from his correspondent in Seville" I think it proper to lay it before you (it is herewith inclosed)[5] supposing either that said dispatch has been intercepted, or that this use may have been made of it without your authority, & at the same time assuring you that I have written No such letters to any private person whatever having during my residence in spain observed a strict rule on this point which I am sure you will approve of.

GWE

RC and enclosed clipping (MHi: Erving Papers). For enclosures, see nn. 2 and 5.

1. *PJM-PS*, 1:237–39.

2. For Erving's nineteen-page account of political developments within the Supreme Junta and the progress of the war in Spain and Portugal, see Erving to Robert Smith, 28 Nov. 1809 (DNA: RG 59, DD, Spain).

3. Erving had been seeking either a leave of absence or the appointment of a successor (Erving to JM, 11 Aug. 1808 [two letters, DNA: RG 59, DD, Spain]; Erving to JM, 5 May 1809, *PJM-PS*, 1:169).

4. Erving's first diplomatic appointment was as consul at London in 1801. He spent part of 1810 in London, returning to the U.S. in August (*PJM-SS*, 1:14 and n. 3, 343 and n. 1; Erving to JM, 5 Aug. 1810).

5. Baltimore newspapers, including the *American & Commercial Daily Advertiser*, 30 Aug. 1809, printed an extract from Erving's dispatch dated 9 July. The enclosed clipping is from another newspaper and is attached to a sheet on which are marginal corrections in Erving's hand. John Graham had reported to JM the possibility of an unauthorized leak of this dispatch (which bears pencil marks corresponding to the printed extract) (Graham to JM, 1 Sept. 1809, *PJM-PS*, 1:348–49 and n. 5).

From David Gelston

DEAR SIR,   NEW YORK November 28th. 1809

I have this day received your letter of the 24th. Mr Forrest called on me yesterday—his vessel has not yet arrived—understanding *the pipe of brandy* was cased I wrote (on its arrival in Boston) to Genl Dearborn, requesting him to ascertain the duties, without opening the case, it is apparently in perfect order. Very truly your's

DAVID GELSTON

RC (DLC).

From Charles Pinckney

DEAR SIR   November 28 1809

I wrote to you a few days agoe stating the nature of the Trade carried on between Amelia & the southern states & how highly advantageous to Great Britain the present nonintercourse act was in enabling her to pour her manufactures in upon us, free *of duty*, to bring them in *her own* Ships & carry away *in them*, all our produce that she wants at her own prices. I did not know whether this state of things was known to you & thought it ought to be communicated as soon as possible—this I did in compliance with the Wishes of our best friends & hope you have long since recieved it.

Knowing how things are here I was not at all surprised at Mr Jackson's late conduct, because I do not see how any other conduct on his part could have procrastinated the negotiations between the two countries, or long continued a state of things so highly advantageous to Great Britain. If he had commenced negotiations seriously, these must in the course of a short time have either ended in a treaty, or (if it was possible to want further conviction) in giving to the American People a final proof that Great Britain would never form an equal treaty with them or forbear invading their neutral rights—either of these results would have been dreadful to her—in the first American Commerce would have been restored to its former extent, energy & enterprise & herself rivalled & outdone not only in every other part of the world, but even in her own ports domestic & colonial—in the second she must have either risqued the consequences of a War, or Embargo perhaps worse to her than War. To avoid this she dispatched Mr Jackson to make a treaty if he could on their *own terms*, but if he could not; at any rate to procrastinate & prevent things coming to a crisis. Failing in his Expectations & seeing that our Government would not listen to improper offers he had but one course to pursue which was at any rate to endeavour to continue the present state as long as possible, by giving such an affront as could not be unnoticed, & to do it in such a way as to make it a personal affair to prevent if possible committing his Government. He expected & no doubt came prepared to be dismissed & to be replaced by another Minister, but all this will take up six Months, in which time he hopes things will remain as they are, & this is the grand object. In that time they will pour in Goods to the amount of Millions on Millions *free of duty*, they will get all our Wheat Cotton, Naval stores & Rice &c &c. they want at their own prices & employ their own Shipping *& have time* to wait Events in Europe.

Convinced that You must be of this Opinion & have been so from the moment it occurred I have taken the liberty of throwing these thoughts on paper on the road to Columbia & of sending them to be forwarded from Charleston, with the assurance that the people of this State will with ardour & unanimity support their Government in every measure they shall concieve the Crisis demands. I hope yourself & friends have enjoyed health & With my best Wishes for your honour & happiness I am always dear sir With great respect & regard Yours Truly

CHARLES PINCKNEY

RC (DLC).

Annual Message to Congress

November 29. 1809.

Fellow Citizens of the Senate & of the House of Representatives.

At the period of our last meeting, I had the satisfaction of communicating an adjustment with one of the principal belligerent Nations, highly important in itself, & still more so, as presaging a more extended Accommodation. It is with deep concern, I am now to inform you, that the favorable prospect has been overclouded, by a refusal of the British Government to abide by the Act of it's Minister Plenipotentiary, & by it's ensuing policy towards the United States, as seen through the communications of the Minister sent to replace him.

Whatever pleas may be urged for a disavowal of engagements formed by Diplomatic Functionaries, in cases where, by the terms of the engagements, a mutual ratification is reserved; or where notice at the time may have been given, of a departure from instructions; or in extraordinary cases, essentially Violating the principles of equity; a disavowal could not have been apprehended in a case, where no such notice or violation existed; where no such ratification was reserved; & more especially where, as is now in proof, an engagement, to be executed without any such ratification, was contemplated by the instructions given, and where it had, with good faith, been carried into immediate execution, on the part of the United States.

These considerations not having restrained the British Government from disavowing the Arrangement, by virtue of which it's Orders in Council were to be revoked, & the event Authorizing the renewal of commercial intercourse, having thus not taken place; it necessarily became a question, of equal urgency & importance, whether the Act prohibiting that intercourse, was not to be considered as remaining in legal force. This question being, after due deliberation, determined in the affirmative, a Proclamation to that effect, was issued. It could not but happen, however, that a return to this state of things, from that which had followed an execution of the arrangement by the U. S. would involve difficulties. With a view to diminish these as much as possible, the instructions from the Secretary of the Treasury, now laid before you,[1] were transmitted to the Collectors of the Several Ports. If in permitting British Vessels to depart, without giving bonds not to proceed to their own ports, it should appear, that the tenor of legal Authority, has not been strictly pursued, it is to be ascribed to the anxious desire which was felt, that no individuals should be injured by so unforeseen an Occurrence: And I rely on the regard of Congress for the equitable interests of our own Citizens, to adopt whatever further provisions may be found requisite, for a general remission of penalties involuntarily incurred.

The recall of the disavowed Minister, having been followed by the Appointment of a Successor, hopes were indulged that the new Mission would contribute to alleviate the disappointment which had been produced, and to remove the causes which had so long embarrassed the good understanding of the two Nations. It could not be doubted, that it would at least, be charged with conciliatory explanations of the step which had been taken, & with proposals to be substituted for the rejected arrangement. Reasonable & Universal as this expectation was, it also has not been fulfil[l]ed. From the first official disclosures of the new Minister, it was found that he had received no authority to enter into explanations, relative to either branch of the Arrangement disavowed; nor any Authority to substitute proposals, as to that branch, which concerned the British Orders in Council: And finally that his proposals with respect to the other branch, the attack on the Frigate Chesapeake, were founded on a presumption, repeatedly declared to be inadmissible by the U. S., that the first step towards adjustment was due from them; the proposals, at the same time, Omitting even a reference to the Officer Answerable for the murderous aggression, & asserting a claim not less contrary to the British laws, & British practice, than to the principles and obligations of the United States.

The correspondence between the Department of State & this Minister will show, how unessentially the features presented in it's commencement, have been varied in it's progress. It will show also, that forgetting the respect due to all Governments, he did not refrain from imputations on this, which required that no further communications should be received from him.[2] The necessity of this step will be made known to His Britannic Majesty, through the Minister Plenipotentiary of the U. S in London— and it would indicate a want of the confidence due to a Government, which so well understands and exacts, what becomes foreign Ministers near it, not to infer that the misconduct of it's own Representative, will be viewed in the same light, in which it has been regarded here. The British Government will learn, at the same time, that a ready attention will be given to communications through any channel which may be substituted. It will be happy, if the change in this respect, should be accompanied by a favorable revision of the unfriendly policy, which has been so long pursued, towards the United States.

With France, the other belligerent whose trespasses on our commercial rights have long been the subject of our just remonstrances, the posture of our relations does not correspond with the measures, taken on the part of the United States, to effect a favorable change. The result of the several communications made to her Government, in pursuance of the Authorities vested by Congress in the Executive, is contained in the correspondence of our Minister at Paris, now laid before you.[3]

By some of the other Belligerents, altho' professing just and Amicable dispositions, injuries materially affecting our commerce, have not been duly controled or repressed. In these cases, the interpositions deemed proper on our part, have not been omitted. But it well deserves the consideration of the Legislature, how far both the safety and the honor of the American flag may be consulted, by adequate provisions against that collusive prostitution of it, by Individuals, unworthy of the American name, which has so much favored the real or pretended suspicions, under which the honest commerce of their fellow Citizens has suffered.

In relation to the Powers on the coast of Barbary, nothing has Occurred which is not of a nature rather to inspire confidence than distrust, as to the continuance of the existing Amity. With our Indian Neighbors, the just & benevolent system, continued towards them, has also preserved peace, and is more and more advancing habits favorable to their civilization and happiness.

From a statement which will be made by the Secretary of War,[4] it will be seen that the fortifications on our maritime frontier, are in many of the Ports compleated; affording the defence which was contemplated; & that a further time will be required to render complete, the works in the Harbour of New York, & in some other places. By the enlargement of the works, and the employment of a greater number of hands at the public Armories, the supply of small arms, of an improving quality, appears to be annually increasing, at a rate, that with those made on private contract, may be expected to go far towards providing for the public exigency.

The act of Congress providing for the equipment of our Vessels of war, having been fully carried into execution, I refer to the statement of the Secretary of the Navy[5] for the information which may be proper on that subject. To that statement is added a view of the transfers of appropriations authorized by the Act of the Session preceding the last, and of the grounds on which the transfers were made.

Whatever may be the course of your deliberations on the subject of our military establishments, I should fail in my duty, in not recommending to your serious attention, the importance of giving to our militia, the great bulwark of our Security, and resource of our power, An Organization, the best adapted to eventual situations, for which the U. S. ought to be prepared.

The sums which had been previously Accumulated in the Treasury, together with the receipts during the year ending on the 30th. of September last (& amounting to more than nine millions of Dollars) have enabled us to fulfill all our engagements, & to defray the current expenses of Government, without recurring to any loan. But the insecurity of our commerce, and the consequent diminution of the public revenue, will probably produce a deficiency in the receipts of the ensuing year, for which and for other details, I refer to the statements which will be transmitted from the Treasury.[6]

In the state, which has been presented, of our affairs with the great parties to a disastrous & protracted War, carried on in a mode equally injurious & unjust to the U. S. as a neutral nation, the wisdom of the National Legislature, will be again summoned to the important decision on the alternatives before them. That these will be met in a spirit, worthy the councils of a Nation, conscious both of it's rectitude, & of it's rights, & careful as well of it's honor, as of it's peace, I have an entire confidence. And that the result will be stamped by a unanimity becoming the Occasion, and be supported by every portion of our citizens, with a patriotism enlightened & invigorated by experience, ought as little to be doubted.

In the midst of the wrongs & vexations experienced from external causes, there is much room for congratulation, on the prosperity & happiness flowing from our situation at Home. The blessing of health has never been more universal. The fruits of the seasons, though in particular

Articles & districts, short of their usual redundancy, are more than sufficient for our wants & our comforts. The face of our country every where presents the evidence of laudable enterprize, of extensive capital, and of durable improvement. In a cultivation of the materials, & the extension of useful manufactures; more especially, in the general application to household fabrics; we behold a rapid diminution of our dependence on foreign supplies. Nor is it unworthy of reflection, that this revolution in our pursuits and habits, is in no slight degree, a consequence of those impolitic & Arbitrary Edicts, by which the contending nations, in endeavoring each of them to obstruct our trade with the other, have so far abridged our means of procuring the productions & manufactures, of which our own are now taking the place.

Recollecting always, that for every advantage which may contribute to distinguish out [sic] lot, from that to which others are doomed by the unhappy spirit of the times, we are indebted to that Divine Providence whose goodness has been so remarkably extended to this rising Nation; it becomes us to cherish a devout gratitude; and to implore from the same Omnipotent Source a blessing on the consultations and measures, about to be undertaken, for the welfare of our beloved Country.

JAMES MADISON

RC and enclosures, two copies (DNA: RG 233, President's Messages; and DNA: RG 46, Legislative Proceedings, 11A-E1, 11A-E3). Both RCs are in handwriting of clerks, dated and signed by JM. Received and ordered printed by both houses of Congress on 29 Nov. House copy referred to the Committee of the Whole (*Annals of Congress*, 11th Cong., 2d sess., 475–78, 684). Sixteen numbered enclosures on Anglo-American relations are printed in *ASP, Foreign Relations*, 3:301–23; some of these are discussed in nn. 1 and 2. Enclosure no. 17, six letters on Franco-American relations, is mentioned in n. 3. The *National Intelligencer*, 29 Nov. 1809, reported that JM "communicated, by Mr. Graham, the following Message to Congress," and thus the president continued the practice instituted by Jefferson of sending his annual message to Congress, where it was read by clerks.

1. Gallatin's circular letter to customs collectors of 9 Aug. 1809 announced the rescinding of JM's 19 Apr. proclamation (*ASP, Foreign Relations*, 3:304).

2. The Francis James Jackson–Robert Smith correspondence between 9 Oct. and 8 Nov. was enclosed. Smith's letter of 8 Nov. took exception to Jackson's intimation on 11 Oct. (repeated later) that the American negotiators knew Erskine had exceeded his instructions and stated that in the light of this "gross insinuation . . . no further communications will be received from you" (ibid., 3:319). Jackson attempted to have the last word by sending a circular to all British consuls in U.S. cities on 13 Nov. explaining his side of the matter. Sympathetic Federalist newspapers reprinted this circular, thus laying Jackson's case before the American people. This action drew the ire of Congress, which passed a joint resolution introduced by Senator William Branch Giles excoriating the British minister for an "aggravated insult and affront to the American people and their Government, as it is evidently an insidious attempt to excite their resentments and distrusts against their own Government, by appealing to them, through false or fallacious disguises, . . . and to excite resentments

and divisions amongst the people" (*Annals of Congress*, 11th Cong., 2d sess., 481, 742–43; *U.S. Statutes at Large*, 2:612).

3. JM enclosed extracts from Armstrong's dispatches of 4 and 16 Sept. 1809, including a translation of Champagny's letter to Armstrong of 22 Aug. announcing French policy with respect to neutral rights. He also included Secretary of State Smith's 1 Dec. 1809 letter to Armstrong (*ASP, Foreign Relations*, 3:324–26).

4. On 19 Dec. William Eustis transmitted his "Report of Fortifications for the defence of the ports and harbors of the United States" (*ASP, Military Affairs*, 1:245–46).

5. On 4 Dec. JM transmitted Paul Hamilton's report on the navy (*ASP, Naval Affairs*, 1:201–5).

6. On 7 Dec. Albert Gallatin submitted his report on the state of the treasury (*ASP, Finance*, 2:373–75).

From Thomas Jefferson

DEAR SIR   MONTICELLO NOV. 30. 09.

I recieved last night yours of the 27th. & rode this morning to Colo. Monroe's. I found him preparing to set out tomorrow morning for Loudon, from whence he will not return till Christmas. I had an hour or two's frank conversation with him. The catastrophe of poor Lewis served to lead us to the point intended. I reminded him that in the letter I wrote to him while in Europe proposing the Government of Orleans,[1] I also suggested that of Louisiana if fears for health should be opposed to the other. I said something on the importance of the post, it's advantages &c. expressed my regret at the curtain which seemed to be drawn between him & his best friends, and my wish to see his talents & integrity engaged in the service of his country again, and that his going into any post would be a signal of reconciliation, on which the body of republicans, who lamented his absence from the public service, would, again rally to him. These are the general heads of what I said to him in the course of our conversation. The sum of his answers was that to accept of that office was incompatible with the respect he owed himself, that he never would act in any office where he should be subordinate to any body but the President himself, or which did not place his responsibility substantially with the President and the nation: that at your accession to the chair, he would have accepted a place in the cabinet, & would have exerted his endeavors most faithfully in support of your fame and measures; that he is not un-ready to serve the public, and especially in the case of any difficult crisis in our affairs; that he is satisfied that such is the deadly hatred of both France & England, and such their self reproach & dread at the spectacle of such a government as ours, that they will spare nothing to destroy it; that nothing but a firm union among the whole body of republicans can save it, & therefore that no schism should be indulged on any ground; that in his present situation he is sincere in his anxieties for the success of the administration, & in his support of it, as far as the limited sphere of his action or influence extends. That his influence to this end had been used with those with whom the world had ascribed to him an influence he did not possess, until, whatever it was, it was lost. (He particularly named J. Randolph who he said had plans of his own on which he took no advice) and that he was now pursuing what he believed his properest occupation, devoting his whole time & faculties to the liberation of his pecuniary embarrasments, which 3. years of close attention he hoped would effect. In order to know more exactly what were the kinds of employ he would accept, I adverted to the information of the papers which came yesterday, that Genl. Hampton was dead,[2] but observed that the military life, in our present state, offered nothing which could operate on the principle of patriotism; he said he would sooner be shot than take a command under Wilkinson. In this sketch I have given truly the substance of his ideas, but not always his own words.[3] On the whole I conclude he would accept a place in the Cabinet, or a military command dependant on the Executive alone; and I rather suppose a diplomatic mission, because it would fall within the scope of his views, & not because he said so, for no allusion was made to any thing of that kind in our conversation. Every thing from him breathed the purest patriotism, involving however a close attention to his own honour & grade, he expressed himself with the utmost devotion to the interests of our own country, and I am satisfied he will pursue them with honor & zeal in any character in which he shall be willing to act.

I have thus gone far beyond the single view of your letter that you may, under any circumstances, form a just estimate of what he would be disposed to do. God bless you, & carry you safely through all your difficulties.

TH: JEFFERSON

RC (DLC: Rives Collection, Madison Papers); FC (DLC: Jefferson Papers).

1. While Monroe was serving as U.S. minister to Great Britain, Jefferson offered him his choice of the governorships of the Louisiana or Orleans territories, which he declined (Jefferson to Monroe, 4 May 1806, Ford, *Writings of Jefferson*, 8:448–49; Monroe to Jefferson, 8 July 1806, Stanislaus M. Hamilton, ed., *The Writings of James Monroe* [7 vols.; New York, 1898–1903], 4:477–78).

2. The *National Intelligencer* for 27 Nov. 1809 carried a report of Hampton's death. "It is with great regret that we state, on the authority of the Whig of Baltimore, the death of General WADE HAMPTON." More accurate information appeared in the Richmond *Enquirer* of 28 Nov. 1809, which reported: "General HAMPTON, left Columbia, [South Carolina] . . . , for New Orleans, on Tuesday, the 7th Instant." Hampton died in 1835.

3. Monroe's recollection of this conversation was rather different, and he told George Hay that he had made it plain to Jefferson that "there was but one proposition which [JM] could have made to me, or I accepted, which was to have invited me into the cabinet in the place next to his own, being that which he had lately held." JM, Monroe further pointed out, "had lost that opportunity" (Monroe to George Hay, 30 Nov. 1809 [NN: Monroe Papers]).

§ From Charles Scott. *30 November 1809, Frankfort*. Sends JM a copy of a letter recently received from Dr. James Speed.[1] Speed, now a resident of lower Louisiana, is a man whose credentials are impeccable. Believes the information Speed relates is "of so Much importance" he is duty bound to reveal contents to JM.

RC (DLC). 1 p. Enclosure not found. Scott was governor of Kentucky, 1808–12.

1. James Speed (1774–1812), born in Charlotte County, Virginia, moved with his family to Kentucky in 1782. He studied medicine at Edinburgh (Thomas Speed, *Records and Memorials of the Speed Family* [Louisville, Ky., 1892], pp. 57, 147).

From William Duane

SIR,   PHILA. 1. Decr. 1809

Every man owes to his country the best services of which he is capable; if in an upright zeal to fulfil this obligation, a man may overate the value of his conceptions, the intention to do good will at once excuse the attempt and apologize for whatever trouble he may give in communicating the result of his reflections.

In the present situation of the national affairs, and considering that the uniform policy of the belligerents is now irrevocably fixt, as well by fear and necessity on the part of Great Britain, as by interest and the pride of triumph on the other, that course which is best adapted to the interests and policy of the United States, tho' it cannot be very well mistaken by men of sober minds, is not so easily pursued directly, as it would be were the attacks upon the nation open instead of insidious—or by other weapons than those of diplomacy and intrigue.

The country has not been more united on any occasion perhaps since the revolution, as on the present occasion; the attack on the Chesapeake, shook the influence of England to its foundations; and had Congress maintained the Embargo, and called forthe the Militia of Massachusetts only to enforce the laws; that influence could never have reared its crest; the Mission of Rose[1] would have been a mission of temporary accommodation at least; and instead of the broken Engagements of Erskine, and the contumacious audacity of Jackson, we should now have had either the open commerce of the World or the applause and respect of mankind as our passport to the friendship of nations after a peace shall have been established.

It is now a matter of the first importance to consider how the nation can best act under the present aspect of human affairs. It is morally certain that a peace whenever it takes place will be followed by an establishment of some fixt rules of law, by which the nations who shall concur in them will be governed in their intercourse with each other; that some code analogous to the principles recognized in the writings of Barlow, Paine, Azuni,[2] and more early asserted by the Armed Neutrality of 1780, tho' not in so enlarged a sense; and that such nations as may either withhold their concurrence, or refuse to maintain them will be placed out of the law of civil society. The first question then is what course ought the United States to pursue in such circumstances?

This question however cannot be determined, until a previous enquiry is made, what can the U. S. do under such circumstances? After this is examined the path appears not to be incumbered with any serious difficulties; and even this question, can be met with perfect confidence and security, if the Representatives of the people do not again abandon the executive; or that the executive determines to support the laws of the land whenever they are established. It is not my intention to say that the Executive did not act with a discretion truly benignant, at the period when Massachusetts appeared to threaten a dissolution of the Union;[3] but I am still convinced, that had the Militia of Masachusetts or only 5000 men been embodied that the government and laws of the Union would have triumphed, and that there neither would have been a life lost nor a factious collusion with the agents of England exhibited since.

What can we now do? This question involves others, and particularly this: are there any means by which the national sentiment can be concentrated so as to bid defiance to every movement or menace of faction. It is not necessary to my present purpose to enter into the discussion of any collateral questions, since my intention is to offer the suggestions of my mind on this point alone. If this point can be accomplished the choice of means and measures afterwards will not be uncertain. If what I conceive proper to be pursued should yet fall short of the extent of advantage which I anticipate, even then we should not in any case be in a worse situation than we are without doing any thing; and if I conceive right all that the most benevolent wishes or the most zealous virtue could desire would be attempted by us.

The policy of the government and the real happiness of the people, have concurred in rendering the nation adverse to the calamitous resort of war. The impossibility of raising large armies, as well as the unexaggerated danger of such establishments have the same operation; and the want of objects sufficiently contiguous to tempt enterprize, damps in a great degree the ardor of those whose military passions would be excited to a dangerous extent, were the temptations nearer at hand. It is impossible for this nation then to go to war, but when the whole people are united, when it is a sentiment of common danger or common resentment. Let me add another reason, the total want of a military system, or speaking largely of military ideas, incapacitates the U. S. from going to war by land.

Under all these difficulties if we were called upon for defence, the sense of danger would supercede the arrangements of policy; and the systems which we are now wholly destitute of, would (tho' with a large purchase of blood) grow out of our dangers; we should as in the Revolution and as Peter the Great acquired his knowlege, learn to conquer by being often defeated. I conceive war may be avoided. The purpose of this address is to suggest my ideas of the means.

Having exhausted all the artifices of Diplomacy, the British government will be governed in her deportment to us, by the prospects which she may have in Europe. She will not abandon her policy of monopoly, unless perhaps for a temporary resting time, as at the peace of Amiens.[4] If there should appear to be a prospect of stirring up another war on the continent, she would again go to war; or so soon as the French should have built a navy equal in number to her own, that moment or before it, war would be again renewed; and we should experience in a more tense tyranny the encrease of those oppressions, for which she has established the precedents within a few years. The Orders of Council ⟨and⟩ the proclamations of 1807 and 1808, would like the rule of 1756, be preached up as the established law of nations; and the leisure of a temporary peace would have quieted down those resentments which now prevail against her tyranny as those which prevailed in the revolution were extinguished by the strange revolution produced by the British Treaty.[5]

It is a very common opinion that if all the nations of Europe were decidedly against England, she would be induced to make peace with us. Those who conceive such ideas, may perhaps know the English policy better than I do; but as I can form no judgment but by my own study and observation; by a residence of several years at the theatre on which they act; by a personal acquaintance with many of the most distinguished men of the age in that country; and by habits and pursuits, well adapted to investigate as well as to acquire a knowlege of their policy.

If the whole of the nations of Europe should, and I am persuaded they must, become hostile to English policy; I am satisfied by reflection, that England will not abate her policy towards the U. States; because as she exists by commerce only, and as we are in truth the most formidable rival in the commercial world; it would be her interest to interrupt if she could not destroy our prosperity; her policy would lead her to do that on a large scale which she has done on a small; she has encouraged the conflagration of our growing factories and would conflagrate our cities and towns; she would not suffer our ships to go to the continent without paying a transit or tribute duty[;] she would [not] suffer our ships to pursue even our accustomed commerce in time of peace; the same policy leads to annihilate our trade altogether; and it is not the want of inclination but of ability that prevents it.

Two all powerful motives impel the U. States to determine now and to satisfy the world of its policy. 1. The national Interests as they concern the body of the nation in their individual situation. 2 The national Interests in their relations with civilized nations. We are now called upon to preserve and to maintain both; and if we lose this time, we shall never again possess occasions so favorable to our fortunes and to the honor of the nation.

All these objects can be obtained in my opinion without war—by a measure founded on the principles of neutrality, as they were asserted in 1780, accompanied by a declaration of Retaliation, which should go to every thing but human life. To exemplify the method in which the government might proceed, I will take the liberty of specifying in a loose way, the particular course and the manner that seems to me best to be adopted in prosecuting the measures.

The outrage on the Chesapeake is in every respect marked by the atrocity of the design and the perpetration, by the contumatious carrying away, several, and hanging of one of the captives; by the unpunished impunity of the authors and perpetrators; and by the repeated insults & refusals of justice which have followed it.

A law of Congress might authorise reprisals, either in that special case, or which would be more decisive in all cases; the seizure of man for man, British subjects for American citizens, and the detention of the persons seized as hostages for the security and safe return of the persons taken unlawfully from on board any american ship. The principle to be extended to ships; ship for ship, dollar for dollar; and in failure of ships or merchandize, the retaliating principle to be extended to every other species of British property; dollar for dollar, together with expences.

The law of Congress recognizing these principles, might be issued with a public Declaration of the intentions of the United States, to be issued by the Executive; wherein the injuries sustained might be set forth, and the long forbearance exhibited; that even now the Govt. of the U States deprecates war, & the destruction of the lives of the unoffending citizens of any country for the offences committed by their rulers; that after repeated efforts had failed to obtain the restoration of the citizens of the U States, without any other effect than a renewal of insult; the Govert. was now disposed to take another recourse, to avoid if possible the greater calamities of war, by taking as hostages wherever found British subjects, in number equal to the number of persons taken from on board the Chesapeake, to the number killed, and to the number maimed; and that those hostages should be detained and put to employments suited to their capacities, and the surplus of whatever they might by their industry acquire to be applied to the support of the injured or the survivers of those who were killed maimed or taken away from on board the Chesapeake, until such time as the British Gover[n]ment should restore those now in their custody and remunerate as might be agreed upon the survivors of the murdered and injured.

The proceedings in the initiatory process of such a course of measures, point themselves out; and I only offer my conceptions because I do not wish to leave the subject incomplete. The minister of the U S. might make a formal demand of the persons, at the court of London, and signify the indisposition of the U S. to resort to an ancient usage that of taking hostages; or this might follow the first requisition; he might in the course of the correspondence, signify that the United States would in future take hostages and make levies on property to the full amount of all illegal captures or detentions made by any nation; and might still strongly and strenuously argue upon the humanity of such a course in preference to the shedding of the blood of the unoffending.

I persuade myself that this recourse would have all the important effects which I set out with assuming as necessary; and other effects equally important. The people of the U. S. would have reason to be proud of another step in national policy towards the avoidance and abolition of war; they would see in the act of taking hostages for the restoration of the captives, a regard to their own security in future; (a regard too little attended to hitherto either in the eye of policy or humanity); they would find the government humane and yet just; faithful to itself and yet more generous than other nations in sparing the blood of the innocent; with regard to foreign nations, it would make every people our friends, because the people of every country are the sufferers and the governors alone are those who do not suffer, our example would then be the touch stone of respect, and esteem would even take place of hostility in the bosom of the very nation that injured us; while the hostages we should have would assure us negociators in the very bosom of the hostile nation whose cries would be respected where our complaints of wrong have only provoked derision; and become the jest of profligate ministers and the topics of their midnight debauches.

There is one more point of view in which this project of retaliation and hostages may be taken. It may be said that it would produce an immediate declaration of war on the part of Great Britain. This would perhaps depend in the first instance on the mode in which the subject should be promulged; or on incidents over which we have no control. I am of opinion that she will yet make war upon us; and I am persuaded as well from the choice of their last Ambassador as well as from the correspondence of his style here with his style in Denmark,[6] that he was interned as the touch stone by which the measure of our patience was to be tried before actual war was resorted to. In this last case then war would not be the Effect of our measure of benevolent policy, but of their intolerable envy and monopoly.

It would then remain to be enquired whether upon their making actual war, that is making war without landing an army or invading our territory, the policy of retaliation and hostages, would not still be a judicious one so long as they should refrain from outrage on our territory. Making war upon our ships at sea, our ships might be authorised to arm for defence; and a declaration to this Effect might be published.

Among the good effects of the retaliation by hostages, the country would soon be cleared of many detestable characters that are now lurking about our cities. Others whose disaffection contributes to sustain that hostility to the government so visible in our cities would be repressed by public opinion or by a sense of danger. The nation once roused by a measure so humane and yet decisive would not suffer the calumny that has been poured forth with impunity.

But the most important consideration in my view is the great probability that it would produce a great effect upon public sentiment in England and compel the administration to restore all our impressed Citizens and to refrain from their capture in future. Should any declaration be issued in such an event, it seems to me that it would be wise to establish the principle as a permanent one, that of taking hostages and sequestrating property in retaliation and declaring that such would be the policy of the U. S. at all times in preference to war.

Such sir are the ideas that present themselves to me, thrown together without reperusal or taking a copy, which my avocations do not admit me the leisure to do. I submit it to your liberality, and offer it as a testimony of my zeal and good intentions, whatever may be the degree of regard to which it is entitled. I am Sir Your Obed Sert

WM DUANE

RC (DLC). Docketed by JM.

1. British diplomat George Henry Rose visited the U.S. from October 1807 to March 1808 on an unsuccessful mission to negotiate a settlement of the *Chesapeake* crisis (Brant, *Madison*, 4:404–14; Mayo, *Instructions to British Ministers*, pp. 235–42, 258–59, 262).

2. Duane referred to the authors of three works advocating neutral rights and freedom of the seas: Fulwar Skipwith and Joel Barlow, *Memoir on Certain Principles of Public Maritime*

Law: Written for the French Government (an appendix to *Joel Barlow to His Fellow Citizens of the United States. Letter II. On Certain Political Measures Proposed to Their Consideration* . . . [Philadelphia, 1801; Shaw and Shoemaker 135]); Thomas Paine, *Compact Maritime* (Washington, 1801; Shaw and Shoemaker 1087); and Domenico Alberto Azuni, *The Maritime Law of Europe*, trans. William Johnson (2 vols.; New York, 1806; Shaw and Shoemaker 9877). All were first published in Paris (*Proceedings of the American Antiquarian Society*, n.s., 70 [1961]: 443). Duane reprinted Barlow's *Letter*, and Samuel Harrison Smith published the English translation of Paine's pamphlet, copies of which Jefferson sent to JM and ten other Virginia Republicans (Jefferson to JM, 12 Feb. 1801 [DLC: Jefferson Papers]).

3. During the embargo crisis of 1808–9 riots occurred in some Massachusetts ports, and the state legislature passed resolutions defying federal enforcement of the law (Malone, *Jefferson and His Time*, 5:652–53).

4. The Peace of Amiens was signed on 25 Mar. 1802 and lasted until May 1803, at which time Great Britain began attacking French commerce without prior warning (Georges Lefebvre, *Napoleon: From 18 Brumaire to Tilsit, 1799–1807*, trans. Henry F. Stockhold [New York, 1969], pp. 110–15, 178).

5. Duane alluded to the partisan support for the Jay treaty in 1795, which to Republicans revealed a pro-British element in the Federalist ranks.

6. In August 1807 Jackson had delivered a demand from the British government to the Prince Royal of Denmark that he surrender the Danish fleet. When the demand was refused, the Royal Navy bombarded Copenhagen between 1 and 5 Sept. 1807.

§ From John Drayton. *1 December 1809, Columbia, South Carolina.* Sends JM a copy of his "first Communication" to the South Carolina legislature [following his inauguration as governor], which relates to "the present Crisis."

RC (DLC). 1 p. Enclosure not found, but a print impression on the cover reveals that Drayton enclosed his *Message from His Excellency the Governor, No. 1, Delivered to the Legislature of South-Carolina, on the 29th November, 1809* (Columbia, 1809; Shaw and Shoemaker 18660). The message recounted the Erskine agreement, its disavowal by Great Britain, the arrival of Erskine's successor, and the fruitless correspondence between Francis James Jackson and the secretary of state. Drayton concluded that Congress "will comport itself with that firmness and dignity which the occasion requires."

§ From Paul Hamilton. *1 December 1809, Navy Department.* Encloses report on condition of "Vessels of Warr & Gun Boats," distinguishing between those commissioned before the navy act of 31 Jan. 1809 and "the Number fitted out under that Act." Also appends reports on expenditures authorized by the act of 3 Mar. regulating the treasury, war, and navy departments.

RC and enclosures (DNA: RG 233, President's Messages); RC and one enclosure (DNA: RG 46, Legislative Proceedings, 11A-E7); letterbook copy (DNA: RG 45, LSP). RC 2 pp. Enclosures with House copy (24 pp.), dated 25 Nov., include a description of the entire American navy, ship by ship, and itemized accounts of warrants drawn on naval appropriations with summaries for each category. Only the report on condition of vessels (1 p.) is filed with Senate copy. RC and enclosures enclosed in JM to Congress, 4 Dec. 1809. RC, report, and summaries of accounts printed in *ASP, Naval Affairs*, 1:201–5.

To Pierre Samuel DuPont de Nemours

DEAR SIR   WASHINGTON December 3. 1809

I have recd. your favor of July 11.[1] with the several setts of Mr. Turgot's valuable works. I thank you much for the one which you were so good as to allot for myself; and have with great pleasure distributed the others according to their destinations. The copy for your son was delivered to Mr. Bauduy his partner in the useful establishment near Wilmington which I hope will be as profitable to the Undertakers, as it is interesting to the public.

I wish I could say more in favor of the efforts in our Republic to establish an adequate system of Education, so requisite to the solidity of its bases. The public attention however has been successfully called to the subject, and would be more animated, if the situation in which we are kept by the war in Europe, & incidents growing out of it among ourselves, did not divert the public feelings & resources. In the mean time it is flattering to find that so much interest is taken in this great object, by our enlightened & benevolent friends, who in the midst of the distractions of their own hemisphere, employ their thoughts for the benefit of ours.

I forward this by one of our Armed Ships; the commander of which is instructed to receive you as a passenger on his return, if circumstances should render the opportunity acceptable to you.[2]

I pray you to be assured of my sensibility to your friendly congratulations, and of my very high esteem & good wishes.

JAMES MADISON

RC (DeGE). JM enclosed a copy of his annual message to Congress and accompanying "documens curieux" (DuPont to JM, 20 Jan. 1810).

1. *PJM-PS*, 1:285–86.
2. DuPont returned to the U.S. in 1815.

To John G. Jackson

SIR,   WASHINGTON Dec: 3. 1809.

I have received your letter of Oct: 29 covering the resolutions of the 119 Regiment of the Virginia Militia.

The Spirit which these resolutions express, is the more to be approved and relied on, as it is the result of an examination into the foreign aggressions committed against the United States, & into the proceedings of the Government in consequence of them. A conviction of the justice of our cause, & a determination to maintain the National rights, as transmitted by the Fathers of the Revolution, form a ground on which faithful Citizens of every political denomination, will never fail to unite their energies at the call of their Country; As these energies are the only foundation on which, next to the favor of Heaven, we ought to rest the security of every thing dear to a free & independent Nation.

Should such a call become necessary, the tender of Service made by yourself, and your companions on the military roll, will doubtless receive the attention due to the patriotism which prompted it.

For the favorable expressions applied to myself, I offer in return, assurances of my respect, & good wishes.

JAMES MADISON

RC (InU: Jackson Collection). In Isaac Coles's hand, signed by JM.

To William Short

DEAR SIR   WASHINGTON Decr. 3. 1809

I duly recd. your favor of Sepr. 15.[1] to which was annexed the copy of Count Romanzoff's letter to you. The latter has been communicated to Mr. Jefferson, and will be placed in the Archives of our Foreign Dept. It is a very pleasing proof of the good will of the Emperor of Russia towards this Country, as well as of the just sentiments he entertains of Mr. Jefferson, and you did very right, in cherishing both by yielding to the request on the subject of the letter of Credence.

The several letters written before & after your sailing from the U. S were all recd. If you did not hear from me in consequence of them by Mr. Coles, it was because I could in that manner best decline a subject on which I did not wish to repeat communications which Mr. Jefferson told me he should particularly make to you, and which I was sure you would understand as expressing my feelings not less than his own.[2]

I send this with public dispatches from the Dept of State for Genl. Armstrong; and I add to it two Gazettes containing the communications just made to Congs. There appears to be a great disappointment among some, produced by the conduct of G. B. & her Minister, and among all, as far as yet appears, no little indignation agst. both.

I thank you for your friendly wishes, and pray you to be assured of mine for your success in whatever may concern your happiness; and of my great esteem & sincere regard.

JAMES MADISON

RC (DLC: Short Papers). Docketed by Short, "recd. from Gl. Armstrong—Jan 10. 1810."

1. *PJM-PS*, 1:379.

2. Earlier in the year Jefferson had explained the background of the Senate's unanimous rejection of Short's nomination for the Russian mission and reassured Short that his personal esteem was undiminished (Jefferson to Short, 8 Mar. 1809, Ford, *Writings of Jefferson*, 9:249–50).

§ From Two Chiefs of the Wyandot Nation. *3 December 1809, Rapids at Lower Sandusky*. Informs JM that the Wyandot chiefs have agreed that their annuities, payable under the 1795 Treaty of Greenville, should be sent on alternate years to the branches of their nation residing at Brownstown and Lower Sandusky. Complains of the difficulties of receiving the annuities at Detroit, where the goods are often damaged and their people are "too easily flattered . . . to part with them for Liquor & other trifles."

RC (DNA: RG 107, LRRS, W-726:4). 2 pp. Signed by Shata-arounyauk (Leather Lips) and Tahauminelia (Bowl), in the presence of William Walker, interpreter. Docketed by a War Department clerk as received 23 Dec. 1809.

To Lafayette

MY DEAR SIR   WASHINGTON Decr. 4. 1809.

I recd. your two favors of June 12.[1] & Sepr. 17.[2] & am extremely concerned that I cannot give you more satisfactory information as to the state of your locations, on which you are about to found such important arrangements. In so distant a situation, delays were always to be counted on. But they have been prolonged by several supervening casualties; and finally by a miscarriage of the particular Mail: which happened to contain the instructions of Mr. Gallatin which were intended as far as he could legally go, to remove some obstacles Mr. Duplantier had met with; and to facilitate the great object of compleating the locations. We shall do all we can to hasten the business to a conclusion, so as to be able to transmit the documents requisite for your purposes at Paris. But knowing by experience that unforeseen incidents may disappoint our best concerted plans, so far as relates to punctuality, in a case involving distant and separate Agencies, I could wish it were possible for you to proceed in your loan, without waiting for the formal consummation of the land titles. I have not heard from Mr. Duplantier since the 25st. of July;[3] in which letter he points out some of his difficulties to which the instructions of Mr. Gallatin were applicable. I shall write to him afresh, by an intelligent gentleman sent on public Business to N. Orleans,[4] whom I shall engage to pay particular attention himself to the subject.[5]

I send a copy of the communications made to Congress now in Session. They will shew the general situation of our affairs, and particularly the recent occurrence with the new British Envoy. We do not distinctly understand what Mr. Champagny means, by a withdrawal of the British Blockades of France; whether it be a removal of all, subsequent as well as prior to the Berlin Decree, and whether with or without Proclamations.[6] From the reference to Chronological order, it would seem, that the Blockades proclaimed prior to the Berlin Decree, and Still considered as in force, ought alone to be within the condition precedent to a repeal of the Berlin Decree. But is it clear, that Blockades of that description now exist? Certain it is that they may be considered as merged, (using a law term) in the Orders of Council. It would simplify the business very much, and according to our ideas, without injury to the Dignity of the Emperor, or the interest of France, if instead of these obscure & controvertible conditions, a direct repeal of his Decrees so far as they are external in operation, were to take place; leaving G. B. either to repeal hers, or to come to an issue with neutrals, or a perseverance in them. Be assured my dear Sir of my great esteem and constant friendship

JAMES MADISON

RC (MWiCA); partial Tr (CSmH: Lafayette Letterbook).

1. *PJM-PS*, 1:241–42.

2. Letter not found.

3. JM originally wrote "21st. of July." Duplantier's letter is dated 25 July 1809 (*PJM-PS*, 1:306).

4. JM entrusted the task to John K. Smith, whom he had just appointed to be navy agent at New Orleans (see Hamilton to JM, 4 Dec. 1809, and n. 1; and Smith to JM, 18 Mar. and 15 May 1810).

5. Partial Tr ends here, except for complimentary close.

6. See David Bailie Warden to JM, 18 Oct. 1809, and n. 2.

To William Pinkney

DEAR SIR   WASHINGTON Decr. 4. 1809

Your favor of Aug. 19.[1] came duly to hand, and I tender my thanks for it. I have very little to add in return for your acceptable observations, especially as the opportunity, happens to be reduced to a very few minutes. Mr. Smith will send you the communications to Congs. with whatever else is important. The career of Mr. Jackson, has been equally short

& singular. His correspondence as far as yet appears, will be viewed as a poor specimen of his talents, as well as of his personal temper, and of the policy of his Govt. Whether pride or prudence will dictate the course of his Govt in relation to him remains to be seen. It would seem as if he does not despond of its approbation; but I think he must have some doubts at least, especially considering the instability of the B. Cabinet & Councils. I have some suspicions also that Mr. Oakley[2] does not carry with him a full sympathy with Mr J's tone towards this Govt. Mr. S. writes you on the subject of Champagny's letter.[3] I am not sorry that it made so early an appearance in the British Gazettes. It certainly behoves G. B. to weigh the consequence of adhering to her system, in case France shd. be found ready to repeal the Berlin Decree, on the sole condition of an annulment of Blockades prior to that date. G. B. will then be at issue with the U. S. on the legality of such Blockades as that of May 1806. from the Weser to Brest.[4] Accept assurances of my great esteem & friendly regard.

JAMES MADISON

RC (NjP: Pinkney Papers). Docketed by Pinkney.

1. *PJM-PS*, 1:335–36.
2. Charles Oakley was secretary to the British legation.
3. See Robert Smith to Pinkney, 1 Dec. 1809, enclosing a copy of Smith's instructions to Armstrong of the same date (DNA: RG 59, IM).
4. Great Britain declared a blockade "of the coast, rivers, and ports, from the river Elbe to the port of Brest" on 16 May 1806. Napoleon's retaliatory Berlin decree, issued 21 Nov. 1806, declared that "the British islands are . . . in a state of blockade" (*ASP, Foreign Relations*, 3:125, 290).

From Paul Hamilton

SIR,   NAVY DEPARTMENT 4 Decr 1809

The death of Mr Keith Spence, late navy agent at New Orleans, having been duly notified to this Department, the public interests require that an immediate appointment be made to that vacancy; and as in that distant agency it is peculiarly necessary that the officer should possess a thorough knowledge of the business which will be confided to him, I beg leave to recommend, to be nominated to that station, Mr John K Smith,[1] of the District of Columbia, who from an intimate acquaintance with the trans-actions of this Department, & his ability & fidelity manifested during a connection of some years with it, affords a well grounded expectation, that the duties of the above agency, if entrusted to him, will be performed to

the advantage of the public. I have the honor to be, Sir, most respectfully Yrs.

PAUL HAMILTON

RC (DLC); letterbook copy (DNA: RG 45, LSP). RC in Goldsborough's hand, signed by
Hamilton; docketed by JM.

1. John K. Smith had recently served as a Navy Department clerk. The act of 3 Mar.
1809 regulating the treasury, war, and navy departments authorized the president to appoint
navy agents for "making contracts, or for the purchase of supplies, or for the disbursement
. . . of monies for . . . the navy." On 7 Mar. JM appointed Keith Spence to the post at New
Orleans. After Spence died, JM nominated Smith on the same day that Hamilton recommended him, and the Senate confirmed him on 6 Dec. Despite Gallatin's reservations concerning his appointment, Smith was still serving in 1816 (Cunningham, *The Process of Government under Jefferson*, p. 330; *U.S. Statutes at Large*, 2:536; *Senate Exec. Proceedings*, 2:120, 129;
Gallatin to JM, 22 Dec. 1809; *ASP, Miscellaneous*, 2:351).

From Nathaniel Vollintine

SIR   WESTON (MASSACHUSETTS) 4 Decr. 1809.
    The high estimation in which I have ever held your Character has in-
duced me to Christen a Child by the Name of James Madison. The town
in which I live has for many years till the last been in the federal Interest,
but by the extra exertions of a few republicans they have a[t] length Obtain'd a Majority. I am induced by no other motive to give you this information, then as a evidence of the veneration & respect I have always had
of your patriotism. I am Sir With the warmest wishes for your health &
happiness your Most Obedt. Sert.

NATHL VOLLINTINE

RC (DLC).

§ To Congress. *4 December 1809*. Transmits report of the secretary of the navy
referred to in the annual message of 29 Nov.

RC and enclosures, two copies (DNA: RG 233, President's Messages; and DNA: RG 46,
Legislative Proceedings, 11A-E7). Each RC 1 p., in a clerk's hand, signed by JM. House
copy dated by JM; Senate copy undated. Received by both houses on 5 Dec. Senate copy
read and tabled; House copy referred to the Ways and Means Committee (*Annals of Congress*,
11th Cong., 2d sess., 480, 694). Printed in *ASP, Naval Affairs*, 1:201-5. For enclosures, see
Paul Hamilton to JM, 1 Dec. 1809, and n.

From William Duane

SIR   PHILA. 5 Decr. 1809

I have revolved for some time in my mind the ideas which in a crude form I have taken the liberty of addressing to you. I presume not to set any higher values on them than liberal intentions and an enthusiastic devotion to the principles and durability of Republican Government, may give them. I neither look for any answer nor do I wish for any thing more than, the gratification of endeavoring to promote what is honorable and glorious to my country.

If this should be acceptable or not intrusive on your time, I should take the liberty of addressing to you my ideas on the institution of a national Bank, the basis of which should be public lands, shares representing acres to a certain amount; the acres to be taken at a limitted period by the holder and the stock to go to the public; or the holder of stock to have his option of Cash for the share in Bank; and the land to become either the object of purchase at the rate of lands at the moment, or to become the representative of new shares: the objects of the plan, would be—1 To unite all the Eastern Bank holders by the tie of property in Southern lands; to make the reduction of Interest to 5 per Cent a part of the establishment, and by combining the shares in Bank with property in land, to cast off the pestilential influence which foreign stock and bank jobbers have on all our national concerns.[1] In fact I have suggested the outline already; to a mind like Mr Gallatin's such a plan would at once present itself in a manner that would give it form and efficacy, and I persuade myself that the useful objects which I have suggested would naturally grow out of it—Objects which I need not describe the vast importance of. I wish however not to be Known as suggesting the subject, because such a matter should stand upon its own foundations without prejudice or partiality to its author—circumstances which too often interfere with human interests & happiness. Excuse this trouble and permit me to subscribe myself your friend & respectful humb St

WM DUANE

RC (DLC). Docketed by JM.

1. Duane's proposal of a land bank was hardly original. It drew on a colonial tradition of using an almost unlimited resource (the public lands) as the capital for a bank scheme (Theodore Thayer, "The Land-Bank System in the American Colonies," *Journal of Economic History*, 13 [1953]: 145–59).

From William Lambert

SIR,   CITY OF WASHINGTON, Decemr. 5th. 1809.

As the inclosed letter to bishop Madison, contains the principles of an useful method, not generally practised, to promote the geography of the United States, permit me to request that you will be pleased to read it with some attention, before you transmit it to him under your frank.

I take this opportunity of acknowledging with gratitude and respect, the favors I have already received from you; and be assured, Sir, that altho' I may not often repeat the *expression* of a due sense of them to you, they have made an impression not easily to be obliterated. I have the honor to be, with great consideration, Sir, Your most obedt. servt:

WILLIAM LAMBERT.[1]

RC (DLC).

1. Lambert, who had been a State Department clerk in the 1790s and was to serve in the same capacity in the War Department, had recently sent Congress a memorial aimed at establishing "a first meridian for the United States of America at the permanent seat of their Government, by which a further dependence on Great Britain . . . may be entirely removed." He was to pursue this goal for several years in conjunction with a campaign to build a national observatory in Washington. Congress took little effective action on either project until 1821, when a joint resolution of 3 Mar. directed the president to take measures for ascertaining the longitude of the Capitol. Lambert then established an observatory in his own home and delivered, on 8 Nov. 1821, a lengthy report that established new values for the latitude and longitude of the Capitol (*ASP, Miscellaneous,* 2:53–71, 753–96; *Annals of Congress,* 11th Cong., 2d sess., 1660–62; Lambert to JM, 19 Feb. 1810; see also Charles O. Paullin, "Early Movements for a National Observatory, 1802–1842," *Records of the Columbia Historical Society,* 25 [1923]: 37, 40–43).

Account with William Thornton

[5 December 1809]

Account between the Honble. James Madison—and Mr. Thornton.

William Thornton Dr:

1806		
Augst. 4.	To a Loan of one hundred and fifty Dollars	$150.—
1807 —	To Interest one year on the above	9.—
	To Interest on fifty Dollars till 1809 from Augst. 4th: 1807 till Decr. 1809. 2 yrs: 3 months	7.50
1805 Octr.	To 120 Bushels of Coals at 28 Cts. ℔r: Bushell	33.60

March 18.	To 196 Bushs: of Coal at 28 Cts.	44:88
	To a set of Dining tables valued by Mr. Worthington Cabinet Maker, whose valuation was delivered to Mrs. Madison	50:00
		$294:98

William Thornton Cr:

1807	By One hundred Dolls: returned in 1807.	$100
1805 —	By four Seasons to Clifden,[1] charged by William Ball to William Thornton	80
1806 —	By three Seasons to Do: charged by Capt. Haskins to William Thornton	40
1809 —	By two Stud Colts by Clifden a Filly by Do.—a Filly by Childers[2]—a Colt by Clifden & Mare by Do.—as ℔r: Valuation of Mr: Gouch $335.04. half of which becomes due to W. T.	167.50
		$387:50

The returns of the labours of the *Vicar of Bray* are not yet made.

(Errors excepted)   WILLIAM THORNTON

City of Washington 5th: Decr: 1809—Received from the Honble: James Madison the above balance of ninety two Dollars 52 Cts: in full—

WILLIAM THORNTON

Ms (DLC). In Thornton's hand. Docketed by JM.

1. Clifden was the most famous of several racehorses that Thornton made available for stud services at his farm near Georgetown. Clifden had a spectacular season at Newmarket as a five-year-old in 1792, and Thornton imported the horse from England in 1799. Thornton's billing accords with the evaluation by Gideon Gooch, the Montpelier farm manager, written on a separate sheet (Bryan, *History of the National Capital*, 1:346; Fairfax Harrison, *Early American Turf Stock, 1730–1830* [2 vols.; Richmond, Va., 1934–35], 2:374–75; Gooch, valuation of horses, n.d. [DLC] [misdated 1804 in *Index to the James Madison Papers*]).

2. Childers is a recurring name in the stud books of eighteenth- and nineteenth-century breeders. Many of the stallions descended from the original champion, "the famous Childers, lately belonging to his grace the Duke of Devonshire" (Harrison, *Early American Turf Stock*, 2:513). JM offered to trade Thornton two horses for his Childers in 1803 (JM to Thornton, 19 Aug. 1803 [DLC: Thornton Papers]).

§ From Willie Blount.[1] *5 December 1809, Knoxville.* Encloses a letter from John Dickinson of Nashville, who seeks the position of attorney for the district of West Tennessee.

RC and enclosure (DNA: RG 59, LAR, 1809–17, filed under "Dickinson"). RC 2 pp. Enclosure is Dickinson to Blount, 26 Nov. 1809 (2 pp.).

1. Willie Blount (1768–1835) served three terms as governor of Tennessee between 1809 and 1815.

§ From the Mississippi Territorial Legislature. *5 December 1809*. Petition requests the appointment of a brigadier general of militia for the Mississippi Territory. Asks that JM name an officer "with as little delay as is consistent with attention to objects of more pressing importance."

RC, two copies (DNA: RG 107, LRRS, H-542:4); FC (Ms-Ar). 1 p. Signed by Speaker Ferdinand L. Claiborne and council president Alexander Montgomery; signed and dated by clerks of both chambers. Enclosed in Ferdinand L. Claiborne to Robert Smith, 25 Nov. 1809, and David Holmes to secretary of war, 6 Dec. 1809 (which recommended Claiborne for the appointment). Printed in Carter, *Territorial Papers, Mississippi*, 6:33. FC dated 24 Nov.

§ John B. Colvin to Richard Forrest. *5 December 1809, Washington*. Provides Forrest with the statement he requested that Forrest had supported JM's election in 1808, that he had assisted Colvin in publishing the Washington *Monitor*, and that he had written articles for that paper in support of the Embargo.

RC (DLC). 1 p. Docketed by JM. On 22 Dec. 1809 JM nominated Forrest to be consul at Tunis. The Senate postponed the nomination, then finally rejected it on 1 May 1810 on the grounds that it was "not expedient, or necessary for the interest of the United States, that a Consul should be appointed, at present, to reside at Tunis." The nomination of Forrest, a reputed Federalist and State Department clerk who was a member of the Madisons' social circle in Washington, was to cause JM some embarrassment, and it became one of the grounds for the increasingly severe criticisms made against JM by Baptist Irvine in the Baltimore *Whig* (*Senate Exec. Proceedings*, 2:132–33, 139, 140, 147, 154; Baltimore *Whig*, 21, 25 Feb. and 25 Apr. 1810).

From Thomas Jefferson

DEAR SIR   MONTICELLO Dec. 7. 09
    The inclosed letter is from Father Richard, the Director of a school at Detroit; & being on a subject in which the departments both of the Treasury & War are concerned, I take the liberty of inclosing it to yourself as the center which may unite these two agencies.[1] The transactions which it alludes to took place in the months of Dec. & Jan. preceding my retirement from office, & as I think it probable they may not have been fully placed on the records of the War office, because they were conducted verbally for the most part, I will give a general statement of them as well as my recollection will enable me. In the neighborhood of Detroit (2. or

3. miles from the town) is a farm, formerly the property of one Ernest,[2] a bankrupt Collector. It is now in possession of the Treasury department, as a pledge for a sum in which he is in default to the government, much beyond the value of the farm. As it is a good one, has proper buildings, & in a proper position for the purpose contemplated, Genl. Dearborne proposed to purchase it for the War department, at it's real value. Mr. Gallatin thought he should ask the sum for which it was hypothecated. I do not remember the last idea in which we all concurred, but I believe it was that, as the Treasury must, in the end, sell it for what it could get, the War department would become a bidder as far as it's real value, & in the mean time would rent it. On this farm we proposed to assemble the following establishments.

1. Father Richard's school. He teaches the children of the inhabitants of Detroit. But the part of the school within our view was that of the young Indian girls instructed by two French females, natives of the place, who devote their whole time, & their own property which was not inconsiderable, to the care & instruction of Indian girls in carding, spinning, weaving, sowing [sic], & the other houshold arts suited to the condition of the poor, & as practised by the white women of that condition. Reading & writing were an incidental part of their education. We proposed that the war departmt. should furnish the farm & houses for the use of the school, gratis, and add 400. D. a year to the funds, & that the benefits of the Institution should be extended to the boys also of the neighboring tribes, who were to be lodged, fed, & instructed there.

2. To establish there the farmer at present employed by the US. to instruct those Indians in the use of the plough & other implements & practises of Agriculture, & in the general management of the farm. This man was to labour the farm himself, & to have the aid of the boys through a principal portion of the day, by which they would contract habits of industry, learn the business of farming, & provide subsistence for the whole institution. Reading & writing were to be a secondary object.

3. To remove thither the Carpenter & Smith at present employed by the US. among the same Indians; with whom such of the boys as had a turn for it should work & learn their trades.

This establishment was recommended by the further circumstance that whenever the Indians come to Detroit on trade or other business, they encamp on or about this farm. This would give them opportunities of seeing their sons & daughters, & their advancement in the useful arts, of seeing & learning from example all the operations & process of a farm, and of always carrying home themselves some additional knolege of these things. It was thought more important to extend the civilized arts, & to introduce a separation of property among the Indians of the country round Detroit than elsewhere, because learning to set a high value on their property, & losing by degrees all other dependance for subsistence, they would deprecate war with us as bringing certain destruction on their property, and would become a barrier for that distant & insulated post against the Indians beyond them. There are, beyond them, some strong tribes, as the Sacs, Foxes Etc. with whom we have as yet had little connection, & slender opportunities of extending to them our benefits & influence. They are therefore ready instruments to be brought into operation on us by a powerful neighbor which still cultivates it's influence over them by nourishing the savage habits, which waste them, rather than by encouraging the civilized arts which would soften, conciliate & preserve them. The whole additional expence to the US. was to be the price of the farm, and an increase of 400. D. in the annual expenditures for these tribes.

This is the sum of my recollections. I cannot answer for their exactitude in all details; but Genl. Dearborne could supply & correct the particulars of my statement. Mr. Gallatin too was so often in consultation on the subject that he must have been informed of the whole plan; & his memory is so much better than mine, that he will be able to make my statement what it should be. Add to this that, I think, I generally informed yourself of our policy & proceedings in the case as we went along: & if I am not mistaken it was one of the articles of a memorandum[3] I left with you of things still in fieri,[4] & which would merit your attention. I have thought it necessary to put you in possession of these facts that you might understand the grounds of father Richard's application,[5] & be enabled to judge for yourself of the expediency of pursuing the plan, or of the means of withdrawing from it with justice to the individuals employed in it's execution. How far we are committed with the Indians themselves in this business will be seen in a speech of mine to them of Jan. 31.[6] filed in the war office, & perhaps something more may have passed to them from the Secretary at War.[7] Always affectionately yours

TH: JEFFERSON

RC and enclosure (DLC); FC (DLC: Jefferson Papers). Enclosure 4 pp.; docketed by Jefferson, "recd Dec. 3" (see n. 1).

1. Jefferson enclosed Gabriel Richard's 9 Nov. 1809 letter. It is similar to Richard's 17 Nov. 1809 letter to JM, discussing the Spring Hill Indian school.

2. Mathew Ernest served as revenue collector at Detroit from 1800 until his removal in 1804 (*Senate Exec. Proceedings*, 1:332, 333; Tarletan Bates to JM, 17 July 1804, Carter, *Territorial Papers, Indiana*, 7:210).

3. Memorandum from Jefferson, Mar. 1809 (*PJM-PS*, 1:1).

4. *In fieri*: pending.

5. In his letter to Jefferson, Father Richard asked the former president to intercede on his behalf with Eustis and JM. "I have neither time nor means to go again to the City of Washington. . . . I Expect that you will be So Good [as] to writ[e] to mr. Eustis that what I require is perfectly corresponding with what was agreed between Govt. & me last January."

6. Jefferson to the chiefs of the Ottawa, Chippewa, Potawatomi, Wyandot, and Shawnee, 31 Jan. 1809 (Lipscomb and Bergh, *Writings of Jefferson*, 16:470–72).

7. The informality of Jefferson's promise to aid the Spring Hill school led to some later difficulties. Father Richard recalled, "it is true that no kind of writing properly Signed, was executed at the time, but minutes of the transaction were kept by mr. Smith the first Clerk in the dept. of war" (Richard to JM, 12 Oct. 1810, Carter, *Territorial Papers, Michigan*, 10:334). These minutes must have been consulted by Eustis, for he wrote Governor Hull on 1 Jan. 1810 that "Four hundred dollars only are to be allowed Mr Richard on the terms originally prescribed" (ibid., 10:305).

§ From Joseph Joshua Dyster. *7 December 1809, Washington*. Tells of his invention, a method "to propel Ships and Vessells of any description up Navigable rivers . . . by means of Steam." His steamboat, however, uses no paddle wheels or oars and makes no "impulse whatever . . . on the Water." Sends this letter by Gideon Granger and seeks an appointment with JM so that "arrangements perhaps may be formed, for carrying this important Object into effect."

RC (DLC). 2 pp. Dyster appears to have been a dilettante with a variety of interests, including poetry (*Four Odes* [Philadelphia, 1816; Shaw and Shoemaker 37484] and *Five Odes* [Philadelphia, 1817; Shaw and Shoemaker 40710]).

§ From Henry Brockholst Livingston. *7 December 1809, New York*. Introduces William Cutting,[1] "a gentleman of the first respectability & connections in this city."

RC (DLC). 1 p. Livingston was an associate justice of the U.S. Supreme Court, 1807–23.

1. William Cutting (1773–1820) married Gertrude Livingston (Henry Brockholst Livingston's second cousin) in 1798 (Florence Van Rensselaer, comp., *The Livingston Family and Its Scottish Origins* [New York, 1949], pp. 84, 86, 93, 98, 114).

From William Duane

SIR,   PHILA. Decr. 8. 1809

I took the liberty of placing before you some few ideas on the subject of an application of the principle of a security in land for an investment of cash in Bank stock, at a reduced interest. It has since occurred to me, that as the impost may probably fall short of the sum requisite for exigency, that a resort to an investiture of land to cover a public loan, would not only enable the administration, to raise an *immense sum*, but to defeat at a stroke the clamour which the enemies of the Government would not fail to raise, in the event of any necessity for a money loan.[1]

It appears to me that the occasion should now be used, to raise a very large sum in that way, so that if the nation should be involved in war, there may be a provision for its calls in advance; for I very much fear there has not been as full a consideration of the necessary amount [of] Expenditures, as would seem to be necessary, among the members of that part of the government who hold the purse; and that the want of a due knowlege of what ought to be done, would cripple the executive to a degree more pernicious than the efforts of an enemy.

My conception of the method of raising a supply I shall take the liberty of stating, merely to explain what I suggest, & not presuming to decide upon its being very excellent much less infallible, but barely giving it as a suggestion which in abler hands may be made something of.

I would raise a sum equal to three or four years of the usual revenue of the United States. This besides being provident in fact, would be a valuable measure on the surface of affairs, indicating the determination to be prepared in earnest for defence.

For every million of dollars to be raised, I would suggest the appropriation of half a million of acres of public lands; the lands to be surveyed in the course of the year ensuing and in ranges after the plan of the Ohio Military lands. The tracts surveyed should be no more than *ten* or 20000 acres in any one section or territory; or each of these tracts should be at least 50 miles apart; and there might be some limit to the right of purchase for any one person of more than a certain number of acres.

It would not be difficult, from an investigation of the sales of public lands for some years past, and other means, to ascertain the progressive rise in various lands before and after survey and sale.

The loan upon lands might be made in such a way as—first to obtain the money at a very low interest.

Secondly—that an option to retain the lands or receive a . . . .[2] per cent stock at the end of six years, or one year after a war; redeemable in . . . . years.

Thirdly the loan when raised to be placed in public funds, so as that what should be over the public demand might be made productive, in either reducing part of the old public debt; or in constructing some great roads or canals, to facilitate intercourse and promote public prosperity.

As the ideas of the principle are all that are necessary, details being superfl[u]ous if the principles are not practicable I think it unnecessary to intrude further upon your time.

I do not look for any answer, if the thoughts are of any use that is all I look for—if not, I am not willing to trespass on you for the mere ceremoney of a note, when I know the paper must reach you. I am, Sir, with respect your Obed Sert

WM DUANE

RC (DLC). Docketed by JM.

1. In his 29 Nov. annual message, JM had remarked on the decline in customs collections, which were the principal source of federal income. The loss of income from duties was reflected in the treasury reports at the close of the 1807–9 fiscal years (30 Sept.) when the treasury balances fell from $8,530,000 to $4,530,964 (*ASP, Finance,* 2:247, 308, 319, 374).

2. Duane's ellipsis points, here and below.

From Paul Hamilton

SIR,   NAVY DEPT. 8 Decr. 1809

Docr. Fraser of South Carolina,[1] whom I take the liberty of mentioning to you for nomination to the Senate as Surgeon in the Navy, is personally known to me, as a gentleman of great professional merit—& his services are now required at Charleston S. C. I have the honor to be with great respect sir yr mo obt.

PAUL HAMILTON

RC (DLC); letterbook copy (DNA: RG 45, LSP). RC in Goldsborough's hand, signed by Hamilton; docketed by JM.

1. JM nominated Alexander Fraser to be a naval surgeon on 12 Dec., and the appointment was confirmed two days later. Fraser was probably the son of Alexander and Mary Grimké Fraser, prominent Charlestonians (*Senate Exec. Proceedings,* 2:129–30; Walter B. Edgar et al., eds., *Biographical Directory of the South Carolina House of Representatives* [3 vols. to date; Columbia, S.C., 1974—], 2:255).

From Alexander McRae

DEAR SIR,   WASHINGTON 8. Decr. 1809

Major Clarke and I had the honor some time ago to receive thro' our friend Mr. Wirt, letters from you, addressed to the American Ministers at London and at Paris.[1] These letters (which I now have with me) were delivered to me sealed, and I am consequently ignorant of their contents; but recollecting as I do the purport of Mr. Wirt's letter addressed to you in our behalf, I presume we were both named in the letters with which you were pleased to honor us.[2] I regret very much, that Majr. Clarke's peculiar situation at this time, will deprive me of the pleasure of his company in the journey I have commenced; but as I am to travel alone, and the commencement of my journey has been inevitably postponed to a period much later than was intended, I have supposed it might be to my advantage to bear letters of more recent date, and in which Major Clarke may not be named as the Companion of my journey.

It is with great reluctance that I trespass in the least degree on your time, at a moment when I am sure your necessary devotion to the public concerns, allows you but little leisure; I flatter myself however, that the deep interest I have, dependent on the success of my journey, will excuse me to you for the freedom I use in making this communication. If it shall be your pleasure to substitute letters of this date, instead of those I have already been honored with, I must in that event beg of you, the favor of information to that effect by the return of the Bearer, and the letters in my possession shall be immediately forwarded to you. With the highest respect & esteem I have the honor to be, Dear Sir, Yr. mo. ob. Servt.

AL: McRae.

RC (DLC). Docketed by JM.

1. Letters not found, but see JM to Pinkney, 8 Dec. 1809.
2. McRae was traveling to Europe in connection with a silk-manufacturing scheme. The scheme failed, causing McRae some embarrassment, which led him, while in Paris, to take on the duties of consul there after John Armstrong removed David Bailie Warden from the post (*PJM-PS*, 1:283–84, 296–97, 323–24; McRae to Monroe, 16 Nov. 1810 [NN: Monroe Papers]). Gov. John Tyler and William Wirt had also made earlier recommendations to JM on behalf of McRae and John Clarke (see *PJM-PS*, 1:137 and n. 2).

From Alexander McRae

8. Decr. 1809.

Al: McRae returns his respects to Mr. Madison.[1] As it will be known on Al: McRae's arrival in Europe, that he passed thro' Washington about this period, he cannot help thinking that letters bearing this date, will be more to his advantage, than letters in the very same words but bearing a much earlier date could be. He therefore avails himself of the permission granted by Mr. Madison, to return the letters with which he has been heretofore honored, and will be indebted for such others, as Mr. Madison may be pleased to substitute in their stead.

RC (DLC). Docketed by JM.

1. JM's acknowledgment of McRae's earlier letter has not been found.

To William Pinkney

private

DEAR SIR   Decr. 8. 1809

The Bearer Mr. McRae, heretofore Lieutenant Governor of Virginia is represented to me as about to visit Europe with views not only creditable to himself, but promising advantage to his Country. I have so far therefore departed from a general rule, as to give him this introduction to you, not doubting that he will receive whatever patronage he may satisfy you, his objects merit. I only add a request, that as I make this letter altogether a private one, and wish to limit its effect to yourself, no reference may be made to it in any with which you may favor Mr. McRae, to others. Accept my friendly respects

JAMES MADISON

RC (NjP: Pinkney Papers). Cover marked by JM, "Mr. McRae." Docketed by Pinkney.

To Robert R. Livingston

DEAR SIR,   WASHINGTON, Dec. 9, 1809

Your favor of the 25th Oct. afforded me much pleasure by the information it gave of the success with which you prosecuted your plan of enlightening your countrymen on the subject of sheep & wool, and of aiding them in the manner of increasing & improving both. I sincerely wish your example may be duly felt in all the states adapted to those objects, and I believe this is the case with all that are members of our Union. In the middle States, I have long been of opinion that we kept on our farms, too many black cattle, and too few sheep, and that a valuable revolution would be found in a reduction of the former, and augmentation of the latter. The motives to it are now greatly strengthened by the additional value given to their fleeces by the merino blood.

I have begun, & regret that I have not been able to go thro' your tract on this subject. Interesting as it is in itself, I perceive that you make it more so by your advantageous manner of treating it. I have disposed of the copies, added to the one you were so obliging as to allot for myself, according to your directions.

Having lately rec'd from England a pamphlet on the subject of merino sheep, said to comprize what is most valuable in the numerous publications lately devoted to that investigation, I send it for your perusal.[1] Having no other copy and not yet read this, I am obliged to offer it as a loan instead of a gift.

Our foreign affairs are so fully before the public, that I have nothing to say in addition. I beg you to accept however a copy of the communications to Congress in a form more convenient for perusal than that of the newspapers.[2] Be pleased to accept Sir, assurances of my high esteem & friendly regards.

JAMES MADISON

Typescript (obtained ca. 1960 from MiD). RC not found. The Detroit Public Library had no record in 1986 that the original was ever part of its manuscript collection, but the carbon copy used for this text carries the note: "Typed copy by Detroit Public Library." The letter's authenticity is established by comparison with Livingston to JM, 25 Oct. 1809 and 8 Jan. 1810.

1. Charles Henry Hunt, *A Practical Treatise of the Merino and Anglo-Merino Breeds of Sheep* (London, 1809) (see William Pinkney to JM, 19 Aug. 1809, *PJM-PS*, 1 : 335, 336 n. 2).

2. *Documents Accompanying the Message of the President* . . . (Washington, 1809; Shaw and Shoemaker 18889). This pamphlet contained the correspondence between Robert Smith and Francis James Jackson that JM submitted with his 29 Nov. 1809 annual message to Congress.

From William Pinkney

DEAR SIR   LONDON Decr. 10th. 1809

Your Letter of the 23d. of October reached me on the 25h. of last Month. That of the 23d. of April[1] was sent to me by Mr. Lee as soon as he arrived in England; and was answered on the 19h. of August.

I see with great pleasure the Ground taken by the Secy. of State in his Correspondence with Mr. Jackson, connected with the probability that our people are recovering from recent Delusion, and will hereafter be disposed to support with Zeal & *Steadiness* the Efforts of their Government to maintain their Honour & Character. Jackson's Course is an extraordinary one—and his *Manner* is little better.

The British Govt. has acted for some Time upon an Opinion that its partizans in America were too numerous & strong to admit of our persevering in any System of Repulsion to British Injustice; and it cannot be denied that Appearances countenanced this humiliating & pernicious Opinion; which has been entertained even by our Friends. My own Confidence in the American people was great; but it was shaken nevertheless. I am re-assured, however, by present Symptoms, and give myself up once more to Hope. The prospect of returning Virtue is cheering; and I trust it is not in Danger of being obscured & deformed by the Recurrence of those detestable Scenes which lately reduced our patriotism to a Problem.

The *new* Ministry (if the late Changes entitle it to be so called)[2] is at least as likely as the last to presume upon our Divisions. I have heard it said that it was impossible to form a Cabinet more unfriendly to us, more effectually steeped and dyed in all those bad principles which have harassed and insulted us. I continue to believe that, as it is now constituted, or even with any Modifications of which it is susceptible, it cannot last; and that it will not chuse to hazard much in maintaini[n]g against the U. S. the late Maritime Innovations.

The people of England are rather better disposed than heretofore to accomodate with us. They seem to have awaked from the flattering Dreams by which their Understandings have been so long abused. Disappointment & Disaster have dissipated the brilliant Expectations of undefined Prosperity which had dazzled them into moral Blindness & had cheated them of their Discretion as well as of their Sense of Justice. In this State of Things America naturally resumes her Importance, and her Rights become again intelligible. Lost as we were to the View of Englishmen during an overpowering Blaze of imaginary Glory and commercial Grandeur, we are once more visible in the sober Light to which Facts have tempered & reduced the Glare of Fiction. The Use of this opportunity depends upon ourselves, and doubtless we shall use it as we ought.

It is, after all, perhaps, to be doubted whether any thing but a general peace (which, if we may judge from the past, it is not unlikely France will soon propose) can remove all Dilemma from our Situation. More Wisdom & Virtue than it wd. be quite reasonable to expect, must be found in the Councils of the two great belligerent parties, before the War in which they are now engaged can become harmless to our Rights. Even if England shd. recall (and I am convinced she could have been, and yet can be, compelled to recall) her foolish orders in Council, her maritime pretensions will still be exuberant, and many of her practices most oppressive. From France we have only to look for what Hostility to England may suggest. Justice and enlightened Policy are out of the Question on both Sides. Upon France, I fear, we have no Means of acting with Effect. Her Ruler sets our ordinary Means at Defiance. We cannot alarm him for his Colonies, his Trade, his Manufactures, his Revenue. He would not probably be moved by our attempts to do so even if they were directed exclusively against himself. He is less likely to be so moved while they comprehend his Enemy. A War with France, I shall always contend, would not help our Case. It would aggravate our Embarrassments in all Respects. Our Interests would be struck to the Heart by it. For our Honour it could do nothing. The Territory of this mighty Power is absolutely invulnerable; and there is no mode in which we could make her feel either physical or moral Coercion. We might as well declare War against the Inhabitants of the Moon or even of the *Georgium Sidus*.[3] When we should have produced the entire Exclusion of our Trade from the whole of Continental Europe &

encreased its Hazards every where, what else could we hope to achieve by Gallantry, or win by Stratagem? Great Britain would go smuggling on as usual; but we could neither fight nor smuggle. We should tire of so absurd a Contest long before it would end (and who shall say when it would end?)—and we should come out of it, after wondering how we got into it, with our Manufactures annihilated by British Competition, our Commerce crippled by an Enemy & smothered by a Friend, our Spirit debased into Listlessness & our Character deeply injured. I beg your pardon for recurring to this Topick; upon which I will not fatigue you with another Word, lest I should persecute you with many.

The Ministry are certainly endeavouring to gain Strength by some Changes. It is said that Ld. Wellesley is trying to bring Mr. Canning back to the Cabinet; and, if so, I see no Reason why he should not succeed. One Statement is that Mr. Canning is to go to the admiralty—another that he is to return to the foreign Department, that Ld. Wellesley is to take the Treasury, & Mr. Perceval to relapse into a mere Chancellor of the Exchequer. It is added that Ld. Camden (President of the Council) and Ld. Westmoreland (Privy Seal) are to go out. If Mr. Canning shd. not join his old Colleagues before the Meeting of parliament he will probably soon fall into the Ranks of opposition, where he will be formidable. There will scarcely be any Scruple in receiving him. If he *should* join his old Colleagues, they will not gain much by him. As a Debater in the House of Commons he would be useful* to them; but his Reputation is not at this Moment in the best possible plight, and his Weight & Connections are almost nothing. I am not sure that they would not lose by him more than they could gain.

If Ld. Grenville & Ld. Grey shd. be recalled to Power, Ld. Holland wd. be likely to have the Station of foreign Secretary (Ld. Grey preferring as it is said the Admiralty).

I believe I have not mentioned to you that Mr. G. H. Rose was to have been the Special Envoy to our Country if Mr Erskine's Arrangement had not been disavowed. I am bound to say that a worse Choice could not be made. Since his Return to England he has, I know, misrepresented & traduced us, with an Industry that is absolutely astonishing, notwithstanding the Cant of Friendship & Respect with which he overwhelms the few Americans who see him.

If I should not meet with a safe opportunity of sending this Letter soon, I will add to it in a P. S. any thing of Interest that may occur. I have the

---

* The only Cabinet Ministers at present in the House of Commons are Mr. Perceval & Mr. Ryder (the Secy of State for the Home-Department & Brother of Ld. Harrowby). The latter Gentn. excites no expectations.

Honour to be—with sincere Respect & Attachment, Dear Sir Your faithful and Obedient Servant

WM. PINKNEY.

RC (DLC: Rives Collection, Madison Papers). Docketed by JM.

1. Pinkney referred to JM's letter of 21 Apr. 1809 (*PJM-PS*, 1:128–29).

2. Perceval had been appointed prime minister to replace the duke of Portland on 4 Oct. His attempts to create a government of national unity were largely unsuccessful. Neither Canning nor Lord Castlereagh would agree to serve together in the same ministry, nor would the leaders of the Whig factions, lords Grey and Grenville, respond positively to Perceval's efforts to enlist their support. Perceval was thus compelled to continue the government with less parliamentary support than his predecessor had. He remained chancellor of the exchequer and first lord of the treasury himself, retained Earl Bathurst and lords Camden, Eldon, Mulgrave, and Westmorland from the previous ministry, shifted Lord Liverpool from the Home Office to the secretaryship for war and the colonies, and appointed Richard Ryder to Liverpool's vacated portfolio. The marquis of Wellesley became the new foreign secretary. The new ministry was not expected to last long (Denis Gray, *Spencer Perceval: The Evangelical Prime Minister, 1762–1812* [Manchester, 1963], pp. 254–77, 471).

3. The astronomer Sir William Herschel originally named the planet now called Uranus *Georgium sidus* (the great star of George) in honor of George III in 1783.

To Thomas Jefferson

DEAR SIR   WASHINGTON Decr. 11. 1809

I duly recd: your two letters of the 26. & 30. Ult. The State of Col. Monroe's mind is very nearly what I had supposed. His willingness to have taken a seat in the Cabinet, is what I had not supposed. I have written to Majr. Neele,[1] according to your suggestion, and shall follow it also as to the distribution of Govr. Lewis's papers when they arrive. Fayette in a letter to me has been equally urgent on the subject of his land titles which are required as the basis of a loan. Owing to delays incident to the distance & the nature of the proceedings in consummating land titles, and more particularly to the miscarriage of a mail containing instructions from Mr. Gallatin, which was long unknown to him, the business has never been compleated. I have renewed my efforts to accelerate it; and have so written to Fayette, by the Ship Jno. Adams, which carries a remittance from the Treasury to Holland, and will touch at France & England for collateral purposes. It was found cheaper to make the remittance in this way, than by Bills of Exch: at their present rate. The papers will tell you what Congs. are about. There is not as yet any appearance, by which their course can be foretold. The Republicans as usual are either not decided, or have different leanings. The Federalists are lying in wait, to spring on any oppy. of checking or diverting the tide now setting so strongly agst. them. The wound recd. by Mr J. G. Jackson, is thought at present to wear a very favorable appearance. As the Ball however remains in him, and the Hip bone, is much broken, it is not certain that he may not be left somewhat of a Cripple.[2] Be assured always of my high & Affecte. esteem

JAMES MADISON

I return the letters from Armstrong and Majr. Neele.

RC (DLC). Docketed by Jefferson, "recd. Dec. 14."

1. JM's letter to James Neely has not been found.
2. John G. Jackson had fought a duel with the North Carolina Federalist congressman Joseph Pearson on 4 Dec. over some remarks printed in the *National Intelligencer* on 24 July 1809. Originally scheduled for 23 Oct. 1809, the duel was postponed until after Congress had reconvened in the fall. Jackson's injuries may have contributed to his decision to retire from politics in the fall of 1810 (Jackson to Dolley Madison, 23 Oct. 1809 [ViU: Breckinridge-Watts Papers]; Brown, *Voice of the New West*, pp. 85–92).

From William Bentley

SIR,   SALEM 11 December, 1809
The inclosed Letter I leave with you. It will be seen by no person, till your pleasure be known.

It is an exact Copy of Gen: John Stark's Letter to me,[1] as he dictated it to his Son in Law, B. F. Stickney,[2] in consequence of a Letter I sent him. Once, when I was at the General's House, his Son Major Caleb Stark was called upon to write a Letter for the General's Signature. The Major, whose manners & accomplishments place him among the best men of our times, wrote a Letter as he would express the thoughts for himself. Upon the reading, the General burst out "Not your words for my Truth—Truth to the man & the matter—Give my own words & my own truth together."

The General is a Favorite Son of Nature. Not a vice has attached to his Character, & he has lived long & much in the world without corruption from it: independant in mind & condition. While every sentence of the General is an Apothegem, the Extract from the Letter of the Son in Law will prove, that the character of the family is not without the Philosophy of Nature.

Extract of a Letter from B. F. Stickney, Son in Law of Gen Stark,

Bow. December. 6. 1809
After an apology for delay, occasioned by the distance from his Father, he says, "The inclosed Letter is submitted to your discretion, to be published, or other-

wise. Since Major Stark has removed to Boston, I have been the General's Clerk. Direct your communications to Pembroke Office, & to my care, by Mail.

"We have made up our minds here, to hear a dreadful roaring of the Sea Lioness, since hearing the late growling of her Whelp. The Pickaroons are skulking into the back ground, & the Lovers of Freedom are preparing themselves to meet any mode of attack, that this voracious Animal may choose.

"Since we conversed together, by paper, or face to face, I have discovered a body of Iron Ore, that from the present appearance is inexhaustible. The Ore is of an excellent kind, & very fortunately situated for Waterfalls, coalwood, & boat-navigation. *This adds one link to the Chain of our National Independence.*["]

With all the respect due to exalted Virtue & condition your devoted Servant

WILLIAM BENTLEY

[Enclosure]

MY FRIEND,   DERRYFIELD 6th. Dcmr. 1809.

I received your letter of the 4th. of November, in which you suggest a wish of an expression of my opinion of President Madison. I have never been so *fortunate* as to have any personal acquaintance with him. But the virtues of Madison have been known to the world, longer than we have been known as a nation. Could my recital of his important services add to their weight, I could freely do it. I think the strongest evidence that we can have of his greatness, & goodness, is, that he was the chosen man of his immediate predecessor, & still retains his confidence. The value of these two great men has appeared as conspicuous in cultivating the arts of peace, as in the conflict for our national Independence.

Peace undoubtedly is our greatest good, as long as peace can be honourable. But I fear if we tip the cup of conciliation any higher, we shall have to drink the dregs. That nation, who has been our secret or open enemy for more than forty years, has now, by their last messenger of insult, heaped the measure of our wrongs: & I think must have prepared the minds of all, that prefer their own country to any other, for the last resort. I think Mr. Madison will not wait for the consent of the Arnolds or Pickerings of our country. Although he has not recommended a declaration of war to Congress, I think he will not suspend it long, without there is an immediate change of measures, with the change of ministry, before he will recommend it with the promptitude that he has dismissed their insulter of Nations.

You are thanked for your numerous presents of Newspapers, pamphlets, &c. &c. Mr. Adams writes like seventy five again.

It can be but a few days before I must leave my country & my friends. I wait the moment with impatience, for although I have spent a long life of enjoyment—life is now a great burthen to me. Conversing with my friends that are about me, or at *a distance, makes life more tolerable.* But it is the greatest consolation I have, that I leave the general government of my country in so good hands. The friend of William Bentley,

JOHN STARK.

RC and enclosure (DLC). Enclosure in a clerk's hand.

1. In his diary Bentley noted that he had forwarded a copy of a "Spirited Letter" from General Stark. "I have left the letter at the president's pleasure & informed Mr. Stickney of this circumstance" (*Diary of William Bentley*, 3:484).

2. Benjamin Franklin Stickney (b. 1775) had married Mary Stark in 1802. He was a justice of the peace in Bow, New Hampshire, and seems to have served in other minor official positions until 1812 when Secretary of War Eustis engaged him to go to Canada to report on the strength of British fortifications there. In March 1812 Stickney was appointed as Indian agent at Fort Wayne, Indiana Territory (J. C. A. Stagg, *Mr. Madison's War: Politics, Diplomacy, and Warfare in the Early American Republic, 1783–1830* [Princeton, N.J., 1983], pp. 228–29; Gayle Thornborough, ed., "Letter Book of the Indian Agency at Fort Wayne, 1809–1815," *Indiana Historical Society Publications*, 21 [1961]: 103).

From George Rogers

SIR,   CARLISLE Decr. 11th. 1809

Being Enlisted as a Soldier In Your Army the 17th. of last March when In a State of Intocsication the Next Day we were Ordered for the Barracks of Carlisle where I have remaind since.[1] My wife with four Small Children Remaind at Lancaster Penns untill Laterly that want Drave her away from it Expecting if She would Come up to the Barracks that She would be releivd By the Coming of Genl. Gensevoort[2] previous To his Coming She pettitioned the Secrty. of War for my Discharge But he wrote to Capt Johnson for to retain me untill I Could Procure a Substitude Genl. Gensevoort I beleive would Give me my Di[s]charge Only for Capt Johnson interfairing. I hope and pray That the Clemency of Your Mercy will be Graciously pleased to Send me my Discharge to Save A Distressed Wife & four Small Children from Distress & want, Which Your Pettitioner will be Ever Bound to pray

GEO ROGERS

RC (DNA: RG 107, LRRS, R-266:4). Postmarked Carlisle, 16 Dec. Docketed by a War Department clerk as received 19 Dec.

1. The recently recruited Sixth Infantry Regiment quartered some companies at Carlisle Barracks in the winter of 1809–10 (*ASP, Military Affairs*, 1:251).

2. Brig. Gen. Peter Gansevoort.

§ From Benjamin Henry Latrobe. *11 December 1809, Washington*. Gives details on construction and repairs of the Capitol wings, President's House, and adjacent roads. Progress on the south wing of the Capitol has been steady, with two capitals finished in the House of Representatives chamber and eight more in advanced stages of completion. A severe hailstorm in June broke "almost all the glass on the south front," and replacements "occasioned a very considerable expense." In the north wing progress has been made in rebuilding the Senate chamber, but the work went slowly owing to "the scarcity of workmen and the difficulty of procuring materials." The appropriation for the President's House has been used to enclose the grounds and gardens, build a carriage house, and prepare the interior "for the accomodation of a family." In estimating requirements for further construction, says there is a critical need for committee rooms in the south wing of the Capitol. Funds for the northwest part of that wing are urgently required, for the cellars are leaking and the appropriation for this section has been postponed until the safety of the entire structure is a concern. Funds are also needed to meet the "terms on which the Italian sculptors, employed on the Capitol are engaged."[1] Postponement of an appropriation for the library and judiciary portions of the north wing forced the work to go on with money moved from a general fund, since those ground-floor offices support the Senate chamber. The east and central portions of the north wing are completed, but the library rooms are in "a state of decay throughout, [so] as to render it dangerous to postpone the work proposed." The President's House was unfinished when the seat of government was moved to Washington in 1800, the surrounding grounds were "covered with rubbish, with the ruins of old brick kilns, and the remains of brick yards and stonecutters sheds." Limited progress was made during Jefferson's tenure, and the interior "is still incomplete." Some timbers of poor quality were used in the construction, and they have rotted. The public road south of the President's House is "in a very bad state, and must certainly be repaired the next season." Total estimated cost of work on the Capitol, President's House, and highways is $103,500. Adds an explanation of how the habit of Congress in appropriating funds at "the late period of the session" impairs efficiency. Workmen are usually engaged on 1 Jan. and those hired later in the season "are few, expensive, and generally inferior hands." Quarry orders are not given out until the "legislative will is known," so that the needed stone is not available until "midsummer, or the beginning of August, and that at a great expense." Common laborers must be engaged during the winter or they are unavailable until July, since they will fish for shad and herring from March until May. "As soon as the fishing season is over the harvest commences, and until the end of the harvest no great exertion which depends upon these numerous classes of our people, can be made." He states the facts so that Congress can know the particulars, "in hope . . . they may have the weight which they merit."

RC, two copies (DNA: RG 233, President's Messages; and DNA: RG 46, Legislative Proceedings, 11A-E2). 9 pp. Both copies in a clerk's hand, signed and corrected by Latrobe. Headed: "The Report of the Surveyor of the public buildings of the U. States." Enclosed in JM to Congress, 16 Dec. 1809. Printed in *ASP, Miscellaneous*, 2:16–18, and in Van Horne, *Papers of Benjamin Henry Latrobe*, 2:794–801.

1. Giuseppe Franzoni and Giovanni Andrei came from Carrara, Italy, to carve the stone-work in the House chamber. Latrobe broke with tradition and designed "corn tassels instead of acanthus leaves for the motif of the capitals" on "the slender fluted columns" (Green, *Washington: A History of the Capital*, 1:37; Van Horne, *Papers of Benjamin Henry Latrobe*, 2:144 n. 2).

From the Georgia General Assembly

IN SENATE, 12th. December 1809.

The foundations of the National Government being laid in the people—the intimate connexion between the people in a Republican Government and their public functionaries—The deep and solemn affection of a people for the Government of their choice—the proud Independence of freemen disdaining a quiet submission to repeated injuries—the long continued outrages and insults which have characterised the conduct of the British Cabinet towards our country, urge the Legislature of Georgia at this momentous crisis to an enunciation of their sentiments.

While with an eye of prudent suspicion we have marked the rapid strides of that imperious Government towards the despotism of the Ocean, we could not but recognize the pointed jealousy of her Orders in Council, which have with undeviating constancy leveled their shafts at the infant, but widely expanding commerce of America.

The Legislature had at one time sympathized in the fond hope of their brethren at large, in the Union, that a character of virtue and integrity sanctioned by the manifestations of a peace-loving community would have entitled them to reciprocal moderation and justice from the Governments of the Old world.

But the steady determination evinced by the two great belligerants of Europe to a continuation of their encroachments, and an unrelenting adherance to their violations of the universally received principles of national law had served entirely to eradicate the fond hope that a steady and virtuous neutrality would be adequate to the maintenance of our rights upon the Ocean; and hence resulted throughout the State of Georgia that animated approbation of the principles of an Embargo, which they deemed best calculated to restore the proud despots of Europe to a sense of Justice and of right; but while indulging in the pleasing expectations that an effect so desirable was about to be produced—while reposing in the grateful retrospection of the virtuous and patriotic policy which had dignified the last administration; and contemplating an equally honorable conduct in the present—we have been roused from a confidence so magnanimous to the recognition of an insult offered to the heads of Department in our Government, in whose hands are entrusted all negotiations with foreign powers—And feeling as we do, that an insult to Officers so high, in whom rests a responsibility so great while in the decent, honorable, rightful and dignified performance of duties incumbent upon them thro' the insolence of a foreign Minister is an insult to the Nation at large—And deeply impressed with the importance of supporting the Executive, in all actions sanctioned by justice where the rights and dignity of our National Government is involved

Be it therefore Resolved by the Senate and House of Representatives of the State of Georgia in General Assembly met, that we conceive the conduct of Francis James Jackson late resident minister from the Court of St. James', to have been highly insulting and censurable, and that with one voice we approve the spirited and decisive manner of the Executive of the United States in refusing further to negotiate with the British Government through the medium of that Minister.

And be it further Resolved that we as Citizens of Georgia, and members of the Union will ever be found in willing readiness to assert the rights and support the dignity of our Country whenever called upon by the proper authority of our National Republic.

And be it further Resolved that his Excellency the Governor be requested to transmit these our Resolutions to our Senators in Congress, to be by them presented to the President of the United States.

Read and unanimously passed.

HEN: MITCHELL
President

Attest.
WILL: ROBERTSON
Secretary

Ms (DLC). Read and unanimously approved in the Georgia House of Representatives and also approved by Gov. David B. Mitchell on 15 Dec. 1809 (see Augusta, Ga., *Mirror of the Times*, 25 Dec. 1809). Certified and signed by the Georgia secretary of state on 3 Feb. 1810. Docketed by JM, with his notation: "approving the Conduct of the Executive of the U. S. towards Mr. Jackson the British Minister Plenipo." JM's reply (not found) was noted by the governor of Georgia in his message to the opening session of the state legislature in November 1810, but the document was tabled and never printed (*Journal of the Senate of Georgia . . . for November and December 1810* [Milledgeville, Ga., 1811; Shaw and Shoemaker 22904], pp. 6, 19).

§ To the House of Representatives. *12 December 1809*. Transmits a "copy of a paper purporting to be a Circular letter from Mr Jackson to the British Consuls" and a paper "purporting to be a copy of a despatch from Mr Canning to Mr Erskine of the 23d Jany last," as they appeared in public prints. Both are submitted in response to a House resolution of 11 Dec.

RC and printed enclosures (DNA: RG 233, President's Messages). RC 1 p. In a clerk's hand, signed by JM. Received and ordered to be printed on 15 Dec. (*Annals of Congress*, 11th Cong., 2d sess., 742–43). Printed, with enclosures, in *ASP, Foreign Relations*, 3:299, 300–301, 323.

§ From David Gelston. *12 December 1809, New York.* Has delivered pipe of brandy to Mr. Forrest and paid the enclosed waybill for $54.11. The Phoenix Insurance Company was consignee.

RC and enclosure (DLC). RC 1 p. Enclosure 1 p.

From William DuBourg

SIR,   ST: MARY'S COLL. OF BALTRE. Decr. 15th. 1809.
Master Todd having communicated to me Mrs. Madison's request that He should visit her at christmas, I have anticipated by a few days that period, in order to give him sufficient time to enjoy himself in his family and be returned for the 27th., the day appointed for our *Commencement.*

Had my health permitted, I would gladly have accompanied him to pay in person to Yr. Exc. the tribute of my respect & my hearty congratulations for his promotion to the first Magistracy, and at the same time to make interest in favor of a beloved brother Major Peter F. DuBourg of Orleans, for the office of Collector of that Port, become vacant by the fraudulous elopement of the late holder of that appointment.[1] But being confined to my room, I must forego this double pleasure and depend on the zeal of my young friend to advocate the cause of my Brother, whose titles to preferment I will only take the liberty of subjoining for your Exc'y's consideration.

Major P. F. DuBourg, a native of St. Domingo, has been a citizen of the U. S. ever Since 1797. He has been in the military Service from the time of the cession, and the Select corps under his command, in the expedition against *Burr* has rendered to government signal services, to which General Wilkinson will bear ample testimony. During four years, after the taking of possession by the U. S. of the Louisiana Territory, He was the only person, who from his Knowledge of the Localities could make the entries of Vessels. By his disinterested exertions, he Saved an immense trouble to the Custom house officers, and without any prospect of remuneration he devoted a valuable part of his time to assist the first Collector Mr. Trist[2] & his unfortunate survivor & Brother in Law. Universally beloved by all parties, He has had the peculiar good fortune of fixing the attention and deserving the approbation & friendship of the Governor and other chiefs, as his friend Mr. Poydras, the representative in Congress of Orleans Territory, will cheerfully certify; and if his petition appears unsupported by the names of the principal officers of the territorial Government, it is not because he doubted obtaining their countenance, but because his natural reserve made him shrink from the part of solicitor in his own cause. To his habits of industry, to his unremitting perseverance, to his experimental Knowledge in business and to the unblemished fairness of his character, by which (much more than by his attractive and conciliating disposition) he has Secured his claims to general confidence, He owes the happiness of having in some measure repaired the wrongs of adverse fortune and of being the support of a numerous train of children and distressed friends, who will share in his gratitude to Yr. Excy. for an appointment which would insure to them all a continuation and extension of blessings. In fine He offers to Government a security of $50,000, or of any greater amount, on the wealthiest Land-holders of the Territory.

It is not without some apprehension of incurring the note of ambitious importunity, I presume, Sir, to repeat my solicitations to yr. Excy. in favor of that worthy Brother. But with a Man endowed with such a share of sensibility & domestic feelings, Brotherly affection cannot but plead my justification. Whatever be the issue of my request, which I am sensible how many preponderating motives can frustrate of its effect, I will at least feel the consciousness of having discharged a sacred duty.

With the most profound respect & gratitude for past favors, I remain, Sir, Yr. Excellency's most humble Servant

WM. DuBourg[3]

RC (DNA: RG 59, LAR, 1809–17, filed under "DuBourg"). Cover marked "Hond. by Mr. J. P. Todd."

1. William Brown.

2. Hore Browse Trist, collector at the port of New Orleans, had died of yellow fever in 1804. He was the son of Elizabeth House Trist, the daughter of Mary House in whose Philadelphia home JM had boarded in the 1780s and early 1790s (*PJM*, 4:251 n. 28).

3. William DuBourg (1766–1833), a Sulpician father and a refugee from Saint-Domingue, was rector of St. Mary's Seminary in Baltimore, where JM's stepson, John Payne Todd, was a pupil. DuBourg later became bishop of New Orleans.

From Thomas Gholson, Jr.

DEAR SIR   15 Decr. 1809.

My limitted circumstances and the claims of an encreasing family, united with a perfect knowledge that the District I represent would not supply my place with any other than an undoubted republican, having induced the determination of my retiring from the Legislature, at farthest, after the expiration of my present term; I was prevailed on by the suggestion of my friend Col: Goodwyn,[1] to tender to you through him, my services in an office which it is expected will shortly be vacant. Col Goodwyn has informed me, that you were pleased to state no other difficulty than that which would probably arise out of the question whether Virginia has not already had her full share of Territorial appointments. As I would be amongst the very last who would either place you under any embarrassment, or who would be the cause of any the slightest complaint against your administration, I beg leave to withdraw the application made yesterday by Col. Goodwyn in my favor, and to assure you of the high regard with which I remain your friend & Obedient Sert.

                                                    THOS: GHOLSON[2]

RC (DLC). Docketed by JM.

1. Peterson Goodwyn (1745–1818), a Revolutionary veteran, represented Dinwiddie County in the Virginia House of Delegates, 1789–1802. He was a Republican congressman, 1803–18 (*Richmond Enquirer*, 26 Feb. 1818).

2. Thomas Gholson, Jr. (d. 1816), a Republican lawyer, served as a delegate from Brunswick County, Virginia, 1806–8, and as a congressman, 1808–16.

From Benjamin Henry Latrobe

SIR,   CAPITOL Decr. 15h. 1809

The alterations which you have been pleased to make in the report submitted to you by me, will be attended to, and fair copies one for the Senate, another for the House of Representatives will be transmitted to You on Monday morning.[1] These copies it has been usual with the late President to send to the house of Congress by a Message.

In respect to the more detailed Specification of the Estimate, I beg leave to submit to You this consideration; that it is almost impossible to make a critically exact distribution of expenditure, *in practice*, of Work to be performed *by the day*, & by the same Workmen, working at *any thing* that shall at any particular time be most advantageously put in hand. Therefore altho' my specification were more minute, it would be impossible to answer for the exactness of the expenditure to each particular object of approbation. When separate Works, such as the North Wing, the South Wing, the President's house, the Highways, are at the same time in hand, it is easy to separate the accounts of expenditure, & this has always been correctly done; but when the Work is so involved as that of the North wing, it is next to impossible. To this Wing *particularly*, I presume your question to apply, as all the other items are separately specified.

But on this particular occasion, I beg to mention another reason why I have stated in one item the amount of appropriation required for the North Wing. In my last report, I had these two items

For the Library & Judiciary	20.000$
For the Senate Chamber,	25.000

Of the Estimate for the *Library & Judiciary*, I proposed to expend from 7 to 10.000$ on the Judiciary, the rest on the Library, which could only be partially completed in that Year. It was impossible to make an exact estimate in this case; & indeed in *no* case, is the estimate for appropriation, an estimate of the ultimate expense, but merely an estimate of what it is possible, under all circumstances of the actual state of the building to expend, *advantageously* in the ensuing season. For while I am employed in pulling down, & rebuilding, no motive whatever would induce me to risk an estimate of *ultimate* cost.

The Senate struck out of that appropriation the item of the Judiciary. Now as the Senate Chamber *could not be built at all*, without building first the court room under it, for which, agreeably to the *letter of the Law* there was not a dollar appropriated, I must have discharged all my Workmen, & awaited the next Session before I could have proceeded. As however the Spirit of the Law required all things to be done, without which the Senate Chamber could not be begun the Courtroom was built out of the General fund for works in the North Wing.

To avoid such inconvenience as has annually grown out of minute specifications & the rejection of individual Items, I have put the whole of the Work of the North wing into one item which, if reduced by Congress, will still leave a remainder applicable to the particular objects of the Estimate.[2]

The same observations apply to the presidents house & grounds, the gross appropriation resulting from the Estimate for which may be applied exactly as You shall direct. I am with highest respect Yrs. faithfully

B HENRY LATROBE.

RC (DLC). Docketed by JM.

1. Latrobe's official report to the president was dated 11 Dec. 1809. JM's alterations to the report have not been found.

2. The largest item in Latrobe's estimate was $40,000 for the "North wing, defraying the expense of completing the court room and the offices of the judiciary on the east side, completing the Senate chamber, and for the library" (*ASP, Miscellaneous*, 2:18).

§ From John Wayles Eppes. *15 December 1809.* Encloses a letter from James P. Preston of Virginia and recommends him for the position of Indian agent in the Louisiana Territory.

RC and enclosure (DNA: RG 59, LAR, 1809–17, filed under "Preston"). RC 1 p. Enclosure is Preston to Eppes, 29 Nov. 1809 (2 pp.). St. George Tucker also wrote to JM on Preston's behalf on 20 Dec. 1809 (ibid.).

To James Dinsmore

SIR   WASHINGTON Der. 16. 1809

In your letter by Mr. Gooch,[1] You suggestd. it as proper not to open a door from the Center room to admit a communication with the Kitchen. As that room will not probably be a permanent Dining room, it was not my intention that such a door should be opened, tho' I forgot to mention it to you. The width of the Sheets of Iron, is 18 inches or so near it as that you may proceed on that calculation. I know not precisely when I shall be able to forward that & the other Articles. Accept my respects

JAMES MADISON

RC (DLC, series 7).

1. Dinsmore to JM, 21 Nov. 1809.

§ To Congress. *16 December 1809.* Transmits report of the surveyor of public buildings.

RC and enclosure, two copies (DNA: RG 233, President's Messages; and DNA: RG 46, Legislative Proceedings, 11A-E2). Each RC 1 p., in a clerk's hand, signed and dated by JM. Received, read, and tabled by the House on 21 Dec. and by the Senate on 22 Dec. (*Annals of Congress*, 11th Cong., 2d sess., 517, 828). For enclosure, see Latrobe to JM, 11 Dec. 1809, and n.

§ To the House of Representatives. *16 December 1809.* In response to a 13 Dec. House resolution, transmits extracts from the correspondence of the U.S. minister at London.

RC and enclosures (DNA: RG 233, President's Messages). RC 1 p. In a clerk's hand, signed and dated by JM. Enclosures (21 pp.) are a "Brief account of an un-official conversation between Mr. Canning and Mr. Pinkney on the 18th. of January 1809, continued on the

22d. of the same month," and extracts from Pinkney to Robert Smith, 28 May and 6, 9, and 23 June 1809. The House, in the 13 Dec. debate on Anglo-American relations, had requested "any despatch from the American Minister in London, relative to the instructions of Mr. Canning to Mr. Erskine, of the 23d day of January, 1809," that in the president's opinion was not "improper to be communicated." JM's message and enclosures were received, read, and ordered to be printed by the House on 18 Dec. (*Annals of Congress*, 11th Cong., 2d sess., 718, 753). Printed, except for the extract from Pinkney's 28 May letter, in *ASP, Foreign Relations*, 3:299–300, 303.

§ To the Senate. *16 December 1809*. In response to a 15 Dec. Senate resolution, transmits copies of the president's correspondence with the governor of Pennsylvania concerning the case of Gideon Olmstead.

RC and enclosures (DNA: RG 46, Legislative Proceedings, 11A-E2). RC 1 p. In a clerk's hand, signed and dated by JM. Enclosures (6 pp.) are copies of Simon Snyder to JM, 6 Apr. 1809, the Pennsylvania "Act relative to certain proceedings in the case of the Prize Sloop Active," 4 Apr. 1809, and JM to Snyder, 13 Apr. 1809 (see *PJM-PS*, 1:105 and n. 1, 114). Received, read, and ordered to be printed on 19 Dec. (*Annals of Congress*, 11th Cong., 2d sess., 515). Printed in *ASP, Miscellaneous*, 2:11–12.

§ From Buckner Thruston and John Pope. *16 December 1809, Senate Chamber*. Encloses recommendations on behalf of John Coburn for the position of governor of the Louisiana Territory. They have also received letters in favor of John Allen for the same position and concur in recommending both men.

RC and enclosures (DNA: RG 59, LAR, 1809–17, filed under "Coburn"). RC 1 p. Enclosures (4 pp.) are two letters signed by citizens of Lexington, Kentucky (see James Taylor to JM, 19 Nov. 1809, n. 2).

§ From an Unidentified Correspondent. *16 December 1809, Portland*. JM's remarks in his annual message to Congress regarding the militia prompted this letter, which might have been sent to Ezekiel Whitman, the Maine district congressman, but "he might not be so sensible of the importance of the subject as you appear to be." Every man should attempt to qualify himself for militia duty, but there is an aversion stemming "from the manner in which military musters are conducted." Urges proper drills, emphasis on marksmanship, and maneuvers with cavalry, artillery, and infantry units combined.

RC (DNA: RG 107, LRRS, A-313:4). 4 pp. Signed "J. H. H." Docketed by a War Department clerk as received 29 Dec. On a separate sheet the writer identifies himself as "a mechanic . . . who has a most ardent desire for the welfare of his country."

§ From William C. C. Claiborne. *17 December 1809, "Near New Orleans."* Informs JM of the death of his second wife from yellow fever.[1] Requests permission to be absent from his post between May and November or December of next year in order to attend to his accounts and to preserve his health.[2] Believes that the territorial legislature will dispatch "all the public Business" within two months of their meeting in January. Warns against the unhealthy location of the governor's residence and advises that it be sold.

RC and duplicate (DLC). 4 pp. Duplicate in a clerk's hand, signed by Claiborne. Printed in Carter, *Territorial Papers, Orleans*, 9:859–60.

1. Claiborne's first wife, Elizabeth Lewis Claiborne, their daughter, Cornelia Tennessee Claiborne, and Claiborne's private secretary as well, had all died of yellow fever in September 1804. In 1806 Claiborne married Clarissa Duralde, who died on 29 Nov. 1809 (Joseph T. Hatfield, *William Claiborne: Jeffersonian Centurion in the American Southwest* [Lafayette, La., 1976], pp. 207–9).
2. JM granted Claiborne's request on 18 Jan. 1810 (Smith to Claiborne, 18 Jan. 1810 [DNA: RG 59, DL]).

From David Bailie Warden

PARIS 18 Dec. 1809.

I have the honor of sending you a file of newspapers which contains an acct. of the late wonderful events that have taken place on the Continent.

Spain is to be attacked with an army of nearly 200,000 men, and will probably be subjugated. Holland is to become a province of france,[1] and the prediction of Smith, in his Wealth of Nations,[2] will doubtless be realised. If the Republican form of Govt. be destroyed, the wealthy merchants, having lost their influence, will transport themselves with their capitals, to some other country. I have written by the Maddison to the Secry. of State on the Subject of Prise causes,[3] giving a detailed acct. of the condemnations, private arrangements, and circumstances that have occurred since the date of my last. It is my endeavour to furnish him with every information of this kind, that I think may be useful; and it would give me much pleasure to know that it is acceptable. I have said so much already on the subject of my appointment, that I dare not renew it at present. I still hope, Sir for your approbation—and shall endeavour to be worthy of it.

D. B. W.

Letterbook copy (MdHi: Warden Papers).

1. In December 1809 Napoleon bullied his brother Louis, king of Holland, into accepting French annexation of Dutch territory along the left bank of the Rhine in order to improve the enforcement of the Continental System. Six months later Louis abdicated, and Holland was finally absorbed into France (Simon Schama, *Patriots and Liberators: Revolution in the Netherlands, 1780–1813* [London, 1977], pp. 602–10; Armstrong to JM, 18 Mar. 1810, and n. 7).
2. "Any public calamity which should destroy the republican form of government," Adam Smith predicted, would force wealthy merchants to "remove both their residence and

their capital to some other country, and the industry and commerce of Holland would soon follow the capitals which supported them" (*An Inquiry into the Nature and Causes of the Wealth of Nations*, ed. Edwin Cannan [New York, 1937], p. 858).

   3. Probably Warden to Robert Smith, 14 Nov. 1809 (DNA: RG 59, CD, Paris).

§ From Oliver Whipple. *18 December 1809, Washington.* Has come to Washington from the District of Maine seeking an appointment and has references from prominent New Englanders, including former president John Adams who has recently declared himself to be JM's "Friend, and the Friend of your Administration, with the most prompt and decided Approbation of your measures." Mentions his support for the administration and declares that he will remain in Washington until the spring, at which time he will return to his home state of Rhode Island.

   RC (DNA: RG 59, LAR, 1809–17, filed under "Whipple"). 2 pp. Oliver Whipple (1743–1813) was the author of *The Historic Progress of Civil and Rational Liberty* (Portsmouth, N.H., 1802; Shaw and Shoemaker 3549), a lengthy poem dedicated to John Adams.

§ From Jeremiah Morrow. *19 December 1809, Senate Chamber.* Encloses a letter from William Sprigg recommending John Coburn for governor of the Louisiana Territory.

   RC and enclosure (DNA: RG 59, LAR, 1809–17, filed under "Coburn"). RC 1 p. Enclosure is Sprigg to Morrow, 3 Dec. 1809 (2 pp.). Morrow was the Republican representative from Ohio, 1803–13. JM received at least one more letter on Coburn's behalf, from Kentucky representative Joseph Desha, dated 11 Feb. 1810 (ibid.).

From Caleb Atwater

DEAR SIR,   SULLIVAN[1] Decr 20th 1809

   Much has been said about the triumph of Federalism in this State,[2] both in and out of it. Having lived in the state a great number of years and having formed a very extensive acquaintance with men belonging to both parties, I think myself qualified to judge pretty correctly in matters relative to our state affairs. And of all the causes which have produced the present disastrous situation of the Republican Party, I must say, that it is almost entirely owing to the appointment of *federal post masters*. Their conduct just before and during our elections has been the most shameful and abandoned. At such times, Republican newspapers and handbills are detained in the Post Offices while Federal Newspapers & lying hand bills fill every bar-room & grog-shop in the State. The evil is so great that it has become truely alarming to every friend to his Country. For several years the Post Master General has appointed such men and such men only to office.[3]

My feelings have been wounded to such a degree that I cannot refrain from laying my complaint before the President of the United States. Such a post master have we had in this town who is at this time recommending one like himself for his successor.

The Post Master says that "Granger is a relation of his, and our petitions & remonstrances will be of no use."

In this county at the last spring election, had the news of the arrangement with Erskine been received in season, the Republicans would have obtained the election. The Federalists had this news on the first day of the election, but the federal post masters detained the newspapers from the Republicans until the election was over and then took the papers from their pockets (belonging to Republicans) which had been in them for three days, and read them aloud. This actually took place in *this town*.

Such conduct Sir, is intolerable. This same man become odious in the eyes of all, is now recommending as a Successor, a man after his own heart. Sir, we cannot feel reconciled to his appointment. We wish to have Mr. William Jennings, a young man of Republican principles and strict integrity appointed.

If we are to be oppressed any longer in this scandalous manner, we wish to know it.

Should we be disappointed in this laudable attempt, the most serious consequences to our Party, and our Country are apprehended.

Nothing but the exigency of the case would have led me to address a letter to the first Magistrate of the Union. It may appear extraordinary to your Excellency, to address a letter to the President, instead of the Post Master General. But Sir, we are insultingly told, that it is of no use to write to "Gid. Granger." I am Sir, with Great Respect your Excellency's humble servt

CALEB ATWATER.[4]

RC (DLC). Docketed by JM. Cover note indicates the letter was posted at Vernon, New York, 24 Dec.

1. JM wrote "(N. York)" under this word. Sullivan is in Madison County, a few miles below Oneida Lake.

2. Federalists had made major gains in the May elections to the New York legislature (JM to Jefferson, 30 May 1809, *PJM-PS*, 1:214 and n. 2).

3. Although JM had held Gideon Granger over in his position from Jefferson's cabinet, the political loyalties of the postmaster general clearly lay with JM's political rivals in the northern states and especially with the Clintonians in New York, who often advocated alliances with the Federalists as an electoral tactic. Granger had supported George Clinton's presidential aspirations in 1808, and he was to support DeWitt Clinton against JM in 1812 (E. Wilder Spaulding, *His Excellency George Clinton: Critic of the Constitution* [New York, 1938], p. 277; Dorothie Bobbé, *DeWitt Clinton* [New York, 1933], p. 187).

4. Caleb Atwater was a lawyer in upstate New York. In 1815 he moved to Ohio, where as a state legislator he advanced public education and internal improvements.

From Benjamin Joy

SIR   BOSTON 20th Decr 1809

Fully persuaded that it is your desire to promote Justice and equity throughout the United States, I beg leave to lay before you the inclosed printed copy of a memorial which has been committed in the House of Representatives to the committee of Claims.[1] I have taken this liberty Sir presuming you would be willing to have a copy by you to refer to when convenient & that you would have the goodness to excuse my thus intruding on you if it was wrong. As I am perhaps unknown to you Sir I shall not attempt to comment on the memorial or say any thing of the distress which many persons here have experienced in consequence of the unfortunate transaction therein mentioned I will only beg to be permitted to say that indubitable proof can be given that the purchasers here were in no measure accessory or in any way knowing to any fraud which might have been committed in Georgia. I am with the Highest Respect Sir your most obedient Humble Servant

BENJN. JOY.[2]

RC (DLC). For enclosure, see n. 1.

1. Joy probably enclosed *To the Honorable, the Senate and House of Representatives of the United States. The Memorial of the Directors of the New-England Mississippi Land Company, Citizens of the State of Massachusetts* (n.p., n.d.; Shaw and Shoemaker 32240). JM's copy of this pamphlet is in the Madison Collection, Rare Book Division, Library of Congress. Joy was one of seven company directors who signed the memorial, which sought a final adjustment of the company's claims to Yazoo lands. Ezekiel Bacon introduced it in the House on 14 Dec. While secretary of state, JM had served on the commission that recommended a compromise settlement, but the matter was still before the Supreme Court during the winter of 1809–10 (*Annals of Congress*, 11th Cong., 2d sess., 729; C. Peter Magrath, *Yazoo: Law and Politics in the New Republic: The Case of* Fletcher v. Peck [New York, 1967], pp. 35–36, 65).

2. Benjamin Joy and his brother George (who had met JM in New York by 1791 and corresponded with him) were sons of the Loyalist exile John Joy. After the Revolution Benjamin Joy returned to his native Boston, served as U.S. consul at Calcutta, 1792–95, then became an investor and real estate developer of Beacon Hill (George Joy to JM, Nov. 1791, *PJM*, 14:92–94 and n. 5; *PJM-PS*, 1:30–31; *Senate Exec. Proceedings*, 1:126; Benjamin Joy to Bartholomew Dandridge, Jr., 4 Nov. 1795 [DLC: Washington Papers]; Harold and James Kirker, *Bulfinch's Boston, 1787–1817* [New York, 1964], pp. 148–49, 161).

From Christopher Ellery

SIR   PROVIDENCE, R. I. December 21st. 1809.

One of the justices of the supreme court, U. S. has this day, left this town on his way to the seat of government, and, as is understood, with the intention of resigning his place on the bench.[1] That such is his intention there is, indeed, no doubt; nor can it be expected that the old gentleman will be diverted from his purpose, so difficult is it to concieve of a motive by which any one could be influenced in deterring him from so wise and necessary a course of proceeding. Upon his resignation, the eye of the President may be directed to the northern district,[2] embracing among other states, Rhode Island, in search of a fit character to succeed him. This state, in many respects, comparatively, unimportant, is in others entitled to consideration—for favor, at least, she may hope. Perhaps an opportunity to extend favor, consistently with public good, may offer in the appointment of a successor to Judge Cushing. On this supposition a gentleman of the bar here, qualified eminently, might be introduced to the attention of the President. There is one of this description, Asher Robbins Esquire,[3] of Newport; but unauthorised to name him, either by his permission, or by my own pretensions to notice, I do not presume further than merely, and I hope respectfully, to suggest, at an early day, that Rhode Island has a man whose merits would be acknowledged in the most elevated judicial station. With sentiments of the highest respect, I have the honor to be, Sir Your most obedient servant

CHRISTR. ELLERY[4]

RC (DNA: RG 59, LAR, 1809–17, filed under "Robbins").

1. William Cushing, the oldest associate justice on the Supreme Court, died in office on 13 Sept. 1810.

2. Cushing's successor on the Supreme Court would have to come from New England, and Ellery's letter was an early maneuver in what became a major campaign over the next ten months to influence JM's choice for the nomination. In this period JM received half a dozen letters supporting Robbins's nomination and many more on behalf of other candidates, particularly Gideon Granger. JM does not appear to have given very serious consideration to Robbins's claims, but eventually he was to offer the nomination to four New Englanders before Joseph Story accepted and was confirmed in 1811 (Morgan D. Dowd, "Justice Joseph Story and the Politics of Appointment," *American Journal of Legal History*, 9 [1965]: 265–85).

3. Asher Robbins (1757–1845) graduated from Yale in 1782 and had been practicing law in Newport, Rhode Island, since 1795. In 1812 JM appointed him U.S. attorney for Rhode Island, and after 1825 he represented his state for fourteen years in the U.S. Senate (*Senate Exec. Proceedings*, 2:310).

4. Christopher Ellery (1768–1840) came from a prominent Rhode Island family, graduated from Yale in 1787, and practiced law in Newport, Rhode Island. Between 1801 and 1805 he served in the U.S. Senate, and in 1804 Jefferson appointed him commissioner of loans at Providence. Ellery was also Robbins's brother-in-law, a fact he later revealed to JM (ibid., 2:7, 10; Ellery to JM, 30 Sept. 1810).

From Albert Gallatin

SIR   TREASURY DEPARTMENT 22d Decer. 1809

Hearing that Mr J. Kilty Smith has been appointed Navy Agent at New Orleans, I think it my duty to state that he was formerly a collector of the internal duties under his uncle Mr Kilty late Supervisor for the district of Maryland;[1] that when he left that office & became a clerk in the Navy department, he was, as appears by the Supervisor's accounts, debtor to the United States in bonds & cash to the amount of about 4,500 dollars; that in the quarter ending on 31 Decer. 1803, the Supervisor assumed the payment of that sum, by crediting in his accounts the collector & charging himself for the same; and that this was at the time assigned as one of the causes of Mr Kilty's delinquency. The Supervisor having charged himself with the amount, it never became my duty or was necessary to investigate minutely the circumstances as they related to Mr Smith: and they may perhaps, by reference to Mr Kilty & to himself, be satisfactorily explained. But the matter, so far as relates to the accounts, being of record in this Department; and one of our appointments in New Orleans[2] having lately proven so unfortunate, I am compelled, tho' with reluctance, to make this communication. With the highest respect Your obedt. Servant

ALBERT GALLATIN

RC (DLC). Docketed by JM.

1. John Kelty (or Kilty) was appointed excise supervisor for Maryland in 1795. John K. Smith was serving as an inspector under him by 1802 and later became a Navy Department clerk (*Senate Exec. Proceedings*, 1:179, 181; *ASP, Miscellaneous*, 1:283; Cunningham, *The Process of Government under Jefferson*, p. 330). On Smith's appointment as navy agent for New Orleans, see Paul Hamilton to JM, 4 Dec. 1809, and n. 1.
2. William Brown.

From Paul Hamilton

SIR,   NAVY DEPARTMENT 22 Decr 1809

Docr Julius R Shumate[1] has been particularly recommended by Mr. Love[2] of the House of Representatives for the appointment of Surgeon's Mate in the Navy—& his services are now wanted at New orleans. I have the honor to be with great respect sir yr mo ob st.

PAUL HAMILTON

RC (DLC); letterbook copy (DNA: RG 45, LSP). RC in Goldsborough's hand, signed by Hamilton; docketed by JM.

1. On 27 Dec. JM nominated Shumate, a resident of Culpeper County, Virginia. The Senate confirmed his appointment on 3 Jan. 1810, and he served until 1812 (*Senate Exec. Proceedings*, 2:134, 136; Callahan, *List of Officers of the Navy*, p. 497).

2. John Love (d. 1822), an Alexandria Republican, represented Fauquier County in the Virginia House of Delegates, 1805–7, and the district composed of Loudoun, Prince William, and Fairfax counties in the U.S. House of Representatives, 1807–11. He served as a state senator, 1816–20 (Swem and Williams, *Register*, p. 399; Stanley B. Parsons, William W. Beach, and Dan Hermann, *United States Congressional Districts, 1788–1841* [Westport, Conn., 1978], p. 130).

§ To the Senate. *22 December 1809.* Submits for ratification a treaty and separate article concluded on 30 Sept. with the Delaware, Potawatomi, Miami, and Eel River Indians, a convention concluded on 26 Oct. with the Wea tribe, and explanatory documents.

RC and enclosures (DNA: RG 46, Executive Proceedings, 11B-C1). RC 1 p. In a clerk's hand, signed by JM. Printed enclosure (8 pp.) is *A Treaty between the United States of America, and the Tribes of Indians Called the Delawares, Putawatimies, Miamies, and Eel River Miamies. December 22d, 1809* (Washington, 1809; Shaw and Shoemaker 19077). Also filed with the RC is a letter from the War Department to William Henry Harrison, 15 July 1809 (2 pp.). Received, read, and tabled on 22 Dec. The Senate unanimously ratified the treaty, separate article, and convention on 2 Jan. 1810 (*Senate Exec. Proceedings*, 2:132–33, 135). Printed in *ASP, Indian Affairs*, 1:760–62.

From Francis Preston

DEAR SIR   ABINGDON. Decr. 23rd 1809

You may remember that about a year or 18 Months ago, I forwarded to you[1] from Richmond some United States Stock in the name of Adam Hope with a power of Attorney to receive the interest thereon. The Certificates I think you informed me last winter you had deposited with Mr Grayham one of the Clerks in the department of State. Mr. Hope has now nominated Mr Sheffey[2] of the house of representatives his Attorney to whom I have written to make application to Mr. Grayham for the papers; but least Mr Grayham may feel some difficulty to give them up I beg the favour of you, should he apply to you on the subject, to direct him to give them to Mr Sheffey.

I hope Sir you enjoy good health for I beleive there never was a time when it was of more importance to your Country than the present—the difficulties and embarrassments our Country is involved in owing to the perfidy of Men and Nations, claim no doubt all your time and attention and the support of the virtuous part of your fellow citizens. The people of this part of the Country view the Conduct of Great Brittain in respect to the late arrangement with Mr Erskine in its proper light, and are devoted to their Country and the administration. I am well satisfied if war shall be the result we shall most promptly engage in it and obey the commands of the Government, yet I presume there are but few here but would rather evade a war if consistent with the honor of our Country altho' there is no part of it that will be more exempt from its evils.

But I can with pride and with truth say I perceive a considerable portion of that spirit and patriotism remaining which actuated us in the revolution, and you may rely on Sir that your measures will be supported in this part of the Country with Zeal. I am Dear Sir with Sincere friendship and high respect your Mo Obet Sert.

FRANS PRESTON [3]

RC (CtLHi).

1. Letter not found, but the list of JM's correspondence probably made by Peter Force (DLC, series 7, container 2) mentions a letter from Preston of 8 June 1808.

2. Daniel Sheffey (1770–1830), a Wytheville Federalist, represented a southwest Virginia constituency, 1809–17, which was part of Preston's former congressional district (Parsons et al., *United States Congressional Districts*, pp. 70, 130).

3. Francis Preston (1765–1836) served with JM in the House of Representatives, 1793–97. He moved to Abingdon in Washington County, resumed his law practice, and was a colonel of volunteers in the War of 1812 (*PJM*, 15:8 n. 9).

§ From Cyrus Griffin. *25 December 1809, Norfolk.* Asks JM to provide for a transfer that would shift his son, John Griffin, "from Michigan to a western or Southern position: he finds the Climate too cold for his Constitution." Since his son is fluent in both French and Spanish, a judicial vacancy "upon or near the Mississippi" might be "advantageous to the public."

RC (DNA: RG 59, LAR, 1809–17, filed under "Griffin"). 2 pp. Postmarked 24 Dec. Printed in Carter, *Territorial Papers, Michigan*, 10:303–4. Jefferson had approved Judge Griffin's transfer from the Indiana Territory to Michigan "agreeably to his own desire" on 23 Dec. 1805 (*Senate Exec. Proceedings*, 2:11; see also John Griffin to JM, 14 Apr. 1809, *PJM-PS*, 1:115 and n. 1).

§ From Levi Lincoln. *25 December 1809, Worcester.* Introduces Major Cogswell,[1] a supporter of administration policies, "from whome you may learn the state of the public spirit in this part of the Country."

RC (DLC). 1 p.

1. Amos Cogswell (1752–1826) rose to the rank of brevet major during the Revolution (*DAR Patriot Index*, p. 142; Francis B. Heitman, *Historical Register of Officers of the Continental Army during the War of the Revolution* [Washington, 1914], p. 163).

To John Stark

SIR   WASHINGTON Decembr. 26. 1809

A very particular friend of your's,[1] who has been much recommended to my esteem, has lately mentioned you to me in a manner of which I avail myself to offer this expression of the sense I have always entertained of your character and of the part you bore as a Hero and a Patriot, in establishing the Independence of our country.

I cannot better render this tribute, than by congratulating you on the happiness you cannot fail to derive from the motives which made you a champion in so glorious a cause; from the gratitude shewn by your fellow citizens for your distinguished services; & especially from the opportunity which a protracted life has given you of witnessing the triumph of republican Institutions so dear to you, in the unrivalled prosperity flowing from them during a trial of more than a fourth of a century.

May your life still be continued as long as it can be a blessing; and may the example it will bequeathe never be lost on those who live after you.

J. M.

FC (DLC). In a clerk's hand; docketed by JM. RC (not found) enclosed in JM to William Bentley, 27 Dec. 1809. Printed in Concord *N.H. Patriot*, 27 Feb. 1810, and other newspapers.

1. William Bentley (see JM to Bentley, 28 Oct. 1809, and n. 1).

To the Vermont General Assembly

WASHINGTON, Dec. 26, 1809.

I have received the address of the General Assembly transmitted to me on the 15th ult. with the impressions which ought to be made by the sentiments expressed in it.

Conscious as I am, how much I owe the high trust with which I am invested, to a partiality in my fellow citizens which overrated my qualifications, I am compelled to mingle my regret that these are not more adequate, with the gratification afforded by the confidence of so respectable a body; and by the tribute which is so justly paid to the success of my illustrious predecessor, under the blessing of Divine Providence in preserving our nation from the wars by which Europe has been so long and so dreadfully afflicted.

Such, nevertheless, has been the extraordinary character of those wars, that it was not possible for the councils of our government, however prudent and pacific, to avoid a participation in the injuries which have been extended to those not parties to them. The United States still experience these unprovoked aggressions; and with the recent addition of circumstances admonishing them to be prepared against more hostile fruits of the reigning policy.

In this conjuncture, it is to be lamented, that any difference of opinion should prevail, with respect to the measures best suited to it, and more particularly, that any measures actually adopted should have been opposed in modes calculated to embolden foreign hopes and experiment, by presenting appearances of internal divisions and weakness. The full strength of every nation requires an union of its citizens. To a government like ours, this truth is peculiarly applicable. If its importance has not heretofore been sufficiently felt on occasions which seemed to demand it, we shall not, I trust, be disappointed of the satisfaction promised by the dawn of a more universal support of the constituted authorities, in the measures for maintaining the national honor and rights.

In this view, the sentiments which animate the Legislature of Vermont are entitled to the warmest commendation; which I sincerely tender, with assurances of my friendly respects and high consideration.

JAMES MADISON

Printed copy (E. P. Walton, ed., *Records of the Governor and Council of the State of Vermont* [8 vols.; Montpelier, Vt., 1873–80], 5:463–64). Addressed to "The Hon. Dudley Chase, Speaker of the House of Representatives of Vermont."

From Sarah W. Lapsley

HON. SIR   PARIS[1] Dec. 26th. 1809.

Pardon the presumption of a female, in troubling you, with this addres⟨s.⟩ I had the misfortune, when an infant to loose my father, Capt. Samuel Lapsley;[2] and with him, the greater part of what, as his Child I had a right to inherit. Amongst the rest was, two Certificates for his faithful services, during the late revolutionary war, containing 2360 dollars. My Mother has repeatedly applied to Congress for relief; but owing to her helpless situation and not being able to make proper statements of our Claim, or for want of suitable persons, to advocate our Cause; we have hitherto not succeeded.[3] But where can the helpless apply, but to those who have it in their power to redress them, the friends of liberty, the patrons of Justice. If Sir, you will be so condescending as to inquire into the merits of our Claim you will find the papers relative to the business, in the hands of the Hon. Benjamin Howard;[4] and if upon investigation, you find our claim to be a Just, one; may I not hope for your Patronage, and assistance;[5] your attention will lay me under infinite obligations, to an unknown friend and benefactor; and will be ever gratefully remembered by

SARAH W. LAPSLEY

RC (DLC).

1. Paris, Kentucky.

2. Samuel Lapsley was a captain in a Virginia regiment, 1777–79 (Heitman, *Historical Register Continental*, p. 340).

3. Lapsley's widow, Margaret, came close to settling the claim in 1800, when the Senate passed a private relief bill for her husband's heirs, but the House of Representatives rejected it (*ASP, Claims*, pp. 241–42).

4. Benjamin Howard (1760–1814) served as a Kentucky congressman, 1807–10. JM appointed him governor of the Louisiana Territory in 1810.

5. Margaret Lapsley had apparently submitted a petition for relief in November 1808 without success, but the House referred the matter again to the Committee of Claims on 9 Jan. 1810. The committee reported that the claim, though reasonable, was barred from further consideration by the statute of limitations, a judgment the House reversed on 9 Mar. A bill for the relief of Margaret Lapsley and five other petitioners was then duly passed by the House on 13 Apr., but Lapsley's name was struck out by a Senate amendment on 1 May. The matter was finally settled in 1813 when Congress voted to pay the claim plus interest from 1783 (*Annals of Congress*, 11th Cong., 2d sess., 655, 657, 663, 676, 678–79, 1531, 1559, 1560, 1761–62, 1794, 2053; *Journal of the House of Representatives of the United States* [9 vols.; Washington, 1826], 7:167, 176, 275, 283; *U.S. Statutes at Large*, 6:119).

From Alexander McRae

SIR,   PHILADELPHIA 26. Decr. 1809

As an American citizen I think it my duty to inform you of the extraordinary and (as I thought) most unwarrantable treatment, which I this day received from his Britannic Majesty's Consul Phineas Bond esqr., at his residence in this place. Before I left Washington, (on my way to Europe) desiring such a protection as the Government of my Country might be pleased to afford me while abroad; I applied for that purpose at the department of State, and had the honor to receive from the Secretary of State, a Passport in unusual Form, presenting me in a distinguished manner, and in terms of high respect, to all to whom it might necessarily be shewn.

I thought it requisite also to super add Testimonials in the usual Form, from the proper Functionaries of the French and British Governments, and for that purpose, my friend Mr. Brent who acts in the Department of State accompanied me to General Turreau's Office, where I was politely received, and had my Passport duly and with promptitude accredited by that Minister. To-day after calling a *fourth* time on His Britannic Majesty's Consul, accompanied each time by my friend Patrick Byrne esqr.,[1] Mr. Bond was pleased to honor me with an interview.

After informing him of my intention, to visit England, France, and other Countries, and (in reply to a cautionary admonition he condescended to give me) "that I intended to leave my politics in America," and to act in whatever Country I might visit during my stay in it, as might become a good citizen of such Country; I presented my Passport, and requested the annexation to it of his certificate, in the customary form. In a Moment he refused it; saying, that the Minister of his Country, Mr. Jackson, was as accessible as he was, and that whatever Mr. Jackson's standing with *this* Government might be, he felt it a duty to refer me to Mr. Jackson, for the Certificate I desired. I replied that I had no feelings of personal enmity against Mr. Jackson, for I was not even acquainted with him; but that it was my duty as an American, to advert to his present peculiar situation with the Government of my Country; that Mr. Jackson himself as a gentleman, reflecting coolly and rationally on the subject, must approve the resolution I had formed, to have no communication with him; and that I could not commit myself, by making any application whatever to him; that if I were to do so, my conduct would expose me to just criticism, and deservedly to severe animadversion: I remarked farther, that the Testimonial for which I applied, was regularly within the scope of Consular authority to grant, and spoke of the dilemma in which I might be involved if it were refused; repeating to him the declaration I had before made, that I could have no communication with Mr. Jackson. He answered (I thought sarcastically) that my feelings were for myself; but they could not regulate *his* conduct, and that he had no doubt my *high* standing in this Country, indicated by the Passport I carried from *my own Country*; "would afford me ample protection in England, without any thing from *him*, or from Mr. *Jackson*." For this expression (the manner of it considered) the Consul certainly deserved a kicking, and perhaps might have received, it had we been elsewhere than in *his own house*. I however, situated as I was, coolly replied, that I intended to act as might become an American citizen, whereever I might go; but that I would have no communication with Mr. *Jackson*. The worthy Consul squinted at Genl. Turreau's signature, and said, *that* would be of no service to me in *England*. I replied, that I had not asked it with a view to derive benefit from it in *England*; but for my protection on the *Continent*, and that I had applied for *his* certificate, to protect me in *England*. *That* he finally refused; after making efforts in four or five different ways to drive me to Jackson, which I as often repelled.

I will sooner starve in a dungeon, than apply to such a Tool, and a miscreant so vile, for any protection he might be able to afford me![2] Unless you should deem it on the information I have given, to be your Official duty, to notice immediately the conduct of Mr. Bond, my wish is (for an obvious reason) that nothing may be said of it 'til after my return. My friend Mr. Byrne shall tomorrow see this letter, and will no doubt if he finds (as he will) my statement to be correct, do me the justice of certifying to that effect. He will at my request, say nothing publicly concerning the contents of the letter, unless you should think it an Official duty to make it's contents public. In the event of your forming such an opinion, I have to beg that it may be immediately announced to me in a letter addressed to me at New-York, where I will remain several days for the pleasure of hearing from you. I have perhaps, as my Interest and Feelings were concerned, attached too much importance to the insolent and insidious conduct of Mr. Bond; but I have thought that as a *Consul*, he was *bound* to comply with the request I made of him; unless he had other reasons for refusing a compliance, than those he assigned, and under that impression I beleived it to be my duty, to trouble you with this communication. With the highest respect and esteem I have the honor to be Sir, Yr. mo. ob. Servt.

AL: McRAE.

I have read the foregoing statement of Alexr McRea Esqr., being present when the conversation took place, between him & Phineas Bond Esqr. British Consul, I feel it to be perfectly correct

P. BYRNE

RC (DLC). Postscript in Byrne's hand. Docketed by JM.

1. Patrick Byrne operated the Sign of the Cock tavern on Front Street in Philadelphia (*Pa. Mag. Hist. and Biog.*, 73 [1949]: 469).

2. In reporting the episode to his government, Francis James Jackson declared that McRae's travel plans were "obscure and mysterious," and he suggested that if McRae should ever arrive in Great Britain, "he will be an object well worthy the attention of the Alien office." The minister further described McRae as a man of about forty years of age, with "very bushy hair, tied long," and well known for his "Jacobinism, and enmity to England" (Jackson to Wellesley, 17 Feb. 1810 [PRO: Foreign Office, ser. 115, Consular Dispatches, vol. 21]).

To William Bentley

SIR   WASHINGTON Decr. 27. 1809

In consequence of your favor of the 11th. instant, I have addressed the few lines inclosed, to General Stark. If the possession of this sincere testimony of my esteem be entirely satisfactory, it may perhaps be as well, that it should not be followed by a publication; the sole object being, to contribute in that form, whatever gratification may be afforded him, by learning the sentiments of one, of whom he has been pleased to think and to speak so favorably. With entire confidence in your judicious estimate of the case, I limit myself to this intimation.[1] Accept assurances of my esteem, and of my friendly respects.

James Madison

RC (owned by Gilman School, Baltimore, Md., 1984); draft (DLC). Enclosed JM to John Stark, 26 Dec. 1809.

1. In the draft, JM first wrote: "I have too much confidence, however, in your judgment, not to limit myself to this intimation." In his diary, Bentley noted receipt of the letter with its enclosure and commented: "The President is very desirous that it should not appear to [be] an electioneering trick which it certainly was not upon the best evidence I can possess, who knew the whole progress of the work & the real occasion & purpose of his writing" (*Diary of William Bentley*, 3:488).

From Isaac A. Coles

Dear Sir   Dec. 29th. 1809

After what has passed in the House of Representatives[1] I feel myself compelled to declare to you, that I never can again be the Bearer of a Message to that Body. It is with feelings the most painful that I make this declaration, which I believe to be due as well to them as to myself—to avoid the Occasions for mortifications & insults which might be offered by some, whose feelings are the most unfriendly, & whose situations place them beyond the reach of resentment; & to avoid too those collisions in Society, under circumstances that would render them peculiarly disagreeable. Influenced by these considerations, & by these only, I cannot but flatter myself that the step which I am about to take, will be viewed by you with indulgence, & that you will Accept the assurances which I now offer you, that in retiring from the situation which I at present Occupy in your family, I carry with me no other feelings than those of the warmest & most respectful Attachment

I. A. Coles

P. S. This morning when I wrote the above, I was under an impression that there had been a decision of the House, on the subject to which it relates; but I have been informed since that the report of the Comtee., was only laid on the Table, to be taken up on a future day.[2] Altho' I would not wish, in appearance even, to avoid a decision of the House by seeming to fly from it; Yet I feel that it has now become my duty to communicate the above, and to add, that I will leave the City as soon as that decision shall be known.[3]

RC (ICHi).

1. While delivering the president's message to Congress on 29 Nov., Coles assaulted the Maryland representative Roger Nelson in the lobby of the Senate chamber. According to one witness to the affair, Samuel Sprigg, Nelson extended his hand in greeting to Coles and Coles responded by striking Nelson in the face. Another witness, James Turner, declared that Coles had seized Nelson by the collar and hit him with "some violence on the forehead or temple." Coles then apparently said to Nelson: "I am willing for this matter to end here; you attacked my character, and I have taken this method to take satisfaction or to chastise you." Nelson denied that he had ever said anything to injure the reputation of Coles. Accounts of the episode were obviously embellished as they circulated. British envoy Francis James Jackson, writing to his brother from Philadelphia on 10 Jan. 1810, reported that Coles had "horsewhipped" a member of Congress (*Annals of Congress*, 11th Cong., 2d sess., 685; *ASP, Miscellaneous*, 2:18–19; Jackson, *The Bath Archives*, 1:79).

2. Two days after the assault Coles sent a letter of apology to the Speaker of the House, but the House appointed a committee to investigate for breach of privilege on 8 Dec. The committee reported on 29 Dec. that the circumstances of the affair could not "be admitted in justification of the act done by Mr. Coles" and that the assault was indeed a breach of privilege. The committee recommended, however, that no further action be taken (*Annals of Congress*, 11th Cong., 2d sess., 705, 987–88).

3. When Coles left Washington, JM evidently gave him a letter for his brother Edward, inviting him to serve JM as his private secretary. Edward Coles at first decided to decline the offer, but James Monroe persuaded him to accept (Edward Coles to JM, 8 Jan. 1810, marked by Coles as not sent [NjP: Coles Papers]).

From William Lewis

Sir   Philadelphia Decr. 30th 1809.

I am about to take a liberty with you which in an ordinary Case I should hardly think myself warranted in doing, but trust you will have the goodness to excuse it when the occasion is known. The friendship which subsisted between the late General Hamilton and myself during his life was great, and his memory is very dear to me. It affords me much pleasure, as well as some others to find, that the Revd. Dr. Mason of New York, has undertaken to give us a History of his life;[1] and the more so, as we have no doubt but that it will be a masterly performance. He is, in many respects furnished with valuable materials but there is one subject on which many well disposed people are mistaken, and on which I am anxious they should be undeceived. It is this; they suppose that in the Convention which formed the Constitution of the United States, General Hamilton was a strenuous advocate for establishing a Monarchy,[2] and yet a little reflection might inform them, that had it been the case, there were not wanting members of that body, who, in the political turmoils which have almost ever since agitated the Country, would with avidity have established the fact beyond the possibility of refutation or even doubt. I always found him in private life, zealously attached to a Republican form of Government; not indeed of too imbecile a Nature to be lasting, but one of sufficient strength to protect itself against the Anarchy and confusion which have ever been too apt to end in Absolute despotism. I should go much too far, were I to expect you to say any thing on this head, and I therefore shall not ask it; but it seems to me, that the end I have in view may be accomplished in another way, and in one which I hope you will think unexceptionable. The able exposition of the Constitution contained in the "Federalist," written as is understood by You, Genl. Hamilton and Mr Jay proves a great deal, but not all that I want, because every honest and sound Statesman, when he finds some measure or other absolutely necessary, will afford all the support in his power to the best one that he can obtain, although it may not in his opinion be so perfect as he had wished for. Another source of information may I am aware be resorted to, which will afford much light; It is this; during a considerable part of the Session of the Convention, Genl. Hamilton *alone* represented the State of New York, and as I believe, the votes were taken by States, the minutes will shew how he voted on most, if not all the questions that were taken; but the same difficulty of Ascertaining his real sentiments still arises; inasmuch as a Man may very honestly vote for a resolution which he does not alltogether like, rather than that it should be entirely lost. I hope however there is one way (perhaps the only one) by which the truth may, with your assistance be completely Ascertained, It is supposed General Hamilton took no very active part in the Convention in the early stages of it's deliberations, nor until the proposed Constitution had received a kind of Skeleton form, and that it was then presented for free and full discussion in all it's parts, when Genl. Hamilton employed many hours in taking a most luminous view of the whole great system, in analizing all it's parts, in approving where he did approve, in disapproving where he could not approve, and in proposing alterations and amendments where he thought them necessary. It is said that his Speech on this occasion excited the Close attention and commanded the Admiration of every member present although it may not in all respects have carried conviction with it, and it is added on Authority apparently correct, that it was taken down by you at great length and with great accuracy. If this was the Case, I am extremely desirous that Dr Mason may be furnished with it, and you will greatly oblige me by letting him have it; since it must incontestibly prove what the real political sentiments of my lamented friend were. Indeed, from the kind and affectionate manner you were pleased to introduce the subject of Genl. Hamilton's family when I saw you last, I can have no doubt of your feeling a pleasure in doing it unless you see an impropriety in it which I do not.

On the subject just mentioned, namely, Genl. Hamilton's family, Dr Mason is much better qualified to give you the necessary information than I was, in answer to the questions you proposed to me at the last time of my seeing you. So far as it may in your opinion be consistent with propriety, but no farther, I earnestly solicit your aid on the interesting subjects which have been mentioned.

The Revd. Dr Mason, who was the friend and companion of Genl. Hamilton during his life, and who reveres his memory since his death, will either present or send this letter to you, and I must beg of you to favour him with a private interview as soon as you can. You will, find him to be, a Man of as strong and enlightened a Mind as perhaps you have ever met. I hope Dr. Mason may have an opportunity of being introduced to Mrs. Madison as I am confident she will be much pleased with him and he will think himself much honored by her acquaintance.

Mrs. Lewis & Miss Durdin beg, that you will be so good as to present their respectful compliments and best regards to Mrs. Madison in which I request to be most heartily united & am dear Sir with great respect and esteem your faithful friend & servant

W: Lewis[3]

RC (DLC).

1. The Reverend John Mitchell Mason (1770–1829) was minister of the Associate Reformed Church in New York and brother-in-law of Senator John Brown of Kentucky. Although Mason opposed Jefferson in 1800, calling him a "confirmed infidel" in a campaign pamphlet, he seems to have been friendly with JM's Republican colleague John Beckley. Mason ministered to Alexander Hamilton after the duel with Aaron Burr, but his plan to write a biography of Hamilton came to nothing (Jacob Van Vechten, *Memoirs of John M. Mason* [New York, 1856], pp. 11, 287; Mason, *The Voice of Warning, to Christians, on the Ensuing Election of a President of the United States* [New York, 1800; Evans 37904], p. 8; Mason, *An Oration, Commemorative of the Late Major-General Alexander Hamilton* [New York, 1804; Shaw and Shoemaker 6731], pp. 37–40; Paul Leicester Ford, *Bibliotheca Hamiltoniana: A List of Books Written by, or Relating to Alexander Hamilton* [1886; New York, 1969 reprint], p. 75; see also JM to Mason, 12 Jan. 1810, and Mason to JM, 29 Jan. 1810; Douglass Adair and Marvin Harvey, "Was Alexander Hamilton a Christian Statesman?" *WMQ*, 3d ser., 12 [1955]: 308–29).

2. No printed version of the Federal Convention debates was available to the public in 1809, but Robert Yates may have allowed associates to see his notes. Yates reported that on 18 June 1787 Hamilton had declared in part, "the British government forms the best model the world ever produced. . . . See the excellency of the British executive—He is placed above temptation" (Yates's notes in Max Farrand, ed., *The Records of the Federal Convention of 1787* [4 vols.; New Haven, 1966], 1:299; for Madison's report, see ibid., 1:288–89).

3. William Lewis (1751–1819), a Philadelphia lawyer, Federalist, and Quaker, had served as U.S. attorney for the district of Pennsylvania from 1789 to 1791 and had sat briefly as a U.S. judge for the eastern district of Pennsylvania in 1791–92. Apparently he and his wife,

Frances Durdin Lewis, had also known Dolley Madison for some years (Harold C. Syrett and Jacob E. Cooke, eds., *The Papers of Alexander Hamilton* [27 vols.; New York, 1961–87], 16:206 n. 4; *PJM*, 14:386 n. 6; Lewis to JM, 30 Nov. 1806 [DLC]).

§ From Robert Fulton. *January 1810.* In January 1809 at Kalorama, Joel Barlow's District of Columbia estate, Fulton demonstrated his torpedo to JM, Jefferson, and members of Congress.[1] Favorable response encourages him to present details of his experiments in France and England, which have enabled him to correct the torpedo's past defects. Asserts that his invention will prevent the necessity of an expensive naval shipbuilding program, with its attendant threat to republicanism, and allow the government to "direct the genius and resources of our country to useful improvements, to the sciences, the arts, education, the amendment of the public mind and morals."[2]

Ms (DNA: RG 45, Naval Records, Subject File B). 100 pp. Undated. Addressed to JM and "the members of both Houses of Congress." Printed as Robert Fulton, *Torpedo War, and Submarine Explosions* (New York, 1810; Shaw and Shoemaker 20177); reprinted in *ASP, Naval Affairs*, 1:211–27. Received by both houses of Congress on 9 Feb. (*Annals of Congress*, 11th Cong., 2d sess., 556, 1402).

1. Fulton here erred on the date of his demonstration of the torpedo. The experiment to which he invited JM and Jefferson was held on 12 Feb. 1809 (Fulton to JM, 9 Feb. 1809 [DLC]; Fulton to Jefferson, 9 Feb. 1809 [DLC: Jefferson Papers]).

2. On 30 Mar. JM signed a bill appropriating $5,000 for Fulton's torpedo experiments. On 14 Feb. 1811 Secretary of the Navy Paul Hamilton reported that Fulton "has not . . . proved that the Government ought to rely upon his system as a means of national defence" but concluded, "it is contemplated to authorize further experiments" to test improvements made by Fulton (*U.S. Statutes at Large*, 2:569; *ASP, Naval Affairs*, 1:234–45).

From Daniel Eccleston

Sir   Lancaster January 1st. 1810

I beg your acceptance of a Medallion of your predecessor General Washington, which I have had struck off to the memory of that *Great Man*, and remain Sir Your Assured Friend

Daniel Beltechazzar Plantagenit Eccleston[1]

RC (DLC). Docketed by JM.

1. Daniel Eccleston (1745–1816), an eccentric English merchant and inventor, sponsored in 1805 a Washington medallion that he sent to Jefferson and other American public men (Edith Tyson, *Daniel Eccleston* [Lancaster, England, 1971], p. 10).

From Robert Patterson

Sir,   Mint of the U. States. Jany 1st. 1810.

I have the honour of laying before you a Report of the operations of the Mint for the last year.

From the Treasurer's statement, herewith transmitted, it will appear, that during this period, there have been issued from the Mint, of gold coins, in half eagles, 33,875 pieces, amounting to 169,375 dollars; of silver coins, in half dollars & dims., 1,450,520 pieces, amounting to 707,376 dollars; & of copper coins, in cents & half cents, 1,377,439 pieces, amounting to 8,001 dollars 53 cents. Making in the whole, Two Millions, eight hundred & sixty one thousand, eight hundred & thirty four pieces of coin, amounting to Eight hundred & eighty four thousand, seven hundred & fifty two dollars, fifty three cents.

The supply of bullion is still abundant; nor is there any apprehension of a deficiency. I have the honour to be, Sir, with sentiments of the most perfect respect & esteem, your obedient faithful servant

R. Patterson[1]

RC and enclosures, two copies (DNA: RG 233, President's Messages; and DNA: RG 46, Legislative Proceedings, 11A-E5); FC (DNA: RG 104, Letters Sent by the Director). Enclosures (2 pp., signed by Benjamin Rush) are quarterly statements of coinage struck in 1809 and an expense account of the Mint for 1809 totaling $20,998.91. RC and enclosures forwarded in JM to Congress, 5 Jan. 1810.

1. Robert Patterson (1743–1824), professor of mathematics at the University of Pennsylvania, was director of the Mint, 1805–24. His subsequent reports to JM, 1810–17, will be summarized in this series.

From David Stone

Hope near Windsor North Carolina

Sir   Jany 1st. 1810.

In compliance with a request of the General Assembly of North Carolina I have the Honor herewith to enclose an address of that body unanimously adopted at their late Session. And permit me to add that it affords me most sincere gratification to be the instrument for conveying to you the undivided approbation of so respectable a portion of your Fellow Citizens—That while our mild institutions have occasion even yet to tolerate the exercise of those hostile or deluded feelings falsely claiming to be American while giving utterance to charges of crimination against our best, our wisest and most enlightened Citizens engaged in the arduous task of preserving the peace, and supporting and defending the Dignity and Interests of the United States against the avarice and ambition of the Nations of Europe there was not found in the Legislature of this State a single individual disposed to withhold a declaration of increasing confidence in our Chief Magistrate, merited by so many important services.

May your Health and Life, daily becoming more precious and valuable to your Country, be prolonged many years in Happiness. I have the honor to be with the most Perfect Esteem your Humble & obedient Servt.

DAVID STONE[1]

[Enclosure]

IN GENERAL ASSEMBLY AT THE CITY OF RALEIGH

SIR   December 23rd. 1809.

The Legislature of North Carolina Assembled for the first time since you were called by the suffrages of your Countrymen to preside over the Councils of their Country, feel it their duty, to the performance of which they chearfully advance, to convey to you their unqualified and Unanimous approbation of the course which you have pursued, and which has so amply protected from injury, the dignity of the American Government.

In times portentous and alarming as the present, when every Salutary and equitable principle seems to be disregarded by the turbulent nations of Europe, the Citizens of the United States, unassisted by that firmness, wisdom and patriotism which have charactarized your public conduct, would indeed, have much to fear; but cheared by the consolatory belief that the American spirit which has hitherto secured to us the benefit of your talents will be always exerted in the advancement of your Country's happiness; we feel no hesitation in pledging ourselves individually and as the Representatives of the Free men of North Carolina, to support with energy, and at the risque of our lives and fortunes, such measures as the General Government shall think proper to pursue, to protect from insult and agrression [*sic*] our common and happy country.

Jos. RIDDICK Spr.
of the Senate.
T. DAVIS Spkr. of the
House of Commons.

RC and enclosure (DLC).

1. David Stone (1770–1818) was governor of North Carolina, 1808–10. He had served as a Republican congressman, 1799–1801, and U.S. senator, 1801–7. He returned to the Senate, 1813–14, where he opposed JM's wartime policies.

§ Presidential Proclamation. *1 January 1810, Washington*. Suspends building regulations laid down in the first and third sections of the act of 17 Oct. 1791 for the city of Washington.[1]

FC (DLC: Commissioners of the District of Columbia Collection, 1791–1869). Fragment.

1. These provisions, requiring the outer walls of all houses to be built of either brick or stone and regulating the height of house walls, had been suspended for two-year intervals by successive presidents since June 1796, on the grounds that their enforcement would inhibit the settlement of mechanics in the District of Columbia.

From Lemuel Sawyer

DEAR SIR,   WASHINGTON 2d. Jany. 1810

Upon the supposition that no one has accepted the office of the Collectorship of New Orleans,[1] I take the liberty of mentioning to you that if no person can be found better qualified, I would be willing to take it. I know it is customary for persons in such cases to procure others to recommend them, but I see no impropriety in my making known to *you* my disposition in that regard, and I trust you will do sufficient justice to my patriotism & sentiments as to beleive, that altho I would endeavour to discharge its duties faithfully, yet I would by no means feel disappointed in the selection of another. My object in this case is not the emoluments of the office merely, but the obtaining a situation in a climate much more congenial to my health than this. My station here would in that case be filled by a person, much better qualified than myself, to take an active support in the measures of your administration, as well as to prove experimentally, the high estimation in which you are professd to be held, by Dr. Sir yr Ob Hule Sert.

                                                 L SAWYER[2]

Please consider this entirely inter nos.

RC (DLC). Docketed by JM.

1. After the customs collector at New Orleans, William Brown, absconded with public funds, JM nominated Thomas Hill Williams to the post on 3 Jan. (William C. C. Claiborne to JM, 19 Nov. 1809; *Senate Exec. Proceedings*, 2:135, 136).
2. Lemuel Sawyer (1777–1852) was a Republican congressman from North Carolina, 1807–13, 1817–23, and 1825–29.

§ From Henry Smith and Others. *2 January 1810, Providence, Rhode Island*. Urges JM to appoint Henry Wheaton, son of Seth Wheaton and recently returned from legal studies in Europe, to the office of district attorney, about to become vacant.

RC (DNA: RG 59, LAR, 1809–17, filed under "Wheaton"). 2 pp. Signed by Smith and four others. In October 1814 JM nominated Henry Wheaton, then editor of the N.Y. *National Advocate* and later to become a noted international lawyer, to the position of judge advocate in the U.S. Army. Wheaton was also to correspond with JM throughout the 1820s (*Senate Exec. Proceedings*, 2:535, 542).

To Congress

January 3. 1810

The Act Authorizing a Detachment of one hundred thousand men from the Militia,[1] will expire on the 30th. of Mar: next. It's early revival is recommended, in order that timely steps may be taken for arrangements, such as the act contemplated.

Without interfering with the modifications rendered necessary by the defects, or the inefficacy of the laws restrictive of commerce and navigation, or with the policy of disallowing to foreign Armed Vessels, the use of our waters; it falls within my duty to recommend also, that in addition to the precautionary measure authorized by that Act, & to the regular troops, for completing the legal establishment of which enlistments are renewed, every necessary provision may be made for a Volunteer force of twenty thousand men, to be enlisted for a short period, and held in a state of Organization and readiness, for actual service, at the shortest warning.

I submit to the consideration of Congress, moreover, the expediency of such a classification & organization of the Militia, as will best ensure prompt & successive aids, from that source, adequate to emergenc[i]es, which may call for them.

It will rest with them also, to determine how far, further provision may be expedient, for putting into Actual service, if necessary, any part of the Naval Armament not now employed.

At a period presenting features in the conduct of foreign Powers towards the United States, which impose on them the necessity of precautionary measures involving expense, it is a happy consideration that such is the solid state of the public credit, that reliance may be justly placed, on any legal provision that may be made for resorting to it, in a convenient form, and to an adequate amount.[2]

JAMES MADISON

RC (DNA: RG 233, President's Messages). In a clerk's hand, signed and dated by JM. Received and referred to committees on 3 Jan. The House committee recommended implementing legislation on 8 Jan. (*Annals of Congress*, 11th Cong., 2d sess., 520, 1089–90, 1159).

1. "An Act authorizing a detachment from the Militia of the United States" of 30 Mar. 1808 (*U.S. Statutes at Large*, 2:478–79).

2. After his dismissal from the cabinet in April 1811, Secretary of State Robert Smith claimed that in sending this message JM had "yielded to [the] importunities" of the congressional critics of Macon's Bill No. 1, who believed that stronger policies were needed. Smith denounced the message as a "half way" measure and declared that he had protested to JM about the "studied ambiguity" of its language (*National Intelligencer*, 2 July 1811).

§ From Phinehas Bean, Jr. *4 January 1810, Newport, New Hampshire.* Blames the distress of his present situation on his political loyalty, which caused his enemies to conspire and plan his financial ruin. Reports his creditors pressed for the sale of his property and "sold it at auction at ¼ Value, as soon as the Law would bear them out." Unless aided by JM he will be sent to prison for debt. Adds copy of recommendation from six citizens testifying to his abilities and fitness for a mercantile position. "May it please your magesty to keep this Epistle in secret for I am the owner of so mutch pride as to not have it known among my enemy's that I apply'd to any person for relief."

RC (DLC). 3 pp.

§ From Peter Crary and Others. *4 January 1810, New York.* Urges JM to appoint Elijah Palmer to be surveyor at the port of Stonington, Connecticut, in the event of the resignation of the incumbent, Jonathan Palmer. Recommends Elijah Palmer for his attachment to the "principles of '76" and as one who has been persecuted for his political beliefs.

RC (DNA: RG 59, LAR, 1809–17, filed under "Palmer"). 3 pp. Signed by Crary and four others. After the death of Jonathan Palmer, JM nominated Elijah Palmer to be surveyor and inspector of the revenue at Stonington on 17 Apr. 1810 (*Senate Exec. Proceedings*, 2:145, 147).

§ To Congress. *5 January 1810.* Transmits the director of the Mint's annual report for 1809.

RC and enclosures, two copies (DNA: RG 233, President's Messages; and DNA: RG 46, Legislative Proceedings, 11A-E5). Each RC 1 p., in a clerk's hand, signed by JM. Received by both houses on 10 Jan. Read and tabled by the Senate on 10 Jan. and by the House on 11 Jan. (*Annals of Congress*, 11th Cong., 2d sess., 526, 1196). Printed in *ASP, Finance*, 2:391. For enclosures, see Robert Patterson to JM, 1 Jan. 1810, and n.

§ From Parke Street. *5 January 1810, Richmond.* Sends JM a process in a lawsuit, which should also be presented to John G. Jackson. As plaintiffs' attorney, the writer asks JM and Jackson for their response to the court as soon as convenient. Payne family is hardly involved, "but it was necessary to make them parties to the suit." The plaintiffs "are indigent," and when JM knows the circumstances, "you will think with me that they have been *injured indeed*, tho' not by Mr Payne."[1]

RC (DLC). 1 p. Street, a Republican, was a commissioner for supervising the presidential election of 1800 and a justice of the peace for Hanover County (*CVSP*, 9:124, 298, 10:87).

1. William G. Payne was one of John G. Jackson's sureties in a breach-of-promise suit that Frances Emelia Triplett brought against Jackson in 1801. The suit discussed by Street apparently concerned Jackson's failure to comply with the courts' decisions in that case (Brown, *Voice of the New West*, pp. 11–12; see also Jackson to JM, 9 Jan. 1810).

From Samuel Huntington

SIR—   CHILLICOTHE Jany. 6th. 1809. [1810]
Agreably to the request of the General Assembly of the State of Ohio, I have the honor to transmit you a certified Copy of their resolution passed the 4th. instant, "on the subject of extinguishing the Indian title to lands within this State," And am With great respect, Sir, your most obedt. Servt.

SAML HUNTINGTON[1]

[Enclosure]

A Resolution on the Subject of extinguishing the Indian title, to lands within this State.

In General Assembly

Whereas, the North western quarter of this state, is inhabited by and subject to, the claims of certain Indian tribes; and while it remains so the settlement and improvement thereof, cannot be effected; and it being of great importance to the United States, as well as to this state that the lands in that part should be open for sale, settlement, and taxation as soon as may be; and in case of war, to be the more easily enabled to defend a coast bordering on the Territory of a Belligerent nation; to secure its local advantages to every part of the State; so far as possible; to avail the United States, and this state of the revenue which will gradually arise from the sale and taxation of that portion of its territory; and to make its jurisdiction and civil government, co-extensive with its geographical bounds. Therefore

Resolved by the General assembly of the State of Ohio, that our senators in Congress be instructed and our representative requested; to use their endeavours to procure by treaty; the extinguishment of the Indian title to the lands within the limits of this state.

Resolved that his excellency the Governor of this State be requested to forward a copy of the foregoing Resolution to each of our senators and representative in Congress, and also a copy to the President of the United States.

EDWARD TIFFEN Speaker of the
House of Representatives
DUNCAN MCARTHUR Speaker

January 4th. 1810   of the Senate

RC and enclosure (DNA: RG 107, LRRS, H-5:5). RC docketed by a War Department clerk as received 18 Jan. 1810. Enclosure in a clerk's hand; attested to by the clerks of the Ohio House and Senate; certified as a correct copy by the secretary of the state of Ohio, 5 Jan. 1810.

1. Samuel Huntington (1765–1818) was an Ohio Republican leader who had held a number of legislative and judicial posts before serving as governor of Ohio between 1808 and 1810.

From William McIntosh and Alexander Cornells

D SIR   TUCKABACHEE SQUARE[1] January 6—1810

It has been four or five years since we was to see you at the seat of Goverment—when we had the pleasure of seeing you—we agreed to ⟨lend?⟩ you a small path for the benefit of a mail path and our Brother white Travellers to pass through[2]—and it has never been made yet, for the Officers that you send here is not Strait people—the first was Mr Bloomfield[3] who came in this Country almost a Beggar. Colonel Hawkins our Agent employed him and said he was a Gentulman and a Straite man—we appointed him to Do this work—and we So Soon found him out to be a Rascall and not a Straite man. The next was Colo Wheton[4] who Came on—and allmost distracted our Chiefs—and done nothing to the road But Hired that Rascall Bloomfield to Carry the mail to Fort Stoddert—and threatning to have a Big road—which the Chiefs thought our father *President* did not use aus [*sic*] well. The next was General Mereweather[5]—who Came on—and Called a few Chiefs together—and said he was sent by you to make a road an Other way. We Told him—to go and make the path agreeably to our Treaty—with our Father the *President* and Secretary of War. When we was with them—and Colonel Hawkins—was not here—when General Mere[we]ather was out at this place—we Told him about It—but we dont think he has Told you of it and now that Rascall Bloomfield is Coming here again we thought proper to Inform you of it.

The first we Knew of Bloomfields working on the Path—He was about twenty five miles this side of the Ocmulgee—he Came to our Public meeting when the nation was together—and it was the day Colonel Hawkins was going home. Colonel Hawkins Brought him in the Square and Told us Bloomfield was sent by the Government of the United States to make the path Good for the mail Horses—and the Chiefs made him Know Answer—and in a day or Two we thought Bloomfield would do as before no Good But cavel—and we would write Colo Hawkins word that he must stop Bloomfield from working on the path—and that he would Let you Know Bloomfields Character—and How he Brought a Waggon—and Cut a large road twenty feet wide. Colonel Hawkins never Stopted him—nor I believe he never told you of it—and we was Obliged to Stop him for every young fealow Knew him to be a Rascall—and not a Strait man—and they would do him some injaurry before long and we dont want to have any of our people interrupting any other people. We want you to Send Some Strait man—and have the path done Good—let him Come to the Chiefs and they will Tell him what to Do and they will have our work done well—the Chiefs will not Refuse you any thing, you ask John B. Chandler Esq.[6] wheather we ever refused him what he asked for—he asked us last winter for Some Bridges—and for Indians and half Breads to Settle on the path we gave him every thing which he asked for and he had it done directly—he is a Good man—and not always Specculating—telling—Lies—and Getting drunk—he does his business well—and such a Man we will Like—and help them. I am sorry that we have to Trouble you with our writing—but we dont think you Know all of this—and we think it our duty to inform you of it—and you will write us word what to do—and send your Letter to Mr Chandler post master—and he will Send it to us—and we Can Get som⟨e ma⟩n to read it—and we will have every thing done that you want.

We want to live freindly—and such men as have been here will always Keep us Confused—we want the path as bad as you—and Let us have some good man—so that we may have the work done well. Our hands are out to our Father *President* and all our Brother Officers. We are your freinds.

Signed—WILLIAM MCINTOSH[7]
Speaker for the path
ALEXANDER CUNNELLS [Cornells][8]
Intreperter and Ch[i]efs of the
Creek Nation

RC (PHi: Daniel Parker Papers). In an unidentified hand. Damaged by removal of seal. Cover bears notation, "Ft. Stoddert Jany 20. 1810." Docketed by a War Department clerk as received 12 Feb. 1810.

1. Tuckabatchee was an old Creek town situated between the Coosa and Tallapoosa rivers in the Mississippi Territory (Lester J. Cappon et al., eds., *Atlas of Early American History: The Revolutionary Era, 1760–1790* [Princeton, N.J., 1976], p. 19).

2. In the autumn of 1805 McIntosh headed a Creek delegation that visited Washington and met President Jefferson and several cabinet members including JM. During their visit the Creeks signed a convention granting the U.S. certain lands within the Creek nation as well as the right to build a "horse path," part of a post road on the Washington to New Orleans mail route (*ASP, Indian Affairs*, 1:698–99; Carter, *Territorial Papers, Mississippi*, 5:395, 396 n. 3, 476; Henry D. Southerland, Jr., and Jerry E. Brown, *The Federal Road through Georgia, the Creek Nation, and Alabama, 1806–1836* [Tuscaloosa, Ala., 1989], pp. 22–32).

3. Samuel F. Bloomfield was a mail contractor and assistant postmaster in the Creek Agency, Georgia (Hawkins to Jefferson, 13 Sept. 1806, Grant, *Letters of Benjamin Hawkins*, 2:507, 509 n. 2).

4. Joseph Wheaton was employed by the Post Office Department as a mail contractor (ibid., 2:497 n. 3).

5. David Meriwether was hired to complete the post road between the Apalachia Shoals and Fort Stoddert (Carter, *Territorial Papers, Mississippi*, 5:518–19).

6. John B. Chandler was awarded a mail contract before he left for the Creek Agency. Jefferson recommended him to Hawkins as "an active, enterprising, intelligent young man" who was a personal friend (Jefferson to Hawkins, 15 Sept. 1808 [DLC: Jefferson Papers]).

7. William McIntosh (ca. 1778–1825), son of a Creek woman and a British army officer, was raised in Coweta in the lower townships of the Creek confederacy and rose to prominence as Hawkins's friend. He advocated cooperation with Americans and was to fight as an ally of the U.S. during the Creek War of 1813–14. He exercised considerable influence as speaker of the Creek National Council until 1824, but the next year he was murdered by a secret Creek tribunal for signing the removal treaty of Indian Springs (Benjamin W. Griffith, Jr., *McIntosh and Weatherford, Creek Indian Leaders* [Tuscaloosa, Ala., 1988], pp. 11, 22–24, 46–47, 98–99, 113, 246–50).

8. Alexander Cornells was an interpreter "of high standing among his chiefs." Hawkins considered his death "a national loss," for he was "the only correct interpreter we have had" (Hawkins to William H. Crawford, 2 Apr. 1816, Grant, *Letters of Benjamin Hawkins*, 2:780).

§ From James H. Blake. *6 January 1810, Washington.* Believes his character has been "much traduced and vilely slandered" to JM and therefore begs him to refer to his testimonials on file in the Department of State.[1] Denies he is a "violent Man," though he admits he had the "misfortune" to be involved in a controversy at Richmond with "one of Jno. Randolphs party." Refers to the sacrifices he has made to support "the cause of Republicanism" and seeks an appointment, since his profession does not enable him to provide for "the pressing demands of a large family."

RC (DNA: RG 59, LAR, 1809–17, filed under "Blake"). 4 pp.

1. James Heighe Blake (1768–1819) was a physician who had resided in Georgetown after 1789. In 1800 he moved to Virginia where he represented Fairfax County in the House of Delegates from 1804 to 1808. He returned to Washington in 1809 and sought office after experiencing financial difficulties. In the summer of 1811 JM gave Blake a recess appointment as a justice of the peace for the District of Columbia, and later, on 21 Dec. 1813, he nominated him to be a collector of the direct tax. The Senate postponed the appointment, then

rejected JM's next nomination of him, on 11 Apr. 1814, to the position of garrison surgeon's mate in the District of Columbia. Blake also held the office of mayor of Washington from 1813 to 1817, and in that capacity he was to farewell JM officially from the nation's capital on 6 Mar. 1817 (Allen C. Clark, "James Heighe Blake, the Third Mayor of the Corporation of Washington [1813–17]," *Records of the Columbia Historical Society*, 24 [1922]: 136–63; *Senate Exec. Proceedings*, 2:187, 189, 441, 443, 526, 527).

§ From the Citizens of Harrison County, Indiana Territory. *Ca. 6 January 1810.* Urges appointment of William Henry Harrison to a second term as territorial governor.

Printed broadside (DNA: RG 46, Territorial Papers of the Senate). Addressed "To the Honorable the President and Senate of the United States." Signed by Nathan Deen and thirty others. Undated. Cover dated Jeffersonville, 6 Jan. Reprinted in Carter, *Territorial Papers, Indiana*, 7:710–11.

§ From the New Jersey Delegation in Congress. *6 January 1810, Washington.* Recommends Bernard Smith, a State Department clerk, for the position of secretary of the Mississippi Territory.

RC (DNA: RG 59, LAR, 1809–17, filed under "Smith"). 1 p. Signed by James Cox and five other members of the New Jersey delegation. Enclosed in Bernard Smith to JM, 8 Jan. 1810 (ibid.). In 1812 JM appointed Smith to be surveyor and inspector of the revenue in New Brunswick (*Senate Exec. Proceedings*, 2:270, 272).

From Alexander McRae

SIR,   NEW-YORK 7th. Jan. 1810.

I fear that the frequency of my communications, on topics principally interesting to myself, may have some tendency to render them irksome to you; but it was my impression, that the Public had, and would properly feel, some concern ('tho I am a private citizen) in the treatment I received at Philadelphia, from Phineas Bond esqr. and I therefore performed what I beleived to be a duty, when I used the freedom of detailing to you, the particulars of that gentleman's very strange conduct towards me.[1] I have been no less surprized at the efforts made by another British Consul at this place, (Colo. Barclay)[2] to compel me to ask of Mr. Jackson, a testimonial necessary for my protection, in his character of British minister.

I have beleived it to be my duty to communicate to you, the substance and the result of this conversation also; and have therefore obtained from Mr. Fay, a lawyer of this City, who was present, a minute and accurate statement of the substance of all that was material, in my conversation with Mr. Barclay; which statement I have now the honor of enclosing for your perusal.[3] Mr. Fay's indisposition, prevented him from handing me the enclosed paper, 'til to-day; or it should have been earlier transmitted to you. If I have acted improperly, in troubling you unnecessarily with these communications, I flatter myself that my sufficient apology will be found, in adverting to the motive which has induced me to give you this trouble. Indeed Sir I am sincere, in offering to you professions of my highest respect and esteem.

AL: McRae.

RC and enclosure (DLC). For enclosure, see n. 3.

1. McRae to JM, 26 Dec. 1809.

2. Thomas Barclay had been appointed consul general for the eastern states of America in 1799 (Mayo, *Instructions to British Ministers*, p. 171).

3. A memorandum (7 pp.), dated 2 Jan. 1810 and signed by Joseph D. Fay, relates a conversation between McRae and Thomas Barclay. Barclay refused, Fay reported, to accredit McRae's passport and asked him to apply to Francis James Jackson for accreditation. The ensuing conversation reached the same conclusion as McRae's talk with Bond in Philadelphia. McRae and Barclay "seperated both evidently warmed, but each to the other very polite."

From Evan Lewis

ESTEEMED FRIEND   WILMINGTON (DEL) 1st. Mo 8th. 1810

I have taken the liberty, of sending thee a copy of the annexed pamphlet[1] as a tribute of respect for our chief-Magistrate in whose talents and integrity, I have placed unlimited confidence, and whose official conduct, in that highly important office has hitherto met my entire approbation, and in this expression of approbation in the measures pursued, or the steps taken by the present administration of the executive department of the general government, I speak, the almost unanimous voice of my fellow citizens of the borough in which I live.

Accept then, esteemed friend, this small production, as the effusions of a heart, which beats in unison with his countrey's good:

The first part, signed Cerus, was written by my Physician, and friend William Baldwin, M D.[2] who has forwardd. one accompanied, with a letter, to our late president Thomas Jefferson Esqr.[3]

At this critical period when the rage for incorporated societies of religeous professor[s] appears to have spread from Maryland to New-york, and Columbia, it appears requisite that the nature and tendency of such incorporations should be understood and examined, before they are adopted:

And I am well assured that the President of the United States will not put his signature to the bill now before the Senate "for incorporating re-ligeous societies in the district of Columbia," even if it should pass both houses of Congress, which I presume it will not.[4]

A knowledge of the judgment thou should form, of the merits of said production after perusing it, would be highly agreable and pleasing to thy friend, as well as the friend of our common countrey.

EVAN LEWIS[5]

RC (DLC). Docketed by JM.

1. Cerus [William Baldwin], *Observations on Infidelity, and the Religious and Political Systems of Europe, Compared with Those of the United States of America: Showing the Incompatibility of Religion with the Despotism of National Churches. . . . To Which Are Added the Essays of Amicus on the Maryland Church-Bill and Quaker's Petition, &c.* (Wilmington, Del., 1809; Shaw and Shoe-maker 17179). On Baldwin's authorship of this pamphlet, see Joseph Ewan, introduction to *Reliquiae Baldwinianae: Selections from the Correspondence of the Late William Baldwin*, comp. William Darlington (1843; New York, 1969 reprint), pp. xiv-xv. Lewis apparently wrote the "Amicus" essays.

2. William Baldwin (1779–1819) received his M.D. from the University of Pennsylvania in 1807 and established a medical practice in Wilmington, Delaware. A botanist, he died in Missouri while accompanying Stephen Harriman Long's expedition to the Rocky Mountains (ibid., pp. xiii-xxiv).

3. Baldwin explained that "these *essays* are now published principally with a view of having them extensively circulated among the *society of Friends* in the eastern part of the state of *Pennsylvania*, who have been too generally prejudiced against the *late Administration*, and whose prejudices still exist, against the *present*" (Baldwin to Jefferson, 7 Jan. 1810 [DLC: Jefferson Papers]; see also Jefferson to Baldwin, 19 Jan. 1810 [ibid.]).

4. On 3 Jan. the Senate amended and then postponed a "bill to incorporate religious societies in the District of Columbia." During the next session JM vetoed bills incorporating an Episcopal church in Alexandria (then in the District of Columbia) and providing relief for a Baptist church in the Mississippi Territory (*Annals of Congress*, 11th Cong., 2d sess., 520–21; ibid., 11th Cong., 3d sess., 982–83, 1097–98).

5. Evan Lewis (1782–1834) was a Quaker antislavery pamphleteer. He published a Phila-delphia monthly journal, *The Friend; or, Advocate of Truth*, 1832–33 (Walter M. Merrill et al., eds., *The Letters of William Lloyd Garrison* [6 vols.; Cambridge, Mass., 1971–81], 1:123 and n. 2).

From Robert R. Livingston

DEAR SIR   CLERMONT 8th. Jany 1810

When I look at the date of your letter, I am actualy asshamed [*sic*] of the time I have kept the pamphlet you were so obliging as to lend me. But the fact is, that it has gone the round of the neighbourhood, every body in this vicinity being infected with the merino influenza, & eagerly seeking whatever may afford them information, or furnish food to their disease.

Having the same feelings myself, I know not how to check them in others, & the rather as I thought you would hardly find leisure as yet to run over the work yourself. I have seen nothing new in it, but a great many proofs of the excellence of Merino mutton, a fact which I had so well assertained by my own experiments, that I have determined to raise none other for my own table. I find it the fattest, the best flavoured, & the most easily kept of any sheep I have ever reared. My shepherd assures me, that the keeping of my common sheep costs pr head twice as much as that of my merinos, & they certainly do not thrive equaly on what they eat. Nor are they heavier when fat (the whethers) than the ½ bred merino. I only regret that I can not supply the demand for rams, or on account of the importunity of my friends, keep the number necessary for the enlargment of my flock.

I thank you for the pamphlet containing the communications. I have read them with particular attention, & am astonished that any American should be found to support the conduct of Ja[c]kson or rather not to take fire at the indignities offered their own government. As for Britain nothing in her conduct surprizes me. A little knowledge of the human heart must convince us that the King & the people of that nation hate, dread, & envy us. And that they will do so till the memory of our having been rebel colonies is entirely lost, & till the sordid spirit peculiar to a nation of Merchants & tradesmen from the days of Carthage to the present æra is extinguished by some great calamity. Jackson would never have been sent had it not been determined to try what indignities we would bear. And I doubt not that he was to have been backed by Congreves arrows[1] as auxilary to the Boston revolutionists. The change of affairs in Europe & Mr Cannings dismissal may possibly make an alteration in their system, but I hope in gods name that it will make none in our preparations for the worst. I am sorry to say that the rage for sinking the national debt a few years earlier (an object of very little moment) has rendered us negligent of much more important duties, & tho we may not be charged with doing "what we ought not to have done" yet we certainly "have left un[done] what we ought to have done."[2] If thirty millions added to our national debt would secure our seaport towns, thirty millions should, when compared with that object, be considered as dust in the ballance. Every town may be defended against a fleet, because guns on shore are more formidable than guns afloat, but it does not follow from this that 100 guns on shore, are equal to 1000 on ship board, but why not have a 1000. & all the militia of the sea coasts artilerists? Nothing is more formidable to ships than bombs, but as their aim is uncertain they must be numerous. And why not numerous? Would any fleet lay within the range of 100 mortars? I hope the torpedoes will not be forgotten, they are a very useful auxilary if sufficiently numerous, & men are trained to the use of them,[3] but neither this, or any other species of defence should be ⟨skived?⟩. What is money to national security, & national honor? Had only ten millions of the money we have paid in discharge of the national debt been applied to the purposes of defence, we might have bid our enemies defiance, & even found resources against their injustice in war itself.[4]

I take the liberty to transmit herewith a few letters for France, which I hope the secretary of State will do me the favor to enclose in his envelope, when occasion occurs. I also enclose a pamphlet for Mr Custis, which being in the line of his pursuits he may possibly find something to amuse him therein. I have the honor to be with the most respectful attatchment Dear Sir Your most Obedient Humble Servant

ROBT R LIVINGSTON

RC (DLC); draft (NHi: Livingston Papers). Stylistic differences between RC and draft have not been noted.

1. "Congreves arrows" were rockets used by British armed forces in the early nineteenth century (Thomas Wilhelm, *A Military Dictionary and Gazetteer* [Philadelphia, 1881], p. 493).

2. Livingston quoted from the general confession in the *Book of Common Prayer*.

3. In the draft Livingston completed this sentence "& a sufficient number employed not less than a thousand for New York."

4. This sentence is not in the draft.

From John G. Jackson

DR. SIR   Jany. 9th. 1810

I have never acquired the legal character of Guardian to my Child—Guardians ad litem[1] can only be appointed by the Courts issuing process against infants; & as there has been no appointment there would be an impropriety in my acknowledging service of the Spa.,[2] which I should not hesitate to do if the act would be legal. Your Mo Obt Servt

J G JACKSON

There can be no objection to acknowledging the service by the defendants of full age.

RC (DLC). Docketed by JM.

1. A *guardian ad litam* is a "special guardian appointed by the court to prosecute or defend, in behalf of an infant or incompetent, a suit to which he is a party" (*Black's Law Dictionary* [5th ed.], p. 635).

2. JM had evidently forwarded to Jackson the subpoena from Parke Street relating to the breach-of-promise suit involving Jackson's illegitimate son, John Jay Jackson, born to Frances Emelia Triplett in February 1800. The suit had been provoked by Jackson's marriage to Mary

Payne, Dolley Madison's sister, sometime before January 1801. After Mary Payne Jackson's death in 1808, Jackson took responsibility for his son and secured his appointment to the U.S. Military Academy in 1815 (Street to JM, 5 Jan. 1810; Brown, *Voice of the New West*, pp. 9, 11–12).

§ To the Senate. *9 January 1810.* Submits for ratification a treaty concluded on 9 Dec. 1809 with the Kickapoo Indians, accompanied by "an extract of a letter from the Governor of the Indiana Territory."

RC and enclosure (DNA: RG 46, Executive Proceedings, 11B-C3). RC 1 p. Surviving enclosure (2 pp.) is an extract from William Henry Harrison to the secretary of war, 10 Dec. 1809. Received and read on 10 Jan. The Senate unanimously ratified the treaty on 5 Mar. (*Senate Exec. Proceedings*, 2:137, 139–40). Printed, with the treaty, in *ASP, Indian Affairs*, 1:762–63.

From John Armstrong

DEAR SIR,   Jan. 10 1810.

In the haste in which I now write, I can do no more than acknowlege the receit of your letter by M. fenwick,[1] and renew my request,[2] that a ship of some kind be sent for me so as to reach France, & the port of Havre if possible, from the 1st. to the 15 of April next.

As London is the theatre of the preliminary Negociation on foot between France & England, Mr. Pinkney will keep you advised of it's progress. Like other attempts of the same kind, it will come to nothing. With the highest respect, I am Sir, Your Most Obedient & ever faithful servt.

                                                    JOHN ARMSTRONG

RC (DLC). Docketed by JM.

1. Letter not found.
2. Armstrong had asked JM to send "a ship Armed or unarmed . . . for me in the spring" (Armstrong to JM, 18 Sept. 1809, *PJM-PS*, 1:383).

From George Logan

MY DEAR FRIEND,   STENTON,[1] Jany: 10th; 1810

As a citizen of the United States, I have for several years viewed with considerable anxiety the future destinies of my country. Every reflecting and candid mind must be sensible of the weakness of a Government deriving its power from popular opinion, rather than from physical force. Such being the situation of the United States: would it not be sound policy in our Government not merely to act with strict justice, but with liberality, and even forbearance, towards other nations?

During the federal administration under Mr: Adams, a desperate faction was anxious to involve our country in a war with France. The people viewing the calamities of war with horror, entrusted the fate of their country in the hands of Men who professed maxims of peace, as the best policy to promote the happiness and prosperity of the United States. This desirable situation of our Country is like to be jeopardized by our republican administration, giving up their sound judgment, founded on deliberate reflection, to the temporary feelings of popular resentment, roused into energy by the clamor of unprincipled demagogues.

The superficial legal education of too many of our young Men in Congress, and their habits of quibble and sophistry in our inferior courts, so debase their minds, as to extinguish that generosity of sentiment and candor, necessary in the character of a national legislator.

Our demands on Spain, respecting french spoliations out of spanish ports; and on account of our claim to West Florida, have been long since declared by the Emperor of France, as totally without foundation. And we have reason to beleive, they never will be granted whether we have to negotiate for them, with the Spanish, or with the French Government.

Our prospects with Great Britain, owing to the inflamed state of the public mind, is more serious—and yet I do not despair; if either or both Nations would substitute a just and magnanimous policy, to suspicion, jealousy and cupidity.

In the present awful crisis of Europe, with the acts and the ambitious views of Bonaparte before us: no man in his senses can doubt of the necessity of the United States preserving peace with Britain.

I was not satisfied with the rejection of Monroes treaty on account of its not having an article, stipulating generally for the protection under the american mercantile flag of french property, and British deserters.[2] The two federal administrations[3] gave up those points, as consistent with the law of nations. The first universally acknowledged by the best writers on the law of nations. The latter, altho not particularly expressed, yet consistent with the spirit and intent of that law, as founded on the immutable principle of doing unto others, as you would expect others to do unto you, is equally binding. Those great national laws which regard the great republick of mankind, cannot justify acts as may promote wickedness, & lessen the general confidence and security in which all have an equal interest; and which all are therefore bound to maintain. For this reason no nation has a right to erect a sanctuary for fugitives, or give protection to such as have forfeited their lives by crimes against the laws of common morality and justice, equally acknowledged by all nations;

because none can without infraction of the universal league of social be-
ings, incite, by prospects of impunity and safety, those practises in another Dominion, which they themselves punish in their own. According
to this fundamental law of nations, What right has the United States to
protect a deserter from the service of [a] foreign nation, whilst in the practice of punishing its own citizens guilty of a similar offence?

My heart mourns on account of the political insanity of my Country—Make use of your power and your influence, as first magistrate of
the United States, to arrest the progress of the destruction of your country—A war with Britain, at once unites us as an ally to Bonaparte, and
will dissolve the union—Arouse my friend; suffer your superior understanding and patriotism to prevail. Banish from our councils that irri-
tability of temper & false honor which has tended to widen the breach.

When I had the pleasure of conversing with you lately at Washington,[4]
you mentioned to me that you had recently given assurances to the British
Government of the desire of the United States to preserve peace between
the two countries; and that you were willing to renew negotiations for
that purpose, in Washington or in London. Confirm this declaration by
immediately sending two or three commissioners of the most respectable characters, to London, for the express purpose of concluding a
treaty of friendship & commerce, equally necessary and beneficial to both
countries.

You have a president in the mission of Mr Jay, by General Washington.
And a yet stronger one in the last mission by Mr Adams to France—an
act of magnanimity which obliterates many of his political blunders.

No man, whatever may be his professions, is more desirous of your
honor and happiness than myself. With sentiments of great respect I am
your real friend

GEO LOGAN

RC (DLC); draft, two copies (PHi). RC docketed by JM.

1. Stenton was Logan's estate near Germantown, Pennsylvania.

2. Logan's terminology minimized the issue of impressment. During the last days of Logan's Senate term (1801–7), Jefferson rejected the treaty that Monroe and Pinkney had negotiated with Great Britain. JM's 3 Feb. 1807 letter to the envoys stressed impressment over
other reasons for rejecting the treaty (Frederick B. Tolles, *George Logan of Philadelphia* [New
York, 1953], p. 279; Madison, *Writings* [Hunt ed.], 7:395–400).

3. In his draft, Logan here crossed through "particularly supported by the mercantile
interest."

4. Logan had visited Washington in December 1809 to talk with JM and Robert Smith
about his fears for the preservation of peace. Evidently dissatisfied with JM's attitude, Logan
decided in 1810 to make a private peace mission to Great Britain (Logan to JM, 14 Jan. 1810;
Tolles, *George Logan*, pp. 285–86).

From John Keemle

Sir,   PHILADA. Jany. 11th. 1810.

The surviving Revolutionary Characters, residing in the City & County of Philada., feeling an anxious solicitude for the welfare of their Country, convened agreeably to public notice, for the purpose of assuring you of their approbation of the measures pursued for repelling the hostile attacks of foreign powers, upon the Neutral & National rights of the United States. In '76 they risked their lives & fortunes for the independance of their Country, & though now less able to do it, still you will percieve by the expression of their sentiments, in the enclosed address, which as Chairman I am instructed to transmit to you, that they are again determined to make any remaining sacrifices, on the same altar; & many of them have sons who would glory in Joining their Fathers in the offering.

The administration of Public affairs by Mr. Jefferson, & yourself has been so perfectly consistent with Republican principles; & with regard to the foreign department so strictly impartial, that it must unite every American with his brother, heart & hand, in rallying round the Goverment of his choice & the object of his affection; while the World cannot but applaud any future course that may be laid out on such ground. With sentiments of the highest respect I am your most Obedt. &c. &c.

JOHN KEEMLE[1]

[Enclosure]

Sir,

At this period of difficulty and danger, to our Country, the surviving Military characters of the late Revolutionary Army and Navy, residing in the City and County of Philadelphia, presume to address you on the existing state of our foreign relations.

It is at once with pride and pleasure, we recognize in you, the enlightened and firm asserter of the rights of America; rights, which the two great Belligerent Powers of Europe have so shamefully and outrageously violated and trampled upon: And we are fully satisfied, that your translation from the most dignified Ministerial Office, to the highest which a free people by their suffrages, can confer, will enable you, to give to the measures, which your Wisdom and experience may suggest, to the assembled representatives of an highly insulted and injured Nation, that direction, on which will ultimately depend, the honor, interest and independance of the United States of America.

Whatever, Sir, may be the result of the repeated and honest appeals, which have been made, by your immediate predecessor, and by yourself since your Election to the Chief Magistracy of the United States, to the sense of Justice, which may yet be presumed to exist, on the part of the two conflicting powers of Europe; we beg you to be convinced, that we entertain too great a regard for the rights, which were atchieved by the valour, Patriotism and blood of an illustrious band of Revolutionary worthies, to meet the event with indifference. Born the heirs of freedom, we shall ever be ready to defend and maintain it; and if we must again unfortunately live, to witness our Country compelled to depart from a state of peace and tranquillity, and assume a Warlike attitude, we shall at least have the consolation to reflect, that by our Goverment, the event will have been unprovoked: And animated by this consideration, with a humble reliance upon the favour of Heaven, we can hope to see the Machinations of foreign intrigue frustrated, the views of Tyrrany blasted, and our unalienable rights transmitted to our latest posterity.

We rejoice, Sir, in the contemplation of the coincidence of sentiments which appears to pervade every political description of American Citizens, with regard to the daring outrages of the Belligerents upon our Neutral rights, by which their public Acts have been distinguished. It is a consolatory reflection, that whatever difference of sentiment may exist, on subjects of Domestic policy, the great Body of the Nation, attached to the principles of the Revolution, will rally round the standard of the Goverment, as we did in the time that tried mens souls, determined to die as freemen, rather than live as slaves, under some Imperious Tyrant, whose will is Law.

When we consider, that, at a Time when the liberties of every other Nation, are rapidly disappearing, under the scourge of unrelenting Tyrrany, the republican Goverment of America, secures to the meanest of its Citizens, every Civil and Religious privilige; when we contempate the old World deluged with the blood of Thousands, the unfortunate victims of insatiable rapacity and lust of power, we are gratefull to the God of Mercies for the blessings which his Providence benignly dispenses to us; implore his future protection: And pray that he may so dispose the hearts of every Goverment, as to secure to a troubled World, the restoration of peace and tranquillity. Under the influence of theese [*sic*] impressions, we, who have borne a part in our late Revolutionary conflict, and assembled to express to you our sentiments, on the present critical state of our Country, with the European powers, beg you to be assured, that allthough we cannot now serve our Country in the field with as much effect, as when the infirmities of age were not felt, as we feel them at present, we are nevertheless as willing now to serve, (should necessity require it) in any station, our advanced state of life will admit.

With fervent prayers for the peace and prosperity of our beloved Country; and with respect and attachment to yourself, we remain &c. &c.

JOHN KEEMLE
Chairman
DAN: BRODHEAD
Secretary
[and 26 others]

RC and enclosure (DLC). Enclosure docketed by JM. Among the signers of the enclosure were such prominent Philadelphians as Alexander Boyd, Blair McClenachan, Gideon Olmstead, and Benjamin Rush.

1. John Keemle (or Keehmle) was a physician who lived at 33 North Fourth Street (James Robinson, *The Philadelphia Directory . . . from the First of March 1810, to the First of March 1811* [Philadelphia, 1811; Shaw and Shoemaker 21062], p. 155).

To John Mitchell Mason

WASHINGTON Jany. 12. 1810

J. Madison presents his respects to Doctor Mason with the promised copy of Mr. Hamilton's observations[1] in the Genl. Convention, on the subject of a federal Constitution as noted at the time.

RC and enclosure (DLC, series 6). Enclosure (14 pp.) is a clerk's transcript of JM's notes on debates at the Federal Convention for 18 June 1787 (printed in Farrand, *Records of the Federal Convention*, 1:282–93). On the last page of the transcript JM wrote, "The above is a literal extract from my notes of the proceedings of the General Convention which met in Philada. in 1787. James Madison / Jany. 12. 1810."

1. On Mason's projected biography of Hamilton, see William Lewis to JM, 30 Dec. 1809, and n. 1.

§ To the House of Representatives. *12 January 1810*. Transmits a report from the secretary of state in response to the House's resolution of 3 Jan. 1810.

RC and enclosures (DNA: RG 233, President's Messages). RC 1 p. In a clerk's hand, signed by JM. Enclosures are Robert Smith's 11 Jan. report (2 pp.) (misdated in *Annals of Congress*) enclosing papers concerning Russian, Swedish, and Danish restrictions on Baltic shipping (8 pp.). Printed in *ASP, Foreign Relations*, 3:327–28. On 3 Jan. the House had requested information "relative to the blockade of the ports of the Baltic by France, and the exclusion of neutral vessels by Russia, Sweden, and Denmark." Received and ordered to be printed on 12 Jan.; referred to committee on foreign relations on 26 Jan.; committee discharged from consideration on 9 Apr. (*Annals of Congress*, 11th Cong., 2d sess., 1091, 1201, 1763).

§ To the House of Representatives. *12 January 1810*. Transmits a report from the secretary of state in response to the House's resolution of 6 Dec. 1809.

RC and enclosures (DNA: RG 233, President's Messages). RC 1 p. In a clerk's hand, signed by JM. Enclosures are Robert Smith's 12 Jan. report (3 pp.) enclosing papers concerning Danish restrictions on Baltic shipping (35 pp.). Printed in *ASP, Foreign Relations*, 3:328–38. On 6 Dec. the House had requested information "respecting seizures, captures, and condemnations of ships and merchandise of the citizens of the United States, under the authority of the Government of Denmark and its dependencies." Received and ordered to be printed on 12 Jan. (*Annals of Congress*, 11th Cong., 2d sess., 699–700, 1200–1201).

§ From Carlo Giuseppe Guglielmo Botta. *12 January 1810, Paris*. Sends a set of his *Storia della guerra dell'Independenza degli Stati Uniti d'America*, an account of the great scenes of the Revolution, inspired by the virtuous American people.

RC (DLC). 1 p. In French, signed "Charles Botta." Botta's work, first published in four volumes in Paris in 1809, was forwarded in David Bailie Warden to JM, 26 Jan. 1810. Botta also sent a copy to Jefferson (Sowerby, *Catalogue of Jefferson's Library*, 1:250–52).

§ From "Mucius" [John Randolph].[1] No. 1. *12 January 1810*. States that he is not a political admirer of JM's but admits that he has found more to approve in JM's administration than he had anticipated. Urges JM to look beyond the partisan divisions in the nation and requests him to consider future policy in the light of the true significance of Gallatin's treasury report to Congress on 17 Dec. 1809. The finances are exhausted and the nation cannot afford defense, therefore the administration is in no position to challenge the belligerent nations of Europe to redress insults of the sort recently offered to Secretary of State Smith by Francis James Jackson. Deplores the influence of the Smith family over national policy and advises JM not to identify himself with the bankrupt policies of his predecessor, Thomas Jefferson. Emphasizes the weakness and the wastefulness of the military and naval establishments and warns JM of the dangers of making erroneous statements about the adequacy of the nation's defenses, as he did in his late message to Congress.

Wishes JM would get rid of the Nonintercourse Act as well as all other measures of economic coercion. The government cannot protect commerce, nor should it tax and ruin agriculture under the pretense that it can do so. Repeats his views about the possible dangers from the "junto" of the Smith family surrounding JM and traces the possible extent of the political influence of the Smiths through their connections with other prominent families. Fears that the "proprietary rule of the *new Lords Baltimore*," by virtue of Elizabeth Patterson's marriage to Jerome Bonaparte, will corrupt American politics and make them subservient to the purposes of France. Napoleon would make use of such "tools" in the national councils, and Senator Giles is sufficiently ambitious and destitute of principle to advance imperial goals in America. Pledges himself to unmask this "French faction in the heart of our country" and begs JM to maintain peace, thus neither destroying the nation's prosperity nor deranging its government. Concludes by quoting the opinions expressed in the *Edinburgh Review*, volume 12 [1808], page 476 [477], that the shock of war would jeopardize "the whole frame of the constitution."

Printed copy (Washington *Spirit of 'Seventy-Six*, 12 Jan. 1810). Reprinted in other newspapers; also printed in *The Letters of Mutius, Addressed to the President of the United States* (Washington, 1810; Shaw and Shoemaker 20555).

1. The essay, probably written in late December 1809, appeared under the signature of "Philo-Laos," a name apparently supplied by the editor of the *Spirit of 'Seventy-Six* and one that Randolph, writing in his second essay as "Mucius," pointed out was a misnomer. As "Mucius" admitted to his readers, he had a "higher respect for his rough, old Roman namesake, than for any Greek, ancient or modern, however polished." By assuming the name of "Mucius," Randolph could have been referring to one of as many as seven notable Romans who were descended from Caius Mucius Scaevola, but it is more than likely that he intended to evoke the spirit of the first of the line for his defiance of King Porsenna, as described by Plutarch, during Porsenna's siege of Rome (*Spirit of 'Seventy-Six*, 26 Jan. 1810; William Smith, ed., *A Dictionary of Greek and Roman Biography and Mythology* [3 vols.; Boston, 1849], 3:304–5, 619–20, 731–33).

From Alfred Madison

DEAR UNCLE   WILLIAMSBURG Janry. 13th. 1810

My duties as a student, combined with a slight indisposition for some time past, have until this time prevented my acknowledgeing the receipt of those pamphlets, which you were good enough to send me.[1] I have read them with peculiar interest; not merely because their contents deeply concerned the welfare of my Country, for at the same time they recalled to my mind some of the fundamental laws laid down by Vattel; & the illustration of general principles by applying them to particular cases, is more clear & satisfactory to the mind, & tends to impress them more permanently upon the memory, than any chain of abstract reasoning. Any communications which you may hereafter think proper to make to me, will be gratefully received, & any papers or books which you may recommend to my consideration will be read with due attention & pleasure.

One of my principal objections to this College, is the great expenses to which its students are necessarily exposed—but this objection is not applicable to Wm & Mary only, it may I think be applied in a greater or less degree to all the principal school⟨s⟩ in Virginia. It appears to me that this circumstance, forms a most formidable barrier to the general diffusion of knowledge throughout the state.

At this critical juncture of our affairs it is thought by many, that War, or measures leading to a war will probably be the result of the deliberations of Congress, consequently there are many young men of my acquaintance ready to become applicants for Commissions in the

Army. Wm. F Pendleton,[2] formerly an assistant teacher in Mr. Girardin's[3] Academy, I am told will certainly apply. He will be highly recommended, & is I think, a young man of much merit & respectability. I am induced to say this, because as it is impossible for the executive to be acquainted with the merits & demerits of each individual, they are compelled sometimes to bestow their favours on the undeserving, & to withhold them from the meritorious, & lest an ignorance of Mr. Pendleton's worth, should form an obstacle to his success, I have made these observations to you.

I have not heard from My Father for some days, but when I did hear he was quite well. With my warmest respects to my Aunt—I re⟨mai⟩n with due affection & esteem Your Nephew

A MADISON

RC (NN). Docketed by JM.

1. JM evidently arranged for some pamphlets to be sent to his nephew, but he does not appear to have enclosed any letter with them in response to Alfred Madison's request of 24 Nov. 1809 (JM to Alfred Madison, 30 Jan. 1810).

2. William F. Pendleton was appointed an ensign in the Twentieth Infantry Regiment in 1812 and remained in the army until 1816 (Heitman, *Historical Register*, 1:782).

3. Louis Hue Girardin (1771–1825) emigrated from France, served as professor of modern languages at the College of William and Mary, 1803–7, and taught schools in Richmond and Albemarle County. He helped to write a continuation of John Daly Burk's *History of Virginia* and corresponded with Jefferson, who bought part of his library (Fillmore Norfleet, *Saint-Mémin in Virginia: Portraits and Biographies* [Richmond, 1942], pp. 166–67; Sowerby, *Catalogue of Jefferson's Library*, 5:192).

From Jonathan Williams

SIR   NEW YORK Jan. 13. 1810

Mr. D. Masson professor at the Military Accademy has presented to our Society a manuscript copy of his lectures on fortification.[1]

This work when compleated will be a transmission of all that is known in the french language into our own, in that condensed and simple shape which is best calculated for the Rudiments of instruction.

I think it my duty towards you, as patron of the society, to transmit it for perusal, and to ask you to put it into the hands of the Secretary of War for the same purpose; his opinion whether it be worthy of publication would much govern mine, and perhaps it might be thought proper for Government to take a certain number of copies, which might decide the question about putting it to press.

The funds of the society would not justify printing it at their expence, unless, either by subscription or some previous assurance, it could be ascertained that the number of copies sold would pay the charge.

The member mentioned in the advertisement prefixed to the included little work was Mr Jefferson and he was so well pleased with it, that he caused a number to be printed and put on the tables of the members of Congress.[2] As I have some reason to believe that it has been imputed to me I think it my duty to declare to you that Mr: Masson wrote it: He has permitted me to let you know this, but he still desires not to be generally known as the author. I have the honor to be with the most perfect respect Sir Your faithfull & obedient Servt

JON WILLIAMS
President USMPS

FC (InU). In a clerk's hand, signed and dated by Williams.

1. Francis Deseré Masson, a refugee from Saint-Domingue, taught topographical drawing and French at West Point from 1803 to 1808. He delivered his lectures on fortifications to the United States Military Philosophical Society in 1807 (George W. Cullum, *Biographical Register of the Officers and Graduates of the U.S. Military Academy at West Point* [2 vols.; New York, 1868], 1:52–53; Sidney Forman, "The United States Military Philosophical Society, 1802–1813," *WMQ*, 3d ser., 2 [1945]: 280).

2. Masson published no works under his own name. Although Williams translated several works on artillery and fortifications, that which he here described has not been found.

¶ To John Tyler. Letter not found. *13 January 1810*. Acknowledged in Tyler to JM, 17 Jan. 1810. Inquires about $300 appropriated to purchase a sword for Gen. William Campbell.

From George Logan

DEAR SIR   STENTON Jany: 14th: 1810
I shall embark for England in about eight days. If you wish to forward any communications to our Minister in London, I shall be happy in being the bearer of them. With sentiments of great respect I am your real friend

GEO LOGAN

RC (DLC).

From John Tyler

SIR;   RICHMOND January 15 1810

I have the honor to introduce to your Notice George Wm: Smith Esqr.[1] our Leiut. Govr: who having business in your City is desirous of being presented to you, whose Character he much respects. You will find him full worthy of your attention as a Patriot and Gentleman.

I greatly fear the hint you have given Congress by your advise to place our Country in a proper State of defence[2] will not be much attended to. Subjects of very inferior consideration seem to engross their time. I am at a loss to know what our National Character is? Certain I am that it is not what it has been even 30 years ago. I believe it is degenerated into a system of Stock-Jobing, Extortion and Usury. I wou'd if I had the power not only interdict the trade with G. B. but I wou'd seize british goods found on Land, Lock up every Store and hold them respo[n]sible for consequences, and if another impressment shou'd take place I wou'd make prisoners of every british Subject in the States. But this wou'd greatly offend the feelings of our Modern Patriots. By the God of Heaven, if we go on in this way our Nation will sink into disgrace and Slavery. Forty Members who cou'd support Jackson,[3] are fit Instruments for any Measure. Perhaps I have gone too far for the present ⟨notions?⟩ therefore will conclude by subscribing my self with considerations of high respect and esteem Yr most obt Servt

JNO: TYLER.

RC (DLC). Docketed by JM.

1. George William Smith (1762–1811) represented Essex County, 1790–93, and the city of Richmond, 1801–2, in the Virginia House of Delegates. Elected to the Council of State in 1807, he twice served as acting governor (following Tyler's and Monroe's resignations). Shortly after he was elected governor, he died in the Richmond theater fire (*WMQ*, 1st ser., 6 [1897–98]: 46; Swem and Williams, *Register*, pp. 73, 429; *CVSP*, 9:616).

2. See JM to Congress, 3 Jan. 1810.

3. William Branch Giles sponsored in the Senate a joint resolution pledging "to stand by and support the executive government in its refusal to receive any further communications from . . . Francis J. Jackson, and to call into action the whole force of the nation . . . to assert and maintain the rights, the honour and the interests of the United States." On 11 Dec. the Senate passed the resolution, 20–4. From 18 Dec. the House hotly debated the resolution and after a nineteen-hour session on 4 Jan. approved it by a 72–41 vote. JM signed the resolution on 12 Jan. (*Annals of Congress*, 11th Cong., 2d sess., 481, 511, 747, 1151–52; *U.S. Statutes at Large*, 2:612).

§ To the Senate. *15 January 1810*. Submits for ratification a treaty concluded on 10 Nov. 1808 and 31 Aug. 1809 with the Great and Little Osage Indians.

RC and enclosure (DNA: RG 46, Executive Proceedings, 11B-C2). RC 1 p. JM evidently enclosed *A Treaty between the United States and the Great and Little Osage Nations of Indians Concluded and Signed at Fort Clark, on the 10th Nov. 1808* (Washington, 1808; Shaw and Shoemaker 16603) and also the explanatory clause added on 31 Aug. 1809 (see *ASP, Indian Affairs,* 1:763–64). The Senate received and read the treaty, then ordered it to be printed on 16 Jan. (see *A Treaty between the United States of America, and the Great and Little Osage Tribes of Indians. January 17th, 1810. Printed by Order of the Senate* (Washington, 1810). The Senate requested further documents on 22 Jan. and unanimously ratified the treaty on 28 Apr. (*Senate Exec. Proceedings,* 2:138, 141, 148).

To David Stone

SIR   [16 January 1810]

I have duly received your letter of the 1st. instant, covering the address by which the General Assembly of N. Carolina have unanamously [*sic*] expressed their approbation of the course pursued by the Ex. of the U. S. in relation to foreign insults & aggressions, and pledged their support of it. I commit the inclosed answer to your favorable attention; offering to you, at the same time, assurances of my sensibility to the very kind terms in which the Act of the Legislature was transmitted, and of my high esteem & friendly regards.

[Enclosure]

To the General Assembly of the State of North Carolina.

Jany. 1810

The Address of the General Assembly, of the 23d. of December, could not but be received with a satisfaction much enhanced by the unanimity with which they approve the course pursued by the Executive of the U. States, for maintaining the Rights of the Nation, and the respect due to its Government.

Whilst the unyie[l]ding injustice of Foreign powers continues to render our situation perplexing, & the preservation of peace more & more uncertain, the Councils of the General Government must find their confidence in the spirit & faculties of the Nation, greatly fortified by the co-operating patriotism of the States. Nor could this resource be more honorably or acceptably pledged than in the example now given.

In the stress which the General Assembly have been pleased to lay on my capacities & endeavors to promote the welfare of our Country I perceive a partiality which claims the return of my Affectionate acknowledgments; along with which I tender assurances of my high consideration & best wishes.

Draft and draft of enclosure (DLC). Addressee of draft not indicated; draft written on verso of draft of enclosure. RC (dated 16 Jan. 1810) and enclosure printed in Richmond *Enquirer*, 13 Feb. 1810.

From Caesar A. Rodney

MY DEAR SIR,   WILMINGTON Jany. 16th. 1809. [1810]

The critical situation of our country necessarily engages the attention of every thinking man in the community. It must more particularly occupy the minds of those to whom the nation has confided any share in the direction & management of its political concerns. The Chief-magistrate of the Union, must feel in a pre-eminent degree, for the public welfare, from the peculiar responsibility attached to his elevated situation; and none can experience more anxious solicitude, than yourself. The uniform patriotism that has animated your conduct, combined with the prudence firmness & wisdom, which have directed your steps, in the path of administration, afford an ample pledge to the country that every care will be taken of its interests & its honor.

We live in an age without precedent in history. A solitary neutral, amid a warring world. All the rules of virtue & morality, which bound together the great families of ma[n]kind, are violated with impunity, as caprice, interest, or ambition direct. The celebrated writers who have civilized the human race; who have taught man the laws of his nature; & have unfolded to sovereigns, the laws by which the conduct of nations should be governed, are no longer respected. Their voice is not heared. We may truly say with Cicero, "*Inter arma silent leg⟨es⟩.*"[1] But the arbitrary orders & decrees of the belligerents, are resounded from the cannon's mouth, in the tone of thunder. Grotius & Puffendorf, Vattel & Burlimqui may be laid on the shelf. They must give place to the novel codes daily published, according to the modern method of promulgation. The subject presents a gloomy prospect to the contemplative mind.

It is in this unexampled state of things, that we are struggling to preserve the moral rules of action, between nations, against the oppressive systems of the contending powers. The task is indeed Herculean. We have sincerely endeavoured, without partiality or prejudice, to support the legitimate rights of Neutrals, when all the great naval powers, were parties to the war. Perhaps, if they were at peace, they would suffer the exercise of no belligerent rights on the ocean. In their present situation, they practice exactly the reverse. They allow no rights of neutrality. When I reflect on the magnitude & difficulty of the undertaking, I lament that the wise measure, recommended by your illustrious predecessor, had not been continued, until the desired effect was produced. I am conscious it would have accomplished the purpose if rigidly enforced. The embargo was the anchor of hope, in such a tempest as the world never before witnessed, and in which it seems to be the will of Providence, that human affairs should now fluctuate. But we were driven from our safe morings, before the storm had subsided. We have been of course buffeted by the waves, & the question presents itself what is best to be done? In this perilous moment, every man should endeavour to preserve the bark. If ever there was a period, which called for unanimity, it is emphatically the present. Every motive of honor patriotism & duty, conspire to urge all good men, to rally round the common standard of the goverment. The crisis ought to efface the distinction of party, & those who on some points have been opposed to the administration, should make a common cause against a common foe. Among the uniform friends of administration, whatever little differences of opinion may have arisen, from the complicated state of affairs, should be reconciled or forgotten. No personal jealousies should be permitted to ruffle the stream of their patriotism. All reasonable sacrifices ought to be made on the altar of accommodation & at the shrine of the Union. By these means the nation would be resolved into a most formidable mass of strenth. Possessing these sentiments, I must acknowledge that I have been disappointed, by the conduct lately manifested by the Federalists in Congress: And I lament to see the business of the Yazous revived,[2] & more especially at such an eventful moment. I fear it will prove a torch of discord: That it will spread a flame not easily extinguished.

England & France have both played a foolish game in relation to this country. They have acted as if they were blind. Either of them by withdrawing their arbit[r]ary orders or decrees might have involved us in a war with the other. And yet neither of them have been willing to take the first step, lest the other might follow in the track. Perhaps it has been the best course they could have pursued for us. It may have, thus long, preserved us from the calamities of war.

From both nations we have received sufficient cause for commencing hostilities. We have thus far avoided them, with either, by the pacific line of conduct adopted. Can we stand on this course any longer with safety? If we cannot, however painful or reluctant the duty, we must yeild to the only alternative. It is not a contest for place, but an arduous conf[l]ict for those rights which God & nature have given an Independent nation. We should be actuated by no narrow or selfish motives in the consideration and decision of this momentous question. If peace can only be preserved by the abandonment of national character, the path is very plain. I am not so ambitious of a contest, as to rush into war on a mere punctilio, more especially in the present state of the world. When every day may produce some unexpected event, and when no human experience can furnish a chart by which to steer. A general peace may take place during this winter. It is true, such a result is not probable, but things cannot, in this age, be calculated by the common arithmetic of human events. If this should happen, the wrongs of neutrals would cease. The war I apprehend will not, nay, cannot last, many years longer. May not our embarking in this late stage on the troubled ocean, have a tendency to prolong it? May we not, in case of peace, be left in the lurch & may not war produce new trammels by alliance or treaty? At all events will it not have a demoralising effect on the country, & be productive of injury to our Republican institutions systems, habits & manners? I cannot subscribe to the doctrine of Lord Kaims[3] & Baccon that a state of peace is unnatural to men, & that it renders them beasts of burthen. But with all my prepossessions in favor of peace, the insults added to the injuries we have sustained, afford I must acknowledge, independent of the novel state of the world, an abundant cause of war. I feel no partialities for England or France. The Emperor & the King in my veiw are equal enemies to free goverment. There was a period when we all felt the cause of Frenchmen as our own, but that has long since passed by.

If we unsheath the sword, I am most decidedly for selecting our foe. We have at least a choice of enemies. The idea of going to war at once with both powers (or in other language with all the world) has ever appeared to my mind preposterous. The opinion sometimes expressed, that one or the other, would soon make peace with us, might prove woe-fully incorrect. At all events it would not afford so fair an opportunity, as if we were not to wage war with all. We should not add any real strenth to our cause by such a policy. Rely on it, those among our opposers who advocate this course, from a nice refined sense of punctilious scruples, have sense eneough to discern, the embarassment which must necessarily ensue.

England is our old & inveterate enemy. She has done us more injury. The impressment of our seamen alone is worse than all we have sustained from France. She is vulnerable by land & water. Her provinces we can conquer & the remnant of her commerce will become a prey to our privateers. In the last war before our allianc⟨e⟩ with France, Marshall states,[4] that we had raised insurance higher than when England was at War with both France & Spain, by the active enterprising spirit of our privateersmen. On this fleet I would rely, much more than our navy. I have heared seafaring men assert that the "Fair American" & the "Holker"[5] did more injury to the British commerce in our last war, than all our thirteen frigates, the principal part of which, were soon captured. It is true the British navy has been greatly increased since that period, & her supremacy on the ocean established. But our privateers would be found on experiment, to have increased in a much greater proportion, than the English Navy.

I have little doubt, but we could get money eneough at home, but if we do not declare war against Europe, I presume we may borrow foreign capital, & leave our domestic, to be applied to manufactures privateers & other purposes.

The experienced mind of Mr. Gallatin can furnish without difficulty, sufficient resources for prosecuting a war, from the ample stores our own country affords.

I would enter into no "entangling alliance" with France, but rely on the fact of our being actually at war with England, to produce in Europe all the benificial effects that could, reasonably, be expected. The reign of British influence will soon be over in this country. The cause will cease, & the effect will of course. I consider England rapidly on the decline, & contemplate her fall as not far distant. She will not suffer our trade to expand its wings & take its accustomed flight, because we interfere with her commerce. This however will render us less able to purchase her manufactures. We have been as busy as bees collecting honey from every coast and clime for her hive. By her mandate we are confined to our own shores. The capital heretofore employed in trade will be invested in manu-factories of various kinds in this country. England is doing by this conduct more to establish manufactures than we could do ourselves. Her excise & her export duties she has strained to the highest pitch. In a few years (as they cannot reduce, but must increase them) in reference to her more important articles, they must amount to a prohibition. Already they fur-nish sufficient inducements to manufacture for ourselves.

As things are, England has little or no interest in the question relative to the Colonial trade; yet she will not acquiesce in the circuitous com-merce between the colony & the mother country.

The period is not favorable for the commencement of a war. The ocean must be covered with our vessels. The East India & Brazil trade must be greatly exposed, unless advice boats were dispatched immediately on the rupture with Jackson. From the time Canning came into power I have suspected, that such was their infatuated policy, they really desired war with us, but did not like to begin it themselves. They wished to throw the odium on us. It is possible they may commence hositilities [sic] when they receive Jackson's budget, & strike without notice. They never could have a fairer opportunity. They have treacherously seduced our commerce abroad, & may now seize on the prey. Our exposed ports ought to be promptly attended to. The winter season will protect many. But New-York & New Orleans require particular attention. If England should at-tack us, it will releive us from all difficulties about commencing war.

I am much pleased with the treatment Jackson received from the government, & highly gratified with the able decorous and dignified style of the correspondence with him. The admirable veiw which Mr. Giles has taken of this subject, for popular instruction & convertion, cannot be excelled or equalled.[6] His speech should be distributed all over the country with every almanack for the new year.

The sentiments expressed by the venerable Dickenson in a letter addressed to me & dated the 16th. of Novr. 1807. are not inapplicable to the present times.

"The infatuated policy of Britain has placed her in such a position, that she seems to think her safety depends on hostility against the world. Perhaps it does. If she is to fall in the contest she will go down with a tremendous crash and dreadful ruin to many others—I turn my eyes from the object witness as I am for more than fifty years of British folly.

"At present let us prepare as well & as quickly as we can, against the most imminent dangers. We ought among other things to have 15. or 20. Gun boats in the Delaware."

The situation of England must be daily becoming more de[s]perate. Previously to the French war her funds were very high. After embarking in a contest which appears likely to prove fatal to herself, but may prove fatal to the liberties of all mankind, her funds experienced a drepression [sic] in the year 99. greater that [sic] at any period during the American war. They have it is true since recovered from a collapse which reduced them to about one half the value they possessed before they plunged into the war with France, but the paroxism may soon return, when their laws can no longer make Bank paper equal to gold & silver coin. In proportion as the annual sums for their expences increase, the ability & resources may diminish.

With a blind old King more than seventy years of age, the heir apparent near Fifty, with a broken constitution, & a little girl[7] of about fourteen the next in succession, the British nation must have, under the present exigences, a hopeful prospect.

When we look round to Buonaparte, who may be styled not merely the Colossus of Europe, but of the world, & who is indebted to England for an extent of power & empire, not only unequalled but unrivalled since the creation of man, we behold a different order of things. Whether we contemplate his character as a warrior or stateman, he has displayed equal talents. He does every thing at the proper time, and fortune seems to crown all his plans with success. What were the conquests of Alexander compared with those, he has atcheived? What the extent of Roman Empire in its most expanded State, or that of his predecessor Charlemagne contrasted with wide limits or range of Buonaparte? His ally the Emperor of all the Russias possesses dominions more extensive than those of Charlemagne or than t⟨he⟩ Empire of Rome. And Russia is his sattilite. His vassal King's & his humbled Emperor's territories, added to those governed immediately in his own name, must furnish him with strenth & resources, the extent of which it would be difficult to calculate.

If this gigantic power, as some of our wise men have predicted, Cyclops like, intends the fate of Ulysses for us, I trust like Ulysses we shall escape by having the sea between us, & by our own wisdom & strenth.

Not to have a war with England or France is a most desirable object, if it can be accomplished consistently with those principles which ought to govern an independent & enlightened nation. I would avoid Scylla & Charybdis too if possible, but in no event would I run upon both. If the trade with Europe were once opened our fast sa[i]ling vessels would carry our produce there, & bring us in return the articles we want.

Will our friends & the great body of congress unite in any system of measures devised on the maturest reflection? It is a glorious occasion, & I trust they will. Yet I have my apprehensions. I submit in confidence the above desultory reflections to your better & more experienced judgment. In a few days I shall repair to my post & have the pleasure of a personal communication. With great esteem I remain Dr. Sir Yours truly & affecy.

C A. RODNEY

RC (DLC: Rives Collection, Madison Papers).

1. "Silent enim leges inter arma": "When arms speak, the laws are silent," Cicero, *Pro T. Annio Milone Oratio*, 4.11 (Cicero, *The Speeches*, trans. N. H. Watts, Loeb Classical Library [Cambridge, Mass., 1931], p. 17).

2. At the time Rodney was writing, the case *Fletcher* v. *Peck* was pending before the U.S. Supreme Court, which on 16 Mar. decided in favor of the New England Yazoo claimants (Magrath, *Yazoo*, pp. 53–54, 70; see also Benjamin Joy to JM, 20 Dec. 1809, and n. 1).

3. Henry Home, Lord Kames.

4. Rodney may have adapted this information from John Marshall's *Life of George Washington*, 3:32–33.

5. During the Revolution the privateers *Fair American* and *Holker* sailed in the Caribbean and in one instance combined to capture four English merchantmen (Edgar Stanton Maclay, *A History of American Privateers* [London, 1900], pp. 214–15).

6. In a speech of 8 Dec. 1809, Senator William Branch Giles defended his resolution approving JM's conduct toward the British envoy Francis James Jackson (*Annals of Congress*, 11th Cong., 2d sess., 484–509).

7. Princess Charlotte Augusta, only child of the Prince of Wales (later George IV), died in 1817.

§ Presidential Proclamation. *16 January 1810, Washington*. On 2 Jan. the president, with the advice and consent of the Senate, ratified and confirmed the treaty concluded at Fort Wayne on 30 Sept. 1809 between the U.S. and the Delaware, Potawatomi, Miami, and Eel River Indians. Requires all officeholders and citizens "faithfully to observe and fulfil" the treaty.

Ms, two copies (DNA: RG 233, President's Messages; and DNA: RG 46, Executive Proceedings, 11B-C1). 7 pp. In a clerk's hand. Enclosed in JM's 28 Feb. message to Congress. Published in *National Intelligencer*, 26 Feb. 1810. The treaty is printed in *ASP, Indian Affairs*, 1:760–61.

§ Presidential Proclamation. *16 January 1810, Washington.* On 2 Jan. the president, with the advice and consent of the Senate, ratified the separate treaty article concluded at Fort Wayne on 30 Sept. 1809 between the U.S. and the Miami and Eel River Indians. Requires all officeholders and citizens "faithfully to observe and fulfil" the article.

Ms, two copies (DNA: RG 233, President's Messages; and DNA: RG 46, Executive Proceedings, 11B-C1). 3 pp. In a clerk's hand. Enclosed in JM's 28 Feb. message to Congress. Published in *National Intelligencer*, 26 Feb. 1810. The separate article is printed in *ASP, Indian Affairs*, 1:761–62.

To John Keemle

[17 January 1810]

Having reced. from you as Chairman the address of the Surviving Revoly. Characters in the City & County of Philada. I return through the same channel, the inclosed answer; tendering you at the same time, my respects & good wishes.

[Enclosure]

To the Surviving Military Characters of the late Revolutionary army & Navy residing in the City & County of Philadelphia.

Jany. 1810

I have recd. fellow Citizens, with particular satisfaction, the Sentiments you have thought fit to address to me at a moment so interesting to the Honor & wellbeing of our Country. The unjust proceedings of Foreign Govts. have long been witnessed by the Nation with feelings repressed only, by a love of peace, & by hopes founded on appeals to those principles of law & right, which have been exemplified in its own conduct. These hopes having continually failed, our situation retains its perplexity, and the preservation of peace becomes more & more uncertain. At such a period, it is a precious consideration that the Govt. of the U. S. instead of having provoked this inauspicious state of our foreign relations, has been as persevering as it has been sincere in efforts to avert it; and that as our wrongs become aggravated, the readiness to maintain our rights becomes more universal. From none was this partriotic [*sic*] spirit more to be looked for, than from those who knowing most experimentally the price paid for our Independence, must be the last to suffer its Attributes to be impaired in its descent to their posterity. A free people, firmly united, in a just cause, can never despond of either inspiring a respect for their rights, or of maintaining them agst. hostile invasions. Should this last alternative, in spite of all our conciliatory endeavors—be forced upon us, it may well be expected, that however the capacity of our revolutionary Champions for active service, may be impaired by the infirmities of age, the deficiency will be amply made up, by the animation given by their former example, & present zeal, to their fellow Citizens who have not before been compelled to rally to the banners & the defence of their Country. Accept assurances of my respect & friendly wishes

Draft and draft of enclosure (DLC). Written on recto and verso of a cover addressed to "The President." RC (dated 17 Jan. 1810) and enclosure printed in Philadelphia *Democratic Press*, 26 Jan. 1810.

From John Tyler

DEAR SIR;   RICHMOND Jany: 17th 1810
    I receiv'd yours of the 13th Instant on the Subject of the 300$ deposited in our Bank for the purchase of a Sword for Genl. Campbell.[1] We found your Letter which enclos'd the Money on which a memorandum on it gave us the information where it was deposited. Will it not be best to draw for the Money in some safe way? or if you chuse to have it enclos'd you will please to signify your desire to your very obt Hble Servt.

JNO: TYLER.

RC (DLC); letterbook copy (Vi: Executive Letterbook).

1. In 1780 the Virginia General Assembly had voted the gift of a sword to Col. William Campbell for his gallantry at the Battle of King's Mountain. Promoted to general, Campbell died less than a year later, but his heir apparently sought the tendered gift. Robert R. Livingston purchased the sword while serving as U.S. minister to France, and in 1802 Governor Monroe arranged for its delivery (*CVSP*, 8:459, 9:340; JM to Monroe, 24 Oct. 1801 [DLC]; Albert Gallatin to JM, 26 Jan. 1810).

From John Wayles Eppes

CONGRESS-HALL January 18th. 1810.

A letter has been received by Mr. Kenan of North Carolina[1] from an officer of the army of good character and veracity stating That of the Troops at Orleans only 950 remain—That of these 520 are on duty and convalescent—That 150 have deserted and about 850 have died since their being stationed there. This extraordinary situation of our force there is attributed to a disobedience of orders from the Secretary at War. It is said with what truth I know not that Genl. Wilkinson against the possitive orders of the Secretary at War, kept the Troops in a swamp below Orleans and absolutely sacrificed them. I have no view in stating to you this circumstance but to put you in possession of information which is now circulating through the House of Representatives and producing some sensibility.[2]

I do not know how far you may be already apprized of the state of public sentiment as to Genl. Wilkinson. Without expressing any opinion on his innocence or guilt and indeed I am unable to pronounce on either, I have no hesitation in saying that he has lost completely the confidence of nine tenths of all persons with whom I am acquainted either here or elsewhere. He hangs like a dead weight upon the administration and so completely has suspicion pervaded the great mass of the community that men of the purest patriotism and best dispositions towards the administration, would if difficulty or danger should occur withold from the public their services if he was to be their commander.

In making to you this communication, I am influenced by no personal feeling of any kind towards Genl. Wilkinson. I wish only to apprize you of what I believe to be the state of public feeling on this subject. It will be easy for you to asscertain by enquiry how far the opinion I have expressed is correct. With great respect I am Yours &ce

JNO: W: EPPES[3]

RC (DLC).

1. Thomas Kenan (1771–1843) was a Republican representative from North Carolina in the Ninth, Tenth, and Eleventh Congresses.

2. The rumors Eppes referred to led Virginian Thomas Newton, Jr., to move resolutions in the House on 22 Jan. and 13 Mar. calling for information on the condition of the "regular force allotted for the defence of New Orleans" and on the "cause or causes of the great mortality" at the Terre aux Boeufs encampment. Over the winter of 1808–9 Brig. Gen. James Wilkinson had been assigned a force of some two thousand regular troops for the defense of the Gulf Coast, but during the following summer approximately half the men in his command died in appalling circumstances produced by bad weather, poor food, unsanitary conditions, and inadequate medical care. At the same time that Newton moved for his

inquiries, Joseph Pearson of North Carolina presented a resolution calling for an investigation of some much earlier allegations about Wilkinson's involvement with Aaron Burr and
his receiving bribes from the agents of foreign governments, particularly Spain. The subsequent inquiries were lengthy and continued into the third session of the Eleventh Congress.
Both resulted in inconclusive verdicts, and Wilkinson survived the scandals until he was
utterly discredited by his conduct during the War of 1812 (*Annals of Congress*, 11th Cong.,
2d sess., 1255–56, 1533, 1606–7, 1727–57, 2288–2379; *ASP, Military Affairs*, 1:268–95;
ASP, Miscellaneous, 2:79–127; Jacobs, *Tarnished Warrior*, pp. 251–65).

    3. John Wayles Eppes (1773–1823), Jefferson's nephew, served as a congressman,
1803–11 and 1813–15, and U.S. senator, 1817–19, from Virginia. His first wife was Jefferson's daughter Maria (1778–1804).

From Benjamin Henry Latrobe

SIR   January 18th. 1810
    In the original design of the senate chamber submitted to and approved
by the late President, it was intended to place a range of seats along the
semicircular wall of the room for the accomodation of members of the
house of Representatives. This design was in the progress of execution
during the summer session, and was observed and remarked upon by several members of the Senate. The result of the conversation which arose
upon the subject, was that a committee was appointed to direct the arrangements of the seats of the senate chamber, which committee ordered
the seats proposed for the members of the house of representatives to be
omitted, & the seats of the senators to be placed the first in order from
the wall.[1]

    During the time which has elapsed since the commencement of the ses-
sion this alteration of the first arrangement having become known to the
members of congress generally has excited feelings, which it is wished to
avoid, and the members of the senate *generally* have a desire that the original order of seats should be restored. But as there is some delicacy felt as
to the manner of reversing the order of the committee of the Senate, and
the expenditures of the public buildings are *by Law placed under the direction
of the President of the United States, I am desired by the Vice President of the
United States* to state to you, that it is *his wish* that the original design
should be restored, and to request your direction on the subject, as my
sanction for so doing. It is my duty to wait upon you to state this wish
but I am the principal witness in a very important cause now before the
court, and cannot depart therefrom. I have therefore desired the Clerk of
the works Mr. Henry S Latrobe to wait upon you with the original docu-

ments and to recieve your directions. The alterations will be very easily effected. I am with the highest respect Yrs.

B HENRY LATROBE Surv.
of the pblic Bldgs U.S.

RC (DLC); letterbook copy (MdHi). RC docketed by JM.

1. For the background to these decisions, see Van Horne, *Papers of Benjamin Henry Latrobe*, 2:752 n. 3.

To George Logan

DEAR SIR   WASHINGTON Jany. 19th 1810

I have received your favour of the 10th. Your anxiety that our country may be kept out of the vortex of war, is honourable to your judgment as a patriot, and to your feeling as a man. The same anxiety is, I sincerely believe, felt by the great body of the nation, & by its public councils; most assuredly by the Executive Branch of them. But the question may be decided for us, by actual hostilities against us, or by proceedings, leaving no choice but between absolute disgrace & resistance by force. May not also manifestations of patience under injuries & indignities, be carried so far, as to invite this very dilemma?

I devoutly wish that the same disposition to cultivate peace by means of justice which exists here, predominated elsewhere, particularly in G. B. But how can this be supposed, whilst she persists in proceedings, which comprise the essence of hostility; whilst she violates towards us rules, which she enforces against us in her own favour; more particularly whilst we see her converting the late reconciliation through one of her Ministers, into a source of fresh difficulties & animosities, thro' another: For in this light must be viewed, her disavowal of Mr. Erskine, and the impressions made thro' his successor. Had the disavowal been deemed essential to her interests, a worse plaister could not have been devised for the wound necessarily inflicted here. But was the disavowal essential to her interests? was it material to them; taking for the test, her own spontaneous change of system, & her own official language? By the former I refur [*sic*] to her orders of April, restricting their original orders against neutrals, to a trade with France and Holland: by the latter, to the conversation of Mr. Canning with Mr. P., in which he abandons, as he could not but do, two of the conditions which had been contemplated; and admits that a non-intercourse law here against Holland was not a sine qua non; So that the arrangement of Mr. E. was disavowed essentially for want of a pledge that our non-intercourse would be continued against France & her dominions. But why disavow absolutely, why at all, on this account? The law was known to be in force against France at the time of the arrangement. It was morally certain that if put in force against France whilst she was pleading the British orders, it would not be withdrawn, if she should persist in her decrees, after being deprived of this plea. And there could be no fair ground to suppose, that the condition would not be pledged & stipulated, if required, as soon as the requisite Authorities here should be together. The disavowal is the more extraordinary, as the arrangement was to be respected till the 20th. of July, and therefore with the addition of four or five weeks only, would have afforded an opportunity of knowing the sense of this Govt. and of supplying all that was wanted to satisfy the British Ultimatum. This course was so obvious, & that pursued so opposite, that we are compelled to look to other motives for an explanation, & to include among these, a disinclination to put an end to differences from which such advantages are extracted by British Commerce & British Cruisers.

Notwithstanding all these grounds of discontent & discouragement, we are ready, as the B. Govt. knows, to join in any new experiment, (& thro' either our diplomatic channel there, or hers here) for a cordial & comprehensive adjustment of matters between the two countries.

Let reparation be made for the acknowledged wrong commited in the case of the Chesapeak, a reparation so cheap to the wrongdoer, yet so material to the honour of the injured party; & let the orders in Council, already repealed as to the avowed object of retaliation, be repealed also as an expedient for substituting an illicit commerce, in place of that to which neutrals have, as such, an incontestible right. The way will then be opened for negotiation at large; and if the B. Govt. would bring into it the same temper as she would find in us; & the same disposition to insist on nothing inconsistent with the rule of doing as she would, or rather as she *will* be done by, the result could not fail to be happy for both.

Permit me to remark that you are under a mistake in supposing that the Treaty concluded by Messr. M. & P. was rejected because it did not provide that free ships should make free goods. It never was required nor expected that such a stipulation should be inserted. As to deserting Seamen, you will find that G. B. practices against us the principles we assert against her, and in fact goes further; that we have always been ready to enter into a convention on that subject founded on reciprocity; and that the documents long since in print show, that we are willing, on the subject of impressment, to put an end to it, by an arrangement, which most certainly would be better for the British Navy, than that offensive resource, & which might be so managed as to leave both parties at liberty to retain their own ideas of right. Let me add that the acceptance of that Treaty would have very little changed the actual situation of things with G. B. The Orders in Council would not have been prevented but rather placed on stronger ground; the case of the Chesapeak, the same as it is; so also the case of impressments, of fa[c]titious[1] blockades &c all as at present, pregnant sources of contention & ill-humour.

From this view of the subject, I cannot but persuade myself, that you will concur in opinion, that if unfortunately, the calamity you so benevolently dread, should visit this hitherto favoured Country, the fault will not lie where you would wish it not to lie. Accept assurances of my esteem & friendship

JAMES MADISON

Jany. 19. P. S. Since I recd. your letter of the 10. and whilst the above was undergoing a copy, yours of the 14th. has come to hand, informing me of your intention to embark in about 8 days for England; an intention I presume suddenly formed as it is not alluded to in your first letter. The Secretary of State will avail himself of your polite offer to take charge of communications to our Minister in London; tho' I fear that your departure may take place before he can be in readiness. I shall myself ask the favor of your attention to a private letter to him, which I shall forward by to-morrow's Mail.

RC (PHi); draft (DLC). RC in the hand of Edward Coles except for JM's signature and postscript; docketed by Logan. Draft in JM's hand, dated 17 Jan., and docketed by JM at a later time, "To Geo: Joy probably." Hence earlier editions described the letter as sent to Joy (Madison, *Letters* [Cong. ed.], 2:465–67; Madison, *Writings* [Hunt ed.], 8:85–89). Postscript not on draft. Minor variations between RC and draft have not been noted.

1. Letter in brackets is here supplied from the draft.

From George Logan

DEAR SIR   [19 January 1810]
In a late Letter I mentioned to you my intention of embarking for England: Some circumstances have since occured which will prevent that event taking place at present.

Two days ago I had some conversation with Mr: Onis. He expresses anxiety that a good understanding should be preserved between Spain & the UStates: he laments that he was not received at Washington; as he had full powers amicably to settle every subject of misunderstanding between the two Governments. He mentioned with regret, that two Letters he wrote some Weeks since to Mr: Smith had not been answered, the latter in his *private capacity*.[1] I am with sentiments of respect your friend

GEO: LOGAN

RC (DLC). Top margin of RC, including dateline, has been clipped. Date determined by JM's docket.

1. Logan referred to Luis de Onís's letters of 20 Oct. and 20 Nov. 1809 to Robert Smith. In the first Onís had sought a "categorical answer in writing" to explain JM's motives for not receiving him as minister from Spain. The second, private, letter called to Smith's attention that JM had agreed Onís could continue communications with the U.S. through the offices of the British minister. Onís wished to know how that promise could be fulfilled after the departure of Francis James Jackson from Washington, and he mentioned that he wished to complain about expeditions against Spanish possessions that were being outfitted in American ports (DNA: RG 59, NFL, Spain).

§ From J. Nichols, Jr. *19 January 1810*, *"Near Boston."* Assures JM that in the event of war "thousands of N. England's hardiest Sons" will "rally round their government." Promises to send to the War Department plans for a "portable battery" for use on riverbanks and shores.

RC (DLC). 2 pp. Docketed by JM.

To William Pinkney

DEAR SIR   Jany. 20. 1810

I received some days ago a letter of the 10th inst. from Doctor Logan, containing observations on the posture & prospect of our foreign relations. Before the answer was out of my hands, I received another dated four days after, in which he merely informed me that he should embark for England in about eight days with an offer to take charge of any communications for you. As his first letter did not glance at any such intention it must be presumed to have been very suddenly formed. And as his last is silent as to the object of the trip, this is left to conjecture. From the anxiety expressed in his first letter for the preservation of peace with England, which appeared to him to be in peculiar danger, and from his known benevolence & zeal on the subje[c]t, it may reasonably be supposed that his views relate, in some form or other, to a mitigation of the hostile tenden[c]ies which distress him; and that his silence may proceed from a wish to give no handle for animadversions of any sort on the step taken by him.

You will receive from the Secretary of State, unless indeed the opportunity fail thro' the shortness of the notice, such communications & ob-

servations as may be thought useful to you. You will find that the perplexity of our situation is amply displayed by the diversity of opinions, &
prolixity of discussion, in Congress. Few are desirous of war; and few are
reconciled to submission; yet the frustration of intermediate courses,
seems to have left scarce any escape from that dilemma. The fate of Mr.
Macon's Bill as it is called is not certain.[1] It will probably pass the House
of Representatives and for aught I know may be concured in by the Senate. If retaliated by G. B it will operate as a non-impo[r]tation Act, and
throw exports into the circuit of the non-intercourse Act: If not retaliated
it may be felt by the British navigation, & thro' that interest, by the Govt.:
since the execution of the law, which relates to the Ship & not to the
merchandise, can not be evaded. With respect to the E. Indies the proposed regulation will have the effect of compelling the admission of a direct and *exclusive* trade for our vessels, or a relinquishment of this market,
for India Goods, farther than they can be smuggled into it. It just appears
that a proposition has been made in the House of Reps., to employ our
Ships of War in convoys, and to permit Merchantmen to Arm.[2] However
plausible the arguments for this experiment, its tendency to hostile collisions is so evident, that I think its success improbable. As a mode of going
into war, it does not seem likely to be generally approved, if war was the
object. The Military preparations which have been recommended, and are
under consideration are what they profess to be, measures of precaution.
They are not only justified, but dictated by the uncertainty attending the
course which G. B. may take, or rather, by the unyielding & unamicable
traits in her cabinet & her countenance. Measures of that sort are also the
more adapted to our situation, as in the event of accomodation with G. B.
they may possibly be wanted in another quarter. The long debates on the
Resolution of Mr. Giles on the subject of Mr. Jackson, have terminated in
affirmative votes, by large majorities.[3] This with the refusal of the Executive to hold communication with him, it is supposed, will produce a crisis
in the British policy towards the U. States; to which the representations
of the angry Minister will doubtless be calculated to give an unfavourable
turn. Should this happen, our precautionary views will have been the
more seasonable. It is most probable however that instead of expressing
resentment by open war, it will appear in more extended depredations on
our commerce, in declining to replace Mr. Jackson; and perhaps in the
course observed with respect to you, in meeting which your own judgement will be the best guide. Should a change in the composition or calculations of the cabinet give a favourable turn to its policy towards this
Country, it is desirable that no time may be lost, in allowing it, its effect.
With this view you will be reminded of the *several* authorities you retain
to meet in negotiation, and of the instructions by which they are to be
exercised:[4] it being always understood that with the exception of some

arrangement touching the orders in Council, reparation for the insult on the Chesapeak, must precede a general negotiation on the questions between the two countries. At present nothing precise can be said as to a condition on our part, for the repeal of the orders in Council; the existing authority in the Executive to pledge one, being expireable with the non-intercourse Act, and no other pledge being provided for. As it is our anxious desire however, if the B. Govt. should adopt just and conciliatory views, that nothing may be omitted that can show our readiness to second them, you may offer a general assurance, that as in the case of the Embargo, and the non-intercourse Acts, any similar power with which the Executive may be cloathed, will be exercised in the same spirit. You will doubtless be somewhat surprised to find among the communications to Congress, and in print too, the confidential conversations with Mr. Canning reserved from such a use by your own request.[5] It was in fact impossible to resist the pointed call for them, without giving umbrage to some, & opportunity for injurious inferences, to others. The difficulty was increased by the connection between those, and other communications necessarily falling within the scope of the rule of compliance in such cases. Finally, there did not appear to be any thing in the conversations which could warrent British complaint of their disclosure, or widen the space between you and the British Ministry.

As it may not be amiss that you should know the sentiments which I had expressed to Dr. Logan, and which, though in answer to his letter written previous to the notification of his intended trip, he will of course carry with him, I enclose a copy of the answer.[6]

The file of news papers from the Department of State will give you the debates on the case of Jackson. I enclose however a speech I have just looked over, in a pamphlet form.[7] Altho' liable to very obvious criticisms of several sorts, it has presented a better analysis of some parts of the subject, than I have observed in any of the speeches.

FC (DLC: Rives Collection, Madison Papers). In the hand of Edward Coles, dated, docketed, and corrected by JM. Enclosures not found, but see nn. 6 and 7.

1. With the impending expiration of the Nonintercourse Act of 1809, Gallatin drafted Macon's Bill No. 1, which would have prohibited British and French ships from entering U.S. ports, permitted U.S. vessels to import goods directly from their place of origin, and allowed the president to rescind discriminatory provisions against either power that ceased to violate American neutrality. The bill passed the House on 29 Jan. but died after a coterie led by Samuel Smith emasculated it in the Senate and conference committees failed to resolve the ensuing deadlock over its terms (Perkins, *Prologue to War*, pp. 239–44).

2. On 19 Jan. William Burwell (Virginia) had proposed a two-part resolution authorizing the arming of merchantmen and requiring the president to use naval convoys for American vessels bearing noncontraband American goods to ports not effectively blockaded in nations that did not enforce restrictions against neutral commerce. The resolution, which at-

tempted to define and protect "lawful" American commerce, underwent some debate over the next three months, but the House, as JM predicted, took no final action before its adjournment (*Annals of Congress*, 11th Cong., 2d sess., 1225–26, 1254, 1403–4, 1463–64, 1482–85, 1789–91).

3. On the 12 Jan. joint resolution approving JM's conduct toward the British envoy Francis James Jackson, see John Tyler to JM, 15 Jan. 1810, and n. 3.

4. In two letters dated 20 Jan. 1810, Robert Smith conveyed to Pinkney JM's instructions that he was authorized to resume negotiations with Great Britain under the powers given to him and James Monroe on 12 May 1806, provided that Great Britain had first given satisfaction for the *Chesapeake* affair (DNA: RG 59, IM).

5. See JM to the House of Representatives, 16 Dec. 1809.

6. JM to Logan, 19 Jan. 1810.

7. Speeches by three House Republicans from the debate on Jackson's conduct were published in pamphlet form. They were those delivered by George Poindexter (Mississippi Territory) on 30 Dec. 1809 and by Thomas Newton (Virginia) and Thomas Sammons (New York) on 3 Jan. 1810 (Shaw and Shoemaker nos. 18410, 20919, and 21274, respectively). It is not known which speech JM chose to enclose to Pinkney.

From Pierre Samuel DuPont de Nemours

MONSIEUR LE PRÉSIDENT,   PARIS 20 janvier 1810.

J'ai reçu avec une vive reconnaissance la lettre dont Votre Excellence m'a honoré le 3 décembre dernier, les marques de bienveillance qu'Elle me donne, et Surtout celle de permettre que je profite d'un des Vaisseaux des Etats Unis que Vous envoyez dans nos Ports pour effectuer mon retour en Amérique quand j'en aurai la possibilité.

Vous rendez justice à mon attachement pour votre Sage nation, pour Son Gouvernement bienfaisant et doux, pour les grandes facilités que Sa position heureusement éloignée des orages de la guerre, et les lumieres qu'elle a déja, lui donnent plus qu'à aucune autre de conserver ces lumieres; et de les augmenter, non Seulement par celles des autres Peuples, mais aussi par l'exemple de leurs fautes et de leurs malheurs. Observer les maladies, c'est apprendre la Santé.

Vos Gazettes et leur liberté Sont un bon moyen d'Instruction: car dans les discussions publiques la Puissance finit par rester à la Raison. Mais cette instruction n'est que pour les Hommes: celle qui manque jusqu'à présent est celle des Enfans. Les Enfans américains Savent lire, c'est un grand point: mais ils n'ont pas encore quoi lire pendant leur enfance, ni même avec quoi apprendre à lire, ou S'amuser à transcrire, de maniere que d'autres idées agréables et utiles entrent dans leurs têtes avec ces deux Sciences: c'est un grand *deficit*. Et ils n'ont aucun examen à Subir Sur le profit qu'ils ont tiré de leurs Lectures.

C'est mon espoir que pendant votre Présidence vous ferez faire au concours ces petits Livres destinés à l'enfance et instituerez les examens qui les leur rendront plus utiles. Il n'en coutera que quelques Prix d'une dépense médiocre.

L'Education qui n'est applicable qu'aux Gens d'un esprit distingué et d'une certaine richesse forme quelques hommes illustres. L'Education qui fonderait, dès le premier âge, la morale Sur la justice et Sur l'interêt bien entendu, et qui embrasserait ensuite les premiers élémens de la Géométrie, de la Mécanique, des Sciences physico-mathématiques, formeront une Nation toute entiere, à la fois équitable et éclairée, et de laquelle Sortirat un bien plus grand nombre d'hommes éminens.

Tous les Enfans naissent avec des dispositions à la Justice, et à la vertu qui n'est que la fille de la justice; et, grace au Ciel encore, à la Compassion qui est la Mere de la Bienfaisance et des bonnes mœurs. *Cent mille hommes*, chez qui l'on n'a pas laissé ces germes précieux S'obliterer, valent mieux pour le bonheur et la puissance de l'Etat que *trois cent mille* qui n'ont appris qu'à manger et boire, et à vouloir leur interêt Sans le calculer.

Sur cent Enfans qui auront cette générale, et raisonnable et morale éducation bonne à tous, il y en aura un qui pourra dans les Sciences ou dans les arts, ou dans une judicieuse administration S'élever très haut et donner un jour des moyens de Subsistance à vingt mille autres. Dans l'état actuel nous n'avons pas un Enfant Sur dix mille qui marque dans la Société. Toutes les Forêts Sont pleines de glands qui perissent inutiles, et auxquels, pour devenir les plus beaux Chesnes, il n'a manqué qu'un peu de terreau.

D'*Aubenton*[1] dit que ce qui rend principalement les animaux beaux et robustes, c'est l'abondante et bonne nourriture de leur enfance. Cela est vrai pour nous comme pour eux; et pour l'esprit, pour la moralité, comme pour le corps. Nous enterrons tous les jours des Socrates, des Newtons, des Locke, des Montesquieu, ignorés de leurs voisins, de leurs Parens et d'eux mêmes. Quant aux Franklin, je conviens que la graine en est fort rare. Celle des autres que je viens de nommer n'est pas très commune: mais il y en a.

Je vous rends mille graces, Monsieur le Président, d'avoir bien voulu m'envoyer votre excellent message et les documens curieux qui l'accompagnent. Je les lis avec beaucoup d'attention, de Satisfaction et d'interêt. Ce Sont les plus hautes affaires de mes Freres adoptifs. Agréez, Monsieur le Président, ma reconnaissance, mon attachement, mon profond respect.

DUPONT (DE NEMOURS)

CONDENSED TRANSLATION

Thanks JM for his letter of 3 December and for his offer of passage to America aboard a public vessel. Freedom of the press in America allows for public discussion, but this means of instruction "is only for grown men." Adequate training for young Americans is lacking. American children are literate but need reading materials; suggests a competition for children's books. A distinctive education based on morality and enlightened self-interest would have salutary effect. For every one hundred children educated on this premise, one leader would result; these special Americans would in turn provide livelihood for twenty thousand others. "Presently we do not have one child out of ten thousand who stands out in society. . . . Every day we bury and forget Socrateses, Newtons, Lockes, and Montesquieus, unrecognized by their neighbors, by their parents, and by themselves."

RC (DLC); draft (DeGE). RC docketed by JM. Draft dated 15 Jan. 1810. Minor variations between RC and draft have not been noted.

1. Louis Jean Marie Daubenton contributed essays on quadrupeds to the comte de Buffon's *Histoire naturelle*. JM commented on those essays when Jefferson was preparing to rebut Buffon and Daubenton in his *Notes on the State of Virginia* (Notes on Buffon's *Histoire naturelle*, ca. May 1786, JM to Jefferson, 12 May and 19 June 1786, *PJM*, 9:34, 47 n. 4, 52, 78).

From William Jarvis

SIR   LISBON 20 Jany. 1810

Having lately, with some pains, been able to obtain a few Merino Sheep, warranted of the best breed in Spain, I hope that you will allow me the honor of presenting you with a Ram & a Ewe.[1] I shall also take the liberty of sending a pair to Mr Jefferson. There are now two or three large vessels bound to Alexandria, in one of which I am in hopes of being able to provide them a passage. As the cost has not been great, I hope Sir that you will do me the favour of their acceptance as a mark of my great veneration & respect. The climate of Virginia being nearer to that of Spain than the more Northern states, I think it not improbable that they will Succeed better there than to the Northward. At all events, they will be so beneficial an acquis[it]ion, should the climate prove favourable, that I think it is well worth the experiment; and I am satisfied that it will not be more fairly made by any persons, than by yourself sir & your patriotic & enlightened predecessor. In point of form the sheep are not better, if so well made, as the common Kind, but their wool is very much thicker, finer & softer. A hilly & arid soil is said to be the best suited to them, and I understand that they will require housing a[t] nights for seven or eight months in the year.

I have been favoured, from the department of State, with your able & patriotic message, to the two branches of the Legislature and the accompanying documents; and as an individual I highly approve of the firm & wise conduct of Government relative to Mr Jackson; and I am happy to add that my sentiments are in unison with the most of my Countrymen here. The unanimity of the Senate on the occasion does honor to that body and is a source of great satisfaction to me. I beleive that had our Countrymen at large discovered more of this disposition at an earlier period, it would have prevented the steps on the part of the British Government, which have led to the present state of things.

Upon a former occasion I expressed a desire of having an appointment in the Brazils,[2] but at forty sir I feel more disposed to content myself with a little than to encounter the risks of an unhealthy climate, in hopes to gain more; and I have entirely relinquished the wish of proceeding there. With sentiments of the highest respect I have the honor to be sir Yr very obliged & Mo: Ob: servt

WM JARVIS

Mrs Jarvis & myself must be allowed to present our respects to your worthy Lady.

RC (DLC: Rives Collection, Madison Papers).

1. France and Spain had long prohibited the export of merino sheep, but during the Peninsular War the Spanish Junta confiscated flocks belonging to defectors and sold them to raise funds. Jarvis bought between three and four thousand sheep for export to the U.S. (Mary Pepperell Sparhawk Jarvis Cutts, "Sketch of Mrs. William Jarvis," ed. Cecil Hampden Cutts Howard, *Essex Institute Historical Collections*, 24 [1887]: 135).

2. In a postscript to his 29 Jan. 1808 letter to JM (DNA: RG 59, CD, Lisbon), Jarvis had sought reassignment to Bahia (or Salvador), Brazil. He left Lisbon in the fall of 1810 and returned to the U.S.

From John Stark

SIR   DERRYFIELD 2 1. Jany 1810

I had the pleasure yesterday of receiving an address from the first magistrate of the only Republic on earth. This letter compliments me highly upon my services as a soldier, and praises my patriotism. It is true I love the country of my birth, for it is not only the country I should choose above all others; but it is the only spot where I could were[1] out the remnant of my days with any satisfaction.

Twice my country has been invaded by foreign enemies, and twice I went with the rest to obtain peace—and when the object was gained, I returned to my farm and my original occupation. I have ever valued peace so high, that I would not sacrifice it for any thing but freedom, yet, submission to insult I never thought the way to gain or support either.

I was pleased with your dismissal of the man[2] the English sent to insult us, because, they will see by the experiment that we are the same nation that we were in 76—grown strong by age, and having gained wisdom by experience.

If the enmity of this British nation is to be feared, their alliance is much more dangerous. For I have fought with them and against them and I found them treacherous and ungenerous as friends, and dishonourable as enemies. I have tried the French likewise, first as enemies and then as friends, and although all the strong parshalities of my youth were against them still I formed a more favourable opinion of them. But let us watch them.

However, among all the dangers that I have been witness of to our country and our "Republican Institutions" perhaps there is none that requires a more watchfull eye than our internal[3] British Faction.

If the communication of the results of my experience can be of any use in the approaching storm, or if any use can be derived from any example of mine—my strongest wish will be gratified.

The few days or weeks of the remainder of my life will be in friendship with James Madison.

JOHN STARK

RC (DLC: Rives Collection, Madison Papers). Cover dated Concord, New Hampshire, 25 Jan. Printed with JM's 26 Dec. 1809 letter to Stark in the Concord *N.H. Patriot*, 27 Feb. 1810, and other newspapers.

1. "Wear" in newspaper copies.
2. Francis James Jackson.
3. "Infernal" in some newspaper copies.

To Albert Gallatin

[ca. 22 January 1810]

A letter from Govr. Tyler answering an enquiry as to the $300 deposited in my hands to pay for the Sword purchased by Chan: Livingston, informs me, that the money was returned to Virga. & lies ready to be applied to its object.[1] That item of course in Mr. L.'s accts. may be struck out, and the charge pd. by a remittance from Va. I do not recollect the cost of the Sword; but if more than $300, the balance will ⟨be⟩ due from Va. not the U. S.

J. M.

RC (DLC). Marked by Gallatin, "For the Auditor." A note on the verso, dated 25 Jan. and signed by Richard Harrison (auditor of the treasury), stated the "Cost of the Swords, as charged by Mr. Livingston," at 1,389 livres, which at 108 sols per dollar, "the rate of exchange adopted in the setlement of his Accts:," amounted to $257.22.

1. See John Tyler to JM, 17 Jan. 1810.

§ To Congress. *22 January 1810.* Transmits "an account of the Contingent expenditures of the Government for the year 1809."

RC and enclosure, two copies (DNA: RG 233, President's Messages; and DNA: RG 46, Legislative Proceedings, 11A-E4). Each RC 1 p. Enclosure (1 p.) is an account signed by Joseph Nourse, register of the treasury, 16 Jan. 1810, showing $2,900 spent for chartering a schooner to return six American seamen from Trinidad, leaving an unexpended balance of $14,110 in the president's contingent fund. Also filed with House copy is Nourse to Gallatin, 26 Dec. 1809. Received by both houses and tabled by the Senate on 22 Jan. Referred to the House Ways and Means Committee on 23 Jan. (*Annals of Congress*, 11th Cong., 2d sess., 531, 1274).

§ To the Senate. *22 January 1810.* Transmits a report of the secretary of the treasury "on the subject of Disbursements in the intercourse with the Barbary Powers" in response to the Senate resolution of 27 Dec. 1809.

RC and enclosures (DNA: RG 46, Legislative Proceedings, 11A-E4). RC 1 p. Enclosures are Gallatin to JM, 16 Jan. 1810 (1 p.), transmitting accounts of expenditures, 1805–9 (153 pp.). Printed in *ASP, Miscellaneous*, 2:20–45.

From George Logan

MY DEAR FRIEND   STENTON Jany: 24th: 1810

By the mail of yesterday I received your obliging Letter of the 17th.[1] Your sentiments in favor of preserving our country in peace, at this momentous crisis, do honour to you as a statesman, and afforded me the most lively satisfaction.

The political and commercial interest of Great Britain, and the UStates, demands, that laying aside mutual jealousy and distrust; we should renew our negotiations with frankness candor, and forbearance. No Man is more sensible of the injurious acts of Britain towards our country, than I am. But we have reason to believe from fatal experience, that irritating acts, regulating & restricting commerce, will not lead to that solid state of peace, necessary to the happiness and prosperity of both countries.

I am disgusted with the miserable policy, and horrid barbarous warfare of the present day. By decrees, orders in council, and commercial restrictions, dastardly attacking the humble cottage, the comforts, the subsistence of unoffending women and children; instead of meeting in open &

honorable conflict the armed battalions of your enemy in the field. I wish my country, disdaining to follow this wretched system of France, & Britain; would remove every obstacle to peace; and appeal to the magnanimity, sound policy, and permanent interest of Great Britain. That country must be sensible, of the importance of our commerce to her, and must see the necessity of sacrifising minor temporary considerations; to extensive and permanent future objects; in which both countries are so deeply interested.

Permit me in deference to your better information, to recommend Mr: Onis to your more particular notice. The glorious cause of his country, which he is sent to represent, merits the good wishes and prayers of every virtuous mind.

Your dispatches for our minister in London entrusted to my care, I will take charge of with pleasure. I expect to take my passage in the British packet, which will sail from NYork, in about two Weeks. I am with sentiments of great respect Your friend

GEO LOGAN

RC (DLC); FC (PHi). FC in the hand of Logan's wife, Deborah Norris Logan.

1. JM's letter was dated 19 Jan.

From the Chairman of the Republican Meeting of Washington County, Maryland

SIR, HAGERSTOWN 25h. January 1810

In compliance with directions from a numerous and respectable Meeting of the Citizens of this County, I have the honor to transmit the enclosed proceedings of that Meeting, and to assure you that they contain their unfeigned sentiments and feelings, and, as I believe, of all the Citizens of the County, with but few exceptions.

I have much pleasure in informing you also, that the Meeting was composed of Citizens of both political parties, and notwithstanding their difference in opinion heretofore with respect to local Measures of the Government, there is not a doubt of their uniting, as on this occasion, in supporting the Constituted Authorities whenever our rights and priviledges as an independent Nation are assailed or threatened, or our Government insulted by any foreign power on Earth. With very high respect I have the honor to be Your Mo. Ob Servt.

N. ROCHESTER[1]

[Enclosure]

At a large and respectable meeting of Citizens of Washington County in the State of Maryland at the Court-House in Hagerstown on Saturday the 20h. January 1810, Nathaniel Rochester Chairman and Samuel Ringgold Secretary,

Messrs. Charles Carroll, Frisby Tilghman, Nathaniel Rochester, John Buchanan, Samuel Ringgold, John Bowles, William Downey, Otho H. Williams, Moses Tubbs, George G. Ross and George C. Smoot were appointed a Committee to draft resolutions in conformity with the object of the meeting, who withdrew, and after a short retirement returned and submited the following resolution,

Whereas in the opinion of this meeting, the present Crisis demands an expression of public feeling on the subject of our foreign relations, and, at a time when all the energies of the Nation may be required, the approving voice of the people is calculated to give confidence to the Government; therefore

Resolve unanimously that we highly approve the Spirited and dignified conduct of the Executive of the United States in repelling the wanton, unprovoked and unparalleled insult offered to the American Government and people, by Francis James Jackson Minister plenipotentiary of his Britanick majesty near the United States, and in declining to receive any further Communications from that functionary whatever may be the consequence.

And having full confidence in the Virtue and patriotism of the constituted authorities, we solemnly pledge ourselves, each to the other, to support the Government in such Measures as may be adopted to protect the interests, avenge the wrongs and maintain the independence of our Common Country, and should the unjust and piratical policy of the Belligerents of Europe terminate in War, we shall not, under existing circumstances deem that event the worst of evils; which after a spirited and appropriate address from Moses Tubbs Esquire, was unanimously adop[t]ed by the Meeting.

Resolved unanimously that the Chairman transmit the above proceedings to the President of the United States, with an assurance that they express the unfeigned sentiments and feelings of the Meeting

By Order
N. ROCHESTER, Chairman
SAML. RINGGOLD[2] Sec⟨y.⟩

RC and enclosure (DLC).

1. Nathaniel Rochester (1752–1831), a wealthy merchant, served as a Madison-Clinton elector in 1808. In 1810 he sold his Maryland holdings and moved to what is now Monroe

County in upstate New York. The city of Rochester, built on lands he purchased, is named in his honor (J. Thomas Scharf, *History of Western Maryland* [2 vols.; 1882; Baltimore, 1968 reprint], 2:1017).

2. Samuel Ringgold (1770–1829) became a brigadier general in the Maryland militia in July 1810 and served as a Republican congressman from Maryland, 1810–15 and 1817–21.

§ Presidential Proclamation. *25 January 1810, Washington.* On 2 Jan. the president, with the advice and consent of the Senate, ratified and confirmed the convention concluded at Vincennes on 26 Oct. 1809 between the U.S. and the Wea Indians. Requires all officeholders and citizens "faithfully to observe and fulfill" the convention.

Ms, two copies (DNA: RG 233, President's Messages; and DNA: RG 46, Executive Proceedings, 11B-C1). 3 pp. In a clerk's hand. Enclosed in JM's 28 Feb. message to Congress. Published in *National Intelligencer*, 23 Feb. 1810. The convention is printed in *ASP, Indian Affairs*, 1:762.

From Albert Gallatin

DEAR SIR   Jany. 26th 1810

Mr Harrison states that the swords purchased by Mr Livingston for the State of Virginia cost 257 dollars & $^{22}/_{100}$. In order to close the business, the easiest mode would be that you should write to Govr. Tyler to remit that sum to the Treasurer of the United States on account of Mr Livingston; which paymt. being passed to his credit will balance that item in his accounts. Govr. Tyler may, I think, obtain a draft from the Bank of Virginia on the Bank of Columbia, by which the remittance can be effected without risk.

A. G.

RC (DLC). Docketed by JM.

From Matthew Lyon

SIR   WASHINGTON Jany 26th. 1810

Had not Mr Brent came in & interupted our Conversation I should have mentioned some applications to me from Kentucky to Solicit the Appointment of Governor of Louisiana Territory Particularly one from John Rowan Esqr[1] in behalf of Joseph H Davies Esqr.[2] Mr Rowan calls Mr Davies an honest federalist, & presumes that you will have no Objection to Call forth tallents such as Mr Davies Possesses in the service of the Nation. Col Posey[3] whose character you must be acquainted with, & a gentleman by the Name of John Allen[4] of Burboun Cy desire to be named to you—supposeing that as Kentucky has had the last Territorial Governor it might be thought too much to ask for an other from there so suddenly I intended to Mention to you My old friend Judge Witherill[5] from Vermont who is now one of the Judges of the Michigan Territory. He is a man eminently calculated for a Station so arduous & difficult as that of Governor of a Territory, a Man of the right sort of Tallents to conciliate & reconcile the People to the Goverment, his family are not Moved to Detroit & would much more Willingly go to the Western Country, his letters to me shew that he would preferr it much. Governor Edwards wishes most sincerely to be transferred to Louisiana as he cannot have the benefit in Illinois of his Property in Slaves, he has Solicited me to use my interest to get him Transferd. & as his Situation would better Suit a Northern Man I intended to have mentioned Judge Witherill to you, I do not think any man in the Nation would better do the duties to be required of him, more effectually serve the Goverment, or give Greater Satisfaction to the people. I am very respectfully your obedt Servt

M Lyon

RC (DNA: RG 59, LAR, 1809–17, filed under "Davies").

1. John Rowan (1773–1843) was a Republican congressman, 1807–9, and U.S. senator, 1825–31, from Kentucky.

2. Joseph Hamilton Daveiss (or Davies; also Davis) (1774–1811), a native of Bedford County, Virginia, was married to John Marshall's sister and had served as U.S. district attorney in Kentucky. Daveiss was one of the first to accuse Aaron Burr of treasonable activities, but his charges were at first discounted because he was a Federalist. He was killed at the Battle of Tippecanoe in November 1811 (William B. Allen, *A History of Kentucky* . . . [Louisville, Ky., 1872], pp. 251–53; Malone, *Jefferson and His Time*, 5:237–38).

3. Thomas Posey (1750–1818) lived at The Wilderness in Spotsylvania County, Virginia, and served in the Continental line during the Revolution. John Dawson defeated him in the 1797 election for JM's vacated seat in the House of Representatives. Posey then settled in Kentucky, where he became active in state politics. Appointed a U.S. senator from Louisiana to fill a vacancy, he served for four months in 1812–13 but lost the subsequent election. JM then appointed him governor of the Indiana Territory (*WMQ*, 1st ser., 6 [1897–98]: 65; Philadelphia *Aurora General Advertiser*, 16 Dec. 1796).

4. John Allen (1749–1816), a native of James City County, Virginia, studied law in Charlottesville under George Nicholas and migrated to Kentucky in 1786. He served on the Bourbon County bench (*Biographical Encyclopedia of Kentucky* [1980 reprint], p. 289).

5. James Witherell (1759–1838) was a Republican congressman from Vermont, 1807–8, and a U.S. judge for the Michigan Territory, 1808–28.

From David Bailie Warden

PARIS, 26 January, 1810.

I have the honor of sending you by Captain Fenwick, a copy of Mr. Bottas' "*Storia della guerra americana*[":][1] this is a solid work, and is well written. The Author has been occupied with it more than three years. I had the honor of writing to you by the Ship *Madison*. I shall not, at present, renew the subject which so deeply interests me. I still hope that you will continue me here as Consul, if political circumstances admit of this appointment. The late orders of the Emperor concerning american vessels and their cargoes in Spain, and at Naples, are extremely hostile, and may prevent any speedy arrangement between this Country and the United States.[2] I trust, Sir, that the Attack of Coleman, and other federal Editors, for my defense of General Armstrong will not injure me in the opinion of the Executive and Senate.[3] As I do not see regular files of American Newspapers, I may not be acquainted with all that has been written against me. I have forwarded, for publication, by General Armstrongs' advice, a copy of the act of my naturalisation, with some remarks on Colemans' attack. The charge of my being a mere tool of the minister, which he so often repeats, will not be believed by those who know my principles, conduct and feelings. I have the honor, Sir, to be, with great respect, Your very obedient and very humble Servt

DAVID BAILIE WARDEN

P. S. Captain Fenwick will present you a Copy of the Imperial Almanack for the present year.

RC and duplicate (DLC); letterbook copy (MdHi: Warden Papers). Postscript omitted in duplicate and letterbook copy.

1. On Warden's enclosure, see Carlo Giuseppe Guglielmo Botta to JM, 12 Jan. 1810, and n.

2. On 19 Dec. 1809 Napoleon ordered the seizure of all American ships and cargoes in Spanish ports occupied by France (Napoleon to the prince of Neuchâtel, 19 Dec. 1809, Plon and Dumaine, *Correspondance de Napoléon Ier*, 20:78).

3. William Coleman, editor of the N.Y. *Evening Post*, attacked John Armstrong for dereliction in obtaining the release of Americans captured at sea and imprisoned in France. His article, "Villains Exposed," called Warden the principal defender of Armstrong, "having been so constituted and appointed by Armstrong himself, in place of some more deserving and proper man." Warden's defense of Armstrong, absolving the American minister of any responsibility for French mistreatment of an American sea captain, was included in the article. After a friend of Warden's threatened Coleman with legal action, the *Post* editor printed a bland but positive statement about Warden. This faint praise in a Federalist newspaper apparently irritated Armstrong, "and he even suspected Warden of working secretly to undermine him." Their relationship was strained thereafter (N.Y. *Evening Post*, 8 Nov. 1809; Skeen, *John Armstrong*, p. 114; Francis C. Haber, *David Bailie Warden: A Bibliographical Sketch* [(Washington), 1954], pp. 12–13).

§ From "Mucius" [John Randolph]. No. 2. *26 January 1810.* Asserts that France has espoused the cause of universal monarchy since the time of Louis XIV and its inherent power is dangerous to the liberties and peace of Europe. Laments that the king of England has been so stupid as "to break down every barrier which wisdom and genius could . . . build up against the universal despotism of the natural enemy of his country." The British Empire was a bulwark for human liberty until it was weakened by the rebellion of the American colonies, but Washington wisely perceived that "it could never be the interest of the United States to swell the power of France" by destroying the maritime strength of Great Britain. Praises Washington at length as a soldier and a statesman but dismisses his successors, John Adams and Thomas Jefferson, as "a rank Englishman" and "a finished Frenchman," respectively. Also insinuates that the appointment of John Quincy Adams as minister to Russia had "too much the appearance of a reward for apostacy" and looked "something like an under-hand mission to the great emperor, through *the little one.*"

Criticizes the secretary of state as "notoriously incompetent" and for his "ignorance" while secretary of the navy; declares that "every independent American" was insulted when JM submitted to the dictates that placed Smith in the State Department. Attacks the second general of the army [Wade Hampton] for his involvement in Yazoo frauds, pronounces James Wilkinson to be in the "last stage of putrefaction," and deplores the fact that the author of the Newburgh letters [John Armstrong] should represent the U.S. in France. Describes Armstrong as a "speculative parricide" and declares, "upon the faith of as respectable a gentleman as any in the United States," that the minister studied the arts of love and politics "in the school of Cambaceres" (which commits the "crime not to be named among Christians!").[1] Urges JM to dismiss them all and stresses the importance of America's remaining at peace with Great Britain.

Points out that JM is both "advanced in life" and "childless," therefore he should think of courting an "honourable fame" for posterity. Denies that Francis James Jackson insulted the U.S. and warns that the people of the nation cannot be driven "into the arms of France." Advises JM that the secretary of the treasury, though fallen from grace, can still be relied on for wisdom and ability in the government. Opposes the "infatuated predilection" of Republicans, such as Smith, Giles, and Varnum, for France; repeats his view that Great Britain, despite the follies of its government, is the last guardian of "the temple of human liberty and human safety." Cannot believe that JM is deceived by Napoleonic "cant of '*the liberty of the seas and commercial peace*'" and argues that France can still threaten the U.S. by retaking New Orleans. Does not believe that the failure of Burr's conspiracy is any guarantee for the security of Louisiana or cause for "public congratulation." The Constitution was destroyed, and the "criminal" escaped.

States that JM can still retrieve the situation and begs him to do his duty by giving his "naked, unbiassed opinion on the state of our affairs" and "what we have to expect." Above all, "save us from the fangs of France," so that Americans do not come to curse the price of their own independence if it should mean subservience to Napoleon's despotism. Admits that he is unwell and that he will be called "*Tory* and *friend of Great Britain,*" but it is his duty to express these opinions.

Printed copy (Washington *Spirit of 'Seventy-Six*, 26 Jan. 1810). Also printed in *Letters of Mutius* (Shaw and Shoemaker 20555).

1. This extraordinary allegation may have been Randolph's revenge for remarks Armstrong had made about the former's "*castrato* voice and *pathic* countenance" in a pamphlet the minister had written in Paris in 1806 (see Skeen, *John Armstrong*, p. 68).

From Willie Blount

Sir,   Knoxville Jany 28th. 1810

John Walker[1] a half breed Cherokee who resides on the eastern side of Highwassee river, in the neighbourhood of the Garrison in the Cherokee Nation, and who is an influential man in his Nation & who conducts himself well has requested me to represent to you that he and some of his friends have a wish to commence a trade to Mobile, and wishes your permission and protection to him and his associates to pass and repass with produce & goods from where he now lives thro' the Creek and Chickasaw Country. His rout will be up Highwassee to the mouth of Amoie, up it so high as to afford convenient portage from that river to Canasaugga, which portage will not exceed nine miles, thence down the navigable waters which lead to the navigable waters of Tombigbe and Mobile. He asks this because it may be that the Creeks and Chickasaws may not like it unless permitted by the President of the United States & thinks if he had his permission to do so that they would not find fault or be the least dissatisfied. I have the honor to be with perfect respect your Obt. Servant

WILLIE BLOUNT

RC (DNA: RG 107, LRRS, B-47:5). Docketed by a War Department clerk as received 22 Feb. 1810. On the cover Secretary of War Eustis has written "File—write Hawkins to give facility to Traders."

1. John Walker, the son of a Loyalist father and a Cherokee mother, rose to prominence as a leader of the eastern band of the Cherokee Indians. Related by marriage to the Indian agent Return Jonathan Meigs, Walker favored rapid acculturation between Indians and whites, and during the War of 1812 he raised a volunteer corps to fight with Andrew Jackson against the Creek Indians. He met JM in March 1816 while visiting Washington as a member of a Cherokee delegation. His subsequent support for the federal government's policy of Indian removal led to his murder after the meeting of the Cherokee National Council in August 1834 (William G. McLoughlin, *Cherokee Renascence in the New Republic* [Princeton, N.J., 1986], pp. 20, 60, 111, 115, 144, 157, 182, 188, 190, 193, 199, 204, 210; Woodward, *The Cherokees*, pp. 133, 169, 171–72, 177).

From Jared Ingersoll

DEAR SIR   PHILADELPHIA January 28t 1810

This Letter will be handed to you by my son Charles,[1] who is already known to you by correspondence and is desirous of the honor of being personally acquainted.

We are anxiously waiting the result of the deliberations of Congress, the general sentiment seems to be in favor of adopting measures to prepare for defence if necessary and then to wait for the intelligence of the temper manifested in the British Cabinet.

I suspect that if Mr. Macons Bill[2] was put to vote in this City, the Majority would be for rejecting it, nor do I believe that party discriminations would influence, or at least not draw the line between yeas & nays, there is I suppose an immense amount of American property abroad, the British possess such a naval Ubiquity, that nothing at Sea can escape their Fangs, when they are tempted to seize, nor are they always, it is said, over scrupulous on these occasions; however the subject is full of difficulty and in my retired way of life I have few means of information on affairs of a political nature. I am With great respect Sir Your obedient Servant

JARED INGERSOLL[3]

RC (DLC).

1. Charles Jared Ingersoll (1782–1862) was a Philadelphia lawyer who had sent JM in 1808 a copy of his widely circulated anti-British pamphlet, *A View of the Rights and Wrongs, Power and Policy, of the United States of America* (Philadelphia, 1808; Shaw and Shoemaker 15302). He later served in the House of Representatives during the Thirteenth Congress, after which JM, in February 1815, appointed him U.S. attorney for Pennsylvania. Ingersoll also became a close friend and frequent correspondent of JM's (Ingersoll to JM, 26 Nov. 1808 [DLC]; William M. Meigs, *The Life of Charles Jared Ingersoll* [Philadelphia, 1900], pp. 67, 88, 97).

2. On Macon's Bill No. 1, see JM to William Pinkney, 20 Jan. 1810, and n. 1.

3. Jared Ingersoll (1749–1822) served with JM in the Continental Congress and at the Federal Convention in 1787. A prominent Philadelphia lawyer, he had consulted JM while representing the plaintiff before the U.S. Supreme Court in *Hylton* v. *U.S.* (*PJM*, 16:219, 224, 231). He was later the Federalist vice-presidential candidate in the election of 1812.

From John Mitchell Mason

SIR,   NEW YORK 29 January 1810

I did myself the honour of calling to pay my respects the evening previous to my leaving Washington, but was not fortunate enough to find you at home.

Your note of the 12th. inst., with its enclosure, was handed to me immediately on my arrival at my own house, which was the latter end of last week. I pray you to accept my thanks for the obliging manner in which you were pleased to communicate so important a document.

In addition to the form of a constitution for the U. States, drawn up by Gen. Hamilton, which you gave me reason to expect when your leisure shall permit, may I, without using und⟨ue⟩ liberty, request such further materials for a co⟨rrect acco⟩unt of the Federal Convention [. . .] the promotion of my general object, as shall accord with your sense of propriety, and your perfect convenience?

I cannot cease to lament that a prior engagement precludes my access to that "curious & interesting" collection of papers which you possess relative to the Convention. If I rightly understood the matter, there is no other difficulty. Whether the gentleman to whom they are promised would consent to my perusal of them, or whether it would be expedient to ask his consent, are questions which I implicitly submit. But I need not express to you, Sir, the sense which I should entertain of the favour, were I allowed to inspect them.

Have the goodness to make my best regards agreeable to Mrs. Madison; and to accept the assurance of the consideration with which I have the honour to be Sir your most obliged hble servt

J. M. Mas⟨on⟩

RC (DLC); partial Tr (NN). RC torn. Docketed by JM. First and last paragraphs omitted from Tr.

From John Tyler

Dear Sir;   Richmond Jany. 29th 1810

Agreeable to your desire I have enclos'd a Draft on the Bank of Columbia for 257$ 22 Cts.[1] The balance remaining in our Bank I suppose may be applied to our State Use; but as I am uninform'd on the Subject except from you, I shall for a while suspend the Application of it.

Nothing new here, but that our assembly has the *Palsy* as well as Congress. However, this week resolutions[2] will be mov'd on the Subject of our *Friend Jackson*; how they will get on I know not, "so thick a mist has closed their visual rays." I am with sentiments of high respect yr very obt Servt.

Jno: Tyler.

RC (DLC).

1. No communication from JM to Tyler requesting the governor to remit this payment to the treasury has been found, but for the likelihood that JM did make the request, see Albert Gallatin to JM, 26 Jan. 1810.

2. The Virginia General Assembly approved joint resolutions—passed by the House of Delegates on 3 Feb. and by the Senate on 7 Feb.—that castigated Francis James Jackson's "unwarrantable and insidious appeal to the nation," declared that the handling of the imbroglio "has confirmed the general assembly of Virginia in the exalted opinion which they entertained of the justice and wisdom, the firmness, decision and patriotism of the present Executive of the United States," and pledged "to support the general government, in all such measures as may be deemed necessary for the defence of the rights, the interests, and the honor of the nation" (*Acts Passed at a General Assembly of the Commonwealth of Virginia, Begun . . . Fourth Day of December, 1809* [Richmond, 1810; Shaw and Shoemaker 21914], pp. 103–4; for earlier versions, see *Journal of the House of Delegates of the Commonwealth of Virginia, Begun . . . Fourth Day of December, 1809* [Richmond, 1810; Shaw and Shoemaker 21915], pp. 94, 99–100, 106; transcript of the House resolutions, 1 Feb. 1810 [ViU: Cabell Papers]; Richmond *Enquirer*, 6 Feb. 1810).

§ From Charles Haumont. *29 January 1810, Sapelo Island.* Fears that the book manuscript [mentioned in his 25 Apr. 1809 letter to JM] that he sent from Savannah on 5 July has miscarried. The president has not acknowledged it; hence his anxiety. His hope was that JM would recommend the work, for since illness and old age now plague him, he needs the benefits derived from a presidential endorsement. Refers to his services on behalf of American independence.

RC (DLC). 1 p. Written in French. Haumont claimed to have served aboard the French vessel *Concorde* during the Revolution (Haumont to JM, 25 Apr. 1809, *PJM-PS*, 1:137).

§ From Robert Williams. *29 January 1810, Lenox Castle, North Carolina.* Seeks appointment for his brother, Marmaduke Williams, who has moved to Madison County, Mississippi Territory. Since Congress is considering a new federal judgeship in that territory, hopes his brother can be considered. "Permit me the liberty to say that his family consists of a wife whom you know, five small children, and about 12 Slaves Clear of all incumbrance with a tract of land in that Country; and . . . he has totally forsaken" the dissipations in which he formerly indulged. Urges JM to act soon, for "no Court of high criminal Jurisdiction, has been holden in that County Since its formation. . . . Hence it is all important Such an appointment Should fall on a Man, whose Situation would inable him to hold the next Court which is by law appointed in april. . . . M Duke Williams would be on the Spot," and neither he nor "any of his Connexions are Concerned in any of the land Speculations in the U States Which is all important a Judge in that particular quarter Should be Clear of."

RC (DNA: RG 59, LAR, 1809–17, filed under "Williams"). 3 pp. Marked "(Private)" by Williams. Printed in Carter, *Territorial Papers, Mississippi*, 6:43–44. Robert Williams was a Republican congressman from North Carolina, 1797–1803, and governor of the Mississippi Territory, 1805–9. Marmaduke Williams succeeded to his brother's congressional seat, 1803–9, and was later active in Alabama state politics (Parsons et al., *United States Congressional Districts*, pp. 54, 55, 111, 112).

§ Executive Pardon. *29 January 1810, Washington.* JM grants "a full and entire pardon" to five enlisted men court-martialed at New Orleans and Terre aux Boeufs between April and July 1809 and sentenced to be "shot to Death."

Tr (DNA: RG 107, LSMA). 1 p.

§ Executive Pardon. *29 January 1810, Washington.* JM grants a general pardon to all army deserters who "shall within four months from the date hereof surrender themselves to the Commanding Officer" of a military post.

Tr (DNA: RG 107, LSMA). 1 p.

¶ From William Cushing. Letter not found. *29 January 1810.* Described as a one-page letter in the lists probably made by Peter Force (DLC, series 7, container 2).

To Alfred Madison

DEAR ALFRED   WASHINGTON Jany 30, 1810.

I have recd two letters from you witht being able sooner to acknowledge either. I shall be glad to hear from you occasionally, and hope you will not infer the contrary from my silence which may otherwise be well explained. I find nothing in the Newspapers last out worth sending you. I will however have the National Intelligencer regularly forwarded to you for the six ensuing months, and it may thence be continued if desired. For the present I enclose a copy of Mr. Fulton's exposition of his Torpedo War.[1] Perhaps a perusal of it may be amusing to the Bishop.[2] Present my affectte respects to him. Your Aunt is well & sends you with mine her affecte wishes.

JAMES MADISON

Typescript (ViU: Launcelot Minor Blackford Collection).

1. On Robert Fulton's *Torpedo War*, see Fulton to JM, Jan. 1810, and n.
2. The Right Reverend James Madison.

From William Eustis

Sir,   WAR DEPARTMENT January 30th. 1810

In obedience to a resolution of the House of Representatives of the 22 Instant,[1] I have the honor to transmit you the following returns, marked A. B & C.

A. Exhibits a General return of the troops of the United states composing the Military peace establishment and the Additional military force, specifying the particular force of each Regiment and Corps, taken from the latest returns received by the Adjutant and Inspector of the Army to the 28th. November 1809, to which is subjoined the present disposition of the General and Field Officers.

B. A return of the regular forces allotted for the defence of New Orleans, comprehending those of the military peace establishment on that station, and the Additional Military force ordered there on the 2d. December 1808.

C. The disposition and effective strength of the Additional Military force ordered for the defence of New Orleans, taken from the latest reports received at the Office of the Adjutant & Inspector of the Army, to which is subjoined a list of resignations, dismissals and deaths of Officers of the Army since the 1st. of January 1809.

The additional force ordered for the defence of New Orleans was detached from the several corps as they had been recruited; and arrived at that place between the 10th. of March and 20th. of April 1809. Leaving a Detachment in the City of New Orleans this Army moved and encamped at Terre au Boeuf on the Mississippi, fifteen miles below New Orleans, on the 8th. of June, where they remained until the month of September. In September they embarked for Natchez and in the month of October encamped near Washington, six miles in the rear of Natchez, at which place they hutted for the winter.

It must have been expected that the sickness and mortality incident to New troops in the summer and autumnal months would be aggravated by their removal to a more southern climate. The whole of this Detachment has been affected with disease; and the number of deaths will be found eventually to exceed those stated in the returns.

Since their removal to their present station, the latest advices state that they are convalescent. I have the honor to be very respectfully Sir Your Ob: Servt.

W. EUSTIS.

RC (DNA: RG 233, President's Messages); FC (PHi: Daniel Parker Papers); letterbook copy (DNA: RG 107, LSP). RC forwarded in JM's 1 Feb. message to the House of Representatives. Printed, with enclosures, in *ASP, Military Affairs*, 1:249–55.

1. For the 22 Jan. House resolution on the Terre aux Boeufs incident, see John Wayles Eppes to JM, 18 Jan. 1810, and n. 2.

§ From Benjamin Smith Barton. *30 January 1810, Philadelphia*. Introduces his nephew, W. P. C. Barton, who holds a naval commission and "will never disgrace the important station in which you have been pleased to place him."

RC (DLC). 1 p. Docketed by JM. Benjamin Smith Barton, the eminent botanist, had recommended William Paul Crillon Barton for appointment as a naval surgeon. JM nominated him in June 1809 (B. S. Barton to JM, 19 Mar. 1809 [DNA: RG 45, Misc. Letters Received]; *Senate Exec. Proceedings*, 2:123, 126).

§ From Albert Gallatin. *30 January 1810, Treasury Department*. Transmits "copies of the instructions issued at several times by this Department with respect to foreign armed Ships or vessels within the waters of the United States" in response to the 18 Jan. resolution of the House of Representatives.

RC and enclosures (DNA: RG 233, President's Messages). RC 1 p. In a clerk's hand, signed by Gallatin. Enclosures 15 pp. Enclosed in JM's 1 Feb. message to the House of Representatives. Printed in *ASP, Foreign Relations*, 3:339–40.

To the Chairman of the Republican Meeting of Washington County, Maryland

SIR   WASHINGTON Jany 31st. 1810

I have recd. your letter of the 25 enclosing the unanimous resolutions of a Meeting of Citizens of Washington County, at Hagers Town on the 20th. instant;[1] approving the course lately taken by the Executive of the U. S. with respect to the British Minister Plenipotentiary, and pledging their support of the Constituted Authorities, in such Measures as may be required by the unjust conduct of the Belligerent Powers. It must be agreeable at all times, to responsible & faithful functionaries, to find their proceedings attended with the confidence & support of their fellow Citizens. And the satisfaction cannot but be increased by unanamity [*sic*] in declarations to that effect. Among the means of commanding respect for our National character & rights, none can be more apposite, than proofs that we are united in maintaining both; and that all hopes will be vain, which contemplate those internal discords & distrusts, from which encouragement might be derived to foreign designs agst. our safety, our honor, or our just interests. Accept my friendly respects.

Draft (DLC).

1. Chairman of the Republican Meeting of Washington County, Maryland, to JM, 25 Jan. 1810.

From William Bentley

SIR,   SALEM 1 February 1810

With the utmost care I conveyed the Letter to General Stark, & tho' my importunity might be troublesome, it obtained for me a great pleasure. On the occasion, I find, the General has not so much of the Philosopher, as of the Good Old man. He felt with extasy, that he had a share in the affections of the man he reverenced as a rich Benefactor of his Country, & like Good Old Simeon, he pronounced, now lettest thou, thy Servant depart in peace. To impart his pleasure, is to enjoy it. To resist the wish of his heart, was to deny him a free draught from his overflowing cup of pleasure.

I have inclosed the Letters, which passed, that the documents might speak for themselves.[1] Let him do as seemeth to him good. He hopes to be useful to his Country, & a more sincere friend, no Country ever had.

I hope, Sir, that you will have a kind opinion of my acquiescence. I never had more pleasure than from the pure flame, as an unknown friend, I had assisted to kindle. Your Letter, Sir, has made a Good man happy. With the highest respect of your public & private Character, Sir, Your devoted Servant,

WILLIAM BENTLEY

RC and enclosures (DLC). RC docketed by JM. Enclosures are a copy of B. F. Stickney to Bentley, 29 Jan. 1810 (2 pp.), and an extract of Bentley's reply of 31 Jan. 1810 (1 p.).

1. In his 29 Jan. letter to Bentley, Stickney acknowledged Bentley's letter to him enclosing JM to John Stark, 26 Dec. 1809. Stickney wrote, "You suggest a doubt of the propriety of printing Mr. Madisons letter 'just at these electionering times.' Mr Madison's letter is so guarded, & so void of political considerations, that I think it removes the objection you mention, (that it may be said that it was written for electionering purposes)." Stickney added that Stark "has expressed a wish to have the correspondence published" but asked Bentley's opinion on the matter. Bentley's reply of 31 Jan. agreed to the publication of Stark's and JM's letters.

§ To the House of Representatives. *1 February 1810.* Transmits a report of the secretary of war in response to House resolution of 22 Jan.

RC and enclosures (DNA: RG 233, President's Messages). RC 1 p. Received by the House and referred to a select committee chaired by Thomas Newton, Jr., on 1 Feb.; ordered to be printed on 2 Feb. (*Annals of Congress*, 11th Cong., 2d sess., 1367, 1368). For enclosures, see Eustis to JM, 30 Jan. 1810, and n.

§ To the House of Representatives. *1 February 1810.* Transmits a report of the secretary of the treasury in response to House resolution of 18 Jan.

RC and enclosures (DNA: RG 233, President's Messages). RC 1 p. Received and tabled on 1 Feb. (*Annals of Congress*, 11th Cong., 2d sess., 1367). Printed in *ASP, Foreign Relations*, 3:338–40. For enclosures, see Gallatin to JM, 30 Jan. 1810, and n.

§ From John Mason and Others. *1 February 1810.* Recommends that Nathan Lufborough and Walter S. Chandler be appointed as magistrates for the northwest part of the county of Washington.

RC (DNA: RG 46, President's Messages, Executive Nominations, 11B-A2). 1 p. Signed by Mason and twenty-one others. On 6 Feb. 1810 JM nominated Lufborough and Chandler to be justices of the peace for Washington County in the District of Columbia. The Senate consented to the appointments on 7 Feb. (*Senate Exec. Proceedings*, 2:139).

§ From George Stevenson.[1] *1 February 1810, Pittsburgh.* Encloses vouchers for medical services he rendered that were disallowed by War Department. Although he admits that "public services should be rendered through regular channels, and by those duly authorized to perform the same," he believes an exception "has been justified by necessity." Precedents for such cases "are to be found in the Annals of our own Government." Under similar circumstances in 1801 his accounts were rejected by Secretary Dearborn, but President Jefferson "with a degree of promptness, highly honorable . . . directed immediate payment."

RC and enclosures (DNA: RG 107, LRRS, S-121:5). RC 3 pp. Docketed by a War Department clerk as received 25 May 1810. Enclosures, marked no. 1 and no. 2, are vouchers for $30 and $20, signed by Lt. Francis W. Small at Fort Fayette, and receipts for both amounts signed by Stevenson. Both enclosures are marked "Disallowed by order of the sect of War."

1. Probably George Stevenson, a veteran of the Revolution who settled in Pittsburgh in 1794. He also served as a major in the Tenth Infantry, 1799–1800 (Syrett and Cooke, *Papers of Hamilton*, 22:145, 146, 24:211 and n. 23).

From Thomas McKean

Private.

SIR, PHILADELPHIA. Febry. 3d. 1810.

Permit me to introduce to your acquaintance Henry Pratt Esquire,[1] an eminent merchant of this city, as my friend, and with whom I have a near family connexion: he is wealthy and a very benovelent [*sic*] citizen, and deservedly esteemed here. Mr; Pratt escorts Miss Elisa Pratt, his daughter, and Sophia Dorothea McKean, my daughter and only child in my family, to pay their respects to Mrs; Madison; for whom as well as yourself, my daughters Yrujo[2] & Sophia have always expressed the greatest regard and gratitude, for the attention you were always pleased to extend to them. They mean to spend a week or two at Washington.

I am now one of the Sovereign People, and have attended particularly the last year to my private affairs, which had been neglected for more than thirty;[3] and having nearly terminated that business, I now design to think of my former friends; for friendship may be compared to a fire, which, if neglected, will soon expire.

The commencement of your Administration has been as propitious as could have been reasonably expected, in a nation composed of not the wisest and best men in the world. You are sufficiently acquainted with the people you rule, to know, that little praise, but much unmerited censure is to be expected from them: An Angel from heaven could not command an universal approbation.

Every occurrence hitherto in the government of the Union meets my approbation, tho' the observations of some Members of Congress on different occasions have given me concern; and perhaps our nation⟨al⟩ affairs might have been managed better, but my greatest surprize is, that they have been managed so well. Tho' in a private station, and in an advanced age, beyond the average of human life (three score & ten) my mind is still too active to forgoe all concern for the happiness of my country; and under as full a consideration as I possess of our present situation, "I think it best to *suffer* crimes we want the power to *punish*."

Present my devoirs to Mrs; Madison, Mr; and Mrs; Cutts & the young folks, and accept my best wishes for your health, fame and fortune. I remain, Your Excellency's Most obedient humble servant

THOS M:KEAN

RC (NN: Emmet Collection). Cover marked, "Favored by Henry Pratt Esq."

1. Henry Pratt (1761–1838) was a prominent Philadelphia merchant who lived at Lemon Hill. He amassed a fortune in shipping, specializing "in the china and crockery trade, and afterward in the grocery business" (Scharf and Westcott, *History of Philadelphia*, 3:2212).

2. McKean's daughter and Dolley Madison's close friend, Sarah McKean, had married Carlos Fernando Martínez de Yrujo, the Spanish minister to the U.S., in 1798 (G. S. Rowe, *Thomas McKean: The Shaping of an American Republicanism* [Boulder, Colo., 1978], p. 300).

3. McKean had served in the Continental Congress with JM, 1781–83, as chief justice of Pennsylvania, 1777–99, and as the Republican governor of Pennsylvania, 1799–1808.

From John R. Smith

SIR   PHILADA: Feby 3d: 1810

Mr. Robert Smith[1] one of the Directors of the Bank of the United States who will hand this letter to you, is one of a Committee appointed by the Bank to proceed to the Seat of Government on the Subject of the renewal of their Charter.[2]

He wishes Sir to pay his personal respects to you, & to communicate his sentiments freely on a Subject much involving the financial interests of the United States & which he is not the less anxious to promote from his very early & continued exertions through our revolutionary Cause.

Not having the honor of a personal acquaintance with you he requested a line from me mentioning his name & the object of his journey & from my knowledge of his truly respectable character & the known liberality with which every thing tending to the public welfare will always be received by you, I have taken the liberty of furnishing him with this letter. With Sentiments of the highest respect I have the honor to be Sir your very obedt: servt.

JNO: R: SMITH[3]

RC (DLC). Docketed by JM.

1. Robert Smith was a merchant with premises at 58 South Front Street (Robinson, *Philadelphia Directory* [1811 ed.], p. 261).

2. The charter of the Bank of the United States was due to expire in 1811. The bank's stockholders, anxious about that prospect, petitioned Congress in 1808 for some reassurance. Gallatin thought their concern premature and urged a delay. His report of 3 Mar. 1809 recommended a renewal of the charter. "Congress then neglected the matter till January 1810, when the House considered it desultorily for a few weeks and in April dropped it" (Bray Hammond, *Banks and Politics in America from the Revolution to the Civil War* [Princeton, N.J., 1957], pp. 209–10).

3. John R. Smith, an attorney who lived at 53 Walnut Street, was the brother of Samuel Harrison Smith, editor of the *National Intelligencer* (Robinson, *Philadelphia Directory* [1811 ed.], p. 260; John R. Smith to JM, 29 Jan. 1808 [DLC]).

To John Mitchell Mason

SIR   WASHINGTON Feby. 5. 1810

I have recd. your letter of the 29th. January. The Form of a Constn. delineated by Genl. Hamilton, & put by him into my hands, being among my papers in Virga. a copy of it cannot be furnished till I shall have made a trip thither. I shall then not fail to make good my promise.[1] The general mass of manuscript materials which I possess relative to the Convention, being under the circumstances intimated to you, I must yield to the restraint they impose;[2] notwithstanding my confidence in your capacities to do justice to them, & the additional motive to comply with your wishes which I might find in the delicacy wth. which they are manifested.[3] Of the various printed Materials, which are connected with your object, I recollect none, that are not probably already known to you, or that do not lie within the sphere of your obvious researches. Should any not within this description occur to me, I shall take a pleasure in referring you to them. Accept my respects.

J. M

Draft (DLC); partial Tr (NN).

   1. JM made a considerable effort to fulfill his promise to Mason, writing to both Jefferson and John Wayles Eppes in the summer of 1810. He did not find the copy of the document Mason sought and evidently wrote two letters to Mason (not found) to inform him of this failure. JM found the copy of Hamilton's plan some years later (JM to Jefferson, 17 July 1810; John Wayles Eppes to JM, 1 Nov. 1810; Mason to JM, 20 Dec. 1810 [DLC]; William Eustis to JM, 28 Apr. 1819 [DLC]; see also Henry D. Gilpin, ed., *The Papers of James Madison* . . . [3 vols.; Washington, 1840], 3: appendix, p. xvi).

   2. Tr ends here.

   3. JM jealously guarded his Federal Convention notes and later declared a desire to have their publication "be a posthumous one" (JM to John G. Jackson, 28 Dec. 1821, Madison, *Writings* [Hunt ed.], 9:71).

§ From the Democratic Meeting of Muskingum County, Ohio. *5 February 1810, Zanesville.* Resolutions express regret at "accumulated aggressions and insults from the Government of Great Britain" in the face of JM's "forbearance and pacific overtures." Meeting approves of president's action regarding Francis James Jackson and declares "fullest confidence in the wisdom and integrity of the constituted authorities of our general Government (the government of our choice)."

Ms (DLC). 3 pp. Signed by Jesse Foulton, chairman, and S. Herrick, secretary. Docketed by JM.

From William Woods

WASHINGTON Feby. 6th. 1810

William Woods Grocer of Baltimore having some time since had the pleasure of Presenting a cheese made in the place where the Noted Mammoth cheese was made to that great and good Man Thos. Jefferson Esqr. late president of the U. S. and also the honour of his Acceptance thereof[1]

   Now presents his best respects to James Maddison President of the United States of America and begs he will please accept of a Cheese Made in the above Neighbourhood as a toke[n] of respect he wishes to Shew him as the Cheif Magistrate of A Great Free and Independant Nation who as an Individual Anticipates by hope that you will fully discharge the all Important duties of your Office so that you may always have the Devine approbation as well as of all good Men and the more so at this Momentous Crisis.

RC (DLC). Docketed by JM.

1. On 1 Jan. 1802 the citizens of Cheshire, Massachusetts, presented Jefferson with a cheese weighing 1,235 pounds as a token of their affection (Malone, *Jefferson and His Time*, 4:106–7).

From Samuel Kercheval

SIR   STEPHENSBURG FREDK. CY VA. Feby 7th. 1810

I have taken the liberty of encloseing to your care, a subscription for the purpose of raising money to enable the Trustees at this place to proceed with the buildings already began.[1]

I am aware Sir, that you are probably too frequently applied to on subjects of this nature, and that such multitudes of applications are disagreeable and even irksome *to you.* I however flatter my self, that you will pardon the trouble this may give you; when I assure you, that nothing but my ardent wish for the success of the institution could induce me to take the liberty of applying to you on a subject of this kind.

If you should deem it proper to patronize the institution, any contributions from either yourself or your friends, will be gratefully received by the Trustees. I have the honor to be Sir Your Most Obt. Sert.

SAML KERCHEVAL[2]
Secy to the Trustees

RC (DLC). Docketed by JM. Enclosure not found.

1. Kercheval had also solicited funds from Jefferson for an academy at Stephensburg (now Stephens City) in Frederick County. He sent a "blank subscription paper" to the former president, who declined to contribute (Kercheval to Jefferson, 28 Sept. 1809, Jefferson to Kercheval, 15 Jan. 1810 [DLC: Jefferson Papers]).

2. Samuel Kercheval (1786–1845) ran for Congress in 1824 and represented Hampshire County in the Virginia House of Delegates, 1828–30 (Samuel Kercheval, *A History of the Valley of Virginia* [4th ed.; Strasburg, Va., 1925], p. 5).

From William Short

The present is merely to acknowlege the reciept & thank you for the kind expressions of your letter of Dec. 3. I shall add nothing more to this letter hoping very soon to have the satisfaction of renewing to you in person the assurance of my sentiments. I informed the sec. of State last summer on receiving his letter that I should return this spring.[1] If there had not been an hope of some amelioration in the relations of the U S. with this country I should have returned in the Winter as you will have been informed by Mr Coles. At the sailing of the Wasp in Septr. the same consideration did not exist, but I was desirous to postpone my voyage to a more favorable season for navigation—& that alone prevented my embarking in that vessel. The season will soon be more favorable—but the difficulties of finding a vessel increase in such a manner that I am hastening now to take my precautions. The J. Adams will be at sea during the worst month of the year, & therefore I decline making use of that vessel. We have just learned that the English have taken the Madison & brought her back to England. Genl. Armstrong thinks therefore that the two vessels now at La Rochelle, which came with passengers & a British passeport for the voyage here will not be respected on the return voyage. Under all these circumstances I am advised to go immediately from hence to England of which an opportunity is furnished me, as I am assured that there will be better & more safe conveyances from thence even [if] the breach be still more widened—on which subject we are impatiently expecting information. Count Pahlen[2] who has passed the winter here, thinks of embarking in April in one of the passenger vessels at La Rochelle—he has no other alternative & therefore is forced notwithstanding the inconvenience apprehended from the number of passengers, & the risk now from the English cruisers. I wish much he may arrive safe, being persuaded you will have every reason to be satisfied with him & his disposition as well as those of his Sovereign of which you have already proofs.

May I ask the favor of you sir to forward the inclosed, & to believe me when I assure you of the perfect respect, & best wishes for your success & happiness, with which I have the honor to be sir, your most obedient & Most humble Servant

W Short

RC (DLC).

1. Short left France for England in February 1810 and returned to the U.S. in July 1810.

2. Count Fedor Petrovich Pahlen (1780–1863) took up his duties as Russian minister to

the U.S. in June 1810 (Nina N. Bashkina et al., eds., *The United States and Russia: The Begin-nings of Relations, 1765–1815* [Washington, 1980], pp. 1113, 1136).

From John Strode

WORTHY SIR   CULPEPER VA. 7th February 1810
In dayly expectation (since the rect. of your favourable Letter of the 26th. of October last) of seeing here the manager of Your Orange Estates (Mr. Gideon Gooch) in order that He and I might have made the proposed Arangements for the debt wherewith You have so long indulged me; but as Yet not having seen or heard from him, have lost all hopes. Otherwise should not have presumed at this critical conjuncture to draw off for a single moment your attention from National concerns—but pray pardon me Sir, I am become most extremely unhappy on the Occasion, the more especially as I have not the money, and hope as you once kindly hinted, that on Security being properly made, you will be good enough to extend your Lenity untill another Crop comes in, or untill I can make sale of something to raise the Money.

I have in the County of Fauquier within 16 or 18 Miles of Falmouth a piece of about 170 Acres of Unincumbered Land which I think will secure that debt as I shall not fail to Lessen it by degrees as expeditiously as I can, a mortgage shall be made to you for that, and our representative in Congress Mr Love, who is an attorney at Law residing at Fauquier Ct. House shall see it duly executed and of record, and note you thereof.

Robert B. Voss esquire[1] my neighbour who has some business at the metropolis has politely offerd to do me the favour, if you please to approach your hand with this Letter, and to bring me an Answer if you have Leisure to honor me with half a line.

Mr Voss has inform'd me that He would gladly beg leave at this portentious time to offer his service to his Country in any department Civil or military, where He can be most usefull, for almost any of those places few are better qualified. He has been educated to and pursued the practice of the Law with Celebrity and at this time has a considerable share thereof at the Bar of this and the neighbouring Counties. He possesses an extraordinary beautifull and productive clear Estate, so that a patriotic view must be his only motive. He is and ever has been a firm republican, but few of our Citizens in this part of the Country in the private walks of life has more Ardently or more effectually on all occasions supported our rights flowing from that political principle than he has done and most un-doubteded [*sic*] will do in all places and times & Occasions where it may fall to his Share. He is Active persevering Spirited & interprising with a high Sence of rectitude & honor. With all due respect & regard I am Sir Yr. most Obdt. hble Sert.

JOHN STRODE

RC (DLC). In an unidentified hand, except for Strode's complimentary close and signature. Cover marked by Strode, "Robert B Voss Esquire."

1. Robert B. Voss was a Culpeper County householder with four dependents. He owned twenty slaves in 1810 (DNA: RG 29, Third Census, Virginia).

To George Clinton

Feby. 8. 1810

J. Madison presents his respects to the Vice President, & incloses a letter inadvertently opened some time since; the error being just now discovered.

RC and enclosure (DNA: RG 46, TP, Indiana). Enclosure (7 pp.) is Elias McNamee to the president of the Senate, 12 Dec. 1809. Enclosure printed in Carter, *Territorial Papers, Indiana*, 7:682–86.

§ From John Wayles Eppes. *8 February 1810, Washington*. Upon learning that Mr. Graham has declined the governor's post in Louisiana has decided to suggest Col. Benjamin Howard as "peculiarly well calculated for a station where military as well as civil Talents may be important." The suggestion is made without Howard's knowledge, but that officer's name came to mind since Louisiana is "a station . . . surrounded by hordes of hostile savages." Howard's early experience as an Indian fighter and as a volunteer with General Wayne affords him "a perfect knowledge of Indians."

RC (DNA: RG 59, LAR, 1809–17, filed under "Howard"). 2 pp. Printed in Carter, *Territorial Papers, Louisiana-Missouri*, 14:374. Shortly after receiving this note, JM may have authorized Eppes to sound out Howard about his accepting the position (see Eppes to JM, ca. 12 Feb. 1810).

§ From an Unidentified Correspondent. *8 February 1810, Philadelphia*. Warns JM to expect "ill treatement" after the return of Francis James Jackson to Great Britain. Offers advice on preparations for war.

RC (DNA: RG 107, LRRS, A-22:5). 1 p. Signed "A friend of this country." Docketed by a War Department clerk as received 12 Feb. 1810.

From Samuel Carswell

SIR   PHILADA. Feby 9th. 1810

An observation has occured to me, on the subject of Mr. Macon's Bill, that I do not recollect having seen, in the debates of Congress, or elsewhere. As, in my opinion, it involves the dearest Interests of our Country, I would consider myself extremely reprehensible, were I to neglect stating it, to Your Excellcy. You will therefore have the goodness, to excuse the liberty I have taken, in addressing you, on the present occasion.

In the Seventh Article, of the Treaty of Cession of the territory of Louisiana, to the United States, by France, it is agreed, "that the French Ships coming directly from France or any of her Colonies, laden with the produce or Manufactures of France or her said Colonies, shall be admitted during the space of Twelve years in the ports of New Orleans, & all other legal ports of entry within the ceded territory, in the same manner as the Ships of the United States coming directly from France, or any of her colonies." This privilege is also extended, to the commerce of Spain.

It appears to me, that Mr. Macon's Bill, in its present shape, is an absolute violation of the above Article, of that treaty, & whether (if it were to pass into a Law) it would not involve the United States in a war with France, or afford that power, a pretext for reclaiming that portion of the territory of the United States, time will discover.

I feel no apprehension, that this will be considered as an improper interference, in Affairs of State, as your own experience of the solicitude, that a friend to his Country entertains for its welfare, will enable you to attribute it, to its proper cause. With the Sentiments of greatest esteem I am Your Ob Hble St

SAML CARSWELL[1]

RC (DLC). Docketed by JM.

1. Samuel Carswell was a merchant with premises at 52 Chestnut Street. In July 1812 JM nominated him to be commissary general for the U.S. Army (Robinson, *Philadelphia Directory* [1811 ed.], p. 56; *Senate Exec. Proceedings*, 2:281).

§ To the House of Representatives. *9 February 1810.* Transmits the secretary of state's report in response to House resolution of 22 Jan.

RC and enclosure (DNA: RG 233, President's Messages). RC 1 p. Enclosure (4 pp.) is a report of 8 Feb. 1810, signed by Robert Smith, concerning American efforts since 1801 to provide free access to Mobile harbor and to protest Spanish duties of 12 percent exacted on U.S. commerce clearing the port. Received and tabled on 9 Feb.; referred to a select committee on 24 Feb. Printed in *ASP, Foreign Relations*, 3:341.

§ From Robert Brent. *9 February 1810, Washington.* Recommends two lieutenants for appointment as military district or regimental paymasters, in accordance with the peace establishment act of 1802. Has consulted secretary of war concerning the vacancies and asks JM "to signify your assent at the foot of this letter" if he approves the nominations.

RC (NjP: Crane Collection). 3 pp. Endorsed by JM, "The appts. approved." Brent was paymaster general of the army, 1808–19 (Heitman, *Historical Register*, 1:242).

§ From "Leontius."[1] No. 1. *9 February 1810.* Warns JM of the dangers of being too mild-mannered and virtuous for his own good. Refers JM to a letter "which bears the mark of genius" and begs him not to disregard its contents as "the raving of one stung with disappointment and brooding over the extinction of ambitious hopes."[2] The letter "contains facts which speak with a force not to be resisted. . . . The character of the men who surround you are [*sic*] eloquently described." Urges JM to "assume a firmness and energy not originally your own, & evince to America and the world that you are not the humble tool of a faction."

Declares that events have rendered irrelevant the differences between Democrats and Federalists. Those who formerly advocated French liberty are now the admirers of French despotism, and Democratic editors have transferred their "love for pure republican institutions" to "one of the most unqualified arbitrary governments that have trampled down the liberties of mankind." Cites the case of those so-called Republicans who justified Napoleon's recent usurpation of the Spanish crown. Cannot believe JM approves of the views and measures of this faction but fears that he is "irresistibly borne along by the tide that bouyed [*sic*] you up to your present elevation." Asserts JM is superior to those who placed him at the head of the administration but he is "excelled by them in all the low arts of intrigue and cunning." Exhorts him therefore to "break the Lilliputian ties by which you are bound, and no longer give your sanction to measures that disgrace the signature of Publius."

Adduces JM's appointment of Robert Smith to the Department of State as evidence of his subservience to a faction. Asks why "the venerable Genevan [Gallatin] was put aside to make way for this mushroom statesman." Claims Robert Smith is "but one among a very numerous connection who pant . . . for power. . . . Even now they look proudly on the presidential seat, and envy you that station." The history of France proves the danger of entrusting too much power to a single family; assumes, despite Napoleon's mistreatment of "an American lady of unparalled beauty"[3] who married his brother, that the French emperor will use her American relatives to advance his interests. The Smith family and their supporters will not be able to resist the temptation of titles and pensions. Warns JM not to be deceived by the recent retirement of one of their number[4] from Congress to his farm in Virginia. Hints that this gentleman aspired to replace Gallatin in the Treasury Department but urges JM to leave him in Virginia and to allow "the shades of retirement [to] thicken around him."

Has no personal quarrel with the Smith family, but will always protest "against abandoning to a few ambitious men, the dearest interests of my country."

Printed copy (Washington *Spirit of 'Seventy-Six*, 9 Feb. 1810).

1. The identity of "Leontius" is uncertain, but the style and the contents of his letter bear obvious similarities to the pieces written by John Randolph under the signature of "Mucius." The use of a Greek pseudonym in an essay that, among other things, lamented the decline of "Roman" virtues in American society might suggest that if Randolph did write this letter, the editor of the *Spirit of 'Seventy-Six* chose his signature, as had been the case with Randolph's first "Mucius" letter published under the signature of "Philo-Laos."

2. See the first letter of "Mucius" to JM under the signature of "Philo-Laos," 12 Jan. 1810.

3. Elizabeth Patterson.

4. Wilson Cary Nicholas.

§ From Thomas B. Johnson. *11 February 1810, New Orleans.* Thanks JM for his "flattering sanction given to the recommendation of my friends" who have urged his reappointment as postmaster at New Orleans. Expresses gratitude for "this mark of your personal approbation."

RC (DLC). 1 p. Johnson was John Quincy Adams's brother-in-law (*PJM-PS*, 1:152 nn.).

From James Campbell and Others

SIR   KNOXVILLE February 12th. 1810

In the Year 1807 the General Assembly of Tennessee established a College in the Vicinity of this Place and at the same time endowed it with the profits arising from the proceeds of the Sale of one half of the Land appropriated by an Act of Congress of the United States for the Support of Two Colleges one in East and the other in West Tennessee.[1] If East Tennessee College had the Necessary buildings Library Apparatus &c. it is believed the funds thus derived from the General Government together with some other funds belonging to the College would be sufficient to defray the expence of conducting the Institution in a manner which would render it immediately as well as highly useful to the public—to procure money sufficient to defray the expence of buildings a Library &c. the Legislature at their last session passed an Act authorising a Lottery of which we are appointed Trustees. In pursuance of the Trust thus reposed in us we have devised a Scheme of the first Class, and are using our best exertions to make Sale of the Tickets. As this Seminary has been thus indirectly endowed by the United States we believe we should not discharge the duty assigned us, if we did not take an early opportunity to solicit your Aid in the Cause of Literature.

We have asked the favor of the Honble. Joseph Anderson one of our Senators[2] to supply your Excellency with as many Tickets as you will have the Goodness to receive.[3] We have the Honor to be With Sentiments of great Respect Your Excellency's Most Obedient Servants

> JAMES CAMPBELL
> H. WHITE
> THOS MCCORRY
> ROBT CRAIGHEAD
> JOHN N. GAMBLE

RC (DLC). Docketed by JM.

1. The 1806 federal law conveying public lands to Tennessee set aside one hundred thousand acres for the endowment of two state colleges (*U.S. Statutes at Large*, 2:382).

2. Joseph Anderson (1757–1837) was a Republican U.S. senator from Tennessee, 1797–1815, and first comptroller of the treasury, 1815–36.

3. No reply from JM to this solicitation has been found, and the East Tennessee College lottery failed. The trustees sent a similar letter to Jefferson, who declined to promote the lottery scheme but set forth his ideas on university buildings and "an academical village" that he later implemented at the University of Virginia (Philip M. Hamer, "The East Tennessee College Lottery," *Tennessee Alumnus*, 9 [1925]: 7–12).

§ From John Wayles Eppes. *Ca. 12 February 1810.* Informs JM that "Colo: Howard will accept the appointment." Suggests that unless the public interest requires an immediate nomination, a delay would be prudent, since Howard is reluctant to deprive his constituents of his vote on important matters still pending before the House.

RC (DLC). 1 p. Dated "Monday Morning." Conjectural date assigned here on the basis that 12 Feb. was the first Monday after 8 Feb., when Eppes had communicated with JM on the subject of Howard's nomination. Benjamin Howard resigned as a congressman from Kentucky on 10 Apr., JM nominated him as governor of the Louisiana Territory on 17 Apr., and the Senate confirmed his appointment the following day (*Senate Exec. Proceedings*, 2:145, 146).

§ From George Harris. *12 February 1810, Philadelphia.* Offers to furnish a plan to fortify and defend the coast at "Small Expence and in a Very Short time." Admits that his understanding of the subject is based on experience in South Carolina and that he has no personal knowledge of ports east of New York. Assumes in New York the requirements of his plan would be more than double what they would be anywhere else. Believes he could execute his plan in New York with three hundred laborers, thirty mechanics, and twenty to thirty large rowboats within twenty to thirty days. Gives an account of his Revolutionary War service in Charleston where he worked on Forts Johnston and Moultrie. In Philadelphia he has been manager of the Schuylkill Bridge and is currently keeping a boardinghouse at 295 Market Street.

RC (DNA: RG 107, LRRS, H-29:5). 4 pp. Docketed by a War Department clerk as received 15 Feb. 1810. JM evidently instructed the secretary of war to obtain details of

Harris's plan, which the latter forwarded on 8 Mar. 1810 (Eustis to Harris, 15 Feb. 1810 [DNA: RG 107, LSMA]).

From Walter Jones

Wednesday [ca. 14 February 1810] ½ after 1. o Clock
CONGRESS HALL.

Mr. Roxas[1] has this moment delivered the inclosed, and proposes waiting upon the president this Evening—he goes in the Carriage with Mrs. La Trobe, and as W. Jones[2] may not be at hand to present him, he conceives he cannot better fulfill the Civility injoined upon him by the Letter of doctor Rush, than by forwarding with his Compliments, the Letter beforehand.

RC and enclosure (DLC). RC dated ca. 6 Feb. 1810 and mistakenly attributed to Joseph Roxas in *Index to the James Madison Papers*. Conjectural date here assigned since the second Wednesday of February 1810 was the fourteenth day of that month. The enclosure, Benjamin Rush to Jones, 6 Feb. 1810, Philadelphia (2 pp.), introduced Joseph Roxas as "a native of the city of Mexico . . . And an enemy to Superstition in Religion. In consequence of the latter, he is a voluntary exile from his native Country."

1. Roxas attended Rush's lectures in Philadelphia during November and December 1809, published an article in a New York medical journal, and in May 1811 established a school of mathematics in New Orleans (George W. Corner, ed., *The Autobiography of Benjamin Rush* . . . [Princeton, N.J., 1948], p. 287 and n. 27).
2. Walter Jones (1745–1815) studied medicine at the University of Edinburgh with Rush, 1766–69. He became acquainted with JM while serving as a Virginia state senator, 1785–87, and representing Northumberland County in the Virginia ratifying convention of 1788. He was a Republican congressman, 1797–99 and 1803–11 (Thomas A. Mason, "'The Luminary of the Northern Neck': Walter Jones, 1745–1815," *Northern Neck of Virginia Historical Magazine*, 35 [1985]: 3978–83).

From Edmund Randolph

MY DEAR SIR   RICHMOND february 14. 1810

Mr. Thomas L. Preston,[1] my son in law, being Edmonia's husband, purposes to visit Washington. I take the opportunity of renewing to you by him my perfect assurances of being ever Your affectionate friend

EDM: RANDOLPH

RC (DLC).

1. Thomas L. Preston (d. 1812) represented Rockbridge County in the Virginia House of Delegates, 1806–11 (Richmond *Enquirer*, 18 Aug. 1812; Swem and Williams, *Register*, p. 419).

§ From Robert Smith. *14 February 1810, Department of State*. Relays to JM for transmittal to House of Representatives copies of various documents related to the House resolution of 5 Feb. requesting the orders and decrees of France and Great Britain "violating the lawful Commerce and Neutral Rights of the United States, except such parts, as may, in his Judgment, require secrecy."

RC and enclosures (DNA: RG 233, President's Messages). RC 2 pp. In a clerk's hand, signed by Smith. For enclosures, see JM's 17 Feb. message to the House. Printed in *ASP, Foreign Relations*, 3:341–43.

From an Unidentified Correspondent

SIR—   WASHINGTON Feby 15th. 1810

I have taken the liberty to call your attention to certain Strictures contained in the 2d & 3d columns of the second page in the inclosed news paper.[1] To you Sir the Nation has a right to look for an honest upright man at the head of the Treasury department.

The People of the United States have not only a right to expect Sir, that the high officer to whom you entrust the management of all the Nations great pecuniary concerns be honest; but they have a right to think that he like Ceasars wife ought to b⟨e⟩ unsuspected.

In the Columns I alude to the Secretary of the Treasury is charged, with haveing made use of "the opportunities his station affords him to spe⟨c⟩ulate in the funds for his individual benefit." With haveing "availed himself of the same opportunities to become proprietor of lands which have been sacrificed by the Artful representations of the man who purchased from the public." With haveing wrongfully drained the Country of hard cash to remit to Holland for the payment of the interest of the Dutch debt. With haveing amassed a fortune of 200,000 dollars in Eight years. This I say Sir is what no American Secretary of the Treasury can honestly do while the law forbids him to be a Merchant—beside all these charges suspicion is excited that the Secretary will for personal considerations favor the bank of the US in obtaining ⟨a⟩ Charter.

The People of ⟨the Uni⟩ted States Sir cannot with patie⟨n⟩ce wait (the issue of a Suit brought for Sland⟨er⟩) for the illucidatio⟨n⟩ of a subject so importan⟨t⟩ to them, they will say with one voice, "if Mr Galatin is the man the writer depicts him, the Nations treasure is not one moment safe in his hands." At this time I know of no one inclined to commence a process of impeachment against him.

In these circumstances there is something in your power ⟨to⟩ do Sir, which will either lead to an establishment of those charges or to the satisfaction of the Nation by ample refutation. It is in your power Sir to order an effectual enquiry for the Author of the publication, and to have him called upon ⟨to⟩ give the clues to the substantiation of those ⟨hi⟩gh ch⟨arg⟩es o⟨r⟩ publicly to renounce them, and if [. . .] prove to be a vile slanderer and a [. . .] of the publ⟨ic?⟩ offices it will be in yo⟨ur power?⟩ to order him per[. . .] station he enjoy⟨s⟩ [. . .].

I am [. . .]

RC (NHi: Gallatin Papers). Docketed by a clerk, "Anonymous to President." The last of the three pages has been heavily damaged. The editors are grateful to the New-York Historical Society Manuscript Department for a reading of the damaged section. Enclosure not found, but see n. 1.

1. The enclosure was an article signed "Camillus" from the Richmond *Va. Argus* of 2 Feb. 1810. The author (probably John B. Colvin, formerly the editor of the Washington *Monitor* who had been employed by Robert Smith in the State Department since 1809) alleged that Gallatin used his post for personal gain. On 19 Feb. New York Federalist Barent Gardenier read the article into the record in the House of Representatives and called for an inquiry, but his proposal was rejected by a 106–7 vote. Some three weeks later Robert Smith inserted a note in the *National Intelligencer* stating that he knew nothing about the attack on Gallatin, that he had no hand in it, and that the article had not originated in the State Department (Brant, *Madison*, 5:131; *Annals of Congress*, 11th Cong., 2d sess., 1414–23; *National Intelligencer*, 14 Mar. 1810).

From Albert Gallatin

SIR,   TREASURY DEPARTMENT February 16th. 1810.

I have the honor to enclose a Statement transmitted by the Collector of Boston, in relation to the ship Arno which entered Tonningen with a forged Sea Letter.[1]

Exclusively of the cases respecting forged marine papers which have from time to time been communicated by the Department of State, one only has come to the knowledge of the Treasury, the particulars of which are explained by the enclosed letter from the Collector of New York, and the papers accompanying the same. I have the honor to be, with the highest respect Sir, Your obedient Servant

ALBERT GALLATIN

RC and enclosures (DNA: RG 233, President's Messages). RC in a clerk's hand, signed by Gallatin. For enclosures, see JM's 17 Feb. message to the House.

1. The *Arno* was carrying a cargo belonging to Stephen Higginson, a prominent Boston merchant and member of the so-called Essex Junto.

From John Barker

Sir   Phia feby. 17. 1810.

I have the honor to send herewith an address and resolutions which were Unanimously adobted by some thousands of the Citizens of the first Congressional District of pensya. in Genaral meeting assembled at the State house yard on the 14th inst.[1]

I have particular Satisfaction in embracing this opportunity to tender to you my Sincere and respectfull good wishes for the prosperity of your admidstration, and that it may as Efectualy promote the honor and best intrest of our Country as your patriotism Can Desire.

Axcept the assurances of my Afectionate respect and beleive me to be personaly and politicaly truely and Sincerely your freind and fellow Citizen

John Barker[2]

[Enclosure]

The Republican Citizens of the first Congressional district of the State of Pennsylvania,[3] Conceive it will not be unacceptable to you as the first magistrate of a free people, to receive the sincere assurances of their confidence & Attachment to the principles which have distinguished your political life; but above all Since you have Succeeded to the chair So happily filled, for two terms, by a man who it is your mutual honour to have been unshaken friends, and who is the ornament of his Country and the pride of his fellow Citizens.

The Citizens of this district can, with the most perfect confidence, with the assurances of the most firm reliance on the wisdom and integrity of your character, declare; that their hearts are with you and their Country, and that they are prepared to partake their full Share of any perils or privations; to perform any portion of personal Service, to voluntarily yield any pecuniary contribution, that the Support of the independence, honour, and interests of the happy nation over which you preside may require.

In common with all good men, in every part of the Union, we have beheld with emotions of delight and an honest pride, the Moderation and dignity, with which national concerns of great difficulty, have been conducted under your guidance; and we Cannot withold the expression of our most cordial approbation of your conduct in the dismissal of that insolent minister Francis James Jackson.

Without presuming to interfere with the rightful authority vested in the chief Magistrate, to conduct the foreign relations of our Country, your fellow citizens of this part of the union, think it correct to affirm, that they have for a long time anticipated, that all the Sacrifices made by this country to the Spirit of peace; that all the measures of policy and negociation So honestly conducted on your part, and that of your predecessor; that the earnest desire of the American government, to maintain a rigid and exemplary neutrality, to consider all nations "in peace friends, and enemies only in War"; [4] that all the forbearance from justifiable retaliation, and confinement to diplomatic demands of honest justice, would in the end prove unavailing; and that the issue must ultimately be to the nerves and Virtues of the Generation that has Succeeded those, who before triumphed over the oppressor of our country.

What the course of policy best calculated to ensure the best result is, we do not venture to Suggest; we confide in the authorities constituted to maintain our national rights and independence, and look every day with growing solicitude for a removal of that anxiety, which is the necessary effect of fluctuating Measures in Congress.

We urge the notice of the measures of Congress as a fact, that Merits the serious regard of those who are constitutionally appointed the rulers of the nation, in the last resort.

We naturally look back upon the progress of events, from the Year 1790 to the present day, and find each Successive year, to have produced new and aggravated grievances, insults and outrages upon our country, our fellow citizens, our property and our flag.

From the experience which we have had, we cannot calculate upon a peace in Europe for many years; and looking to the progressive growth of wrongs, from trivial to the most enormous injuries; we ask ourselves; and submit to the consideration of Your [sic] Sir, whether forbearance might not become crime, in Submitting to any further aggravation of wrongs and insults; but above all, we respectfully submit, whether the effect of further sufferance, may not be as fatal to the confidence of the people in their Government, as the measures that have been pursued have been unavailing.

We Submit it to our government, whether measures which only operate in favour of depravity and the enemies of our Country, and to the disadvantage of the Virtuous part of the Community, may not ultimately, if perservered in, prove more dangerous to public morals and public interest, than any other course of measures which could be pursued.

We have addressed you Sir, in the language and Spirit of a reverential affection; the boldness of our address, will not we are persuaded be misconstrued. We think it full time that the whole people should declare, that they are ready to Maintain, at every hazard, the Government of their choice, the Chief Magistrate and their representatives, who are faithful to the independence of the nation and its most Sacred rights, and to express a hope, that their Government will not longer suffer them, to be outraged with impunity.

Attest.   JOHN BARKER
FREDK WOLBERT Secy   Chairman

Resolutions unanimously adobted by the Citizens of the first Congressional District of the State of Pennsylvania at a District meeting, held on the 14th. Day of February AD 1810 at the State house in the City of Philadelphia in pursuance to public Notice.

1. Resolved, As the opinion of this meeting, that the conduct of the Executive of the United States in treating with the Government of Great Britain, and every other foreign government and their Agents, has been Moderate dignified and such as Comports with the sincerity and good faith of the chief Magistrate of a free, Neutral and independent Nation.

2. Resolved. That in the various Acts of perfidy insult and outrage upon our Citizens property flag and Country Committed by Great Britain; We Se[e] no prospect of obtaining Justice or redress by diplomatic Negociation.

3. Resolved. That we consider the outrage committed upon the Chesapeake, as an Authorised and deliberate Act of hostility on the part of the British Government; and that the various artifices and frauds combined with breach of faith and Contumelious insult displayed by the Ministers of Great Britain Constitute Acts of War calling for immediate attonement or immediate retaliation.

4. Resolved. That the proclamation of the King and privy Council of Great Britain inviting our Citizens to break the Laws of our Country was an interference in our internal government which would in itself justify a declaration of War.

5. Resolved. That the proposition of the British government, to enforce our Laws by its Navy, was an insideous attempt to represent the American government as unable to carry into effect the Laws which it passed, and to wheedle us into a war to Maintain British domination on the Ocean.

6. Resolved. That Savage Nations are justly condemned for Murdering

their prisoners; And the Barbary powers for putting them to hard labor; but it was reserved for the British government to refine upon Cruelty so far as to seize upon Citizens of a friendly and Neutral Nation, And compel them to fight against and Murder their fellow countrymen their friends their fathers and their brothers.

7. Resolved. That in dismissing a Supercilious and insolent Minister, called Francis James Jackson the Executive of the United States has Maintained the dignity of the Chief Magistrate of a free and independent People and that the great Mass of the Citizens in our opinion is ready to rally under the National Standard whenever the Congress shall respond to the feelings and spirit of the People.

8. Resolved. As the Opinion of this Meeting, that looking back to the period of the Revolution we see a strong similarity in the circumstances and causes, of the wrongs and injuries which we had then and subsequently have suffered, and that the injuries and insults murderings and plunder the tyranny over our Commerce and the limitation of its Direction without a British Licence imperiously call upon our government to take such measures as may be best calculated to assert and secure the rights of the Nation either by resistance and the force of Arms or by entering into engagements similar to those of the Armed Neutrality of 1780 for maintaining neutral rights and the freedom of the Seas.

9. Resolved. That the commerce of the United States ever has and ever shall under Providence be conducted without a British Licence and without the protection of the British Navy.

10. Resolved That we recommend it to our representatives in Congress to propose, that in Order to assure the restoration of our fellow Citizens impressed into the British Navy a Law be enacted Authorizing the seizure of an equal number of British Subjects, with those detained in British bondage; to be treated as hostages and put to useful employments according to their Capacities during their detention or till the restoration of our fellow citizens tyrannically impressed; and that our Representatives in Congress be requested to propose as a fundamental Law of the Land a provision of the same import to continue to all future times and be extended to all foreign Nations.

11. Resolved—That as Citizens of a free Nation having a right to express our Opinions on Public Measures under discussion, we do deprecate and protest against the ruinous, weak and inadequate projects contained in Certain propositions offered to Congress by the Chairman of the Committee of foreign relations.[5]

12. Resolved, That the Militia is the Army of the Constitution and the bulwark of the Republic; And that it ought to be properly organized, disciplined, armed and Uniformed.

13. Resolved. That our Chairman be requested to transmit, as soon as possible a Copy of the preceeding address and resolutions, to the President of the United States and a Copy of the Resolutions to each of the Senators of this State and the Representatives of this District in Congress.

Attest   JOHN BARKER
FREDK WOLBERT Secy   Chairman

RC and enclosure (DLC).

1. Reports of the meeting and its proceedings were printed in the Philadelphia *Aurora General Advertiser* on 15 and 16 Feb. 1810. With reference to JM's dispute with Pennsylvania governor Simon Snyder over the Olmstead affair, the *Aurora* declared that the meeting also passed an additional resolution condemning the governor for "*calling out an armed force to oppose the constituted authority of the general government*," a claim that was later disputed by the organizers of the meeting (see *PJM-PS*, 1:102–5; Higginbotham, *Keystone in the Democratic Arch*, p. 210).

2. John Barker was mayor of Philadelphia, 1808–10 (*Pa. Mag. Hist. and Biog.*, 49 [1925]: 92).

3. The first congressional district of Pennsylvania included Delaware County and the city and county of Philadelphia (Parsons et al., *United States Congressional Districts*, p. 116).

4. The meeting seems to have paraphrased the last line of the penultimate paragraph of the Declaration of Independence (see Boyd, *Papers of Jefferson*, 1:432).

5. Nathaniel Macon. On Macon's Bill No. 1, see JM to William Pinkney, 20 Jan. 1810, and n. 1.

§ To the House of Representatives. *17 February 1810*. Transmits reports from the secretaries of state and of the treasury in response to a House resolution of 5 Feb.

Printed copy (*ASP, Foreign Relations*, 3:341); enclosures (DNA: RG 233, President's Messages). RC not found. Enclosures are Robert Smith to JM, 14 Feb. 1810, and Gallatin to JM, 16 Feb. 1810, transmitting information requested by the House on French and British commercial restrictions. Besides the correspondence printed in *ASP, Foreign Relations*, 3:301, 324, 342–43, the enclosures include extracts from David Gelston to Gallatin, 22 Feb. 1808, enclosing Jan H. C. Heineken to Gelston, 19 Feb. 1808; Levett Harris to Sylvanus Bourne, 17 July 1809, enclosing a list of papers belonging to the ship *Aurora*; George R. Curtis to Bourne, 25 Aug. 1809; and various documents relating to the ships *Aurora, Jane, Georgia*, and *Arno*. Received and ordered to be printed on 19 Feb. (*Annals of Congress*, 11th Cong., 2d sess., 1374, 1423–26).

§ To the Senate. *17 February 1810*. Transmits report of the secretary of the treasury in response to a Senate resolution of 12 Feb.

RC and enclosures (DNA: RG 46, Legislative Proceedings, 11A-E4). RC 1 p. Enclosures are Gallatin to JM, 16 Feb. 1810 (1 p.), forwarding statements on duties on imports from the Mediterranean (2 pp.). On 12 Feb. the Senate had requested information on revenue generated since 1804 by the act protecting U.S. commerce and seamen against the Barbary powers. Received, read, and tabled on 19 Feb. (*Annals of Congress*, 11th Cong., 2d sess., 556–57, 575). Printed in *ASP, Finance*, 2:404–6.

From John Francis Mercer

DEAR SIR   WEST RIVER[1] Fb. 18th. 1810.

When in Baltimore a few days since, a French Emigrant of distinction gave me some details relative to a conspicuous personage lately arriv'd there from Spain, apparently in the capacity of Captain & Owner of a Privateer but who I beleive holds the Commission of General in the service of Joseph Buonaparte—his Vessell is gone but he remains, having landed some Spaniards & Frenchmen who are Agents of the Buonaparte's & who have gone into our back Country, where One of them has employ'd himself in a manner that may be ultimately interesting to our Government.[2] I requested this Gentleman to commit any information he had relative to these Intriguers, determind to convey it to the Government, that if they thought proper they might have an eye to them.

At a moment so critical as the present I deem it a duty to communicate any movements that tend to commit the peace & safety of the Country & if you shoud find in this nothing interesting, still I hope you will receive it as a proof of my sollicitude for the honor & prosperity of yr administration & of the pleasure I feel in repeating the assurance of the sincere attachment & respect with which I am Dr. Sir Yr. Ob. hb Sert.

JOHN FR: MERCER[3]

RC (DLC).

1. Mercer's Cedar Park estate was located on the West River inlet on Chesapeake Bay, about fifteen miles south of Annapolis.

2. Mercer's informant probably was referring to José Desmolard, who arrived in Baltimore from Norfolk early in 1810 to head a Bonapartist organization entrusted with the task of revolutionizing the Spanish-American colonies (see John Rydjord, "Napoleon and the Independence of New Spain," in *New Spain and the Anglo-American West*, ed. George P. Hammond [2 vols.; 1932; Los Angeles, 1969 reprint], 1:289–312).

3. John Francis Mercer (1759–1821) had known JM while serving as a Virginia delegate in the Continental Congress, 1782–85, a Maryland delegate in the Federal Convention of 1787, and a Republican congressman, 1791–94. He was governor of Maryland, 1801–3.

From Landon Carter

SIR VA. CLEVE 19. Febry 1810

Altho the subject of this Letter interests me individually, it yet involves public convenience enough to apologise in some sort for my intrusion, at this time of your deepest engagements. The present period points the attention of high commissioned characters to domestic structures, to such a degree, that I entertain a hope you will afford me your influencial patronage. I was indeed preparing to present myself before you but I am infirm and so much in the habit of indulgence as to dread a journey in the Winter season; unless induced to it by large prospects.

I have on hand—complete—a new constructed Lock, which in its plan baffles all attempt to enter by any other means than with its legitimate key. It is of plain, simple structure, as may be imagined from the agent of execution being a negroe carpenter, the number of whose ideas are very limited; and of course is chiefly of wood. I think the general utility of such a thing makes fit it should be exhibited, while Gentlemen are assembled from all parts of the nation, that it may be speedily disseminated. You have in your power to acquire a general sense of the estimation such an object will obtain and will perhaps consent to spare as much time as to write your ideas respecting the prospects of demand for permits under patent: Perhaps indeed Congress might be willing to make it a public property by purchase: It would suit me better, to sell out at once and the Public Would derive benefit from that mode as it would be a mean to bring it into a readier circulation.

The Locks now in use have wards contrived to obstruct the passage of Keys not accomodated with slit notches adapted to them; while the bolt is left free to be shot by any instrument which can be made to elude them: It is therefore that every attempt to vary the wards and the figure of the key is overcome by the ingenuity of man: The motion of the key, as respects the wards, also affords an opportunity, by impression, to mark the arrangement so as to imitate the key perfectly.

In my lock the wards connect with the bolt so as to hold it stationary untill the key arranges them to let it pass, and that arrangement is layed out after sections in the key ordered as fancy directs: The Lock therefore may be said to be made to the key & chance alone, hanging upon Millions of changes, can produce a key to the lock. My key consists of two parts, One to cooperate with the wards, having no horisontal motion, the other to force the driver upon the bolt. The slightest inequality in a key made as a copy, exact as may be to the eye, will effect the corresponding ward so as to leave it in the way, & no means exists to know which or how many are involved. Thus it may be seen that all the functions of the key are required to open the lock & it therefore cannot be picked—and those functions are so ordered as to cast the copier into the wide region of chance to find his purpose.

As no invention can be altogether original but that some similar Idea had prior existence, so do not I pretend to such unity in the present case: The arrangement of the same ideas may be new & more effective in operation; which is all that can be expected from the Inventor. If I can know the probable time Congress will adjourn I could regulate my motions accordingly; to you I shall be indebted for some information.

Under a full impression you will pardon me for giving you this trouble I will conclude with a repetition of my request that you will honor me with your patronage. I am mo: respectfully Sir yr. Obt.

L. CARTER[1]

P. S. My address—mail to K. G. Cthouse

RC (DLC).

1. Landon Carter (1751–1811) of Cleve in King George County served in the Virginia House of Delegates, 1780–81 (Lucien Beverley Howry, "Some Carters of 'Cleve,' King George County, and Their Descendants," *VMHB*, 44 [1936]: 343; Swem and Williams, *Register*, p. 357).

From William Jarvis

SIR   LISBON 19th. feby 1810

I had the honor to address you the 20th. Ultimo and in that letter begged that you would do me the favour to accept of a Marino Ram & Ewe. They are warranted of the best breed in Spain & a Certificate of their being such will be inclosed to Nicholas Gilman Esqr.[1] I shall however take the liberty to inclose you the best of all vouchers, a sample of the wool I took from their backs, which I found superior to a sample of the best imported Spanish wool, brought from England as a sample. Beside the pair for you & the pair for your worthy predecessor seven rams & two ewes go in the same vessel; but Colo. Gilman is desired that those four be selected from the whole. The two rams I should recommend have the inner part of the end of the horns (the tips of which are sawed off) notched; and the two youngest ewes which are also the largest. The latter may be known by having one or two of their lambs teeth still in. Should any of those die you will please to direct that others be selected, or take sir any others that may be more agreeable; my preference to those being only that they were the Youngest. The Rams as well as the ewes are all marked in both ears & five of the former have a small brand mark thus ⊔ on the left side of the face on which the hair does not grow, the other two have a brand mark round the nose just above the nostrils. The first is about an inch & a half to two inches long. The ewes are branded round the nose just like the two rams; but it is scarcely perceptible in two of them. In case of the absence of Colo. Gilman Messrs. James H. Hooe[2] & John Muncaster[3] will take charge of the sheep; who have the particular ear marks. Perhaps however it will be better to send on board & select yours sir & Mr Jefferson's, while on board.

Let me again add sir that I am happy to have it in my power to send you an animal so useful, & so worthy of your enlightened patriotism and hope that your Love of your Country will plead[4] my apology for the liberty I have taken.

I must [ask] the favour of your taking charge of Mr Jefferson's pair untill his instructions regarding them is known. A Bill of Lading of both go inclosed. With entire Respect I am sir Yr. Mo: devoted Hble servt

WM JARVIS

The Captain refusing to take them unless he had the promise of two lambs, of any yeaned on the passage and being desirous of affording a proof of my regard to Messrs Hooe & Muncaster I have promised them t⟨w⟩o likewise, if as many are yeaned, which I must pray you to consent to the fulfillment of, should you choose those which have yeaned.

RC and enclosures (DLC: Rives Collection, Madison Papers). RC docketed by JM. Enclosures (2 pp.) are bills of lading for the sheep to be carried aboard the *Diana*, William Lewis, master. On the verso of each bill of lading Jarvis wrote: "In case of the death on the passage, of any of the Sheep specified in this Bill of Lading the Skin is to be taken off the Carcase from the tip of the Nose to the extremity of the Heels—the hind feet & part of the legs as high as the first Joint above the Hoofs to remain attached to the Skin, which is to be dried & delivered to James Madison Esqr."

1. Nicholas Gilman (1755–1814) was a New Hampshire congressman, 1789–97, and Republican U.S. senator, 1805–14.

2. James Hewitt Hooe was a merchant in Alexandria, Virginia. JM had met him in 1795 and introduced him to Monroe. A Madison-Clinton elector in 1808, Hooe represented Fairfax County in the Virginia House of Delegates, 1809–10, and received consignments of merino sheep from Jarvis for JM and Jefferson (*PJM*, 16:162 and n. 1; Hooe to JM, 4 May 1810 and 13 Oct. 1810).

3. John Muncaster had served in the militia of Fairfax County, Virginia (*CVSP*, 6:554).

4. Jarvis wrote "prove" at the bottom of the page but "plead" at the top of the next page.

From William Lambert

Sir,   City of Washington, February, 19th. 1810.

I have the honor to inclose for your perusal, the last letter I have received from bishop Madison, by which you will perceive the strong interest that truly valuable man takes in the object and completion of my undertaking to fix a first meridian for the U. S. Other communications having a similar tendency, are now before the Select Committee of Congress to whom my papers have been referred. From what Mr. Pitkin,[1] the chairman of that Committee mentioned to me, they seem anxious to learn the sentiments of the President and the heads of departments concerning the utility of the object. I have no hesitation in avowing my belief, that *every* member of the administration, and particularly, such of them as are *native* citizens, will carry into effect with pleasure, any favorable plan which the national Legislature may adopt to lessen our dependence on a foreign Country, and to patronize such branches of science as may tend to promote the honor and advantage of the U. S. There is no doubt with me, that if Congress fulfil their duty, the Executive will do theirs.

One of the members of this Committee asked me a few days ago, what I expected for myself? I told him, that my principal object was to extricate the people of this Country from a state of dependence on a foreign nation, which I considered to be unnecessary and degrading; and that in the memorial accompanying my abstract of calculations, nothing was said about pecuniary emolument to me. An unexpected delay has already taken place, unfavorable to me, in my present Situation; and it appears that there is a probability of much longer procrastination; whether this proceeds from *two* objects referred to the Commee., (the magnetic variation, and the establishment of a first meridian), or any other Cause, I cannot pretend to determine.

I intend to shew the inclosed to the Secretaries of State and of the Navy. The business of the latter department seems to be more connected with the plan I have proposed, than of any other under the government. I have the honor to be, with great respect, Sir, Your most obedt. servant,

WILLIAM LAMBERT.

RC (DLC). Enclosure not found.

1. Timothy Pitkin was a Federalist congressman from Connecticut, 1805–19. On 28 Mar. 1810 he reported from committee a recommendation that the president "be authorized to cause the longitude of the City of Washington, from the observatory at Greenwich, in England, to be ascertained with the greatest possible degree of accuracy." Pitkin supported Lambert's proposal, but the House tabled his recommendation and took no action until 1821 (*Annals of Congress*, 11th Cong., 2d sess., 1660–62; Lambert to JM, 5 Dec. 1809, n. 1).

From George Logan

My Dear Sir   New York Feby 19th 1810

Since my arrival here, I have had a conversation with Mr Jackson. Whilst he regrets, his being dismissed; he assures me, that he does not consider it will be a cause of rupture with his Government; and that his representations to his Court have been to allay, not increase the present unhappy difficulties between the two countries. Whilst in Philadelphia he had an opportunity of seeing the wealth, industry, and extensive internal commerce of that State; which he highly admired. And I am satisfied from his observations respecting the UStates, that he considers our friendship of importance to his own Country.[1]

I expect to embark in the morning. Accept assurances of my esteem & Friendship

Geo Logan

RC (DLC); draft (PHi).

1. Logan sought letters of introduction from Jackson to George Canning and Lord Wellesley. Warned by Phineas Bond, the British consul at Philadelphia, that Logan was preparing for "his old trade of diplomatic adventuring," Jackson declined to give him the letters (Tolles, *George Logan*, p. 288).

§ From Richard M. Johnson.[1] *19 February 1810, Washington.* Recommends John Monroe of Lexington for nomination as a territorial judge in Mississippi in the event that the position is created.

RC (DNA: RG 59, LAR, 1809–17, filed under "Monroe"). 1 p.

1. Richard M. Johnson was a Republican representative from Kentucky, 1807–19. He recommended John Monroe again to JM—for nomination as U.S. attorney in Ohio—on 24 Oct. 1810 (ibid.).

§ From J. Aaron Emanuel Vonhalle. *19 February 1810, Fort McHenry.* Informs JM that in the "greatest Distress" he enlisted five months ago as a soldier in Capt. George Armistead's company but now seeks a discharge.

RC (DNA: RG 107, LRRS, V-7:5). 1 p. A second letter from Vonhalle to JM, 20 Feb. 1810 (ibid.; 1 p.), adding that his family wished him to return to his native Prussia, is docketed by a War Department clerk as received 22 Feb. 1810.

§ From an Unidentified Correspondent. *20 February 1810, New Haven.* Advocates the establishment of "*privileged corps*" of engineers to defend the seacoast from attack by armed vessels in lieu of the volunteers called for by JM.[1]

RC (DNA: RG 107, LRRS, A-26:5). 1 p. Signed "A Native American." Docketed by a War Department clerk as received 26 Feb. 1810.

1. The House committee that acted on JM's 3 Jan. 1810 message calling for "a volunteer force of twenty thousand men" had recommended implementing legislation on 8 Jan. (*Annals of Congress*, 11th Cong., 2d sess., 1159).

To John Barker

SIR   WASHINGTON Feby 21. 1810.

I have recd. your letter of the 17th. covering the Address & Resolutions adopted in the first Congressional District of the State of Penna. and avail myself of the same channel, for conveying an answer to the former. I tender at the same time, my acknowledgments for your kind expressions, and assurances of my respect & good wishes.

[Enclosure]

To the Republican Citizens of the 1st. Congressional District of the State of Penna.

I have recd., fellow Citizens, your address of the 14th. inst: with the impressions which its assurances of approbation & attachment could not fail to make; and with every participation in your sensibility to the extraordinary circumstances which continue to distinguish our foreign relations.

You do no more than justice as well to my predecessor as to myself, in referring the course which has been pursued, to a steady purpose, of witholding from each Belligerent, a pretext for disturbing our rightful intercourse with the other, by observing towards both, the strictest impartiality, in exercising our neutral rights, and in fulfilling our neutral Obligations. This unexceptionable conduct, which ought to have shielded us from aggressions of every sort, has been followed by a perseverance in multiplying them, which no appeals to Law, to reason, or to that policy which alone accords with the true interest of Nations, as of individuals, have succeeded in averting or arresting.

In this State of things, it lies with the Legislative Councils, to decide on the measures adapted to it.[1] That their decisions, will duly consult the sense of the Nation, and faithfully pursue its best interests, is what I feel great satisfaction in presuming; as I do, in witnessing the patriotism, which, in your example, unites with a manly expression of your particular sentiments, a confidence in the Constituted Authorities, and a determination to support them. Accept, fellow Citizens, my respects & friendly wishes.

WASHINGTON Feby. 21. 1810

Draft (DLC).

1. There is some evidence that JM by this time was weary of receiving and answering all the addresses sent to him. In a lengthy editorial entitled *"Addresses! Addresses!!"* on 5 Feb. 1810, the *National Intelligencer* complained of the "pernicious tendency of complimentary *Addresses to the Chief Magistrate.*" The editorialist even wished that other Republican newspapers would censure these productions on the grounds that their organization suggested they were intended as "instruments of preferment" and, as such, they "neither inspire respect for their authors or the man to whom they are addressed."

Developing the theme, the writer declared that "no one since the corrupt & courtly days of the Stuarts, received more of these *distinguished honors*, seasoned too with every ingredient that could gratify the palate of the epicure, than John Adams," and the author then inquired rhetorically as to what had been the fate of the second president. (JM, it might be recalled, had been greatly disturbed by the manner in which John Adams had responded to similar addresses in the late 1790s, and he had at that time denounced Adams's conduct as "the most grotesque scene in the tragicomedy" of the Quasi-War with France [JM to Jefferson, 10 June 1798, *PJM*, 17:150].) The editorialist contended, moreover, that such addresses were unnecessary, particularly in a society where there already existed adequate means for the expression of public opinion and the very structure of the republic itself provided for "infusing into the government the wishes of the people" at regular and prescribed intervals. Drawing upon a distinction that would have been approved by the authors of *The Federalist*, the editorialist reminded his readers that the U.S. was "a *representative* government" and not "a pure democracy" and that accordingly "all rational liberty must depend on the vigorous maintena[n]ce" of the former condition as opposed to the latter.

In this context, the writer argued that while the people certainly had the right to address their representatives, it was inappropriate for them to approach the executive, "the fountain of office," in the same way, and that by doing so, they exposed the chief magistrate to "peculiar difficulties." The addresses invariably censured a foreign power in bold and warm language. "A congenial answer is expected. It is received. It is couched in terms of firmness; but it has none of the fire of the address," even though "*reflecting* men" should "see that it would be unworthy of the President to indulge in angry passions on such, or indeed on any occasion." The result, the editorialist complained, was "a *general* disappointment," and "it is inferred that the Executive govt. wants nerve." This inference was unjust, since "the bulk of the people do not reflect that, it rests with another department of the govt. to take the decided steps that lead to war, and that if the Chief Magistrate should even be of opinion that such, or any other vigorous measure ought to be taken, yet that this conviction does not diminish the respect he owes to his station, his personal character, or to the very nation which has ⟨sir?⟩ed us; they do not, in fine, reflect that the constitution has enjoined upon the government the duty of *acting*, and not of *coining words*, of which, God knows, we have already to our shame more than enough."

Memorandum to Albert Gallatin

[ca. 21 February 1810]

The sea-letter, as its name & its address, import are meant to verify the ship on the High seas. As *Belligerents* alone have a right to such a verification, is not the Document unnecessary when there is no belligerent. If the verifying papers, intended for the Jurisdiction at the port of destination be not at present suitable or sufficient, should not some other more appropriate than the sea letter, be provided?[1]

J. M.

Ms (PPRF). In JM's hand. Undated. Conjectural date assigned on the basis of the evidence in n. 1.

1. In his annual message on 29 Nov. 1809, JM had recommended that Congress consider measures to protect the American flag from fraudulent use, and the House of Representatives responded on 1 Dec. by instructing the Committee of Commerce and Manufactures to consider the expediency of "registering anew" all American-owned or American-built vessels and also of prohibiting the use of sea letters by any vessels "not registered or licensed according to law, or not owned by citizens of the United States." The committee chairman, Thomas Newton, duly reported a bill on 19 Jan. 1810 to restrict the future use of sea letters as a means of identifying American-owned vessels, unless such vessels were registered. The bill passed the House on 8 Feb. and was sent to the Senate where James A. Bayard, on 19 Feb., referred it to the treasury for comment. Gallatin endorsed the bill, as did many congressmen, on the grounds that it would help prevent abuse of the American flag. JM, apparently, had some reservations about the measure, but an amended version of the bill passed both houses of Congress by 21 Mar. and was signed into law five days later (*Annals of Congress*, 11th Cong., 2d sess., 556, 584, 588, 594, 595, 596, 600, 611, 686–87, 1225, 1378, 1379–81, 1385, 1533, 1535, 1584, 1605–6, 2529; Gallatin to Bayard, 20 Feb. 1810, *Papers of Gallatin* [microfilm ed.], reel 20).

From Willie Blount

SIR   KNOXVILLE February 21st. 1810

Feeling a warm interest in the Welfare of the United States, a respect for you, and a desire to assist in bringing men of Talents and Worth in aid of your Administration of the affairs of the people of the United States, are reasons why I take the liberty of recommending to your Notice and Consideration a worthy and respectable Man Col. John McKee,[1] at present at Natchez who will feel himself highly gratified to be honored with an appointment under the general government to be confered by you. He is a Man of good Education, possessing a liberal and well cultivated mind, correct in his habits, and second to no man in point of integrity. I have known him upwards of seventeen years intimately, and never knew or heard of his having done a little thing; but frequently the reverse; and in no instance did I ever know him to depart from the Conduct of a Gentleman, and such is my opinion of him that I have no hesitation in believing and saying that his Conduct will at all times hereafter be correct, be his situation what it may. I have his own authority for saying, and I believe him: that he "never injured in thought, word, or Deed, any member of the present Executive Council; and if honored with an appointment by the President of the United States, that he will discharge his duty with zeal, fidelity, integrity, and with such judgment as Nature has given." He is capable of being useful and desirous of having an Opportunity afforded of being so. No Doubt need be entertained of his Talents, Integrity, Love of Country, Respect for the Administrators of the Government of the United States, or of his faithfulness to the Constitution. Hundreds of Men and more in this Country, where he is and has been long known, and tried, would have pleasure in saying the same of him. He has been employed as you know in Character of agent amongst the Southern tribes of Indians; and the people of this Country, who have known his Conduct in Discharge of his Duty feel sensible of his worth, and are desirous for his being in appointment; in that agency they believe he promoted the interest of the United States in general, of this State in particular; and we are convinced that he gave such general satisfaction to the Indians that he possesses now and has uniformly possessed their confidence in as great a degree, if not greater, than any other man in this Country.

He feels sensible that no part of his Conduct in discharge of his duties as agent ever was by the Government, viewed as exceptionable; and believes that he was removed from appointment through the influence and misrepresentation of some persons who have never yet so openly ⟨avowed?⟩ themselves as to enable him to be certain who they are; and never has been able to understand why he was removed. A Removal under such circumstances is extreemely grating to his feelings as it would be to any Man who had any of the nicer kind.

He would be a very valuable man to the United States in Indian Agency west of the Mississippi, as he possesses a very conciliatory cast of Mind and Manners; I presume such a man is much wanted there. He has talents integrity and firmness enough to make a very valuable feild Officer in the Army of the United States. He Would fill an Executive office in a Territorial Government with Dignity and Benifit; or discharge the duties of secretary in a Territory as well as any man; and in short I view him qualified to discharge the duties of any office in the gift of the Executive of the United States to be acted on in the Western Country, and believe his appointment to office would be satisfactory to the people. I have too much respect for you, and for myself; too great a desire to see office filled with men of Talents and integrity, and too great a desire for the prosperity of the United States, to trifle with the feelings or interest of either the one or the other in recommending any man as fit for office, of whom I could not safely say, that he is qualified to fill it with Utility to the Government and Credit to himself. Mr. Andrew Moore of Virginia, Mr. McKee of Kentuckey, Messrs. Miller, Rhea and Weakley of Tennessee, and the Senators of Tennessee, have a personal acquaintance with Colonel McKee, to whom I beg leave to refer you. I have the honor to be with perfect respect Your Obt Servant

(Signed)   WILLIE BLOUNT

RC (DNA: RG 94, Letters Received, filed under "McKee"). In a clerk's hand. Marked "Duplicate." Postmarked "Ten June." Marked by JM "Secy of War."

1. John McKee (1771–1832), a native of Virginia, began a long and complex career in the southwestern borderlands in 1792 when territorial governor William Blount appointed him to negotiate a boundary line with the Cherokee Indians. In 1799 Secretary of War James McHenry named him as agent to the Choctaw, but he was removed from this post in 1802, probably because Jefferson suspected him of involvement in the Blount conspiracy in the late 1790s. McKee's lifelong interest in attempting to extract personal advantage from the confusion of Spanish, Indian, and American rivalries in the Southwest led him to befriend Aaron Burr and James Wilkinson and thus into a degree of involvement in their various projects. Both men approached McKee about the possibility of his raising forces for expeditions against Mexico, and McKee subsequently appeared as a witness on Burr's behalf during his trial in Richmond in 1807. While residing near Natchez in 1810, McKee was drawn into the problems of West and East Florida when the Spanish governor, Vicente Folch, overwhelmed by the difficulties of dealing with the filibustering schemes of the Kemper brothers and Joseph Kennedy, sounded him out on the possibility of delivering Spanish territory directly to the U.S. McKee then traveled to Washington where he met with JM in January 1811, and together with Gen. George Mathews of Georgia they discussed ways in which the Spanish territories could be incorporated into the U.S. For the next two years McKee was associated with Mathews in the abortive American attempts to annex portions of West and East Florida, and he also organized volunteer corps of Chickasaw and Choctaw Indians to serve with Andrew Jackson's forces against the Creek Indians in 1814. At that time too, McKee regained his former position as agent to the Choctaw, and after 1818 he participated in many of the negotiations that led to the final cession of the Choctaw lands east of the Mississippi in the 1830 treaty of Dancing Rabbit Creek. In 1821 he settled in Alabama and served three terms in the House of Representatives between 1823 and 1829 (Carter, *Territorial Papers, Southwest*, 4:62; ibid., *Mississippi*, 5:42, 58–59, 146, 154, 6:443, 447; William S. Coker and Thomas D. Watson, *Indian Traders of the Southeastern Spanish Borderlands: Panton, Leslie & Company and John Forbes & Company, 1783–1847* [Pensacola, Fla., 1986], pp. 227–31; *Annals of Congress*, 5th Cong., 2d sess., 673 and appendix at 2347; *ASP, Miscellaneous*, 1:593–95; Isaac J. Cox, *The West Florida Controversy, 1798–1813: A Study in American Diplomacy* [Baltimore, 1918], pp. 480–81, 522–26, 550; Rembert W. Patrick, *Florida Fiasco: Rampant Rebels on the Georgia-Florida Border, 1810–1815* [Athens, Ga., 1954], pp. 14–16, 36–39, 72, 306–7).

§ From "Clitus."[1] *21 February 1810*. Informs JM that those Republicans who supported George Clinton in the last presidential election did so from "the purest motives." These men judged JM by the presence of "Quids, sycophants and Yazoomen" among his supporters and predicted that his administration would be characterized by "*indecision* and *quidism*." Warns JM to take care that his acts do not verify these predictions and alludes to the recent nomination of Richard Forrest, a man known for his "toryism." Reminds JM that he was elected by adherents of "'the glorious spirit of whigism,'" and "you must adhere to the principles which raised you, or you will . . . be sent to your 'Sabine farm'" at the end of four years. Adds a postscript complaining that the executive levees and drawing room ceremonies instituted by JM are "galling to plain republican feelings. . . . A rough clad farmer could find no footing" at these occasions, and "no gentleman is even admitted in boots; it being a law, that silk stockings and shoes, &c are requisite passports to the wearer." Concludes that "at this rate, *home manufactures* are not much encouraged at Washington!" Urges JM to discontinue these ceremonies and to "imitate the excellent Jefferson; and let it not be said that when we lost him, we left our mainstay."

Printed copy (Baltimore *Whig*, 21 Feb. 1810).

1. According to Plutarch, Clitus was a Macedonian general and friend of Alexander the Great. Alexander killed him in a drunken rage after Clitus accused the king of preferring the company of conquered, foreign-born barbarians to that of free-born, native Greeks (Plutarch, *Alexander*, ch. 50, *Plutarch's Lives*, Loeb Classical Library [11 vols.; London, 1914–26], 7:369–75).

§ From William Foster, Jr. *21 February 1810, Boston*. Solicits an appointment in Spain, Portugal, Italy, or South America on the basis of his knowledge of French and Spanish and his acquaintance with several New England political figures.

RC (DNA: RG 59, LAR, 1809–17, filed under "Foster"). 2 pp. The folder containing Foster's letter also has an undated sheet bearing JM's notation: "Wm. Foster jr. was named by Mr. Adams to the Senate who concurred; but no commission was issued. He was of the State of Massachusetts." On the verso is Jefferson's docket, "Foster, Wm. junr. to be Commerl. Agent Morlaix," indicating that the sheet is misfiled. JM evidently sent this explanatory note to Jefferson in January 1802 along with a letter he had received from William Foster, Sr., inquiring about the failure of his son to receive his commission for the post of commercial agent at Morlaix to which he had been nominated by President John Adams on 18 Feb. 1801. The Jefferson administration apparently treated Foster as one of President Adams's "midnight appointments" (William Foster, Sr., to JM, 14 Jan. 1802 [ibid., 1801–9; docketed by Jefferson as received 25 Jan. 1802; *Senate Exec. Proceedings*, 1:382, 385).

From John Martin Baker

SIR,   CAGLIARI February 22d: 1810.

I have now the Honor Most Respectfully to make known, that I arrived in this City on the thirteenth of the present Month. On yesterday I had an Audience with His Majesty the King of Sardinia, who has requested me Sir, to present to you his best compliments: I beg leave Sir, to mention that I had a long conference with His Majesty, in which he was pleased to Express his Sentiments in every thing friendly towards the United States, and a desire in that of an Encreasing and more intimate Commercial intercourse. Should you sir, consider a Commercial treaty important or Necessary, I beg leave to offer myself, and pray you Sir to be pleased to consider me in such Agency. His Majesty, as well as Chevalier Rossi, the Minister of State have given me Assurances that should the Navy of the United States, when in the Mediterranean, require a supply of Provission from this Island, they would be received friendly, treated with favor, and Supplied in whatsoever their wants, that the Island can Afford. I beg leave to be permitted the liberty Sir, to State, that The Honorable the Secretary of the Navy was pleased to promise me the appointment of Navy Agent for Minorca:[1] Should the Honorable Secretary, deem it more expedient for the United States Squadron to rendezvous, or to provission at this Island, and not at Minorca—I have the Honor Sir, to Solicit the appointment of Navy Agent for Sardinia. Praying Yours, and the Honorable the Secretary's Consideration in my behalf—I have the Honor to be, with the Highest Respect and Gratitude—Sir Your Most Obedient Humble Servant

JOHN MARTIN BAKER.[2]

RC (NN); duplicate, triplicate (DLC). All copies docketed by JM.

1. Baker was referring to a promise made to him by Robert Smith in 1807 (James A. Field, Jr., *America and the Mediterranean World, 1776–1882* [Princeton, N.J., 1969], pp. 105–6).

2. John Martin Baker of New York served as U.S. consul for Minorca, Iviza, and Majorca, 1803–7, and from 1807 at Tarragona, where he was still serving in 1816 (*Senate Exec. Proceedings*, 1:441, 442, 2:60, 63; *ASP, Miscellaneous*, 2:315).

From Albert Gallatin

TREASURY DEPARTMENT 22d February 1810

In obedience to the Resolution of the Senate of the Sixteenth instant,[1] the Secretary of the Treasury respectfully reports to the President of the United States

That exports to and imports from the ports of France have not been nor are now permitted in the execution of the Act "to interdict the commercial intercourse between the United States and Great Britain and France and their dependencies and for other purposes"

That exports to and imports from the ports of Great Britain were, in conformity with the Proclamation of the President of the 19th day of April 1809 announcing that the British orders in Council would be withdrawn on the 10th day of June ensuing, permitted from the said 10th day of June and until the 9th day of August ensuing.

That the President having, by his Proclamation of the 9th day of August 1809, announced that the British orders in Council were not withdrawn on the tenth day of June preceding, and consequently that the trade renewable on the event of the said orders being withdrawn was to be considered as under the operation of the several acts by which such trade was suspended, information thereof was immediately transmitted to the several collectors by a circular dated also "August 9th 1809" copy of which is herewith transmitted, and also of a postscript directed to the Collectors on the Lakes.

That the collectors were informed by that circular (which has already been laid by the President before the Congress at the opening of the present session) that the Act above mentioned was in every respect applicable to Great Britain and her dependencies; but that the President had also directed a suspension of seizures & prosecutions in certain cases, arising from acts which would, in conformity with his Proclamation of the 19th day of April preceding, have been considered as lawful; and that in such cases the vessels and cargoes might be admitted to entry.

That no other instructions but those contained in the said circular have been given on that subject to the collectors; and that if any collector has knowingly admitted to an entry goods the growth and manufacture of Great Britain or France, in any other case but those enumerated in the circular above mentioned, such act is unknown to this Department & would be considered as a high breach of duty. All which is respectfully Submitted

ALBERT GALLATIN

RC and enclosure (DNA: RG 46, Legislative Proceedings, 11A-E4). Enclosure (4 pp.) is a copy of a Treasury Department circular to customs collectors dated 9 Aug. 1809 (printed in *ASP, Commerce and Navigation*, 1:818–19). RC and enclosure included in JM's message to the Senate, 22 Feb. 1810.

1. The Senate resolution requested information on the enforcement of the Nonintercourse Act and on the instructions under which the collectors acted (*Annals of Congress*, 11th Cong., 2d sess., 573–74).

From Samuel Huntington

SIR—   CHILICOTHA Febry. 22d. 1810.

Agreably to the request of the General Assembly of the State of Ohio, I have the honor to transmit you their Resolution of the 19th. Instant approbating the measures of the General Government—and am with high respect your most obedt. Servt.

SAML. HUNTINGTON

[Enclosure]

In General Assembly.

Resolved by the general Assembly of the state of Ohio, that we highly approve the Candid, firm, and dignified Conduct of the executive of the United States during the important, and dificult negotiations with the belligerent powers, in the recess of Congress—especially in warding against the insidious artifice of the british court in their late nefarious breach of political faith and national honour in refusing to ratify the solemn engagements entered into by their accredited minister: Also that we highly applaud the spirit and patriotism manifested by Congress on the same occasion. And while those to whom our dearest rights are committed profess a spirit of reconciliation on terms honourable to the sovereignty of a free people, with full confidence we rely on our national council, to adopt such measures as will prove to the world that we regard no consequences in maintaining our honour and independance.

Resolved unanimously that we pledge our lives, our fortunes, and all our energies in the Support of all Just, necessary, and efficient measures which Congress may deem expedient, for securing our injured rights, insulted sovereignty, and independance.

Resolved that the Governor be requested to forward Copies of the foregoing resolutions to the President of the United States, the president of the Senate, the Speaker of the house of Representatives, and to our Senators and Representatives in Congress.

EDWARD TIFFIN Speaker of the
house of Representatives
DUNCAN MCARTHUR Speaker
Feby. 19th. 1810   of the Senate

RC and enclosure (DLC). Enclosure in a clerk's hand; docketed by JM. Attested to by the clerks of the Ohio House and Senate and certified as a correct copy by the secretary of the state of Ohio, 22 Feb. 1810. On 5 Feb. the *National Intelligencer* had published an earlier version of the resolutions, passed by the Ohio House of Representatives on 16 Jan.

From the Republican Meeting
of Cecil County, Maryland

SIR, [22 February 1810]

Whilst faction with unblushing opposition to the constituted authorities of our country, stalks abroad in the persons of the advocates for national submission, and the adherents of Mr. Jackson; the republicans of Cecil county who have assembled at Elkton to commemorate the birth-day of the illustrious *Washington*, think it a duty that they owe to themselves and their country, to assure you that you possess their unequivocal approbation of your private and political conduct, and that they are determined to support the government of their choice at the risque of their lives and fortunes. We properly appreciate our chartered right of freely discussing the measures of government, but valuable as this privilege is, we would draw a line between those who do not approve of all the measures of your administration, and those who attempt to palliate, nay, justify foreign aggression and insult, and who losing sight of all sense of national honour openly adulate a discarded minister.

The present unhappy commercial war has drawn us into a most awful crisis, from which we believe we can only be extricated by the most prompt and energetic measures of the general government. We dread an European peace before our rights and just claims are recognized, and we believe that if we do not at this time establish the dignity of our national character by heroic firmness, and our commercial rights by express and well defined treaties, the opportunity will be ever lost.

We regret that our claims, reasonable, equitable and just, have not been clearly stated, and in the most plain language, not only as a source of correct information to the citizens of these U. States; but, as a *sine qua non* to the rulers of Europe; and with an express declaration by our national legislature, that upon such claims being recognized by either of the belligerents, the whole energies of our country shall be called forth to maintain the contract, and that we will declare out of our protection the persons who may be detected in violating the treaty.

We believe with General Washington "*It is our true policy to steer clear of permanent alliances with any portion of the foreign world;*"[1] that we understand our own interests, and are capable of managing our own national concerns; and when the protection of any power is necessary we shall know how to ask it, but what sir, is our boasted independence if we are the sport of orders and decrees, and of what consequence is it to us as a nation, which of the belligerents shall first acknowledge our rights by a manly unreserved treaty? Let Great Britain, if the expression pleases her, fight for her "own existence," and may heaven grant her success—Let France contend against coalitions formed to blot her from the map of Europe, and may she be victorious; but, there cannot be any sound reason why *we* should be involved in the hostilities of these nations, nor to use another sentiment of the immortal Washington, "*why we should forego the advantages of our own peculiar situation, why we should quit our own to stand upon foreign ground, why by interweaving our destiny with that of any part of Europe, we should entangle our peace and prosperity in the toils of European ambition, rivalship, interest, humor or caprice.*"[2] We wish to assure you sir, that the general government has nothing to dread from the disaffected; they are clamorous, but not numerous, and it is only owing we believe to the temporising indecision of congress, that they are not left in a minority too inconsiderable to be entitled even to the name of a party.

Should hostilities commence between the United States and Great Britain; much as we shall regret the necessity, yet one desirable result will follow, it will unite the friends of our republican form of government by whatever names they may be distinguished, and such characters as were deemed *tories* during our *revolutionary struggle* will be indebted to political justice for a mere legal distinction; and while some of the advocates for our national degradation & submission, will fly from our shores to join the standard of our enemies; others will become victims of their treason, and the pitiful residue will skulk into retirement to escape from the penalties of the law, and to conceal themselves from an offended people.

The great body of our citizens know the value of liberty, and how important it is that they should submit to every sacrafice to preserve their independence and to hand it down unimpaired to posterity. Our country is rich, our population great, our resources many, and with grateful recollection of Thomas Jefferson our late president, we can boast that we are unincumbered with debt and our credit high. The American people have not been called upon to gratify the waste of an extravagant administration; and this assures to you, that when there is real necessity, they will cheerfully grant the reasonable requisition of an enlightened, virtuous and patriotic government.

Continue then sir in the path you have trod, to defend the honour and the rights of the United States, and you may confidently rely upon the virtue and resources of the American people.

We are sir in behalf of our constituents, and personally with sentiments of the highest respect, Your obt. humble servants,

DANL. SHERIDINE,
Chairman.

JAMES SEWALL, *Sec'ry.*

Printed copy (Baltimore *Whig*, 15 Mar. 1810).

1. The quotation is from George Washington's Farewell Address of 1796 (Fitzpatrick, *Writings of Washington*, 35:234).

2. Ibid.

§ To the Senate. *22 February 1810.* Transmits a report from the secretary of the treasury in compliance with a Senate resolution of 16 Feb. 1810.

RC and enclosures (DNA: RG 46, Legislative Proceedings, 11A-E4). RC 1 p. For enclosures, see Gallatin to JM, 22 Feb. 1810. Received, read, and tabled on 23 Feb. (*Annals of Congress*, 11th Cong., 2d sess., 573–74, 584). Printed in *ASP, Commerce and Navigation*, 1:818–19.

§ From Francis Hall. *22 February 1810, "Citizen Office," New York.* Sends JM an account showing $25 due for two and one-half years' subscription to the N.Y. *American Citizen.*

RC (DLC). 1 p.

§ From Hugh Holmes. *23 February 1810, Winchester.* Asks JM to find a position in one of the territories for Henry Daingerfield.[1] "Because he is your *distant relation* and a *Virginian* I feel a confidence that you will render a service to him which he deserves and thereby a greater One to your Country." The secretaryship in Mississippi would be appropriate, since Daingerfield is "the bosom friend" of the governor.

RC (DNA: RG 59, LAR, 1809–17, filed under "Daingerfield"). 4 pp. Printed in Carter, *Territorial Papers, Mississippi*, 6:49–50. Holmes was a judge of the Virginia General Court and brother of Gov. David Holmes of Mississippi. JM also received a letter on Daingerfield's behalf from Lawrence Augustine Washington, a nephew of George Washington, dated 18 Mar. 1810 (printed ibid., 6:53).

1. Henry Daingerfield (1771–1815) of Winchester, Frederick County, was a grandson of JM's aunt, Elizabeth Madison Willis Beale. He received a recess appointment as secretary of the Mississippi Territory on 30 June 1810 and served in that office until his death (*VMHB*, 32 [1924]: 135; *WMQ*, 1st ser., 6 [1897–98]: 207; Carter, *Territorial Papers, Mississippi*, 6:75 n. 72, 514 n. 89; *Senate Exec. Proceedings*, 2:159, 161).

To Landon Carter

SIR   WASHINGTON Feby. 24. 1810

I have duly recd. your letter of the 19th. on the subject of a newly invented Lock. From the description of it, it would seem to be a useful subs[t]itute for the common locks. Its value however necessarily depends on so many circumstances which influence a general preference, in such cases, & which are so well understood by yourself, that with your better knowledge of the merits of your invention, you can I am persuaded, better estimate its success, than I can pretend to do. I may venture however to intimate an Opinion that it would not be well to calculate on a purchase of your right by Congress, who have in no case exercised such a mode of encouraging useful inventions. The duration of their Session, being a matter of mere conjecture, I can no other wise answer your inquiry on that point, than by saying that there is at present, no appearance of its being very soon brought to a close. Accept my respects.

James Madison

Photocopy of RC (ViU: Launcelot Minor Blackford Collection).

§ From an Unidentified Correspondent. *24 February 1810, Charleston.* Criticizes the decision of the Jefferson administration to reduce the naturalization period for foreigners to four years. "Experience teaches us daily, that there is but little confidence to be placed in them." Argues that foreigners may be "received among us" and permitted to hold land and conduct business, but they should "never . . . be permited to vote at Elections, or be Eligible, to take a Seat in the legaslative Councils, or to hold a commission in the militia." Complains about "influential foreignrs" congregating in large cities and seaport towns where they show "no modesty" and "find fault with evry thing." Declares that the Charleston militia is officered "in many Instances, by Scotchmen & Irish &c," while "men who were looked up to during the revolution . . . are discarded." Urges JM to restore the period for naturalization to not less than fourteen years.

RC (NN). 3 pp. Signed "a Carolinian and Charlestonian." Postmarked 12 May.

From Winfield Scott

Sir,   February 27th. 1810.

One who's had the honor to be presented to you in person, but does not flatter himself he yet retains a place in your memory, respectfully solicits your first moments' leisure, from matters of greater importance, to the consideration of his case.

If it be true in the œconomy of Nature, that not even a sparrow falls without the consent of Him who ruleth above, so neither, perhaps, should a punishment be inflicted, however slight, on the humblest of those over whom you preside, without your knowledge and approbation.

Genl. Hampton, informs me, he has done me the favor to forward for your consideration the proceedings of a late General Court Martial, which, Suspended me from my military functions;[1] under the idea, you might, probably, restore me to command. It is contrary, both to my principles and profession, to solicit mercy for myself. Yet, Sir, if after looking over my case, you shall be pleased to restore me, to my place, among our country's defenders, the act would certainly record itself on my heart as its most grateful impression.

I will take the liberty, to add, only one idea of solicitation. Should war in a short time, grow, out of our foreign relations, my Sentence will inflict a pang upon my feelings, not contemplated by the Court. For, after, the sacrifices I have made, to prepare for Such an event, to remain an idle Spectator when it shall happen, would be to my soul the worst of tortures. To guard against which, I will entreat you, Sir, to interpose your authority, and let me in for a share of the glorious hazard. With Sentiments, of the highest personal reverence, and official respect, I have the honor to be, Sir, yr: Obt: Sert.

WINFIELD SCOTT.
Capt: U. S. L. A.

RC (PHi: Daniel Parker Papers).

1. In January 1810 Winfield Scott, a captain in the Light Artillery, had been court-martialed in Washington, Mississippi Territory, on two charges of conduct unbecoming an officer and a gentleman. The first charge related to Scott's speaking disrespectfully of Brig. Gen. James Wilkinson by calling him a "traitor" and "a liar and a scoundrel." The second involved his withholding improperly some $400 remitted to him for the payment of the men in his company. The court found Scott guilty on both counts, though on the second charge they acquitted him of "all fraudulent intentions in detaining the pay of his men." Scott was suspended from his rank and pay for twelve months. He served out his sentence in Virginia and returned to the army in the fall of 1811 (Winfield Scott, *Memoirs of Lieut.-General Scott, Ll.D.* [2 vols.; New York, 1864], 1:37–43).

From Gideon Granger

DR: SIR.   Feb: 28. 1810

My long acquaintance with Stanley Griswold Esqr[1] and the Solicitude of his numerous acquaintance—emboldens me to depart from a rule to which I have generally conformd.—Of not interfering to reccommend any candidates for Office.

Mr: Griswold and myself were educated at the same time at Yale College and our acquaintance has continued ever since. He is a man of Science, and has ever sustained the character of An upright faithful Citizen devoted to the liberties of his Country. It was owing to him that New-Hampshire was revolutionized & the unfortunate dispute between him & Govr Hull has most essentially injured his affairs. He has read law with Judge Huntington.[2]

I⟨t is,⟩ Sir, my firm beleif that should it be the pleasure of the President to bestow on him a territorial Judgeship, he would be an useful & faithful Officer and that his appointt Would be highly pleasing to all the leading Republicans of New England. With great Esteem & Respect Yours

G GRANGER

RC (DNA: RG 59, LAR, 1809–17, filed under "Griswold").

1. Stanley Griswold (1763–1815), a 1786 graduate of Yale College, had been a clergyman in Connecticut and the editor of a Republican newspaper in New Hampshire. He served as secretary of the Michigan Territory, 1805–8, until a quarrel with Gov. William Hull forced his resignation. He moved to Ohio, was appointed a U.S. senator in 1809 to fill a vacancy, but was not a candidate in the subsequent election. JM received three other letters from New England political leaders supporting Griswold's candidacy for office as well as letters from John G. Jackson and Jeremiah Morrow. JM nominated Griswold on 9 Mar. 1810 to an Illinois territorial judgeship, and the Senate confirmed the appointment one week later (Jonathan Robinson to JM, 26 Feb. 1810, John G. Jackson to JM, 1 Mar. 1810, Elisha Mathewson to JM, 2 Mar. 1810, Obadiah German and Uriah Tracy to JM, 2 Mar. 1810, Jeremiah Morrow to JM, 7 Mar. 1810 [DNA: RG 59, LAR, 1809–17]; *Senate Exec. Proceedings*, 2:140, 141).
    2. Samuel Huntington (1731–1796), a signer of the Declaration of Independence and president of the Continental Congress, was a judge of the superior court of Connecticut after 1773 and served as chief justice in 1784. He was the uncle of his namesake, Samuel Huntington, who had served on the Ohio Supreme Court and was currently governor of Ohio.

§ To Congress. *28 February 1810.* Transmits copies of the treaties concluded with the Delaware, Potawatomi, Miami, Eel River, and Wea Indians "for the extinguishment of their title to the lands therein described." Recommends implementing legislation.

RC and enclosures, two copies (DNA: RG 233, President's Messages; and DNA: RG 46, Executive Proceedings, 11B-C1). Each RC 1 p., in a clerk's hand, signed by JM. Received, read, and tabled by the House on 1 Mar. and by the Senate on 2 Mar. House copy referred to the Ways and Means Committee 3 Mar. JM signed the appropriations act for executing the Indian treaties on 1 May (*Annals of Congress*, 11th Cong., 2d sess., 589, 1469, 1479; *U.S. Statutes at Large*, 2:607–8). For enclosures, see JM's two presidential proclamations of 16 Jan. and one of 25 Jan. 1810.

From the Georgia Delegation in the House of Representatives

SIR   WASHINGTON 1st March 1810

A Bill having passed both branches of the Legislature authorising the Appointment of an additional Judge in the Mississippi Territory,[1] we beg to ask that it may be filled by Obediah Jones Esqr,[2] at present a Judge in the Illinois Territory. We would also solicit the appointment of Attorney in behalf of the United States in that district, for John W Walker Esqr,[3] a young Gentleman of talents & respectability.

Our sensibility on the subject of the Yazoo claim[4] will plead an apology for what may be considered an improper interference in a Matter which belongs to another department of the Government. We have the honor to be & &

H COBB
WM W BIBB
G M TROUP
D: SMELT.

RC (DNA: RG 59, LAR, 1809–17, filed under "Jones").

1. On 2 Mar. JM signed "An Act for the appointment of an additional judge, and extending the right of suffrage to the citizens of Madison county, in the Mississippi territory" (*U.S. Statutes at Large*, 2:563–64).

2. The delegation had previously recommended Obadiah Jones of Georgia for a territorial judgeship. While serving as a federal judge in the Illinois Territory, 1809–10, he had made known his desire to return to the South. JM nominated Jones for the Mississippi post on 5 Mar., and the Senate confirmed the appointment the next day (William H. Crawford to JM, 18 Feb. 1809, and enclosure, Carter, *Territorial Papers, Mississippi*, 5:701–2; Crawford to JM, 3 Mar. 1809, *PJM-PS*, 1:13–14; Jones to Crawford, 22 Oct. 1809, Carter, *Territorial Papers, Illinois*, 16:60–62; *Senate Exec. Proceedings*, 2:119, 120, 139, 140).

3. John Williams Walker (1783–1823), a native of Amelia County, Virginia, graduated from the College of New Jersey (Princeton) in 1806. A rising young Republican lawyer, he became involved in Alabama territorial politics and was elected to the U.S. Senate upon statehood in 1819.

4. Howell Cobb, William Wyatt Bibb, George M. Troup, and Dennis Smelt—Georgia's Eleventh Congress delegation in the House of Representatives—opposed the New England Mississippi Land Company's claim, which the Supreme Court upheld on 16 Mar. in *Fletcher v. Peck* (Magrath, *Yazoo*, pp. 83, 86–87).

§ From William H. Crawford. *1 March 1810, Senate Chamber*. Obadiah Jones has authorized Crawford "to accept of the appointment in his name, if it should be made," to the Mississippi territorial judgeship "& in his name to sign a resignation of his present appointment" of judge in the Illinois Territory.

RC (DNA: RG 59, LAR, 1809–17, filed under "Jones"). 1 p. Printed in Carter, *Territorial Papers, Illinois*, 16:81. Crawford was a U.S. senator from Georgia, 1807–13, U.S. minister to France, 1814–15, secretary of war, 1815–16, and secretary of the treasury, 1816–25.

§ From Joseph Wheaton. *1 March 1810, Washington*. Seeks appointment as store-keeper of the Washington Navy Yard.

RC (DNA: RG 59, LAR, 1809–17, filed under "Wheaton"). 1 p. Wheaton had been sergeant at arms of the House of Representatives from 1789 to 1809, when he lost his position to Thomas Dunn of Maryland. He was to correspond frequently with JM between 1811 and

1824, and in October 1814 JM nominated him for the post of deputy quartermaster general in the U.S. Army. The Senate rejected the nomination on 30 Jan. 1815 (*Senate Exec. Proceedings*, 2:543, 604, 606).

§ From Willis Alston. *2 March 1810, Representatives Chamber*. Encloses a letter he has detained for some time while waiting to see if the bill for an additional judgeship in the Mississippi Territory would pass.

RC (DNA: RG 59, LAR, 1809–17, filed under "Alston"). 1 p. Alston served as a Republican congressman from North Carolina between 1799 and 1815 and again from 1825 to 1831. Enclosure was probably Marmaduke Williams to JM, 6 Jan. 1810 (ibid.; 1 p.), seeking an appointment to a judicial position in the Mississippi Territory. JM also received letters written on 2 and 3 Mar. from three other members of the North Carolina congressional delegation, Jesse Franklin, James Holland, and Nathaniel Macon, advocating the claims of either Marmaduke Williams or his cousin John Williams for the Mississippi judgeship (ibid.).

From Isaac Hite

DR. SIR   BELLE-GROVE[1] March 3d. 1810
Urged by a benevolent disposition to Oblige a very worthy man I hope you will excuse the liberty I now take in again soliciting you for an office for our mutual friend Henry Dangerfield. As the object of his wished for attainment & his reasons for the application can best be disclosed by his letter to me on the subject I have enclosed it for your perusal. I sincerely hope the appointment may ⟨have?⟩ your concurrence which will I assure you be a high gratification to your friend

ISAAC HITE[2]

RC and enclosure (DNA: RG 59, LAR, 1809–17, filed under "Daingerfield"). Enclosure is Daingerfield's letter to Hite, 26 Feb. 1810 (2 pp.; printed in Carter, *Territorial Papers, Mississippi*, 6:50–51).

1. Belle Grove was Hite's estate near Middletown in Frederick County, Virginia. Shortly after their wedding in 1794, JM and his bride had visited Old Hall, which antedated Belle Grove on the site (JM to Jefferson, 5 Oct. 1794, *PJM*, 15:360 and n. 3).
2. Isaac Hite (1758–1836) had married JM's sister Nelly in 1783 (*WMQ*, 1st ser., 10 [1901–2]: 120).

§ From Samuel McKee.[1] *3 March 1810, Washington*. Encloses a letter from John Boyle recommending Thomas Montgomery for a judicial position in the Louisiana Territory. Forwards Boyle's letter now in the hope that Montgomery might be appointed to a vacancy in the judiciary of the Mississippi Territory.

RC and enclosure (DNA: RG 59, LAR, 1809–17, filed under "Montgomery"). RC 2 pp.
Enclosure is John Boyle to JM, 29 Jan. 1810 (2 pp.).

1. Samuel McKee was a Republican representative from Kentucky, 1809–17.

From William C. C. Claiborne

DEAR SIR,   NEW ORLEANS March 4th. 1810.
I take the liberty to enclose you the Names of the ten Citizens, nominated by the House of Representatives of this Territory, for the ensuing
Legislative Council, and to furnish you with some information respecting them.[1]

Messrs. Thomas Urquhart, Etienne Boré, Jean Noel Destrehan, Manuel Andry & Arnaud Beauvais, are Natives of Louisiana; Messrs. Jean
Blanque, Matarin Guerin, Magloire Guishard & Felix Bernard are natives
of France, and Henry Bry is a native of Switzerland.

Mr. Thomas Urquhart resides in New-Orleans; He is a well informed
Merchant, in high Credit, & enjoying an independent fortune; He is president of the Louisiana Bank, & of the New-Orleans Insurance Company;
he is also a Member of the House of Representatives of the Territory, & is
now, & has been for the last three years, Speaker of that branch of the
Legislature. Mr. Urquhart supports a most amiable Character in private
life, & discharges with great fidelity the public Trusts reposed in him: Mr.
Urquhart considers the English as his native language, but the french
seems alike familiar to him.

Mr. Etienne Boré resides about six miles above New Orleans; He is a
wealthy Sugar Plantor, and esteemed a very honest Man. Immediately
after the Cession of Louisiana to the United States, Mr. Boré was a strenuous advocate for a State authority; and was much dissatisfied with the
Government which Congress thought proper to prescribe for this Territory. But he has of late years, seemed to be better contented with the state
of things, & acted the part of an excellent Citizen. Mr. Boré is a man in
years, perhaps 67, and is held in high estimation by his Neighbours: He
speaks french only.

Mr. Jean N. Destrehan resides about twenty five miles above New Orleans, & is also a wealthy Sugar Plantor. Alike with Mr. Boré he was once
a great advocate for a State authority, but seems now to be very friendly
to the existing Government. Mr. Destrehan supports a very fair reputation, and possesses handsome Talents: He speaks a little English. Manuel
Andry is also a wealthy Sugar Plantor, & resides thirty six miles above
New Orleans; he has for the last four years been a member of the House

of Representatives, & is at this time Colonel Commandant of the Militia of his County. Mr. Andry is a man of integrity; has received a good education, & is much esteemed by his neighbours. Mr. A. Speaks french only. Mr. Arnaud Beauvais is a Cotton Plantor & resides at Pointe Coupée; He is at present a member of the House of Representatives; is a young man of great Integrity, & I believe much esteemed in his County; he speaks french & English.

Mr. Jean Blanque came to Louisiana with the Colonial Prefect Mr. Laussat, & was attached to his family. On the departure of Mr. Laussat Mr. Blanque was named by him as Consol or Commercial Agent for france at New-Orleans, but was never recognized as such, either by the *General* or *local Government*. Mr. Blanque resides near New Orleans, & is a merchant in high Credit; About three years ago he married a very beautiful Creole Lady, possessing a large estate, & connected with one of the most numerous & respectable family's in the County of Orleans. Mr. Blanque is a man of Genius & Education, & possesses considerable influence in the City & vicinity of New Orleans; he is a member of the City Council, a Director of the Louisiana Bank, & has been for the last three years a member of the House of Representatives of the Territory. Mr. Blanque is much disliked by most of the native Americans residing in & near New Orleans; His attachments are supposed to be wholly foreign, & they consider him a dangerous man. Mr. Blanque has, *I am persuaded strong partialities for his native Country, France*: But I should be wanting in Candour, were I not to add, that his conduct has not (in my opinion) been such, as to justify the fears & the prejudices, which some of my Countrymen here, feel of & towards him.

Mr. Matharin Guerin, resides on a little Farm about two miles below New Orleans; he has passed, the last twenty years in Louisiana, & is esteemed an honest man & an excellent Citizen; He is a Member of the present Council, & *the only one that has been renominated.*

Mr. Guishard is a farmer & resides about twelve miles below New-Orleans; He has passed the last twelve or thirteen years in Louisiana, and has been for three years past a member of the House of Representatives; he is a man of excellent understanding, & esteemed a worthy member of Society.

Mr. Felix Bernard came to Louisiana about twenty or twenty five years ago; he is a farmer and resides nearly opposite to Baton Rouge. Mr. Bernard has been a Member of the House of Representatives for the last five years, & is esteemed an honest man.

Mr. Henry Bry is a Farmer & resides in the County of Ouachitta. For some time he acted as Judge of his Parish & his conduct was correct. Mr. Bry is at present a Member of the House of Representatives; Mr. Bry is a man of information and esteemed a worthy Citizen; He Speaks french & English.

You will have observed, that there are five natives of Louisiana & five Foreigners in nomination. I have thought Sir, that it might not be proper wholly to exclude the foreigners from the Council; but that it would be politic to give the natives a decided preference.

The Characters of the Foreigners in nomination are alike respectable; but the former *services* of Mr. Guerin, & the proof which his *renomination* affords, that those services are approved, give him the strongest claim for patronage. I will therefore take the liberty to recommend Messrs. ["]*Thomas Urquhart, Matharin Guerin, Manuel Andry, Arnaud Beauvais,* & *Etienne Boré.*" Mr. Destrehan & Mr. Boré are Brothers in Laws; it might perhaps be best not to Commission both; The appointment of Mr. Boré, would I beleive, be most satisfactory.[2]

The period of service of the members of the present Legislative Council expires (I beleive) in January next. I have the honor to be Sir, With great respect & esteem Yo: Mo: obt. Servt.

WILLIAM C. C. CLAIBORNE

RC and enclosure (DNA: RG 59, LAR, 1809–17). RC filed under "Boré." Enclosure, 2 pp., filed under "Beauvais," is a report of the 12 Feb. election of ten candidates for the Legislative Council, signed by Eligius Fromentin, clerk of the Orleans Territory House of Representatives (printed in Carter, *Territorial Papers, Orleans*, 9:872).

1. The Orleans territorial reorganizational act of 1805 created a House of Representatives and reduced the Legislative Council from thirteen to five members. The president appointed councillors from a list of ten nominated by the legislature to serve five years (Edwin A. Davis, *Louisiana: A Narrative History* [Baton Rouge, La., 1971], p. 168).

2. JM opted for Destrehan instead of Boré. On 17 Apr. he nominated Destrehan, Urquhart, Guerin, Andry, and Beauvais. The Senate confirmed the appointments the following day (*Senate Exec. Proceedings*, 2:145, 146).

To the Republican Meeting of Cecil County, Maryland

March 5th, 1810.

To the Republicans of Cecil county, who were convened in Elkton, Feb. 22, 1810.

I have received fellow citizens your address of the above date. The period and the circumstances which have called forth this expression of your sentiments, are truly interesting, as well to the character as to the rights of the nation: and it affords satisfaction to find, in the meeting formed by you, a harmony with so many others, in approving the measures which have been pursued in reference to both. In a government founded on the principles, and organized in the form, which distinguish that of the U. States, discord alone, on points of vital importance, can render the nation weak in itself, or deprive it of that respect which guarantees its peace and security. With a union of its citizens, a government thus identified with the nation, may be considered as the strongest in the world; the participation of every individual in the rights and welfare of the whole, adding the greatest moral, to the greatest physical strength of which political society is susceptible.

For your kind assurances of regard and confidence, I return my thanks and my friendly wishes.

JAMES MADISON.

Printed copy (Baltimore *Whig*, 15 Mar. 1810).

From the Democratic Association of Gloucester County, New Jersey

[5 March 1810]

At the Annual meeting of the Democratic Association of the County of Gloucester in the state of New Jersey held at Woodbury on the 5th Day of March AD 1810.

Whereas it is the bounden duty of all good Citizens to come forward in defence of their government when it is insulted and Abused by any foreign Agent or Domestic Traitor. Therefore Resolved that the Conduct of Francis James Jackson the late British minister towards the American Government was Base and Insolent in the extreme and only equalled by his Outrageous conduct to the Danish Government at the time he had the savage cruelty to cause a Considerable part of the City of Copenhagen to be destroyed and a large proportion of its innocent Inhabitants to be murdered by the British fleet.

Resolved that the Conduct of the President of the United States in dismissing Francis James Jackson late minister from the King of Great Britain and Spurning him from his presence was dignified and Honorable to himself and to the united States and meets our warmest Approbation.

Resolved That should Great Britain in consequence of the dismissal of her late minister by our Government take any hostile steps against our Common Country we will stand by our Government and give it all the support that shall be in our Power.

Resolved that the President of the association shall transmit a fair Copy of the foregoing preamble and Resolutions signed by himself and Counter signed by the Secretary to the Honorable Thomas Newbold[1] Esquire one of our Representatives in Congress with a Request that he will present the same to the President of the United States.

THOMAS HENDRY, President.

CHARLES OGDEN Secretary

Ms (DLC). Docketed by JM.

1. Thomas Newbold (1760–1823) was a Republican representative from New Jersey, 1807–13.

§ From David Gelston. *5 March 1810, New York*. Has received JM's letter of 1 Mar. [not found] with its enclosure. Encloses the receipt. Has directed that the paper be discontinued.

RC and enclosure (DLC). RC 1 p. Enclosure (1 p.) is a receipt dated 4 Mar. 1810 for $10, "being the amount of the Years subscription to the American Citizen Sent to the President of the United states to the present date," signed by Francis Hall for James Cheetham, editor of the N.Y. *American Citizen*.

¶ From Eléonor-François-Elie, Marquis de Moustier. Letter not found. *5 March 1810*. Cited in duplicate dated 2 Aug. 1810. Suggests appointment of P. F. Fauche as U.S. consul at Gothenburg.

From Hezekiah Hall

DEAR SIR   CITY GOAL March 6 1810

I am confineed in this goal for the want of bail. I will Relate the circumstance to you. I owed Mr Jacob Boarer six $6. He Ishew a warrent aginst me and put it in Mr Gorge Loyde Hands to collect and Loyde came to me in Mr Miles shop in order to serve a warrent on me and I tolde Him to stand off in the Presence of Mr Miles & His wife. Without any hesitation [he] drew out a cow Hide whip out of His cane [and] Rushed on me. I Had a Hansaw in my Hand at the time and struck Him over the Head. After thay combat was over I paide the money to Mr Boarer. Theay next day a wirt was serve on me for sat and batterry and fr the want of bail I am in goal this is make 12 Days I am in confinement. Be pleased to Help me in grate trouble and disstress and your compliance will oblige Your Umble Scervt

I am the Person Hezekiah Hall that carred letters from the gum [s]prings tavern to your farms and from your farmes to motesellar in the year 1807 H

HEZ HALL

RC (DLC). Punctuation has been added for the sake of clarity.

§ From Michael Weyer. *7 March 1810, Cumberland, Allegany County, Maryland.* Lists for JM "Statutes &c. noted in the holy Scriptures" with relevance to "Some Particular affairs of our time."

RC (DLC). 4 pp.

From [John H. Douglass]

SIR   NEW YORK March 8th 1810.

I wrote you several letters previous to and pending your Election communicating important information which has proved true relative to the proceedings of certain men in the state to defeat your Election under the annonymous signature of Hancock[1] that information came principally from Mr Keteltas[2] whose talents and integrity broke up the whole scheme and drove the Clintonian hypocrites from their purpose this Gentleman has more efficient force than any man here, and has been basely treated by all parties for his truly Republican principles—I verily believe he has it in his power to turn the scale at the ensuing Election. If he would accept of the Office of Governor of Upper Louisiana, you could not make a more popular Appointment—he has been in that Country and was appointed Attorney General, by General Wilkinson. He is a man of great worth & Independence of mind and holds it as a principle that the Office should look for the man and not the man for the Office and that the actions of men and not their professions should recomend them to places of trust, therefore will never solicit the recommendation of others, particularly those who he has raised to power, by his tallents and virtues.
Yours &c Sincerely

NB Mr K has lately returned from the seat of Government of this state with a possession of sufficient knowledge to serve his Country if that Country is deserving of his further services, which can only be proven by his Country's giving him some distinguished place in the gift of those to whome she has confided her best interest his wish is retirement and thus end his days without further sacrifice of himself and family—regardless of all honours & profits he has refused offers from the present Administration in this State, his reasons are I dare say of the purest kind.

RC (DNA: RG 59, LAR, 1809–17, filed under "Keteltas"). Unsigned.

1. On the twenty letters written to JM between 7 Feb. 1808 and 22 Apr. 1809, signed variously "H.," "J. H. D.," or "Hancock," see *PJM-PS*, 1:134 n. 4.

2. For the early career of William Keteltas (ca. 1764–1812) as a lawyer and a prominent member of the Tammany and Democratic societies of New York City, see Mary-Jo Kline, ed., *Political Correspondence and Public Papers of Aaron Burr* (2 vols.; Princeton, N.J., 1983), 2:629–30 nn. 1, 3. Keteltas had supported JM's candidacy for the presidency in 1808 by attacking the ambition and intrigues of DeWitt Clinton in his pamphlet *Political Hipocrites Unmasked and Exposed* (New York, 1808; Shaw and Shoemaker 15371).

§ From William H. Crawford. *8 March 1810, Senate Chamber*. Sends Obadiah Jones's resignation as judge of the Illinois Territory and acceptance of appointment as judge of the Mississippi Territory.

RC (DNA: RG 59, LAR, 1809–17, filed under "Jones"). 1 p. Printed in Carter, *Territorial Papers, Illinois*, 16:82. Enclosure not found.

§ From George Harris. *8 March 1810*. Describes in considerable detail a gunboat and other weapons devised to destroy invading naval force. "Now pleas Your Exellency I have Indevoured, to give the outlines of my Defence of a Turtle war—with your permistion I Shall give it that Name, as allmost Every part resembles, a turtle or its Shell. . . . My moddles are all ready—and your Excellency Will pleas to Direct, in what manor they Shall be Sent forward to you, a box or trunk 3 feet long 16 Inchis wide one foot Deep will Contain them, and the weight will not accead 50 or 60 weight."

RC and enclosures (DNA: RG 107, LRRS, H-92:5). RC 8 pp. Docketed by a War Department clerk as received 26 Apr. 1810. Enclosures (8 pp.) are drawings of proposed weapons.

§ Presidential Proclamation. *8 March 1810, Washington*. On 5 Mar. the president, with the advice and consent of the Senate, ratified and confirmed the treaty concluded at Vincennes on 9 Dec. 1809 between the U.S. and the Kickapoo Indians. Requires all officeholders and citizens "faithfully to observe and fulfil" the treaty.

Printed copy (DNA: RG 233, President's Messages). Enclosed in JM's 15 Mar. message to Congress. Published in *National Intelligencer*, 14 Mar. 1810. The treaty is printed in *ASP, Indian Affairs*, 1:762–63.

§ From William Hull. *9 March 1810, Detroit*. Recommends Harris H. Hickman for collectorship at the port of Michilimackinac, to replace the late George Hoffman. "Mr. Hickman's connection with my family" makes it delicate to mention the gentleman's abilities, "which peculiarly qualify him for the office," but he is known personally to Jonathan Robinson and Peter B. Porter in Congress.

RC (DNA: RG 59, LAR, 1809–17, filed under "Hickman"). 1 p. Printed in Carter, *Territorial Papers, Michigan*, 10:311–12. JM nominated Hickman for the collectorship on 17 Apr., but the Senate rejected the nomination on 1 May. In 1812 JM appointed him a captain of infantry (*Senate Exec. Proceedings*, 2:146, 154–55, 226).

From Lafayette

MY DEAR SIR   PARIS 10h March 1810
 I Have Received By the John Adams Your kind Letter of the 4h december and Wish it Was in My power to Announce a Happy Change of European Measures. The frigate Has Not Yet Been Sent Back from England. Mr. de Champagny's Note, promised Several Weeks Ago is still Expected—and Altho' the Motive for delay, that the Emperor is taken Up With Matrimonial preparations,[1] Appears frivolous, it is Consistent With all other informations About Him. My Sentiments on American Affairs and the Conduct of Both Belligerent[s], My particular disapprobation and Grief With.Respect to the one I Should the Most Wish to Behave Well are So obvious that No Expression Could Add to Your Conviction. The few Services I May Render are Not So important and decisive as to deserve a formal Mention. Whatever intelligence I Can Collect is of Course Communicated to Gnl. Armstrong. He Will, No doubt, Write by Count palhen the Amiable Envoy from Russia to Whom and to His Brother I Entrust this Letter.[2] I shall therefore, With Grateful Confidence, Come to the private Concerns Upon Which, Amidst Your public Avocations, You are pleased to Bestow an Attention So friendly and So Momentous to me. But instead of Repeating What I am obliged to write to Mr. duplantier, I Believe I Save Some of Your time By the inclosed duplicate of My Letter to Him Which I Beg You Will Have the Goodness to forward With Such instructions and Modifications as You and Mr. Gallatin May think proper. I Have thought it Useful to Give Him a full View of My present Situation and state of informations, to impress Him With the Necessity to forward those documents and Legal titles the Want of Which I feel in a Manner Equally forcible and Urgent. Nor Could I Refrain, While His Concern in My Behalf discovers to Him Uncommon Embarassments and Wants Exhorbitant to Give Him Some details Which, if they don't Rescue me Wholly from Blame, are However in a Measure Explanatory and Apologetic. Words Could Not Give an Adequate idea of the Lively profound Sentiments of Gratitude I feel for You, My dear Sir, for Mr. Jefferson,

and Mr. Gallatin Whose Kindness to Me Has Made Him a Benevolent Associate of My two old friends. I am Sensible of the impropriety to Give You Additional troubles. Yet I Have So Severely Experienced the Want of Complete documents and titles that I Cannot Help Mentionning How important it is to Send them as Soon as possible, and for fear of Accidents By Several Opportunities.

I am much obliged to Mr. Humbolt[3] for the Acquaintance of Count palhen and His Brother. They possess Every Qualification that Must, in the United States, insure to them General Affection and Esteem. With the Most Grateful Attachement and Respect I am Your Constant Affectionate friend

LAFAYETTE

Permit me to Suggest an idea to Be Attended to only in the Case of My documents and titles Not Being in Your Hands at the time of the Sailing of the Next Vessel. Informations as positive as they Could Be Had, Under official Seals and Names, Might perhaps in a Measure Make Up for the deficiency of Regular drafts and patents Which However, it is Very desirable to be able to present in their Complete form.

RC (PHi). Docketed by JM. Enclosure not found.

1. On 1 Apr. Napoleon married Marie-Louise, the daughter of Emperor Francis I of Austria.

2. Count Fedor Pahlen's brother, the Russian general Pavel Petrovich Pahlen, may have been in Paris at the time Lafayette was writing (Fedor Pahlen to Count Nikolai P. Rumiantsev, 30 June 1810, Bashkina et al., *The United States and Russia*, pp. 672, 673 nn. 1, 4).

3. When Baron von Humboldt returned from his Latin American scientific expedition in 1804, he stopped in the U.S., and JM gave him a safe-conduct pass. He took residence in Paris to begin publication of his scientific findings and was active in Parisian intellectual and court circles until his departure in 1827 (pass for Baron von Humboldt, 23 June 1804 [DNA: RG 59, DL]).

§ From William Tatham.[1] *10 March 1810, Norfolk.* Transmits enclosures for JM's perusal but reminds him that "these uncountenanced pursuits" cannot continue "unless some respectable appointment in the power and inclination of the executive can afford me means wherewith my leisure hours may be thus employed." A plan to present JM with "some very extensive results of my topographical researches" is in abeyance for lack of funds, "an irrecoverable loss to the community."

RC and enclosures (DLC). RC 2 pp. Printed in Elizabeth Gregory McPherson, ed., "Letters of William Tatham (Second Installment)," *WMQ*, 2d ser., 16 (1936): 387–88. Enclosures are a description of a variety of engineering and optical devices, headed "Inestimable Apparatus" (7 pp.), and a prospectus for a manuscript entitled "Lessons in Public administration" (13 pp.). JM forwarded the enclosures for evaluation to Secretary of War Eustis, who reported that he had examined Tatham's "philosophical apparatus" and was "of opinion that it is not expedient to purchase them" for the War Department (Eustis to JM, 12 Apr. 1810 [DLC]).

1. William Tatham (1752–1819), who was to conduct a largely one-sided correspondence with JM, was born in England and immigrated to Virginia in 1769. He entered into mercantile ventures, fought in the Revolution, and moved to North Carolina where he served in the legislature in 1787. He returned to England in 1796 where he was employed as superintendent of the London docks, but he came back to the U.S. in 1805, at which time James Monroe gave him a letter of introduction to JM. As part of an endless quest for office and patronage, Tatham wrote and published extensively on canals, irrigation, agriculture, commerce, and topography, and he briefly held the position of military storekeeper at Richmond in 1817. His last years were spent in poverty. He was killed when passing (possibly intentionally) in front of a cannon during the celebration of Washington's birthday in 1819 (Monroe to JM, 25 Sept. 1804 [DLC, series 7, container 1]; see also G. Melvin Herndon, *William Tatham, 1752–1819: American Versatile* [Johnson City, Tenn., 1973]).

From Charles Scott

SIR   FRANKFORT KENTUCKY March 12th. 1810

I have the honor to transmit to your Excellency the enclosed Copy of an Act of the Legislature of this State, at their last Session.[1]

The subject is interesting to its Citizens. I trust their unwillingness to incur the Charges of the extinguishment of the Indian title in the act refered to; and the motives of which it is founded will be duly appreciated and considered. The large extent of Territory given up by the parent State to the General Government, on mere patriotic motives, seem to furnish some claim to an unincumbered enjoyment to the portion reserved.

The object of the price in the extinguishment of the Indian title (to the contemplated Lands), though insignificant as it regards the United States, becomes considerable in the estimation of this State; when taken into view with the circumstance mentioned; especially when it is also considered that however wise or just the recognition of the Indian title may have been in the General Government, it does not seem clear, that Virginia viewed that title as subsisting at the time of the Confederation. No State in the Union, I can venture to pronounce, is more attached to the Federal Government than this, and it would be to me a matter of infinite regret that any circumstance should tend to weaken that affection. What ever may be your decision on this subject, I have reason to hope a becoming deference will be evinced. I have to request of your Excellency that I may be instructed as to your views and intentions with respect to the proposed treaty that I may know how to act.[2] I am with high respect Yr. Mo. Obt. Servt.

CHS. SCOTT

RC and enclosure (DNA: RG 107, LRRS, S-108:5). RC in a clerk's hand, signed by Scott. Postmarked Frankfort, 1 Apr. Enclosure 2 pp. (see n. 1).

1. The enclosure is a copy of "An Act concerning the extinguishment of the Indian claim to certain lands within this Commonwealth," passed by the Kentucky General Assembly and signed by Governor Scott on 15 Jan. 1810. The act empowered the governor to negotiate with the federal government regarding the costs incurred in extinguishing Indian claims and permitted the governor to appoint an agent to attend future treaty-making councils with Indians. The agent was to be "vested with all necessary powers, except that of rendering this commonwealth in any wise liable for the payment of money."

2. Eustis informed Scott on 7 May 1810 that JM had decided, "from considerations which have been explained to the Delegation of Kentucky," not to incur "during the present year, any expenditures on account of the extinguishment of Indian Titles" (DNA: RG 107, LSMA).

§ To the Senate. *14 March 1810.* In response to a Senate resolution of 22 Jan., transmits a report of the secretary of war.

Printed copy (*ASP, Indian Affairs*, 1:764); enclosures (DNA: RG 46, Executive Proceedings, 11B-C2). RC not found. Enclosures are Eustis's report of 13 Mar. (1 p.) (FC, PHi: Daniel Parker Papers; letterbook copy, DNA: RG 107, LSP) and documents relating to the treaty concluded on 10 Nov. 1808 and 31 Aug. 1809 with the Great and Little Osage Indians (12 pp.). Printed in *ASP, Indian Affairs*, 1:764–67.

From David S. Garland

SIR   CONGRESS HALL March 15th. 1810

Many of the Citizens of Virginia are interested in the Lands North of the Ohio and between the Rivers Scioto and little Miami, which wer[e] reserved by that State to sattisfy Bountys due to the Officers and Soldiers of the Virginia line on Continental establishment.

The Warrants are daily issuing by the Executive of Virginia and are Sold in the Markett fare below their real Value in consequence of their being no good Land on which they can at this time be located.

But there is a tract of Country of about Twentyfive Miles Square within the reservation aforesaid to which the Indian claim is not extinguished, which is said to be Land of good quaility, and I presume wou'd be suffi-cient to sattisfy all the Warrants of that description that are not Located. Cou'd the Indian claim to the aforesaid Land be extinguished it wou'd contribute much to the advancement of the Interest of those who are now intitled to Warrants and wou'd be no more than justice, those who Ob-tained their Warrants at an early period had good Land to Locate them on, and those that are now Obtaining Warrants are equally intitled.

I presume that the Extinguishing the Indian claim is within the range

of Executive duties: I therefore take the liberty of requesting your attention to that subject.

You will pardon the liberty which I have taken in making to you this
inofficial Communication for I know of no Other way in which the Object
can be Obtained. With sentiments of the highest respect & esteeme I am
Yr. M. O. H. Servant

DAVID S. GARLAND [1]

RC (DNA: RG 107, LRRS, G-39:5). Docketed by a War Department clerk as received
16 Mar. 1810.

1. David Shepherd Garland (1769–1841), of Amherst County, Virginia, succeeded Wilson Cary Nicholas as a Republican congressman in the twenty-first Virginia congressional
district, 1810–11.

§ To Congress. *15 March 1810*. Submits for consideration copies of the ratified
treaty with the Kickapoo Indians "for the extinguishment of their title to certain
lands within the Indiana Territory, involving conditions which require Legislative
provision."

RC and enclosure (DNA: RG 233, President's Messages); RC (DNA: RG 46, Legislative
Proceedings, 11A-E2). Each RC 1 p., in a clerk's hand, signed by JM. Received by both
houses and tabled by the Senate on 16 Mar. House copy referred to Ways and Means Committee on 17 Mar. The appropriations act of 1 May for implementing Indian treaties awarded
a permanent annuity of $500 to the Kickapoo (*Annals of Congress*, 11th Cong., 2d sess.,
600–601, 1563; *U.S. Statutes at Large*, 2:608). The treaty is printed in *ASP, Indian Affairs*,
1:762–63. For enclosure, see Presidential Proclamation, 8 Mar. 1810.

From William L. Madison

UNITED STATES FRIGATE, UNITED STATES,
DEAR UNCLE   OFF NORFOLK March 16th 1810

Since my return to Norfolk from Madison, I have yielded to the wish
of my Father in consenting to quit the Navy, provided I can obtain a
Commission in the Army. My Father informs me that he has written on
to Washington, and thro' Mr. Dawson receiv'd a promise of a Commission
for me, in the Artillery. I hope in acting thus, I shall meet your approbation without incuring the censure of fickelness; for altho it wears much
the appearance of fickelness, to desire a change of situations in so short a
time, yet when in compliance with the wish of a Father, it ought at least
to be excusable, if not entirely blameless. I hope you will not attribute my
willingness to quit the Navy, to any dislike to my particular situation on
board this Ship, for I am confident let my situation be what it may, I shall

never serve under an Officer whom I esteem more than Captain Decatur; but it is more because my Father is averse to my being in the Navy than that I am anxious to quit it. Perhaps there are more advantages to be derived in the Army, than the Navy. In the Army, promotion is comparatively quick, in the Navy it must necessarily be slow. Let the merit of a Midshipman be what it may, he is compelled to serve at least three years before he can be qualifyed for promotion, at the expiration of that time, there will be a number in service equal to him in point of merit and much older in the dates of their warrants; would it not be great injustice then, to promote him before those whose claim to promotion is infinitely greater than his? Could it be, I should not wish it. Then the probability is, that five or six years would be as soon as it could be expected. But in the Army a man of merit has to encounter none of these difficulties, he is soon qualifyed, and there is greater room for promotion. I should be truly sorry were you to infer from what I have written that I am actuated by a wish for premature promotion in my present conduct; So far from it, I would not accept promotion were it offered me unless perfectly sensible of my ability to answer the responsibility attach'd to a Lieutenant. I have stated to you the only reasons by which I am actuated, if they appear to you not entitled to that consequence which I have given them, and that my situation here is better than in the Army, I have not the smallest doubt but that my Father will willingly consent to my remaining here.

Captain Decatur expects to sail from this port about the first of April on a cruize, before we return here, it is probable we shall visit the principal of our northern ports, and particularly Philadelphia. Should I succeed in my application, I should like to remain in this Ship until after this cruize. My Father informs me that all my friends at the Mountains are well, and particularly my Grand-Mother who has enjoyed uncommonly good health. Remember me with gratitude to Aunt Madison and believe me your affectionate Nephew

WILLIAM L. MADISON[1]

RC (NN). Docketed by JM.

1. William L. Madison (1789–1812), JM's nephew, was one of William and Frances Madison's ten children. He had been appointed a midshipman on 16 Jan. 1809 (*WMQ*, 1st ser., 6 [1897–98]: 116; Callahan, *List of Officers of the Navy*, p. 346).

From John Armstrong

Private

DEAR SIR, PARIS 18 March 1810

This will be handed to you by Count Pahlen who goes out as I beleive with every disposition to please and be pleased. He is a respectable young man.

If report says true, (for I know nothing of it officially) you will soon have a new Minister from this country. This is a Diaplomatic Cadet, who is for the first time put on horseback. He is the son in law of your old acquaintance Laforest,[1] and the son of the Count de Moustier, whom we knew as a Minister from Louis 16th. at New York.[2] They who know him, say he is a chip of the old block, which is not saying much for his discretion. What seems to confirm this suspicion is, that he has quarrelled with all the Ministers he has been with, and is not now on speaking-terms with his father & mother in law. P.[3] has refused to go back with him, which is another proof that things are not as they ought to be. Perhaps as the E.[4] likes to tread on the heels of English policy with regard to us, he may have selected de Moustier as the person coming nearest to Jackson & most likely to obtain the same sort of eclàt. This opinion has the air of ridicule, but in this age of wonderful things and astonishing calculations, it may turn out to be sober, and *serious* truth. I need not say that these details are for yourself—nor would I do so, but that almost everything personal in my letters has some how or other got abroad. E.g. I said something two years ago in a public letter about one Hunt,[5] who was then, as he is now, engaged in buying up titles to Western lands. This was put in his way, & he insinuates by some high officer of the Government, and takes it as a ground of justification for sweeping all the gutters & sinks of Paris for filth to throw at me in revenge. Warden also has been told that I wrote against his permanant appointment as Consul here, and though not yet an open enemy, soon will become such. This I regret, because in discharging What I beleived to be my duty to the public, I did not intend to injure M. W. nor M. H.—the injury, if there was any to them, was incidental, and not to be avoided but at the expence of a duty to the State. This however is reasoning that will not satisfy them & I must of course look out for other arguments which When employed, will but widen the breach between us. Having thus mentioned Warden's place I must add, that I understand from M. J. Russel of providence that he was the person destined for it when our foreign relations should admit a permanant appointment. This gave me great pleasure because it exactly corresponded with a view of my own Viz: to leave him chargé d'affaires if I quitted Paris before a successor arrived. He is by much the most fit man that I have seen here and is disposed to remain in either capacity.

The Emperor who was born to keep the world awondering, is now on the point, as you will see by the journals, of marrying the grand neice of Marie Antoinette. Of the political effects of this connexion, you can judge as well as any body. It will no doubt bring with it some important changes, but that of the most interest to the world is, that Bonaparte's power will now be encreased with the whole weight of Austria. Whether this will tend to quiet or distract mankind, is the question? A degree of power which puts a man hors d'insult, ought to make him mild, generous & benevolent—and that such may be the effect in the present case, is devoutly to be wished.

In relation to our business, I can add nothing to the contents of my public letters. M. C's letter of Feb.[6] is a new proof of the correctness of your estimate of European diaplomacy.

Holland has concluded a treaty in which she has saved her nominal independance.[7] Beleive me with the most respectful consideration your obliged & faithful hum servt.

J ARMSTRONG.

RC (DLC). Docketed by JM.

1. Antoine-René-Charles-Mathurin, comte de La Forest, had held a variety of consular and vice-consular positions in Savannah, Charleston, and New York after 1783. He was the French consul general at Philadelphia between 1792 and 1794 (Abraham P. Nasatir and Gary Elwyn Monell, *French Consuls in the United States: A Calendar of Their Correspondence in the Archives Nationales* [Washington, 1967], pp. 560–61).

2. In January and February of 1810 Napoleon seemed disposed to negotiate a new commercial treaty with the U.S. but found that Armstrong was only interested in discussing the problem of French spoliations on American shipping. In an effort to outmaneuver the American minister, Napoleon, in late February, decided to send Clément-Edouard Moustier on a short mission to Washington to raise the matter directly with JM and his administration. After about six weeks in the U.S., Moustier was to return to Paris, as Napoleon did not then intend to replace Turreau as his minister in Washington. Moustier's father, Eléonor-François-Elie, marquis de Moustier, had served as French minister to the U.S. in 1788–90, at which time he had openly offended American sensibilities by his liaison with the marquise de Bréhan. After 1793 the elder Moustier was in exile, either in Prussia or in England, and did not return to France until 1815, while his son commenced his diplomatic career in Napoleon's service. Napoleon aborted Moustier's mission to the U.S. in April 1810 and sent him instead to Morlaix to arrange prisoner of war exchanges with Great Britain. Six months later, in September 1810, Napoleon appointed Louis-Barbé-Charles Sérurier to replace Turreau as French minister to the U.S. (Napoleon to Champagny, 22 Feb. 1810, Napoleon to Denis Decrès, 20 Apr. 1810, Plon and Dumaine, *Correspondance de Napoléon Ier*, 20:237, 297; JM to Jefferson, 8 Dec. 1788, *PJM*, 11:383; Clifford L. Egan, *Neither Peace nor War: Franco-American Relations, 1803–1812* [Baton Rouge, La., 1983], pp. 114, 137).

3. JM later interlined here in pencil "Pichon."

4. JM later interlined here in pencil "Emperor."

5. Seth Hunt (1780–1846), son of an army officer from Massachusetts, purchased the claims of British grantees in the Mississippi Territory. He had also been appointed by James Wilkinson as commandant at Ste. Genevieve in the Louisiana Territory in 1804 but later

quarreled with Wilkinson (Carter, *Territorial Papers, Mississippi*, 6:489 n. 28; Mann, *A Yankee Jeffersonian*, p. 272 n. 34). On his relations with Armstrong and David Bailie Warden, see Skeen, *John Armstrong*, pp. 114–15.

6. Champagny to Armstrong, 14 Feb. 1810 (printed in *ASP, Foreign Relations*, 3:380–81).

7. Under a treaty signed in Paris on 16 Mar. 1810, Louis Bonaparte, king of Holland, was forced to accept the French occupation of Dutch territory south of the rivers Maas and Waal as well as the presence of French forces in all port towns to close them off to English trade. The treaty also required the confiscation of all goods carried into Dutch ports in American vessels during the previous year (Schama, *Patriots and Liberators*, pp. 605–6; Alexandre de Clercq, ed., *Recueil des traités de la France* [23 vols.; Paris, 1880–1917], 2:328–30).

From Richard Peters

DEAR SIR   BELMONT[1] March 18. 1810
   The enclosed contains Letters to several of the French *Savans* who, with great Civility, & some very profitable Attention, have corresponded with our Philadelphia Agricultural Society. I have sent Letters thro' private Conveyances; & have Reason to believe they have miscarried, owing to the Uncertainty of such Conveyances. I take the Liberty of requesting you to have the Letter to Genl Armstrong sent with the public Despatches, when an Occasion offers. I am not sufficiently acquainted with the Officers in public Departments, to ask even this small Favour. If I have outlived most of my old Friends, I have the greater Necessity to take all Advantages of the *Remnant saved*. Being persuaded that this Request will give you more Pleasure than Trouble, I have with the more Confidence made it: Especially as it is of public Benefit to keep up such Reciprocations of Good-Will. I am very truly & affectionately your obedt Servt

RICHARD PETERS[2]

RC (DLC).

1. Peters's estate, Belmont, stood on the west bank of the Schuylkill River in Philadelphia.

2. Richard Peters (1744–1828), a federal district judge for Pennsylvania, was a long-standing friend and correspondent of JM's. He conducted experiments in scientific farming, helped to found the Philadelphia Society for Promoting Agriculture in 1785, and served as its first president.

From John K. Smith

NEW ORLEANS march 18th 1810

I have the honor to enclose you in a tin Case five Certificates & plats of Land located for the marquis Lafayette.[1] I received from the Register 6 Certificates but delivered one to Mr Duplantier who wished to alter the location.

There remains now 2520 acres for which Certificates are to be returned & which will be immediately attended to—the location for 2,000 acres is already fixed upon & Mr Duplantier says he will have it in his power to select when he goes up the Country (which he intends to do next week) the 520 acres which were originally located adjacent to this place but for which no land could be found beyond the Six hundred yards ceded as Commons to the City of N Orleans by Congress.[2]

Mr Duplantier states that he would give for these lands 50,000$ in Cash—they are however worth much more & he will when the remaining plats & Certs. are ready give you full information as to the Situation & value of the whole. I have the honor to be with high respect sir your Ob St.

J. K SMITH

RC (DLC).

1. The enclosures were among those forwarded by JM in his 18 May 1810 letter to Lafayette.

2. JM may have asked the treasury secretary to investigate this matter. Mounted immediately behind the RC is a separate sheet bearing the following notation in Gallatin's hand: "From a survey made by Charles Trudeau in 1798 by order of Govr. Carondelet; copy of which dated 1806 is deposited at the Treasury, it appears that between the boundary line of the six hundred yards given to the Corporation, and Bayou St. John, and between Gravier's line & that of the concessions made to Morand, Latille, Le Breton, Suares & Vidal, there were at least 500 acres vacant land interrupted only by a small concession to Carlos Guadiola. Have any new claims been discovered which prevent the execution of Gen. La Fayette's location. This on account of its value ought to be strictly examined before it is abandoned. A. G." (later docketed by JM, "see letter from J. K. Smith of March 18. 1810").

§ From Nathaniel Macon. *18 March 1810, Washington.* Francis Xavier Martin will accept appointment to fill vacancy created by the death of one of the Orleans territorial judges [John Thompson]. Has known Martin, a native of France, as a North Carolina lawyer from 1781 until he became a judge in the Mississippi Territory [in 1809].

RC (DNA: RG 59, LAR, 1809–17, filed under "Martin"). 2 pp. Macon was a Republican congressman from North Carolina, 1791–1815. JM nominated Martin for the Orleans territorial judgeship on 19 Mar. (*Senate Exec. Proceedings*, 2:119, 120, 142; see also Jefferson to JM, 16 Apr. 1810, and n. 2).

§ From William C. C. Claiborne and Thomas B. Robertson. *19 March 1810, New Orleans*. The resignation of Philip Grymes as U.S. attorney for the Orleans district has created a vacancy, which must be filled by "a Citizen of competent talents, and correct principles." They recommend "Tully Robinson (late of Virginia) who has resided in this Territory about twelve months."

RC (DNA: RG 59, LAR, 1809–17, filed under "Robinson"). 1 p. Printed in Carter, *Territorial Papers, Orleans*, 9:877–78. JM nominated Robinson (formerly a major in the army) on 17 Apr., and the Senate confirmed the appointment the following day (*Senate Exec. Proceedings*, 2:94, 95, 145, 146).

§ From Benjamin Day. *19 March 1810, Fredericksburg*. Has received JM's letter of 12 Mar. [not found] and states Mr. Maury's account as requested. Anthony Buck will call on JM to receive the $19.37 due.

RC (DLC). 1 p. Cover marked "Favoured by Mr. Buck." Endorsed by Buck on 29 Mar., "Recd payment." Docketed by JM.

§ From Samuel Hanson of Samuel.[1] *19 March 1810*. Addresses JM not to "deprecate the Sentence of Mr. Hamilton" in dismissing him from his position following a court of inquiry but to regain JM's good opinion. Believes that the court of inquiry found some of the charges against him to be not only "unfounded" but also "vexatious & malicious"; complains that the secretary of the navy neglected to investigate the evidence. Lacks now the means of supporting a large family and must depend on JM's patronage. "For the length and freedom of this address, your amiable Lady must be responsible—Since it is owing to her benevolent communication of your Good wishes for me that I have been tempted to take the liberty" of writing this letter.

RC (DLC). 12 pp. Docketed by JM.

1. Samuel Hanson of Samuel (ca. 1752–1830), a native of Maryland and a member of the General Assembly of Maryland from 1781 to 1784, had moved in 1787 to Alexandria, Virginia, where he received an appointment as surveyor in 1789. He resigned that position in 1793 following a dispute with the collector, Charles Lee, and then served for the next eight years as cashier of the Bank of Columbia. During this period he also edited two Georgetown newspapers. Hanson was dismissed from his cashier's position in 1801, at which time he received a "midnight appointment" as notary public for Washington from President John Adams. He subsequently solicited employment from JM and in 1804 finally received the position of purser at the Washington Navy Yard. In this post he complained of being "uniformly oppressed" by the accountant of the Navy Department, and Secretary Paul Hamilton dismissed him in 1810 after a court of inquiry had examined his accounts, a decision which Hanson then appealed to JM for the next year (Edward C. Papenfuse et al., eds., *A Biographical Dictionary of the Maryland Legislature, 1635–1789* [2 vols.; Baltimore, 1979–85], 1:409; *Senate Exec. Proceedings*, 1:11, 14, 388, 390; John Fitzgerald to Alexander Hamilton, July 1793 and 20 Nov. 1793, Syrett and Cooke, *Papers of Hamilton*, 15:155, 156 n. 3, 403 and n. 1; Hanson to JM, 9 May 1802, 6 Oct. 1803, and 16 Apr. 1811 [DLC]).

From Lafayette

MY DEAR SIR   PARIS 20h March [1810]

The John Adams By Whom I Have Received Your Kind Letter of the 4h december is Not Yet Returned from England. I Heartily Wish She May Carry Such Arrangements as Will Have Settled the differences With one Belligerent and Must Enable Gnl. Armstrong to Call Upon the declarations Made By the other. There is for me Every Motive to Wish this tardive Recourse to Honest and Sound policy Had first taken place in france. But Since the Emperor Seems determined to Wait for the Recall of the British orders of Council I Eagerly Expect and Shall More Joyfully Welcome the Good Tidings from that Quarter. I Hope it is Superfluous to Express My feelings at the Universal Seizure of American property.[1] My Informations Could not Be More Minute, nor of a Later date than those from General Armstrong. I am for Obvious Reasons Every Day More Attached to My plan of Retirements—But Should Much Lament My distance from Affairs Where the U. S. are Concerned Was it Not Evident that Bonaparte Cannot, in Essential points, Be influenced. I Have Had, in My Endeavours to Render Service, Many Opportunities to know that the fine Men About Him disapprove that part of His System and Conduct. That He May See What is Right, Adopt it, and Repair What Has Been Wrong is my most fervent Wish. His Attention is Now Wholly taken Up With the preparations for the Marriage Which Connects Him, By the Nearest ties of Consanguinity With the House of Austria and Every Branch of the House of Bourbon. The political State of Europe Will of Course Be Related in the Ministerial dispaches. I shall therefore Confine Myself to observations Relative to My private Concerns. Permit me, My dear friend, to Request Your Reading a Long Letter to Mr. duplantier, Which I inclose duplicate to Guard Against Any Accident of the Louisiana Mail. The Last Accounts I Have Received, the pressure of My pecuniary Embarassments, the Necessity and Urgency to obtain documents and Legal titles are there So fully Explained that I Will not trouble You With Repetitions. Yet, while I most Respectfully Aknowledge that the Gift of Congress Surpasses Every Hopes I Could form, While I am penetrated With Gratitude to My friends, and While in this Rescue from Ruin, and Expectation of Wealth I particularly Enjoy the Source to Which I am Endebted for it, I am forced to insist Upon the Speedy and Multiplied transmission of those papers Without Which No Loan Can Be Effected. I Could not Refrain, in the Letter to M. duplantier, from a few Explanations Which if they don't Wholly Justify the Exhorbitance of My debts May at Least Some What Lessen the Blame. Permit me to Hope that Mr. Gallatin Whose kindness I feel Most Gratefully and Whose Opinion I Much Value Will not Be a Stranger to this Apologetic

Attempt. I indulged in details Still More particular With our friend
Jefferson Who Has Now More time to Spare. Permit me to inclose My
packet to Him.[2] I offer You the Best Wishes, Grateful Affection, and High
Respect of Your old friend

LAFAYETTE

RC (PHi). Docketed by JM. For surviving enclosure, see n. 2.

1. In retaliation for the Nonintercourse Act of 1 Mar. 1809, Napoleon had been steadily
increasing his seizures of American vessels. Three days after Lafayette wrote to JM the
policy was to culminate in the Decree of Rambouillet, which authorized the confiscation of
all American ships entering French ports, regardless of whether or not they had already
touched at British ports (*ASP, Foreign Relations*, 3:384).

2. Lafayette enclosed his 20 Feb. 1810 letter to Jefferson (DLC: Jefferson Papers; printed
in Chinard, *Letters of Lafayette and Jefferson*, pp. 296–300), which JM forwarded in his 25 May
letter to Jefferson (see also Jefferson's Epistolary Record [DLC: Jefferson Papers]).

From James Turner

SIR   SENATE CHAMBER 20th. March 1810
I was requested by Oliver Fitts Esquire Attorney General of the State
of North Carolina to inform You that he would willingly Accept the Appointment of Judge in the Mississippi Territory,[1] having thoughts of removing to that country.

Mr. Fitts is a gentleman of Education Character & talents, and the office
he holds in the State is an evidence that his legal Acquirements are Such
as to qualify him for Such an appointment.

As a vacancy is Occasioned by the removal of Judge Martin to the Orleans Terry. I should be glad if Mr. Fitts Could be appointed. I am with
Much esteem Your Obdt Servt.

J. TURNER[2]

RC (DNA: RG 59, LAR, 1809–17, filed under "Fitts").

1. An act of 2 Mar. had created a new Mississippi territorial judgeship, to which JM had
appointed Obadiah Jones. On 19 Mar. the other Mississippi judgeship became vacant when
Francis Xavier Martin was shifted to the Orleans Territory. JM nominated Fitts on 17 Apr.,
and the Senate confirmed the appointment the following day (Georgia Delegation in the
House of Representatives to JM, 1 Mar. 1810, and nn. 1, 2; *Senate Exec. Proceedings*, 2:142,
145, 146).

2. James Turner was a Republican U.S. senator from North Carolina, 1805–16. On 21
Mar. 1810 JM received letters supporting Fitts's candidacy from Jesse Franklin and Nathaniel
Macon, Republican senator and representative respectively from North Carolina. Another
North Carolina representative, Willis Alston, sent JM a further letter on Fitts's behalf on
16 Apr. 1810 (DNA: RG 59, LAR, 1809–17; printed in Carter, *Territorial Papers, Mississippi*,
6:54, 60).

§ To Congress. *20 March 1810*. Submits a return of the militia, "as received by the Department of War from the several States and Territories."

RC and enclosure (DNA: RG 46, Legislative Proceedings, 11A-E6); RC (DNA: RG 233, President's Messages). Each RC 1 p., in a clerk's hand, signed by JM. Enclosure (1 p., 16" × 52") is Eustis's 16 Mar. report of returns, by states and territories, of numbers of militia members (totaling 684,335) and equipment. Received and tabled by the Senate on 20 Mar. and by the House on 21 Mar. (*Annals of Congress*, 11th Cong., 2d sess., 612, 1605). Printed in *ASP, Military Affairs*, 1:258–62.

§ From James T. Johnson. *20 March 1810, Baltimore*. Describes himself as an orphan placed under the guardianship of a "miserly ould uncle" who neglected his education and failed to curb his "idle propensityes." The recent death of his uncle, however, has arrested his career of dissipation and rendered his future prospects "gloumy." Requests appointment as a midshipman, as he desires to spend the rest of his days in the service of his country.

RC (DNA: RG 45, Misc. Letters Received). 2 pp.

From an Unidentified Correspondent

SIR   PHILADA. March 21. 1810

I have taken the liberty of forwarding to you a copy of the Democratic Press[1] containing the Letter from Colonel Frederick Evans, Member of the State Legislature from the Democratic County of Northumberland, to Wm Duane Lt. Colonel of the Rifle regiment[2] in the Standing Army of the United States and Commandant of the troops at the old Lazaretto near fort Miflin to give you some idea of the estimation in which your Military officer is held in this State by the firmest republicans.

It will be worth your attention to make some enquiry respecting this officer who is now become so obnoxious to the republicans of this State that unless something is done we will really have to turn ours; to the source from whence he derived his power. Is it I will ask the President of the U States proper to keep in Commission a Lieut. Colonel who abuses in the vilest manner all the Constituted Authorities of the State from the Executive & Legislative down to the appointments made by the Governor. Is such conduct as Willm. Duane is Guilty of not sufficient to require an investigation in to his conduct—for my part I think it sufficient to justify the President for removing him from office—& I can assure Mr Madison that this is the opinion of 19 twentieths of the Democrats of this commonwealth & tha⟨t⟩ if he places any reliance on the Aurora he may rest satisfied that it is a broken stick on which he depends. The Aurora is held in this state in the same Estimation that the Abandoned James Cheethams paper[3] is held in the state of New York.

It is allmost insufferable that such Cowardly Poltroon as Duane should be paid by the United States about 2000 Dollars pr. An for abusing and Reviling the Democrats of this state. But you will find shortly that Unless, the Feds support the Aurora it will fall to the ground—with the assistance of the U States 2000$ pr. Ann. I am Sir your sincere friend & fellow REPUBLICAN

RC (DNA: RG 107, LRRS, A-39:5). Docketed by a War Department clerk as received 27 Apr. 1810.

1. The 21 Mar. issue of the Philadelphia *Democratic Press* contained a letter from Frederick Evans to William Duane, editor of the "apostate paper called the *Aurora*." Evans was responding to allegations printed in the Philadelphia *Aurora General Advertiser* of 8 Mar. to the effect that Evans, as the brother-in-law of Pennsylvania governor Simon Snyder, was at the center of a faction in the Pennsylvania state legislature promoting measures to produce "civil war" between the federal government and the state in the aftermath of the Olmstead affair of 1809. Evans denied the charges and further stated that he was "*no relation whatever to Governor Snyder either by blood or marriage.*"

2. In 1808 Jefferson had awarded Duane his commission, which he resigned on 31 July 1810. In 1813 JM appointed him adjutant general of the fourth military district (*Senate Exec. Proceedings*, 2:101, 106, 371, 380; Heitman, *Historical Register*, 1:385).

3. James Cheetham was editor of the N.Y. *American Citizen*.

§ From Etienne Harries. *21 March 1810, Paris*. Requests JM's aid in delivery of mail to and from New Orleans, since his own efforts have been unavailing. Asks that M. L. Rousset of New Orleans be advised that he can send letters to Harries by addressing them to JM's office.

RC (DLC). 2 pp. In French. Docketed by JM.

§ From Jared Ingersoll. *21 March 1810, Philadelphia*. Introduces his son Joseph.

RC (DLC). 1 p. Fragment. Lower portion of page, including signature, is missing.

From John B. C. Lucas

SIR,   ST. LOUIS March 22d. 1810.

It has been my Misfortune from the commencement of the Sitting of the Board of Commissioners, for ascertaining Titles and adjusting Claims to Land in the Territory of Louisiana until this present time to be one of those who entertained and entertains opinions the least favorable to land

Claimants, this is a fact that I should undertake to prove by transcripts of various parts of the proceedings of the Board, was Not Mr gallatin allready possessed of full information on that head; this, Sir, is more than Sufficient to account for the Libellous petition that has been Signed in this territory against me, and which I suppose has been presented to you by Col. John Smith T.[1] The Bounds of a Letter do Not permit me to enter into the details Necessary to prove the correctness of the opinions I have given as Land commissioner, suffice it to say that it cannot be suspected that I have been biassed by partiality for french Men or by bribery, had these things taken place you probably would Not have heard of any complaints against me either as Judge or commissioner. Lest however these should be considered as mere surmises I wish that an inquiry into my official conduct may take place.[2] I have the honor to be, Sir, Most respectfully your very humble svt.

John B. C. Lucas

RC (DLC).

1. John Smith, who placed a T. after his name to identify himself as a Tennessean, was an early settler in the Ste. Genevieve district of the Louisiana Territory where he became heavily involved in both lead mining and speculation in old Spanish land claims. In territorial politics Smith T. supported James Wilkinson during his governorship, but he was dismissed in 1807 from his local judicial and militia offices by acting governor Frederick Bates who suspected him of involvement with Aaron Burr. As one of the three commissioners appointed to settle disputed land claims, Lucas earned the hostility of Smith T. and other land claimants because of his opposition to the wholesale confirmation of Spanish land titles. In August 1809 Smith T. and others organized a convention at Ste. Genevieve to petition Congress to establish a more generous land policy and to remove Lucas from office as well. In St. Louis two months later, Smith T. was appointed to go to Washington to lobby on behalf of the claimants (William E. Foley, *A History of Missouri, 1673 to 1820*, vol. 1 of *A History of Missouri*, ed. William Parrish [Columbia, Mo., 1971], pp. 101–2, 103, 121, 123, 124, 142–43; Lucas to Gallatin, 19 Oct. 1809, Carter, *Territorial Papers, Louisiana-Missouri*, 14:335; see also Inhabitants of the Louisiana Territory to JM, ca. 10 Oct. 1809).

2. JM ignored or was unaware of the criticism, for he had already nominated Lucas for a second term on 19 Mar. The Senate confirmed the appointment two days later (*Senate Exec. Proceedings*, 2:142).

From William Pinkney

Dear Sir   London. 23d. March 1810.

I had intended to write you a very tedious Letter; but I have no longer Time to do so—as it is now near 2. OClock in the Morning and Lieut. Elliott leaves Town at 10. A.M.

My official Letter of the 21t. Inst.[1] will apprize you of the Course finally taken by this Government in Consequence of Mr. Jackson's Affair. I do not presume to anticipate your Judgment upon it. It certainly is not what I wished, &, at one Time, expected; but I am persuaded that it is meant to be Conciliatory. I have laboured earnestly to produce such a Result as I believed wd. be more acceptable. Why I have failed I do not precisely know—and I will not harrass you with Conjectures. The Result, such as it is, will I am sure be used in the wisest Manner for the Honour & prosperity of our Country.

It is doubtful whether there will be any Change of Administration here. Partial Changes *in* Administration are very likely.

I think I can say with Certainty that a more friendly Disposition towards the U. S. exists in this Country at present than for a long Time past.

I had the Honour to receive your Letter of the 4h. of December, by Lieut Elliott—and am very much obliged to you for it. Presuming upon your Indulgence I will write again by the first opportunity. Mr. Oakeley[2] will I think set out for America very soon; and I take for granted will be the *Chargé d'Affaires.*

With sincere and anxious Wishes for your Health and Happiness and for the Honour & Strength of your Government—believe me to be Dear Sir your faithful Friend and Obedient Servant

WM PINKNEY

RC (DLC: Rives Collection, Madison Papers). Docketed by JM.

1. Pinkney to Robert Smith, 21 Mar. 1810 (*ASP, Foreign Relations,* 3:351–52). In this letter, Pinkney reported—on the basis of correspondence and several conversations with Lord Wellesley—that the Perceval ministry was unlikely to send a new minister to Washington in the immediate future to replace Jackson and that JM therefore could not expect to receive any proposals for arrangements on the *Chesapeake* affair and the orders in council.

2. Charles Oakley was secretary at the British legation in Washington when Jackson's recall was demanded. While Jackson tarried in America for several months, Oakley returned to London late in 1809. Instead of Oakley, John Philip Morier was appointed secretary of the British legation circa 14 Apr. 1810, and he served as chargé d'affaires at Washington until the arrival of Augustus John Foster in July 1811 (Mayo, *Instructions to British Ministers,* pp. 302–3 and n. 4).

From Lafayette

MY DEAR SIR   PARIS 24h March 1810

The Letters intended for the John Adams Are Gone an other Way. I Will not However Miss the Opportunity of the frigate. It is probable, after she is Arrived from England, Gnl. Armstrong Will Have to detain

Her a few days, and By that time More May be Said on the Situation of American Affairs With Respect to Both Belligerents. My feelings and Wishes You Well Know. What information May Be obtained Will Be Given at the Last Moment. While the talk of the day is Upon the Match Which ⟨Connects⟩ By So Many ties of Consanguinity the families of Bonaparte, Austria, and Bourbon, My Mind is Anxiously Bent on the public Concerns of the U. S. Both Sides of the Channel, and the State of American property Under the Last Measures. But I Will to day only offer My Best thanks for Your Kind Letter By the John Adams. It Gives me the Hope to Receive, through the Next Opportunity, the titles and documents which are to Complete Your friendly Work. Indeed, My dear friend, the Want of them is Now Severely felt. The Munificent Gift of Congress I Had no Right to depend Upon. Its Extent, as is Confirmed By the last intelligences, Surpasses Any Expectations the Most Sanguine Hope or Aspiring Wish Could Have formed. Words are Not Equal to My Sense of My obligations to My friends. But While this Grateful Confidence and the Ressources founded Upon it Have for Several Years preserved and Supported me it Has Become impossible to postpone Any longer My Complete Liberation. This pecuniary Situation Appears So Unaccountable that I Could not Refrain from offering, in the inclosed letter, Some Explanation for it. I Have Sent a Much Longer one to our friend Jefferson who Now Has time to Read My Apologies.[1] You Will Conceive the Want I feel to lay Before Him, You, and Mr. Gallatin the observations Which if they don't Wholly Explain a Way do in a Measure Soften the Blame Which My Budget is Apt to incur. Be it as it May, and Whatever Share in it is allowed to the Singularity of My Adventures, it is a fact that I Have Been Saved from Ruin and a fortune insured to My family By the Generosity of Congress and the Exertions of My Excellent friends. But a fact Not Less Evident is that the only Way to prevent the first part of that Good Work from Being defeated is to Send me immediately the titles and documents Without Which a Loan Cannot Be effected. I Beg Your pardon, My dear friend, for troubling You With So Many details of My personal Affairs. The liberty I take is founded on Grateful and Experienced Reliance on Your Kindness to Me. I Beg You to present My Best Compliments and thanks to Mr. Gallatin. Remember to our friends about You. Permit me to Request Your forwarding the inclosed to Mr. duplantier if You Approve it. I am With Most Affectionate Respect Your old Constant friend

LAFAYETTE

RC (PHi). Docketed by JM. For surviving enclosures, see n. 1.

1. Lafayette enclosed his letters to Jefferson of 18 Nov. 1809 and 24 Mar. 1810 and also, apparently, a manuscript in French, "Compte rendu sur la fortune de Général Lafayette à

différentes époques de sa vie" (DLC: Jefferson Papers; printed in Chinard, *Letters of Lafayette and Jefferson*, pp. 293–96, 302–3, 303–15), which JM forwarded in his 15 June letter to Jefferson (see also Jefferson's Epistolary Record [DLC: Jefferson Papers]). The manuscript recounted Lafayette's vicissitudes in America and Europe from 1777 to the present. His personal expenses during the American Revolution came to 1,033,000 livres; confiscations during the French Revolution, aid to relatives, and other expenses after 1789 added a burden in excess of three million livres. To carry on his family obligations since his release by the Austrians, he borrowed 520,000 livres secured by his Louisiana land grants. His situation was now so desperate that he must obtain the patents or face complete ruin.

§ From John Wayles Eppes. *24 March 1810, Congress Hall.* Has learned from William Branch Giles that Mr. Dublois, "who is soliciting the appointment of purser was dismissed from the Navy yard under the Federal administration for peculation—That he practiced actual fraud on the workmen and on the public." If an appointment has not yet been made, perhaps JM can ascertain if the charges can be supported by evidence. To remove a Republican and appoint such a "violent Federalist" would bring "serious disappointment and mortification to your Republican friends." Mr. Brent has the evidence proving the charges against Dublois. A postscript states that Dr. Eustis now has these papers.

RC (DLC). 3 pp.

§ From Samuel Hanson of Samuel. *24 March 1810, Washington.* Disavows "any Animadversions, either oral or printed," that may be made in consequence of his dismissal. Cannot be responsible for his friends who think he was harshly treated, "especially, as some of them, being Fœderalists, will, *of course*, be gratified with any opportunity . . . of censuring the present Administration." If Secretary Hamilton had investigated the charges "with unbiassed precision . . . it is impossible that, at an advanced age; I should have been Sacrificed, as I have been, to a confederacy of unprincipled & fraudulent Agents." Asks to be permitted "an opportunity of vindication" should any unfavorable report reach JM.

RC (DLC). 3 pp.

From Thomas Jefferson

DEAR SIR   MONTICELLO Mar. 25. 10.

You knew, I believe that the society of Agriculture of Paris had sent me a plough which they supposed the best ever made in Europe.[1] They at the same time requested me to send them one of ours with my mould board.[2] I have made one for them which every body agrees to be the handsomest & of the most promising appearance they have ever seen, and I have five at work on my own farms, than which we have never seen ploughs work better or easier. I have taken as a model the ploughs we got through Dr.

Logan (you & myself) a dozen years ago,[3] & fixed my mould board to it. But how to get it to Paris I know not, unless you can favor it with a passage in some public vessel. It is a present, & therefore no matter of merchandise. Can you encourage me for this purpose to send it to Washington, Baltimore, Philadelphia or New York? taking into account that I set out for Bedford[4] tomorrow, not to return under two or three weeks, & consequently that your answer will have to lie here unopened to that time. Jarvis writes me he has sent us a pair of Merino sheep, each, to arrive at Alexandria.[5] Whether he has designated them individually I do not know; but as they are so liable to accidents by the way I propose that we make them a common stock not to be divided till there be a pair for each, should any have died. We are suffering by drought, & our river is so low as to be scarcely boatable. It would take very unusual quantities of rain to ensure it's usual state through the ensuing summer. Wheat looks well generally. It is believed the fruit has been all killed in the bud by the late extraordinary cold weather. Mine is untouched, tho I apprehend that a very heavy white frost which reached the top of the hill last night may have killed the blossoms of an Apricot which has been in bloom about a week. A very few peach blossoms are yet open. Always affectionately yours.

TH: JEFFERSON

RC (DLC); FC (DLC: Jefferson Papers).

1. In 1808 the Agricultural Society of the Seine had sent Jefferson "one of Guillaume's famous ploughs, famous for taking but half the moving power of their best ploughs before used" (Jefferson to John Taylor, 23 June 1808, Jefferson to Robert Fulton, 16 Apr. 1810, Betts, *Jefferson's Garden Book*, pp. 372, 435).

2. Jefferson had been experimenting with the "mouldboard of least resistance" since 1788. He sent a model of his mouldboard to the Agricultural Society of the Seine, which awarded him a gold medal in recognition of his improvements in plow design (Edwin Morris Betts, ed., *Thomas Jefferson's Farm Book* [1953; Charlottesville, Va., 1976 reprint], pp. 47–49).

3. Jefferson had arranged to have plows made for JM from a design by George Logan (JM to Jefferson, 12 Apr. and 30 July 1793, *PJM*, 15:7, 8 n. 11, 49).

4. Jefferson's Poplar Forest estate was in Bedford County.

5. William Jarvis shipped thirteen Spanish merino sheep from Portugal to Alexandria, Virginia (Jarvis to JM, 20 Jan. 1810, and n. 1, 19 Feb. 1810, and n. 2; James H. Hooe to JM, 4 May 1810; Jarvis to Jefferson, 20 Jan. and 19 Feb. 1810, Hooe to Jefferson, 4 May 1810, Betts, *Jefferson's Farm Book*, pp. 125–26, 127–28).

From Jared Mansfield

SIR,   CINCINNATI March 26th. 1810.

I received, not long since, a letter from the Secretary at War requiring me to rejoin the Corps of Engineers, in which I have the honor to hold a commission of Lieut. Colonel.

In respect to this requisition, I would beg leave to observe, that I have never voluntarily absented myself, for an hour, from that Corps. My acceptance of the office of Surveyor General, proposed to me without any solicitation on my part, was the result of a condition implied, if not explicitly made by the late chief magistrate, that I should retain my rank in that Corps without any emoluments. My subsequent promotion, & various other circumstances evince, that it was not only the intention of the President, that I should hold my place among the Engineers, but derive all the advantages (emoluments excepted) of one actually in service. Though I feel the strongest impulse of gratitude for the many favours gratuitously conferred on me, I cannot consider the retention of my place in the Engineer Corps, otherwise than as a matter of right. For the President, who is at the head of the Corps, can order any individual of it, on any service, at his own discretion. When thus detached he cannot be supposed to be liable to other calls, or those of the ordinary service; nor does it belong to him to make a choice of the kind of service, in which he shall be engaged; unless it be previously submitted to his volition.

As an Officer of the U. States, in either capacity, I will cheerfully obey any orders or directions, which I may receive from my Superiors, but if it be left to my own choice to determine whether I shall hold my present situation, or remove to the Corps of Engineers, it would follow, I should suppose, that my Own convenience, as well as the public interest, be allowed, as a Motive for my determination. Now under the circumstances of the business of this office at present, & of the situation of myself, & family, if called on for an immediate decision, there is no alternative; for it would be impossible for me to be prompt in the Obedience of military orders, unless by a dereliction of plans of public service just commenced, & a total derangement of my private concerns. The Amount of orders to me for immediate service, is to allow me no choice. My passionate fondness for the Engineer Department, & the expectations, I have cherished of devoting the latter parts of my life to scientific pursuits for public advantage, must be sacrificed to an impossible condition. It is true, the Secretary at War does not require an immediate compliance with his orders, & in this I must do justice to the delicate consideration, he has afforded to this subject. But a state of suspence, is, of all others, the most unpleasant, & this to me is rendered more so, as I do not know in what light the Government views this matter, or what motives may have given rise to the requisition, except, that in the present situation of National affairs, the public service requires the aid of every individual of the Corps of Engineers. I am far from wishing even if the laws should render that Corps more numerous, for any length of time to come, to hold a place nominally, as heretofore; but since that has been the case for 6 or 7 years, I cannot perceive any great disadvantage arising from a continuation of this arrangement for a few Months. I think, a longer time, than from this to Midsummer, will not be necessary for me. It was my expectation, that this point could be decided before now, but it has been found impracticable. I must, therefore, crave your indulgence, so far as, to allow me, 4 months from this date, for the purpose of deciding on the point of holding, or resigning my commission in the Corps of Engineers.[1] At the expiration of that time, if I hold my commission, I shall be prepared to obey Military Orders. At present, it would be impossible, without sacrifices of health, property & responsibility on my part, & I believe of the public interest as connected with a due exe[c]ution of the service in which I am engaged. I have the honor to be With the most profound respect Your Obt. Humle. Sert.

> JARED MANSFIELD[2]
> Survr. Genl. & Lieut. Col.
> of Engineers

RC (DNA: RG 107, LRRS, M-108:5). Docketed by a War Department clerk as received 28 Apr. 1810.

1. JM granted Mansfield the four months' indulgence he requested (Eustis to Mansfield, 28 Apr. 1810 [DNA: RG 107, LSMA]).

2. Jared Mansfield (1759–1830), commissioned a captain in the Corps of Engineers in 1802, was professor of mathematics and natural and experimental philosophy at the U.S. Military Academy, 1802–3 and 1812–28. As surveyor general of the U.S., 1803–12, he surveyed Ohio and the Northwest Territory. He resigned from the Corps of Engineers on 23 July 1810 (Charlotte W. Dudley, "Jared Mansfield: United States Surveyor General," *Ohio History*, 85 [1976]: 231–46; Heitman, *Historical Register*, 1:688).

To the House of Representatives

March 27th 1810

In consequence of your Resolution of the 26th instant,[1] an enquiry has been made into the correspondence of our Minister at the Court of London with the Department of State; from which it appears that no official communication has been received from him, since his receipt of the letter of November 23d last, from the Secretary of State. A letter of Jany. 4th 1810,[2] has been received from that Minister by Mr. Smith; but being stated to be private and unofficial, and involving moreover personal considerations of a delicate nature, a copy is considered as not within the purview of the call made by the House.

> JAMES MADISON

RC (DNA: RG 233, President's Messages). In a clerk's hand, signed by JM. Received on 27 Mar., read and tabled on 28 Mar.

1. On 26 Mar. Federalist Edward Livermore (New York) proposed a resolution requesting the president to send to the House any letters or dispatches written by William Pinkney
in London since Pinkney's receipt of Secretary of State Robert Smith's 23 Nov. 1809 letter
justifying the dismissal of Francis James Jackson from Washington. Livermore declared that
his purpose was to ascertain whether the British government had disapproved of Jackson's
conduct and whether it would send a new minister to the U.S. After some debate, the House
passed the resolution by 109 to 14, and Livermore and Erastus Root (New York) were appointed to wait on the president (*Annals of Congress*, 11th Cong., 2d sess., 1622–25).

2. Pinkney's private letter to Robert Smith of 4 Jan. 1810 has not been found, but on
12 Mar. the *National Intelligencer* mentioned that its contents had "explicitly" stated that "the
British minister [Lord Wellesley] did not attempt to vindicate Mr. Jackson; on the contrary,
he admitted that he was in the wrong, that he must return, and that a successor would be
sent out to the United States." Upon receiving the letter, Robert Smith drafted a note of
acknowledgment. Mentioning that he was "really anxious that the U. S. should avoid the
vortex of the present war," Smith declared his "peculiar pleasure" in learning that the
"Marquis Wellesley had so cordially conferred with you and especially that he had not vindicated Mr. Jackson. This very agreeable intelligence contained in your letter, came most
seasonally. It was of course mentioned in conversation by the President & myself to some
of our friends (Members of Congress). They communicated it to others and, as you will
perceive, it has found its way to the press in various forms. It, however, had administered
great & general consolation inasmuch as it has been considered an indication of a disposition
on the part of the Br. Govt. to accommodate amicably the existing points of difference between the two countries. And we are at this moment indulging the pleasing expectation of
receiving from you the result of your conferences with Lord Wellesley. An arrangement
formal or informal be assured will be highly acceptable" (Bernard C. Steiner, ed., "Some
Papers of Robert Smith, Secretary of the Navy 1801–1809 and of State 1809–1811," *Md.
Historical Magazine*, 20 [1925]: 145).

From Charles Scott

SIR,   March 27th, 1810.
    I have the honor to transmit herewith, the copy of a Resolution, passed
[by] both houses of the General Assembly, at their last session. I am with
sentiments, Of high esteem, Your obedient servant.

                                                    CHS SCOTT

[Enclosure]

IN GENERAL ASSEMBLY—JANUARY 22nd 1810
RESOLVED by the General Assembly, That the indecorous, and unbecoming style used by Mr. Jackson, his Britannic Majesty's minister near
the United States, in his correspondence with the Secretary of state, and
above all, his insulting imputations against the veracity and integrity of
our government, were such as fully authorised the refusal, on the part of
the Executive, any longer to recognize his diplomatic character.
    RESOLVED, That the insidious appeal made by the said Jackson to the

people of the United States, under the disguise of a circular, addressed to the members of the diplomatic corps in the United States deserves the execration of every patriotic citizen.

RESOLVED, That the General Assembly view with entire approbation, the conduct of our government in dismissing said Jackson, and that whatever may be the consequences resulting therefrom, the state of Kentucky will be ready to meet them, and will most cordially co-operate in the support of such measures as may be necessary to secure the interests, and maintain the honor and dignity of the nation.

RESOLVED, That copies of the foregoing resolutions be transmitted to the President of the United States, and to each of our Senators and Representatives in Congress.

RC and enclosure (DLC: Madison Collection, Rare Book Division; Shaw and Shoemaker 20487). Printed copy, signed by Scott.

§ From Joseph Desha. *27 March 1810*. Recommends George Poindexter[1] for the vacant federal judgeship in the Mississippi Territory.

RC (DNA: RG 59, LAR, 1809–17, filed under "Poindexter"). 1 p. Printed in Carter, *Territorial Papers, Mississippi*, 6:56. Joseph Desha (1768–1842) was a Republican congressman from Kentucky, 1807–19.

1. George Poindexter (1779–1835) served as delegate to Congress from the Mississippi Territory, 1807–13. JM was to receive two other letters from members of the House on his behalf; one was from Adam Seybert and eight other Pennsylvania representatives, dated 29 Mar., and the other was from Robert Witherspoon and four other South Carolina representatives, dated 4 Apr. (printed ibid., 6:57, 58–59).

From Joseph Anderson

SIR   SENATE CHAMBER 29th March 1810.
In the Course of the communication which Judge Thruston[1] and I had with you, on Monday evening, he mentioned a resolution[2] which had been passed by the Legislature of the Mississipi Territory in relation to Mr Poindexter. The resolution has been handed to me this morning—with a request that I would transmit it to you. Accept Sir assurance of my high and Sincere respect, and Esteem

JOS: ANDERSON

RC and enclosure (DLC).

1. Buckner Thruston (1764–1845) was a Republican U.S. senator from Kentucky, 1805–9, and a circuit court judge in the District of Columbia, 1809–45.

2. Anderson enclosed a clipping, evidently from a Natchez newspaper, with three resolutions approved by the Mississippi Territory House of Representatives on 3 Mar. 1809. The
first resolution expressed confidence in territorial delegate George Poindexter. The second
requested him to seek the passage of laws to confirm Spanish land titles in the territory, to
open a post road from St. Stephens on the Tombigbee River to the town of Liberty in Amite
County, and to establish an Indian factory in Washington County. The third directed that
the above resolutions should be sent to the newspapers for publication.

From Samuel Carswell

RESPECTED SIR,   PHILADA. March 29th. 1810

I have the pleasure to acknowledge the Receipt of your favor of the
23rd. of Feby.[1] & the arrival of the Hams, for which accept my sincere
thanks.

I understand that the Collector of the Customs at New-York[2] has seized
some late importations of British Merchandize. It is an act that gives perfect satisfaction to all the regular importers & American Merchants & it is
to be hoped that it will not stop at seizure, but that the requisitions of the
Law be fully satisfied. The remittance of the penalty by the Secretary of
the Treasury in the cases of this nature that have already occured has been
much censured. If the Laws were violated by our own Citizens there
would be the *shadow* of a reason for exercising lenity, but when they are
trampled upon by the Agents of a foreign nation (for it is to be observed
that ever since the commencement of the restrictions on our trade with
England the Shiper has almost invariably been the Consignee) when they
are made subservient to the base purpose of speculation & that, to the
disadvantage of the honest Merchant & the revenue of the Country the
utmost severity ought to be used.

Formerly when unprincipled men wished to introduce articles prohibited by the Laws they had recourse to smugling, but now more impudent
& daring they violate them openly concluding perhaps that their temerity
will preserve them from punishment.

These things certainly speak the sentiments of foreigners with regard to
our national character & it is time to convince them that the virtues that
once so greatly distinguished it are *not* lost in commercial cupidity.

A few days since there was a trial in our district Court between the
United States & a British Agent for commiting a fraud on the revenue.
The jury brought in a verdict in favor of the United States for upwards of
12.400 Dollars. A few more such examples will convince these people of
the error of their judgment on our system of government, that it is not too
weak to punish injustice.

I am so sensible that the discussion of whatever relates to the welfare of the Country over whose Interests you preside is your best pleasure that I think it unnecessary to offer an apology for the length of this letter: tho, the matter which it contains may not inform your mind it will not fail to interest your heart as it possesses in so eminent a degree the spirit that dictated it. Accept Dear Sir my best wishes for your health & happiness.

SAML CARSWELL

RC (DLC). Docketed by JM.

1. Letter not found.
2. David Gelston.

§ To the Senate. *30 March 1810.* In response to the Senate's resolution of 22 Mar., transmits a report of the secretary of state.

Tr and Tr of enclosures (DNA: RG 46, Transcribed Reports and Communications from the Executive, vol. 4). Tr 1 p. Enclosures are copies of Robert Smith to JM, 29 Mar. 1810 (1 p.), transmitting State Department correspondence (17 pp.), requested by the Senate on 22 Mar., relating to the detention of the Danish ship *Mercator* in 1800. Received and read on 2 Apr. (*Annals of Congress*, 11th Cong., 2d sess., 614, 636). Printed in *ASP, Foreign Relations*, 3:344–47.

§ From Charles Harris. *30 March 1810, Savannah.* Encloses letter from "an old, infirm, meritorious & truly unfortunate french officer [who] has enclosed and dedicated to you a work which he hopes may meet your approbation." Asks JM to write a letter to the veteran, which he would forward.

RC and enclosure (DLC). RC 1 p. Enclosure (2 pp., in French) is Charles Haumont to JM, 1 Apr. 1810. Haumont wrote that he was afraid the letter and manuscript (a French-English grammar) he sent JM had been lost in the State Department. He reminded the president of his wartime service to America and entreated JM to help him find relief from his indigent situation. JM arranged for the return of Haumont's manuscript (JM to John Graham, 25 July 1810).

§ From Joseph Young. *April 1810, No. 53 Catharine Street, New York.* Relates a theory on circulation of blood. Has published a treatise on the physical cause of all motion, the astronomical part of which the "Gnosti machi" have attacked. Appeals to "those of more Liberallity, and discernment." Sends a volume of the treatise with a manuscript appendix and asks JM to submit it to William Eustis and Joel Barlow. Hopes for JM's patronage as well, should it meet with his approval. Will assign copyright of the treatise to the editor of the *National Intelligencer* if he will publish it. If this proposal is rejected, asks that his papers be returned "to wait for a more favourable opportunity."

RC (DLC). 2 pp. The enclosure (not found) was probably Young's *A New Physical System of Astronomy* . . . (New York, [1800]; Evans 39158).

§ John D. Lewis and Others to Robert Smith. *1 April 1810.* The petitioners, Americans residing in Malta, urge that John Hudden Lander, "an Englishman by birth," be appointed to replace the present consul,[1] who is "negligent & inattentive in his Office" and who "neither speaks, writes, or understands the English language." As Malta is a rendezvous for the Royal Navy, the interests of American seamen there "require consular interference."

Ms (DNA: RG 59, LAR, 1809–17, filed under "Lander"). 2 pp. Signed by Lewis and eight others. Enclosed in Lewis to William Jones, 17 Apr. 1810 (DNA: RG 59, ML). Both Lewis's letter and the memorial were forwarded by Jones in a letter to Robert Smith, 17 July 1810 (ibid.), in which Jones added his protests about the failure of the American consul at Malta to protect American seamen from impressment. Jones suggested that the administration consider retaliatory measures against British seamen in American ports. In reply, Smith promised Jones that he would forward his "very Interesting" letter and its enclosures to JM, who was spending the summer at Montpelier (Smith to Jones, 21 July 1810 (DNA: RG 59, DL). A pencil note on the last page of the Ms, in JM's hand, is apparently the president's response to Smith: "(For?) the person recommended to act for the present as Agent for Seamen, which might perhaps be known from Capt. Jones, it may be best, under present circumstances, to subs[t]itute him in that character, for Pulis. Among the objections to a Consular appt. of Lander are the uncertainty (whether) the B. Govt. wd. sanction it at Malta; and the repugnance to ask what wd be deemed a favor."

1. Joseph Pulis had been nominated by Jefferson to be consul at Malta on 6 Jan. 1802 (*Senate Exec. Proceedings,* 1:402).

To Thomas Jefferson

DEAR SIR   WASHINGTON April 2. 1810
Yours of the 25th. Mar: has been duly recd. Every thing is so uncertain at this moment with respect to our approaching relations to France & G. B: that I can only say that a conveyance of your plow to the Former will be favored as much as possible, and that I will endeavor to have more definite information on the subject ready at Monticello for your return from Bedford. I am glad to learn that your plow succeeds so well in practice. I always supposed that wd. be the case, when the soil was sufficiently dry. My apprehension was, that the obtuseness of the Angles made by the Mould Board, & the line of draught, might too much increase the resistance & subject the plow moreover to be clogged, by a degree of moisture not having the same effect with the ordinary plows. Your experiments will soon have decided this point. Your proposal as to the Merinos expected from Jarvis accords precisely with my ideas. I submit as a supplement, in case the pairs shd be designated and a loss be sustained by either of us, that it be repaired by the first increase from the pair of the other. Be assured always of my high & affecte. respects

JAMES MADISON

RC (DLC). Docketed by Jefferson, "recd. Apr. 15."

§ From Napoleon. *3 April 1810, Paris*. Announces his recent marriage to Marie-Louise, archduchess of Austria.[1]

RC (DNA: RG 59, Communications from Heads of Foreign States); FC (AAE: Political Correspondence, U.S., 63:72). RC 1 p. Written in French; in a clerk's hand, signed by Napoleon. FC addressed "Au Président du Congrès des Etats-unis."

1. JM offered his "Cordial congratulations" in response on 3 Nov. 1810 (AAE: Political Correspondence, U.S., 63:260).

§ To the House of Representatives. *4 April 1810*. Transmits report of the secretary of state in compliance with the House resolution of 26 Mar.

RC and enclosures (DNA: RG 233, President's Messages). RC 1 p. Enclosures are Robert Smith's 4 Apr. report (2 pp.), transmitting an abstract of returns on impressment of 903 American seamen by the British navy between 1 Oct. 1807 and 31 Mar. 1809 (1 p.) and an extract of G. T. Ladico, consular agent at Port Mahon, to Smith, 10 Dec. 1809 (2 pp.). Read and tabled on 5 Apr. Printed in *ASP, Foreign Relations*, 3:347–48.

Proposal to Renew Nonintercourse

[ca. 5 April 1810]

Re-enact the Non-Intercourse; with a proviso that its operation shall not commence untill the   day of   [1] Unless in the meantime either G. B. or Fr. shall have repealed &c. its Edicts &c., & the other shall fail to do the same; in which case it shall be lawful for the P. by proclamation, to fix an earlier day on which the Act shall go into operation, towards the Nation so failing to revoke &c.[2]

Ms (NHi: Gallatin Papers). In JM's hand, written in pencil on a small slip of paper. Undated. Conjectural date assigned on basis of evidence in n. 2. Docketed by Gallatin, "Mr Madison's proposition / 1810."

1. Left blank by JM.
2. This proposal seems to have been JM's response to the situation arising from the failure of the House of Representatives and Senate to reconcile their disagreements over Macon's Bill No. 1. The House had voted to reject the Senate amendments to the bill on 31 Mar.; the same day, John Randolph of Roanoke had moved for the immediate repeal of the Nonintercourse Act. The House committee on foreign relations met on 5 and 6 Apr., and it is likely that JM then drafted this proposal for Gallatin to transmit to its members. According to Nathaniel Macon, the committee considered and rejected at this time a modification of the Nonintercourse Act before it reported to the House, on 7 Apr., a measure apparently drafted by John Taylor of South Carolina and subsequently known as Macon's Bill No. 2. Macon

disavowed all responsibility for the bill (*Annals of Congress*, 11th Cong., 2d sess., 1701–5, 1763; Macon to Joseph H. Nicholson, 6 and 10 Apr. 1810 [DLC: Nicholson Papers]).

From John Roane

April 7th 1810

J Roane[1] presents to Mr Madison a few bottles of wine, made of the native grape of Virginia; & also a little cyder, the product of a newly discovered seedling apple, both bottled about 6 weeks ago, the latter, too early for spring clarification. Without experience in the art of wine making, J Roane offers this, as evidence, that our grapes possess qualities, worthy the attention of skilful managers. The cyder proves the great variety of that liquor, which, might be made, from a judicious selection of apples. It never sparkles. A South Carolina paper of the past winter, furnishes some useful hints on fermenting wine, from which, experiments shall be made the ensuing fall. Such productions greatly assist the unskilful operator.

Would it be presumption to add, an opinion, that within our land, may be found, not only necessaries, but all the comforts & luxuries of life, by suitable application, & perseverance?

RC (DLC). Docketed by JM.

1. John Roane (1766–1838) represented King William County in the Virginia House of Delegates, 1788–90 and 1792. He was a Republican congressman, 1809–15, 1827–31, and 1835–37. Judge Spencer Roane was his cousin (*WMQ*, 1st ser., 18 [1909–10]: 275).

§ From William Eustis. *9 April 1810*, *War Department*. Through a spelling error the president appointed Henry M. Gilman, instead of Henry M. Gilham, as an ensign in the Seventh Infantry in May 1808. Since Gilham's acceptance was not received until 5 Jan. 1809, his name was never sent to the Senate, but he has done service and drawn pay. Asks JM to nominate Gilham to correct the error.

RC (DLC); FC (PHi: Daniel Parker Papers); letterbook copy (DNA: RG 107, LSP). RC 1 p. In a clerk's hand, signed by Eustis. JM followed Eustis's recommendation, but the Senate rejected Gilham on 26 Apr. (*Senate Exec. Proceedings*, 2:147).

§ From Jesse Kersey.[1] *9 April 1810*, *Downingtown*. Feels an interest in JM's welfare, "having been in thy company some months past" when the Senate was discussing the status of some Cuban emigrants. Sends a pamphlet written "to reform the habits of our Country and that in relation to an evil which is now rendering Miserable many thousands of our fellow Creatures." Mentions in a postscript that the author is an "obscure Character" but "respectable in his own neighbourhood," and Kersey would be happy to see his ideas "spread over the Continent of America & particularly among the influential part of the community."

RC (DLC). 1 p. Enclosure not found.

1. Jesse Kersey (1768–1845) was a prominent Quaker minister who resided at Downingtown in Chester County, some thirty miles outside Philadelphia. He was involved in antislavery activities and discussed the problems of emancipation with JM in a meeting on 1 June 1814. He also opposed the War of 1812 and visited Washington, probably sometime in the second half of 1812, to call on JM "to embrace the first opening to close the contest" (Jesse Kersey, *A Narrative of the Early Life, Travels, and Gospel Labors of Jesse Kersey* . . . [Philadelphia, 1851], pp. 74, 195–96).

From Samuel Blodget

RESPECTED SIR   11th of April [1810]

On observing to several friends in Congress (who are in favour of a renewal of the Charter to the Bank U S & on the terms *They have offerd to Congress as they are expressed in the report through a committee Published this day* in the National intelligencer)[1]

That a much better plan could be carried into effect *with or without the junction with the Old Bank*, I was called on for a Sketch of a Bill which for the importance of the subject, I have taken the Liberty to enclose for your inspection, well knowing that it is still imperfect. My reason for altering the Share to *300* Dollrs.[2] is that it may answer for a remittance *at one hundred Pounds Sterling* the Share to serve hereafter in *lieu of Specie* remittances, & this hint I derived from conversation with Alexr Barring, when he was last in this City. $444. dollrs will be *the lowest price* of this stock in Europe as soon as the Law is passed, for it is now at 35 pr Cent advance, *and on the apprehension of a disolution of the Bank*, the highest rate of our shares in London has been 55 pr Cent advance *soon after the last sales U S @ 45 pr Cent*. I am with unalterable esteem & respect your Obedt Servant

S BLODGET[3]

RC (DLC). Enclosure not found.

1. On 19 Feb. a House of Representatives committee recommended renewal of the charter of the Bank of the United States. Implementing legislation was presented on 7 Apr., printed in the *National Intelligencer* on 11 Apr., and debated in the House on 13 Apr. Charter renewal then languished until January 1811, when single-vote majorities defeated bills in both houses (*Annals of Congress*, 11th Cong., 2d sess., 1413, 1762–63, 1795–1817; Hammond, *Banks and Politics in America*, p. 210; see also John R. Smith to JM, 3 Feb. 1810, and n. 2).

2. In the pending legislation, the issue price of newly authorized shares was left blank at the first reading (*National Intelligencer*, 11 Apr. 1810).

3. Samuel Blodget (1757–1814) designed the first Bank of the United States building in Philadelphia and from 1792 had been investing in Washington, D.C., real estate. His wife, Rebecca Smith Blodget, had appealed to JM on behalf of Aaron Burr in a letter of circa 11 Mar. 1809 (*PJM-PS*, 1:32–34).

Cherokee National Council to Return J. Meigs

FRIEND AND BROTHER,   OUSTENNALLIGH,[1] April 11th, 1810

I now acquaint you with the result of the Council of the deputies of the whole Cherokee Nation held at this place according to my appointment.

On meeting the Chiefs I had convened I delivered the Speeches suitable to the occasion, they have received them gladly, and resolved to hold them fast: they have now united their hearts and minds in brotherly love and in a determination to observe sacredly the treaties concluded with General Washington;[2] although he has left us for better abode; yet we feel assured, that he has left behind him traces both clear and strong of his former transactions.

The country left to us by our Ancestors has been diminished by repeated sales to a tract barely sufficient for us to stand on, and not more than adequate to the purpose of supporting our posterity. We hope that the aforesaid treaties will protect us in the possession of it, and the remembrance of them keep the sky clear all around us.

Some of our people have gone across the Missisippi without the consent or approbation of the Nation,[3] although Our Father the President in his Speech required that they should obtain it previous to their removing.

We hope that the advice of former Presidents, encouraging our people to apply their minds to improvement in Agriculture and the arts, may be continued, that their knowledge in these arts may be extended: and we rest assured that the General Government will not attend to or be influenced by any straggling part of the Nation, to accede to any new arrangement of our Country that may be proposed, contrary to the Will and consent of the main body of the Nation.

We request that you will forward these communications to Our Father, to which we add our intreaties, that he will cause his white children and their property to be kept separate from his Red children by the lines drawn at our former treaties, which we trust he will guarantee: even brothers of the same mother when they are arrived at the years of manhood they find it more agreeable, and sometimes necessary to preserve a good understanding between them, that their respective properties be kept apart, not interfering the one with the other.

You are continually endeavoring to remove the intruders off our lands, they put you to a great deal of trouble, for you are no sooner gone than they or others return to their former place of abode, we hope that you would find some means of rendering your exertions on this account more effectual, as you will thereby save yourself much trouble and make the minds of our people easy.

We must also inform you that the Chickasaws are very unjustly laying claim to that part of our country bordering on the Muscle shoals—the treaties we have already mentioned will sufficiently shew the little foundation they have to support there [*sic*] claim, as our boundaries are therein particularly specified.

Respecting the navigation of the Mobile it is out of our power to grant it: because the right of navigating this river does not rest with us alone.[4]

Our former treaties were concluded and confirmed by your beloved President General Washington and Our beloved Man the Little Turkey,[5] they were both sincere in their engagements, they directed us to look to the rising sun, by it to be guided and not by the moon, now both their Spirits have fled from our abodes, and gone to the habitation of the Great Spirit to receive the reward of their integrity—we remember with gratitude their benevolent labors, and hold fast their words.

This we send you to transmit to the Secretary of War as the unanimous Speech of the Cherokee nation, as represented by their Chiefs and deputies in Council assembled.

BLACK × FOX
[and thirty-eight
other principal chiefs]

RC (DNA: RG 107, LRRS, M-155:5); Tr (DNA: RG 75, Records of the Cherokee Indian Agency in Tennessee). RC enclosed in Return J. Meigs to William Eustis, 20 July 1810. Docketed by Meigs as an "Address to be Sent to the President of the U. States done in Cherokee National Council at Eustinalee 11th. April 1810." Docketed by a War Department clerk as received 2 Aug. 1810.

1. Oustanarle, or more commonly Ustanali, located on the Coosawattee River a few miles above its junction with the Conasauga River, became the principal town of the Upper Town Cherokee after 1788. It is now the site of Calhoun, Georgia (Woodward, *The Cherokees*, pp. 109, 111).

2. On the 1791 Treaty of Holston, whereby the Cherokee surrendered the lands of east Tennessee, a cession not accepted by the Lower Town Cherokee until the 1794 treaty at Tellico Blockhouse, see McLoughlin, *Cherokee Renascence*, pp. 23–25.

3. In 1808 some of the Lower Town Cherokee, or Chickamauga, led by Stone Carrier, proposed to divide the Cherokee Nation by ceding their lands to the U.S. in exchange for new grants farther west. The division was opposed by the Upper Towns but favored by Cherokee agent Return J. Meigs and President Jefferson, with the latter indicating his support for the plan in an address to the Cherokee on 9 Jan. 1809. It is evident that the state government of Tennessee then attempted to press JM over the winter of 1809–10 to follow

through with the removal of the Lower Town Cherokee, but JM seems to have been reluctant to act on the issue. He did not, however, make his position clear until March 1811 (Meigs to Eustis, 14 Feb. 1810 [DNA: RG 75, Records of the Cherokee Indian Agency in Tennessee]; Joseph Anderson and others to JM, 1 Mar. 1811 [DNA: RG 107, LRRS, A-110:5]; Mc-Loughlin, *Cherokee Renascence*, pp. 146–60).

4. In March 1810 Eustis had instructed Meigs to obtain Cherokee consent to access rights on the rivers flowing through their lands for whites wishing to trade at Mobile Bay (Mc-Loughlin, *Cherokee Renascence*, pp. 163–64).

5. Little Turkey was the principal chief of the Upper Town Cherokee from 1788 until his death in 1802, when he was succeeded by Black Fox (Woodward, *The Cherokees*, pp. 103, 109, 113).

From Levi Lincoln

DEAR SIR   WORCESTER April 12 1810

Permit me to congratulate you on the happy result of the recent elections in this State & in New Hampshire.[1] Firmness, steadiness & united persevering efforts by the friends to the national government will complete our triumph, break down & scatter to the winds the mad & hopeless cause of the Northern Confederacy.

I am informed that Judge Cushing is about resigning his seat as Judge of the Supreme Court of the U. States. I need not state to you how important it is in the opinion of republicans that his successor should be a gentleman of tried & undeviating attachment to the principles & policy which mark your's & your Predecessor's administration of the national government. It will form in some degree a countervailing action to that overgrown yet still encreasing influence in which federalism is intrenched in this State. Your [*sic*] are sufficiently acquainted with the prominent legal characters in this judicial District. Mr Bidwell's[2] standing in society, patriotism, professional qualifications are known to you. Please to excuse the liberty I have taken. My apology is the importance of the subject; my only motive the general welfare.

Let me ask you to make my grateful recollections acceptable to Mrs Madison, & believe me to be with the highest esteem & most sincere attachment your most Obedient Humble Servant,

LEVI LINCOLN[3]

RC (DLC).

1. The post-Embargo recovery of the New England Republicans led to Elbridge Gerry's defeating the Federalist incumbent, Christopher Gore, in the Massachusetts gubernatorial election, while in New Hampshire the Republicans elected John Langdon to the governorship and won control of the state legislature (*National Intelligencer*, 18 Apr. 1810; Lynn W. Turner, *William Plumer of New Hampshire, 1759–1850* [Chapel Hill, N.C., 1962], p. 195).

2. Barnabas Bidwell was a Republican congressman from Massachusetts, 1805–7. Jefferson had encouraged him to replace John Randolph as floor leader and administration spokesman, but he resigned and served as attorney general of Massachusetts until 30 Aug. 1810. When an investigation of his accounts as treasurer of Berkshire County since 1791 exposed a shortage of about $10,000, he fled to Canada (Cunningham, *The Process of Government under Jefferson*, p. 189).

3. Levi Lincoln (1749–1820) had served in Jefferson's cabinet as acting secretary of state until JM took up his duties in May 1801 and as attorney general, 1801–4. Lieutenant governor of Massachusetts, 1807–8, he was an unsuccessful candidate for governor in 1809. After Associate Supreme Court Justice William Cushing died in September 1810, JM offered Lincoln the vacant seat on the court only to receive Lincoln's refusal. Undeterred, JM placed Lincoln's name in nomination before the Senate on 2 Jan. 1811 but still could not persuade him to accept (JM to Lincoln, 20 Oct. 1810; Lincoln to JM, 27 Nov. 1810 and 20 Jan. 1811 [DLC]; *Senate Exec. Proceedings*, 2:159).

From Caspar Wistar, Jr.

Dr. Sir,   Philada. Apl. 12. 1810

The letter which accompanies this was written at my request by one of my patients who lately commanded a Vessel in the London Trade. His communications respecting the subjects to which this letter refers appeared so interesting that I requested him to give me a statement in writing. Altho it is very probable that you have more full information, yet as it is possible that your communications may not include the same facts, I determined to forward them to you. This act of duty as a citizen is particularly agreeable to me as it affords me an opportunity of assuring you of my most sincere & respectful attachment

Caspar Wistar Junr.[1]

P. S. In compliance with the wish of the writer I have cut off his signature but I believe him intitled to full credit.

RC (DLC). Docketed by JM. Enclosure not found.

1. Caspar Wistar, Jr. (1761–1818), professor of anatomy at the University of Pennsylvania, was a long-standing friend and correspondent of JM's. A leading member of the American Philosophical Society, he served as its president from 1815.

¶ To John K. Smith. Letter not found. *12 April 1810*. Acknowledged in Smith to JM, 15 May 1810. Requests information about Lafayette's Louisiana lands.

§ From Lyman Spalding. *13 April 1810, Portsmouth*. Encloses the Portsmouth bill of mortality for 1809.

RC (DLC); enclosure (DLC: Madison Collection, Rare Book Division). RC 1 p. Enclosure is Spalding's *Bill of Mortality, for Portsmouth, New Hampshire, for A.D. 1809* (n.p., [1810]; Shaw and Shoemaker 21125). Spalding, a 1797 graduate of Harvard Medical School, published the Portsmouth bills of mortality, 1800–1813, and founded the U.S. Pharmacopoeia in 1820.

From William A. Burwell

Dr Sir,   WASHINGTON April 16th 1810.

By a resolution of this House an adjournment will take place on the 23d.[1] I am personally extremely anxious to get home, every consideration conspires to render me impatient, but I think from the prospect which the last intelligence from Europe presents us, much good might result from the arrival of the J. A.[2] There are also several questions of great national Moment which would probably be decided—if the Session shall be protracted for 10 days. I have thought it right to suggest to you the propriety of advising by a message the continuance of the Session. I should not mention this circumstance except that I believe without such a step C. will adjourn on the 23d. & should you think the measure adviseable the earlier the better, because the members are dispersing very fast. Yours with great respect

W. A BURWELL[3]

RC (DLC).

1. The resolution Burwell referred to had been passed on 30 Mar. 1810. The session, in fact, ended on 1 May (*Annals of Congress*, 11th Cong., 2d sess., 1693, 2054).

2. On 15 Apr. 1810 the *National Intelligencer* printed a report from the London *Morning Chronicle* of 7 Feb. to the effect that Lord Wellesley and William Pinkney had amicably settled the disputes between Great Britain and the U.S. and that the frigate *John Adams* had been detained in order to carry a treaty to Washington. The report also declared that there would be changes in the British government and that a new British minister would be sent to the U.S.

3. William Armisted Burwell (1780–1821) represented Franklin County in the Virginia House of Delegates, 1804–6, while serving as President Jefferson's private secretary. He was a Republican congressman, 1806–21 (Swem and Williams, *Register*, pp. 70, 354).

From William Duane

Sir,   PHILA. April 16, 1810

My son Wm. J. Duane will have the honor to present you this note, going to Washington on a matter of business his own wishes and my desire would not suffer me to scruple taking this liberty of making him known to you.

He goes to Washington with the View of prosecuting an undertaking which I formerly contemplated, the publication of an Edition of the laws of the U. S. upon a plan of which I had the honor, once personally and once by letter,[1] to present to your attention. Any support which the undertaking may be entitled to, and which you may consider yourself fairly authorised to bestow is all he seeks, and which given to him will be most grateful to, Sir, your most obedt and respectful Sert

WM DUANE

RC (DLC).

1. Duane had proposed to JM the publication of "an Edition of the Laws of the U States in a neat form, perfectly corresponding with the ideas of an index and arrangement which you were pleased to mention to me about two years ago" (Duane to JM, 8 Feb. 1808 [DLC]). This proposal eventually succeeded when his son, William John Duane, and John Bioren published *Laws of the United States of America, from the 4th of March, 1789, to the 4th of March, 1815* . . . (5 vols.; Philadelphia, 1815; Shaw and Shoemaker 36275).

From Thomas Jefferson

DEAR SIR   MONTICELLO Apr. 16. 10.

On my return from Bedford I found in our post office your favor of the 2d. inst. as also the inclosed letter from mr. Martin, formerly of N. C. recommended to us by mr. Blackledge.[1] I dare say you will recollect more of him than I do. I remember that his being a native French man, educated I believe to the law there, very long a resident of this country and become a respectable lawyer with us, were circumstances which made us wish we could have then employed him at N. O. I know nothing of him however but what you learned from the same source, & I inclose his letter that you may see that emploiment would be agreed to on his part.[2] I have at the same time recieved an offer from mr. Fulton to lend me his dynamometer, mine having been lost.[3] I have concluded therefore to keep the plough till I can determine it's comparative merit by that instrument. The mould-board which I first made, with a square toe, was liable to the objection you make of accumulating too much earth on it when in a damp state, & of making the plough too long. By making it, on the same principles, with a sharp toe, it has shortened the plough 9. I. & got rid of the great hollow on which the earth made it's lodgment. It is now as short & light as the plough we got from Philadelphia, which indeed was my model, with only the substitution of a much superior mould board. I have certainly never seen a plough do better work or move so easily. Still the instrument alone can ascertain it's merit mathematically. Our spring is wonderfully backward. We have had asparagus only two days. The fruit has escaped better than was believed. It is killed only in low places. We easily agree as to the Merinos: but had nothing happened would they not have been here? Ever your's affectionately

TH: JEFFERSON

RC and enclosure (DLC); FC (DLC: Jefferson Papers). Enclosure (3 pp.) is Francis Xavier Martin to Jefferson, 11 Feb. 1810 (see n. 2).

1. William Blackledge, a Republican congressman from North Carolina, 1803–9 and 1811–13, had recommended Martin for a territorial judgeship (Blackledge to JM, 12 Dec. 1808, Carter, *Territorial Papers, Orleans*, 9:810–11).

2. JM had already nominated Martin—who had served for the past year as a judge in the Mississippi Territory—for the Orleans territorial judgeship on 19 Mar. In his letter to Jefferson, Martin complained, "My Situation in the Mississippi is So very uncomfortable & the emoluments of office So Scanty . . . that it was expedient to Seek employment in the City of New Orleans, as an attorney, or return to Carolina." The death of John Thompson, the Orleans territorial judge, caused Martin to solicit Jefferson's "powerful aid." Martin wrote a similar letter to Robert Smith on 15 Feb. (ibid., 9:867; see also Nathaniel Macon to JM, 18 Mar. 1810, and n.).

3. Jefferson accepted Robert Fulton's offer to lend him a dynamometer for his plow experiment. A friend in Paris had previously sent Jefferson a dynamometer, which was lost during his move from Washington to Monticello (Jefferson to Fulton, 16 Apr. 1810, Lipscomb and Bergh, *Writings of Jefferson*, 19:172–73).

§ From "Mucius" [John Randolph]. No. 3. *17 April 1810*. Has no desire to discuss the details of the correspondence between Francis James Jackson and Robert Smith but hints that Smith and his brother, as well as "*other members* of the family compact," would not be averse to a war with Great Britain in order to conceal evidence of their financial peculation. Declares JM to be "a prisoner of state in your own palace" and that "consultations are held upon you, by the Smiths, the Giles's, and the Leibs, in which your present interest and future fame are alike disregarded." Attacks the "simpering, self-applauding" secretary of state for his lack of ability and deplores the want of talent in the public councils generally. Congress is scarcely capable of conducting the nation's affairs in time of peace; the "same dull, spiritless, incapacity" seems to pervade the state legislatures. Asks if JM could, therefore, trust himself "to carry on war with any power superior to the corsairs of Barbary." "Time-serving, and electioneering, and jobbing, and chaffering and bargaining for offices and contracts, are the order of the day," though the people themselves "*have not degenerated*." They could be embarked on a war "to screen the embezzlers of their substance" and "to achieve the guilty purposes of the blackest ambition."

Both "commerce" and "sentiment" dictate that the U.S. should prefer the cause of Great Britain to that of France. Wishes that the power of "the modern Zingis [Napoleon] rested on no firmer basis than the prayers of his Gallo-American votaries." But Napoleon engages talents in his service that are "not less appalling than the tremendous physical force which he wields," though "when *he* employs blockheads, it is not in his own councils, but in those of other nations." Yet to cope with Napoleon once every obstacle to French power has been removed, the U.S. must rely on the "empty garrulity," "frothy nonsense," and "pert loquacity" of the statesmen presently in the House of Representatives. These are "fearful odds!" yet "our patriotic legislators" are astonished that "neither words, nor proclamations, nor resolutions" have succeeded in bringing the European belligerents "to a just sense of their transgressions."

Suggests that JM consider whether "the most lofty language and pretensions" of the U.S. "comport with the resources of second, and third-rate powers" and whether its policies ought not to be governed more by circumstances. Asks whether there are "any rights so absolute as not to be limited and modified by the posture of affairs and the existing state of things." Relates a lengthy anecdote to support his view that nations and men should "husband [their] threats" until in "some condition to execute them." Apologizes for addressing JM in a style so "familiar" but excuses himself by noting that folly as well as the "'lie circumstantial and countercheck quarrelsome'" are in fashion in both Congress and "the first political circle in the country."

Concludes that the U.S. is not disgraced if its gunboats are not a match for the Royal Navy and if General Wilkinson and his forces hardly equal "Bonaparte at the head of his legions." Knows that this is "damnable heresy," but heresy thrives on persecution. Many would now agree that the U.S. ought to pursue its interests, and there is "no absolute necessity for hanging ourselves . . . out of spite, because we are thwarted in argument." Returns to his theme of "the history, character and connexions of the 'family compact'" and promises JM he will devote many hours of labor to the subject in order to present "such a body of evidence in relation to these people and their designs, as no man claiming the character of common prudence, or foresight ever ventured to resist."

Printed copy (Washington *Spirit of 'Seventy-Six*, 17 Apr. 1810). Also printed in *Letters of Mutius* (Shaw and Shoemaker 20555).

§ From "Tammany." *18 April 1810.* Warns that the nation depends on JM to save the ship of state and the "democratic party" from shipwreck. Alludes to the "bank question" and the report that JM considers it to be "settled." Asks what this might mean: that because a Federalist majority once voted for the bank the Federalists can determine the meaning of the Constitution? Reminds JM that he argued against such reasoning in his earlier speeches against the Bank of the United States. Such sophistry will turn the Constitution into "a nose of wax." Points out that the same logic could settle the constitutionality of the Sedition Law, about which JM "made no little pother in your famous report in the Virginia Assembly." But since no Republican Congress ever officially protested against the Sedition Law—and neither did Jefferson or JM—does such acquiescence render it constitutional? Is the Constitution "like the cameleon [*sic*], which changes its hue according to the times and positions in which it may be viewed?"

JM "once thought and spoke differently." Time has not changed the validity of

JM's earlier arguments on the bank question, and he is "committed in a thousand ways" on the subject; his speeches are "before the world" as is his report in the Virginia legislature. Should the present bank bill pass Congress and JM give it his sanction, his "fame will be blasted forever." No excuses about the question being "*settled*" will conceal his inconsistency or save him from "eternal odium and reproach." His change of opinion, moreover, could not be attributed to ignorance but only to "'corruption's soul-dejecting arts.'"

Supposes JM might have been "the victim of slander." But if JM has changed his views because he now follows "federal precedents" and "the petty-fogging rules of courts," then the Republicans struggled for their principles in vain and politics is "nought but a contest for loaves and fishes,—an ignoble squabble between *ins* and *outs*." Concludes by warning that liberty has often been lost by "avarice, by intrigue, by timidity, by all the corruption which peace and commerce are too apt to engender!" "Must we too, after passing through the red sea of revolution, perish in the desert?"

Printed copy (Baltimore *Whig*, 18 Apr. 1810).

From John Lambert

DEAR SIR,   WASHINGTON April 19th. 1810.

Inclosed is a graft of the St. Germain Pare, of which I sent Mrs. Madison a sample some time ago. If you have a pare stock growing in the Garden, or walks around the Presidents House, would you not wish to propagate the fruite. I expect to have some of them sound and good when I get home. They begin to mellow in Novbr. and last until May. I am your most Obdt Humbl. Servt.

JOHN LAMBERT [1]

RC (DLC).

1. John Lambert was a U.S. senator from New Jersey, 1809–15.

Madison and the Collapse of the Spanish-American Empire
The West Florida Crisis of 1810
20 April 1810

EDITORIAL NOTE

The letter of Samuel Fulton to JM, 20 April 1810, introduces one of the more dramatic developments JM witnessed during his terms as secretary of state and president of the United States—the revolutions for independence in the Spanish-American colonies. At the beginning of 1808 Spain still ruled an American empire stretching from California to Cape Horn; twenty years later it retained only Cuba and Puerto Rico. Admittedly, many of the important events in this transformation of the New World were to occur during the administrations of JM's successors, but there were several occasions between 1809 and 1817 when JM himself had to confront the problems and opportunities presented to the United States by the disintegration of the Spanish Empire. Insofar as JM's reactions and decisions involved Spanish territories close to the United States, such as the Floridas, they were of considerable significance and importance. Further afield, his measures often had a less immediate impact, but they did in many instances anticipate the policies of later presidents toward the region that became Latin America.

Unfortunately, it is not possible within the limitations of this edition of JM's papers to provide a complete record of all the documentary material that influenced or reflected his responses to the collapse of the Spanish Empire. The primary concern of this edition must always be with the documents addressed to, or issuing from, the president himself. Readers of these volumes should be aware, though, that not even a full and comprehensive publication of this presidential material will explain in all cases the range of considerations governing JM's policies toward Spain and its colonial possessions. For this reason JM's personal papers must be supplemented with a wide variety of public and private manuscripts as well as with material published in the newspapers of the times. Under these circumstances, the editors can do no more than present JM's own papers in ways that elucidate this larger documentary context as efficiently as possible, thereby indicating some of the additional historical sources where important evidence bearing on JM's conduct may be found.

The crisis of Spanish authority in the New World was precipitated by Napoleon's decision to seize and imprison the Bourbon monarch, Ferdinand VII, in order to replace him with Joseph Bonaparte as king of Spain and the Indies. This act of usurpation led, in May 1808, to the outbreak of popular insurrection in Spain where initially the resistance was conducted by a coalition of provincial juntas acting in the name of a legitimist Supreme Junta in Seville. As French armies advanced throughout Spain in the summer of 1809, this latter body retreated to Cadiz and in January 1810 relinquished its authority to a regency, entrusting its five members with the task of reorganizing the rebellion by summoning a *cortes* (parliament) in which both Spain and its American colonies would be represented. At the same time a similar array of insurrectionary juntas emerged in the Spanish-American colonies. These bodies, like their metropolitan counterparts, justified their resistance in terms of their loyalty to Ferdinand VII, but their members were usually native-born *criollos* with their own grievances against the *peninsulares*—the class of soldiers and officials who had ruled them in the name of Madrid. The leaders of the colonial juntas, as it proved, had no desire to perpetuate their traditionally subordinate roles in the empire, and as they resolved to reject the pretensions of Joseph Bonaparte as *El Rey Intruso*, they also adopted policies that led them toward autonomy, if not outright independence, from the mother country.

In this context, the events of greatest importance in shaping JM's policies toward the Spanish Empire occurred in Venezuela. The *cabildo* of Caracas, fearing that the resistance in Spain had become too weak to prevent Joseph Bonaparte from asserting a claim to rule the empire, repudiated the authority of the Cadiz regency on 19 April 1810. This revolt provoked further disturbances and led to the establishment of autonomous ruling juntas in Caracas and in many other towns throughout the viceroyalty of New Granada. In the months thereafter similar developments took place in Buenos Aires and Chile, while in New Spain (Mexico) the discontent that had been building up since the displacement of viceroy José de Iturrigay in 1808 finally erupted in the Hidalgo revolt of September 1810. Closer to the United States, events in the Floridas also seemed likely to follow the patterns that were emerging in Spain's larger and more populous colonies, and as JM later remarked to Jefferson, it was in West Florida that the crisis of the Spanish Empire finally came "home to our feelings and our interests." The prospect of an autonomous or an insurrectionary West Florida, however, was not one that JM was prepared to tolerate. To prevent it he tried, at first, to pursue a course of action to incorporate the province into the United States with the consent of its leading settlers, but when that effort failed, he quickly decided on the more drastic alternative of simply annexing parts of the territory by presidential proclamation late in October 1810 (Mathew Arnold Hœvel to JM, 29 Sept. 1810; JM to Jefferson, 19 Oct. 1810).

The background to these decisions was long and complicated. As early as 1803, the United States had asserted that West Florida, as far eastward as the Perdido River, had been included in the Louisiana Purchase; and shortly after France had transferred the Louisiana territory to the American government, the Jefferson administration advanced a further claim for Spanish East Florida on the grounds that its acquisition would be adequate compensation for spoliation claims against Spain dating back to the Quasi-War of the late 1790s. Jefferson then devoted the next four years to some complex, if not tortuous, diplomacy to acquire both of the Floridas before the more serious crisis over maritime rights with Great Britain after the summer of 1807 came to claim most of his attention for the remainder of his presidency. JM's role in these events will be covered in the secretary of state series of this edition, and here it is sufficient merely to note that JM, while fully accepting the claim that West Florida had been part of the Louisiana Purchase, was never quite so driven to acquire the Floridas as rapidly as Jefferson seems to have been. Certainly, he never doubted that the United States would ultimately succeed in taking the Spanish territories along the Gulf Coast, but he was prepared to be flexible about the time and the means by which this outcome might be reached. As he remarked in 1805 in order to acquit the Jefferson administration of the charge of pursuing the Floridas with an ill-disguised greed: "When the [Florida] pear is ripe, it will fall of its own accord" (Turreau to Talleyrand, 2 July 1805 [AAE: Political Correspondence, U.S., vol. 58]).

In this respect JM's administration inherited the diplomatic goals of its predecessor, but after JM took office himself in March 1809 he found that he lacked both the opportunities and the resources to pursue the Floridas as Jefferson had done. Events in Spain after May 1808 made it impossible to negotiate with any authority that could wield effective power in the matter, while the $2 million appropriation voted by Congress in the Mobile Act of 1805—cash intended to be used to enlist French support for the transfer of the Floridas from Spain to the United States—had expired. Yet domestic as well as diplomatic pressures continued to evolve in ways that kept the Florida question before JM's attention, and in this context the relationships between the Spanish and the American communities on the southwest frontier were to have some bearing on the manner in which the president responded to events throughout the summer and fall of 1810.

Many of the inhabitants of West Florida, particularly in the areas west of the Pearl River and around the town of Baton Rouge, were of American origin, and like other Spanish colonial subjects they had grievances against weak, corrupt, and inefficient rule from Madrid. Their opinions on this score were reinforced from the states and territories north of the boundary line on the thirty-first parallel, where United States citizens resented having to pay duties to Spanish officials to gain access to the sea from the interior rivers flowing to the coast. This last complaint had been the subject of petitions during the second session of the Eleventh Congress from Tennessee and the Mississippi Territory, whose settlers demanded free navigation on the Tombigbee and Alabama rivers. In response, JM did not deny that the United States had long claimed a "natural right" for Americans to use the rivers in question, but he declined to take the matter up at that time, pointing out as he did so the risks of "controversies with the Creeks & Spaniards" (*Annals of Congress*, 11th Cong., 2d sess., 1257, 1443, 1761; JM to the House of Representatives, 9 Feb. 1810; *National Intelligencer*, 20 June 1810).

JM's reaction here strongly suggests, therefore, that his handling of the West Florida problem was governed much more by his assessment of international developments than it was by any sympathy he felt for the desires and needs of settlers on the southwest frontier. And indeed, all the evidence after the commencement of JM's administration in March 1809, if not from an earlier time as well, reinforces the conclusion that JM had always assumed that the solution to the Florida issue would be reached through negotiations in Paris, London, and Madrid rather than by unilateral action on the part of the United States. And although JM was not particularly anxious to recognize Joseph Bonaparte's usurpation of the Spanish throne, he could not afford to ignore the probability that the Bourbon cause in Spain would fail and that Napoleon would eventually come to dominate the government in Madrid. For this reason, if for no other, JM had decided in August 1809 that it was inexpedient to receive Luis de Onís as minister from the Supreme Junta in Spain (JM to Jefferson, 24 Apr. 1809, *PJM-PS*, 1:135–36; JM to Caesar A. Rodney, 22 Oct. 1809, and n. 2).

But as JM awaited the outcome of events in Europe, his hand was forced by the even more rapid pace of developments in the Americas. In the early days of June 1810 news reached the United States about the uprisings in Venezuela after 19 April, and newspapers began to publish translations of the manifestos issued by the Caracas junta to justify its repudiation of the Cadiz regency. In Washington the *National Intelligencer* printed several of these documents, including one on 13 June 1810 under the headline of "Spanish America Declared Independent," which was attributed, probably incorrectly, to the "supreme government of Caraccas." The administration newspaper then presented its readers with a "declaration of independence" for Spanish America. Its contents renounced allegiance to any authority in Spain and did so in language that was more than a little redolent of a similar document issued in the United States on 4 July 1776. The manifesto concluded that the people of Spanish America should declare themselves to be "free sovereign and independent" and called upon their governments to secure their "happiness and give [them] a place of honor and respect among the independent nations of the earth."

That JM gave some credence to these Venezuelan documents is suggested by the fact that the very same day Secretary of State Smith sent a note to William Pinkney in London, declaring that the "Colonial relation of Spanish America to their parent Country" was evidently on the point of dissolution. The minister was therefore instructed to remind the British government of the American claim to West Florida and to warn it as well that any British policies based on a contrary supposition "will necessarily be regarded as unjust and unfriendly." This instruction, Smith added, was based on JM's belief that "the connection of Great Britain with Spain will have been terminated by events in Europe." Developments in Spain and Venezuela, moreover, continued to occupy the president's mind when he met the next day, 14 June, with William C. C. Claiborne, the governor of Orleans Territory. Claiborne had long before planned his journey to Washington for personal and business reasons, but together the two men began to take the decisive steps in JM's efforts to acquire West Florida for the United States (Smith to Pinkney, 13 June 1810 [DNA: RG 59, IM]; Claiborne to JM, 17 Dec. 1809).

Claiborne was thoroughly familiar with the difficulties of dealing with Spanish authorities on the Gulf Coast, and he had long urged the administration in Washington to take an aggressive line to incorporate both of the Floridas into the United States. As a result of his meeting with JM, the governor composed a letter, "under the sanction of the president" as Robert Smith later put it, to his friend territorial judge William Wykoff, Jr. The letter instructed Wykoff what to do in case the settlers in West Florida should show signs of wanting to imitate the Venezuelan rebels. Assuming that Spain itself had "yielded to Bonaparte" and that the people of the Floridas were about to be "assailed by a Host of Intriguers" advising them on the merits of future connections with France and Great Britain, Claiborne stated that any connection with a foreign power or the formation of "an independent Government" was "out of the question!" Reminding Wykoff of his own opinion—which was also the opinion of JM—that Florida both by nature and by right should belong to the United States, Claiborne told the judge to seek out the "most influential" settlers around Baton Rouge in order to give their views "a right direction." Among the men he named for this purpose were some who were known to, or who had corresponded with, JM, and they included Philip Hickey, Samuel Fulton, and William Barrow. To encourage them to "scout every thing like French or English influence," Claiborne hinted that the time was now right for the United States to make good on its long-standing claim to West Florida. Wykoff's task was to obtain from the settlers a request for the United States to do so, preferably "thro' the medium of a Convention of Delegates, named by the people." The judge was further directed to use his discretion in the matter and to send confidential communications to Washington, where Claiborne anticipated he would remain "until the last of October" (Claiborne to Wykoff, 14 June 1810 [DNA: RG 59, TP, Orleans]; Smith to David Holmes, 21 July 1810 [DNA: RG 59, TP, Mississippi]).

Since a majority of the American-born settlers in West Florida resided in the districts adjacent to the Mississippi River, Wykoff's prospects for finding a receptive audience around Baton Rouge for JM's views were not unreasonable. But as Claiborne reminded the judge, the American claim to the province extended to the Perdido River, and it would be harder to mobilize comparable support for JM's plans in the more remote regions to the east. Wykoff was instructed to think about preparing "the minds of some of the more influential characters in the vicinity of Mobile," but Claiborne himself was clearly uncertain how this might best be achieved. A few days later, however, the administration settled on a way to deal with the problem. Possibly recalling that both Claiborne and James Wilkinson had hinted in May 1809 that the Spanish governor of West Florida, Vicente Folch, might be persuaded to deliver his province to the United States should Napoleon finally conquer Spain, the secretary of state wrote to Georgia senator William Harris Crawford on 20 June, requesting him in confidence to find an agent to go "without delay into East Florida, and also into West Florida, as far as pensacola" to encourage the population there to accept the idea of joining the United States. Crawford did not receive this letter until late in July, but he lost no time in selecting George Mathews, a former Georgia governor, for the assignment. JM later declared himself to be "perfectly satisfied" with Crawford's choice. By the end of June 1810, therefore, JM had set in motion policies designed to settle the West Florida problem once and for all by incorporating the region into the United States (Wilkinson to JM, 1 May 1809, *PJM-PS*, 1:155–56; Claiborne to Smith, 21 Apr. and 14 May 1809, Rowland, *Claiborne Letter Books*, 4:342–44, 351–54; JM to Smith, 17 July 1810, and n. 4; Crawford to Smith, 20 Sept. 1810 [DNA: RG 59, ML]; Smith to Crawford, 20 June and 2 Oct. 1810 [DNA: RG 59, DL]).

As the president made these decisions with respect to West Florida, he further decided that it was appropriate to respond to developments in some of the other Spanish-American colonies as well. In the last week of May JM called to Washington the New England merchant William Shaler and asked him to undertake "confidential" missions to Cuba and New Spain. The presidential summons may have been prompted by rumors that officials in Havana had just reduced the duties imposed on American ships and goods and that the establishment of independent governments on both the island and the mainland was a likely consequence of the ongoing French conquest of Spain. Shaler had already made the acquaintance of JM earlier in the year, and he was, by virtue of his travels in California, Chile, Guatemala, and Mexico, one of the few Americans who could claim any extensive knowledge of Spanish America (*National Intelligencer*, 16 and 25 May 1810; Smith to Shaler, 24 and 29 May 1810 [PHi: Shaler Family Papers]).

But JM wanted Shaler to do more than merely gather information, important though that would be to inform future administration policies. More significantly, the president directed his agent to engage in some delicate diplomacy with the as yet unknown leaders in the emerging successor states of the disintegrating Spanish Empire. In particular, Shaler was to persuade the new Spanish-American leaders in both Cuba and New Spain not to adhere to the positions that the metropolitan regime in Madrid had taken in its disputes with the United States over the boundaries of the Louisiana Purchase and West Florida. And with respect to Cuba, JM also instructed Shaler to renew an initiative that the Jefferson administration had assigned to James Wilkinson in January 1809 only to see the general mishandle it—namely, to "feel the pulse of Cuba as to an estimate of the inducements to a[n] . . . incorporation of that island with the United States in comparison with those of an adherence to the Spanish Main." Cuba, though, was of less immediate importance to the president than the future events on the mainland, and he told Shaler to pass through Havana and then lose no time in going to Veracruz in order to repair "to the place where the local authority of Mexico may reside." After he had carried out all these duties successfully, Shaler was finally authorized to explain to the new Spanish-American leaders "the mutual advantages of a commerce with the United States" based on "liberal and *stable* regulations" (Smith to Shaler, 16 June 1810, John Graham to Shaler, 15 and 21 June 1810 [PHi: Shaler Family Papers]; Smith to Shaler, 18 June 1810 [PHi: William Shaler Papers]).

No sooner had Shaler left Washington to make his arrangements, however, than the same newspapers that had been reporting the April rebellion in Venezuela also announced that the Caracas junta had sent diplomatic agents to both Great Britain and the United States. The agents to the latter, Juan Vicente Bolívar and Telésforo d'Orea, arrived in Baltimore in early June, and approximately two weeks later they were received by Secretary of State Robert Smith, JM's longtime friend William Thornton, and, if the dispatches of Onís are to be believed, even by JM himself. No question of the formal recognition of these agents arose at this time, though the administration seems to have made no objection to their efforts to purchase arms and supplies for their Venezuelan compatriots. Their very presence in the country, however, undoubtedly persuaded JM of the desirability of the administration's having some additional agents in Spanish America to keep it abreast of developments. Should any of the Spanish colonies in South America actually make "a political separation from the parent Country," it would be undeniably useful to have Americans on the spot—as in the case of Cuba and New Spain—both to gather information and "to promote the most friendly relations and the most liberal intercourse" with the United States. At the end of June, therefore, JM and Robert Smith decided that they should send confidential missions to Buenos Aires and Venezuela, and they chose Maltby Gelston and Robert K. Lowry, respectively, for the tasks. Gelston and Lowry were designated, as Shaler had also been, as agents for commerce and seamen. This was done in case any of the Americans should encounter the well-known reluctance of Spanish officials to grant formal recognition to the representatives of any foreign power in their colonies, but the instructions to all three agents made it plain that they were to operate as consuls as far as they could possibly do so (Onís to marqués de las Hormazas, 19 and 24 June 1810 [AHN: Archivo de Ministero de Estado, legajo 5636, photocopies in DLC]; Smith to JM, 23 June 1810?; JM to Smith, 17 July 1810, nn. 2, 4; Gallatin to JM, 15 Aug. 1810; JM to Gallatin, 22 Aug. 1810).

The results of these decisions and the subsequent missions were mixed. Gelston declined his assignment and had to be replaced in August 1810 by Joel Roberts Poinsett, who was later to distinguish himself by his participation in the independence movement in Chile. Shaler arrived in Havana on 1 August, and he lost no time in making contacts among the more important officials and settlers. He found far less enthusiasm for any sort of Cuban connection with the United States than the administration would have liked. His informants were particularly skeptical of the ability of the United States to defend the island in the event of an American war with Great Britain, and they generally believed that their fate remained very much tied to that of New Spain itself. With the captain general, Don Salvador de Muro y Salazar, marqués de Someruelos, Shaler fared no better. The marqués was prepared to meet with Shaler but would not otherwise recognize him in any capacity, nor would he grant him a passport for Veracruz on the mainland. The New Englander therefore found himself stuck in Havana, from where he penned his voluminous and informative dispatches for more than a year before Someruelos finally became so suspicious of his activities that he expelled him in November 1811 (marqués de Someruelos to Shaler, 7 Aug. 1810 [PHi: Shaler Family Papers]; Shaler to Smith, 5, 9, and 12 Aug. 1810 [DNA: RG 59, Communications from Special Agents]; JM to Gallatin, 22 Aug. 1810; Graham to JM, 27 Aug. 1810, n. 1).

Lowry, on the other hand, reached Venezuela in late August 1810 and remained there until December 1812. He arrived just in time to announce that he had been preceded several weeks earlier by the colonial secretary to the British governor of Curaçao, a Colonel Robertson, and that Robertson on 3 September had successfully negotiated a commercial agreement reducing by one-quarter the duties charged on British exports and imports in Venezuelan customhouses. Lowry was understandably chagrined by this development, which he predicted would extend British influence throughout Venezuela in ways "highly injurious" to American commercial prospects. He was able to compensate for the setback to some extent, however, by obtaining from the Caracas junta copies of Onís's correspondence with the recently displaced Spanish colonial officials. Among these documents was an angry and indiscreet letter Onís had written to the captain general of Caracas in February 1810. The minister of the Supreme Junta, ever fearful that JM was on the point of recognizing Joseph Bonaparte as king of Spain, hinted that Great Britain should be persuaded to send troops and vessels "near to Louisiana" in order to divide western North America into "two or three republics" and thus reduce the United States to "a state of perfect nullity." JM promptly attempted to turn the document to advantage by sending it to Congress in January 1811 in an effort to obtain legislative authority to occupy Spanish East Florida, thereby extending the scope of the policies he had commenced six months earlier (Lowry to Smith, 6 Sept. [two letters], 1 Oct., and 30 Nov. 1810 [DNA: RG 59, CD, La Guaira]; see also ASP, Foreign Relations, 3:404; Annals of Congress, 11th Cong., 3d sess., 370, 375).

As for the more immediately important missions of Wykoff and Mathews to West Florida, however, very little can now be known with any certainty. Mathews evidently began his task immediately after meeting with Crawford in late July. He headed for Pensacola only to find his entry to the town prevented "by the prevalence of a contagious fever." He then went to Mobile where he met with Vicente Folch, to whom he explained the president's views. The Spanish governor accepted Mathews's argument that there was a "unity of interest between the U S.

& the Spanish provinces in America" to the extent that neither party would wish any other European nation to obtain "a footing in the New world," but otherwise he seemed uninterested in discussing the idea that West Florida might become part of the United States. Mathews next departed for St. Augustine, and in January 1811 he came to Washington to report his findings to JM. On that occasion the president gave him further instructions about the resumption of his mission to the Mobile region and also renewed his discretion, depending on "the precise state of things there and of the real disposition of the Spanish Governor," to extend it into East Florida as well. Documentary material relating to the manner in which Mathews fulfilled these instructions in 1811 will be included in subsequent volumes of JM's papers. His conduct was to create so many difficulties, though, that by the early months of 1812 JM decided that he had no choice but to disavow all knowledge of his agent's deeds (Crawford to Smith, 1 Nov. 1810 [DNA: RG 59, ML]; Smith to Mathews and John McKee, 26 Jan. 1811 [DNA: RG 59, DL]).

Even less, unfortunately, is known about Wykoff's mission to Baton Rouge. It is clear that the judge received his instructions from Claiborne and that he exchanged letters with him over the summer of 1810, a correspondence the governor later reminded Wykoff "always" to regard as confidential since there were "persons who would gladly learn the whole contents of [the] letters" in order to injure the government. It is probably safe to assume that Wykoff did contact the American settlers mentioned in Claiborne's 14 June letter to him, though the effect of his activities in this regard more than likely merely reinforced developments already under way in the region in response to the anticipated demise of Spanish authority. In any event, as the judge reported on 24 July to Orleans territorial secretary Thomas B. Robertson, "the people in the different districts of [West Florida] have voted their electors, who met on the 14th [July] and voted their Representatives, who are to assemble in convention." This convention duly assembled at St. Johns Plains near Baton Rouge on 25 July, and its fourteen members included four of the American settlers—William Barrow, Philip Hickey, Thomas Lilley, and George Mather—who had been recommended to the judge by Claiborne (Claiborne to Wykoff, 26 Mar. 1811, Rowland, *Claiborne Letter Books*, 5:189–90; Wykoff to Thomas B. Robertson, 24 July 1810 [PHi: Daniel Parker Papers], enclosed in Graham to JM, 24 Aug. 1810).

Assuming that Wykoff and Mathews had commenced the task of giving events in West Florida "a right direction," JM retired for the summer to Montpelier, where he decided, on 17 July, that the role of keeping "a wakeful eye to occurrences & appearances" in the region should be assigned to Mississippi territorial governor David Holmes. At the same time JM also requested Robert Smith to instruct Holmes to mobilize his territorial militia and thus have it in readiness to "take care of the rights & interests of the U. S." in the event "either of foreign interference with W. F. or of internal convulsions." Smith drew up the necessary orders four days later. JM's choice of Holmes was a logical one. Like Claiborne, he was a Virginian whom JM had long known, and in the absence of Claiborne himself on the Atlantic coast over the summer, he was now the most important American political leader close to the Spanish province. Holmes's subsequent letters to the secretary of state were probably the single most important source of information about the situation in West Florida that JM was to receive, both during his summer vacation in Virginia and after his return to Washington on 6 October 1810 (JM to Smith, 17 July 1810, and n. 4).

In addition to reports from Holmes, JM also received news about West Florida from his cabinet colleagues, the executive department clerks, and from some of his less regular correspondents as well. Their letters, as may be seen in this volume, reflected considerable anxiety about the potential for disorder in the Spanish province as the convention at St. Johns Plains met and deliberated. The organizers of the convention justified their activities, as did many of the juntas in the Spanish-American colonies at this time, merely as a movement to redress local grievances and to provide for the better defense of the loyal subjects of Ferdinand VII. It was widely believed, however, that the final decisions of the convention would be more radical than the stated intentions of its membership, and there were clearly considerable differences of opinion throughout the province about its future allegiance in the event of the total collapse of Spanish authority. A majority of the convention's members, according to Holmes, had no goal other than the incorporation of West Florida into the United States, but in the absence of more specific assurances than either he or Wykoff were ever able to give them about how JM would respond to any actions they might take, they were fearful of the possible consequences of Spanish revenge. They therefore hesitated to renounce their loyalty to the Spanish crown and embarked instead on a two-month period of negotiation with the local commander at Baton Rouge, Carlos Dehault Delassus, over such matters as judicial reform and control of the militia. This reluctance on the part of the convention's members to act decisively in turn inspired rumors that their behavior was encouraging the machinations of a "British party" believed to be working for a transfer of the province to Great Britain (John Smith to JM, 7 Aug. 1810, enclosure; David Holmes to Robert Smith, 31 July and 8 Aug. 1810 [DNA: RG 59, TP, Mississippi]).

For his part, JM was always mindful of the danger that Great Britain would exploit Spanish weakness for commercial and diplomatic advantage. As will be seen, both he and his cabinet colleagues regarded the trade concessions granted by the Caracas junta to British merchants in September 1810 as an extremely ominous development, and they were apprehensive about British designs on Cuba as well. Nonetheless, on the basis of the early reports Holmes sent to Robert Smith, JM seems to have had few doubts that the work of the West Florida convention would eventually result in an invitation to the United States to exercise its claims to rule the province. While at Montpelier the president did at one point consult the secretary of war about the circumstances under which he might have to employ military force in the region, but this inquiry was prompted more by a concern that developments there could encourage unauthorized filibustering expeditions to oust the Spanish officials than it was by any fears of an immediate foreign invasion or intervention. At the time he made the inquiry to Eustis about the possibility of using military force, JM was receiving reports that members of the Caller, Kemper, and Kennedy families, all of whom had plotted to overthrow Spanish rule in the past, were engaged in forming an association for the purpose of attacking the garrison at Mobile. JM, who doubtless did not wish such activities to interfere with the tasks he had assigned to Wykoff and Mathews, immediately gave orders to civil and military officials to repress all signs of filibustering, but on reflection he decided that the threat was more apparent than real. He therefore waited for events to take their course and probably expected little of importance to happen before Claiborne was ready to return to New Orleans at the end of October (John R. Bedford to JM, 4 July and 26 Aug. 1810; Harry Toulmin to JM, 28 July and 31 Oct. 1810; JM to Eustis, 10 and 30 Aug. and 7 Sept. 1810; JM to Graham, 10 and 24 Aug. 1810; Eustis to JM, 19 Aug. and 14 Sept. 1810; Graham to JM, 3 and 29 Aug. and 3 Sept. 1810; George W. Erving to JM, 2 Sept. and 20 Oct. 1810; JM to Toulmin, 5 Sept. 1810; Gallatin to JM, 17 Sept. 1810; JM to William Pinkney, 30 Oct. 1810).

If JM did so calculate, his plans were upset by the West Florida convention itself. The men gathered at St. Johns Plains were less worried by the prospect of filibustering schemes than they were fearful of the consequences of the uncertainty that would result from the outcome of their deliberations remaining too long in suspense. In this context, their most important decisions were prompted by their distrust of the Spanish officials at Baton Rouge, especially Delassus, his secretary, Raphael Crocker, and his deputy commander, Tomaso Estevan; and, as a consequence, the relationship between the two groups of men quickly developed into an elaborate charade of mutual deceit and duplicity. No sooner had the convention delegates announced at the end of July that they wished to discuss with Delassus plans for the defense of West Florida and for the reform of its local administration than they immediately suspended these deliberations until after the middle of August in order to explore the possibility of incorporating the province into the United States. Governor Holmes, who wished to obtain his own information on "the real wishes and intentions of the convention," had dispatched an agent, Joshua G. Baker, to Baton Rouge in early August; and on his return to the Mississippi Territory approximately two weeks later, Baker was accompanied by delegate William Barrow. On behalf of the convention, Barrow inquired of the governor whether he had the authority to act "under any circumstances that might arise" and take West Florida under American "protection." Holmes replied that he had received no instructions to take "any active part" in the affairs of the province, though as he did so he did not try to disguise his sympathy with Barrow's request (Journal of the West Florida Convention, entry for 27 July 1810 [DLC: West Florida Miscellany]; Holmes to Smith, 21 Aug. 1810 [DNA: RG 59, TP, Mississippi]).

This response, as Barrow's correspondence with John R. Bedford would suggest, however, was less than the convention had hoped for, and the members evidently concluded that for the moment they had no other option but to go on with their discussions with Delassus. It is quite likely, though, that the convention expected Delassus to reject their demands for change, and once he had done so they would then have to consider how to use his relcalcitrance to justify bolder actions on their part. But Delassus, well aware of the weakness of his position, sought instead to gain time, and he did so by granting the convention the substance of its requests, subjecting them only to the provisos that the government continue in the name of Ferdinand VII and that any changes be approved by his superior, the captain general in Cuba. This uneasy agreement was embodied in an address issued by the convention to the inhabitants of Baton Rouge on 22 August, but the delegates were apparently both surprised by the apparent willingness of Delassus to meet their terms and extremely wary of the conditions he attached to them. They doubted that the commandant could be trusted to keep his word and concluded that his ultimate purpose was to wait for Folch to summon troops from Cuba, after which he would repudiate his concessions and crush the assembly by force (Barrow to Bedford, 5 Aug. 1810, enclosed in Bedford to JM, 26 Aug. 1810; Journal of the West Florida Convention, entries for 13–15 and 22 Aug. 1810 [DLC: West Florida Miscellany]; Graham to JM, 24 Aug. 1810, nn. 1 and 2, and 21 Sept. 1810, n. 1; Thomas B. Robertson to Smith, 26 Aug. 1810 [DNA: RG 59, TP, Orleans]; Holmes to Smith, 8 and 21 Aug. and 12 Sept. 1810 [DNA: RG 59, TP, Mississippi]).

Acting on these suspicions, the convention remained in session until 29 August, passing ordinances to secure its control over the militia and all local offices as well as granting itself the authority to borrow money on the credit and revenue of the province "whenever the public service may require." The delegates then adjourned their proceedings until 1 November, partly to implement the measures they had already adopted and partly to broaden the base of their support by arranging for the election of additional members to represent the more remote eastern districts of the province. For the period of their recess, they appointed a three-man committee to act for them in dealings with the Spanish authorities, and they further authorized their president, John Rhea, to summon any six delegates to exercise full powers "in case of emergency." For the next three weeks, both the Spanish officials and the convention members continued to operate on the basis of their mutual distrust. Delassus delayed carrying out some of the details of the agreement he had made on 22 August, and he was frequently reported as having declared that he did not consider himself bound by its terms. For their part, the delegates went about the task of reorganizing the militia and the local government, all the while proclaiming their undying loyalty to the person of Ferdinand VII. On 20 September the local militia commander, Philemon Thomas, finally intercepted letters from Delassus to Folch in which the beleaguered Baton Rouge commandant requested military assistance to help put down the insurrection of the self-appointed officers who had usurped his authority. Two days later John Rhea convened a meeting of half a dozen convention delegates at St. Francisville to decide on the settlers' response. The delegates promptly passed resolutions condemning Delassus as "unworthy of their confidence" and stripping him of all his executive powers. They then instructed Thomas to gather his available militia forces and seize the Spanish fort at Baton Rouge, a task he accomplished with relatively little difficulty in the early morning hours of 23 September. Three days later, ten of the convention members reassembled at Baton Rouge and declared West Florida to be independent from Spain (Journal of the West Florida Convention, entries for 24, 25, 27–29 Aug., 22, 25, 26 Sept. 1810 [DLC: West Florida Miscellany]).

By taking this last course of action, however, the convention was not rejecting the possibility of joining the United States. It was merely adopting a different tactic to achieve that very goal. Even as the delegates gathered again on 22 September and authorized the seizure of the fort at Baton Rouge, they also took the step of informing Governor Holmes of their purposes, including their intention "in a day or two" of making "an unqualified declaration of Independence" as evidence of their "unalterable determination to assert [their] rights as an integral part of the United States." If Holmes could respond to this advance notice by putting "into motion . . . any body of militia . . . to favor [their] views" and perhaps even send down some gunboats "to the neighborhood of Baton Rouge" in order to "para-lise . . . the Dons," so much the better. True to their word, the convention members forwarded Holmes a copy of their declaration of independence on 26 September, and John Rhea requested that the governor send it to JM on the grounds that he and his fellow delegates believed it was administration policy to take the province "under immediate & special protection, as an integral & inalienable portion of the United States." Implicit in this action was the assumption that the convention's declaration of independence would serve to acquit the United States government of any suspicion that it had conspired with the delegates to subvert the legitimate governing authorities in West Florida and that if JM was to recognize its deeds in that light, he would then be free to disregard the Spanish claim to the province altogether. The president could thereafter negotiate with the newly independent republic the terms of its entry into the United States (John Rhea to Holmes, 22 Sept. 1810 [DLC: West Florida Miscellany]; Rhea to Holmes, 26 Sept. 1810 [DNA: RG 59, TP, Mississippi]; see also Fulwar Skipwith to JM, 5 Dec. 1810, and Skipwith to Graham, 23 Dec. 1810, 14 Jan. 1811 [DLC: West Florida Miscellany]).

That JM did not share this view of the convention's conduct quickly became apparent as reports of its actions began to reach Washington after the third week in October. In a postscript to the *National Intelligencer* of 19 October there appeared an extract from a 25 September letter written by R. Davidson to a friend of Governor Holmes's, Abner L. Duncan, describing the seizure of the fort at Baton Rouge and mentioning that it had been necessary for the convention forces to place Delassus in irons and "to knock him down with the butt end of a musket." Copies of this letter were included in Holmes's reports of 26 September and 3 October to Robert Smith, though neither letter has any docket to indicate the date of its receipt in the State Department, and the enclosures to only the second of these letters can now be located in the National Archives. A comparison of the contents of the Davidson letter with the *National Intelligencer* postscript on 19 October leaves no doubt, however, that Holmes's letter of 26 September and its enclosures must have been the source for the story in the administration newspaper. JM's reaction was one of bewilderment. Uncertain as to what the news might mean, he hesitated about responding and, as he confessed to Jefferson, wondered whether he even could act at all without consulting Congress beforehand (Holmes to Smith, 26 Sept. and 3 Oct. 1810 [DNA: RG 59, TP, Mississippi]; JM to Jefferson, 19 Oct. 1810).

Holmes's next letter of 3 October, which included a copy of the West Florida declaration of independence, compelled the president to clarify his thoughts, however. It arrived in the capital, according to Joseph Gales, Jr., who recorded the event in his diary, on 25 October, and the cabinet immediately went into "close session for at least three hours thereupon." There was, without doubt, much for the cabinet to discuss, for the contents of Holmes's letter would have alarmed JM greatly. It began with the governor's announcement that the administration's instructions of 21 July for him to mobilize the Mississippi militia had not been put in the mail until 1 August and that they had not reached him until 29 September. The delay, as Holmes pointed out, was both unexpected and "regrettable," since it meant he had no troops "for any service that [might] be called for" as JM had intended. Even worse was the news from West Florida itself, where events, the governor reported, had "assumed a Very serious and determined aspect." Not only had the convention seized a Spanish fort and declared West Florida independent, but the population of the lower portions of the province was described as being "inimical to the New Order of things" and quite likely to attack the convention should Governor Folch decide to send forces from Pensacola. Furthermore, the adherents of Spain were said to be negotiating with the local Indians for support, and there was widespread fear of slave insurrection as well. Confessing that he was uncertain how these developments might affect the American claim to West Florida, the governor asked JM to send him "special instructions" for his guidance (Holmes to Smith, 3 Oct. 1810 [DNA: RG 59, TP, Mississippi]; "Recollections of the Civil History of the War of 1812," *Historical Magazine*, 3d ser., 3 [1874–75]: 158).

The president, however, had already been thinking for some time about problems in the Spanish-American colonies. On 14 October the administration received the first of Lowry's dispatches from Venezuela, including the report of the commercial concessions the Caracas junta had recently granted to British traders. JM was more than a little alarmed, and according to Joseph Gales, Jr., who called at the executive mansion three days later to pay his respects as the new editor of the *National Intelligencer*, he was convinced that Great Britain was meddling improperly in the province's affairs. When Gales raised the subject of West Florida in the belief that Americans in the adjacent territories were about to become similarly involved in affairs there, JM obliquely remarked that "he imagined measures had been adopted" to prevent this. The president, however, did voice his concern that elements in the West Florida population—whom he described as "the British party, together with the refugees from justice, deserters from the United States Army, and land-jobbers"—might form a majority that was unwilling to see the province come under American jurisdiction ("Recollections of . . . the War of 1812," p. 157; *National Intelligencer*, 15 Oct. 1810).

Any confidence JM retained after this meeting with Gales that Holmes could still respond with "any service that [might] be called for" in West Florida, however, was simply destroyed by the news arriving in the week after 19 October. If the account of the seizure of the fort at Baton Rouge had perplexed the president, the report of the emergence of a "self created independent Government" claiming the authority to form treaties, establish commerce, and provide for the common defense on the Gulf Coast—while Holmes was just starting to mobilize his militia forces—could only have struck him as disastrous. This development raised serious questions, which, if not settled at once, would ultimately invalidate the American claim to West Florida altogether (Presidential Proclamation, 27 Oct. 1810, and n. 2).

The president therefore acted. Immediately after the cabinet meeting on 25 October, a proclamation was drafted for the annexation of West Florida justifying the policy on the grounds that it had always been part of the Louisiana colony and should have been transferred to the United States in 1803. Its occupation was now justified, the president asserted, in order to forestall "events ultimately contravening the views" of both Spain and the United States and to prevent threats to "the tranquility and security of our adjoining territories" as well. Among these last concerns, the proclamation specifically mentioned the creation of "new facilities given to violations of our Revenue and Commercial laws." It is not difficult to surmise what was bothering the president here. If, as he told Joseph Gales, Jr., he had been concerned about British agents who had recently negotiated a commercial agreement with "the independent party" in Venezuela in order to give an "eclat" to "British commercial favors" and thus "strengthen their party" there, it did not take much imagination for him to think what British agents might make of the new opportunities presented by an independent West Florida. The final version of the proclamation was therefore perfected on 26 October and given to Claiborne the next day. The governor then promptly left Washington to supervise the operations required to give it effect (ibid.; "Recollections of . . . the War of 1812," p. 157).

The proclamation was to remain a secret until JM revealed it to Congress in his annual message on 5 December 1810. By then Claiborne had already commenced the business of extending American authority over West Florida, and JM was able to present the world with the fait accompli that the Spanish province, as far as the Perdido River but excluding the town of Mobile, was now part of the United States. Admittedly, the acquisition of this much of West Florida did not come about in ways that JM either had anticipated or would have liked. There is no reason to doubt that he would have preferred to have received an invitation from the convention at St. Johns Plains and then responded to it after consulting with members of Congress when they had assembled in Washington at the end of the year. That this did not occur was due, in part at least, to a feeling among the convention members that JM had failed to give them sufficiently explicit indications about his ultimate intentions. For his part, though, JM probably believed that he could not have intervened in West Florida more overtly than he did without incurring the risk of serious diplomatic and political consequences. In the resulting confusion, the West Florida convention acted to precipitate a solution, and JM's annexation proclamation was the president's response to a situation that was otherwise threatening to escape his control.

(Secondary sources used for this note: Stanley Clisby Arthur, *The Story of the West Florida Rebellion* [St. Francisville, La., 1935]; Leslie Bethell, ed., *The Cambridge History of Latin America* [5 vols. to date; Cambridge, 1984—], vol. 3: *From Independence to c. 1870*; Philip C. Brooks, *Diplomacy and the Borderlands: The Adams-Onís Treaty of 1819* [Berkeley, Calif., 1939]; Thomas D. Clark and John D. W. Guice, *Frontiers in Conflict: The Old Southwest, 1795–1830* [Albuquerque, 1989]; Cox, "The Pan-American Policy of Jefferson and Wilkinson," *Mississippi Valley Historical Review*, 1 [1914–15]: 212–39; Cox, *The West Florida Controversy*; Clifford L. Egan, "The United States, France, and West Florida, 1803–1807," *Fla. His-*

torical Quarterly, 47 [1968–69]: 227–52; Philip S. Foner, *A History of Cuba and Its Relations with the United States* [2 vols.; New York, 1962]; Humbert B. Fuller, *The Purchase of Florida: Its History and Diplomacy* [Cleveland, 1906]; Charles C. Griffin, *The United States and the Disruption of the Spanish Empire, 1810–1822* [New York, 1937]; John S. Kendall, ed., "Documents concerning the West Florida Revolution, 1810," *La. Historical Quarterly*, 17 [1934]: 81–95, 306–14, 474–501; John Lynch, *The Spanish-American Revolutions, 1808–1826* [New York, 1973]; Roy F. Nichols, "William Shaler: New England Apostle of Rational Liberty," *New England Quarterly*, 9 [1936]: 71–96; James A. Padgett, ed., "Official Records of the West Florida Revolution and Republic," *La. Historical Quarterly*, 21 [1938]: 685–805; Grady D. Price, "The United States and West Florida, 1803–1812" [Ph.D. diss., TxU, 1939]; William Spence Robertson, *France and Latin-American Independence* [Baltimore, 1939]; John Rydjord, *Foreign Interest in the Independence of New Spain: An Introduction to the War for Independence* [Durham, N.C., 1935]; Arthur P. Whitaker, *The United States and the Independence of Latin America, 1800–1830* [Baltimore, 1941]; and Henry M. Wriston, *Executive Agents in American Foreign Relations* [Baltimore, 1929].)

From Samuel Fulton

SIR,   WEST FLORIDA, BATON ROUGE 20 Apl 1810

On my quittal of the Service in the year Eighteen hundred and three I had the Honour of addressing you[1] on the Subject of my quitting a foreign Service, and offring it to my Native Country. Some Short time after I had the Honour of receiving from you an answer[2] Informing me that nothing Could be Done at that moment nor untill a new organization would take place. About five years past I became a Spanish Subject and have [done] evry thing in my power to merit the Confidence of the Government as I would wish to do under what ever Government I may recide; I have organized the Millitia of the Provence over whom I act, as Adgt. Gnl. and Commandt. of their Cavelry. Some of your Generals have assured me that they have never Seen Millitia under better Subordination in any part of the United States.

Seeing the unhappy Situation of old Spa⟨in I⟩ have But Little hopes that She can hold out much Longer against the Colossal power of Bonaparte, Should She fall we must of Course Change our Masters here; the Choise would be General, in favour of the Government over which you have the Hono⟨ur⟩ to Preside. Should the President & Congress jud⟨ge⟩ Wright to take possession of this Detatch provin⟨ce⟩ I will make to reclaime of you that friendship and Service which you so Generously offerd me when I had the pleasure of seeing you in Phillidelphia In the year 1795, But not at the Expence of an ancient Veteran.

Possibly my Knowledge of the Local Situation of this Country; the Charecters & Manners & Languages of the people might render my Services usefull to the Government. I have the Honour to remain your Very obedt. Servt

S. FULTON[3]

RC (NN). Headed by Fulton, "Samuel Fulton formerly Lieutanant Colol. In the Service of France; To Mr. James Maddison President of the United States of America." Docketed by JM.

1. Probably Fulton to JM, 10 Aug. 1802 (DNA: RG 59, LAR, 1801–9).
2. Letter not found.
3. Samuel Fulton was a military adventurer who had entered French service in 1793, becoming actively involved in the intrigues of Citizen Genet and George Rogers Clark against Spanish territory in Florida and Louisiana. He had met JM in 1795 and left for France in May 1796, carrying with him JM's letters and State Department correspondence to James Monroe in Paris. Fulton continued to serve in the French army in Europe and Saint-Domingue but resigned his commission after hearing of the Louisiana Purchase while on a furlough in New Orleans. His repeated applications to JM for an army commission or any position, preferably on the southwestern borderlands, were unsuccessful. He settled at Baton Rouge by 1804, married the Spanish governor's daughter, and commanded the Spanish militia in West Florida. American leaders of the movement for self-government met at his house in Baton Rouge, and he became lieutenant colonel of the Louisiana territorial militia (*PJM*, 16:304 n. 6; Fulton to Jefferson, 29 Apr. 1801, Monroe to Jefferson, n.d. [received 26 Aug. 1801] [DNA: RG 59, LAR, 1801–9]; Fulton to JM, 12 Oct. 1812, and enclosure [NN]; Cox, *The West Florida Controversy*, pp. 342, 380).

To Thomas Jefferson

DEAR SIR   WASHINGTON Apl. 23. 1810

Yours of the 16th. has been recd. It is not improbable that there will be an early occasion to send for public purposes, a ship to G. B. & France; & that Norfolk will be the port of Departure. I recommend therefore that your plow be lodged there as soon as may be, with the proper instructions to your Agent. It may not be amiss to include in them a discretion to forward the plow to any other port, if he shd. learn in time, that another is substituted for Norfolk. Congs. remain in the unhinged state which has latterly marked their proceedings; with the exception only, that a majority in the H. of R. have stuck together so far as to pass a Bill providing for a conditional repeal by either of the Belligts. of their Edicts; laying in the mean time, an addition of 50 perCt. to the present duties on imports from G. B. & F.[1] What the Senate will do with the Bill is rendered utterly uncertain by the policy which seems to prevail in that Branch. Our last authentic information from G. B. is of the 28. Feby. & from France of the

2d. of Feby. The information in both cases, has an aspect rather promising; but far from being definite; and subsequent accts. thro' the ordinary channels, do not favor a reliance on general professions or appearances. Bonaparte, does not seem to have yet attended to the distinction between the external & internal character of his Decrees; and to be bending his Augmented faculties for annihilating British Commerce with the Contt. with which our corrupt traders have confounded the Amn. Flag. And it will be a hard matter for Wellesley, shd. he be well disposed, to drag his AntiAmerican Colleagues into a change of policy; supported as they will be by the speeches & proceedings of Congs. From those the inference will be that one party prefers submission of our Trade to British regulation, and the other confesses the impossibil[it]y of resisting it. Without a change of Ministry, of which there is some prospect, it wd. be imprudent to count on any radical change of policy. For the moment, I understand that the Merchts. will not avail themselves of the unshackled trade they have been contending for; a voluntary Embargo being produced by the certainty of a glutted Market, in England, and the apprehension of Brit: Blockades, and French confiscations. The experiment about to be made will probably open too late the eyes of the people, to the expediency & efficacy of the means which they have suffered to be taken out of the hands of the Govt. and to be incapacitated for future use. The Merinos are not yet heard of. Be assured of my constant & Affe. respects.

JAMES MADISON

RC (DLC). Docketed by Jefferson, "recd Apr. 26."

1. On 1 May 1810 Congress passed, and JM signed, the measure known as Macon's Bill No. 2. Its provisions excluded armed belligerent vessels from American ports but otherwise imposed no restraints on trade with France and Great Britain. In the event of one of the belligerents' removing its restrictions on neutral trade before 3 Mar. 1811, the president was authorized, after a period of three months, to impose nonintercourse on the other if it had failed to lift its restrictions as well. The House provision for a 50 percent additional duty on British and French goods was dropped in the final version (*Annals of Congress*, 11th Cong., 2d sess., 1915, 2051; *U.S. Statutes at Large*, 2:605–6).

From Jesse Waln

DEAR SIR   PHILADELPHIA April 23rd 1810
  Previous to my departure from Canton I received a small Package from Poonqua Winchong[1] for Mrs Maddison, he has lately visited this Country and appears to be greatly pleased by the civilities received from you— have the goodness to present my best Compliments to Mrs Maddison and

tell her I shall forward the Package by the first safe opportunity. With great Respect Your Obedient Servt.

JESSE WALN[2]

RC (DLC). Docketed by JM.

1. John Jacob Astor had induced Punqua Wingchong, a Cantonese shopkeeper, to impersonate a mandarin merchant seeking to return to China. In July 1808 JM, Gallatin, and Jefferson had arranged for his passport and allowed a ship of his choice to sail from New York, exempted from the Embargo. Punqua chose Astor's ship the *Beaver*, which returned to the U.S. after repeal of the Embargo with a cargo valued at more than $200,000 (Punqua Wingchong to JM, 5 Feb. 1809 [NHi]; Porter, *John Jacob Astor*, 1:143–49, 420–28).

2. Jesse Waln (d. 1848), with his cousin and business partner Robert, traded extensively with the East Indies and China. His firm's headquarters were "at Waln's wharf, near Spruce Street" in Philadelphia (Scharf and Westcott, *History of Philadelphia*, 3:2213, 2215).

§ From Josiah Jackson. *23 April 1810.* Reports that his father-in-law, Henry Madison, "as well as the rest of us were much g[r]atifyed in the short answer" [not found] JM sent. The old gentleman "is still in tolerable Health except a giddiness in the Head that causes a staggering." His own family includes eight living children; in addition, "We have had about the same number of Blacks to raise." While educating his family and making a living "on a thin Soil," Jackson has accumulated only about $1,000 with which to purchase land for his children. In his neighborhood "the rich & dureble soils are precured [*sic*] by the more moneyed men." No member of his family has "ventured yet over the blue ridge . . . to settle," and since JM is well informed, seeks his advice "where good soil may be precured with a small sum of money (not out of reach)." JM's reply should be directed to Charlotte Court House.

RC (DLC). 3 pp. Docketed by JM. Jackson had previously written JM on 1 June 1809 (*PJM-PS*, 1:217–19).

§ From Joseph H. Macklefrith. *23 April 1810, Fort McHenry.* Rumors that provisional army is to be disbanded prompts this request for a discharge from the Fifth Infantry Regiment. Macklefrith (a sergeant) must properly care for his family. If the country were endangered or lacked an army, "I should prefer the Cause of my Country to that of my family but its to the reverse."

RC (DNA: RG 107, LRRS, M-177:5). 3 pp. Docketed by a War Department clerk as received 28 Apr. 1810.

From William Bentley

Permit me to say, that in asking a Letter to Gen Stark, It never entered
my thoughts to answer any Public purpose.[1] But I may say with truth,
                Gen Stark's Letter has saved New England.
The bitterest invectives are from this conviction, but they soon cease. Still
the conviction is sure, "And they gnaw their tongues for pain."[2]
Assured that I speak the sense of all N E, I remain with the highest
honour of your public & private Character your devoted Servant
                                                WILLIAM BENTLEY.

RC (DLC).

1. In his diary entry for 1 Mar. 1810, Bentley noted the local publication of Stark's 21 Jan.
letter to JM. Then on 9 Mar. Bentley wrote: "Gen. Stark has been much insulted, as well as
President Madison, for the publication of a correspondence between these two patriots
which has done wonders in New England in confirming the patriots in their duty. The
Opposition fear the final success" (*Diary of William Bentley*, 3:502, 503).

2. Rev. 16:10.

§ From Christopher Ellery. *24 April 1810, Providence.* Recommends Henry Wheaton for the position of marshal of Rhode Island.

RC (DLC). 1 p.

From Joel Barlow

DEAR SIR   KALORAMA 25 April 1810

Mr. Carey who is probably well known to you desires an interview with
you on the subject of Mr. Tench Cox whose present office will probably
be vacated by the passing of the Bill respecting a quartermaster's department.[1] Mr. Cox's political character, his official talents & his mode of conducting the office he now holds are doubtless much better known to you
than to me. But his domestic affairs are somewhat within my knowledge,
his family is large & now at the most expensive time of life. I believe a
great degree of distress would follow his being dismissed from his office,
unless that of the projected department of quartermaster could be given
him. With great respect & attachment yr. obt. Sert.

                                                J. BARLOW

RC (DLC).

1. Secretary of War Eustis favored a reform of his department that would create a quartermaster general to handle purchases previously left to the purveyor of public supplies, Tench Coxe. On 16 Apr. the Senate had passed a bill to implement that proposal, and Coxe believed his political enemy, Senator Michael Leib of Pennsylvania, was excessively eager to see it become law. Coxe asked his friend Mathew Carey to intervene on his behalf, but Congress adjourned without further action on the bill. Leib reopened the issue when Congress reconvened, but Coxe survived as purveyor until the position was abolished in 1812 (Jacob E. Cooke, *Tench Coxe and the Early Republic* [Chapel Hill, N.C., 1978], pp. 470–72, 478–79; see also Coxe to JM, 28 Apr. 1810).

§ From "Tammany." *25 April 1810.* Reminds JM that the American people placed him at the helm of government so that he might "steer it aright." Urges him to "active duties" since "inaction does not befit your station." Warns JM of intrigue in Washington and attacks "Mutius Randolph" for his third essay claiming that the Smith family has "imprisoned [you] in your own palace." "Mutius" is an "incoherent writer," out to deceive JM, but his subject matter—"the misunderstanding between Gallatin and others"—is "notorious at Washington."[1] Admits that Gallatin might not have been very well treated at the outset of JM's administration, but he has sought and taken his revenge. Accuses Gallatin of using his "capacity for business" to dictate a policy of submission to Great Britain, and only the London newspapers [publishing Erskine's diplomatic correspondence] have unmasked the "deformity of his apostacy."

Points to the "universal discontent" created after a five-month session of Congress that accomplished "*nothing*" and criticizes JM for his "equivocal" conduct and messages. Some thought JM meant war, others thought he meant peace, while Gallatin's treasury reports were "calculated to inspire fears in the breasts of ignorant men, who know not how to estimate our resources." Hence Congress abandoned the nation's rights and instead sat down to consult the interests of English stockholders in the recharter of the Bank of the United States. Thinks Gallatin's "*Swiss venality*"[2] is equal to the task of reconciling the renewal of the bank charter with "the former professions of the democratic party" but points out that JM will incur the blame and censure for this.

Believes the people will not "patiently suffer" Gallatin to usurp the duties of the president. "Though we do not desire the vulture to rule us, yet we naturally despise the log." Warns that Gallatin will drag JM "to destruction." Reminds JM that he has received some hints of the people's attitude toward ceremonies and office seeking in Washington in the "reception of Dick Forrest's nomination by the senate." Advises JM to heed these and other warnings as the people "cannot be long deceived. They will compare profession with practice."

Printed copy (Baltimore *Whig*, 25 Apr. 1810).

1. At the conclusion of the essay by "Tammany," the editor of the Baltimore *Whig* added a footnote to deny rumors that either Robert or Samuel Smith had any responsibility for instigating the attacks on Gallatin that had appeared in the paper.

2. In a footnote to the essay, "Tammany" reported that Gallatin had recently been giving "dinners upon dinners" to groups of congressmen—"an unusual thing with him"—in an effort to persuade them to vote for the recharter of the Bank of the United States.

§ To the House of Representatives. *27 April 1810.* Transmits a report of the secretary of state in compliance with the House resolution of 23 Apr.[1]

RC and enclosures (DNA: RG 233, President's Messages). RC 1 p. In a clerk's hand, signed by JM. Enclosures are Robert Smith's 26 Apr. report (2 pp.) on U.S. consular and commercial agents in foreign countries, "together with the Salaries and compensations that have been allowed to the Consuls residing at Algiers, Tripoli, Tunis and Morocco" (2 pp.). Received, read, and tabled on 27 Apr. Printed in *ASP, Commerce and Navigation,* 1:819–20.

1. The House resolution of 23 Apr. requested "a statement of the several consular or commercial agents" of the U.S. "together with the salaries or compensation, if any, allowed to them, respectively." Four days after the receipt of JM's message, Congress, on 1 May, passed a bill to fix "the compensation of public ministers, and of Consuls residing on the coast of Barbary." JM signed the bill, but according to Robert Smith's later recollection he had such "strong objections" to it that he "utterly disregarded its provisions." Smith added that JM deemed it inexpedient either to veto it or to recommend its modification, and instead "at a late period of the session" he "pressed me much to prevail upon some member to introduce, with that view, a bill into Congress." Smith declined on the grounds that he "had powerful objections to every kind of private intermeddling with the business of members of the Legislature and especially to such secret modes of recommending public measures to the consideration of Congress." JM received this response "with great perturbation and was evidently much displeased" (*Annals of Congress,* 11th Cong., 2d sess., 1946; *U.S. Statutes at Large,* 2:608–10; *National Intelligencer,* 2 July 1811).

From Tench Coxe

SIR   PHILADELPHIA April 28th. 1810

As it is possible, that the bill to create a quartermasters department may become a law, and its operation upon my situation will be the most unexpected & inconvenient, I do myself the honor to submit myself to your consideration as a candidate for the office of Deputy Quarter Master at this place. I shall be willing, to obtain subsistence for myself & family, to perform any or *all* of the present duties of Purveyor of public Supplies and any of the duties of the newly created office, as they may be required of it under the third section, for the Salary of fifteen Hundred dollars, which is proposed for it.

Accustomed to procure the public supplies in the last three very difficult years, and intimate from my seventeenth year with the freighting of vessels and waggons, I trust I can justify the appointment by an union of all the labors of the purveyor and of a proper quarter master, within the view of the law.

I hope, for reasons, which appear to me very strong, that the bill will not pass. I have offered them, in a hasty note, to the consideration of Mr. Eppes, who is chairman of the Committee of ways & means. They were suddenly sketched this evening from an apprehension that the bill might be yet taken up; and, as an executive officer, I wish them respectfully submitted to the Head, & the proper & other branches of the Executive Government. Tho I am indeed too deeply interested in the case, yet I trust I have not at all forgotten, that love of truth, which has been my polar star in every public disquisition. The bill, in my humble opinion, will induce solemn ills. If it should be adopted, I hope that a Union of all the laborious duties I have ventured to suggest in the preceding paragraph, which I think no other ⟨preposed?⟩ man will undertake, will occasion the public service to be effectually, tho less advantageously executed. I have the honor to be, with sincere wishes for your public and personal health, Sir your most respectful servant

TENCH COXE

RC (DNA: RG 59, LAR, 1809–17, filed under "Coxe").

§ From George Joy. *28 April 1810, Copenhagen.* The French minister at Copenhagen, Didelot,[1] gave Joy the enclosed papers relating to "a claim or rather a pretension of the heirs of the late Mr. Gerard (first Minister of France to the U.S.) to Some lands or the value of them presented to him by the Illinois & Wabash Company." The enclosed note of Gérard de Rayneval, brother of the deceased minister, shows that Monroe was convinced of the lawfulness of the claim, and Talleyrand had instructed Bernadotte[2] to support it. When the latter did not proceed to his post, Chaumont was entrusted with the claim and with a letter to Jefferson on the subject. Assumes that knowledge of this transaction prevented Congress from making a grant to Gérard similar to those it made to Lafayette and d'Estaing.

Cannot say how far current political considerations would enter into the question, but when Didelot raised the matter a few weeks ago Joy told him that the U.S. was not disposed to blend its old Revolutionary War friends with the present generation and that recent difficulties would not obliterate any obligations contracted to those individuals. Also mentioned to Didelot that in one of the last dispatches Joy received from JM there was "by Some accident an enveloppe on which you had written in pencil instructions to one of the clerks to Send another parcel to Genl. *laFayette*; which I had no doubt contained like my own the printed Communications to Congress & a letter from yourself [not found], & if the lands in question, as I understood at that Time, were Similarly Situated to those voted to *Lafayette*; I presumed he might at any time get possession of them or Sell them."

Is aware that the Constitution forbids American ministers from accepting gifts from foreign governments, but there is nothing to prevent the U.S. from granting that indulgence to other nations. Points out that Didelot is so "modest" and so well regarded that it is "hard to believe him a frenchman." Thinks Didelot's support will be useful to him and has no doubt that Didelot is well disposed to the U.S. Has communicated this to Adams in the correspondence of which Joy enclosed copies in his letter to Smith of 23 Mar.

Discusses recent French decrees and "the late treaty between France & Holland." Declares that Napoleon had "no retreat provided England yielded to a certain point" but was surprised to learn that Didelot believed the emperor would "accept of Something Short of what had been looked for from England; that he was desireous of backing out, & would do it by any decent avenue." Told Didelot that he considered this "very precarious" and understood it to be JM's opinion also. Will not recapitulate their discussions of the value of the property under sequestration but thinks that recent events look "propitious." Has always applauded "the patience & perseverance with which you have pursued what I consider the only legitimate course of redress."

Has received no letters "from you, from Mr. *Pinkney*, or from the Secretary of State Since I left *London*. The last I have from you is of the 16th. March 1809" [not found]. Adds in a postscript that he would appreciate an early opinion respecting Gérard's case and mentions that he is thinking of going to Holland in the summer.

RC and three enclosures (DLC). RC 10 pp. In a clerk's hand, signed by Joy. Marked "(Copy) 1st. via Gottenburg." Docketed by JM. Enclosures are: "Extracts of letters & papers relating to Illinois and Wabash land Companies," 20 Aug. 1779–2 May 1803 (6 pp.), including copy of a letter signed by James Wilson, Silas Deane, and William Murray to Conrad Alexander Gérard, 24 Aug. 1779, presenting him with stock in the Illinois and Wabash Company; Le Ray de Chaumont to Jefferson, 8 May 1807 (3 pp.; in French); memorandum by Joseph-Mathias Gérard de Rayneval on lands granted to Conrad Alexander Gérard, undated but probably written between 1807 and 1809 (4 pp.; in French; described as C. A. Gérard, claim to western land, and misdated 8 May 1807 in the *Index to the James Madison Papers*).

1. François-Charles-Luce Didelot, French minister to Denmark, 1807–11, had married Alexandrine-Sophie Gérard de Rayneval, the sister of Joseph-Mathias Gérard de Rayneval and Conrad Alexander Gérard, in 1790 (*Dictionnaire de Biographie Française*, 11:263, 15:1210, 1211, 1243).

2. In 1803 Napoleon had appointed Jean-Baptiste Bernadotte (later Karl XIV of Sweden) to be French minister to the U.S., but Bernadotte renounced the position after learning of the sale of Louisiana and the resumption of war between France and Great Britain (Dunbar Plunket Barton, *The Amazing Career of Bernadotte, 1763–1844* [Boston, 1929], pp. 149–53).

From Henry Dearborn

DEAR SIR,   BOSTON April 30th. 1810
With this you will receive a thing called a sermon, in which you will see exhibited a correct picture of New Engld. Federalism, excepting one strong feature, which the painter has not exhibited, viz. a deep rooted hostility to our present sistem of Government but he deserves great credit for having given a correct picture of the veracity, Charity, & candor of his party.[1] Whether we shall succeed in obtaining a Republican majority in our Legislature or not, is uncertain,[2] I think the chances about eaqual.

We are now anxious to hear the result of the Newyork Elections. Mrs. Dearborn joins me in the most friendly & respectfull salutations to your self & Mrs. Madison.

H. DEARBORN.

RC (DLC). Docketed by JM.

1. JM's reaction to Dearborn's enclosure (see JM to Dearborn, 7 May 1810) leaves little doubt that it was David Osgood's *A Discourse Delivered at Cambridge in the Hearing of the University, April 8, 1810* (Cambridge, Mass., 1810; Shaw and Shoemaker 20966). Taking 2 Samuel 15:6, "So Absalom stole the hearts of the men of Israel," as his text, Osgood told the story of David and Absalom as a parable for the times. George Washington was David, Jefferson was Absalom, while JM was cast in the role of "Ahitophel, the Machiavel of the age" (p. 5). In case his audience missed the point, Osgood made his message explicit by concluding with a severe critique of Republican foreign policy, in which JM was depicted as a tool of Napoleon. The students of Harvard, on 9 Apr., passed a vote of thanks to Osgood for his "impressive and valuable discourse."

2. At the time Dearborn wrote, the state of parties in the Massachusetts General Court after the recent elections was uncertain. The final partisan identity of General Court members for the sessions of 1810 and 1811 was 302 Federalists, 264 Republicans, and 76 of unknown political affiliation. A sufficient number of the latter members voted with the Republicans to enable them to elect a Speaker of the House and thus control the sessions of 1810 and 1811 (James M. Banner, Jr., *To the Hartford Convention: The Federalists and the Origins of Party Politics in Massachusetts, 1789–1815* [New York, 1970], pp. 362, 367).

§ To the House of Representatives. *1 May 1810.* Transmits a report from the secretary of state in compliance with the House resolution of 30 Apr.

RC and enclosures (DNA: RG 233, President's Messages). RC 1 p. Enclosures (13 pp.) are Robert Smith's 1 May report on relations with Great Britain and France and six appendixes containing extracts from diplomatic correspondence. Received, read, and tabled on 1 May. Printed in *Annals of Congress*, 11th Cong., 2d sess., 2028–31. On 30 Apr. the House had requested information on French or British responses to American protests over commercial decrees and orders in council (ibid., 2018, 2021).

From Albert Gallatin

DEAR SIR   2 May 1810

The Senate having rejected the nominations of Hickman & Wilkinson,[1] I beg leave to submit the following in their stead vizt.

Samuel Abbott of Michigan to be Collector of the district of Michillimakinac & Inspector of the revenue for the port of Michillimakinac[2]

Denison Darling of Mississippi territory (whose nomination you had withdrawn & sent in its place that of Wilkinson) to be Collector of the district of Mobile and Inspector of the revenue for the port of Mobile.[3]

The absolute incapacity of John Pooler[4] Comr. of Loans for Georgia renders his removal necessary; and Charles Harris of Georgia is warmly recommended by the two Georgia Senators as a proper successor. Respectfully Your obedt. Sert.

ALBERT GALLATIN

RC (DLC). Docketed by JM.

1. On 1 May the Senate had rejected JM's nominations of Harris H. Hickman and James B. Wilkinson, the general's son, for the positions of collector and inspector of the revenue at Michilimackinac and Mobile, respectively (*Senate Exec. Proceedings*, 2:146, 147, 154–55).

2. JM's nomination of Abbott for the positions on 7 Jan. 1811 was confirmed by the Senate on 12 Jan. 1811 (ibid., 2:160, 162).

3. JM nominated Addin Lewis for the Mobile positions on 5 Feb. 1811 (ibid., 2:165, 166).

4. Jefferson had appointed Pooler on 14 Nov. 1808. JM replaced him with Robert Habersham, whose nomination he sent to the Senate on 7 Jan. 1811 (ibid., 2:85, 88, 159, 161).

§ From "Tammany." *2 May 1810.* Sends JM a "valedictory note,—having resolved to retire from a fruitless political contest." Warns JM against the flattery of those legislators who submitted to France and Great Britain and who will attend this evening's levee marking the end of "the present ignoble congress." JM must bear responsibility for the state of the country. He was elected "to perform the active and provident duties of a father and guardian of the United States—not to remain in the criminal, imbecile and inglorious *neutrality* of king *Log.*"

Asks, "before the American people," whether JM fulfilled his duties during the last session of Congress, whether he tried to prevent "submission" to the European belligerents, whether he recommended proper measures to Congress, and whether he warned that body and the people that "national extinction" was preferable to "national degradation." JM must answer these questions in the negative, having neglected the national interest for the "trifles of the *drawingroom.*" Points out that JM has tolerated "dangerous schisms" in his cabinet and allowed one of his secretaries [Gallatin] to pluck the reins from his feeble hands. As a result the nation is insulted with impunity. Predicts there will be no change until future elections return "an independent congress" and "bring a more energetic and manly tenant into the *white house.*" Declares that the people will not accept "the contemptible blank of a neutral president" and that if JM cannot govern more effectively he will lose their "confidence and respect."

Entreats JM to reflect on "our wretched and dishonorable" situation as well as on his own reputation. Concludes by urging JM to "chuse some sort of characteristic feature by which you will be hereafter distinguished from the crowd, and saved from oblivion."

Printed copy (Baltimore *Whig*, 2 May 1810).

From Albert Gallatin

[3 May 1810]

I have the honor to enclose the copy of an Act for the relief of Arthur St. Clair,[1] and a letter from the Comptroller of the Treasury on the same subject.

The phraseology of the Act being different from that adopted in other similar cases, the authority of the President is necessary in order that the money may be paid: and the whole or part will be paid in conformity with his decision.

RC (DLC). Lower portion of RC, including complimentary close, signature, and probably dateline, has been clipped. Docketed by JM, "Treasury Dept / May 3. 1810." Enclosures not found.

1. Arthur St. Clair claimed that he advanced $1,800 from personal funds for reenlistments in the Continental army in 1776. He was the Federalist governor of the Northwest Territory, 1787–1802. Republicans in the territory charged him with financial and legal improprieties, and after he delivered a speech denouncing statehood for Ohio, Jefferson dismissed him. St. Clair believed that Republicans in Congress blocked his reimbursement. He had lost his fortune by 1810, when a private act awarded him $2,000 provided he would "sign a release of all claim for further remuneration from the government for services rendered, or money advanced by him, during the revolutionary war" (ASP, Claims, pp. 375–76; Malone, Jefferson and His Time, 4:243–44; U.S. Statutes at Large, 6:94–95).

To [the Comptroller of the Treasury?]

May 3. 1810

In pursuance of the Act of Congress, passed May 1. 1810, entitled "An Act for the relief of Arthur St. Clair,["] I hereby direct that the sum of two thousand Dollars be paid to him, out of the monies, and on the conditions, stated in the said Act.

JAMES MADISON

RC (DNA: RG 217, Manning File).

From James H. Hooe

SIR,   ALEXANDRIA May 4. 1810.

I received a Letter some weeks ago from Mr. William Jarvis of Lisbon, in which he advised me of his having shiped to my address by the Ship

Diana Capt. Lewis, for this port, some Merino Sheep, a pair of which were intended for you, & one other pair for Mr. Jefferson.[1]

I have now the honor & satisfaction to advise you, that this Ship has arrived in the River and about ten miles below the Town, where she is at present detained in consequence of being run a ground last night. I have just seen the Captain & he informs me, the Sheep are safe, with the exception of one Ewe, which died on the passage. I have not yet determined what Steps it may be most adviseable to take for the safety of the Sheep, but they ought certainly to be brought on shore as speedily as possible.

Particular Sheep were pointed out by Mr Jarvis, in his Letter to me, which were intende⟨d⟩ for yourself and Mr. Jefferson, but he has desired that you shoud make a choice, if more agreable, out of the whole.

It will give me pleasure to receive the instructions of your Excellency, with regard to these Sheep, and with regard to those of Mr Jefferson, shoud it be your pleasure to make a disposition of them. I have the honor to be, with due Consideration & Respect Sir Yr. Mt Obt Servt

J H: HOOE

RC (DLC). Docketed by JM.

1. See William Jarvis to JM, 20 Jan. 1810, and n. 1, and 19 Feb. 1810.

§ From John Rhea. *4 May 1810, Washington.* Encloses a copy of his circular letter to his constituents.

RC (DLC); enclosure (DLC: Madison Collection, Rare Book Division). RC 1 p. Enclosure (3 pp.) is Rhea's 20 Apr. 1810 printed letter to his constituents (reprinted in Cunningham, *Circular Letters of Congressmen*, 2:687–93), which quoted extensively from JM's 29 Nov. 1809 annual message to Congress. Rhea was a Republican congressman from Tennessee, 1803–15 and 1817–23.

From John Armstrong

Private
DEAR SIR,   PARIS 6 May 1810

I have just been informed that M. Bowdoin (before he left Paris) in conjunction with M. Skipwith & by means which I shall take care to investigate, did obtain from an Irish ex-priest of the name of Somers a deposition, in which an attempt is made to implicate me in a land Speculation, connected with the then intended purchase of the Floridas, and conducted by Mess. Parker, OMealy and le Ray de Chaumont.[1] This deposition was multiplied by several copies, one of which was inserted on the Consular Register of this place—which, by the way, forms the true reason why that Register has been so unwarrantably witheld by Skipwith and Barnet.[2] Another of these copies was, as I understand, sent to you, when Secretary of State, to be presented to the President. It is this last circumstance that gives me a right to trouble you with anything on this Subject and in particular to request, that a copy of this deposition, if in the office, or otherwise within your reach, may be forwarded to me. I venture to say in advance, that I will cover with infamy the fabricators of this calumny: they are Assassins, and deserve no pity. I have got hold of this through the leakiness of a fellow of the name of Hunt, whom I mentioned in my last. I am dear Sir with the truest Attachment & respect Your Most Obedt. & very hum. servt.

J Armstrong

RC (DLC). Cover marked by Armstrong, "By M. Ronaldson," and, in another hand, "Recd at Bordeaux May 14—brought by the George Dyer that sailed from Bordeaux June 6." Postmarked New York, 9 Aug. Docketed by JM, "Recd. Aug. 15. 1810."

1. James Bowdoin, U.S. minister to Spain, 1804–8, and Armstrong had served as commissioners at Paris in abortive negotiations with the Spanish government concerning spoliations and the acquisition of Florida. Bowdoin quarreled with Armstrong and in May 1806 told Jefferson that Armstrong was involved in a scheme for the purchase of three million acres of Florida land. Bowdoin sent Jefferson a deposition by Charles M. Somers, an Irishman working in Paris as a translator, which implicated Armstrong in the scheme with the American speculators Daniel Parker and Michael O'Mealy. Jefferson ignored Bowdoin's charges against Armstrong and never told JM of them. JM later assured Armstrong that nothing in Bowdoin's letter to Jefferson implicated the American minister "in any land speculation whatever" and that neither JM nor Jefferson had withdrawn "a particle from the perfect confidence felt by both in your honor & integrity" (Skeen, *John Armstrong*, pp. 80–81, 83–84; JM to Armstrong, 29 Oct. 1810; see also Egan, "The United States, France, and West Florida, 1803–1807," *Fla. Historical Quarterly*, 47 [1968–69]: 247 n. 67).

2. Fulwar Skipwith (1765–1839) had served in France in various capacities—as James Monroe's personal secretary in 1794–95 and thereafter as commercial agent for the U.S. and consul general in Paris. In April 1806 he commenced a bitter dispute with John Armstrong over his compensation for the services that he and Isaac Cox Barnet, American consul at Le Havre, had rendered to Americans who had spoliation claims against the French government. Skipwith returned to the U.S. in September 1808, settling first in Virginia and then in West Florida, where he was elected governor after settlers in the province had declared its independence from Spain on 26 Sept. 1810. After Skipwith's departure from France, Armstrong had pressed Barnet to hand over two volumes of consular registers on the grounds that they were essential for official business, but as the minister admitted to JM, he also wished to examine them for documents that were critical of his own conduct in Paris (Skeen, *John Armstrong*, pp. 63–72; Henry Bartholomew Cox, *The Parisian American: Fulwar Skipwith of Virginia* [Washington, 1964], pp. 95–114).

From George Logan

MY DEAR FRIEND   LONDON May 6th: 1810

Since my arrival in London I have had an opportunity of conversing with several members of this Government, and with private Citizens of distinction; and am happy to inform you, that a general anxiety prevails to preserve peace with the UStates. Mr: Pinkney our Minister is much esteemed, and considered here as fully competent to negotiate a treaty, should he receive liberal, & full powers for that purpose.

You will find by the public papers, as well as from the information of Mr Short, that the foreign, as well as domestic affairs of Great Britain are in a deplorable situation. The patriotic cause in Spain is considered desperate: in some measure to be attributed to the policy of this Government uniting with the Junta to support the form and abuses of the Spanish monarchy. In this situation of Spain, would it not be prudent for the UStates to wait the probable event of Spanish America forming an independent Government, and receive a minister from that quarter, rather than from Ferdenand: who I believe will never be restored to the Crown: even should the Patriots be successful in driving the French out of their Country.

With respect to France, and our affairs with that Kingdom, my friend Mr Short who has politely taken charge of this Letter, will give you the most accurate information, having lately been in Paris.[1]

I expect to return to America in Sepr next. Accept assurances of my great respect and friendship—

GEO LOGAN

RC (DLC).

1. Short later gave this letter to George W. Erving to forward to JM (Short to JM, 19 June 1810; Erving to JM, 5 Aug. 1810).

To Henry Dearborn

[. . .][1]   May 7. 1810

I have recd. your favor of the 30th. Ult: accompanied by the Discourse of one of your D. D's.[2] This is the most signal instance I have seen, of a prostitution of the sacred functions. If such be the religion, morality, & citizenship of the federal clergy & colleges, it is not to be wondered that the pious & patriotic people of N. England are forsaking such guides, and rallying to the Republican Standard. We remain without authentic information either from London or Paris. The return of the Public Vessel daily looked for will probably relieve us from the suspense; altho it is possible that as in the case of preceding expectations, we may find a continuance only of disappointments. Mrs. M. offers her affectionate respects to Mrs. Dearborn. Be pleased to tender mine also, & to be assured yourself of my great esteem & friendly regards

RC (MHi). Docketed by Dearborn. Signature clipped. Headed "*No. 39.*"

1. Salutation cut away when signature was clipped from verso.
2. Doctors of divinity. JM referred to the publication that Dearborn had sent with his letter of 30 Apr. 1810.

To Thomas Jefferson

DEAR SIR   WASHINGTON May 7. 1810

The inclosed letter from Jarvis[1] accompanied one to me on the subject of the Merinos. I learn that they have arrived safe; but the vessel is aground a few miles below Alexanda. Jos: Doherty[2] is gone to bring them up, making the selections warranted by Mr. Jarvis. As the means I shall employ to have my pair conveyed to Virga. will suffice for yours, it will be unnecessary for you to attend to the matter till you hear of their arrival in Orange. Altho' there have been several late arrivals from England We remain in the dark as to what has passed between Wellesly & P.[3] The same as to the F. Govt. & A.[4] You will notice the footing on which Congress has left our relations with these powers. Unless G. B. should apprehend an attempt from F. to revive our non-intercourse agst. her, she has every earthly motive to continue her restrictions agst. us. She has our trade in spite of F. as far as she can make it suit her interest, and our acquiescence in cutting it off from the rest of the world, as far as she may wish to distress her adversaries, to cramp our growth as rivals, or to prevent our interference with her smuggling Monopoly. N. England & N. Y. are rallying to the Repubn. ranks. In N. Y. every branch of the Govt. is again sound.[5] The Election in Massts. now going on, will probably have a like issue with their late one. There is some danger however, from the federal artifice, of pushing the fedl. Towns to their maximum of Reps. Boston is to send 40. Yrs. always most affectly.

JAMES MADISON

RC (DLC). Docketed by Jefferson, "recd. May 9."

1. Jarvis to Jefferson, 19 Feb. 1810 (printed in Betts, *Jefferson's Farm Book*, pp. 125–26).
2. Joseph Dougherty, a Washington resident and formerly Jefferson's coachman, acted as JM's agent for the delivery of the merino sheep sent by William Jarvis from Portugal.

3. William Pinkney.

4. John Armstrong.

5. The *National Intelligencer* reported on 7 and 9 May a "decisive victory of the republican interest" in New York on the basis of Daniel D. Tompkins's reelection as governor and a Republican majority in the assembly.

Account with Joseph Dougherty

[ca. 7 May 1810]

Four Spanish Merino Sheep to Jos. Dougherty Dr.

May 7th. —10   D. cts

To freight from Lisbon to Alexa. va.	24—00
To 5 per. cent. primage	1—20
To freight from below Alexa. to Washington	2—50
To customhouse permits	0—40
To one Dollar for each sheep, claimed by the person that had the care of them on the passage	4—00
To tavern expences two and half Days in Alexa.	4—25

Dolls.   36. .35

Received the above from Mr. Madison

JOS. DOUGHERTY

Ms (DLC: Jefferson Papers). In Dougherty's hand. Enclosed in JM to Jefferson, 22 June 1810.

From Robert S. Bickley

SIR   UNION HOTEL, GEO: TOWN 8th May 1810

It has been represented to me by my friend Doctr. Seybert[1] & other Gentn. Members of Congress, that it was understood the Hotel could be purchased for about ten thousand Dollars, in consequence of which the sum appropriated was only twenty thousand Drs.[2]

The bill Authorises the President to buy or build an house for public Offices, I believe it cannot be denied that it was the general wish of the friends of the bill that the President should purchase the Hotel and Altho' it cost me in the present state thirty six thousand Dollars independent of the lots attached to it, I am disposed to meet the general Wish of the Gentn. & the inhabitants of the City of Washington, and will therefore

Accept the Sum of ten thousand Dollars for the building & the lots attached to it. A clear and indisputable title will be given.

If this sum meets your approbation I pray you to inform me as I am detained in the City only on this Accot. I am with great respect—Yr obedt Servt.

ROBT. S. BICKLEY[3]

RC (DLC).

1. Adam Seybert of Philadelphia had been elected to replace Benjamin Say in the Eleventh Congress and took his seat in the House of Representatives in November 1809. He subsequently served as a Republican representative from Pennsylvania in the Twelfth, Thirteenth, and Fifteenth Congresses.

2. Congress had passed a law, signed by JM on 28 Apr. 1810, authorizing the president to "erect, or procure by purchase" a building suitable for the accommodation of the Post Office and Patent Office (*Annals of Congress*, 11th Cong., 2d sess., 1771–72; *U.S. Statutes at Large*, 2:589–90).

3. Robert S. Bickley of Philadelphia had acquired title to property and an uncompleted building known as Blodget's Hotel in the District of Columbia by holding the winning ticket in Federal Lottery No. 2 in the 1790s. Lengthy legal proceedings between 1798 and 1813 were necessary to confirm Bickley's title to the property he was now trying to sell (Bryan, *History of the National Capital*, 1:228–30).

From Stephen Sayre

SIR.   BORDENTON 12th May. 1810.

Mr Newbold,[1] one of the Deputies of this State has lately called on me. He says he had the honor of waiting on you, expressly to remind you, that tho' hitherto unnoticed, you aught, in justice, to all the principles of good policy, & rules of common equity, place me in some situation of independence.

I have done every thing in my power to discharge the debts I had contracted, under the full belief, that they would have been honorably paid by the government, to whose interest I sacrifised my own; but the sum is too far above the means of an individual—the whole I obtained from Congress was not equal to one demand, made on me since the act, improperly intitled, *for Relief*[2]—I have paid the exact proportion of that demand but am liable to pay the whole.

If you do not, very shortly, enable me to discharge the rest I must submit to be disgraced under the State act of Insolvency—my own honor, & justice, to my creditors, will compel me to show, that I fall under the weight of expenditure for the nation. When Mr Jefferson came first into office he promised one of my friends who stated my case to him—to provide for me—he has not done it—my just claims will reach you as his successor—the delay of justice is a denial of it. You were pleased to encourage Mr N. in the hope, that you will remember me. Let me have the satisfaction of a short note, to support the hopes of independence. Can you reconcile it to the common feelings of humanity, or the principles of good policy, to suffer a man to fall into disgrace, who has thro' a long life of integrity, & high standing, with the greatest Characters in England, & the principal powers of Europe, while you are the chief in the Government, who in honor, & justice, aught to protect him. Living in retirement, I hear of nothing in your gift till other applicants are at your door. Please to remember an old & faithful Servant—he will not disgrace the government or yourself. I am respectfully—

STEPHEN SAYRE

RC (DLC). Docketed by JM.

1. Thomas Newbold, a Republican congressman from New Jersey, 1807–13, first tried to aid Sayre early in 1809, when JM apparently asked what Sayre expected of him. Sayre used that opening to insist that he was qualified to be a paymaster, quartermaster, or dock inspector. "I want nothing, if I can't render essential service" (Sayre to JM, 20 Jan. 1809 [DLC]).

2. In 1807 Congress had passed a relief act for Sayre, awarding him £333 plus thirty years' interest for diplomatic services performed in 1777 (*U.S. Statutes at Large*, 6:65; see also Sayre to JM, 16 May 1801, *PJM-SS*, 1:186–87 and nn.).

From Thomas Jefferson

DEAR SIR   MONTICELLO May 13. 10

I thank you for your promised attention to my portion of the Merinos, and if there be any expences of transportation Etc & you will be so good as to advance my portion of them with yours & notify the amount it shall be promptly remitted. What shall we do with them? I have been so disgusted with the scandalous extortions lately practised in the sale of these animals, & with the ascription of patriotism & praise to the sellers, as if the thousands of Dollars apiece they have not been ashamed to recieve were not reward enough, that I am disposed to consider, as right, whatever is the reverse of what they have done. Since fortune has put the occasion upon us, is it not incumbent on us so to dispense this benefit to the farmers of our country, as to put to shame those who, forgetting their own wealth & the honest simplicity of the farmers, have thought them fit objects of the shaving art, and to excite, by a better example, the condemnation due to theirs? No sentiment is more acknoleged in the family of

Agricolists, than that the few who can afford it should incur the risk & expence of all new improvements, & give the benefit freely to the many of more restricted circumstances. The question then recurs, What are we to do with them? I shall be willing to concur with you in any plan you shall approve, and in order that we may have some proposition to begin upon, I will throw out a first idea, to be modified, or postponed to whatever you shall think better.

Give all the full blooded males we can raise to the different counties of our state, one to each, as fast as we can furnish them. And as there must be some rule of priority, for the distribution, let us begin with our own counties, which are contiguous & nearly central to the state, & proceed, circle after circle, till we have given a ram to every county. This will take about 7. years, if we add to the full descendants those which will have past to the 4th. generation from common ewes. To make the benefit of a single male as general as practicable to the county, we may ask some known character in each county to have a small society formed which shall recieve the animal & prescribe rules for his care & government. We should retain ourselves all the fullblooded ewes, that they may enable us the sooner to furnish a male to every county. When all shall have been provided with rams, we may, in a year or two more, be in a condition to give an ewe also to every county, if it be thought necessary. But I suppose it will not, as four generations from their full blooded ram will give them the pure race from common ewes.

In the mean time we shall not be without a profit indemnifying our trouble & expence. For if, of our present stock of common ewes, we place with the ram as many as he may be competent to, suppose 50. we may sell the male lambs of every year for such reasonable price as, in addition to the wool, will pay for the maintenance of the flock. The 1st. year they will be ½ bloods, the 2d. ¾ the 3d. ⅞ & the 4th. fullblooded, if we take care, in selling annually half the ewes also, to keep those of highest blood. This will be a fund for kindnesses to our friends, as well as for indemnification to ourselves; & our whole state may thus, from this small stock, so dispensed, be filled in a very few years, with this valuable race, & more satisfaction result to ourselves than money ever administered to the bosom of a shaver. There will be danger that what is here proposed, tho' but an act of ordinary duty, may be perverted into one of ostentation. But malice will always find bad motives for good actions. Shall we therefore never do good? It may also be used to commit us with those on whose example it will truly be a reproof. We may guard against this perhaps by a proper reserve, developing our purpose only by it's execution. 'Vive, vale, et si quid novisti rectius istis Candidus imperti. Si non, his utere mecum.[']¹

TH: JEFFERSON

RC and enclosure (DLC); FC (DLC: Jefferson Papers). Jefferson enclosed a paper (1 p.) with two tables. The first calculated over a seven-year cycle that "from 2. full blooded ewes & their female descendants will proceed annually the following numbers [totaling 34] either of rams or ewes separately, or double the number in the aggregate." The second table estimated that over a seven-year period "from 100. common ewes & their female descendants will proceed annually the following number [601] of either rams or ewes separ[a]tely, or the double in the aggregate of ½ breeds, ¾, ⅞ and full."

1. "Live long, farewell. If you know something better than these precepts, pass it on, my good fellow. If not, join me in following these," Horace, *Epistles*, 1.6.67–68 (*Horace: Satires, Epistles, and Ars Poetica*, Loeb Classical Library [1970 reprint], p. 291).

From David Parish

Sir   Philada. the 13th May 1810.

Agreably to the Conversation I had the honor of holding with You some months ago, I beg leave to inform You that I shall embark for Europe in Eight or ten days, & be glad to take Charge of the Deeds you wish to transmit to General LaFayette with whom I propose spending Some days at La Grange in July or August.[1]

It will give me real pleasure to execute any Commands you may have for England Holland & France.

I beg you will accept my best thanks for the Attention & Civility I have experienced from you during my Stay in America, & beleive me to remain with the highest Regard Sir, Your most obedt. & very hble Servt.

DAVID PARISH[2]

RC (DLC).

1. Parish carried JM's 18 and 19 May 1810 letters to Lafayette.
2. David Parish (d. 1826), the son of a former American consul in Hamburg, John Parish, became involved in banking and land speculation on a large scale while affiliated with the Dutch firm of Hope and Company. He served the firm in Philadelphia, 1806–10, and helped negotiate a loan for Lafayette with Baring Brothers, the London bankers. He promoted the sale of Lafayette's Louisiana claims to the Barings and to his father in Amsterdam. Parish returned to America in 1811 and arranged a critical war loan to the U.S. in 1813 (Lutz, "Lafayette's Louisiana Estate," *La. Studies*, 6 [1967]: 358; Chinard, *Letters of Lafayette and Jefferson*, pp. 242, 319; Philip G. Walters and Raymond Walters, Jr., "The American Career of David Parish," *Journal of Economic History*, 4 [1944]: 150–54, 157, 160–61).

From John Mason

SIR   INDIAN TRADE OFFICE 14th. May 1810

I had the honour to intimate to you in conversation the other day that remonstrances had been made by some of the agents for Indian Trade in the Upper Mississippi against the facility with which british Traders obtained licences to trade in that quarter.

On that subject, it has occurred to me to be my duty to communicate to you Sir a letter lately received from the agent at Fort Madison. Mr. Johnson[1] the writer—tho' not of much acquirement is a man of good sense and as I beleive of strict truth. With high Respect & &

J M sup

Letterbook copy (DNA: RG 75, Letters Sent by Superintendent of Indian Trade).

1. The letter from John W. Johnson—factor for Indian trade at Fort Madison, located fifteen miles above the juncture of the Mississippi and Des Moines rivers in the Louisiana Territory—has not been found.

From John K. Smith

SIR,   NEW ORLEANS 15th. may 1810.

I have had the honor to receive your letter of the 12th. ulto. Mr. Duplantier being absent at Batton Rouge & not being expected to return for some time I applied to Mr. Derbigney his friend agent & attorney upon the Subject of your letter. His memo. in writing I enclose & also a plat & some observations explanatory which I obtained from B. Lafon a Surveyor of this place who is a man of talents & may I believe (where his own interest is not concerned) be depended upon.[1]

None of the claims upon these Vacant lands adjacent to the City have yet been decided upon by the Board of Comrs. nor will they possibly for some time. Should a decision be pressed I shall be informed of it & will apprize the agent on the part of the US who will with myself attend to scrutinize the claims.

From all the information I can get it appears that there is not 500 acres even including the lands upon which claims are presented & as the last act of Congress requires that it Should be located not less than 500 acres it results that it will be requisite & for the Interest of Genl. Lafayette that Congress should grant to him all the Vacant lands adjoining N. Orleans not including the 600 yards from fortifications granted to the Corporation nor any in front of the City upon the Levee.

I shall communicate with Mr. Duplantier upon his return & in the mean time I shall take every step in my power to possess myself of information on the Subject. I have the honor to be with the greatest resp[ect] yr mo. Ob St.

J. K SMITH

[Enclosure]

Copy

Mr. Derbigney's memo. (in pencil)

⟨"⟩Mr. Duplantier gave up all idea of locating any land for Genl. Lafayette behind the 600 yards granted to the Corporation

1st. because the line of a claim filed by Mr. Jno B. Macarty & to all appearance perfectly good runs from the Mississipi & strikes the Canal Carondelet within a very short distance of the said 600 yards so as to leave no room for 500 acres.

2dy. because should there be room ⟨to locate 500 acres in⟩ that part they ⟨are⟩ not worth locating being nothing but swamps."[2]

RC and enclosures, two copies (DNA: RG 49, Special Acts; and DLC). Second enclosure 3 pp.; docketed by Smith, "Memo. / B. Lafon—lands adjacent to N Orleans / Genl. Lafayettes claim" (see n. 1). A folder of plats is filed with the records of Lafayette's Louisiana land claims (DNA: RG 49, Special Acts), but the editors were unable to identify the plat enclosed by Smith. RC (DLC) marked "Copy"; docketed by JM. Smith apparently sent the copy of the RC and enclosures in his 14 July 1810 letter to JM to replace originals he feared had been lost.

1. Smith enclosed a copy of a 12 May 1810 memorandum, apparently by Bartholomew Lafon. The writer stated that he had delivered to Lafayette plats for lands surveyed in 1805 "in the back part of the city of New-Orleans, and measuring in the whole 959. Superficial arpents," but since he could not "find 1000. arpents in one tract, my operation had no effect." Congress then amended its grant to "not less than 500. acres," and he was asked to make a new survey. He located "two lots of 500. arpents each" and presented the claims to the land office on 8 Apr. 1806. For reasons not clear to him, Lafayette's agents gave up this grant. Subsequently, other vacant land was surveyed, amounting to 447 arpents but including a tract claimed by the city. The tract claimed by the city "could be Sold for more than $500,000." Part of the remainder needed draining, but once "dried up—it has a value of from $25000 to 30.000. . . . The corporation of New Orleans is already very rich, and the Congress should be very wrong to encrease their property as it would be increasing their influence already to[o] powerful against individuals."

2. Words torn or obscured on damaged enclosure have been supplied from the copy (DLC).

To Lafayette

MY DEAR SIR   WASHINGTON May 18. 1810

Mr. Parish having given me notice of his intention to embark in a few days for Europe, with an expectation of seeing you in July or August, I could not wish for a more favorable conveyance for the Patents herewith inclosed. They cover about ⅔ of the land allotted to you by the Act of Congress. The residue of the locations is not yet compleated, but Mr. Duplantier continues to be occupied with the task. He intimates that the present cash price of the actual locations is about $50,000. with every prospect of an approaching rise in value. I am very sorry to learn from him that a difficulty has arisen with respect to the important location contemplated in the vicinity of the Town of N. Orleans. Untill I receive the further information for which I have written, I can form no opinion on the subject. You may be assured that what so nearly concerns your interest, & your expectations will engage all the attention which can flow from the great esteem & sincere affection, of which I beg you to accept My assurances.

JAMES MADISON

RC (NIC: Dean Collection). Enclosed eight land patents (see JM to Lafayette, 19 May 1810; David Parish to JM, 21 May 1810).

From Robert S. Bickley

SIR   UNION HOTEL, GEORGE TOWN 18th May 1810

The communication made to you yesterday by Mr. Granger appears to me very extraordinary, After the explinations that took place between that Gentn & Myself. As to the title, permit me to remark that the only possible difficulty arose in Mr. Blodget's not recording the Deed for two lots he purchased from Mr. Burns in the usual time required by the law of the State, but this difficulty is now done away by the return of Mr. Van Ness[1] & his Lady who are willing to make a conveyance at any moment they may be required, in my Note to you Sir on the 8th. inst: I stated that I would take for the Hotel & Lots attached to it, the Sum of ten thousand Dolls. it could not be supposed that I ment to convey any property but that in which the title was completely vested in me, Mr. Granger now makes a difficulty respecting a lot No 14 which does not belong to me or ever did & this I stated to him expressly, Altho' the lots attached to the building in the Decree of the Court are more than ever can be wanted by the United States I was induced to include them in my offer in order to

Close a most unfortunate & ruinous concern, that originally originated with the Commissioners appointed by the Government. It is not possible there ever can be a more complete title & this Mr. Granger is very sensible of, but why he should make these difficulties I am at a loss to Know, unless it is done with a view to prevent a purchase which I am bold to say is the best ever Offered to the United States.

I have at the solicitation of several Members of Congress made this Offer & have attended here eight or ten days for an Answer, after going thro' an examination of all the papers relative to the title & satisfied Mr. Granger, I am now told that unless lot No 14 is purchased by me & given to the United States, that the purchase cannot be made, this is the most extraordinary proceeding I ever heard. It rests with you Sir to determine, which I pray you to do as soon as possible, as I am only waiting your answer.[2] With the Highest respect for Yourself I am Yr obedt Servt.

ROBT. S. BICKLEY

RC (DLC).

1. John Peter Van Ness (1770–1846) was born in New York, studied law at Columbia, and then served as a Republican representative from New York in Congress, 1801–3. In 1802 he married Marcia Burnes, the daughter of a substantial local property holder, David Burnes (d. 1799) of Georgetown, and settled permanently in Washington. He rose to the rank of major general of the District of Columbia militia in 1813, held many business and civic positions, and served as mayor of Washington, 1830–34 (Allen C. Clark, "General John Peter Van Ness, a Mayor of the City of Washington, His Wife, Marcia, and Her Father, David Burnes," *Records of the Columbia Historical Society*, 22 [1919]: 125–204).

2. On 25 May the *National Intelligencer* reported that JM had ordered the purchase of "the unfinished building known by the name of Blodget's Hotel."

§ From James Ogilvie. *18 May 1810, Augusta.* Thanks JM for his "friendly letter [not found] . . . in reply to one which I took the liberty to address to you from Portland."[1] Plans to spend several months in Kentucky, in "seclusion & solitary study," to work on a series of orations: "'The Progress & Prospects of society in the U.S.'—'The Licentiousness of the Press & the most eligible & probably efficient corrective of this fundamental evil'—And 'The nature, effects and tendencies of moral Fiction.'" Asks JM to suggest further topics "to be illustrated from the Rostrum." Encloses for JM's perusal "a little hasty publication," mentioning that he reveres the memory of Charles Brown and knows his biographer Allen.[2] Also encloses a "little effusion" [not found] which he hopes Dolley Madison will read.

RC (DLC). 4 pp. Docketed by JM. For surviving enclosure, see n. 2.

1. Ogilvie to JM, 20 June 1809 (DLC). James Ogilvie (1760–1820) emigrated from Scotland in 1779 and taught school in Virginia. He visited JM in 1799. He wrote several pamphlets and traveled widely as an orator (Walter Jones to JM, 27 July 1799, *PJM*, 17:255–56 and n. 1).

2. Ogilvie evidently enclosed a one-page printed circular letter by "A Stranger" inviting subscriptions to support the publication of the "memoirs of the life of *C. B. BROWN* deceased to which will be annexed copious selections from his writings" (DLC: Madison Collection, Rare Book Division). This circular was probably an early notice for the projected biography of Charles Brockden Brown by Paul Allen, an assistant editor for Joseph Dennie's Philadelphia *Port Folio*. Allen failed to complete the biography, and he relinquished his contract in 1814 to William Dunlap, who published *The Life of Charles Brockden Brown* in Philadelphia in 1815. A volume of Allen's uncompleted biography was published under the title of *The Late Charles Brockden Brown* in 1976 (see Robert E. Hemenway and Joseph Katz, eds., *The Late Charles Brockden Brown* [Columbia, S.C., 1976], pp. vii–xxix).

§ From William Tatham. *18 May 1810, Norfolk.* Gratefully acknowledges receipt of JM's friendly reply[1] to his 10 Mar. letter. He is recuperating from a long illness. Since last seeing JM in Washington, has never heard from Gallatin concerning his ideas on "the Coastwise improvement of the revenue powers." About 10 Mar. he also wrote to the secretary of the navy regarding "Maritime improvements . . . far superior to the Torpedo."[2] Trusts JM will protect his interests. Meanwhile, he has "nearly matured my surveys of perhaps eighty miles of the most material . . . parts of our Country" for the War Department archives.

RC (DLC). 3 pp. Printed in McPherson, "Letters of William Tatham," *WMQ*, 2d ser., 16 (1936): 388–89.

1. Letter not found. Possibly JM had expressed some interest in acquiring Tatham's collection of topographical materials (Herndon, *William Tatham*, p. 242).

2. See Tatham to Paul Hamilton, 10 Mar. 1810 (DNA: RG 45, Misc. Letters Received).

§ From William Tatham. *18 May 1810, Norfolk.* The same mail that brought JM's letter [not found] also carried one from London, telling of the death of Miss Tatham, the writer's cousin, at Hornby Castle, the seat of John Marsden. "As sole heir on my Mothers side," he may inherit an annual income of £5,000 and from Miss Tatham "the Peerages of Morville, L'Engleys, and Barony of Askham," to which the duke of Norfolk assured him he is entitled.[1] His American citizenship will "work no injury to my rights." If he takes a seat in the House of Lords, the U.S. would gain "a fixed, & long proved, friend, in the British Counsels." Intends to write Lord Erskine and "to our *best national friend* the old Duke of Norfolk."

RC (DLC). 3 pp. Marked "(*Private letter*)." Printed in McPherson, "Letters of William Tatham," *WMQ*, 2d ser., 16 (1936): 389–90.

1. Tatham was related to a titled family on his mother's side, but no evidence has been found that he was entitled to the peerages he mentioned (Herndon, *William Tatham*, pp. 4, 242).

To Lafayette

MY DEAR SIR   May 19. 1810

Since the packet, inclosing 8 Patents was sent to the Mail, I have obtained a ninth, which I forward without delay that [it][1] may overtake the others Yrs. &c &c

JAMES MADISON

RC (NIC: Dean Collection).

1. Word supplied here was either clipped from margin or omitted by JM.

§ From Benjamin Smith Barton. *20 May 1810, Philadelphia.* Has initiated at his personal expense a scientific expedition into the Northwest Territory "and the adjacent British settlements." Thomas Nuttall leads the party, which is already, "I presume, at Detroit, without any passport." An unanticipated difficulty arose owing to Nuttall's British citizenship. Secretary of State Robert Smith has been uncooperative, in contrast to David Erskine, who gave "a full and generous protection" to a French scientist in 1807. Regrets necessity of troubling JM, but the matter has become urgent. "I have lost every chance of getting a protection from the British minister; and it will require every exertion on my part to forward, in time to be useful, that from the A. government, *even if obtained.*"[1]

RC, appendix, and enclosure (DLC). RC 4 pp. The appended letter, Barton to JM, 21 May 1810 (1 p.), states that the enclosure was received after first letter was written and that, based on JM's knowledge of him, Barton still hopes to receive "some kind of letter of facility"; in any case, he will reapply to the British minister for a passport. Enclosure, Richard Forrest to Barton, 17 May 1810 (1 p.), cites State Department regulation "not to grant a Passport to any other, than an American Citizen."

1. No official response to this request has been located, but according to later testimony by Barton, he was able to obtain "a special passport from the president of the United States" (Jeanette E. Graustein, *Thomas Nuttall, Naturalist: Explorations in America, 1808–1841* [Cambridge, Mass., 1967], pp. 39, 410).

§ From David Gelston. *21 May 1810, New York.* Has received a letter from John Martin Baker at Cagliari by the ship *Charles and Harriet.* Baker has sent for JM "a cheese, a box citron, some olives &ca.," which Gelston will ship at the first opportunity.

RC (DLC). 1 p.

§ From David Parish. *21 May 1810, Philadelphia.* Has received from JM the two packets for transmittal to "our mutual worthy friend General LaFayette containing Nine Land patents." Hopes "to have the pleasure of delivering them into his own hands at La Grange in August."

RC (DLC). 1 p.

To William Pinkney

Dear Sir   Washington May 23d 1810

You will learn from the Department of State, as you must have anticipated, our surprise that the answer of Lord Wellesley, to your very just and able view of the case of Jackson,[1] corresponded so little with the impressions of that Minister manifested in your first interviews with him. The date of the answer best explains the change; as it shows that time was taken for obtaining intelligence from this country, and adapting the policy of the answer to the position taken by the advocates of Jackson. And it must have happened that the intelligence prevailing at that date was of the sort most likely to mislead. The elections which have since taken place in the Eastern States, and which have been materially influenced by the affair of Jackson and the spirit of party connected with it, are the strongest of proofs, that the measure of the Executive coincided with the feelings of the Nation. In every point of view the answer is unworthy of the source from which it comes.

From the manner in which the vacancy left by Jackson is provided for,[2] it is infered that a sacrifice is meant of the respect belonging to this Government, either to the pride of the British Government, or to the feelings of those who have taken side with it against their own. On either supposition, it is necessary to counteract the ignoble purpose. You will accordingly find that on ascertaining the substitution of a Chargé, to be an intentional degradation of the diplomatic intercourse on the part of Great Britain, it is deemed proper that no higher functionary should represent the United States at London. I sincerely wish, on every account, that the views of the British Govt. in this instance, may not be such as are denoted by appearances, or that, on finding the tendency of them they may be changed. However the fact may turn out, you will of course not lose sight of the expediency of mingling in every step you take, as much of moderation, and even of conciliation, as can be justifiable; and will, in particular, if the present dispatches should find you in actual negociation, be governed by the result of it, in determining the question of your devolving your trust on a Secretary of Legation.

The Act of Congress transmitted from the Department of State, will inform you of the footing on which our relations to the Belligerent powers were finally placed.[3] The experiment now to be made, of a commerce with both, unrestricted by our laws, has resulted from causes which you will collect from the debates, and from your own reflections. The new form of appeal to the policy of Great Britain and France on the subject of the Decrees and Orders, will most engage your attention. However feeble it may appear, it is possible that one or other of those powers may allow it more effect than was produced by the overtures heretofore tried. As far as pride may have influenced the reception of these, it will be the less in the way, as the law in its present form may be regarded by each of the parties, if it so pleases, not as a coercion or a threat to itself, but as a promise of attack on the other. G. Britain indeed may conceive that she has now a compleat interest in perpetuating the actual state of things, which gives her the full enjoyment of our trade and enables her to cut it off with every part of the World; at the same time that it increases the chance of such resentments in France at the inequality, as may lead to hostilities with the United States. But on the other hand, this very inequality, which France would confirm by a state of hostilities with the U. States, may become a motive with her to turn the tables on G. Britain by compelling her either to revoke her orders, or to lose the commerce of this Country. An apprehension that France may take this politic course would be a rational motive with the B. Govt. to get the start of her. Nor is this the only apprehension that merits attention. Among the inducements to the experiment of an unrestricted commerce now made, were two which contributed essentially to the majority of votes in its favor; first a general hope, favored by daily accounts from England, that an adjustment of differences there, and thence in France, would render the measure safe & proper;[4] second, a willingness in not a few, to teach the advocates for an open trade, under actual circumstances, the folly, as well as degradation of their policy. At the next meeting of Congress, it will be found, according to present appearances, that instead of an adjustment with either of the Belligerents, there is an increased obstinacy in both; and that the inconveniences of the Embargo, and non-intercourse, have been exchanged for the greater sacrifices as well as disgrace, resulting from a submission to the predatory systems in force. It will not be wonderful therefore, if the passive spirit which marked the late Session of Congress, should at the next meeting be roused to the opposite point; more especially as the tone of the Nation has never been as low as that of its Representatives, and as it is rising already under the losses sustained by our Commerce in the Contenental ports, and by the fall of prices in our produce at home, under a limitation of the market, to Great Britain. Cotton I perceive is down at 10 or 11 cents in Georgia. The great mass of Tobacco is in a similar situation. And the effect must soon be general, with the exception of a few articles which do not at present, glut the British demand. Whether considerations like these will make any favorable impression on the British Cabinet, you will be the first to know. Whatever confidence I may have in the justness of them, I must forget all that has past before I can indulge very favorable expectations. Every new occasion seems to countenance the belief, that there lurks in the British Cabinet, a hostile feeling towards this Country, which will never be eradicated during the present Reign; nor overruled, whilst it exists, but by some dreadful pressure from external or internal causes.

With respect to the French Govt. we are taught by experience to be equally distrustful. It will have however the same opportunity presented to it, with the British Govt., of comparing the actual state of things, with that which would be produced by a repeal of its Decrees; and it is not easy to find any plausible motive to continue the former as preferable to the latter. A worse state of things, than the actual one, could not exist for France, unless her preference be for a state of War. If she be sincere either in her late propositions relative to a chronological revocation of illegal Edicts against Neutrals, or to a pledge from the United States not to submit to those of Great Britain, she aught at once to embrace the arrangment held out by Congress; the renewal of a non-intercourse with Great Britain being the very species of resistance most analogous to her professed views.

I propose to commit this to the care of Mr. Parish who is about embarking at Philadelphia for England; and finding that I have missed a day in my computation of the opportunity, I must abruptly conclude with assurances of my great esteem and friendly respects

FC (DLC: Rives Collection, Madison Papers). In the hand of Edward Coles. Marked "(duplicate)," docketed, and corrected by JM. Signature clipped.

1. Pinkney to Lord Wellesley, 2 Jan. 1810 (*ASP, Foreign Relations*, 3:352–55).
2. In his 14 Mar. 1810 letter to Pinkney, Lord Wellesley announced that British diplomacy in Washington henceforth would be conducted by "a person properly qualified to carry on the ordinary intercourse between the two Governments," i.e., a chargé d'affaires rather than a diplomat of ministerial rank. In a 22 May 1810 letter to Pinkney probably drafted by JM, Secretary of State Robert Smith declared that if a chargé should represent Great Britain for an extended period of time, Pinkney could reciprocate by withdrawing from London and leaving a chargé in his place, provided he was not at the time engaged in negotiations authorized by his instructions of 20 Jan. 1810 (ibid., 3:355–56, 358–59).
3. Macon's Bill No. 2.
4. See William A. Burwell to JM, 16 Apr. 1810, and n. 2.

From Paul Hamilton

SIR,   NAVY DEPARTMENT 23rd May 1810

In the Navy Estimate for the year 1810, it was stated to Congress, that for keeping in a state of repair the frigates & other Vessels now in commission, the sum of 150,000 Dollars would be required; & that for repairing the frigates & other vessels & gunboats in ordinary, there would be required the further sum of 450,000. Congress appropriated 150,000 only; & the Department having in this, as in every preceding case, presumed that the amount stated in the annual Estimate, would be appropriated, & favorable opportunities of making purchases occurring, commenced preparations for placing the frigates in ordinary in a state of perfect repair—& proceeded so far in such preparatory arrangements & purchases of valuable and necessary materials that the balance left of the 150,000, after applying a considerable amount to the discharge of debts incurred during the year 1809, has been exhausted; & debts to the amount stated in the accompanying paper A, have been incurred under the head of "Repairs." These preparations were made & these debts incurred in the full faith (which was strengthened by the passage of a navy Bill on the part of the Senate, & which I had strong assurances would pass the House of Representatives) that Congress would appropriate the 450,000$ called for in the Estimate.

As early as the probability, that the 450,000 would not be appropriated, could be ascertained or foreseen by me, I addressed to the navy agents circular instructions, copy of which is herewith transmitted, requiring them to incur no further expence whatever on account of repairs; and since the rising of Congress, I have been endeavouring to retrench the expences as far as possible. These retrenchments will, it is confidently hoped, so far reduce the expences, that after paying off the debts incurred we shall not require a sum exceeding 74000$ to defray every expence under the head of Repairs during the present year.

Thus circumstanced I have to submit to you, Sir, the propriety of a transfer of funds in aid of the fund for Repairs. The appropriation for Provisions can spare 150,000$, which sum it appears to me the public service requires; but the sum of 100,000 dollars will answer all our present purposes.

I enclose the form of a transfer which, in the event of your determining to make it, will require your signature. I have the honor to be with great respect sir yr ob st

PAUL HAMILTON

[Enclosure A]

A.

Statement of Debts due under the Head of "Repairs of Vessels."

For bills drawn by the agent at New orleans	12 000
For bills drawn by the agent of Kentucky cordage & other articles	12 000
Requisition of agent at Charleston S. C. expence of fitting out 3 gun boats	5 100
Requisition of agent at Norfolk Virga.	6 000
Requisition of agent at Boston	5 500
Requisition of agent at Philaa.—cable for frigate President & other articles	4 500

Repairing the Vesuvius at N orleans, commenced without my knowledge	3 000
Navy Yard Washington, due to Mechanics who have been repairing the frigate Congress	12 000
Cordage furnished by Chalmers & Parrott, say	10 000
Timber delivered by captns. Terbell & Somers repairs of Congress &c	6 000
Dollars	76 100

Unavoidable Expences.

The expence of employing the Mechanics in this Navy Yard, the number of which has been considerably reduced, is estimated at 32,000$. during the present year	32 000
The expence of mechanics at other Yards	10 000
For Contingencies which can not be foreseen	31 900
Dolls	73 900

	76 100
	73 900
Amount necessary to ⎱ be transferred ⎰	150,000 Doll's

[Enclosure B]

Circular to the Navy Agents.

Sir   Navy Department 22d. March 1810.

In the confident expectation, that Congress would authorize the Repair of our frigates, and make an adequate appropriation therefor, I have been progressing in my preparatory arrangements to accomplish that object: So far indeed have we progressed, as to straiten very much the appropriation made exclusively for the frigates and other vessels in Commission. It appears now very uncertain, whether Congress will authorize the repair of the frigates, and it becomes proper to take every precautionary measure for the relief of our funds.

I have therefore to request that you will *incur no expence whatever* under the head "of Repairs of vessels" without previous special instructions from me—and you will be pleased to apprize all our Commanders of the indispensible necessity of avoiding every such expence—and attending particularly to this direction. I am respectfully Sir yrs.

Paul Hamilton

[Enclosure C]

In pursuance of the Authority vested in the President of the United States by the Act of Congress passed on the 3d. day of March 1809, intituled "An Act further to amend the several Acts for the establishment and regulation of the Treasury War & Navy Departments" I do hereby direct that out of the balance of the appropriations for Provisions for the use of the Navy of the United States there be applied One hundred thousand Dollars to Repairs of Vessels. Given under my hand this 24th day of May in the Year of our Lord 1810.

RC and enclosures A and B (DLC); letterbook copy and copies of enclosures A and C (DNA: RG 45, LSP). RC in Goldsborough's hand, signed by Hamilton. RC and enclosed circular letter docketed by JM. Enclosure A filed at November 1809 (DLC).

From Samuel Smith

[BALTIMORE, 24 May 1810]

. . . The situation of our country is indeed very critical, but I cannot yet believe that Denmark will be coerced to receive french troops in Holstein. Sweden has the most friendly disposition towards us—indeed I would suppose American property to be perfectly safe in her Ports. . . .[1]

Printed extract (Robert C. Black Catalogue No. 104 [1965], item 133). Also mentioned as a one-page letter in the lists probably made by Peter Force (DLC, series 7, container 2).

1. Smith was evidently reacting to reports that France would attempt to close the Baltic to neutral vessels. Accounts from Sweden, as printed in London newspapers in April 1810, announced that French troops had entered Holstein as a preliminary to taking possession of all Denmark to the "Northern extremity of Jutland." The French minister in Sweden was also expected to seek the imposition of "new and severe restrictions" on Swedish commerce (*National Intelligencer*, 23 May 1810).

§ From Robert Patton.[1] *24 May 1810, Philadelphia.* Encloses at the request of Dolley Madison bills amounting to $381.30 for expenses incurred in purchasing and delivering a pair of gray horses. The horses are "not as elegant as the others," but they were "the best I could find of the colour."

RC (DLC). 1 p. Patton probably enclosed Jehiel Tuttle to Patton, 24 Apr. 1810 (DLC), which was a receipt for a pair of gray horses. In his 31 May 1810 letter to JM (DLC), Patton acknowledged receipt of a draft on the Bank of Pennsylvania for $381.30 to settle this account.

1. Robert Patton (d. 1814) served as postmaster of Philadelphia from 1789 until his death. He had negotiated the purchase of a coach for JM a year earlier (Scharf and Westcott, *History of Philadelphia*, 1:576; *ASP, Miscellaneous*, 1:296; Benjamin Henry Latrobe to JM, 24 July 1809, *PJM-PS*, 1:302 and n. 1).

To Thomas Jefferson

DEAR SIR   WASHINGTON May 25. 1810

I have duly recd. your favor of the 13th. The general idea of disposing of the supernumerary Merino Rams for the public benefit had occurred to me. The mode you propose for the purpose seems well calculated for it. But as it will be most proper as you suggest, to let our views, be developed to the public, by the execution of them, there will be time for further consideration. When the Sheep came into my hands, they were so infected with the scab, that I found it necessary, in order to quicken & ensure their cure, to apply the Mercurial ointment. I hope they are already well. One of the Ewes has just dropt. a Ewe lamb, which is also doing well. I expect my overseer every day, to conduct them to Orange. As he will have a Waggon with him, the trip I hope may be so managed as to avoid injury to his Charge.

A former Natl. Intellr. will have given you our last communications from G. B. That of this morning exhibits our prospects on the side of F.[1] The late confiscations by Bonaparte, comprize robbery, theft, & breach of trust, and exceed in turpitude any of his enormities, not wasting human blood. This scene on the continent, and the effect of English Monopoly, on the value of our produce, are breaking the charm attached to what is called free trade, foolishly by some, & wickedly by others. We are looking hourly, for the "John Adams." There is a *possibility*, that the negociations on foot at Paris, may vary our prospects there. The change, wd. be better perhaps, if the last act of Congs. were in the hands of Armstrong;[2] which puts our trade on the worst possible footing for France; but at the same time, puts it in the option of her, to revive the Non-intercourse agst. England. There is a *possibility* also that the views of the latter may be somewhat affected by the recent elections; it being pretty certain that the change in the tone of Wellesley from that first manifested to Pinkney, was in part at least, produced by the intermediate intelligence from the U. S. which flattered a fallacious reliance on the British party here.

You receive by this Mail a letter from Fayette.[3] An open one from him to Duplantier, shews equally the enormity of his debts, (800,000 frs.) and the extravagance of his expectations. I have forwarded him deeds for 9,000 Acres located near Pt. Coupé, & stated by Duplantier, as worth abt

$50,000, at an immediate Cash price; of course intrinsically worth much more. I learn with much concern, that some difficulty, not yet explained is likely to defeat altogether, the location near the City of Orleans, which was the main dependence of Fayette. Yrs. always & affecly

JAMES MADISON

RC (DLC). Docketed by Jefferson, "recd May 27."

1. On 25 May the *National Intelligencer* published French foreign minister Champagny's 14 Feb. 1810 letter to John Armstrong (reprinted in *ASP, Foreign Relations*, 3:380–81), justifying condemnation of American ships as a retaliation against the Nonintercourse Act: "American vessels have been seized, because the Americans have seized French vessels."

2. Armstrong first learned of Macon's Bill No. 2 when he read the *National Intelligencer* and hastened to show this unofficial version to Champagny, because it had arrived in Paris "at a moment of extreme vaccilation between the old system of exclusion and the new one of licenses" (Armstrong to Robert Smith, 10 July 1810 [DNA: RG 59, DD, France]).

3. JM forwarded Lafayette's 20 Feb. 1810 letter to Jefferson (DLC: Jefferson Papers; printed in Chinard, *Letters of Lafayette and Jefferson*, pp. 296–300), which Lafayette had enclosed in his 20 Mar. letter to JM (see also Jefferson's Epistolary Record [DLC: Jefferson Papers]).

From John Armstrong

Private.

DEAR SIR,   PARIS 25 May 1810.

You will find in one of the last journals two Notes from M. de Rochefoucauld, the French Ambassador in Holland; to the Prussian Minister there—Baron Knoblesdorf. The object of these is to enable Prussia to negociate a loan of 40,000,000 frs. with which she proposes to pay off the old Score due to France. In other times, this would have been considered an extraordinary State Paper. An additional guarantee to Prussia is said to be on the tapis Viz: a Matrimonial connexion between a prince of Prussia and Mademoiselle Bonaparte, the oldest daughter of Lucien Bonaparte.

The Journals will also inform you of a change of Ministers in Denmark. The Bernstorfs are displaced and M. Rosencrantz and others (beleived to have less of the Anglo-mania) are substituted for them.

There was a report some weeks past of a rising discontent between this country and Russia, founded on the new successions to the Crown in Sweden. A conspiracy to subvert this, in favor of a son of the late King, was said to have been discovered, and was pretty distinctly attributed to Russia.[1] It however matters very little, whether the cause assigned, was real, or pretended, as the report is not less ominous, on either supposition. A Minister of the Russian Cabinet, Prince Alexis Kourakan, is now here

& professedly, for the purpose of offering the felicitations of his Master on the late Imperial Wedding.

My other letters by Messrs. Ronaldson[2] & Bailey leave me little if anything to add on the subject of our business here. The Imperial Decree of the 23d of March[3] sufficiently indicates it's own cause, though from the personal explanations given to me, it would appear to have been less the result of the law itself, than of it's non-execution, which was construed, and with some plausability, into a partiality for English Commerce. "My wishes and interests" said the Emperor the other day, "both lead to a free & a friendly connexion with the U. S. but I cannot see with indifference, on the part of this power, measures which expresly favor the trade of my enemy. Such is their non-intercourse law, which, if faithfully executed, would not be equal in it's operation, but which, so far from being thus executed, has been violated openly, and with impunity, from it's date to the present day and certainly much to my prejudice and greatly to the advantage of British Commerce." The error in this reasoning is in not going farther back for premises. I am Dear Sir, with the greatest respect and attachment, Your Most Obedient & faithful Servant

JOHN ARMSTRONG.

P. S. I mentioned in a late letter that the information I had two years ago given to you concerning the business here of a M. Hunt, had been communicated to him & had excited in him the most malignant conduct towards me. ⟨Trying?⟩ to prevent censure from falling on the innocent, I hasten to inform you, that M. Hunt has told his friend here, that *M. Gallatin* was the person who had informed him.

RC (DLC). Marked "*Duplicate.*" Docketed by JM.

1. Armstrong was probably referring to Prince Gustav of Vasa, son of Gustav IV Adolf, who had been overthrown in 1809 and succeeded by his great-uncle, Karl XIII. Because Karl XIII had no heir, the Diet of Sweden had elected as crown prince in 1809 the Norwegian prince Christian August, who adopted the Swedish name of Karl August. Karl August's accidental death three days after Armstrong wrote set in motion the events that led to one of Napoleon's marshals, Bernadotte, becoming king of Sweden (Franklin D. Scott, *Sweden: The Nation's History* [Minneapolis, 1977], pp. 295–300, 302).

2. James Ronaldson was born in Scotland and settled in Philadelphia where he engaged in textile and typefounding businesses. He was visiting France in 1809–10 and later became the first president of the Franklin Institute of Pennsylvania (Mann, *A Yankee Jeffersonian*, p. 268 n. 5).

3. The Decree of Rambouillet.

From Thomas Jefferson

DEAR SIR   MONTICELLO May 25. 10.

I inclose you the extract of a letter from Govr. Tyler which will explain itself, and I do it on the same principle on which I have sometimes done the same thing before, that whenever you are called on to select, you may have under consideration all those who may properly be thought of & the grounds of their pretensions. From what I can learn Griffin cannot stand it long,[1] and really the state has suffered long enough by having such a cypher in so important an office, and infinitely the more from the want of any counterpoise to the rancorous hatred which Marshal bears to the government of his country, & from the cunning & sophistry within which he is able to enshroud himself. It will be difficult to find a character of firmness enough to preserve his independance on the same bench with Marshall. Tyler, I am certain, would do it. He is an able & well read lawyer about 59. years of age: he was popular as a judge, & is remarkeably so as a governor, for his incorruptible integrity, which no circumstances have ever been able to turn from it's course. Indeed I think there is scarcely a person in the state so solidly popular, or who would be so much approved for that place. A milk & water character in that office would be seen as a calamity. Tyler having been the former state judge of that court too, and removed to make way for so wretched a fool as Griffin has a kind of right of reclamation, with the advantage of repeated elections by the legislature, as Admiralty judge, circuit judge & Governor. But of all these things you will judge fairly between him & his competitors. You have seen in the papers that Livingston has served a writ on me, stating damages at 100,000. D.[2] The ground is not yet explained, but it is understood to be the batture. I have engaged Wirt, Hay, & Wickham as counsel. I shall soon look into my papers to make a state of the case to enable them to plead: and as much of our proceedings was never committed to writing, and my memory cannot be trusted, it is probable I shall have to appeal to that of my associates in the proceedings. I believe that what I did was in harmony with the opinions of all the members of the administration, verbally expressed altho' not in writing. I have been delighted to see the effect of Monroe's late visit to Washington on his mind.[3] There appears to be the most perfect reconciliation & cordiality established towards yourself. I think him now inclined to rejoin us with zeal. The only embarrasment will be from his late friends. But I think he has firmness of mind enough to act independently as to them. The next session of our legislature will shew. We are suffering under a most severe drought of now 3. weeks continuance. Late sown wheat is yellow. But the oats suffer especially. In speaking of Livingston's suit, I omitted to observe that it is little doubted that his knolege of Marshall's character has induced him to bring this action. His twistifications in the case of Marbury, in that of Burr, & the late Yazoo case, shew how dexterously he can reconcile law to his personal biasses: and nobody seems to doubt that he is ready prepared to decide that Livingston's right to the batture is unquestionable, and that I am bound to pay for it with my private fortune. Ever affectionately your's.

TH: JEFFERSON

[Enclosure]

'My present station is a tedious insignificant one, & has but one good trait in it, & that is this, it gives me not power enough to do mischief in any other way than by the sin of neglect, which I avoid as much as possible by a constant attendance on the duties of my office; & if I retire without exciting envy or ill nature, tho' with a shattered fortune, I shall be content. Long have I neglected my private concerns in the engagement of those of the public, & also those of a social kind. Having had 21. children to bring up, besides my own, which took away so much of my life from a fair chance of encreasing my estate, so that I am much the worse, having got behind hand. However my eldest son has graduated as a Doctor of medecine, my 2d is now commencing the practice of law, leaving a son & daughter to promote as well as I can; & my object is to fall into some little public emploiment, if I live my time out here (or sooner) which may enable me to divide my estate among my children, after paying what I owe, and so glide off this scene of trouble as quiet as I can. Judge Griffin is in a low state of health and holds *my old office*, which Genl. Washington gave him because I was not for the new federal government without previous amendments, and of course could not be trusted in the British debt cases. This kind of conduct began the strong distinction which has embittered the cup of life, & in a great measure produced a spirit of retaliation when the republicans prevailed. But the British influence had the best share of the above policy in the beginning. I never did apply for an office, but I really hope the President will chance to think of me, now & then, in case of accidents, & if any opportunity offers, lay me down softly on a bed of roses, in my latter days, for I have been on thorns long enough.'

RC and enclosure (DLC: Rives Collection, Madison Papers); FC (DLC: Jefferson Papers). Enclosure is an extract, in Jefferson's hand, from John Tyler to Jefferson, 12 May 1810 (RC, DLC: Jefferson Papers).

1. Cyrus Griffin, the federal district judge for Virginia, died on 14 Dec. 1810. John Tyler, then serving his third term as governor of Virginia, had been a judge of the Virginia High Court of Admiralty, 1776–88, and of the Supreme Court of Appeals, 1788–1808. On 2 Jan. 1811 JM appointed Tyler as Griffin's successor (*Senate Exec. Proceedings*, 2:159).

2. Edward Livingston sued Jefferson in the federal circuit court at Richmond seeking personal damages for an alleged trespass during Jefferson's presidency. The litigation stemmed from Jefferson's controversial 1807 order for Livingston's eviction from the Batture

Ste. Marie adjacent to the New Orleans waterfront. On 5 Dec. 1811 John Marshall—serving on the circuit court, as Supreme Court justices did by geographic assignment in that era—concurred with John Tyler in dismissing Livingston's suit (Dargo, *Jefferson's Louisiana*, pp. 59–98; Malone, *Jefferson and His Time*, 6:55–73).

3. In April 1810 Monroe had returned to public life with his election from Albemarle County to the Virginia House of Delegates. At that time he had delivered a widely reported speech declaring that "Mr. Madison is a republican, and so am I. As long as he acts in consistence with the interests of his country, I will go along with him. When otherwise, you cannot wish me to countenance him." Then, in the first week of May, Monroe visited Washington to settle his diplomatic accounts. While there, he called on JM and reported that "the President recd. me with great kindness, as did the heads of departments. Indeed I had proofs of kindness from every one, many of whom, I did not expect it. It shows that they think I have been pushed too hard, for any errors imputed to me" (Richmond *Enquirer*, 10 Apr. 1810; Monroe to John Taylor, 9 May 1810, *Proceedings of the Massachusetts Historical Society*, 3d ser., 42 [1908–9]: 328).

From William Lambert

SIR,   CITY OF WASHINGTON, May 25th. 1810.

I have the honor to inclose for your acceptance, a printed copy of an ode which I have composed for the fourth of July, in the present year, to which some alterations and additions have been made since the last anniversary of American independence. That part which relates particularly to yourself, you will be pleased to receive as a testimonial of sincere respect, without a tincture of sycophantic adulation. I have likewise attempted to do justice to the character of Mr. Jefferson, and to show the esteem I have for him. When we look back to the fourth of July 1776, as the birth day of our independence, we naturally recur to events and circumstances relating to the revolutionary war; and this, I trust, may be done, without offence to the government or subjects of that kingdom from which we are now separated. This ode, in a more imperfect state, has met with the approbation of Mr. Barlow. I am, Sir, with great respect, Your most obedt. servant,

WILLIAM LAMBERT.

RC (DLC); enclosure (DLC: Madison Collection, Rare Book Division). Enclosure is Lambert's printed *Ode for the Fourth of July, 1810* (1 p.).

From David Bailie Warden

Sir,   Paris, 25 may, 1810.

I have the honor of sending you the inclosed newspapers and *brochures*. I am, at present, much occupied with the business of Prize-Causes. I have thought it a duty to make a defence of several cases not represented here by any Agent. The Court, though it regularly confiscates the property in every American case that comes before them, continues to ratify contracts between the captors and captured. I have transmitted, to the Secretary of State, a detailed statement of their proceedings.[1] It will give me great pleasure to know that my conduct meets your Approbation. I have the honor to be, Sir, with the greatest respect, Your very obedt and very humb Servt

                                            David Bailie Warden

RC (DLC). Enclosures not found.

1. See Warden to Robert Smith, 24 May 1810 (DNA: RG 59, CD, Paris).

§ From John B. Chandler. *25 May 1810, Georgetown*. Sends gifts from the "Speker" of the Creek Nation, who asked that JM be informed "that he manufacterd the Pipe and his Wife the Pouch."

RC (DLC). 1 p.

§ From William Tatham. *25 May 1810, Norfolk*. Sends JM papers "on the defence of Lynnhaven Bay, the Chesapeake, Norfolk, &c," including a paper "which contemplates a co-operation by Fire rafts." Lists seven more communications he will complete "if encouraged to do so," ranging from field fortifications to an inland canal system. Asks for JM's assistance, as he is without income and the administration has neglected him.

RC and enclosures (DNA: RG 107, LRRS, T-81:5). RC 3 pp.; enclosures 60 pp. JM evidently deposited this material in the War Department after he returned to Washington from his summer vacation (see the entry for 6 Oct. 1810 in Registers of Letters Received by the Secretary of War [DNA: RG 107]).

From William Davy

Sir!   Philadelphia May 26h. 1810

My Son entrusted to me, the Care of procuring & forwarding to You, four Volumes of Syms's Embassy to Pegue including the Drawings.[1] I hope you will receive them safe by the Mail.

After your Perusal, the Secretary of State, will be so good, as to take Charge of, & return these Volumes to me, as they are obtained from a private Library.

My Son sailed for Calcutta the 24h Instant.[2] With Sentiments of profound Respect I have the honour to be Your Excellency's Most Obt Hble Servt.

WILLIAM DAVY[3]

RC (DLC).

1. Michael Symes, *An Account of an Embassy to the Kingdom of Ava, Sent by the Governor-General of India in the Year 1795* (2d ed.; 4 vols.; London, 1800). Ava and Pegu were Burmese city-states.

2. JM gave John B. Davy a recess appointment as consul at Rangoon. The Senate confirmed the appointment on 12 Jan. 1811 (*Senate Exec. Proceedings*, 2:160, 162).

3. William Davy was a merchant with premises at 356 High Street. In 1816 JM appointed him consul at Hull, England (Robinson, *Philadelphia Directory* [1811 ed.], p. 78; *Senate Exec. Proceedings*, 3:61, 68).

§ Memorandum from Tench Coxe. *Ca. 26 May 1810*. Discusses the need to encourage American manufactures and encloses some observations[1] on a treasury report on the same subject. Lists merchandise now imported that might be produced in America (linen, iron, hemp, liquors), since European sources are likely to be cut off by war. Also stresses the need to encourage manufactures that will supply the means of national defense. Believes that those sections of the treasury report relating to military supply will have influence in Europe and suggests that a "special and well executed comment" on this matter "would be of great use to us abroad, by inspiring caution and respect."

Ms (DLC). 6 pp. In Coxe's hand. Undated. Date assigned on the basis of JM's docket, "May 1810," and the date of the enclosure (see n. 1).

1. Coxe evidently enclosed an essay, "Cursory Thoughts on Public Affairs," printed in the Philadelphia *Democratic Press*, 25 May 1810. The article is now in JM's portfolio of newspaper clippings (DLC, series 7, container 3). Both the essay and Coxe's memorandum were probably written as a comment on Gallatin's report of 17 Apr. 1810 on domestic manufactures (see *ASP, Finance*, 2:425–39).

¶ To Armand Duplantier. Letter not found. *26 May 1810*. Acknowledged in Duplantier to JM, 21 July 1810. Makes inquiries about the surveys of Lafayette's Louisiana lands.

From Albert Gallatin

Dear Sir May 28th 1810

I enclose for your signature an authority[1] in the usual form empowering me to negotiate a loan with the Bank of the United States, if you approve of the terms which I had proposed & which have been accepted.[2] The correspondence with the Bank is enclosed.[3]

If the Charter is not renewed, a loan to the same amount (3,750,000 dollars) must be negotiated in 1811, to repay this.

If the Charter is renewed, nothing more will be necessary than annually to renew the loan (to which there will be no objection on their part) whilst our finances continue in their present situation. It is presumable that if we remain both as to receipts & expenditures in statu quo, no other measure will be necessary to enable us to go on. As this would simplify & facilitate the subsequent annual operations of Government, I have preferred that mode to that of issuing new stock by sale or subscription. To which must also be added that as the sum borrowed will be applied to the payment of 3,750,000 dollars exchd. six per cent stock, the amount of stock at market being diminished by that sum, & no new stock being issued in lieu thereof; the operation will tend to enhance the prices of stock, & thus facilitate the means of obtaining another loan on good terms next year, if that should be necessary. With great respect Your obedt. Servant

ALBERT GALLATIN

RC (DLC). Docketed by JM. For enclosures, see nn. 1 and 3.

1. A copy of the authority, dated 28 May 1810, permitting Gallatin to borrow up to $3,750,000, is located in the Senate records (DNA: RG 46, Legislative Proceedings, 11A-F2; see also *ASP, Finance*, 2:449).

2. In his annual report on the state of the finances, submitted to the House of Representatives on 8 Dec. 1809, Gallatin had reported that the budget for the coming year, including repayments on the public debt, could not be balanced unless Congress either cut military and naval expenditures by nearly 50 percent or authorized a loan to make up the deficit. In response, Congress passed a bill on 1 May 1810 authorizing the secretary of the treasury to negotiate a loan not exceeding the amount of public debt to be repaid in 1810, a sum that Gallatin had estimated at about $3,750,000 (*ASP, Finance*, 2:373–75; *Annals of Congress*, 11th Cong., 2d sess., 1762, 1947, 1955; *U.S. Statutes at Large*, 2:610–11).

3. See Gallatin to the president and directors of the Bank of the United States, 3 May 1810 (reproduced in *Papers of Gallatin* [microfilm ed.], reel 21).

From Thomas Macon

DEAR SIR   ORANGE 28th. May 1810

My Son Madison is now about nineteen years of age. He has lived the last three years in a retail Store in Fredericksburg. Free from every natural prejudice I beleive I may say he is a very promising young Man. I wish this fall to get him in a whole sail store in New York. For the first year I would pay his board and find him his cloths, & as I have no acquaintances in New York I find considerable dificulty in procuring him a situation there. If it would be attended with no trouble to you, and if you have any friend in New York that could procure him a place in a whole saile Store there you would render me a very great favour: Madison is acquainted with accounts, writes a tollerable good hand, and is well spoken off [*sic*] by all that is acquainted with him, for his attention to business and morral good conduct.

Your Mother is now at my house and very well. She has informed me of your wish respecting the bacon. When I was in Hanover about six weeks ago, my Father informed me that he had applications for all the bacon he could spare, that he had reserved a part for you,[1] but as he was in doubt whether you wanted or not, he observed he would waite a week or two longer, and if he did not hear from you he should conclude you did not want, and that he should dispose of it. I have no doubt but before this it is all disposed of. I am Dear Sir your Most Obt. St

THOMAS MACON[2]

RC (DLC). Cover dated "Orange C h / June 5th." Docketed by JM.

1. William Macon wrote JM on 14 June 1809 about supplying him with bacon (*PJM-PS*, 1:251–52).

2. Thomas Macon (1765–1838) of Somerset in Orange County, Virginia, married JM's sister Sarah Catlett Madison (1764–1843) in 1790. Madison Macon was one of their seven sons (Madison Family Tree, *PJM*, 1: following p. 212).

¶ To John K. Smith. Letter not found. *28 May 1810*. Acknowledged in Smith to JM, 14 July 1810. Makes inquiries about the surveys of Lafayette's Louisiana lands.

From Thomas Jefferson

DEAR SIR   MONTICELLO May 30. 10.

In the action brought against me by Edward Livingston, the counsel employed, Wirt & Hay (Wickham declining) desire me to furnish them with the grounds of defence, with as little delay as possible. The papers relating to the batture in the offices of State, the Treasury & war, will undoubtedly be needed to exhibit facts. I am now engaged on this subject, and not to give you unnecessary trouble I write to the Secretaries of State, Treasury & War directly, not doubting you will approve of their communicating what is necessary on the assurance of the papers being faithfully & promptly returnd, after extracting material parts. One article I am obliged to trouble yourself for; to wit Moreau de l'Isle's Memoir[1] which I have never read; & yet am sure it is too able not to be the most important I can consult. Will you be so good as to furnish me a printed copy if it has been printed or to lend the M. S. if not printed. I have copies of all the opinions printed before 1809. Poydras shewed me an argument of his[2] in which I recollect that I thought there was one sound & *new* view. I have now forgotten it, & have no copy. Your's affectionately

TH: JEFFERSON

P. S. No rain since the 3d. inst. Every thing getting desperate.

RC (DLC); FC (DLC: Jefferson Papers).

1. See Caesar A. Rodney to JM, 17 Oct. 1809, n. 2.
2. Julien Poydras de Lalande was the author of *A Defence of the Right of the Public to the Batture of New Orleans* (Washington, 1809; Shaw and Shoemaker 18438) and *Further Observations in Support of the Right of the Public* . . . (Washington, 1809; Shaw and Shoemaker 18439). Two congressional speeches delivered by Poydras in 1810 on the subject of the batture were also published as pamphlets (Shaw and Shoemaker 21128 and 21129).

¶ To James Leander Cathcart. Letter not found. *30 May 1810.* Acknowledged in Cathcart to JM, 13 Aug. 1810. Orders wine.

¶ To Anthony Charles Cazenove. Letter not found. *30 May 1810.* Acknowledged in Cazenove to JM, 6 June 1810. Transmits an enclosure to be forwarded to Madeira.

From George Washington Parke Custis

ARLINGTON HOUSE 31st May 1810

Beleiving that whatever concerns the Domestic Interests of our Country will readily obtain a portion of yr Excellency's notice, & esteem, I have sent for Yr inspection, a *Rambuillet Merino*, lately received as a present, from Chancellor Livingston, of New York.

Having been formerly honoured, with yr correspondence on matters, touching our rural interests, I have been induced, to take the present liberty, from the idea, that such subjects, are yet prominent in yr affections.

I have further prepared, either for yr private cabinet, or for that of the Government House, some Specimens of the most celebrated Foreign, & Domestic Wools, selected from the best Authorities, & duly labelled, & arranged, to which is added an Index Explanatory.

In perusing these samples, you will observe at once, the perfection of European science, & emprove[me]nt, & the indigenal product, of our clime, improved by the hand of Nature.

Our Country, can no longer be said to need foreign resources, while she can boast such native riches. If such is the simple effort of Nature alone, what may we not expect, when Science, zeal, & Industry, shall contribute their aid. I trust that my Countrymen, will unite their energies in support of the noble, & generous cause of Independence, that holy right, for which our Fathers fought, & which their Posterity should preserve, & I trust that under whatever circumstances of Political change, we shall continue to cherish the spirit of Domestic oeconomy, as the source of Individual wealth, & National Prosperity.

I am happy to learn, that you carry your years so well. Of the number of Statesmen, & Soldiers, who atcheived the Revolution, how many have been stricken from the list of mortality, Yet has the hand of Fate, been lenient withall, for most have lived, to see the benefits, resulting from their goodly work, & beheld an Empire of Reason, proudly arise amid the oppressions, of a suffering World. May the last of Republics, long be preserved in the pure & benevolent spirit of her Constitution, & Laws; Great within herself, may she stand as a monument of virtue, amid the storms of conflicting empires, & present to future ages the inestimable blessings of Rational Liberty. I have the honour to remain With perfect Respect Yr Excellency's Obt. & H Sert

GEORGE W P CUSTIS

RC (DLC).

§ From James M. Henry. *1 June 1810, Pointe à Pitre, Guadeloupe*. Has moved to this island for health reasons, after living in the south of France for three years. When JM wrote him a few years ago concerning an appointment at Jamaica, the state of his health forbade acceptance of the office. Has written secretary of state that he would now be willing to serve as consul at Guadeloupe.

RC (ViU). 2 pp. Docketed by JM. Jefferson had appointed Henry as agent for distressed and impressed seamen in Jamaica, but he declined the post (JM to Henry, 25 Mar. and 20 July 1805 [DNA: RG 59, IC]). On the same day that he wrote JM, Henry wrote Robert Smith concerning the consulship at Guadeloupe (DNA: RG 59, LAR, 1809–17). He was not appointed.

¶ From William C. C. Claiborne. Letter not found. *1 June 1810*. Calendared as a one-page letter in the lists probably made by Peter Force (DLC, series 7, container 2).

Dolley Madison to an Unidentified Correspondent

3d. June — 10.

I am about to take a liberty my good friend, which *must remain a secret*. It is to invite you to visit Washington *immediately*. I have deliberated for the last Two weeks, on the propriety of my doing this and on finding that you are not likely to be made acquainted with the *necessity* for *your aid*, I determine to act consistant with that regard & friendship I feel for you & which I know you deserve.

Come then, as soon as possible to my Husband who will not call, tho he wishes for you, every day.

D. P. MADISON

RC (NjGbS).

To Thomas Jefferson

DEAR SIR　　　　　　　　　　　　　　WASHINGTON June 4. 1810.

I have recd. your two letters of the 25. & 30. Ult. I have not yet seen any of the Secretaries to whom you have written on the subject of the papers relating to the Batture. I take for granted they will readily comply with your request. Mr. Gallatin is absent on a visit to his Farm in the Western parts of Pennsa. But his chief Clk will I presume be able to furnish the papers, if any, lying in that Dept. The Argument of Moreau de Lislet has never been printed; nor, as I believe, fully translated. The Original Manuscript, if not in the hands of Mr. Rodney, will be forwarded from the Dept. of State. What Poydras has said on the subject is herewith inclosed. Altho' the ground to be taken in the suit agst. you, is not disclosed, I think it not difficult to conjecture it. The Act of Congs. will be represented as Unconstitutional, and the case of the Batture as not within its scope; and these misconstructions as too obvious to be resolvable into Official error of Judgment. In any event there will be the chance of an Obiter Opinion of the Court, on the Merits of the case, st⟨reng⟩thening the cause of Livingston. Till I recd. your letter, I had scarcely yeilded my belief that a suit had been really instituted. If the Judiciary shd. lend itself for such a purpose, it cannot fail I think, to draw down on itself the unbounded indignation of the Nation, and a change of the Constitution, under that feeling, carried perhaps too far in the opposite direction. In a Governmt. whose vital principle, is responsibility, it never will be allowed that the Legislative & Executive Depts. should be compleatly subjected to the Judiciary, in which that characteristic principle is so faintly seen. My overseer left this on friday at noon, with our Merinoes under his charge. He will write to you on his arrival, that *when you chuse*, you may send to have them divided & your share removed. He will concur in any mode of division that may be preferred. That the result may be as equal as possible, I wd propose, that the owner of the Ewe with a lamb, should furnish the other party, with the first Ewe lamb that may follow from the same Ewe. I suggest this on the supposition that the other Ewe is not with lamb, a point which is not absolutely certain.

The John Adams Still keeps us in suspence; & when she arrives, will probably increase, rather than remove the perplexity of our situation.

The drought here is equal to what you experience, and I find by newspaper paragraphs, that it is nearly universal. We had a slight shower on wednesday evening, and as much this morning as lays the dust; but the effect of both together will not be sensible. Yrs. always & most Affectly

JAMES MADISON

RC (DLC). Docketed by Jefferson, "recd. June 6."

§ Draft of Robert Smith to John Armstrong. *5 June 1810, Department of State.*[1] Acknowledges letters and enclosures from Armstrong received on 21 May. Protests strongly against France's decision to seize American vessels as announced in the letter from the duc de Cadore to Armstrong [14 Feb. 1810]. Describes French policy as "an act of violence, which under existing circumstances is scarcely less than an act of war [and] necessarily required an explanation which would satisfy not only the United States but the world." Asserts that the U.S. has always resisted the British orders in council and that the right of doing so by the municipal prohibition of trade is a "lawful exercise of sovereign power," which the French government can neither complain of nor justly construe "into a cause of warlike reprisal." The U.S. has likewise resisted the decrees of France, which had "assumed a prescriptive power over the policy of the United States, as reprehensible as the attempt of the British government to levy contributions on our trade was obnoxious."

Denies that the U.S. has singled out French vessels for seizure in the manner complained of by Cadore and adds, "Had France interdicted to our vessels all the ports within the sphere of her influence, and had she given a warning of equal duration with that given by our law, there would have been no cause of complaint on the part of the United States."[2] Points out that it has always been possible for France to avoid American trade restrictions merely by modifying or annulling its own decrees. The U.S. has already made propositions to this effect to France, and "they were not accepted." Instead, French policy has been calculated to produce results other than that of "a good understanding between the two countries." The recent act of Congress [Macon's Bill No. 2] gives the French emperor the opportunity to establish "the most amicable relations" with the U.S. Let him withdraw or modify his decrees, restore American property, and "a law of the United States exists, which authorises the president to promote the best possible understanding with France, and to impose a system of exclusion against the ships and merchandise of Great Britain in the event of her failing to conform to the same just terms of conciliation." As American trade restrictions are not now in force, France no longer has "a solitary reasonable pretext for procrastinating the delivery of American property." Instructs Armstrong to present these observations to the French government.

Printed copy (*National Intelligencer*, 2 July 1811). Included in Smith's defense of his conduct as secretary of state. Described as a "*Copy of the draught of the letter proposed to be sent to Gen. Armstrong*," which was "laid before the President for his approbation." Dated "June —, 1810."

1. According to Smith, JM "objected to the sending" of this letter and, instead of the "animadversions" it contained, "directed the insertion of simply the following section" into the draft: "As the 'John Adams' is daily expected, and as your further communications by her will better enable me to adapt to the actual state of our affairs with the French government the observations proper to be made in relation to their seizure of our property and to the letter of the Duke of Cadore of the 14th Feb. it is by the President deemed expedient *not to make, at this time, any such animadversions*. I cannot, however, forbear informing *you*, that a high indignation is felt by the President, as well as by the public, at this act of violence on our property, and at the outrage, both in the language and in the matter, of the letter of the Duke of Cadore, so justly pourtrayed [*sic*] in your note to him of the 10th of March" (ibid., emphasis added by Smith). For the remainder of the revised instructions to Armstrong, which directed him to advise the French government that "by putting in force, agreeably to the terms of this statute [Macon's Bill No. 2], the non-intercourse against Great Britain the very species of resistance would be made which France has been constantly representing as most efficacious," see Smith to Armstrong, 5 June 1810 (DNA: RG 59, IM; printed in *ASP, Foreign Relations*, 3:384–85). For JM's response to the news conveyed by the *John Adams*, see Madison's Draft of Robert Smith to John Armstrong, 5 July 1810.

2. The *National Intelligencer*, on 9 July 1811, expressed doubts about whether Smith had been as wholly responsible for this draft as he claimed. The administration newspaper conceded, however, that the president had rejected the draft and cited this sentence as one of the "particular passages and expressions which may help to account for its unfavorable reception by Mr. Madison." The comment continued: "What! *no cause* of complaint! The United States, it is true, could not complain of it as a violation of their *neutral* rights and nation[al] sovereignty, obnoxious to the resentment of the other belligerent: but would it be consistent with friendship, with liberality, with reciprocity, with the spirit of common intercourse among civilized nations?"

From Anthony Charles Cazenove

A. C. Cazenove[1] has the honour of acknowledging the receipt of Mr. Madison's note of the 30th. Ulto. with an inclosure for Madeira, which will go per brig Columbia expected to sail tomorrow, now detained for want of seamen; to inform him that an other vessel will sail from hence for that port in 8 or 10 days, & he will be happy in forwarding by her any letter Mr. Madison may be pleased to intrust to his care.

As agent in this place of Messrs. Murdoch Yuille Us. & Co. he takes the liberty of assuring Mr. Madison that, if he will at any time favour him with an order for some of their wine, every care shall be taken that he will be pleased with it.

RC (DLC).

1. Anthony Charles Cazenove (1775–1852) fled from the revolution in Geneva in 1794. He entered a business partnership with Albert Gallatin and lived at New Geneva in Fayette County, Pennsylvania, 1795–97. He became a U.S. citizen and established himself as a merchant at Alexandria, Virginia, in 1797. He handled wine purchases for JM, 1810–21 (John Askling, ed., "Autobiographical Sketch of Anthony-Charles Cazenove, Political Refugee, Merchant, and Banker, 1775–1852," *VMHB*, 78 [1970]: 295–307).

From Caesar A. Rodney

MY DEAR SIR, WILMINGTON June 7. 1810.

The delicate situation of Mrs. Rodney at the death of her father compelled me to return home & has since detained me. She was however confined the evening before last & has presented me a daughter. In a few days I trust she will be in a situation to leave, and I shall promptly repair to Washington. Private business of considerable consequence, & of a pressing nature in Philadelphia will claim a moments attention. This would have been transacted before, but I could not leave home. In the course of next week I shall certainly see you, & sooner if possible.

The merchants of Philada. who are generally considered the most prudent and cautious, have, since the non-intercourse expired, sent out more ships with the most valuable cargoes, than perhaps ever passed down the Delaware within the same period of time. The experiment will be fairly made, between an embargo, & a free trade as it has been improperly termed. Much I fear that the rash adventurers will be taught a dear lesson. The cargo of one ship (Woodrop Simms) was valued at half a million of dollars. A large fleet of them lay at New-Castle for several weeks waiting for orders. Their owners were uncertain whether they would permit them to sail, or not. They at len[g]th directed their departure.

I regret extremely that Mr. Gallatin has been obliged to leave you for any time, but flatter myself that he will not be detained long, by his private affairs. With great esteem & respect I remain Dear Sir, Yours Truly & affectionately

C. A. RODNEY

RC (DLC). Docketed by JM.

From Samuel Smith

SIR,   BALTIMORE 7th. June 1810

I hope & believe that I am not interested in the late Surrender of the American property by the King of Holland to the Emperor of France.[1] I therefore may be permitted to give my Opinion on the Course that the U. S. ought to pursue, being (as to Interest) unbiassed.

Holland has by a Solemn treaty transferred all the American property in her Ports to the Emperor of France. Holland then has, *by a Solemn And public Act*, Seized on the property of American Citizens, who (under the faith of treaty & of her laws) entered her Ports and has delivered it to a foreign Prince to be by him used for his purposes. Retaliation on the Citizens of Holland who may have property in the U. S. is just, (if Retaliation Can in any Case be just)—I believe that the Subjects of Holland have property in our funds of the Old Debt & the Louisiana Debt[2] to at least the Amount of fifteen Million, they also hold a large proportion of Bank Stock, and this ought to be Seized & Sequestered until Restitution be made for all the American property Seized in Holland—this Cannot be done without a law, and it is to be presumed that the proprietors will transfer all their property in the funds before the next meeting of Congress. Is it possible to Avoid this? Could a Stop be put to all transfers of Stock as well Stock of the U. S. as Bank Stock owned by foreigners? If it Can (but I fear it cannot) it certainly ought to be done, and yet there is a danger to be apprehended, to wit—that the power of the Emperor (extending as it does over all Europe) may be exerted to Seize American property in all the Ports of the Continent. I have Stated what I concieve to be a just retaliation, and to which there Can I presume be little Objection either as to Justice or Policy, but may this Retaliation not be Carried further? France Considers Holland, Naples, & Spain by Cadores letter[3] & her own Acts, as a part of her Power, and whatever Act France directs is Obeyed by those Subordinate Kingdoms. Is it not then fair & Just to consider them as One power? If it is, then the Act of One is the Act of the whole—and the Dutch property may be applied to reimburse the American Sufferers in Naples & St. Sebastians, and there will be enough to pay the whole. In the losses at Naples I am interested, my house[4] have had Seized to the Amount of about $31.000. This may (but I do not think it does) Influence my Mind. I consider it a trifle, yet Sir, we are frequently influenced without being at all Conscious thereof. I have taken the liberty to throw out those undigested Observation[s] for your consideration—your better judgement and more liesure will direct the proper Course to be pursued upon this important Subject. I only request that those Observations may be considered as for yourself *only*. I have the honor to be—Your friend & Servt

S. SMITH

RC (DLC). Docketed by JM.

1. See John Armstrong to JM, 18 Mar. 1810, n. 7.

2. Hope and Company of Amsterdam were major handlers of American loans in Europe and, with Baring Brothers of London, financed the Louisiana Purchase (Alexander DeConde, *This Affair of Louisiana* [New York, 1976], pp. 172–73).

3. In his 14 Feb. 1810 letter to John Armstrong, French foreign minister Jean-Baptiste Nompère de Champagny, duc de Cadore, declared that Napoleon retaliated against the Nonintercourse Act "not only in his territory, but likewise in the countries which are under his influence. In the ports of Holland, of Spain, of Italy, and of Naples, American vessels have been seized, because the Americans have seized French vessels" (*ASP, Foreign Relations,* 3:380).

4. Smith and Buchanan was Smith's trading partnership with James A. Buchanan (Cassell, *Merchant Congressman in the Young Republic,* p. 107).

Account with St. Mary's College

[7 June 1810]

Dr. his Excellency James Madison for Master John P Todd

1810.   College Charges as specified in the Prospectus[1]

June.	7.	Mending Linen Stockings &c	3 "	
		Doctor's fees and Medicines	4 "	
		Paper Slates Quills &c	3 "	
		Postage and Penny Post Commission	" 46½	
		Six Months board and Tuition in Advance	115	125 46½

1809.		Classic Books.		
Novem.	10.	2 vol. Mathematical Manual	2 "	
	"	Telemachus	1 25	
		Wanostrocht's Recueil	1 25.	
		Atlas	6 50.	
Decem.	14.	1 Case of Mathematical Instruments	7 "	
1810				
January	16.	Rasgos Historicos	1 "	
April	2.	Juvenalis Delphini	3 12½.	22 12½

Expenses foreign to the Pension, which, &c.

1810.		Clothing.		
february	24.	Mending Clothes to this Day	1 12½.	
April.	14.	Do. Do. Do.	1 68¾	
	"	1 pr. of Boots bottomed	2 25.	
May	27.	Mending Clothes	" 37½	
	"	2 Night Drawers $2. 1 Bathing Do. 75d.	2 75.	8 18¾

1810		Extra-money advanced.		
January	11.	Money advanced him this Day	4 "	
	24.	Do. Do. Do.	5 "	
february	2.	Money advanced him to buy a great-Coat	8 "	
		D. Do. to pay his Washer-woman	5 "	
March	8.	Money advanced him	5 "	
		Do. Do. to pay his Washer-woman	2 50	
March	24.	Money advanced him at his Demand	3 50	
April	18.	Check at his order to pay his Taylor	27 "	
	23.	Money advanced him at his Demand	6 "	
May	9.	Do. Do.	10 "	
	19.	Do. Do. to pay his Washer-woman	7 50	83 50

239.27¾

Jnl. No 13   Added Mr. Godefroy's bill for 1
pa. 200   qt. endg. 15 Decbr. pap. clay.
                   mod.   15.00.
                   Do. Mr. Forster's Do. for 2 qrs.
                     endg. 12th. march 1810 paper
                     & ink   21.50.
                   Do. Mr. Bullets Do for 1 qr.
                     ending 11th february 1810   12."
                   Entrance omitted in all Mr.
                     Godefroy's preceeding Accts.   5."

Ms (MdBS: Account Book, 1809–11).

1. On 1 Dec. 1805 JM and Dolley Madison had enrolled Dolley's son, John Payne Todd, then thirteen years old, at St. Mary's College in Baltimore. Founded in 1791 as a seminary, that institution became a college in 1799 and a university in 1805 (JM to Dolley Madison, Nov. 1805 [MHi]; Scharf, *History of Baltimore*, 1 : 234). Subsequent accounts from the college will be summarized.

To Thomas Jefferson

DEAR SIR   WASHINGTON June 8. 1810

Since I rendered the account of our Merinos sent on by My Overseer, I have learnt, that Mr. Hooe of Alexanda. considers the lamb yeaned after their arrival, as allotted to him by the intention of Mr. Jarvis. I have not yet investigated the merits of his claim, by comparing what he may have recd. from Mr. J. with the language of Mr. J's letter to me; but I think it very possible that the claim will be entitled to attention. Mr. J. mentions in a postscript to me,[1] that the Capt: had refused to take charge of the Sheep without a promise of two lambs in case they should drop on the passage, and that as a proof of his regard to Mr. Hooe & his partner, he wished him a like advantage, desiring that I would contribute to fulfil the engagemts. in case the Ewe chosen by me *should have yeaned*. It is probable that his letter to you contained a similar clause, or that he relied on a communication of the one in mine. According to the strict expression, Mr. Hooe, is evidently barred of a claim to the lamb in question, as it had not been yeaned at the time the Ewe came into my possession. But as it seems to have been the general intention of Mr. J. that his Alexa. friends should have the benefit of the actual pregnancies, leaving us the future increase only, & that he took for granted as he might well do, from the season of the voyage, that the lambs, if any, would drop before it was over, I do not think we ought to avail ourselves of the letter of the donation. Another question occurs between the Capt of the Vessel & Messrs. Hooe &c, and if the meaning of the postscript to me be not controuled by other explanations, the Capt: seems to have in strictness a priority of claim. But as the promise to him seems to have been extorted, and to be unsupported by strict construction, I should be disposed to favor the title of the others, which rests on the same friendly intentions with our own. As soon as I come to an understanding on the matter with the other parties I will write you more definitely. I have thought it proper to say this much at present, in order that the division between us may be suspended, or so made as to be consistent with the pending question. Always & affectly Yours

JAMES MADISON

RC (DLC). Docketed by Jefferson, "recd June 10."

1. See Jarvis to JM, 19 Feb. 1810.

§ From William Dunn. *8 June 1810, Richmond.* Implores JM to send him money so that he can extricate himself from debt and save his character from ruin. "You are surrounded with all the pomp and Splender this world can afford thousands at your command three or four hundred dollers you would Scarcely miss out of your coffers."

RC (DLC). 2 pp.

¶ To Thomas Macon. Letter not found. *8 June 1810.* Acknowledged in Macon to JM, 13 June 1810. Suggests two cities other than New York where Madison Macon could gain commercial experience.

From Simon Snyder

SIR,   LANCASTER June 9th. 1810

In compliance with the request of the General Assembly, of the commonwealth of Pennsylvania I have the honor to transmit to You a copy of certain resolutions adopted at their last Session. With high respect & consideration Your Obt. Svt.

SIMON SNYDER

[Enclosure]

In the General Assembly of the Commonwealth of Pennsylvania

Whereas the Legislature of Pennsylvania at their last Session, made so explicit an avowal of their sentiments respecting the foreign relations of the United States; gave so firm a pledge of support to the General Government, that uncommon events alone could have rendered correspondent declarations by their successors, useful, or necessary, but the conduct of Great Britain & the insolence of her minister plenipotentiary, has produced a crisis that has excited public feeling & anxiety to such an unexampled height, that the general assembly of this commonwealth cannot hesitate to renew the solemn expression of devotion to their country, & of resentment against the governments, under whose order the rights, dignity, & honor of the United States, have been violated & insulted: Therefore,

Resolved, by the Senate & House of Representatives of the Commonwealth of Pennsylvania That they unequivocally approve the pacific & liberal measures, which the administration of the United States has so zealously pursued, for obtaining an adjustment of the existing differences between this country and the governments of Great Britain and France.

Resolved, That whilst with sincere pleasure they thus bear testimony to the upright & honorable conduct of their own government, they view the refusal on the part of France, to accomodate the differences between the two nations, as a flagrant disregard of our national rights, & they cannot hesitate to pronounce the violation on the part of Great Britain, of a solemn & reciprocal engagement, & her subsequent failure to clothe her minister with adequate powers to adjust with our government the disputes that had arisen prior to that event as well as those thereby produced, to be such a manifestation of determined hostility; as must arouse the spirit, & nerve the arm of every american to resent the insults, & to resist the outrages thus wantonly heaped upon an unoffending nation.

Resolved, That when in the opinion of our national councils, an appeal to the patriotism & force of the american people becomes necessary, the general assembly of this commonwealth pledge themselves to co-operate with the general government, to sustain the rights, honor, & reputation, & to avenge the wrongs and insults of their country.

Resolved, That the governor of this commonwealth be requested to transmit a copy of these resolutions to the president of the United States and a copy to each of the Senators and Representatives from Pennsylvania, in the Congress of the United States.

> JOHN WEBER, Speaker of the
> House of Representatives.
> P. C. LANE, Speaker of the Senate.

Approved, the nineteenth day of March one thousand eight hundred & ten.

> SIMON SNYDER

RC and enclosure (DLC). In a clerk's hand. RC signed by Snyder. Enclosure marked "Copy." An earlier version of the resolutions, as passed by the Pennsylvania House of Representatives, had been printed in the *National Intelligencer* on 24 Jan. 1810.

From Elbridge Gerry

DEAR SIR,   CAMBRIDGE 13th June 1810

From some circumstances which have come to my knowledge, I am induced to think, that measures are adopted to shake the confidence of Government, in their district attorney, George Blake Esqr.[1] If so, the grounds are said to be, his having had in his office, a brother, & his having associated with native & foreign gentlemen, of *different politicks*. I regret exceedingly, that reports of this kind are in circulation, in regard to republicans; because it will be said that they are in these habits, for the purpose of placing themselves or their friends in office, & that they are as much influenced by ambition & competition, as other people.

That Mr Blake, of all others, should be censured for countenancing his political opponents, is extraordinary: seeing that his public measures have exposed him to the resentments of the *illiberal* part of them, beyond any gentleman in this State. *Such* for years have refused to admit him into any of their circles, or even Assemblies of amusements: a mark of indignation confined, I beleive to himself alone, & yet, as a gentleman his character is as high as that of any man in Boston, or in this State. Besides, his profession, of which he is at the head, unavoidably connects him at the first judicial Courts with the most prominent characters at the bar, & with foreign clients, resident or transient, of every nation. Perhaps I speak feelingly on the subject: for if he is culpable for associating with Gentlemen, because not of his politicks, I am equally so, & justify it in my mind, by an abhorrence of that illiberality & intollerance, which has ere marked the conduct of many of our political adversaries. If Mr Blake's association with his brother, an affectionate friend & a man of the first talents & respectability, *in a law office* had been disagreable to Government, a circumstance which may, but which I had no reason to beleive did exist; a hint to him from any one, or to Mr Blake himself from any of the executive departments, would have removed the difficulty.

Mr Blake in his district office has laboured abundantly, night & day, & in consequence of the numerous embargo causes, has been litterally a slave—in supporting officially, as well as privately that measure, & the dignity of the federal Government generally, he has confronted its adversaries, & increased beyond bounds, their pointed indignation: of all which I presume, Sir, your excellency must have had full proof.

I pray you, Sir, to consider this voluntary address, in a matter which may be unfounded, but which beleived, struck my mind with regret & astonishment, as a measure flowing from a regard to Justice, & the promotion of harmony amongst the friends of Government: & from a wish to render unsuccessful, the arts & intrigues too much practised, at the present day. I have the honor to be dear Sir with the highest sentiments of esteem & respect Your excellency's obedt Sert

E GERRY

RC (DLC).

1. George Blake had been appointed district attorney for Massachusetts in 1801 and was still serving in 1829 (*PJM-SS*, 1:479, 480 n. 2).

From Thomas Macon

DEAR SIR   ORANGE 13 June 1810

I have received your favour of the 8 Inst. I am very sensible of the obligation I am under to you for the trouble which your willing to take in favour of my Son. I have no particular preferance in favour of New York over the two Citys which you have mentioned further than it was Madisons choice & I would have wished to have gratifyed him in it. If it is necessary to pay more than his board & cloths I will very cheearfully do it, as in all probability much of his future prosperity may depend on the manner in which the two or three next years of his life is spent. If it was equally convenient I would not wish him to go on untill about the beginning of the fall. Your sheep got safe home with the increase of a lamb. The drouth has been very great in this part of the country for several weeks past, notwithstanding the crop of wheat is as promising, as ever was seen. It has been most severely felt on the crops of oats and grass, and unless there should come very soon very seasonable weather there must be very short crops of oats & Hay. My Family unites with me in there best wish to you & Mrs. Madison & I am Dear Sir your Most Ob St

THOMAS MACON

RC (DLC). Docketed by JM.

From William Pinkney

DEAR SIR.   LONDON. 13. June 1810.

As Mr. Erving leaves Town early in the Morning and it is now past Midnight I have scarcely Time to do more than acknowledge the Receipt of your kind Letter by Dr Logan. In a few Days I will trouble you with a Letter of some Length. The newspapers will apprize you of the Violence & Injustice of France towards the U. S. I hope it will be found possible (at least until England does us Justice) to avoid War with France. The Conduct of France is absolutely unintelligible; and has no Excuse either in Right or Policy—but still England does not profit of the occasion!! The orders in Council seem still *to be in Favour*—and the late act of Congress is not calculated to make them otherwise. The *Elections*, however, are cheering—and may counteract the Effect of that proceeding.

As Mr. Erving has his Account to settle, with the Secretary of State, as Agent for Claims in this Country, will you suffer me to repeat my Testimony in Favour of his Zeal Industry & ability in the Execution of his Trust on that occasion? I have a sincere and affectionate Regard for Mr. Erving; but I am sure that I am not influenced by my Friendship when I say that there could not have been a more deserving officer. I do not know how far it may be regular or possible to allow his Charge of a Commission on the money that passed through his Hands; but it is certain that he merits it. I thought so formerly when his Services were fresh in my Knowledge.

I send to the Secretary of State the last No. of the Ed. Review. You will find Walsh's pamphlet reviewed in it.[1] The Praise of that most injudicious Book is by Jeffrey—the residue of the article by a young Gentleman of London. Believe me to be—with sincere Respect & Attachment Dear Sir—Your faithful & Ob Servt.

                                                  WM PINKNEY

RC (DLC). Docketed by JM.

1. Robert Walsh, Jr., a Baltimore Federalist, had served as Pinkney's secretary in London, and Pinkney introduced him to JM (Pinkney to JM, 4 May 1809, *PJM-PS*, 1:166–67 and n. 1). In *A Letter on the Genius and Dispositions of the French Government, Including a View of the Taxation of the French Empire* . . . (Baltimore, 1810; Shaw and Shoemaker 21934), Walsh pleaded for American sympathy toward England and insisted that Napoleon was an enemy of the U.S.: "The people of this country he detests and despises" (p. 225). In the lead article of the April *Edinburgh Review*, 16 (1810): 1–30, that journal's Whig editor, Francis Jeffrey, praised the London edition of Walsh's work: "We must all learn to love the Americans, if they send us many such pamphlets as the present." An advocate of Anglo-American reconciliation, Jeffrey acted on his own advice and married an American during a visit to the U.S. in 1813, when he also met JM.

From Jonathan Williams

I took the liberty last fall of submitting to your inspection, as our Patron, Mr Massons Lectures on Fortification which he had presented to the U. S. Mily. Philo: Society.[1] Besides the satisfaction of producing in our own Language the french improvements in this art, I was desirous of knowing whether you thought the Subject worthy of publication and dissemination.

Brigadier General Morton of the New York Artillery,[2] and one of our Members, has since translated an Essay by Mr de L'Espinasse,[3] which displays the late improvements in the use of Artillery in Battle, made during the Campaigns in Italy by the then first Consul of France. This Essay does not I believe exist in the English Language, and it is in my estimation of the highest importance, since it shows in a neat and perspicuous manner the principal Causes of the success that has attended the french Arms. The General is disposed to publish this, under the auspices of the Society, at his own Expence, and if I could have reason to hope that the sale would pay the expence I would publish Mr Massons Lectures with it. These works coming out in conjunction would show, in addition to what has been already published, that our Society is not altogether useless, and to evince this I feel myself strongly stimulated by my zeal for the Institution. I pray you to return the Copy, and if it be attended with your Remarks I shall be highly gratified.

I would not again trouble you on the subject of the Military Academy if it were not to express the regret arising from two circumstances which I formerly intimated to you, and which I think are clearly ascertained, by the repeated failure of every attempt in its favour, to be decided Facts. 1st. Those Members of both Houses of Congress who wish to augment the establishments at Washington are determined to oppose everything relating to the Institution unless its removal to Washington be a preliminary condition. 2d. The opposite party are equally determined to oppose everything relating to the Institution if it be not so absolutely fixed elsewhere, as forever to prevent its removal to that City. This is confirmed by what has been told me by an honourable Senator; "if the Site of the academy be left to the President" (as was proposed in the Bill presented last session) "he will fix it at Washington, and therefore I (of course his party) would oppose it, although I had no other objection to the Bill."[4]

I communicated to the Secretary of War sometime since, a proposition made to me by Governor Tompkins; it was this, To grant to the United States all the state ground on the east side of staaten Island bordering the whole extent of the Narrows and including all the Works that have been erected there, *gratis*, on condition of its being accepted as a site for the

military academy. Taking into view the objects of the Institution, uncon-
nected with any other consideration, I cannot hesitate in saying that I
think this would be an excellent position & the proposed terms of the
grant would operate as a Gift to the Institution of the cost of these Works,
for if the United States would appropriate their value to the Academy
taking the amount from the Fortification Fund there would be an ample
provision for a permanent establishment without (in effect) any expence
whatever: But unfortunately the Legislature of this State[5] will not be in
session 'till February, and Congress must dissolve on the 4th of March.
From these and other considerations I totally dispair of any alteration in
the System that will raise the academy to that State which the honour of
the Nation and the advantage of the Army indisputably require, and convinced as I am that under its present want of necessary Buildings, requisite professors, and almost everything that should constitute a seminary
of military Science, neither Benefit to the public nor honour to myself can
be derived from it, I hope to be permitted to view the present session as
the last in which I shall be required, personally, to superintend this inadequate Establishment.

I think myself bound to express my sentiments thus early that they may
not hereafter appear to be devoid of due reflection; but I beseech you to
be persuaded Sir, that in every way that I can aid the administration and
serve the public, I shall always be ready within the compass of my limited
Talents to testify the warmest Zeal; on the other hand whenever it appears
to my mind impossible to render such services as the end in view indis-
pensibly requires, or to give such satisfaction to the Government and the
public at large as from ostensible circumstances they might reasonably
expect, I shall feel it to be my duty to acquiesce in my inability, rather
than vainly persist in useless Efforts. I have the honour to be With the
greatest deference & Respect Sir Your devoted & obedient servant

JONA WILLIAMS

RC (DNA: RG 107, LRRS, W-101:5); FC (NWM); draft (InU: Jonathan Williams Papers). RC docketed by a War Department clerk as received 20 June 1810, with a notation:
"The Lectures were return'd to Col. Williams on the 25th. of June 1810." FC in a clerk's
hand, corrected by Williams. Draft, dated June 1810, is heavily emended. Minor variations
between the copies have not been noted.

1. Williams to JM, 13 Jan. 1810.
2. Jacob Morton (1761–1836) graduated from the College of New Jersey at Princeton in
1778 and became a Federalist leader in New York City politics. He served as a brigadier
general with the New York militia in the War of 1812 (Richard A. Harrison, *Princetonians,
1776–1783: A Biographical Dictionary* [Princeton, N.J., 1981], pp. 236–39).
3. Augustin de Lespinasse, *Essai sur l'organisation de l'arme de l'artillerie* (Paris, 1800). No
English translation of this work has been found.
4. Williams was most likely referring to Jefferson's 18 Mar. 1808 message to Congress

recommending that the Military Academy be expanded, reformed, and relocated in Washington. These proposals were supported with a report written by Williams on the state of the academy at West Point. A bill implementing Jefferson's recommendations was introduced in the Senate ten days later but then postponed indefinitely, and the matter was not taken up again until JM requested Congress to do so in his annual message on 5 Dec. 1810 (*ASP, Military Affairs*, 1:228–30; *Annals of Congress*, 10th Cong., 1st sess., 176–77, 360–61).

5. The FC and draft here include an additional clause: "whose assent to the Governors proposition is necessary before it can be acted upon by the Government of the U. S."

§ From James Fenner. *13 June 1810, Providence.* Reports that Justice William Cushing will resign from the Supreme Court and suggests Barnabas Bidwell be nominated as his replacement. Bidwell's appointment would "gratify our friends in New England, and afford no cause for censure to our Enemies."

RC (DNA: RG 59, LAR, 1809–17, filed under "Bidwell"). 1 p. Fenner was the Republican governor of Rhode Island, 1807–11.

§ From William Nicholson Jeffers. *13 June 1810, Cincinnati, Ohio.* Circumstances prevented his traveling to France, and a member of Senate has told him the office to which he previously aspired is still vacant. Hopes JM can act while Senate is in recess. Demands from a numerous family require that he find "any office, of Small Emolument."

RC (DNA: RG 59, ML). 1 p.

From Thomas Jefferson

DEAR SIR   MONTICELLO June 14. 10.

Mr. Thweatt[1] my particular friend and connection expecting that an excursion he is to make will put it in his power to pay his respects to you personally, en passant, and being desirous to do so, I with pleasure present him to you as a gentleman of perfect worth, and of sincere zeal in those political principles which you & I have so steadily cultivated. His energy in their support has been often felt by our friends as well as opponents in Petersburg & it's vicinity. I pray you to accept with favor his & my devoirs and to be assured of my constant affection & respect.

TH: JEFFERSON

FC (MHi).

1. Archibald Thweatt married Lucy Eppes, Jefferson's niece and John Wayles Eppes's sister. He served on the Prince George County Republican Committee in 1800 and represented Chesterfield County in the Virginia House of Delegates, 1813–15 and 1816–18 (*VMHB*, 3 [1895–96]: 396; *CVSP*, 9:80; Swem and Williams, *Register*, p. 438).

To Thomas Jefferson

DEAR SIR   WASHINGTON June 15. 1810

The inclosed letters[1] were brought, together with the separate Packet now forwarded, by the John Adams. The official communications received by her, from F. & G. B. you will find in the Natl. Intelligencer of this date.[2] The Editor I perceive passes over the obnoxious refusal of G. B. to comply with the reasonable course of putting an end to the predatory Edicts of both Nations; and it is not improbable that a like sensibility to the atrocity of the F. Govt. may divert the public attention from what would otherwise strike it with due force.[3]

RC (DLC). Incomplete (see n. 3). Docketed by Jefferson, "recd June 17."

1. JM enclosed Lafayette to Jefferson, 18 Nov. 1809 and 24 Mar. 1810, and Lafayette's "Compte rendu" (DLC: Jefferson Papers; printed in Chinard, *Letters of Lafayette and Jefferson*, pp. 293–96, 302–3, 303–15), which Lafayette had sent in his 24 Mar. 1810 letter to JM (see also Jefferson's Epistolary Record [DLC: Jefferson Papers]).

2. The *National Intelligencer* 14 June supplement and 15 June issue contained correspondence between Pinkney and Wellesley, Armstrong and Champagny, and other letters from London and Paris dated from 25 Jan. to 15 Apr. (partially printed in *ASP, Foreign Relations*, 3:349–57). Those letters, commented the editor, Samuel Harrison Smith, "add little to the information previously received" and dashed the hope that the *John Adams* would not return "with such unwelcome intelligence. But even that hope is now dissipated; and nothing remains but the manifestation of the naked purpose of the French government to pursue what it considers its line of interest, without regarding our interests or rights."

3. Paragraph ends here. Lower part of page has been clipped.

From Edmund Randolph

MY DEAR SIR   RICHMOND June 15. 1810.

This is the first letter, which I have written, since my convalescence after the dreadful attack from a hemiplegia, with which by a kind of sympathy with my poor wife,[1] I was afflicted in a few weeks from her death. It happily affected no faculty of my mind, and has not taken away the sanguine hope, that altho' I require in rough ground the aid of a crutch, I may be restored to the free use of my legs.

I write now, in reference to my friend the Governor. Judge Griffin is so much reduced by a longstanding disease, and seems so little able to resist a great flux of blood, which seized him about a week ago, that I cannot forbear indulging my friendship for Mr Tyler by saying to you, that he was long conversant in the admiralty practice, and I have from a review of his situation, after the expiration of his triennium presumed, that it would be grateful to him even now to return to the bench.

I have been urged by my children to restrict my future practice at the bar to a smaller compass than heretofore, from a belief, that I ought to rest from promiscuous professional labour. To their advice I shall submit, and pursue the gratification of my literary appetite[2] at the loss of a flattering income. Under all circumstances, I shall pray for your happiness and fame; being my dear sir your affectionate friend

EDM: RANDOLPH

RC (DLC).

1. Elizabeth Nicholas Randolph died on 6 Mar. She suffered a stroke in October 1809 that left her partially paralyzed (John J. Reardon, *Edmund Randolph: A Biography* [New York, 1974], p. 360).

2. Randolph was writing a history of Virginia. Never published in his lifetime, his manuscript was later destroyed by fire. The history is known only from an incomplete copy (Edmund Randolph, *History of Virginia*, ed. Arthur H. Shaffer [Charlottesville, Va., 1970], pp. xxxvii-xlix).

¶ To James Leander Cathcart. Letter not found. *15 June 1810*. Acknowledged in Cathcart to JM, 13 Aug. 1810. Orders wine.

¶ To Anthony Charles Cazenove. Letter not found. *15 June 1810*. Acknowledged in Cazenove to JM, 19 June 1810. Orders wine and transmits an enclosure to be forwarded to James Leander Cathcart in Madeira.

From Samuel Carswell

SIR,　　　　　　　　　　　　　　　　　PHILADA. June 16th. 1810

In consequence of a conversation that lately passed, betwixt the post-Master of this place, (Mr. Patton) & myself, I take the liberty, of addressing you at the present time. He says he is fearful, that a late Law of Congress, will compel him, to keep the post-Office open, on the Sabbath.[1]

The necessity of enforceing the Law, & the consequences that will result therefrom, are what I purpose to submit to your consideration.

I am well convinced, that but a very small portion of the community, desire it, & they must necessarily be the less moral, & consequently, less respectable part of Society. They certainly are not more industrious, nor more pressed with business, than their fellow Citizens; the same portion of time, then, that is alloted to the one, to discharge the common occupations of life, will serve the other. I hope & think that a majority against the measure, proportionably large, with that in this District, prevails throughout the Union. Were the contrary the case, that reason would not justify it. I confess that I am not so zealous a republican, as to advocate an evil, because it is approved by a majority of opinions, or to suppose, that the approbation of the majority, will change its nature.

I am sorry, that Congress should have passed such a Law, as it is an absolute infraction, of one of the links, in the chain that unites & renders society happy. It is hard to expect virtue in a people, when those who are selected for the guardians of virtue, shew so great a disregard, for it. They did not consider, that a man, *worthy* of the Office, would consider it, an insuperable objection. Honest men, who will accept of public trusts, are sufficiently scarce, without raising obstacles, that will keep them back. Should the Law be enforced, it is the purpose of Mr. Patton, to retire from the office, which will be, an irreparable loss, to the mercantile Interest of this place, as he has discharged his duty, with the greatest ability & fidelity. In such a case, from his long & well established character, I would recommend him, as a very suitable person, to fill the Office, of Surveyor of this port. But I hope it will not be necessary for him, to leave his present situation, as he can be much more useful in *it*. With Sentiments of the greatest esteem I am Your ob Hble St

SAML CARSWELL

RC (DLC). Docketed by JM.

1. On 30 Apr. JM signed the Post Office Act, which required postmasters "at all reasonable hours, on every day of the week, to deliver, on demand, any letter, paper or packet, to the person entitled to or authorized to receive the same." Despite prolonged objections on religious grounds, Sunday postal service survived for more than a century, until Progressive labor legislation terminated it in 1912 (*U.S. Statutes at Large*, 2:595, 604; John R. Bodo, *The Protestant Clergy and Public Issues, 1812–1848* [Princeton, N.J., 1954], pp. 39–43; Clyde Kelly, *United States Postal Policy* [New York, 1931], p. 201).

From David Bailie Warden

SIR,   PARIS, 16 June, 1810.

I have the honor of sending you copies of some of my memoirs in defense of american vessels and cargoes. A considerable number of american Cases still remain to be adjudged by the Council of Prizes. As there is no Agent to represent them, I think it is my duty to make a defence. I trust that my zeal and industry in this business, and in the discharge of my Consular duties will meet your approbation and that you will be pleased to continue me in office.[1] It would be fortunate indeed to be protected by a President whose talents and patriotism I so highly venerate, and to whose administration I feel so strongly attached. I am, Sir, with great respect, Your very obedient and very humble Servant

DAVID BAILIE WARDEN.

RC (DLC); letterbook copy (MdHi: Warden Papers). Enclosures not found.

1. Warden continued his quest for a permanent consular appointment until JM acquiesced and nominated him for the post on 1 Mar. 1811 (*Senate Exec. Proceedings*, 2:173).

¶ To William Jarvis. Letters not found. *17 June 1810* (two letters). Acknowledged in Jarvis to JM, 26 Aug. 1810. Expresses his gratitude on the receipt of the merinos sent by Jarvis and discusses the arrangements for the disposition of the lamb born since their arrival (see JM to Jefferson, 2 July 1810). Also places an order for old wine.

From Thomas Boylston Adams

SIR.   QUINCY June 18th. 1810.

Since the departure of my Brother, Mr. John Q Adams, upon his Mission to Russia, and while he was yet at sea, I had the pleasure to receive from him a list of names, comprizing the circle of his particular friends to whom he requested I would present, in his name, and as a small token of his respect, a set of Lectures on Rhetorick & Oratory, delivered during the period of his Professorship at Harvard University.[1] I have the honor, at this late hour, of complying with the injunctions of my Brother, when I transmit to The President of the United States, and ask his acceptance of a copy of these Lectures. Unforeseen delays have prevented an earlier discharge of this duty. I have the honor to be, very respectfully, Your Obedient Servant

THOMAS BOYLSTON ADAMS.[2]

RC (DLC).

1. John Quincy Adams, *Lectures on Rhetoric and Oratory, Delivered to the Classes of Senior and Junior Sophisters in Harvard University* (2 vols.; Cambridge, Mass., 1810; Shaw and Shoemaker 19304).

2. Thomas Boylston Adams (1772–1832) graduated from Harvard in 1790 and served as chargé d'affaires at The Hague and secretary of legation at Berlin, circa 1795–99, when his brother, John Quincy Adams, was U.S. minister in those capitals. He practiced law in Philadelphia, settled in Quincy, Massachusetts, by 1806, and later served as a judge of the court of common pleas in Norfolk County (Joseph Jerry Perling, *Presidents' Sons: The Prestige of Name in a Democracy* [New York, 1947], pp. 25–29).

From Tench Coxe

SIR   PHILADELPHIA June 18 1810

It would be a matter of surprize to you, if you were to learn that any person, who ever felt a solicitude for the public happiness & safety, were easy in the recent state of our foreign affairs. The provision in the treaty* between France & Holland,[1] the complicated but consolidated power of France in Germany, which far exceeds that of the imperial & electoral family of Austria, at any period, the general progress and consolidation of the French power, and all the circumstances of the times, bring to my mind a paper I had the honor to submit to the late President upon the dangers to our country from abroad and the strength with which those dangers admonished us to arm our whole free population. The date, I think on memory, was about the month of April 1807.[2] The enclosed paper I beg leave to submit, as bearing upon the same Subject—particularly the last paragraph.[3]

I am deeply sorry to perceive that our affairs have issued, with France in the way I have feared. Alternately alarmed for her safety and extravagant in success, always irritable in her councils, & irregular also from the unsettled nature of her various governments during twenty eventful years, she has gone into one energetic or hasty step and another till the kingdoms of the old world are nearly all sent from their foundations and our Situation has become painful, in various views, suffering in extreme and full of danger.

To insure the prevention of vital evils is the first object. The general armament of the country has long appeared to me the great & *only* means. The resistance of the Blacks of St. Domingo is a proof of power of an armed people, however rude and ignorant. Spain has stood longer on that ground than Austria or Prussia.

Permit me, Sir, to ask your perusal of the paper of 1807, to which I have refer'd, and your consideration of its suggestions in connexion with the present time.

It will not render things better between us, that the Marquis of Wellesley has conceded the question of the right to retaliate, in his recent correspondence with Mr. Pinckney. I have the honor to be, Sir your most respectful h. Servt.

TENCH COXE

* dismembring the Dutch Country on the avowed ground of a rule drawn from *the French constitution.*

RC and enclosure (DLC). For enclosure, see n. 3.

1. See John Armstrong to JM, 18 Mar. 1810, n. 7.

2. In his letter to Jefferson of January 1807 (received 24 Jan.), Coxe enclosed his essay "Opinion on Arming the Militia for Defense" (DLC: Jefferson Papers; see also Cooke, *Tench Coxe*, pp. 430–31 n. 38).

3. Coxe enclosed a clipping of an essay entitled "The Public Safety," which appeared under the signature "Z" in the Philadelphia *Democratic Press* on 18 June 1810. The essay advocated the diversification of the American economy and stressed that the public defense required a "universal militia, armed and embodied." The last paragraph, marked in ink, argued that for the cost of eighteen ships of the line and eighteen frigates, the U.S. could purchase enough cannon, muskets, and rifles to arm every man and militia unit in the nation. The article is now in JM's portfolio of newspaper clippings (DLC, series 7, container 3).

From Wilson Cary Nicholas

My Dear Sir   Warren June 19. 1810

When I was in Richmond lately, it was said Judge Griffin, wou'd probably, never be able to take his seat on the bench again. Will you pardon me if I take the liberty to place before you the name of a Gentn. as his successor, with whom you are as well acquainted as I am? I am far from expecting or wishing more than that, his fitness for the office, shou'd be decided by a comparison with others who may be thought of or proposed to you. Mr. Peter Carr is the person I mean. His capacity, his improvement, honor & independence are known to you. Mr. Carr was bred a lawyer and obtained a licence to practice which he did for a short time. Whether he has law learning enough to satisfy the public expectation I doubt. For myself I had rather be judged by such a man than a mere lawyer. In this case I beg you to be assured it is my sincere wish, you shou'd do, not only what will best promote the public interest, but that such an appointment shou'd be made as will give the most general satisfaction. My writing to you upon this subject shall not be known to Mr. Carr or any other person, but yourself. I am perfectly convinced it wou'd give you pleasure to give him this office, if you believe him qualified for it. If you believe any other person wou'd better serve the public, of course that person will and ought to be nominated by you. No consideration of personal friendship cou'd ever induce me to wish you to do an act that wou'd either give discontent, or in any manner discredit an administration, that I most anxiously wish shou'd in all things do honor to you, and be most useful to the public. I am with the greatest respect Dear Sir Your hum. Servt.

                                                          W. C. Nicholas

RC (DLC: Rives Collection, Madison Papers). Docketed by JM.

From William Short

DEAR SIR　　　　　　　　　　　　　　　LIVERPOOL June 19—10

I have already acknowleged & thanked you for your favor of　　[1] recieved in France. I came to this country with the intention of embarking
in the April packet from Falmouth. I was dissuaded from this, & have
since been disappointed in the vessel I expected from hence whither I
came to embark. I am now waiting for the return of a Ship which is recommended to me as a peculiarly good one. In the mean time Mr Erving
intending to sail in a small despatch vessel which goes in a day or two &
purposing to wait on you immediately on his arrival, I have thought it best
to transfer to his care two letters for you which Dr. Logan committed to
mine in London. You will find them here inclosed.[2] When I received them
I had hopes of being in America before this time. I shall regret the delay
those letters have met with if it should occasion any inconvenience to the
writer or to yourself. I take the liberty of putting under your cover ⟨a
letter⟩ for our mutual friend[3] which I ask the favor of you to forward to
him—& to believe me your very obedt. servt.

W: SHORT

RC (DLC).

1. Short here left a blank space but referred to JM's 3 Dec. 1809 letter to him, which he
had acknowledged in his 7 Feb. 1810 letter to JM.

2. One of the letters that Short gave to George W. Erving was George Logan to JM,
6 May 1810.

3. Short to Jefferson, 19 June 1810 (MHi), which JM forwarded in his 15 Aug. 1810
letter to Jefferson (see also Jefferson's Epistolary Record [DLC: Jefferson Papers]).

§ From Anthony Charles Cazenove. *19 June 1810, Alexandria*. Acknowledges JM's
15 June letter ordering a pipe of Messrs. Murdoch's best wine, which with the
enclosure for James Leander Cathcart will be forwarded to Madeira by a vessel
sailing at the end of the week.

RC (DLC). 1 p.

From John Dawson

DEAR SIR　　　　　　　　　　　　FREDERICKSBURG. June 20. 1810.

It is reported that congress will be convend during the summer.[1] I will
thank you for information on this point, thereby to govern my summer
movements, as well as upon any other. With much Esteem Your friend

J DAWSON.

RC (DLC).

1. Several newspapers printed a report to this effect. The source of the story was given as the N.Y. *Evening Post*, which made the claim shortly after the frigate *John Adams* returned to the U.S. with the latest news from Europe (see *Alexandria Daily Gazette*, 20 June 1810).

§ From Robert Gilman and Others. *21 June 1810, Baltimore.* Petition of Baltimore merchants recommends Robert K. Lowry as a fit person to be sent to Caracas as a consul or commercial agent.

RC (DNA: RG 59, LAR, 1809–17, filed under "Lowry"). 1 p. Signed by Gilman and eight others, including James Calhoun, Thomas Hollins, Isaac McKim, James Purviance, and "S Smith & Buchanan."

To Thomas Jefferson

DEAR SIR   WASHINGTON June 22. 1810

I inclose an authentication of the blood of our Merinos, as translated from the Original by Mr. Graham: also a state of the charges incident to their passages &c. The half falling to your share, of course, may be left for any convenient occasion of being replaced. You need not trouble yourself to remit it hither.

On the first publication of the dispatches by the J. Adams, so strong a feeling was produced by Armstrong's picture of the French robbery, that the attitude in which England was placed by the correspondence between P. & Wellesley was overlooked. The public attention is beginning to fix itself on the proof it affords that the original sin agst. Neutrals lies with G. B. & that whilst she acknowledges it, she persists in it.

I am preparing for a departure from this place immediately after the 4th. July. Having been deprived of the Spring visit to My Farm, I wish to commence the sooner the fall recess. Be assured of my highest & most Affee. esteem

JAMES MADISON

Have you recd. a Copy of Coopers (the Pena. Judge) masterly opinion on the question whether the sentence of a foreign Admiralty court in a prize Cause, be conclusive evidence in a Suit here between the Underwriter & Insured. It is a most *thorough*, investigation, and irrefragable disproof, of the B. Doctrine on the subject, as adopted by a decision of the Supreme Court of the U. S.? If you are without a Copy I will provide & forward one.[1]

RC and first enclosure (DLC); second enclosure (DLC: Jefferson Papers). RC docketed by Jefferson, "recd June 24." First enclosure (2 pp.) is John Graham's translation of a notarized certificate of the bloodlines of forty merino rams and twenty-six ewes, signed by Celestino de Cordova and attested by Placido Lorenzo Gonzales de Valcarcel, 28 Dec. 1809, at Badajoz; docketed by Jefferson, "Merino Sheep. (authenticated &c)." For second enclosure, see Account with Joseph Dougherty, ca. 7 May 1810.

1. Jefferson did receive a copy of Thomas Cooper's dissent in *Dempsey* v. *Insurance Company of Pennsylvania*, published in pamphlet form by Alexander J. Dallas in 1810. Cooper, sitting on the Pennsylvania Court of Errors and Appeals, had argued against the doctrine adopted in 1808 by the U.S. Supreme Court in *Croudson et al.* v. *Leonard*, which accepted the ruling of a Barbados vice-admiralty court that the American brig *Fame* had attempted to breach the British blockade of Martinique and thus became a lawful prize (*The Opinion of Judge Cooper, on the Effect of a Sentence, of a Foreign Court of Admiralty* [Philadelphia, 1810; Shaw and Shoemaker 19858]; Dumas Malone, *The Public Life of Thomas Cooper, 1783–1839* [New Haven, 1926], pp. 195–97).

From George Hite

SIR   CHAS. TOWN June 22nd 1810

As I enclosed you the extract of Mr. Pickering's letter to his friend, I thought it best to enclose you the justification.[1] I have been prevented from preparing it sooner in consequence of my absence from home, & an unavoidable attention to my own business. That health & happiness may await you is the wish of your Friend

GEO HITE

RC (DLC). Enclosure not found.

1. No letter from Hite to JM enclosing such an extract has been found. He apparently sent JM a newspaper clipping related to the 1810 controversy involving charges that Timothy Pickering had used public funds "for the laudable purpose of accommodating his federal friends, and furthering the federal elections to the eastward—*which money is not accounted for*." These charges were made in a handbill that had circulated throughout New York during the April elections. Federalist congressman James Emott of Poughkeepsie asked Pickering to respond, and the *Poughkeepsie Journal* subsequently published copies of the handbill as well as copies of the correspondence between Pickering and Emott and between Pickering and treasury secretary Gallatin and treasury comptroller Duvall to show that Pickering's accounts with the State Department were in order (Gerard H. Clarfield, *Timothy Pickering and the American Republic* [Pittsburgh, 1980], p. 244; Octavius Pickering and Charles W. Upham, eds., *The Life of Timothy Pickering* [4 vols.; Boston, 1867–73], 4:162–68).

From Robert Smith

Saturday [23 June 1810?]

Mr Lowry is a good Republican, of unblemished Character—understands the French & Spanish languages—a regular bred Merchant—about 30 years of age—his talents good.

R SMITH

RC (DLC). In pencil. Addressed to "The President." Dated 1809 in the *Index to the James Madison Papers*. Conjectural date assigned on the basis that Lowry probably traveled to Washington after 21 June and evidently had left the capital to make arrangements to go to Venezuela by the first week in July (see Robert Gilman and others to JM, 21 June 1810; JM to Robert Smith, 17 July 1810, and nn. 2, 3).

From Fontaine Maury

DEAR SIR FREDERICKSBURG 25 June 1810

Having good reasons to believe that unfair, and unfounded, representations have, or will be made to the Executive, with a view to injure the reputation of my Brother James in his Official Character, I take the Liberty to address you on that Subject, and to request you to Suspend any Opinion thereon, untill time can be given for investigation, which I am persuaded will terminate honorably to the accused, and Satisfactorily to yourself. I pray you to excuse the Liberty I have taken, and to be assured that nothing Short of a Conviction of innocence on the one part, and interested views on the other, would have induced me to trouble you on a Subject of this Sort. With Sentiments of high Esteem I have the honor to remain Your Mo Obt st

FONTAINE MAURY[1]

RC (DLC); FC (ViU: Maury Family Papers). FC written on the verso of a copy of Richard Forrest to Fontaine Maury, 5 June 1810, which warned that "great efforts are making to injure [James Maury's] well earned Reputation as a Public Officer, and altho' our worthy President is not of a Character to abandon a Man on Slight Grounds, yet it May not be amiss for you and your Brother to know of the Efforts that have been made and that are Still making to injure him."

1. Fontaine Maury (1761–1824) managed the Fredericksburg end of the family importing business until 1801. Thereafter he appears to have been engaged in a variety of business and commission activities. His brother James had been appointed U.S. consul at Liverpool in 1790 (*PJM*, 12:88 n. 2; *PJM-SS*, 1:192, 224; Fontaine Maury to JM, 1 June 1802 [DLC]).

§ From Aaron H. Palmer. *25 June 1810, New York.* Encloses a letter and a parcel for Dolley Madison.

RC (DLC). 1 p. Enclosures not found.

From Samuel R. Trevett and Others

SIR [ca. 26 June 1810]

Under a full impression of the impropriety of trespassing on the valuable time of your Excy. & aware that it too frequently happens you are troubled with trivial applications we hope you will pardon us while we briefly state to you the reasons which have induced us to adopt the resolutions, a Copy of which we have now the honor to enclose.

It cannot have escaped the knowledge of your Excellency how very unpleasant a situation property to a large amount (belonging to Citizens of the U:S) has been placed in by the late edicts of some of the Governments of Europe and we feel the fullest confidence no one more than your Excy. would wish the interest of real Americans to be properly represented in these troublesome and unsettled times when every day produces some important change.

From such information as we have collected it appears that R. G. Gardner Esqe.[1] the person last known to our government as Consul for this Port, died about Six Years past and that since then a Mr. Erth who we beleive was authorised by Mr. Gardner, officiated for some time, on the death of Mr. Erth Mr. R. Dickson[2] the subject of the resolutions submitted to your Excy. took possession of the Seal of the Consulate & has without a shadow of authority as he himself acknowledges continued to grant the customary Certificates as acting Consul for the United States.

We do not wish to trouble your Excellency with all the circumstances within our knowledge which have induced us to adopt these resolutions. We presume the circumstances of Mr. Dickson being a subject of the King of Great Britain and the acknowledged Agent for the Governor of the Island of Anholt now in possession of the British will convince you of the propriety of our proceedings and form an apology for our thus trespassing on your time.

We take the liberty under all those circumstances, and at a time when the property of the honest & real American is Jeopardized by the number of false papers (which is, particularly in this quarter unfortunately too great) to request that if it meet your approbation you will be pleased to appoint some proper person to the office of Consul for this Port, that the interest of so large a body of your fellow Citizens as are now here (& the number likely to encrease) may be properly represented. With sentiments of respect we beg leave to subscribe ourselves your friends and fellow Citizens. *Signed*

SAML. R. TREVETT

[and forty-seven others]

[Enclosure]

Port of Gothenburg

At an adjourned Meeting of American Gentlemen held at the house of Mr. Tod June 26th. 1810, the following Resolutions were adopted.

1st. Resolved, that this Meeting neither collectively or individually will give any sanction to Mr. Robert Dickson for acting as American Consul.

2nd. Resolved, that in all cases where consular certificates of an Agent regularly appointed ought to be taken, We will not apply to Mr. Dickson for any such documents, but will adopt the measures pointed out by the laws of the United States in cases like the present where no Consul has been appointed.

3rd. Resolved, that as in measures of this nature it is of the utmost importance not only that they should be adopted with prudence & caution but that it appear on their face they have been submitted to the consideration of a large majority of the American Interest, That three Copies of these Resolutions be made out signed by each individual, one Copy Sent to Mr. Dickson, one to the Government here & one to our own government. Signed

SAML. R. TREVETT

[and forty-six others]

RC and enclosure (DNA: RG 59, LAR, 1809–17, filed under "Dickson"). Both marked duplicate; in a clerk's hand. On a separate half sheet, JM wrote in pencil: "Besides disarming this usurper, some penal animadversion ought to make an example of him. If his offence be such as is made public, a prosecution would, doubtless, lie agst. him under the Sweedish laws, and the aid of the Govt. might be asked, as was done in the case of the fabricated documents in G. B. If there be a Consul in Sweeden, he may be instructed on the subject. If there be none, an appointment becomes proper. The diplomatic channels at Petersburg & Paris are also open to the Sweedish Govt. ⟨If?⟩ the offender be a public agent under British Govt. that also ought to co-operate in punishing so scandolous & pestilent an outrage."

1. Robert C. Gardner had been nominated by Jefferson to be consul at Gothenburg on 27 Apr. 1802 (*Senate Exec. Proceedings*, 1:422–23).

2. Trevett's concern about Dickson had been conveyed to Robert Smith by a mercantile firm in Boston in February 1810. It is not clear if either JM or Smith took any action at that time, but the receipt of Trevett's letter may have prompted the announcement in the *National Intelligencer* on 31 Aug. 1810 that Dickson had usurped the functions of the consul's office in Gothenburg and was acting as an agent for the governor of Anholt in privateering schemes (James D. Harris to Robert Smith, 21 Feb. 1810 [DNA: RG 59, ML]).

§ From Charles Haumont. *26 June 1810, Sapelo Island.* Apologizes for troubling JM again about his manuscript, which he fears has been lost. Mentions that he heard about three weeks ago that there was a letter addressed to him from JM [not found] in the post office in McIntosh County. Begs JM to instruct the postmaster general to locate the manuscript and forward it to Charles Harris at Savannah.

RC and translation (DNA: RG 59, ML). RC 2 pp., written in French. Translation 2 pp., in Haumont's hand.

From Thomas Jefferson

Dear Sir   Monticello June 27. 10.

Your letters of the 8th. 15th. & 22d. are now to be acknoleged. I should consider the debt to mr. Hooe as made incumbent on us by the wish of our Donor, and shall chearfully acquiesce in any arrangement you make on that subject. I have accordingly suspended sending for my portion till further information from you. Dougherty's bill shall be duly attended to. I have recieved a copy of Judge Cooper's opinion but have not yet read it. I shall do it with pleasure because I am sure it is able. There is not a stronger head in the US. than his. I hardly know whether I ought to trouble you with reading such a letter as the inclosed. The last half page is all that is material for you. The rest is an account of the country of Oppalousa. I know nothing of the writer, & take no interest in his application.[1] Our sufferings from drought have been extreme. The rains of the last month were but 2. I. and of this month the same, till the one now falling which has already given us 6/10 and promises more, perhaps too much, for we had just begun our harvest. If not injured by rain it will generally be as fine a one as we have ever seen. Corn, tho' lower than ever known, has still time to yield a good crop. This rain will enable every one to pitch his tobo. crop. It's result must depend on the length of the fall as well as the intermediate seasons. It is very unpromising at present. The present rain is too late for the oats. Very little will be high enough to cut. At length Gr. Br. has been forced to pull off her mask and shew that her real object is the exclusive use of the ocean. Her good sense is overruled by her avarice, & that of Bonaparte by his own haughty & tyrannical temper. A return to embargo could alone save us. Always yours affectionately

Th: Jefferson

Be so good as to return the inclosed.

RC (DLC); FC (DLC: Jefferson Papers). Postscript not on FC.

1. Jefferson evidently enclosed a 6 May letter to him (not found) from William Garrard at "Appelousas," which he recorded as having been received on 10 June (Jefferson's Epistolary Record [DLC: Jefferson Papers]).

§ From "Cassius." *29 June 1810*. Declares he is a friend to JM and the administration but fears that JM's confidence has been abused by "a set of political earwigs." Criticizes JM's appointments of Buckner Thruston and Benjamin Howard on the grounds that it is wrong for the executive to remove men from Congress by naming them to office. The executive should respect the separation of powers and not touch men in their "legislative character." Congressmen distracted from their legislative duties by the prospect of appointments "cease to be the agents of the people" and become "the Tools of the Executive." Points to the example of the British House of Commons, where members are corrupted by ministerial "bribes and pensions and offices." Does not mean to insinuate that JM has corrupt motives but warns that dangerous precedents are being set.

Printed copy (Richmond *Enquirer*, 29 June 1810).

¶ To David Gelston. Letter not found. *29 June 1810*. Acknowledged in Gelston to JM, 11 July 1810. Sends $20 to cover various expenses and forwards a box of hams for Robert R. Livingston.

From John Bassette

DEAR SIR,   [ca. 1 July 1810]

At the instance of the Honorable Stephen Van Rensselaer[1] and several individuals of the New York Historical Society, I have been induced to undertake, and have now compleated the Translation of Dr Van Der Donk's *Natural* and *Topographical* History of New-Netherland.[2] As that gentleman comprehends under the appellation of New-Netherland, the States, lying between the great South and North rivers, and consequently bounds that Country on Virginia.

I have therefore entertained thoughts of adding by way of an appendix a Translation of De Laet's History of the originall Discoveries and settlements of the last mentioned Colony.[3]

The object of this Letter is, to beg the favor of you to inform me by post, whether the Virginians are in possession of any Dutch accounts relative to their Country; if so, it may be unnecessary to trouble myself or the Public with a Translation of De Laet. Being unacquainted with any gentleman in the Southern States who could give me any information on the subject; I hope it will not be considered as arrogant in me to request it from him, whom God has elevated to the most conspicuous and honorable station in our Country; and who being a native of Virginia, is best qualified to Answer me Satisfactor⟨ily⟩ on this head.

A line addressed to John Bassette DD. late a Minister of the reformed Dutch Church in Albany, will be gratefully acknowledged. I am with highest sentiments of respect, your very humble Servant.

JOHN BASSET⟨TE⟩ [4]

RC (DLC). Undated. Conjectural date assigned on basis of contents of JM to Jefferson, 7 July 1810, and Jefferson to JM, 13 July 1810. Docketed by JM.

1. Stephen Van Rensselaer (1764–1839), eighth patroon of the Van Rensselaer family estates, was much respected for his devotion to agricultural, educational, and philanthropic causes in New York. As a New York Federalist leader and militia general, however, his public career was often controversial. He commanded the American forces during the unsuccessful invasion of Canada at the Battle of Queenstown Heights in October 1812, and he later served in the House of Representatives between 1822 and 1829. In 1825 he cast one of the crucial votes in the House election that made John Quincy Adams president (Harrison, *Princetonians, 1776–1783*, pp. 379–88).

2. Adriaen van der Donck, *Beschryvinge van Nieuvv-Nederlant . . . begrijpende de nature, aert, gelegentheyt en vrucht-baerheyt van het selve land* (2d ed.; Amsterdam, 1656), later translated as "Description of the New Netherlands" (*Collections of the New-York Historical Society*, 2d ser., 1 [1841]: 125–242). The preface (p. 128) to this translation mentioned that a text had been prepared by Bassette many years earlier but had not been published for want of funds. The translation published in 1841 was made by Jeremiah Johnson.

3. Joannes de Laet, *Nieuwe wereldt, ofte Beschryvinghe van West Indien* (Leyden, 1625), later translated as "Extracts from the New World; or, A Description of the West Indies" (*Collections of the New-York Historical Society*, 2d ser., 1 [1841]: 281–316). From the editorial note accompanying this publication (pp. 287–88), it is evident that Bassette was not responsible for the translation of the text.

4. John Bassette (or Bassett) (1764–1824), a graduate of the colleges of Columbia, Yale, and Williams, had been a minister in Albany between 1787 and 1804. After 1804 he taught theology at the New Brunswick Theological Seminary, and from 1811 to his death he served as minister to the congregation at Gravesend and Bushwick, New York (Peter N. Vanden-Berge, ed., *Historical Directory of the Reformed Church in America, 1628–1978* [Grand Rapids, 1978], pp. 7–8).

To Thomas Jefferson

DEAR SIR   WASHINGTON July 2. 1810

I have recd. your favor of the 27th. by which I find you have suspended the sending for your portion of the Merinos. I have not yet come to an eclaircissemt. with Mr. Hooe. I learn however that a reexamination of the tenor of Mr. J's letter to him, has induced an abandonment of his pretensions to the Lamb. Still I am rather inclined to think that they are not altogether without foundation; & have written to Mr. Jarvis in terms not inconsistent with that idea. As the Lamb whether it remain with us, or fall to the lot of Mr. H. must be kept with the Ewe for a considerable time, would it not be best for a division to be made at once, as doubling the security of the germ agst. casualties. A single day, whilst they are all together, might put an end to it. To whichever of us the Ewe having the lamb might fall the lamb might remain a common property, if not finally delivered over to Mr. H. As it has not been proved that the other Ewe may not be barren, it may be understood if you do not object, that in that event, the first Ewe lamb from the other, shall make up for the defect. We have had latterly favorable rains here. They are too late however for Oats not in moist or rich lands. The Wheat harvest will be good in this quarter. In N. Y. it will be very scanty; very moderate in Pena. & on the Eastern shore of Maryland the drought & H. fly, have in a manner destroyed the crop. Yrs. as always

JAMES MADISON

The return of Guarrants letter in my next.

RC (DLC). Docketed by Jefferson, "recd July 5."

From William Bentley

SIR,   SALEM, July 2. 1810. MASS USA.

Your approbation is among my highest pleasures, especially of my actions, which are in the fullest consent with my purest convictions, & with assurances of the best consequences.

Having lately had an interview with Gen. Stark, at his home in Derryfield, I thought it would not be displeasing to you to hear from him. I reached his house on 31 May, after having spent the morning with Col Thornton,[1] & having visited the monument of his Father, who signed the declaration of our Independance. He died at Merrimac in 1803, aged 89 years. Upon the Stone opposite to the House is written "The Honest Man.["] I found Gen. Stark at home, & in his usual good humour after political events which please him. He repeated with the fondness of age, his War stories. He was very free in his sarcasms upon the prevailing Superstition, in which he included every thing in religion, not practical, & hoped his Chaplain, as he called me, was not addicted to it. He had read Paine & Palmer,[2] but his independant mind had gathered little from the history of Religion, tho' much from his own good habits. His historical researches are few, & often careless, but he spends the enthusiasm of a strong mind upon Virtue & Patriotism, & he feels the Roman definitions, without having heard of them. His conversation has not refinement, but deep interest. Said he "I flatter no man, I dare not flatter myself. And he who attempts to flatter me disputes with me. And I have as much pride in my opinions as any man. For they are the heart & soul of me.["] Besides the Scetches of him from his Son in Law, Capt Stickney, the Major, Caleb Stark, intends a history of Gen Stark after his decease, should he survive his Father. The Major is a Merchant, in Boston, & a man of accomplished manner & good understanding. The Gen. observing upon the Embargo, & the resistance of the Merchants, to whose habits he has no indulgence from inclination, or his manner of life, observed "The Worst Embargo upon our Country would be upon our plows & our spinning wheels. We should have no Embargo at home. We should dispise to give any nation any advantage over us from anything; it could possess. A Free people will never think themselves dependant upon any other people for any thing. They will exchange, but not purchase—they will be the better by it, or not have it at all.["]

I have always wished to obtain a portrait of my Hero. And being told that he would refuse the liberty of taking it, at a former visit, I asked his leave, & told him what I had heard. He replied "I would not give a penny for it, but if it can please a friend, he shall have it.["] I carried with me a female pupil, who took it with her pencil, during our conversation; but she observed to me afterwards, "Sir, he kept you upon the roar, but I never caught one smile from himself. I saw eve[r]y other emotion, a tell tale!" This young female is a Cousin of Mr Crowninshield, who died at Washington. Mr Jefferson accepted some early proofs of her talents. The Original is as large as life, & is known by all the friends of the General among us. A Copy of the size inclosed has been sent to the General. The Original, in red chalk, is to be engraved, & painted in oil.

I carried, from the pen of my pupil, a Map of Massachusetts addressed to the General, & a figure of the Atele[3] Belzebuth.

under this mischievous Monkey was written,

"The British Agent, or the Climbing Monkey caught by the Tail."

The General had before left with me some emblems of our political Characters & Affairs, which I had promised, at some future time, to display in his own humour. He has all the Accent of his Ancestors, who are described by Belnap,[4] & as if he was immediately from their native country. He expresses all the warmth of his Soul, upon the President of the United States. He cannot dissemble.

Sir,

I have repeatedly sent to Philadelphia, to my Bookseller for Bp. Madison's Map of Virginia.[5] He says he believes, it is not published, as it is not in that City. I have had repeated notices from the most worthy Bishop, but dare not send to him, lest It might be supposed that I sent to the Author, & intended a tax upon his generosity. I want it for a Foreigner, A man of Letters, who is able & willing to pay for it. I wish to know how to obtain it.

A literary friend informs me that he has had repeated interviews with Mr Burr at Hamburg. That not a word had passed upon his affairs in America, but that he had displayed a rich knowledge of the progress & of the resources of our Country. With the Greatest respect of your public & private virtues, & of your preeminent qualifications for the highest honours of my Country, Sir your devoted Servant,

WILLIAM BENTLEY.

RC (DLC). Enclosed drawing not found.

1. Col. James Thornton was the son of Dr. Matthew Thornton, a delegate to the Continental Congress who did not reach Philadelphia until November 1776 but achieved immortality as a late "signer."

2. Elihu Palmer (1764–1806), president of the Theistical Society of New York, was the author of several deistical tracts, including *Principles of Nature* and *Prospect; or, View of the Moral World* (Sowerby, *Catalogue of Jefferson's Library*, 2:179, 5:333–34).

3. Atel: foul, terrible (*OED*).

4. Stark's life and times were traced throughout Jeremy Belknap's *The History of New-Hampshire* (3 vols.; Philadelphia and Boston, 1784–92; Evans 18344, 23166, 24088).

5. Bishop James Madison's *Map of Virginia from Actual Surveys* was engraved in 1807 and was known as "Madison's Map" for the two decades when it was considered the authoritative edition (Earl G. Swem, "Maps relating to Virginia," *Bulletin of the Virginia State Library*, 7 [1914]: 84).

To Robert R. Livingston

DEAR SIR   WASHINGTON July 3. 1810

It has been my wish to find some specimen of manufacture within my domestic precincts worthy of being presented to your daughter Mrs. Livingston.[1] Delay has not relieved me from the mortification of betraying the poverty of our resources, by resorting to Mrs. M's Smokehouse; from which are forwarded a few Virginia Hams, in a *Box addressed to the care of the Collector at N. Y. Mr. Gelston. If they should prove such as are sometimes prepared, they may, as a variety, be not altogether unacceptable. I pray you, in having them delivered, to express to Mrs. Livingston the respect & thankfulness, of which I have given so deficient a proof, & to be assured, yourself, of my high esteem & regard.

JAMES MADISON

* The Box contains 2 dozen, & Mr. G. is requested to forward it to Clermont; but perhaps it may be well for some direction to go thence to him.

RC (NHi: Robert R. Livingston Papers).

1. Early in 1809 Livingston had sent JM a roll of cloth as a gift from his daughter, Mrs. Edward P. Livingston, explaining that the wool was "carded, spun, & wove in her house" (R. R. Livingston to JM, 17 and 24 Jan. 1809 [DLC]; JM to R. R. Livingston, 13 Mar. 1809, *PJM-PS*, 1:37–38).

From John R. Bedford

Sir,   Nashville July 4th. 1810

Inclosed, I forward You the copy of a letter from one of the most opulent inhabitants of West Florida. This letter, together with a personal knowledge of many of the inhabitants of that Province, impresses me with a strong belief, that a revolution of some kind may be attempted in that country, before a great while. It has been suggested to me from other sources, that two plans have been thought of. One, to disclaim all subordination or allegiance to the mother country, or the Usurper, and become associated with the other Spanish American Provinces, which might co-[o]perate to form an Independent Government and a new Nation—the other, to declare themselves independent of the World and institute a government within themselves upon economical & liberal principles, with the view at present, to endure no longer, than it may be reciprocally eligible to become an integral part of the U. States.

I feel considerably assured that it is the wish of a large majority of these people to become American Citizens—and that they would not adopt & persue any measures calculated to embarrass & jeopardise that event.

It is therefore desireable to ascertain, if practicable, if either of the above suggested plans is any wise calculated to create obstacles to the future acquisition of these provinces by the U. States. Should you feel free to communicate on this subject, it will be received with great satisfaction—and my best exertions will be to influence events in that country most conducive to the interests of my own. For I have no local or peculiar interest in that country, nor in any other than this, where I have been bred from early youth.

This note, from an obscure & private individual, may perhaps be considered intrusive & therefore neglected. I too, would deem it such, & would not Obtrude it, if not actuated by conscious & earnest zeal for the interests of my country—and a wish to aid the emancipation of these people, as well as the acquisition of these provinces, which are so important; & to some parts of our territory, so essential.

The author of the letter, of which a copy is hereto annexed, is a native of North Carolina, and an American in principle—exclusively an agriculturalist from his youth and an *honest man*. He became reconciled to settle in that country 9 years ago from a positive confidence, that the U. States would speedily acquire it. His attachments, cautiously manifested to the principles of our government, have rendered him somewhat an object of suspicion & jealousy several years ago, with the immediate officers of that Government. From the malice of which, he has been secured perhaps only, by his popularity grounded on his own probity & worth—and by that ascendency which superior opulence obtains in all countries. I am very Respectfully Your Obt. Servt.

J. R. BEDFORD[1]

N. B. The following copy is communicated in the strictest confidence to you, fearful my worthy friend might become the victim of unchecked & relentless tyranny.

[Enclosure]

[William Barrow to Bedford]

MY OLD FRIEND,   WEST FLORIDA June 4th. 1810

I am this day at leisure & have just been perusing your friendly letters, which bring the alarming situation of our country seriously to my reflection. I do assure you, my friend, at this moment, I feel more alarmed at our situation than I ever did since I lived in West Florida. We are here quite at a loss what to do. I fear our Government [. . .] is quite done—and we have no hope from the U. States claiming us & taking this country into possession. We have no able men to advise with, and what is best to do in justice to our situation and we are so much divided in politics. Now, my old friend, I as one who feel interested in our present situation, beg the favor of you to call on some of your ablest men & state the situation of our country to them—and get their advice, what is best for us to do in our present distressed situation. I wish to act so that it will be just & right for our own Safety & honor. Be so good as to consult men of talents & honor—as I know such are with you & that they are your friends. I assure you I have not the pleasure of being acquainted with that kind of men here. We are so much divided who is best to rule us, that I wish to have the best advice, possible to be had—as it is not my wish to do wrong—nor, give wrong advice. I have lost all hope of the U. States taking possession of us. Be so good as to write me fully on the subject, and that, as soon as possible you can give the best advice. I remain your friend & Hble Servt.

WM. BARROW[2]

RC and enclosure (DLC). Enclosure marked "(Copy)"; in Bedford's hand.

1. John Robertson Bedford (1782–1827) was a native of Mecklenburg County, Virginia, whose family moved to Rutherford County, Tennessee, in 1795. He studied and practiced medicine but also became increasingly involved in trade with New Orleans. In March 1814 JM appointed him as tax assessor for the fifth collection district of Tennessee (*Tenn. Historical Magazine*, 5 [1919]: 41–43, 108; *Senate Exec. Proceedings*, 2:511, 513).

2. William Barrow was born in North Carolina in 1765 and settled in the Feliciana district of West Florida under a Spanish grant in 1798. After his participation in the convention that declared West Florida independent of Spain, Barrow was elected, in November 1810, to the house of representatives in the newly established republic (Arthur, *Story of the West Florida Rebellion*, pp. 57, 128).

§ From William Nelson. *4 July 1810, Williamsburg*. Reports a rumor of the death of Judge Cyrus Griffin and suggests St. George Tucker for the vacancy.

RC (DNA: RG 59, LAR, 1809–17, filed under "Tucker"). 2 pp. Nelson was a judge of the General Court of Virginia, 1791–1813 (*PJM*, 6:500 n. 2).

§ From the Nelson Artillery Cadettes. *4 July 1810, Lovingston*. Cites resolutions, passed unanimously at 4 July meeting, condemning Great Britain and France for violating American neutral rights and expressing confidence in JM.

Ms (DLC). 2 pp. Signed by George W. Varnum, commandant, and attested by Thomas E. Fortune, secretary. Docketed by JM. Enclosed in Varnum to Robert Smith, 7 Aug. 1810 (DLC).

§ From Thomas Newell. *4 July 1810, Zanesville*. Complains that he has received neither pay nor land for his Revolutionary War service. A "Practical Surveyor . . . acquainted with Book Keeping," he requests employment to support his family.

RC (DNA: RG 107, LRRS, N-69:5). 2 pp.

To Simon Snyder

SIR   WASHINGTON July 5. 1810

I have duly received your letter of June 9. covering the Resolutions of the General Assembly of the Commonwealth of Pennsylvania, adopted at their last session.

The principles & purposes avowed in these Resolutions, are such as were to be expected from a State which has given so many proofs of its readiness to maintain the rights & honor of the Nation, against foreign aggressions and insults.

In this renewed pledge of their co-operation whenever, in the opinion of the National Councils, an appeal to the patriotism & force of the

Amn. people becomes necessary, the Genl. Assembly, afford an example, equally animating to those charged with the interests of the Union, & worthy the emulation of every member of it.

Accept, Sir assurances of my high respect

Draft (DLC).

Madison's Draft of Robert Smith to John Armstrong

GENL A.   DEPARTMT. OF STATE July 5. 1810
    I avail myself of the oppy. by Mr.   to forward copies of my several letters lately written to you; & to add the present.
    The arrival of the J. Adams brought your letters of the following dates .[1] From that of the 16th. April, it appears that the seizures of Amn. property lately made, had been followed up by its actual sale, & that the proceeds had been deposited in the Emperors Caisse prive. You have presented in such just colours the enormity of the outrage, that I have only to signify to you that the P entirely approves the step taken by you, & that he does not doubt that it will be followed by yourself, or the person succeeding to the duty, with any further interpositions which may be deemed advisable. He instructs you, particularly, to make the F Govt. sensible of the deep impression made here by so signal an aggression on the principles of justice & of good faith, & to demand every reparation of which the case is susceptible. If it be not the purpose of the F. Govt. to renoun⟨ce⟩ every idea of friendly adjustment with the U. S. it wd. seem impossible but that a reconsideration of this violent proceeding, must lead to a redress of it, as a preliminary to a general accomodation of the differences between the two Nations.
    At the date of the last communications from Mr. P. he had not obtained from the B. Govt. an acceptance of the condition on which the F. Govt. was willing to concur in putting an end to all the illegal Edicts of both agst. our neutral commerce. Should he have afterwards succeeded, you will of course on receiving the fact, immediately claim from the F. G. the fulfilment of its promise; and by transmitting it to Mr. P. co-operate with him in compleating the removal of all the illegal obstructions to our commerce.
    Among the documents now sent, is another copy of the Act of Congs. repealing the non-intercourse law; but authorizing a renewal of it, agst. G. B. in case F shall repeal her Edicts; & G. B. refuse to follow the example; & vice versa. You have been already informed that the P. is ready

to exercise the power vested in him for such a purpose, as soon as the occasion shall arise. Should the other experiment in the hands of Mr. P. have failed, you will make the Act of Congs. and the disposition of the P. the subject of a formal communication to the F. Govt. and it is not easy to conceive any grounds even specious on which the overture specified in the Act can be declined.

If the non-intercourse law, in any of its modifications, was objectionable to the Emperor of the French, that law no longer exists.

If he be ready, as has been declared in the letter of the D. de Cadore of Feby. 14, to do justice to the U. S. in the case of a pledge on their part, not to submit to the B. Edicts, the opportunity for making good the declaration is now furnished.[2] Instead of submission, the P. is ready, by renewing the Non-intercourse agst. G. B. to oppose to her orders in Council a measure of a character, which ought to satisfy every reasonable expectation. Should it be necessary for you to meet the question, whether the non-intercourse will be renewed agst. G. B. in case she should not comprehend in a repeal of her Edicts, her Blockades, not consistent with the L. of Nations, you may, if found necessary, let it be understood that a repeal of the illegal Blockades, prior to the Berlin Decree, namely that of May 1806, will be included in the condition required of G. B.: that particular blockade having been avowed to be comprehended in & of course identified with the orders in Council.

With respect to Blockades, of subsequent date or not agst. France, you will press the reasonableness of leaving them, together with future blockades not warranted by pub. law, to be proceeded agst. by the U. S in the manner they may chuse to adopt. As has been heretofore stated to you, a satisfactory provision for restoring the property lately surprized & seized by the order or at the instance of the F. Govt. must be combined with a repeal of the F Edicts, with a view to a non-intercourse with G. B.: such a provision being an indispensible evidence[3] of the just purposes of F. towards the U. S. And you will moreover be careful, in arranging such a provision for that particular case of spoliations, not to weaken the ground on which a redress of others may be justly pursued.

If the Act, in legalizing a free trade with both the Belligts.; witht. guarding agst. Bsh. interruptions of it with F. whilst F. can not materially interrupt it with G. B, be complained of as leaving the trade on the worst possible footing for F. & on the best possible one for G. B, the F G. may be reminded of the other feature of the Act which puts it in their own power to obtain either an interruption of our trade with G. B. or a re⟨call⟩ of her interruption of it with F.

Among the considns. which belong to this subject it may be remarked, that it might have been reasonably ⟨ex⟩pected by the U. S. that a repeal of the F. decrees, would have resulted from the B. Order in Council of Apl.

1809. This order, expressly revoked the preceding orders of Novr. 1807 heretofore urged by F. in justification of her Decrees, & was not only different in its extent and in its details, but was essentially different in its policy & object. The object of the orders of 1807, was by cutting off all commercial supplies, to retort on her Enemies, the distress, which the French Decree was intended to inflict on G. B. The object of the Order of Apl. 1809. was if not avowedly, most certainly, not to deprive F. of such supplies; but by arresting those from neutral sources, to favor a surreptitious monopoly to B. Traders.[4] In order to counteract this object, it was the manifest interest of F. to have favored the rival & cheaper supplies thro' neutrals; instead of which she has co-operated with the monopolizing views of G. B. by a rigorous exclusion of neutrals from her ports. She has in fact reversed the operation originally professed by her Decrees. Instead of annoying her enemy, at the expence of a friend, she annoys a friend for the benefit of her enemy.

Should the F. Govt. accede to the overture contained in the Act of Congs. by repealing or so modifying its Decrees as that they will cease to violate our neutral rights, you will transmit the repeal properly authenticated, to Mr. P. by a special messenger if necessary; and hasten & ensure the receipt of it here, by engaging a vessel if no equivalent conveyance shd. offer, to bring it directly from F. and sending several copies to Mr. P. to be forwarded from B. Ports.

Draft (DLC). In pencil in JM's hand. JM's draft, with minor revisions, was the basis for Robert Smith's letter to John Armstrong of 5 July 1810 (letterbook copy, DNA: RG 59, IM; printed in *ASP, Foreign Relations*, 3:385–86). Minor differences between the draft and the final version have not been noted.

1. In the State Department letterbook copy a clerk supplied the dates of 1, 4, 7, and 16 Apr.

2. In his letter of 14 Feb. 1810 the duc de Cadore had stipulated that if the U.S., through its minister in Paris, could "enter into an engagement that the American vessels will not submit to the orders in council of England of November, 1807, nor to any decree of blockade, unless this blockade should be real, [he was] authorized to conclude every species of convention tending to renew the treaty of commerce with America, and in which all the measures proper to consolidate the commerce and the prosperity of the Americans shall be provided for" (*ASP, Foreign Relations*, 3:381).

3. Text from this point to the end of the paragraph is continued on a separate page.

4. In the final version of the instruction this sentence reads: "The policy of the order of April, 1809, if not avowedly, was most certainly to prevent such supplies, by shutting out those only which might flow from neutral sources, in order thereby to favor a surreptitious monopoly to British traders" (ibid., 3:386).

¶ To Thomas Cooper. Letter not found. *Ca. 5 July 1810*. Acknowledged in Cooper to JM, 9 July 1810. Congratulates Cooper for his dissenting opinion in *Dempsey* v. *Insurance Company of Pennsylvania*.

§ From Benjamin Henry Latrobe. *6 July 1810, Washington*. Expresses views about that part of the law appropriating $20,000 for public buildings which relates to the "fireproofs" to be erected in the public building west of the President's House.[1] Observes that the only security that can be attained in safeguarding records from fire is against "fire from without," since it is evident that in the case of "persons using the rooms, & writing within them by open fire places, . . . the only security is in the care with which the fires are extinguished or covered in their absence." "If however a fireproof deposit of papers were so constructed as to be warmed, as a security against damp, by covered flues, and if it were ventilated by tubes passing through the Walls, and if no persons were permitted to introduce fire into it; it would then be perfectly adapted to its purpose." The building west of the President's House is well constructed and capable of being vaulted without unduly interrupting public business. The cost of vaulting one set of rooms, using iron doors and shutters and stone door frames, would not exceed $1,750, and two sets of rooms could be completed during the month of August. His proposals, if approved, could be executed by contract, and they are the cheapest and best way to comply with the law.

Letterbook copy (MdHi). 4 pp. Reproduced in Thomas E. Jeffrey, ed., *The Papers of Benjamin Henry Latrobe* (microfiche ed.; Clifton, N.J., 1976), fiche 75.

1. Under the law approved on 28 Apr. 1810, the president was authorized to erect or purchase a building to accommodate the Post Office and Patent Office, to order the removal of the city post office and the offices of the superintendent and surveyor of the city of Washington from the public building west of the President's House, and to order the construction in the latter building of "as many fire-proof rooms as shall be sufficient for the convenient deposit of all the public papers and records of the United States, belonging to, or in the custody of the state, war or navy departments." An appropriation of $20,000 was made for these purposes (*U.S. Statutes at Large*, 2:589–90).

To Andrew Ellicott

DEAR SIR   WASHINGTON July 7. 1810

Your favor of Novr. 8. was duly received. I must trust to your own friendly inferences, for an apology for so long a delay in acknowledging it.

I found that there were in the Navy Office three Sheets of Gaulds Survey referred to in your letter. They are now in my hands. I find also, among the Charts handed over by Mr. Jefferson: one, on a large scale, of the Coasts of W. Florida, & Louisiana, from Sawaney River to 94°. 30′. W. Longitude, describing the entrance of the Mississippi, the Bay of Mobille, Pensacola Harbor &c, as surveyed by G. Gauld, in 1764, 5, 6, 7, 8, 9. 70 & 71. under direction of the Admiralty, and published in 1803, by W. Faden Geographer to the P. of Wales. As the publication is of later date than that of the Charts belonging to you, you may perhaps not have seen it.

You are aware I presume that Mr. Patterson of Philada. was made the pivot of the general plan for effecting a survey of our Coast. As Mr. Gallatin, to whose department the business falls, is just about visiting Philada. on his way to N. York, I have desired him to see Mr. Patterson, and if a consultation with him should lead to any result requiring a communication with you, to write to you accordingly. Should you not hear from him, therefore, you will conclude that for the present at least, your attention need not be diverted from other objects. Accept my friendly respects

JAMES MADISON

RC (DLC: Andrew Ellicott Papers).

To Albert Gallatin

July 7. 1810

A nephew of J. M. with the approbation of his father, is desirous of finishing a mercantile education, begun at Fredericksburg about a year & a half ago, in the Counting House of some respectable Merchant in N. York. The youth is about 19 or 20 years of age, believed to be of amiable temper and of virtuous habits. His father is willing to conform to the conditions usual in such cases.

J. M. will be much obliged to Mr. Gallatin, if [he] will be so good as to make enquiry, during his trip to N. Y. as to the most eligible situation to be had there for J. M. Macon, the name of the young man, in case his preference of N. Y. should continue, and drop a line to Orange Court House Virginia on the subject.

RC (NHi: Gallatin Papers). Docketed by Gallatin.

To Thomas Jefferson

DEAR SIR   WASHINGTON July 7. 1810

Not knowing where I could be enabled to answer the inclosed,[1] with so much confidence in the fact, as in your acquaintance with the historical antiquities of Virginia, I take the liberty of asking whether I may not say to Mr. Bassette, that no such accounts as he enquires after, are known to exist. As he seems desirous of an early answer you will oblige me by a few lines as soon as convenient.

RC (DLC). Lower part of page, including complimentary close and signature, has been clipped. Docketed by Jefferson, "recd. July 12."

1. John Bassette to JM, ca. 1 July 1810.

From John Strode

WORTHY SIR   CULPEPER 7 July 1810

On the 31 March last I executed my penal Bond to you for the Sum of £320.13.10 and left it for you in the hands of Doctr Isaac Winston[1] and yesterday executed a mortgage Deed to You as a further Surety for the payment, which on my Sacred honor if God permit shall be either proved or Acknowledged at the Next Fauquir Court. The reason this Sum was delay'd so long I was in hope that I could ere now have made you a handsome payment but alas! it is not in my power as yet. The Security is not so large as I wd. have wisht. It is intrinsically worth much more, but such is the extreme Scarcity of Money that property will not at this time bring but Very little. However I shall make yr. Claim less and less from time to time as it is in my power. Be increasing felicity yours is indeed the Ardent prayer of Yr. ever gratefull humble Servant

JOHN ST[R]ODE

Herewith is a Copy of the Mortgaged Deed.

RC and enclosure (DLC). Postmarked 19 July at Fredericksburg, Virginia. Docketed by JM. Enclosure is a copy of a mortgage deed dated 6 July 1810 for land in Fauquier County, Virginia.

1. Dr. Isaac Winston was the son of Capt. Isaac Winston and Lucy Coles Winston, Dolley Madison's aunt (Clayton Torrence, ed., *The Edward Pleasants Valentine Papers* . . . [4 vols.; Richmond, 1927], 3:1622–23).

§ From Barent Gardenier. *7 July 1810, New York.* Proposes the establishment of an office in New York City for the collection and securing of moneys owed by traders and others in the country to merchants and others in the city. Establishes a scale of fees for the services offered.

RC (DLC: Madison Collection, Rare Book Division). A three-page printed circular letter. Addressed to JM and signed by Gardenier.

§ Presidential Proclamation.[1] *7 July 1810, Washington.* Announces a sale for the disposal of the "quarter Sections of land adjacent [to] the old Indian boundary line, in the Indiana Territory, and East of the second principal Meridian," to be held at Jeffersonville, Indiana Territory, on the [third Monday] in [November] 1810. Issues the proclamation in conformity with the authority conferred by the following acts: the second section of "An Act making provision for the disposal of the public lands, situated between the United States military Tract and the Connecticut Reserve," passed 3 Mar. 1807; the third section of "An act providing for the Sale of certain lands in the Indiana Territory," passed 30 Apr. 1810; and the first section of "An Act concerning the Sale of the Lands of the United States," passed 31 Mar. 1808.

Draft (DNA: RG 49, Records of the General Land Office, Jeffersonville, Ind., Registrar and Receiver Letters, vol. 19, sect. D). 4 pp. In a clerk's hand. Printed in Carter, *Territorial Papers, Indiana*, 8:30–32.

1. The proclamation resulted from a letter sent by Samuel Gwathmey of the Jeffersonville Land Office to Gallatin, 15 June 1810, inquiring about the disposal of some remaining fractions of public land in the Indiana Territory. Gallatin directed a clerk to draw up a proclamation for the public sale of the lands. A draft was ready by 5 July 1810, evidently submitted to JM two days later, and then forwarded by Gallatin to Gwathmey on 10 July (ibid., 8:24–25, 33).

¶ From Richard Forrest. Letter not found. *7 July 1810.* Described as a one-page letter in the lists probably made by Peter Force (DLC, series 7, container 2).

To William Bentley

SIR   WASHINGTON July 8. 1810

I have received your favor of the 2d. inst: accompanied by a likeness of General Stark. I thank you for both. The latter, in its execution, seems to do so much credit to the talent of your pupil, that I, the more readily, confide in its likeness; and shall place it by the side of others, whose originals are known to have inspired the General with that esteem of which they are worthy.

The circumstances related in your letter coincide with the more important anecdotes recorded of this patriot & hero, in shewing a mind made of Nature's best stuff, and fashioned in a mould seldom used by her.

I regret that I cannot supply you with a copy of Bishop Madison's Map of Virginia, for your friend. The inclosed Newspaper will refer you to the source whence one may be procured. Accept assurances of my esteem & friendly respects.

JAMES MADISON

RC (NjP: Crane Collection).

From Thomas Cooper

Sir   Philadelphia July 9th 1810

Col. Patten of the post office here, was so good as to hand me your obliging letter relating to my opinion on an Insurance Case.[1] I hasten to acknowledge the receipt of your favour, and to express my high satisfaction at the approbation you have thought fit to bestow. It is approbation of the only kind worth having; laudari a laudato viro.[2] I remain with sentiments of great respect Sir Your obliged friend and Servant

                                                        Thomas Cooper

RC (DLC). Attached to the verso is a clipping from the *Northumberland Gazette* of 31 July 1810 with Cooper's instructions of 17 May 1810 on gathering data for the 1810 census (see Cooper to JM, 14 Sept. 1810, n. 7).

1. See JM to Jefferson, 22 June 1810, and n. 1.
2. "To be praised by one who has himself been praised," Cicero, *Letters to His Friends*, 5.12.7 (Loeb Classical Library [3 vols.; London, 1972], 1:375).

§ From William Tatham. *10 July 1810, Norfolk.* Believes it is important to add to his former communications the enclosed statement of facts concerning the legal right of the public to "the Desart" at Cape Henry. Is continuing his topographical work. Relates that his family is in distressed circumstances.

RC and enclosure (DLC). RC 2 pp. Printed in McPherson, "Letters of William Tatham," *WMQ*, 2d ser., 16 (1936): 391. Enclosure (undated, 8 pp.) is a "Statement *Concerning a tract of Land called 'the Desert,' situated on, and adjoining to, Cape Henry, at the enterance of the Chesapeake Bay; many years reserved for public use; and of great importance to the United States.*"

From William Eustis

Sir,   WAR DEPARTMENT July 11. 1810.

I have the honor to enclose a return exhibiting the several posts & stations occupied by the troops with their numbers & commanding officers.

No further information has been received from Governor Harrison. In a conversation with a gentleman well acquainted with the country & with the state disposition & power of the Indians I have been encouraged to believe they will not commence hostilities: the movement of the troops on the Western waters will nevertheless be calculated to meet the emergency. I am with perfect respect Sir, your obedt. Servt.

                                                        W. Eustis

RC (DLC); letterbook copy (DNA: RG 107, LSP). Enclosure not found.

From David Gelston

DEAR SIR,   NEW YORK July 11th. 1810
Your letter of 29th ultimo with $20. I have recieved, the box of hams I have forwarded to Chancellor Livingston. The sundry payments made are stated at foot, receipts enclosed, the bal: $2.46 will remain in your favor in Y/a. My son says he does not recollect the cost of *the book* it was however a mere trifle, very truly yours

DAVID GELSTON

30 May	pd.	duties on goods	5.79
6 July	"	Mer: Ad:	10 —
9 "	"	fret. hams	1.50
" "	"	cartg "	.25
			17.54
		to y/a	2.46
			$20.00

RC and enclosures (DLC). Enclosures are receipts from Joseph P. Meeks for $1.50 for freight of hams and from John Latham for $10 for a subscription to the N.Y. *Mercantile Advertiser*.

From the Bunker Hill Association

SIR;   BOSTON 12th. July 1810.
We have the honour to address you, in conformity to a Vote of the general Committee of the "Bunker Hill Association," and request you to accept a Copy of the Oration delivered on the 4th of July last.[1]

In commemorating the feelings and principles which led to the glorious event of our revolution, it is peculiarly congenial to our grateful sensibility on this occasion, to render homage to the virtues of those Patriots who contributed thereto, and to express individually our personal respect for your Character, and our ardent wishes that you may enjoy the satisfaction of seeing our Country flourish in peace and union, under the happy influence of your wise and salutary administration. We are Sir, Your faithful fellow Citizens & most Obedient Servants

BENJAMIN HOMANS ⎫
J. E. SMITH   ⎬ Committee.
WILLIAM BLAGROVE ⎭

RC (DLC). Docketed by JM.

1. Daniel Waldo Lincoln, *An Oration, Pronounced at Boston, on the Fourth Day of July, 1810, before the "Bunker-Hill Association"* (Boston, 1810; Shaw and Shoemaker 20572).

From William Eustis

SIR,   WAR DEPARTMENT July 12. 1810.

I have the honor to enclose a copy of a Letter received from Governor Harrison by which it will appear that we are relieved from any apprehension of hostilities on the part of the Indians.[1] With the highest respect I am Sir, your obedt. servt.

W. EUSTIS

[Enclosure]

§ William Henry Harrison to William Eustis. *26 June 1810, Vincennes.* Reports information he has received from a deputation of Potawatomi Indians about a council held at St. Joseph where the Delaware and other Indians refused to join forces with the Prophet.[2] Was informed that the Prophet intended to engage all the tribes on the Mississippi to join his confederacy and to attack Detroit, Fort Wayne, Chicago, St. Louis, and Vincennes, but he now thinks that the Prophet's influence is limited to "the War-Chiefs, or those who are heads of small bands." Relates the "consummate villainy" of the Prophet in trying to incite younger men to murder the principal chiefs of all the tribes in order to unite the Indians and thus prevent further land sales to whites. Is convinced that the Prophet is "inspired by the Superintendant of Indian Affairs for Upper Canada, rather than [by] the Great Spirit, from whom he pretends to derive his authority." Has sent an emissary (Mr. DuBois) to the Prophet and has mustered two companies of militia but will not keep them in service after the return of DuBois "unless the Accounts brought by him should be very different from what I expect them to be."

RC and enclosure (DLC); FC and FC of enclosure (PHi: Daniel Parker Papers); letterbook copy (DNA: RG 107, LSP). RC docketed by JM. Enclosure (6 pp.) in a clerk's hand; marked "(Copy)"; docketed by JM; printed in Esarey, *Messages and Letters of William Henry Harrison*, Indiana Historical Collections, 1:433–36.

1. At a later time, JM wrote in the left margin of the RC, "see his letter of June 26. 1810."
2. Lalawethika, or the Prophet (1775–1836), was born of Creek-Shawnee parentage and passed most of his early life in Ohio. Reputedly an alcoholic, he aspired to the status of medicine man but without much apparent success before the winter of 1804–5 when he experienced a spiritual crisis and fell into a prolonged trance. He awoke to preach a message of cultural revitalization, based on an amalgam of reformed Indian custom and Christianity, which stressed that Indians should avoid contact with American settlers and their way of life. In 1808 he and his followers moved from Ohio to the juncture of the Tippecanoe and Wabash rivers where they established a community (Prophetstown) that became a focal point of Indian dissatisfaction in the Northwest with the expansionist policies of the U.S. (R. David Edmunds, *The Shawnee Prophet* [Lincoln, Nebr., 1983], pp. 28–86).

From Tobias Lear

(Private)

My dear Sir,   Algiers, July 12th 1810.

It is a long time since I have had the honor to address a letter to you personally; but I hope you will not impute my silence to a want of respect, or to a forgetfulness of your favor and friendship; for I can most truly assure you that it has not been owing to either; but more to an apprehension of intruding upon your time, which must of late, have been very much occupied, and which is too precious to be employ'd in keeping up an uninteresting correspondence. Your exaltation to the Chair of Government, in which I rejoice most sincerely, has also had its weight in preventing my writing, when it might seem that I would rather write to the President of the United States, than to Mr. Madison.

The present fair opportunity of writing cannot be passed over, if it were only to assure you of my sincere attachment and grateful remembrance; but it is also to express my ardent desire to return to my native Country; or to find some other employment more congenial with my feelings and disposition. Since I have been in Barbary I have served my Country with all the ability and integrity which I possess; and I hope not without usefulness. My only son has long felt the want of that attention which a parent only can bestow; and has now advanced to that time of life when it is peculiarly necessary to guide and direct him towards his future pursuits. An aged Parent also demands the consoling sight of her son. For your kind attention to them, as far as you could give it, they speak with gratitude; and for that, as well as for the other favors you have always shewn me, my heart answers with acknowledgement most warm and sincere.

As my letter to The Hone. the Secretary of State, which goes by this occasion (the Brig Blanchy, which brought out part of our annuities last year) will give a full detail of all occurrences here,[1] I shall not trouble you with anything of a public, or a political nature in this.

I take the liberty of sending by this Vessel, for yourself; or to be distributed in a way you may judge most beneficial, fifteen measures (about 20 bushels) of the wheat of this Country, for seed—Eight Male sheep of the best breed we have here—a Barrel containing some cuttings of the best grape Vines; and a basket containing the seed of a tree, called here the *Gegub*, a species of thorn, which may be useful for hedges, as the seed springs up most readily wherever sown, or drop'd; and the tree, if suffered to attain its full size, is as large as a common pear tree. Its growth is rapid. If any good can be done for my Country by any of these, I shall feel peculiarly gratified in having contributed my mite.

To your highly respected and beloved predecessor, I beg to be remembered, when occasion may offer, in terms of the warmest attachment and respect. I hope once more to have the satisfaction of seeing him, as well as yourself, face to face. Mrs. Lear has written a few lines to Mrs. Madison,[2] which I take the liberty to enclose; and beg her acceptance of my best respects, and sincere prayers for her health and happiness. Receive, my dear Sir, the assurances of invariable attachment and esteem with which I am always Your faithful friend & Obedt Set

TOBIAS LEAR.[3]

RC (DLC). Docketed by JM.

1. See Lear to Robert Smith, 16 July 1810, covering a dispatch of 14 July (not found) (DNA: RG 59, CD, Algiers).

2. Letter not found.

3. Tobias Lear (1762–1816), a native of New Hampshire and a graduate of Harvard, had served as private secretary to George Washington. From 1803 to 1812 he held the position of consul general at Algiers; he returned to the U.S. in 1813. In 1814 JM appointed him to be accountant to the Department of War (*PJM-SS*, 1:13 n. 5; *Senate Exec. Proceedings*, 1:453, 2:531).

From Horatio Gates Spafford

HOND. & ESTEEMED FRIEND—   ALBANY, N. Y., 7 Mo. 12, 1810.

I take the liberty to address one of these Letters to thee,[1] because I can but suppose thou must feel an interest in every undertaking which interests & affects the community. Placed, as thou art, at the civil head of a Nation of Freemen, thy fatherly goodwill embraces, I trust, an anxious regard for the whole—& while I thus regard thee, I could but wish to engage thy attention to what is doing here. I rejoice at the elevation of good men, & congratulate thee, most devoutly, on the return of this State, to Republicanism: having myself, the fullest confidence in the wisdom & integrity of our Rulers. But, in the triumph, or defeat, of *parties*, I have nothing to do, as a party-man. I am an American; & simply wish for Rulers of American principles. Sensibly & deeply impressed with the trials of these times, I cannot forbear expressing my sense of our wrongs, & my general approbation of the measures of our Rulers—while I tender thee my best wishes for thine & the general welfare.

My endeavors, here, are generously patronized by the Government, & I contemplate extending my plan, by individual States, through the Union. Would it be impolitic, or would it be just & politic both, for the General Government to relieve me in the expense of Postage? My Correspondence has yielded to the Govt., at least 1000 dollars, with 3 years. Pray let me hear from thee, & rest assured of the cordial esteem of, thy friend,

H. G. SPAFFORD.[2]

RC (DLC); enclosure (DLC: Madison Collection, Rare Book Division). For enclosure, see n. 1.

1. Spafford enclosed a printed circular letter (1 p.), dated "7 Mo. 4, 1810," addressed to JM and mistakenly docketed by him "Sepr. 12. 1810." The letter appealed for further information and subscriptions to permit the completion and publication of "Spafford's Gazetteer, of the State of New-York." Spafford announced that because of delays in receiving the latest census returns, his manuscript would not be sent to the press until "early next winter."

2. Horatio Gates Spafford (1778–1832) was a member of the New-York Historical Society and the author of the text *General Geography, and Rudiments of Useful Knowledge* (Hudson, N.Y., 1809).

¶ From [Robert Smith?]. Letter not found. *Ca. 12 July 1810*. Mentioned in JM to Smith, 17 July 1810. Forwards letters from Gov. David Holmes and Robert K. Lowry and a copy of his reply to Lowry.

From Thomas Jefferson

DEAR SIR   MONTICELLO July 13. 10.

I return you mr. Bassette's letter & think you may safely tell him we possess no Dutch accounts of Virginia. We have De Laët; but it is a folio volume of Latin, & I have no doubt a good translation will sell well. I have not examined De Bry's collection[1] to see if that contains any Dutch account. That is in 3. folio volumes of Latin, and certainly will not take off one single reader from mr. Bassette's work. I have not sent for my Merinos till you should have settled the claims of others on them. If the lamb is to remain ours, it will be at your choice to keep it or not, returning the first ewe lamb in exchange. I come perfectly into your idea that if any accident shall put either of us out of the breed, the other shall put him in again with either a male or female of full blood or both if necessary, & this to be indefinite in point of time, because even after we have a tolerable stock, a total loss is not unexampled. In the mean time I am inclosing a lot of 5. or 6. acres with a fence dog-proof, on a plan of mr. Randolph's taking only half the rails a common fence does, with some more labour, so as to be on the whole about equal in expence. I have recieved every thing I could desire in Livingston's case except Moreau's Memoire. Wirt, Hay & Tazewell are engaged in the defence. They desired of me to furnish them the grounds of defence. This has obliged me to study the case thoroughly, to place all the points on paper, with my own views of them & the authorities in their support. This is the more tedious, as the authorities being in few hands, & being in Latin, French, & Spanish entirely, are obliged to be copied in the body of the work. It has raised my rough draught to 8. sheets of letter paper. It is cruel to propose to you to read this, and yet I have three reasons for doing so. 1. The suit is an attack on the administration, and in a delicate point. I do not think myself free therefore to urge or omit any point of defence they would disapprove; & therefore I think to submit it also to mr. Smith & mr. Gallatin. 2. I know how much it will gain by such views as you will suggest. 3. I think it will be a great satisfaction to you to see how clear a case it is. A clearer never came before a court. I have a trip to Bedford on hand, but shall defer it till I have copied this, which will take me 8. or 10. days, at 2. or 3. hours a day given to it, shall have sent it to you for perusal & followed it myself to pay my respects to you. My absence will be of a month. I have a pair of Shepherd's dogs for Dr. Thornton. He desired me to send them to mr. Gooch's your overseer who would keep them till mr. Barry or your waggon would be going to Washington. But as you will probably have a rider coming weekly to Montpelier, & the dogs lead well both, I should think he might carry them conveniently for a small premium from the doctor. I shall send them when I send for the sheep. They are most valuable dogs. Their sagacity is almost human, and qualifies them to be taught any thing you please. Accept my affectionate salutations for mrs. Madison & yourself.

Th: Jefferson

RC (DLC); FC (DLC: Jefferson Papers). Cover of RC dated Milton, 17 July.

1. Theodor de Bry, *Collectiones Peregrinationum in Indiam Orientalem et Indiam Occidentalem* (3 vols.; Frankfort and Oppenheim, 1590–1619). For Jefferson's set of these volumes, see Sowerby, *Catalogue of Jefferson's Library*, 4:167–76.

From John K. Smith

Sir,   New Orleans July 14th 1810

I have the honor to acknowledge the receipt of your letter of the 28th may.

Mr Duplantier has at length returned & is now with me. He has received two letters from Genl. Lafayette under *blank* covers from you— upon seeing your letters to me & my answer of the 15th. may he agrees that nothing can now be done in the location of the remaining 500 acres adjacent to the City for the reasons stated in my letter of the 15th. may. Mr Brown[1] agent for land claims is of the same opinion.

My letter of the 15th. may was sent by the Fort Stoddert mail—fearing that it may have miscarried I enclose Copies of the letter & accompanying papers except the plat of Mr Lafon of which I could not keep a Copy. I do not believe from the information I have Obtained that the Claims of McCarty & others upon the lands adjacent to the City are Valid & I have ascertained that these lands not including the 600 yards granted to the Corporation are worth at least 30,000$ my opinion & information upon these points are in Contradiction to the Opinion Contained in Mr. Derbigneys note.

Mr. Duplantier while absent located the rem[ainin]g 2000 acres of land adjoining his former locations—the Certificates for which are daily expected & will be forwarded. I shall have great satisfaction in attending to your future Commands & am with the highest respect Sir your Obt. St.

J. K SMITH

Mr. Duplantier will write to you by this mail.

RC (DLC). For enclosures, see Smith to JM, 15 May 1810, n.

1. James Brown had been agent for land claims at New Orleans since 1805 (Carter, *Territorial Papers, Orleans*, 9:468–69).

From William Eustis

SIR,   WAR-DEPARTMENT, 16th. July 1810

Doubtful of the propriety of issuing the order, I have the honor to enclose for your consideration & decision the letter of General Wilkinson, requesting that certain Officers may be ordered to the Seat of Government for the purpose therein mentioned.[1]

The objections appear to be, first, the expense. Secondly several of the Officers are on duty from which they cannot be released without injury to the service. Thirdly. As the Government necessarily becomes a party to any charges or imputations, alledged against a public Officer, it would seem that the Government should be represented at the taking of testimony. In the present instance, there is no Court, no constituted authority, or legal provision, under which an agent on the part of government may be appointed, nor any specification of the points on which evidence is to be required.

From an expression in the letter of the General, "that he should unwillingly exercise his own authority in his own case," it appears, that he considers himself, as having a right to command, and it has become necessary that this also should be determined, lest the expression unanswered might be construed into an acknowledgment of such right. When Genl. Wilkinson was recalled from the Western Army & had surrendered the command of it, to General Hampton; it was understood by me, that his Command ceased. The Command of the other Districts, with the exception of such posts as received their Orders immediately from the War-Office, had been assigned to other Officers, and it was supposed that Genl. Wilkinson could not, without special instructions, exercise any command whatever.

In the hope that the occasion will be deemed justifiable of this intrusion upon your retirement—I have the honor to remain with perfect respect, Sir, Your obedient servant,

W. EUSTIS.

RC and enclosures (DLC); letterbook copy (DNA: RG 107, LSP). RC in a clerk's hand, signed by Eustis; docketed by JM. Enclosures are a copy of Wilkinson to Eustis, 14 July 1810 (1 p.), and a copy of a list of fourteen witnesses (1 p.) (see n. 1).

1. Throughout March and April 1810, Wilkinson's conduct had been under investigation by committees of the House of Representatives seeking evidence about his dealings with Burr and his role in the scandal at Terre aux Boeufs. Wilkinson, on 24 June, had requested a court of inquiry, but JM refused to grant it. In response, Wilkinson demanded that Eustis order to Washington fourteen officers he had named as witnesses to substantiate "various facts and circumstances essential to the repulsion of the greatest misrepresentation" and hinted that he would issue the necessary orders himself if Eustis did not comply. JM again denied Wilkinson's request (Eustis to Wilkinson, 28 June 1810, and John Smith to Wilkinson, 9 Aug. 1810 [DNA: RG 107, LSMA]; Jacobs, *Tarnished Warrior*, pp. 263–65).

From William Eustis

SIR,   WAR DEPARTMENT July 16th. 1810.

Agreeably to the request of Colo. Simonds,[1] I have the honor to enclose his Letter on the subject of his double rations. Altho' it does not appear that General Wilkinson was authorised to assure the Colo. that he would be entitled to the allowance, reliance was undoubtedly had on the promise, and to be obliged to refund what has been received under such circumstances is considered by the officers peculiarly hard upon them. By the regulations lately adopted it is presumed such cases will not occur in future. Should the allowance in the present Instance be made by the president, his signature under the word allowed at the bottom of the Letter will be sufficient.[2] With the greatest respect

W. EUSTIS

FC (PHi: Daniel Parker Papers); letterbook copy (DNA: RG 107, LSP). Enclosure not found.

1. Jonas Simonds was colonel of the Sixth Infantry Regiment, 1808–15 (Heitman, *Historical Register*, 1:887).
2. See JM to Eustis, 20 July 1810.

From Albert Gallatin

DEAR SIR   WASHINGTON July 16th 1810
It appears that a depreciation of the paper currency of Norway has taken place which requires, for the purpose of calculating the duties, the interference of the President. I enclose for that purpose an Act for your signature; which, if you approve, please to return under cover to Mr Duvall,[1] as I expect to leave this for New York to morrow. I also enclose for your approbation a recommendation of keeper of light house.

Nothing new, the West Florida business excepted which may require some decision before the meeting of Congress. I have received the papers for Mr Gelston;[2] but as he is not a merchant, I apprehend that he will refuse going unless his expences are paid. With sincere attachement Your's respectfully

ALBERT GALLATIN

RC (DLC). Docketed by JM. Enclosures not found, but see n. 1.

1. See JM's proclamation of 19 July 1810.
2. Gallatin referred to Maltby Gelston, son of New York collector David Gelston. As Gallatin predicted, Gelston declined the position of commercial agent to Buenos Aires (Brant, *Madison*, 5:172; Gallatin to JM, 15 Aug. 1810).

¶ To James Monroe. Letter not found. *16 July 1810*. Acknowledged in Monroe to JM, 25 July 1810. Concerns the employment of Bizet, a French gardener.

To Thomas Jefferson

DEAR SIR   MONTPELIER July 17. 1810
Among the papers relating to the Convention of 1787. communicated to you, that copies in your hands might double the security agst. destructive casualties, was a delineation of Hamilton's plan of a Constitution in his own writing. On looking for it among the Debates &c, which were returned to me, this particular paper does not appear.[1] I conclude there-

fore that it had not then been copied, or was at the time in some separate situation. I am very sorry to trouble you on such a subject, but being under an engagement to furnish a Copy of that project,[2] I must ask the favor of you to see whether it be not among your papers; & if so, to forward it by the mail.

I reached home on wednesday last;[3] and have since been somewhat indisposed. My fever has left me, and if as I hope, it was the effect of fatigue only, I consider myself as again well. I am not, however, without sensations which make me apprehensive that if bile was not the sole cause, it was a partial one, & that it has not yet been entirely removed. Be assured of my affectionate respects & best wishes

JAMES MADISON

RC (DLC). Docketed by Jefferson, "recd. July 19."

1. At a later time, JM placed an asterisk here and noted in the left margin, "*afterwards found."

2. See JM to John Mitchell Mason, 5 Feb. 1810, and n. 1.

3. JM had left Washington on Monday, 9 July (*National Intelligencer*, 11 July 1810).

To Robert Smith

DEAR SIR   MONTPELIER July 17. 1810.

The letter from Govr. Holmes,[1] with that from Mr. Lowry[2] & copy of the answer,[3] which were inclosed to me, are now returned.

I think Govr. Holmes should be encouraged in keeping a wakeful eye to occurrences & appearances in W. Florida, and in transmitting information concerning them. It will be well for him also to be attentive to the means of having his Militia in a state for any service that may be called for. In the event either of foreign interference with W. F. or of internal convulsions, more especially if threatening the neighboring tranquility, it will be proper to take care of the rights & interests of the U. S. by every measure within the limits of the Ex. Authority. Will it not be adviseable to apprize Govr. H. confidentially, of the course adopted as to W. F. and to have his co-operation in diffusing the impressions we wish to be made there?[4]

The anecdote related by Mr. L. is interesting in several respects. I take for granted that the papers to be sent him from the Dept. of State will be adapted to the unsettled State of things in Caraccas; yet I do not recollect to have recd. for signature any Commission varied from the ordinary consular form. Accept my respects & friendly wishes

JAMES MADISON

RC (DNA: RG 59, ML). For enclosures, see nn. 1–3.

1. David Holmes's 20 June 1810 letter to Robert Smith (DNA: RG 59, TP, Mississippi) discussed the political situation in West Florida. Holmes reported that Spanish authority in the province had virtually collapsed, to the point that the resulting "sense of common danger [had] induced some of the inhabitants to establish a kind of neighbourhood police" whose operations were both "inefficient" and "unjust." The "mixed nature" of the population had, moreover, led to the development of parties favoring American, British, and Spanish interests, and, until recently, there had also been a French party. The "American party" wished to see the province become part of the U.S., but Holmes believed its members hesitated to act from fear of the consequences of failure. He also stated, though, that they would rather take the risk than be subjected to any other power or the "perils of anarchy." The British party wished for the protection of Great Britain, while many of the French party had recently removed to Orleans Territory after having been ordered to leave the country. Holmes further noted that "a great portion of the population of West Florida consist[ed] of slaves, and persons without character, or the means of procuring a comfortable living." These facts led him to ask what would be the effect of a "state of Anarchy and confusion" upon the adjacent territories of the U.S., and he predicted that should the "respectable" and "well disposed" portions of the community be overcome in any struggle, "we shall be placed in a very unpleasant if not in a precarious situation as respects our slaves." Holmes concluded by observing that Great Britain was the only foreign power likely to interfere in West Florida, and he assumed that the U.S. must be "considered in some degree interested" in the outcome.

2. In his 10 July 1810 letter to Robert Smith, Robert Lowry, agent-designate to the revolutionary junta at Caracas, reported that he would be ready to leave by the end of the month (DNA: RG 59, CD, La Guaira; printed in William R. Manning, ed., *Diplomatic Correspondence of the United States concerning the Independence of the Latin-American Nations* [3 vols.; New York, 1925], 2:1144). Lowry also related conversations he had in Baltimore with two agents from Caracas, Juan Vicente Bolívar and Telésforo d'Orea. The former told Lowry that he had placed orders for muskets to be sent to Caracas, while the latter mentioned a meeting he had attended the previous week in Philadelphia with Francis James Jackson, Luis de Onís, Juan Bautisa Bernabeu, and the recently displaced Spanish governor from Caracas. The Spanish officials believed that Great Britain would probably not favor their cause to the extent that they had hoped, especially if the revolutionaries in Caracas should repudiate totally the authority of Ferdinand VII.

3. Robert Smith to Robert Lowry, 12 July 1810, acknowledged receipt of Lowry's letter of 10 July and informed him that papers for his mission would be ready by 20 July (copy, DLC) (1 p.; in John Graham's hand; docketed by JM).

4. See Robert Smith to David Holmes, 21 July 1810 (letterbook copy, DNA: RG 59, DL), where Smith instructed Holmes to have the territorial militia of Mississippi ready for service in the event of "foreign interference" or "internal convulsions" in West Florida. Smith also sent to Holmes a copy of portions of William C. C. Claiborne's 14 June letter to William Wykoff, Jr., authorizing Wykoff to go to Baton Rouge to assure the West Florida settlers of "the friendly disposition of the American Government" and to encourage them to form a convention to determine the future of the region. Claiborne's letter, Smith declared, had been "written under a sanction from the president." Smith further enclosed "some instructions issued from this department, marked A," which were subsequently indentified by Clarence E. Carter as a letter written to Wykoff by the secretary of state on 20 June. These informed Holmes of the selection of an agent for the "confidential purpose of proceeding without delay into East Florida, and also into West Florida, as far as pensacola for the pur-

pose of diffusing the inpression that the United States cherish the sincerest good will towards the people of the Floridas as neighbours . . . and that in the event of a political separation from the parent Country, their incorporation into our Union would coincide with the sentiments and the policy of the United States" (see copy of Smith to Holmes, 21 July 1810, and enclosures [DNA: RG 59, TP, Orleans]; enclosure "A" reprinted as Smith to Wykoff, 20 June 1810, in Carter, *Territorial Papers, Orleans*, 9:883–84).

The obvious differences, if not total incompatibility, between these two sets of instructions, supposedly written to Wykoff within the space of one week, require some explanation. Assuming that Smith was not trying to confuse Holmes about the nature of Wykoff's mission, it is plausible to suggest that his 20 June letter was not, as Carter claimed, to Wykoff but was, instead, the enclosure in his letter of the same day to William Harris Crawford requesting the senator to select "a gentleman of honor & discretion qualified to execute a trust of . . . interest & delicacy" (ibid., 9:885). Neither the RC of Smith's letter to Crawford nor its enclosed "letter of instruction" has been located, but it would seem that State Department clerks, in fulfilling JM's request to inform Holmes of the administration's policy toward West Florida, sent the Mississippi governor a copy of the latter along with the extracts from Claiborne's 14 June letter to Wykoff.

From the Chickasaw Nation

FATHER   CHICKASAWS 17th. July 1810

You told us in writing when you were about to Establish a Factory among us, that we should have goods at the same price they were then sold to the Cherokees at Tellico;[1] we have found a very great Difference from the first begining of the Chickasaw Factory in the price of goods here & at Tellico & we have to pay higher every year, so much so, that we suppose the goods will get so high that it would be more to our Interest to pack such goods as we want from Mobille; which we shall be under the necessity of doing if the price of goods is not lowered at the Chickasaw Factory.

FATHER

Please to inform us? whether there is so great a Differance in the prices of goods purchased annually by the United states, for the Chickasaw Factory as we have to pay, one year after an other in succession? Whether it is your advice to your Factor to Charge us mor[e] for goods every year? or whether your Factor does it of his own accord, to fill his own Coffers, & Cheat you out of what he extorts from us.

FATHER

We would be extremely glad to have these few quest[i]ons resolved so as to relieve our minds from that Doubt we Cannot help entertaining, of your orders to the Factor to sell goods so high to us.

The Factor trims all the heads & shanks of our Deer & Beaver skins &

no allowance made in the price of goods for this reduction of the weight of skins—all which we Humbly submit to your Decission.

> CINUSUBEE MINGO, his mark ×
> ATTASHEMICO, his mark ×
> EMATTA HA MICO, his mark ×
> MINGO MATTAHA, his mark ×
> WM. COLBERT, his mark ×
> GEORGE COLBERT, his mark ×
> WM. MCGILBERY his mark ×
> PIOHOLAUGHTA his mark ×
> PAISAUGHSTUBBEE his mark ×
> MCKLUSH HOPIA his mark ×
> FUNNY MINGO MASTUBBEE mark ×

FATHER,

I have one favour to ask of you, that is that you will please to grant permission for my self & four other headmen with an Interpreter to go to the City of washington next fall, on business of importance which can be better done when we are present than by writing

> his
> GEORGE × COLBERT[2]
> mark

N: B Please a[n]swer this request as early as practicable & oblige your friend[3]

> G C

RC (DNA: RG 107, LRRS, C-199:5). Headed: "A talk from the King Headmen & Warriors of the Chickasaw Nation to James Madison Esqr. President of the United States." Docketed by a War Department clerk as received 30 Aug. 1810 (but see Eustis to JM, 26 Aug. 1810, and n. 2).

1. On the establishment of the Chickasaw Bluffs Trading House in 1802 and the subsequent trade in pelts, see Arrell M. Gibson, *The Chickasaws* (Norman, Okla., 1971), pp. 94–95.

2. George Colbert (ca. 1764–1839) and his brother William were sons of a Scots trader, James Logan Colbert, who had settled in the Chickasaw Nation in 1729, married three Chickasaw women, and become a substantial slaveholder as well as the owner of a store and a ferry across the Tennessee River in northwest Alabama. The Colberts emerged as one of the most prominent families of mixed blood who increasingly dominated Chickasaw affairs in the early nineteenth century. In 1805 George Colbert received a payment of $1,000 from the U.S. for his services in arranging a land cession, and during the War of 1812 the Colbert brothers allied Chickasaw forces with Andrew Jackson's army in the campaigns against the Creek Indians (*ASP, Indian Affairs*, 1:697; Gibson, *The Chickasaws*, pp. 65–66, 80, 96–101).

3. JM sent the letter to the secretary of war, who referred it to John Mason, superintendent of Indian trade, for consideration and a response (Eustis to JM, 26 Aug. 1810; John Smith to Mason, 4 Sept. 1810 [DNA: RG 107, LSMA]).

From George Logan

Dear Sir   London July 17th: 1810

The Government of the Unite[d] States in renewing commerce with the Belligerants, has done our country great honor as by this magnanimous act, we offer to both nations, another opportunity to do us justice, and to restore our friendship. It has powerfully strengthened our friends in this country—and whatever may be the feelings of the administration; even the ministry in private conversation, and in parliament, profess a desire to preserve peace with the United States. This sentiment is general amongst every class of citizens, which I have witnessed in several instances. I lately attended the annual meeting of the agricultural society of Surry; above eighty gentlemen of the first characters in the county were present. At dinner the two members of parliament for the county presided, when they proposed the following toast, which was drank with great acclamation "Dr. Logan, and may harmony be restored between Breat [*sic*] Britain and the United States equally honorable and beneficial to both countries." I am just returned from the annual agricultural meetings of the Duke of Bedford at Woburn; and of Mr: Coke at Holkham; both attended by many of the first nobility and gentry in the kingdom. At the first a universal desire was expressed to preserve peace with the UStates. At the latter a sentiment of that kind was drank by three hundred & forty persons at table; on this occasion partaking of the hospitality of Mr: Coke; among whom were the Duke of Bedford Sir John Sinclair Sir Joseph Banks &c. Mr: Coke has presented me with a new improved drilling machine, which he makes use of himself, and thinks being introduced among us, it will be of service to the United States.

As to public affairs I am a stranger to what is passing between Mr: Pinkney and the Marquis Wellesley. As a private citizen, I have not thought it proper to enquire into the negotiation. But as your Friend I have considered it my duty to remove some prejudices respecting your attachment to France—as that you would rather make a sacrifice to France, than to seek peace with England. I have also expressed an earnest desire that the remaining shadow of the orders in council should be removed, to ensure the success of the negotiation so auspiciously commenced by the two governments. Accept assurances of my highest esteem & friendship

Geo Logan

P. S. I expect to embark in September for the UStates.

RC (DLC); draft (PHi). RC docketed by JM. Draft dated July 1810. Postscript not on draft.

¶ To William Eustis. Letter not found. *17 July 1810*. Acknowledged in Eustis to JM, 29 July 1810. Inquires about orders given to U.S. Army troops marching to Pittsburgh.

To Daniel Eccleston

SIR   VIRGINIA July 18. 1810.

I have duly recd. the Medallion of General Washington accompanying your favor of Jany. 1; and return my thanks for it. The high veneration in which his Memory is held in his own Country, renders such tokens of respect to it, in others, at once grateful in themselves, and just titles to esteem in those, who looking beyond a national horizon, can do justice to the worthies & benefactors of Mankind, wherever seen, or however distant. Accept my friendly respects

JAMES MADISON

RC (Central Public Library, Lancaster, England); draft (DLC). Draft undated; docketed by JM, "1810"; dated ca. January 1810 in *Index to the James Madison Papers*.

From Elizabeth House Trist
18 July 1810

EDITORIAL NOTE

The following is the opening letter in a series of exchanges between JM and Elizabeth House Trist that took place over the summer of 1810 and culminated in a meeting in Washington, D.C., on or shortly after 18 October 1810. JM had long known Elizabeth House Trist, having first met her during the 1780s when he had boarded in the Philadelphia home of her mother, Mary Stretch House. At that time Elizabeth House Trist was the wife of Nicholas Trist, a young British army officer whom she had married in June 1774. Their son, Hore Browse Trist, had been born in February 1775. With the birth of his son, Nicholas Trist decided to resign his army commission in order to settle in America with his family, and by 1777 he had taken up lands in British West Florida where he endeavored to arrange for his wife and son to join him. The difficulties of the Revolution delayed the reunification of the family, and Elizabeth House Trist was unable to make plans to go to her husband until the end of 1783. She traveled to Pittsburgh in order to make the river journey to the Gulf Coast, only to learn that Nicholas Trist had died in February 1784. After struggling to settle his affairs, she returned to Philadelphia in August 1785 (JM to Jefferson, 3 Oct. 1785, *PJM*, 8:376).

During and after these unhappy events both JM and Jefferson remained on friendly terms with the House family. In 1798 Hore Browse Trist purchased property in Albemarle County, Virginia, where he also encouraged his close friend, Dr. William Bache (the grandson of Benjamin Franklin), to settle with him. The following year he married Mary Louisa Brown of Philadelphia, and in 1800 their first son, Nicholas Philip Trist—who was later to become JM's secretary—was born. Misfortune continued to plague the family, however. By 1802 Hore Browse Trist was near bankruptcy, brought about in part by his own mismanagement and in part by several bank failures that had occurred in 1800. He resolved in 1802 to recoup his fortunes by taking up his father's old claims, now located in the recently created Mississippi Territory where Jefferson gave him the appointment of revenue collector at Natchez. With the transfer of the Louisiana Purchase to the United States in December 1803, however, the president conferred on him the more important position of collector at the port of New Orleans.

In 1804 the Trist household, including Elizabeth House Trist, moved to New Orleans, but Hore Browse Trist died of yellow fever within two months of their arrival, leaving a widow with two young children. Jefferson then gave the vacant New Orleans collectorship to William Brown, Trist's brother-in-law, while Trist's widow, Mary Brown Trist, subsequently married Philip Livingston Jones, a prominent member of a New Orleans faction at odds with the administration of Orleans territorial governor William C. C. Claiborne. Elizabeth House Trist did not entirely approve of her daughter-in-law's choice for a second husband, and this may have contributed to her decision, sometime in 1808, to return to Virginia, where she resided for the remainder of her life (Claiborne to Jefferson, 1 June 1807, Carter, *Territorial Papers, Orleans*, 9:743).

Unfortunately for the family, however, William Brown, in addition to his duties as collector, had purchased two sugar plantations, along with a sizable number of slaves, and he was soon in financial difficulty. These circumstances probably influenced his decisions in 1808 and 1809 to sell portions of his plantations to Philip Livingston Jones, subject to the provision that Brown would pay $8,090 toward the support of Mary Jones's two children by her marriage to Hore Browse Trist. Still worse was to follow. William Brown, finally overwhelmed by financial troubles, absconded in November 1809 with public money to the amount of $150,000, and within the month, on 14 December 1809, Philip Livingston Jones died while returning to New Orleans from Philadelphia where he had been seeking funds to complete his purchase of portions of Brown's plantations.

Inevitably, the United States government began proceedings against William Brown in order to obtain his assets to satisfy the public claims against him, and the task of setting the business in motion fell to the district attorney, Philip Grymes. As he did so, however, Grymes seized the assets of both William Brown and Philip Livingston Jones on the grounds that the latter had no valid title to the property of the former and that the United States, by law, had a prior right to all of Brown's property anyway. Understandably distressed by these developments, Mary Jones brought suit in May 1810 in the New Orleans superior court, where a jury found that her late husband's title to Brown's plantations was "good," but Grymes, undeterred by this verdict, continued with his task throughout 1810 (Elizabeth House Trist to JM, 7 Aug. 1810, and enclosures).

It was at this point that Elizabeth House Trist wrote to JM on 18 July, bitterly protesting against the conduct of Grymes and requesting JM to take steps to counteract it. On looking into the matter, JM concluded that Grymes had the law on his side, though he did write to Gallatin to suggest, as he told Elizabeth House Trist, that the Treasury Department should consult "the interest & accomodation" of Mary Jones "as far as may be permitted by fidelity to the public rights." The news that William Brown had been arrested in a London theater, however, encouraged Elizabeth House Trist to hope that JM could yet retrieve her family's fortunes from Brown's assets, though JM's response was clearly intended to warn her not to expect too much on that account. Evidently dissatisfied with this answer, Elizabeth House Trist decided to see JM personally while she was returning to Virginia from a visit to friends in Philadelphia. The two met in the third week of October 1810, but it proved to be an awkward and embarrassing reunion. Elizabeth House Trist left the meeting after she concluded that JM did not appear to be sufficiently responsive to the concerns of her daughter-in-law and her grandchildren (JM to Elizabeth House Trist, 25 July and ca. 5 Sept. 1810; JM to Gallatin, 26 July 1810; Gallatin to JM, 21 Aug. 1810, n. 1; Elizabeth House Trist to JM, 27 Aug. 1810).

(Secondary source used for this note: Jane Flaherty Wells, "Thomas Jefferson's Neighbors: Hore Browse Trist of 'Birdwood' and Dr. William Bache of 'Franklin,'" *Magazine of Albemarle County History*, 49 [1989]: 1–13.)

DR SIR   [18 July 1810]

However unfortunate and miserable no personal consideration wou'd induce me to trouble you—but as the first magistrate of my country I appeal to you in behalf of those who have a claim on me to support with my best energy their rights and duty impels me to the task, tis not for favor or indulgence I solicit but an impartial investigation into the conduct of Mr Grimes by whoes chicanery my daughter and her children will be totally ruind unless the Goverment counteracts his proceedings and does that justice which I am confident will ever be their intention to perform I can not explain to you better the nature of my appeal than by subjoining an extract from my daughters letter of the 6th June recd yesterday,[1] the emotions it has occasion'd unfits me for any thing more. Knowing I was in the country she enclosed my letter under cover to Mrs Bache for her perusal and some papers relating to her claim which Mrs. B. informd me that she had taken the liberty to send on to Mr Gallitan. From the commencement of the unhappy period which gave Mr Grimes the power has he done every thing to teaze and distress that wretched family and from the constant agitation of Spirits Marys health is greatly impaird and I fear much, we shall have her loss to deplore goodness honor and prudence have mark'⟨d⟩ her deportment thro life and if she is taken I shall pray that her Sons may go als[o] and then I shall have nothing to bind me to a world so replete with unhappiness.

I have this moment lea[r]nd that the papers have announc⟨ed⟩ your departure for Virginia if you shou'd visit at Monticello I will thank you to mention the [*sic*] this affair to Mr Jefferson and Mrs Randolph as they have always felt an interest in the family with respects to Mrs Madison &c

Tr (PPAmP). In the hand of Elizabeth House Trist; copied in her letter to Catharine Wistar Bache dated "Wednesday noon." Date of Tr assigned on the assumption that the RC (not found) was the letter of 18 July acknowledged in JM to Elizabeth House Trist, 25 July 1810.

1. Extract not found.

¶ To William Thornton. Letter not found. *Ca. 18 July 1810*. Acknowledged in Thornton to JM, 27 July 1810. Encloses a letter to be forwarded to Daniel Eccleston.

From John Smith

SIR, WAR DEPARTMENT, July 19th. 1810.

I have the honor, in the absence of the Secretary of War, to enclose a Copy of Governor Harrison's dispatch of the 4th. inst. A like Copy will be transmitted to the Secretary at New York. I am, Sir, with perfect respect, your ob. servt:

(signed.) JNO. SMITH, C. C.

[First Enclosure]

§ William Henry Harrison to William Eustis. *4 July 1810, Vincennes*. Reports the return of Messrs. Brouillet and DuBois from Prophetstown and encloses a deposition from the former.[1] States that DuBois was well received by the Prophet, who denied any intention of going to war but who also asserted that "the Indians had been cheated of their lands, that no sale was good unless made by all the Tribes." DuBois suggested that the Prophet visit Vincennes, but he declined, "alleging that he had been ill-treated when he was there before." Mentions that DuBois talked with some of the Kickapoo tribe as well as with the Wea and Eel River tribes, all of whom feared there would be war and that they might be involved, but Harrison endorses DuBois's view that the defection of the Potawatomi and other Indians at the recent council has "for the present, entirely frustrated the prophets designs." Refers to reports that the Prophet will assassinate the Potawatomi chief, Winnemac, but Harrison suspects there are persons in Vincennes fomenting the Prophet's discontent and encouraging him to oppose U.S. policies. Reiterates his long-standing opposition to the Prophet's claim that the Indians consider all their lands as common property, defends his conduct in negotiating recent treaties, and agrees with Jefferson that the Miami Nation "are the only rightful Claimants of all the unpurchased lands from the Ohio to the Illinois and Mississippi Rivers." Dismisses the Prophet's grievances as "mere pretence, suggested to [him] by British Partizans & Emmissaries." Believes the signatories to the 1809 treaty at Fort Wayne are satisfied with its terms.[2]

Letterbook copy (DNA: RG 107, LSP); enclosures (DLC). First enclosure (4 pp.) in a clerk's hand; marked "(Copy)"; docketed by JM; printed in Esarey, *Messages and Letters of William Henry Harrison*, Indiana Historical Collections, 1:438–40. For second enclosure, see n. 1.

1. Harrison enclosed a copy of a deposition signed by Michel Brouillet describing his mission to Prophetstown, 30 June 1810 (3 pp.; in a clerk's hand; docketed by JM; printed ibid., 1:436–38).
2. The RC of Harrison's letter closes with a sentence not included on the copy sent to JM: "Captain Posey has not yet arrived as soon as he comes I shall dismiss the two Companies of Militia" (DNA: RG 107, LRRS, H-142:5).

§ Presidential Proclamation. *19 July 1810, Montpelier, Virginia.* Instructs customs collectors, under section 61 of "An Act to regulate the collection of duties on imports and tonnage, passed 2 March 1799," to estimate the value of the Norwegian dollar, now circulating "with a considerable depreciation," in order to levy duties on goods and merchandise imported from Norway. Directs that the value of the dollar is to be calculated at "such rate as may appear to be its real value at the time when the goods, wares, and merchandize were shipped from the said country."

Printed copy (Baltimore *Federal Republican and Commercial Gazette*, 7 Sept. 1810).

To William Eustis

DEAR SIR   MONTPELIER July 20. 1810
I have recd. your letter of the 16th. answering one from Genl. Wilkinson of the 14th. of which a copy was inclosed.

Your objections to his request seem to evince the irregularity of it. Nor do I perceive its importance to his object. As the examination of the Officers, if present, being ex. parte, wd. of course be without cross examinations, their testimony may be taken where they are, with the same degree of weight; and on whatever points and questions Genl. W. may prescribe. It is true that new questions might grow out of unforeseen answers to previous ones, and that in the presence of Genl. W. these might be conducted more satisfactorily by himself, than otherwise. But it is not presumable that in an exparte proceeding, the difference would be material, and pretty certain that it would not be sufficient to justify a course without precedent, and forming one which might be found not a little perplexing. If the Officers named by him, could be brought to Washington, without inconvenience to the public, and in a way so incidental as never to be drawn into precedent, the accomodation to the wishes of the General would doubtless be agreeable to all of us. But this it appears, is out of the question.

The expression in his letter which you quote, suggests questions, which I had supposed, were precluded by considerations such as you state. Can any order, going directly from the War Office, altho' to any inferior Officer, be interfered with by a superior? In ordinary cases this does not happen, because the order would pass thro' the latter. In the case before us it does happen. If the interference be not allowable, and all the commands have been specially disposed of, there seems to be no room for his. If a strict right to interfere resulted from his rank, notwithstanding any immediate orders to Officers under him, Still it would seem irregular, not to say indecorous, to interfere without a previous resort to the sanction of the Department. The tendency of the remark in the letter of Genl. W. seems to be [to] draw out an explanation, how far he is or is not to be considered in the light of a suspended Officer; and consequently how far on the one supposition he ought to be kept in inactivity at the Seat of Govt: and, on the other, why he is not allowed an immediate trial. If this explanation be the object, and is to be given, the true one seems to be, that he is no otherwise suspended in his Command than as the effect necessarily results, from his being called to the seat of Govt. and from the several Military commands being vested for the time being in others. I am aware of the real difficulty & awkwardness incident to the peculiarity of the case; and as I not only make these observations in haste, but also without the accurate knowledge of military rules you possess, I wish them to have no effect, beyond your concurrence in them.

I return the letter from Col. Simonds with the signature required. Accept my respects & best wishes

JAMES MADISON

RC (PHi: Daniel Parker Papers).

¶ To John Bassette. Letter not found. *Ca. 20 July 1810*. Mentioned in JM to Jefferson, 24 July 1810. Replies to Bassette's inquiry about Dutch accounts of early Virginia history.

To Albert Gallatin

DEAR SIR   MONTPELIER July 21. 1810

I recd. your favor written the day before your intended departure from Washington, and complied with its contents.

The inclosed letter from Dr. Bache,[1] has just come to hand. I can not do better with it, than to give you an opportunity of extending to a distressed family, whatever accomodations may be permitted, by fidelity to the public interest. You will be the better judge of the case, as a report of it from Grymes, or his successor, will doubtless have been forwarded to you.

We must allow Gelston, his reasonable expences at least. Every thing relating to Spanish America, is too important to be subjected to a Minute Œconomy; or even to unnecessary delays. Accept my respects & best wishes

JAMES MADISON

RC (NHi: Gallatin Papers). Cover marked "*private*" by JM.

1. Letter not found. William Bache's letter related Mary Jones's complaints about the conduct of Philip Grymes, U.S. attorney at New Orleans (see Elizabeth House Trist to JM, 18 July 1810; JM to Trist, 25 July 1810; and JM to Gallatin, 26 July 1810).

From Armand Duplantier

SIR   NEW ORLEANS 21st July 1810.

I have received duplicate copies of a letter from General La Fayette, which you had the goodness to send me; Mr. Smith informed me that you had done me the honor to write to me at the same time: if so, the letter must have miscarried, for I did not receive it.

Since I forwarded to your Excellency the last five Surveys, I have located two thousand acres more, the certificates whereof would have been ready by this time, if the survayor had not omitted to send with the plats the attestation required by law. As soon as that omission shall be corrected, I will have them dispatched for Washington.

I have to this day kept 500 acres to be located, if possible, in the neighbourhood of this place, though I despair ever to find room for them. Mr. Smith, in my absence, wrote to you on this subject; & I find, from his communication to me of his information to you thereupon; that his Statement was perfectly conformable to what I take to be the true Situation of things. The only chance I may have to take possession of any portion of grant in that neighbourhood, would be that Congress should authorize Genl. La Fayette to locate any quantity of land in this vicinity, Say not less than fifty acres in a tract. Such loc⟨ation would?⟩ in⟨deed⟩ however small, be infinitely more valuable than any other.

The lands which I have hitherto located, are undoubtedly the best that could be found in the whole territory: so much so that, even now, if they were exposed for sale, none would not fetch less than five Dollars pr. acre & many would yield more. Some of the persons, who had begun Settlements on lands located for Genl. La Fayette, would be disposed to contract the obligation of clearing some more, on condition to remain there three or four years longer. I did not venture to enter into any such agreement before consulting your pleasure, & being previously authorised to that purpose. I have only given my consent to their continuing there untill further orders; because I think it to be for the advantage of Genl. La Fayette, as these Settlements always attract notice, & recommend the land. Your instructions on this subject will be thankfully received.

The General, in his last letters, shows much impatience to know the true situation of his landed property in this country, & to be furnished with the necessary plans, for the satisfaction of those who have made advances to him. He desires me to forward to him those titles; but every thing [. . .] with you, so that I have to request you to have the goodness of sending him copies of the necessary Documents. He seems still to depend on a location of great value in the vicinity of Canal Carondelet: some persons coming from this country appear to have kept up his wishes in this particular, notwithstanding I wrote to him that I entertained no such hope, & that such land as could be had there was but of small value, very low, & subject to be overflowed. I write to him again on that subject, and pray you to be so good as to cause my letter to be forwarded to him.

If the General is compelled to sell some part of his land, I am confident that by granting a credit of one, two, three and four years, some thousand acres may be sold advantageously, perhaps at the rate of ten Dollars pr. acre, on account of the settlements, and that the persons who actually reside on them, for fear of being ousted, would ask the preference. I am very respectfully Sir Your most obedt. humble servant

Du⟨PLANTIER⟩

P. S. I have just now been favoured with your letter of the 26th. may last. Your Excellency will find in this an answer to its contents.

RC (DNA: RG 49, Special Acts, Lafayette Grant, La.).

From Paul Hamilton

SIR NAVY DEPARTT July 23d. 1810

I enclose for your information copies of letters relating to another outrage on our Flag.[1] Some of the Gun Boats on the Orleans station having become unfit for service, I judged it expedient to replace them by one of our most active brigs of a depth of draft convenient in the waters of that Territory. For this purpose the Vixen was selected, and it being necessary that, on that distant station, the officers to be employed should be men whose experience and character entitle them to confidence, Lieutt. Trippe[2] was ordered to take command of that Vessel. Mr. Poindexter returning from his duties in Congress with his family, and a Son of the Attorney general,[3] for the benefit of his health took passage with Mr. Trippe by permission from this Department. As I have recalled Lieutt. Trippe for the purpose of a scrutiny into his conduct which strikes me as being exceptionable in two particulars, I will not at present trouble you with any comments on it; but on the behaviour of the Commander of the british vessel I cannot but observe, that it appears from the statements given to have been unjustifiable and outrageous. In forming this opinion I beg that I may not be understood as intending to dispute the right of one Ship of War firing to bring to another not known to be friendly. This right is admitted, and the frequent deceptions practiced by false colors warrant the propriety of the practice; but as it must have been discovered before the second shot was fired that our Vessel bore up, and was boarded by the british boat, on no principle of justice or humanity ought any firing to have taken place until sufficient time had been allowed for the boat to return and make report. Adopting a different course of conduct constitutes, in my judgment, an outrage purposely intended. If the statements given are correct, it was impossible for the british Commander to have reason to suspect the character of our Vessel; and the unmanly evasion that the Shot was not intended to take effect, proves nothing more than the meanness of the man who was guilty of it. As this affair occasions much talk here, and will no doubt become the subject of much newspaper animadversion I have thought it not amiss to give a view of it in the Intelligencer[4] to prevent if possible misrepresentations.

It has been reported here that since you left us you have been seriously indisposed: if this has been the case, I sincerely hope that before this you have been completely restored to health; and that with Mrs. Madison you are enjoying with very high relish, the leisure, rest, and every other blessing which your retreat affords. Be pleased to present my best respects to Mrs. M. and be yourself assured that I am with the greatest attachment and truth yrs.

PAUL HAMILTON

RC and enclosures (DLC). RC docketed by JM. Enclosures are copies, in a clerk's hand, of John Trippe to Hamilton, 30 June 1810 (3 pp.), with notes dated 24 June exchanged between Trippe and the commander of HMS *Moselle* (1 p.); and George Poindexter to Hamilton, 30 June 1810 (3 pp.).

1. The episode here described by Hamilton occurred on 24 June 1810.
2. John Trippe, who had entered the navy as a midshipman in 1799 and had been a lieutenant since 1807, died on 9 July 1810 (Callahan, *List of Officers of the Navy*, p. 551).
3. Caesar A. Rodney's son was slightly wounded during the encounter (Poindexter to Hamilton, 30 June 1810).
4. Hamilton's account appeared in the *National Intelligencer* of 23 July. It included Poindexter's 30 June letter to Hamilton, described as "a letter from a gentleman of great respectability . . . to his friend in this city."

§ From Seth Pease. *23 July 1810, Washington*. Resigns his position as surveyor of lands south of Tennessee.

RC (DNA: RG 49, Records of the General Land Office, Letters Received from the Surveyor General of Mississippi, 1803–9). 1 p. Verso readdressed by JM to Gallatin and dated Orange Court House, 27 July. Printed in Carter, *Territorial Papers, Mississippi*, 6:84).

To the Bunker Hill Association

MONTPELIER July 24. 1810.

J. Madison presents his respects to Benjamin Homans, J. E. Smith, & William Blagrove, Esqrs. from whom he has received the copy of Mr. Lincoln's Oration delivered on the 4th. of July; and returns his thanks for the polite attention, to which he is indebted for this opportunity of expressing the pleasure he has felt in perusing a performance equally distinguished for its polished eloquence, and its animated patriotism.

RC (NjP: Crane Collection).

To Thomas Jefferson

DEAR SIR   [ca. 24 July 1810]

Yours of the 13th. was duly recd. I have answer'd Bassette's Enquiry on the ground you have been so good as to furnish. Whether the lamb from the Merino Ewe is to remain ours or not, I think no time should now be lost in sending for your share, the season being at hand when the Ewes will be in heat; and as care will be taken of the lambs whenever they may drop, it will be best that they should drop early. It may make a year's difference in the maturity for breeding. I can not account for your not getting Moreau's Memoire. I have given a hint for it now to be sent from the Dept. of State.[1] His view of the case ought certainly to be comprized in your examination of [it].[2] I shall peruse this when recd. with pleasure; tho' not for all the reasons you enumerate, & for some which you do not; & I shall be particularly happy in the visit with which you flatter me. I see no convenient oppy. of sending on the Dogs to Dr. T. till my Waggon goes in Novr. In the mean time they will be duly attended to by G. Gooch if committed to his custody. Be assured of my constant & affectionate attacht.

JAMES MADISON

RC (DLC). Undated. Date assigned on the basis of Jefferson's docket, "recd. July 26. 10," and the information in n. 1.

1. The nature of JM's hint is unclear, though presumably he wrote a letter to Robert Smith at this time (not found), requesting him to forward the memoir to Jefferson. On 26 July 1810 Robert Smith instructed John Graham to "give the President the requisite information respecting the Memorial of Moreau de Lislet" (DNA: RG 59, ML). Graham wrote to JM the next day, reporting that the memoir was "not in this Dept." (Graham to JM, 27 July 1810).

2. JM wrote "of" again here. At a later time the word "it" was inserted in an unknown hand.

¶ From Benjamin Henry Latrobe. Letter not found. *24 July 1810.* Calendared as a two-page letter in the lists probably kept by Peter Force (DLC, series 7, container 2).

To John Graham

DEAR SIR   MONTPELIER July 25. 1810

The writer of the inclosed letter,[1] sent ⟨me⟩ a long time ago, a most voluminous manuscript in French on the subject of F. & English grammer, with a wish that I might approve & patronize its publication. Having neither time nor competency to decide on the merits of the work, it was examined by a Critical judge on such subjects; who discouraged the experiment of printing it, tho' he did justice to the ingenuity of the Author. The manuscript was sent back, with a letter referring to these sentiments.[2] It appears that either by misdirection or mistake, the packet, instead of going to Savanna, has been lodged at McIntosh Ct. House, and that complaint is made of the difficulty of obtaining it. The complaint is rather a proof that Grammarians as well as Poets belong to a genus irritabile, than that any wrong has been committed. Understanding however, that Mr. Haumont is old, respectable, and belonged to the French army which aided our Revolution, I wish he may be gratified by a direction from the General post office, that the packet, which is franked, be sent by the post master in McIntosh, to the post office in Savanna. Will you be so obliging as to intimate as much to Mr. Bradley[3] and to explain the occasion of this trouble to him. Accept my friendly respects & best wishes

JAMES MADISON

RC (DNA: RG 59, ML). Docketed by Graham.

1. Charles Haumont to JM, 26 June 1810.
2. JM's letter to Haumont has not been found.
3. Abraham Bradley, assistant postmaster general at Washington (Bryan, *History of the National Capital*, 1:350).

To Horatio Gates Spafford

SIR   [ca. 25 July 1810]

I have recd. your favor of July 7.[1] accompanied by your printed circular on the subject of your proposed Gazetteer of the State of N. York. It is certainly a commendable undertaking, and I wish you success in it. An extension of it to all the States would proportionally extend the value of the Work. It is an inconveniency incident to publications of this kind in our Country, that its rapid growth, and multiplied changes, soon call for new Editions improving & superseding the former, and consequently arresting the profits of the Authors. On the other hand, the public equally gains by this circumstance, which promotes an accumulation of statistical materials particularly interesting to the science of political Œconomy. Its patronage therefore may be considered as the more due in such cases. Whether the particular aid you wish for ought to be afforded, is a question which Congress alone have the authority to decide. For myself, I am restrained from being even a Subscriber, by a general rule, enforced by experience, and not departed from but in very peculiar cases. You will oblige me however, without entering my name on your list, to have two copies, with the price of them, forwarded to me at Washington as soon as the work you have in hand issues from the Press.[2] Accept my friendly respects.

JAMES MADISON

RC (NjMoHP: Spafford Collection). Undated. Conjectural date assigned on basis of comparison of the contents with Spafford to JM, 12 July 1810. Docketed by Spafford, with his note, "Ansd., & with 2 Gazetteers, 8.28,'13."

1. JM referred to Spafford's letter of 12 July 1810.

2. Spafford's *A Gazetteer of the State of New-York* was published in Albany by Solomon Southwick in 1813 (Shaw and Shoemaker 29836). Spafford's docket suggests that he forwarded two copies to JM.

To Elizabeth House Trist

DEAR MADAM   MONTPELIER July 25. 1810

I recd. after my arrival here your favor of the 18th. The substance of Mrs. Jones's letter had been previously sent ⟨to⟩ me by Dr. Bache, and I lost no time in forwarding it to Mr. Gallatin, whose disposition will doubtless concur with Mr. Duvall's & mine, in consulting the interest & accomodation of your daughter, as far as may be permitted by fidelity to the public rights. This, it would be superfluous to remark to you, is a law paramount with Executive Authorities, to that of friendship or benevolence, and in some insta⟨nces⟩ even to their own ideas of justice & equity. As Mr. Grymes is no longer in office,[1] and his explanations have not been recd. it is neither necessary nor proper to pass judgment on the charges ag⟨ainst⟩ him. With perfect confidence in the Sincerity of Mrs. J's statem⟨ents⟩ and in the accuracy of them where proceeding from her personal knowledge, it is but just to keep in mind, that it would be dif⟨fi⟩cult for a public Officer, strictly adhering to his duty, to avoid, under the circumstances of such a case, an appearance of insensi⟨bi⟩lity or even severity, not only in her eyes, but in those of her ⟨sym⟩pathizing friends. Accept Dear Madam, assurances of my respect and ⟨best⟩ wishes.

JAMES MADISON

RC (ViU). Edge of RC damaged.

1. Philip Grymes had resigned as district attorney on 18 Mar., but he promised to "continue to discharge the Duties of the Office so as that the U. States shall not sustain any Injury for the want of a prosecuting Atty in this District" (Grymes to Robert Smith, 18 Mar. 1810, Carter, *Territorial Papers, Orleans*, 9:877).

From James Monroe

I wished to obtain an interview with Bizet[1] before I answer'd your favor of the 16th., that I might communicate to you something decisive relative to its object. Owing to his engagments at some distance, and to an injury which he lately received in blowing a rock, I could not see him till today, when I explain fully your wishes respecting his services. He seemed to be much gratified at the proposed employment, and very willing to undertake it, provided he should be able to execute it to your satisfaction. He mentiond that he had some engagments, the completion of which would take him about a fortnight, and that the necessity he was under to give a portion of his time to his family, would he feard, form an additional obstacle; but that he would wait on & confer personally with you on the subject. I encouraged him in this step, because I thought that it would lead to a more satisfactory arrang'ment with him, after he had seen the ground, and you had heard what he had to say on that subject, and of his proposed services, should you think proper to employ him, than it would be possible for me to make, under existing circumstances. He will be with you in the commencment of the ensuing week. He is an honest hard working man, with much information in his branch of business, but his vision is too imperfect to allow him to embrace distant objects, which is of importance in certain kinds of improv'ment. Add to which, that altho his education was good, the employment hitherto given him has been calculated rather to contract than enlarge his knowledge, of the ornamental kind. I was desirous of fixing with him the price to be paid for his services, in case you engaged him but he declined it, untill after he had seen the ground & made some estimate of the time requisite to complete the business, as of its interference with his prospects here. He receives I understand a dolr. pr. day for his services in this neighbourhood. Mrs. Monroe and our daughter who is with us, desire me to present their best regards to Mrs. Madison, to which I beg to add mine. I am dear Sir with great respect & esteem yr friend & servant

JAS MONROE

RC (DLC: Rives Collection, Madison Papers).

1. Bizet (or Beazee) was a French gardener (Hunt-Jones, *Dolley and the "Great Little Madison,"* p. 74).

¶ From Richard Forrest. Letter not found. *25 July 1810.* Calendared as a two-page letter in the lists probably kept by Peter Force (DLC, series 7, container 2).

To Albert Gallatin

DEAR SIR   MONTPELIER July 26. 1810
I inclosed to you, a few days ago a letter from Docr. Bache stating the complaints of Mrs. Jones, agst. the proceedings of the District Attorney at N. O. I have just recd. & inclose one from Mrs. Trist which is more full on the same subject. I am aware, that the business may lie, rather with the Controler, than with you; but it is not amiss that it should be under your view also. As Grymes' explanations have not been recd. as he is personally obnoxious to that family, and as one of his Accusers is E. Jones,[1] whose personal animosity is embittered by his political, it would be very unfair, as it is now unnecessary, to pass judgment on his conduct. It is easy to perceive that more was expected from him, than might be consistent with his public duty; tho' it is to be presumed also, that a reciprocity of ill-will might tempt him to do less. If the property should, as I take to be of course, soon be exposed again to sale, Mrs. J. will have the oppy. of which she thinks she has been deprived, of becoming the purchaser. I remain without information from abroad. We are at length relieved from the apprehension of an Indian war, which at one moment Govr. Harrisons intelligence as to the arrangements of the Prophet, rendered highly probable. The several Tribes, towards the lakes, who had entered into his views, failed him at the critical moment. Mrs. Madison tenders her best respects to Mrs. Gallatin. Be pleased to add mine; & to be assured yourself of my esteem & my friendly wishes

JAMES MADISON

RC (NHi: Gallatin Papers). Docketed by Gallatin.

1. Evan Jones, a planter and merchant who had been U.S. consul at New Orleans before 1803, was also the uncle of Philip Livingston Jones, second husband of Mary Brown Trist. He subsequently became notorious for his sympathy to Aaron Burr and for his opposition to territorial governor Claiborne (Carter, *Territorial Papers, Orleans*, 9:82, 246, 308–9, 345, 489; *PJM-SS*, 1:185 n. 8).

To Paul Hamilton

DEAR SIR   MONTPELIER July 26. 1810
I have recd. yours of the 23. inclosing the report of the incident to Lt. Trippe on his way to N. Orleans. The conduct of the British commander, appears to have been highly reproachful; whatever may be the light in which that of Lt. Trippe ought to be viewed. The right of one Ship of war towards another not avowing or displaying hostility, can not extend

beyond the means necessary to verify the Flag. These means, as sanctioned by usage, may fairly be used on one side, & honorably admitted by the other. This test evidently condemns the second Shot, as wanton & inhuman. The firing from the boat, must have been sheer impudence. Had the Boat been American & the Ship British, the former would doubtless have been sent to the bottom without a parley. I observe that Lt. T. in his *official* note falls into an error, but too common, of designating H. *Britannic* Majesty, by the simple title "His Majesty." This on the High seas, or any where out of the British Dominions, is the language of a British subject; not of a member of an Independent State, who can not know one Majesty from another, a British, French, Danish or any other, but by the distinctive epithet prefixed. You will be pleased to communicate to the Secretary of State, the circumstances of this case, that he may give the proper instruction to Mr. Pinkney relative to it.[1]

I am much obliged by the interest you are so good as to take in my health. I was shortly & slightly indisposed a few days after I got home, owing I conjecture to bile contracted either at Washington, or by some exposure to the sun, which I did not shun on the journey. I hope I am now freed from it.

Altho' your letter is silent with respect to your projected ramble in this direction, I cherish the expectation of being able to welcome you, 'ere long, to Montpelier, where I shall see you with particular pleasure. I regret that we can not flatter ourselves with the same favor from Mrs. Hamilton & the young ladies; to whom our joint & best respects are tendered. Accept, for yourself, assurances of my great esteem with my affectionate salutations.

JAMES MADISON

RC (DLC: Gideon Welles Papers, Records of the Navy Department).

1. No such communication from Robert Smith to William Pinkney has been found.

To Robert Smith

DEAR SIR   MONTPELIER July 26. 1810

I return herewith the letters from Vanderhorst,[1] & Bernabeu.[2] It would have been better if Lowry had more carefully concealed his destination.[3] The case of the Spanish Goods landed from the French privateer, must be decided by the result of the judicial enquiry into the character of the latter.[4] If equipped from our jurisdiction, the capture gives a claim to restitution. If not so equipped, the law as it stands in relation to prize goods brought into the U. S. must decide on the course to be pursued. It would seem proper to transmit the representation of Bernabeu, to the Collector & the District Attorney, with a request to the latter to do what may be right in the cases.

I find by a letter from the Secretary of the Navy, that another insult to our National Flag, has been offered by a British Commander. I have desired him to communicate to you the circumstances of the case; on which you will please to found whatever instruction to Mr. Pinkney, they may render proper. Accept my respects & best wishes.

JAMES MADISON

RC (DNA: RG 59, ML). Docketed by John Graham, with his notation: "write to Mr P touching the affair of the Vixen."

1. Elias Vander Horst had been consul at Bristol since 1792. JM had probably been reading his 24 May 1810 dispatch to the State Department, reporting on a growing grain shortage in Great Britain as well as on the efforts of American merchants to trade with Great Britain in both American and Spanish goods (DNA: RG 59, CD, Bristol).

2. Juan Bautisa Bernabeu to Robert Smith, 17 and 18 July 1810 (DNA: RG 59, NFL, Spain).

3. In his 17 July letter, Bernabeu—the Spanish consul at Baltimore—referred to rumors that JM had appointed Robert K. Lowry as commercial agent at Caracas. Bernabeu pointed out that not only were such agents not permitted in Spain's American provinces but that Lowry would certainly not be admitted to Caracas, which was then in a state of insurrection. Hinting that Lowry's appointment would harm relations with Spain, Bernabeu requested the State Department to inform him whether there was any truth to the rumors.

4. On 18 July, Bernabeu complained of the activities of a French privateer, *La Revanche du Cerf*, which, he stated, had berthed at Norfolk, Virginia, with items seized from Spanish vessels. He requested the State Department to give orders to collectors in U.S. ports to detain similarly seized Spanish property until it could be reclaimed by its owners.

From Thomas Jefferson

DEAR SIR   MONTICELLO July 26. 10

Your's of the 17th. & that by the last mail are recieved. I have carefully searched among my papers for that of Hamilton which is the subject of your letter, but certainly have it not. If I ever had it (which I should doubt) I must have returned it. I say I doubt having had it because I find it in your Conventional debates under date of June 18. where it is copied at full length, being so entered I presume in your Original manuscript. Having it in that, I do not suppose I should have wanted his original. I presume you have your MS. of the debates with you. If you have not, drop me a line and I will copy it from my copy.

I hope I shall be ready to send you my statement of the case of the batture by Tuesday's post, and shall follow it myself within two or three days. I am obliged to send a copy also to my counsel the moment I can finish it, being ruled to plead before the 15th. prox. and Wirt being to leave Richmd. the 28th. inst. But our plea will be amendable should your own suggestions or those of Mr. Gallatin, Smith or Rodney render it adviseable. I extremely lament the not having been able to see Moreau's Memoir. I wrote to mr. Graham for it, & he to mr. Rodney. The latter wrote me in reply that he supposed it was among his papers at Washington & would send it to me on his return to that place; but that may be distant. I am afraid of taking false or untenable ground; tho my investigation of the subject gives me confidence that a stronger case never came before a court. I shall finish in a day or two the dog-proof inclosure for my sheep and will then send for them if I find my prospect of seeing you at Montpelier retarded. One of the dogs, the male, intended for Washington, died on the very day I wrote to you. The other shall be sent to mr. Gooch. Affectionately yours'

TH: JEFFERSON

RC (DLC); FC (DLC: Jefferson Papers).

From John Smith

SIR   WAR DEPARTMENT July 26th. 1810

I have the honor of transmitting herewith a copy of Govr. Harrison's letter of the 11th. Inst. and of stating that a similar copy will, by this day's mail, be forwarded to the Secretary of War at New York, to follow him from thence to Boston, should he have proceeded for that place. I am with perfect respect Sir, Your Ob. servt

JNO. SMITH, C. C.

[Enclosure]

§ William Henry Harrison to William Eustis. *11 July 1810, Vincennes.* Has received a letter from John Johnston, Indian agent at Fort Wayne, which confirms his own views "on the subject of the hostile combination of Indians, against the United States." Also promises further and more convincing "proofs of the hostility of the Prophet & his followers." Last week the Prophet sent four canoes to the Wea village at Terre Haute. Four Kickapoo Indians, in one of these canoes, came within sixteen miles of Vincennes and stole five horses, greatly alarming the local people. Has prevented a pursuit of the thieves as he suspects that a larger party of Indians were planning an ambush. Is trying to bring the Prophet "to reason" but fears that the settlers will kill indiscriminately in revenge, thus uniting "all the Tribes . . .

against us in six months." The two militia companies have been dismissed so that the men could tend to the harvest, but Harrison now thinks their services will be necessary.

FC (PHi: Daniel Parker Papers); letterbook copy (DNA: RG 107, LSP); enclosure (DLC). Enclosure (4 pp.) in a clerk's hand; docketed by JM; printed in Esarey, *Messages and Letters of William Henry Harrison*, Indiana Historical Collections, 1:444–45).

From John Graham

DEAR SIR   DEPT OF STATE 27th July 1810

I am requested by Mr Smith to forward to you the inclosed Papers which I have this Moment received from him.[1] He also desires me to say that he accompanies Mrs Smith to Bath, and will be there on Sunday next.

The Memoire of Moreau de Lislet is not in this Dept. I wrote to Mr Rodney for it so far back as the 10th June—at the request of Mr Jefferson and as I have not heared from him in reply, I presume he has sent it to Mr Jefferson. I beg to refer to a Copy of my Letter, inclosed. I do so as I understand the Mail is closing. With the Most Sincere & Respectful attachment I am Sir your most obt Sert

JOHN GRAHAM

RC and enclosure (DLC). RC docketed by JM. Enclosure is a press copy of John Graham to Caesar A. Rodney, 10 June 1810 (1 p.). For other enclosures, see n. 1.

1. On 26 July 1810 Robert Smith instructed John Graham to forward to JM the following papers: the memoir of Moreau de Lislet; copies of the "Communications prepared for Gov. Holms"; the "dispatch from Mr [John Quincy] Adams"; and the "packet from Mr Onis" (DNA: RG 59, ML). Graham might also have included a letter from William Jones to Robert Smith, 17 July 1810, and its enclosures (see John D. Lewis and others to Robert Smith, 1 Apr. 1810, and n.).

From William Thornton

SIR   CITY OF WASHINGTON 27th. July 1810

I had the honor of your Note acknowledging the receipt of the Medallion, and shall take the earliest opportunity of forwarding your Letter to England. I am very unwilling to trouble you, but I have received two Letters from Mr. Joseph Cerneau a French Citizen of the U. States, resident in New York, who wishes to send a Vessel to France but is afraid of the Rambouillet Decree; and solicits any kind of protection. I applied to the Secy of State for one, but the Reasons given for a refusal were so cogent that on repeating them to him he seems perfectly satisfied. He states however that some passengers wish to go to France, and he is willing to take in our Seamen who are desirous of returning from France, on the usual Terms. He thinks an Authority to receive them would probably serve him. The Secy of State being now absent at Bath, and the Communication thither tedious, Mr. Graham advised me to write to you, as the Secy would no doubt refer the Subject to you if present. Though I have not much acquaintance with Mr. Cerneau, and only in my official Capacity I think so favourably of him as to subject myself to the necessity of apologizing for intruding on your time in his behalf. Any permission to authorize an Agreement accordg. to law to bring our Seamen might perhaps render him an essential Service as well as some of our Country men, and without committing in the slightest degree the dignity of our Government. With the highest respect & consideration—

WILLIAM THORNTON.

RC (DLC). Docketed by JM.

§ From John Drayton. *27 July 1810, Charleston.* Sends JM a British cannonball and shot taken from the old palmetto battery at Fort Moultrie and encloses a letter on the subject.

RC and enclosure (DLC). RC 3 pp. Enclosure (1 p.) is Richard Bohun Baker to Drayton, 20 July 1810.

From Richard Law and Others

CHRISTIANSAND July 28th 1810

The Memorial of the Undersign'd Citizens of the United States, Masters & Supercargoes of American Vessels detained in different Ports of Norway, respectfully represent,

That your Memorialists whilst in the pursuit of a lawful Commerce, having in their possession every requisite document from the regular constituted authorities of their Country, and also the necessary certificates from the foreign Consuls residing at their respective Ports of clearance, to prove the perfect neutrality of the property under their charge, and the legality of their pursuits, & having the fullest confidence that all whom they should meet on that great high Road of Nations, would treat them

443

with becoming respect, while alike unsuspicious of Insult or Injury, Hindrance or Molestation, & by no means prepared to resist either, have been most shamefully and unjustly impeded in the prosecution of their respective voyages by armed vessels bearing the Flag, & pretending to act under authority from the King of Denmark and are now detained in different inhospitable Ports of Norway.

Your Memorialists feel it their indispensible duty to represent to your Excellency, that on their arrival in Port, most of them have been kept as prisoners on board their own vessels, & every kind of communication with their friends, their Countrymen, and even with their Consul strictly prohibited until they and their Crews have gone through an insulting and vexatious series of interrogations, & cross examinations, all their papers & vessels' documents translated, & themselves and Crews then re-examined & sworn, which generally takes up from twelve to fifteen days, during which time the most vilainous arts are practiced upon their seamen, tempting them with bribes to the amount of thousands of dollars, & where these have failed, threatening them with punishment in order to extort false testimony from them against the Vessels to which they respectively belong. Your Memorialists are unwilling to awaken any improper jealousies or give any false colouring to the conduct of these people, yet they feel it a duty which they owe to their own Government, who are honorably treating with every mark of Civility & respect, the Flag & subjects of every nation to State, that the American flag and Citizens are treated here with the greatest disrespect and abuse, and even the seal and signature of the highest Officers of the United States, with contempt. Hundreds, perhaps thousands of our transatlantic Friends and employers are now no doubt harrassed & greatly perplexed in consequence of the unjust detention of their property in this Country by a Nation who pretends to be in a State of amity with them, yet every day wafting into their harbours fresh spoils without the shadow of a pretext—whilst your memorialists on the spot are denied the common privilege allowed in most other Countries of having such legal or other proper advice as might be useful to them under their present embarrassed circumstances, & confined to a circle of people whose sole aim is to benefit themselves by their misfortunes, & who use every mean to injure & deride them, from one petty Court to another your Memorialists are transferred merely as caprice may actuate, their vessels decaying, & hundreds of useful Mariners detained from their families and homes, some through dire necessity obliged to seek active employ for their immediate support. Deplorable indeed would have been the situation of your memorialists, but for the judicious appointment of Peter Isaacksen Esqr. to the American Consulate at Christiansand, a Gentleman who at all hazards as regards his own comforts, & to the utmost extent of a large fortune, came forward in the handsomest manner with pecuniary means and friendly advice to every fair trading American. To Mr. Isaacksen the United States owe much, and your Memorialists flatter themselves that they will amply remunerate him for the daily sacrifices he is making in consequence of his unlimited confidence in the characteristic of the Nation he now represents, & to whose service he devoted the whole of his time and extensive means, which were formerly engaged in active & lucrative Commerce, at the same time your Memorialists beg leave to notice the embarrassing situation in which he is placed in consequence of his Office; the number of captures already made this season and which are daily increasing, & the frequent & necessary demands for advice, assistance, and pecuniary aid, are quite too much for the attention of any one Man, added to all this the whole Privateering Interest have combined against him, yet he remains unshaken in his fidelity to the trust reposed in him.

Your Memorialists now therefore take the liberty of respectfully suggesting to your Excellency the propriety of immediately dispatching out a person fully authorized by the Government to demand the restoration of American property so unwarrantably detained not only in Norway but also in different Ports of Denmark.[1] Mr. Isaacksen although doing every thing in his power as Consul for the United States, is nevertheless a Danish subject, & therefore *cannot* make such a remonstrance to the Court of Denmark, as a person expressly impowered by the American Government and unshackled by any allegiance to this, would be at liberty to do, and if your Memorialists are rightly informed, this Gentlemen had once already been checked in a measure of this kind, by being informed his powers as Consul did not extend to affairs of Diplomacy. The approbation of the American Government to the conduct of Mr. Isaacksen (which he so highly deserves) would also in the opinion of your Memorialists be of considerable service and would no doubt be peculiarly satisfactory to that Gentleman's feelings in his present disagreeable situation. Your Memorialists could then no longer be told insultingly that "they are Englishmen under false papers, for that even their own Government disapproves the conduct of their Consul here, in affording us protection or else ere this they would have sanctioned it."

Your Memorialists utterly deny the charge of being any other than real Americans, or of Sailing under any protection but the American Flag and the faith which they supposed might be safely placed in those Powers who profess to be on terms of amity with, and have never received the least cause of provocation from the United States.

Your Memorialists beg leave to refer your Excellency to a list of the vessels to which they respectively belong, accompan⟨y⟩ing this, together with the date of their respective clearances from the United States and hope your Excellency will direct the necessary enquiries to be made at the different Custom house⟨s⟩ for the truth of what your Memorialists advance on this hea⟨d.⟩ Your Memorialists also beg leave to state to your Excellency that some of their Countrymen have seen the Register of the Ship Commerce of Philadelphia, which vessel was condemned by the high Court of Admiralty at Christiana last year, in the possession of a Swedish Gentleman, who purchased the Ship at Public Auction, and her Register privately, from the Captain of the Privateer who captured her; by what means this Document was obtained from the Court or what has become of the Registers of the other American Vessels condemned there, they have not been able to learn. This is the conduct practiced by those very people whose principal charge against the Americans who are captured, is, that they are from England with false papers! The mode of what is here called a trial of those Vessels which are captured is of itself ruinous, if even a final liberation take place. Some of your Memorialists, have been detained upwards of two months and their papers are not yet laid before the Court at this place, and even after the decision of this Court the Captors have it in their power to make a delay of eight weeks before the papers are forwarded to the high Court at Copenhagen. That Court tardy always to an extreme in its operations will be rendered still so by the great number of appeal Cases arising from the many Americans already captured, so that your Memorialists see no prospect whatever of getting through it in less than six and probably more than twelve months, this joined with the preceding delay will be dreadful, the Cargoes during this time perishing in the Vessels, not being able to discharge them. All this is also exclusive of the heavy expences of from five to ten & even twenty thousand dollars which accompany an appeal to the upper Court, & which the Americans have as yet been invariably obliged to pay. In this unjustifiable delay the Captors have several objects in view, one of which is in hopes of some political change that will enable them to make prizes of the Vessels, and another, expecting to extort a large sum by way of an inducement for them to relinquish the appeal, knowing at the same time that they will be exonerated from any of the expences. The decissions of the upper Court have been always to that effect. The amount of property already detained, your memorialists consider not only embarrassing to the owners in America, but also highly alarming in a National point of view. Your Memorialists feel themselves authorized to state that what comes under their own immediate observation alone exceeds several millions of dollars, and the amount hourly increasing.

Your Memorialists have thus laid before your Excellency a plain & candid statement of their situations without the least exaggeration or colouring, for it requires none, not doubting but that your Excellency will direct such measures as will be best for supporting the Honor & dignity of the American character, & affording protection to its Citizens, which as such we consider ourselves entitled to call for, Hoping that your Excellency will take the Situation of your Memorialists into immediate consideration, as the immense property under their charge they consider in a very perilous situation, & which a few months may possibly make irrecoverably lost. And your Memorialists as is duty will ever pray

RICHD LAW[2]

[and twenty-five others]

Ms (DNA: RG 76, Denmark Convention, Powers of Attorney). Enclosed in Isaac Stone, William Bell, Jr., John Simson, and William L. Hodge to JM (ibid., 2 pp.). Enclosed list of vessels not found.

1. On 4 Nov. 1810 JM sounded out William Jones to see whether he would accept a "temporary" diplomatic appointment to Denmark. After Jones declined, JM nominated George W. Erving on 12 Dec. 1810 to be special minister to the court of Denmark "with the subject of spoliations committed under the Danish flag on the commerce of the United States" (Robert Smith to Jones, 4 and 9 Nov. 1810 [PHi: William Jones Papers]; *Senate Exec. Proceedings*, 2:156).

2. Richard Law of New York was the master of the ship *Egeria*, which was captured on 14 May 1810 while bound from New York to St. Petersburg. When Erving commenced his mission a year later, Law's case was still pending in Copenhagen, as were also the cases of sixteen other signatories to the memorial sent to JM (see *ASP, Foreign Relations*, 3:521–36).

From Harry Toulmin

DEAR SIR   FORT STODDERT, 28th July 1810

Placed as you are in the highest station to which the good sense of a republican nation can elevate an individual; fully occupied, no doubt, if not burthened with concerns highly interesting to a large portion of the globe; I have felt reluctant to intrude myself and my own little circle on your attention. And although from the peculiar local position of this settlement, surrounded by indians, cut off and entirely detatched from & unknown to the main body of the territory of which it is a part, adjacent to the province of an European power, bearing daily oppressions from it, and yet in physical strength its superior, altho' from these circumstances there is perhaps a fairer field open to unprincipled intrigue & restless ambition than in any spot of equal extent, although the difficulty of revolt from government or defiance of its authority is less, and prospect of indemnity is greater, than in any other community professing to be civilized; although the peace of the United States & the integrity of their territories & dominion may more easily be brought into jeopardy, by the people of this country than by the same number of people in any other part of the continent, & although from these considerations, I have at all times been deeply impressed with the importance of a really efficient government on this insulated frontier, and have viewed the concerns of this settlement (poor & contemptible* as it is) as having a bearing on the general interests of the empire, very disproportioned to its magnitude; yet I never could suffer myself to have the presumption to imagine that similar views of us, and our concerns & our relations to the general government, ever could be entertained at a distance. And indeed, the circumstance of our being totally unrepresented in the congress of the United States (—for the Mississippi delegate[1] represents us about as much as the Middlesex members represented the American colonies in the British parliament) cannot but have a tendency to place us in a point of insignificance even below that which a mere regard to our numbers would leave us in.

Far, however, am I from mentioning these circumstances as affording the slightest ground of complaint. I speak of them merely as the natural result of our peculiar situation, & as at once accounting for my not troubling the chief of the general government with frequent reports of our situation, as well as of forming the foundation of my apology, in case I should even in the present instance, be regarded as unnecessarily intruding upon your attention.

By the last mail I mentioned to my friend Mr Graham some fears which I had that every thing was not going on right here, and likewise sent him a copy of a formal complaint on the subject of a projected expedition against the Spanish settlements, which had been made by the Governor of West Florida to Coll. Sparks the commanding officer at this post, and of which I had previously transmitted a copy to Govr. Holmes.[2] At first I thought it an idle fear. On my going lately up into our settlement, though evevery [sic] one stoutly denied knowing any thing of it; yet I was led from some circumstances to suspect that there had been some such scheme in agitation, but that it was possibly abandoned.

Under these impressions I wrote to Mr Graham. But I have since become satisfied that it exists, that it has been long in contemplation, & that it is the present intention to carry it into execution.

At first I had supposed that a mere predatory incursion was the object: but I am now convinced that a conquest of the country is anticipated, but whether the ultimate object really be an unconditional submission to the authority of the United States, or the formation of a new government under the protection of some foreign power; I have no data on which to form a satisfactory conclusion. The probability is that no definite plan has been adopted by the bulk of the partizans.

About 10 days since I went up to our old court house to examine into the case of a man accused of murder, when being at the house of a friend

* I used to estimate our numbers at 2,000. They are now supposed to amount to nearly 10,000.

and several other persons being present, Mr Kennedy (an attorney at law and lately commissioned a Major of the Militia, and who was supposed at Mobile to be the prime mover of the projected expedition) having called upon me; I made some allusion to the alarms which I understood existed in Mobille as to an attack from this country, and added, that whenever an expedition to take possession of Florida should be undertaken by the American government, he might count upon me as one who would serve as a soldier in it. Upon this he observed, that there was no law of the United States which prohibited such an expedition: that the act of congress related merely to fitting out military expeditions, against the dominions of any foreign prince or state,[3] & that inasmuch as the president had rejected the ambassador of the Spanish Junta, and had declared that he would not receive an ambassador from King Joseph; the province of Florida could not be considered as belonging to any foreign prince or state, and consequently an expedition against that province, would not come within the provisions of the act of congress.

Though I was well satisfied from this of the turn which his mind had taken; I was not a little surprised when on monday last he called upon me, and very openly avowed the existence of an association for the purpose of taking possession of Mobile or Florida (for I do not recollect which term was used) and after completing the conquest, making a tender of it to the United States. He told me that in a few days he was to set out for Georgia and was taking letters from Coll. Carson (a young lawyer who is a member of the Council and was lately appointed Colonel of the militia of this (Baldwin) county) and Mr Sewell, Register of the land office to Mr Crawford & Mr Tait, Senators from the State of Georgia, to enquire whether if the people of this country took possession of Florida and were ready to deliver it up to the United States, they would receive their countenance in Congress.

Mr Kennedy observed that if those gentlemen gave any favourable assurances, the enterprize would be carried into immediate execution: that it had been neglected too long: that it was necessary that something should be done: that the expedition had been many months in contemplation: that a society for the purpose had long been formed: that it consisted of upwards of 400 members, and that the toasts given at the different meetings on the 4th. of July were intended to stir up the people, who would no doubt, generally & heartily engage in it.

He remarked that he had been considered at Mobile as at the head of the expedition, but that it was in fact Coll. James Caller. I replied that this must be impossible as Col. Caller was the man who, three or four years ago, by communicating it to me, broke up a similar expedition projected by his brother Coll. John Caller, then Colonel of Washington County. He answered that such it was true, was then the effect, but that it was not the intention of Coll. Caller, who had communicated the affair to me merely to sound my inclinations on the subject.

I observed that it was impossible that the Georgia senators could countenance the enterprize, that the law was plain, and that the consequence must be either a separation from the Union or a vigorous prosecution of the offenders in the courts of justice.

He replied that as to a division of the Union we were too few in number for such an event to be the consequence; and that as to prosecutions for the offence, the parties would be tried among ourselves. I reminded him that the officers concerned in the administration of justice, were bound by their oaths to enforce the laws actually existing. He replied that he was well aware of it and could not expect any thing from me incompatible with my official obligations: that he & I, it was true, had been of different opinions, but that of my patriotism he could never entertain a doubt: that their reliance would be on the ultimate favourable indulgence of the United States; of which he should consider that assurances from the Georgia senators of a disposition to exert themselves to be a sufficient pledge. He added that the expedition at any rate must do some good: that it wd show government that we would have the navigation of the river, and that this was absolutely necessary as it was evident that they would never give it to us.

On this I remarked that I had feared that the government of the United States had not been in the habit of seeing the urgency of this object in a point of view sufficiently strong, that I had entertained serious apprehensions on the subject, and really wished that every means could be taken, short of a violation of the laws, to impress the minds of the general government with a sense of the importance of the free navigation of these rivers, but that I would never consent to do evil that good might come.

His whole manner indicated a sanguine calculation upon general support, and a perfect confidence in the success of the enterprize. His full persuasion of impunity has no real connection with any reliance on what he calls my patriotism. It results either from a belief that the United States will be compelled to wink at the outrage in order to preserve their own territory: or it may be nothing more than the natural result of past experience, as he has more than once been acquitted on serious charges, where I thought the proof of guilt was clear as day light.

Mr Kennedy mentioned also that Mr Caller meant to write to Govr. Holmes and to apprize him of their intentions: and informed me that as to himself he expected to return from Georgia about the middle of September. Not having been in habits of much intercourse with Mr Kennedy, I was much surprized at the freedom of this communication, & could only impute it to a confident & I hope extravagant calculation on the infallible operation of their plans. A similar communication I find was made to some of the military officers, and to a very intelligent citizen, whose report of it I inclose. Overtures were also lately made by a Justice of the peace to another respectable citizen residing here, who was assured that a body of men was possitively engaged, that they hoped to have the countenance of government—but that *at any rate they were determined not to be cramped.*

As this plan it seems has been some time in agitation, it is probable that many appointments in the militia have been made with reference to it. There are some arrangements which have heretofore appeared to me inexplicable which are rendered perfectly intelligible by this Conspiracy: and as the militia officers of this country have been in the habit of exercising very extraordinary powers; it was a matter of infinite importance that the friends of the expedition should monopolize as great a number of militia commissions as possible. It is true that the power of appointment nominally resides in the governor: but it results from the remoteness & insulated nature of our situation, that all the powers of government are practically possessed by the people, or rather are exercised by the few who by popular intrigues & by devoting themselves to the business are enabled to procure themselves to be elected to the territorial legislature.

It is probably in a great measure with a view to this expedition that the leaders in it have been extremely solicitous to prevent a division of our territory, although it was unquestionably the wish of the great body of the settlement.

They readily foresaw that no progress could be made in such a project, whilst a federal governor and federal judges were stationed in the midst of them.

To remove another obstacle, a very dexterous manuvre has been made to prevent the holding of a superior court, and the extreme anxiety to establish the doctrine that under existing circumstances no court could be held has probably resulted from more than mere private reluctance to comply with pecuniary obligations.

As to the probable issue of this business, I am by no means satisfied. If it has really gone to the length that Kennedy asserts, and if the people be really so generally well affected to it (though I believe that no individual should be condemned on his testimony alone); I believe that the enterprize will be carried into effect and that with a moderate share of conduct and courage, it will be successful. As to its depending at all on any assurances from Georgia, I do not believe it. It may be politic to hold out the idea to the people & by and by to make a declaration that such assurances have been received. Or it may be nothing more than a scheme to provide for the leaders a decent way to retreat out of the conspiracy, in case, it should be thought too hazardous. But I cannot conceive that the projectors of the enterprize really mean to let it rest on a contingency so precarious.

As to their success, if they should really persevere; the few troops which are in this country cannot stop them, nor indeed, do I see how the military commander could step forward by virtue of any authority with which he is invested. Besides this the insurgents may cross the line at some point entirely out of the observation of Fort Stoddert: and when they get to Mobile, if they have any thing of the energy of desperadoes, they may enforce a surrender from the Spanish officers, notwithsg the Spanish troops & the 4 or 500 Indians whom they have to protect them. It is possible indeed that the Invaders may have confederates at Mobile: but I do not conceive that they have any connection with the revolutionists in New Feliciana, (on the Mississi) as there is no intercourse between that country & this.

But I do not believe that there is any thing like such unanimity among the people of this country as Kennedy seemed to calculate upon. I even believe that the greater part of the old tories, true to their original principles, are disposed to remain submissive subjects of the *powers that be*. The other old settlers have generally property, and few of them will be disposed to risque that for the sake of pre-eminence. As to the new comers, who are numerous and generally needy, I am not much acquainted with them. There [*sic*] are mostly from Georgia & are settled on the public lands and certainly ought in prudence not to provoke an enforcement upon them of the provisions of the law to prevent settlements being made unauthorized. They are besides acquainted only by report with Spanish oppression and are not likely very soon to be materially affected by it. For these reasons I am not without the hope, that the current may still be turned. Perhaps indeed it is already turned, & this disclosure might be made to me by Kennedy merely to enable them to have a decent way of getting out of the scrape.

I shall, however, use all the exertions I can to ward off the meditated blow, but I must rely on argument & persuasion merely. If there were public meetings, I should fear nothing. But every thing here is done by private intrigue & as the people are exceedingly scattered, it is hard to see many of them at a time.

Should the goverment deem any step necessary either to quiet the Spanish governt here, or to deter our own people, or to oppose their progress if needful; it is desirable that [I] may be advised of it as speedily as possible.

Any communications with which you may be pleased to honour me will come most speedily by the Georgia route. I have the honour to be, with the highest respect, dear Sir Your obliged & most obedt Servt

HARRY TOULMIN[4]

P. S. Since writing: I have recd from Captn Gaines who is near St Stephens, a copy of the toasts, and the inclosed letter to myself.

I have not time before the Mail goes to copy it, or to review what I have written.

RC and enclosures (DNA: RG 107, LRRS, T-76:5). RC docketed by a War Department clerk as received 10 Sept. 1810 (but see JM to Gallatin, 22 Aug. 1810, and n. 6). Enclosures are a memorandum by a citizen near Fort Stoddert (1 p.); E. P. Gaines to Toulmin, 27 July 1810 (3 pp.); and "Toasts—given out at a Carousal of certain Citizens in the Eastern part of the Mississippi Territory" (4 pp.).

1. George Poindexter.

2. Francisco Maximilian de St. Maxent to Richard Sparks, 25 June 1810 (printed in Carter, *Territorial Papers, Mississippi*, 6:77).

3. Toulmin was referring to section 5 of the 1794 act "in addition to the act for the punishment of certain crimes against the United States" (*U.S. Statutes at Large*, 1:384).

4. Harry Toulmin (1767–1823), an English Unitarian minister and political radical, had met JM in 1793, shortly after immigrating to the U.S. He settled in Kentucky, where he served briefly as president of Transylvania Seminary and then as secretary to the commonwealth, 1796–1804. In 1804 Jefferson appointed him as judge of the superior court for the eastern district of the Mississippi Territory, a position he held until 1819. He also published a number of works on a wide range of subjects, from travel to law, religion, and poetry (Marion Tinling and Godfrey Davies, eds., *The Western Country in 1793: Reports on Kentucky and Virginia by Harry Toulmin* [San Marino, Calif., 1948], pp. v-xv; *PJM*, 15:6 n. 1).

From William Eustis

Sir,   New London Connt. July 29th. 1810.

Having left the post road on a visit to West Point with Governor Tompkins who persuaded me, as in the event I really found, that it facilitated my journey I have not found a convenient opportunity to acknowlege your Letter of the 17th instant. The order for the march of the 6th Regt from Carlisle to Pittsburg has not been countermanded, a delay in their movement has arisen from the difficulty of procuring waggons in the midst of harvest. On the receipt of the Letter of Govr. Harrison the Agent was informed that he might wait untill they could be had on reasonable terms, and the emergency having abated the Regt will move by easy marches. The two companies of rifle & dragoons were countermanded & will remain at Carlisle for further orders. The universal enquiry is, what is to be done, and the question is already answered in the mind of the enquirers before it is asked. In this part of the country the attack on the vixen helps out the answer. To morrow I expect to be in Newport, where Major Porter[1] expects some directions, and after two days I shall be in Boston, to take up the Letters by mail, and receive any instructions which may have been forwarded. With entire respect

W. Eustis

RC (DLC).

1. Maj. Moses Porter of the U.S. Artillery (Heitman, *Historical Register*, 1:800).

To David Gelston

Dear Sir   July 30. 1810

If this should happen to arrive before the sailing of the Hornet, be so good as to forward the packet for Mr. Pinkney[1] by that opportunity; if not in time for that, by any safe one next offering from your port. If no early oppy. should offer for London, it will be nearly as well to send it to Liverpool, endorsing in this case, "to the care of Mr. Maury Consul of the U.S." Accept my respects & good wishes.

JAMES MADISON

RC (NEh: Long Island Collection).

1. No communication from JM to Pinkney during the summer of 1810 has been found.

From Albert Gallatin

Dear Sir   NEW YORK 30th July 1810

On enquiring respecting a proper situation in a mercantile house for your nephew, and after consulting with some friends, I find that in order to make a proper selection, some information is wanted as to his particular object and as to his acquirements.

Exclusively of retailers, West India & coasting traders &ca., there are two distinct species of Merchants on a large scale vizt. importers of goods principally of British manufacture for the consumption of the country, and men employed chiefly in navigation. The last class, which is rather considered as the first, trades to all parts of the Globe, occasionally importing from India, China &a., but is more particularly concerned in freight, & exportation of foreign and domestic produce. To make a complete & great Merchant engaged in various & extensive speculations, this is the best school; but the theatre or permanent residence must be New York or some other large sea-port; and if the field be more vast, the success is more uncertain. Importers whether for themselves or on commission being confined to a certain branch, a better knowledge of the quality of merchandize will be obtained, but less variegated knowledge. In that respect, therefore I would decide according to the ultimate object of the young gentleman and of his friends, & wish therefore to be informed of it.

As in the present state of commerce, there are more candidates for occupation, than there is employment, some knowledge of Mr Macon's acquirements is wanted. Does he write a good mercantile hand? is he already a good accountant? does he understand book keeping? &ca. Generally what branches of the elementary commercial knowledge has he already acquired? and what must he still learn?

It is also asked, considering his age, for what length of time he intends to engage himself? and I will add another query, whether politics or nation will be an objection?

Besides receiving a short answer from you, I wish that the young man would write to me a letter on the subject, which will be the best means of conveying to me just notions of his wishes & acquirements.

It would be easy to place *your* nephew in many mercantile houses: but it would be unnecessary for him to come here unless one can be selected where he may learn, & where some pains will be taken to teach him what he ought & what he wants to know. I need not say that a selection is not in that respect easy, most merchants being the worst possible teachers of their trade; & generally leaving young men to find out as well as they can what is useful and no secret, keeping them designedly from the knowledge of the most important matters, and employing them chiefly in transcribing and on errands.

Mrs. Gallatin requests to be affectionately remembered to Mrs Madison. I find it impracticable to take my intended trip to Niagara. I have succeeded in purchasing bills on Amsterdam, which tho' done at a dear rate (ten per cent loss) appeared preferable to sending specie. The Hornet will not go to Holland & sails day after to morrow for Havre. With respect and attachment Your's

ALBERT GALLATIN

Your letter of 21st is received.

RC (DLC).

From Abigail Adams

SIR   QUINCY August 1st 18010 [*sic*]

I take the Liberty of addressing you in behalf of my son, now at st petersburgh, and to ask of you, permission for his return to his native Country. I hope you may have already received, through the Secretary of State, his own request to this effect.

From Several Letters which I have received from Mrs Adams, I have been led to think their Situation very unpleasent, as it respected their domestic Establishment, and I am now confirmed in the fact; by a Letter recently received from him.

The outfit and sallery allowed by Congress, for a public Minister; is altogether so inadequate to the Stile, and Manner of living, required, as indispensable at the Court of st petersburgh, that inevitable ruin must be the concequence to himself and family.

To quote his own words—"you can judge how congenial it is to my habits, and disposition to find extravagance and dissipation become a public duty. You will readily conceive the embarrassment in which I find myself and of the desire which I feel to get out of a situation irksome beyond expression."[1]

I will allow sir that there are Situations and circumstances in which a Country may be placed, when it becomes the duty of a good citizen to hazard, not only property, but even his Life, to Serve and save it.

In that School I was trained, but those days I hope have passed. I have too much confidence in your wisdom and justice to imagine that you would require a sacrifice not only of the most valuable Season of Life for active pursuits, but Subject a gentleman whom you have honourd with your confidence to pecuniary embarrssments which would prevent his future usefullness.

In making this request, I am not insensible to the honor done mr Adams, by your repeated nomination of him to this Embassy. Whatever confidence you have been pleased to repose in him, I trust will never be forfeited by him.

The[2] expence attendent upon this Mission, was I presume as unknown to you, as to him, however readily you might be disposed to consider his Situation, I presume their is no way to extricate him, but by allowing him as speedily as possible to return to America.

I Should not so earnestly make this request if the circumstances of his Father would enable him, to aid in Supporting him there, but after near fifty years devoted to public Service, a rigid œconomy is necessary for us, to preserve that independence; which asks no favours; and Solicits no recompence.

As this is the only opportunity I have ever had of addressing you sir, permit me to Say that I entertain a high respect for your person, and Character, and to add my best wishes for the Success, and prosperity of your administration. I am Sir your Humble Servant

ABIGAIL ADAMS

RC (DNA: RG 59, DD, Russia); FC (MHi: Adams Family Papers). To the RC JM attached the following note, which was apparently an instruction to the State Department:

"The answer has intimated to Mrs. A. that the Sey. of State will let her son, know that as it was not intended to subject him to the sacrifices he finds unavoidable, his retiring from them, will not impair the sentiments which led to his appointmt. To the letters of recredence to be forwarded, will of course be added a commission for a provisional functionary of Chargé or S. of L. An offer of this seems due to Mr. Harris." Minor variations between the RC and FC have not been noted.

1. John Quincy Adams to Abigail Adams, 8 Feb. 1810 (Worthington Chauncey Ford, ed., *Writings of John Quincy Adams* [7 vols.; New York, 1913–17], 3:396).

2. The following paragraph is not in the FC.

From John Smith

SIR   WAR DEPARTMENT Augt. 2d. 1810.

I have the honor to enclose you Copy of a Letter just received from Governor Harrison. A Similar Copy will be forwarded to the Secretary of War by this day's Mail. I am, with perfect respect, Sir, &c. &c. &c.

                           (signed.)—JNO. SMITH, C. C.

[Enclosure]

§ William Henry Harrison to William Eustis. *18 July 1810, Vincennes.* Has received a report from an emissary he sent to the Miami Indians to ascertain their loyalty as well as to obtain their consent to the treaty negotiated with the Kickapoo Indians [see JM to the Senate, 9 Jan. 1810]. The Miami did not give "a final and positive answer . . . on the latter subject," but Harrison believes their chiefs, with one exception, to be loyal to the U.S. Intends tomorrow to send an interpreter to the Prophet to invite him and others to visit JM in order to give the Indians an idea of the strength of the U.S. and thus deter them from hostilities. Believes that the Sac and Fox Indians are already hostile and will strike whenever the Prophet or the British Indian agent at Fort Malden should "give the signal." Adds in a postscript that the defection of the Wyandot Indians to the Prophet is less complete than he had previously reported and is confined to those from Sandusky.

FC (PHi: Daniel Parker Papers); letterbook copy (DNA: RG 107, LSP); enclosure (DLC). FC marked "(Copy)." Enclosure (3 pp.) in a clerk's hand; docketed by JM; printed in Esarey, *Messages and Letters of William Henry Harrison*, Indiana Historical Collections, 1:446–47.

§ From Eléonor-François-Elie, Marquis de Moustier. *2 August 1810, Well Walk, Hampstead, Middlesex County.* Recommends P. F. Fauche[1] for post of U.S. consul in Gothenburg.

RC (DLC). 2 pp. In French. Marked by Moustier as duplicate of his letter of 5 Mar. Docketed by JM.

1. Peter Francis Fauche, a Swiss merchant residing in Gothenburg, Sweden, had written to JM as early as 29 Jan. 1809 for a consular appointment (DNA: RG 59, LAR, 1809–17).

From John Graham

DEAR SIR   DEPT OF STATE 3d August 1810

I had the Honor to receive your Letter of the 26th Ult:[1] and immediately called on Mr Bradley, who promised to direct that the Letter for Mr Haumont should be sent on to Savanna.

Of the inclosed communications from Governor Holmes[2] and Mr Robertson,[3] we have taken Copies for the Secretary of State as the Mail goes to Bath on Tuesday.

I beg to be presented to Mrs Madison and to assure you of the sincere & Respectful attachment of Your Most Obt Sert

JOHN GRAHAM

RC (DLC). Docketed by JM. Enclosures not found, but see nn. 2 and 3.

1. Graham referred to JM's letter of 25 July 1810.

2. Probably Holmes to Robert Smith, 11 July 1810 (DNA: RG 59, TP, Mississippi), in which Holmes reported that the settlers in West Florida were determined to bring about a change in their government. Holmes also described a meeting, held on 1 July 1810 of a "considerable number" of the inhabitants of the Feliciana district of West Florida, who "by an almost unanimous voice" adopted a prearranged plan for security against "both Foreign invasion and internal disturbances." The meeting then elected four delegates—John Rhea, John Johnston, William Barrow, and John Mills, "all of them wealthy and respectable Men"—to communicate with settlers throughout West Florida in order to persuade them to adopt a similar course of action and thus create a council with "general powers" to promote the good of the province. Holmes stated that the meeting did not discuss the status of Spanish officials in West Florida, but he mentioned that it was "tacitly understood" that the new council would "suffer them to remain in office provided they acknowledged the new authority and consented to be controlled and regulated thereby." The governor added that "you may readily conjecture how this business will ultimately eventuate" and that he regarded the proceedings as "incipient to the more decisive and important Measure of asking the protection of the United States."

3. Probably Thomas B. Robertson to Robert Smith, 6 July 1810 (printed in Carter, *Territorial Papers, Orleans*, 9:888–89). Robertson, the secretary of Orleans Territory, in addition to reporting on events in the territory, discussed rumors that "the people of West Florida . . . appear to be preparing to throw off their dependence on Spain." He believed the rumors to be true, adding that "the News from the Province of Venezuela which has just arrived, will have a tendency to hasten the event."

From Paul Hamilton

DEAR SIR   NAVY DEPARTT. August 3d. 1810

I have been favored with your letter of the 26th. ult., and conformably to your desire have forwarded to Mr. Smith, for the purpose mentioned, copies of the papers stating the aggression on the Vixen. I subjoin an extract of a letter I have received from Mr. Gaillard,[1] a Senator in Congress for South Carolina, relative to the illicit introduction of Slaves; and believing that I could correctly estimate what would be your determination on the subject, I have ventured to issue orders to our Vessels stationed at Charleston, Savannah and St. Mary's, founded on and in conformity to the Act of Congress of the 2d. March 1807. prohibiting the introduction of Slaves. I have, moreover, dispatched the brig Syren to New Orleans where great infractions of this law are practiced, and have directed Capt Tarbell her commander to observe such instructions, respecting this business, as he may receive from the Governor of that Territory. I have also written to the Governor apprizing him of the Orders and instructions given to Capt Tarbell.

The existence of a disposition in so many parts of our Union, as we have for some time past witnessed, to violate every law which clashes with individual interest cannot but give pain to every mind anxious for the welfare of our Country, and it furnishes cause for fearful presages, that, at no distant period, all respect for our excellent institutions may be effaced from the minds of the Community, and a foundation laid for some awful change.

I thank you heartily, my good Sir, for your hospitable and obliging invitation, and assure you that very few occurrences could afford me so much pleasure as that of spending some time with you at your Seat. I am endeavouring to get my business into such a state as to enable me to take some recreation, and if I succeed, I will certainly have the happiness of visiting you.

Be pleased to accept for you and Mrs. Madison the united best wishes of my family and self; and be assured that I am with sincere respect and affectionate attachment yrs.

Paul Hamilton

Extract from Mr. Gaillards letter.

"Knowing that the President has the power of employing our armed vessels to prevent the introduction of Slaves into the United States, and having received the most authentic information that they are bringing them into the Country, I feel it to be my duty to apprize you of it, and through you, the President."

RC (DLC).

1. John Gaillard served as a Republican senator from South Carolina, 1804–26.

From John Armstrong

Dear Sir,   Paris 5 August 1810.

Nothing can better illustrate the opinions I have frequently had the honor to give on the subject of our differences with France, than the history of the revocation of the Berlin and Milan decrees, announced in my official letter of this date to M. Smith.[1] On the 27th. Ultimo advices were received from England stating, that on the arrival of the John Adams, Congress had been called and that the object of this extra-Session was known to be a declaration of War against France. The excitement produced by this report was greater than I had expected, though I well knew that such a report, if credited at all, would not fail to produce one of considerable seriousness and extent. Repeated messages were sent to me to know, what I had heard and what I believed? I disguised nothing—I answered that I knew the writers to be respectable men and likely, from their connexion with the United States, to be well-informed; that I had myself seen the letters; that I beleived the extra-Session a probable measure and that if it did take place, it could only be for the purpose which had been suggested, as the Presidents powers were competent to any course of conduct, short of declaring war. Petry[2] was of the same opinion and, no doubt, most honestly so. To these circumstances, light as they appear, is owing the *revocation*, which abundantly proves two things—

1st. that though France has no objection to frighten, she has no disposition to fight the U. S. Her ambition, gigantic and terrible as it certainly is, is travelling another road & will find full occupation for twenty years to come, in establishing her dominion over Europe &c. &c.

2d. that sick of expedients, by which she has lost both character & money, & under which her people are fast impoverishing—she would now return to a degree of justice, moderation and good sense. To the first of these, her disposition is however less strong than it ought to be, and I much fear that on the present occasion, she will content herself by coming within the mere letter of your late law & instructions, that is—that she will revoke her decrees, and make her seizures a subject of future Negociation. It will be for you to decide, how far good faith will furnish an obedience to the injunctions of the Act of Congress,[3] should England refuse to annul, or so to modify, her orders in Council, as to leave your Maratime rights unmolested. That circumstances may exist that shall enable you, on the soundest principles, to dispense with these obligations, cannot be doubted, and be assured, that should such circumstances arise, I will not fail to communicate them to you.

I subjoin to this letter another measure of the Council of Commerce, which is however still in discussion. It is a new tariff of duties which is not less than 50 per cent of the market price of the Article. It matters not to tell them, that this avidity will defeat itself by Keeping the Articles enumerated out of the market, or, (what is still worse) by smuggling them into it. They answer, that if on experiment, such should be the effect, it will be time enough to alter it. I have no doubt therefore but that this new tariff will be adopted. As good is sometimes brought out of evil, it strikes me that we may turn this very tariff to Account. By applying it to the St. Sebastian Seizures,[4] he will have half the Amt. he now has, & will, at the same time, recover in some degree his character for justice, & thus re-inspire us with a confidence, which can alone fill his ports with our Commerce. If this idea, presented as it may be, in conjunction with the ill-effects of an opposite policy, does not bring about some degree of reparation, I almost despair of obtaining any, at the present moment.

Burr is yet here but in uneasy circumstances.[5] A pass-port for the U. S. which he requested, has been refused—under the beleif, as my informant states, that his real destination was South America or *England*.

I hope to sail from Bordeaux on the 1st. day of October. With the highest respect, I am Sir, Your Most Obed. h. Servant

JOHN ARMSTRONG

P. S. The Emperor leaves this in a few days for Amsterdam.

P. S.   [post 15 August 1810]
I sub-join a copy of the tariff mentioned in what goes before. You will perceive that pot ashes & tobacco are not among the enumerated articles. The first, is however a mere omission, the other, is purposely excluded, as is evident from the text of the New licenses intended for our trade.[6] These admit all articles, (excepting tobacco), the produce of *Asia*, or *of any ci-devant Dutch or French Island*, or *of the U. S.*

My fears with regard to the operation here of the 3d. Sect. of your late Law[7] are verified. The declaration of a French Capt. whose Ship had been seized under the Non-intercourse Act at New York—has been transmitted to the Emperor who sent it to the Duke of Cadore, who sent to me the Substance of it. I have given a verbal explanation, which I hope may have the effect of preventing any new proof of ill-temper or Caprice & in this I have ventured to say, that the bonds given in this case or in any other of a similar Character, would be cancelled, unless the conduct of the Emp. towards his Citizens & their property, made that measure impracticable.

I thought it proper to communicate to M. P. the substance of what I knew with regard to Ouverard's[8] overtures to the English Govt. expecting to know from him in return, whether the B. Minister had made (to him) any prior intimation of these. It appears by his Answer, that he knew nothing of them & Lord Wellesly has even made him believe, that none such were ever made. It is however true that L. W. did as late as the 23d. of April, suggest (thro' Mr. McKenzie) that the British Govt. wished to receive all overtures from that of France thro' *accredited Agents*, directly alluding to those which had been made thro' Agents of a different character. Can any one believe, that the Emp. would have fixed such a stigma upon any Minister of his Govt. wantonly & without foundation, & even one which begets suspicions (as this has done) of his own good faith towards the U. S. &c.? It is quite impossible. That he might put upon the Minister the whole blame of an act in which he had participated, is not impossible—but, that he should charge upon him an Act, which had no existence, & which almost necessarily involved himself—is quite impossible. The concealment therefore employed by G. B. & the disguises also, are of a character truly unfriendly. The truth perhaps is, that Old Rose[9] Ld. Liverpool[10] & the King, chose to take the basis presented by Ouverard, into more consideration than could hastily be given to it—a conjecture which derives strength from some information obtained by M. McRae, when in London, on this subject, & which proves, that the business was not entirely unknown there to people *out of the Cabinet*. By the way, I am assured, that the Emperor has been in direct & personal correspondence with the B. Gt. within a fort-night. Whether it is meant that I should know more than this fact, or whether the communication of that, has been made to excite my suspicions or my curiosity, I do not know—but judging from the channel through which I get it, I am apt to believe that the communication was ordered. On the 15 Inst. occurred the Emperor's birth-day. (You know that there being no Saint Napoleon on the Calendar, he made one, & displacing the Virgin Mary, gave him her day). The Diaplomatic Corps were received & many others. On introducing to him a young man of Phil. (a Mr. Craig) who had recently come from England, he asked him, what was the opinion in London—would the B. Gt. give up their Orders & blockades or not? Craig answered (not very directly) that it was hoped they would. "Yes" he replied "I have set them the example and they ought to follow it, and if they do not, the Cannon of the Republic should make them. They (cannon) alone command the respect of nations." Tho' the Circle was uncommonly large & the time given to it's reception very short, he came twice to me & asked me many questions all of which were personal, excepting one viz: at what time Congress would meet? & this he repeated. I understand that Arcambal[11] & Fourcroy[12] are appointed to the consulates of New-York & Charlestown to make an experiment of the new system of licenses. I shall present a Note on this new system before I leave Paris. As it now stands, it is quite ridiculous—& none but madmen will meddle with it. J. A. Morton[13] is the only american here that I have heard of, who is mean enough to take one of these licenses.

RC and enclosure (DLC). Second postscript misfiled under 15 Aug. 1809 in the Madison Papers (DLC). Enclosure (1 p.) is a printed copy of a French customs decree dated at Trianon, 5 Aug. 1810.

1. Armstrong had forwarded a copy of a letter from the duc de Cadore communicating Napoleon's announcement that the Berlin and Milan decrees "are revoked, and that from the 1. Nover., they will cease to be in force, it being understood that in consequence of this declaration the English shall revoke their Orders in Council, and renounce the new principles of Blockades which they have att⟨empted⟩ to establish; or that the United States, conformably to [the terms of Macon's Bill No. 2], shall Cause their rights to be respected by the English" (Armstrong to Robert Smith, 5 Aug. 1810 [DNA: RG 59, DD, France]; English translation of Cadore to Armstrong, 5 Aug. 1810 [DLC: Rives Collection, Madison Papers]).

2. Jean-Baptiste Petry, an official in the French foreign ministry, had formerly held a number of consular positions in the U.S. between 1783 and 1798 (Nasatir and Monell, *French Consuls*, p. 567).

3. Macon's Bill No. 2.

4. See David Bailie Warden to JM, 26 Jan. 1810, n. 2.

5. On Aaron Burr's unsuccessful attempts between March and July 1810 to interest Napoleon in plans to expel Spain and Great Britain from their American colonies, see Kline, *Papers of Burr*, 2:1099–1123.

6. After learning by June 1810 of the repeal of the Nonintercourse Act, Napoleon had to adjust his commercial system to the resumption of American trade. He established at this time a new *conseil du commerce*, while in the 5 July decree of St. Cloud he issued new customs regulations, including a license scheme to permit a restricted number of American merchants to import enumerated colonial products into France (Frank E. Melvin, *Napoleon's Navigation System: A Study of Trade Control during the Continental Blockade* [New York, 1919], pp. 165–78).

7. Armstrong referred to the third section of the Nonintercourse Act of March 1809, which stipulated the penalty of seizure and condemnation for any vessel and its cargo illegally entering American ports after 20 May 1809 (*U.S. Statutes at Large*, 2:529).

8. Gabriel-Julien Ouvrard (1770–1846), a French banker and speculator, had recently been sent to London by the French minister of police, Joseph Fouché, duc d'Otrante, on an unauthorized mission to sound out the prospects for peace. When Napoleon heard of these activities in July 1810, he imprisoned Ouvrard and dismissed Fouché. Armstrong was cynical about the emperor's reaction because he knew that Napoleon had made similar unofficial efforts to obtain peace earlier in the year through the agency of a Dutch banker, Pierre-César Labouchère (Hubert Cole, *Fouché: The Unprincipled Patriot* [London, 1971], pp. 191–200).

9. George Rose was vice president of the Board of Trade and father of George Henry Rose, the British diplomat with whom JM had been unable to negotiate a settlement of the *Chesapeake* affair in 1808.

10. Robert Banks Jenkinson, second earl of Liverpool, was secretary for war and the colonies in the Perceval ministry.

11. Louis Arcambal had held consular appointments in New York, Rhode Island, Norfolk, and Baltimore between 1794 and 1804 (Nasatir and Monell, *French Consuls*, pp. 549, 550, 551).

12. M. Fourcroy was French consul at Charleston (ibid., p. 552).

13. John A. Morton was an American merchant, evidently trading out of Bordeaux (Mann, *A Yankee Jeffersonian*, pp. 106, 137).

From George W. Erving

Private

DEAR SIR   PHILA Augt. 5. 1810

In my last letters to Mr Smith I mentioned my intention of returning to the United States; pursuant to which, after about a month passed with Mr Pinkney in London I embarked at Liverpool on the 23d June, and arrived at N. York on the 1st instt. It was my purpose to proceed to Washington without any delay, but I was induced to stay a day at N. York for the pleasure of conversing with Mr Gallatin.

I have in charge two dispatches from Mr Pinkney, which (in case of my going immediately to Washington) he requested me to deliver, or (otherwise) that I woud send by the post; Mr Gallatin being of opinion that this latter mode, will from hence, be perfectly safe, & as I have great need of some short repose, the dispatches in question will be sent forward by this nights mail.

The news of the "Non-intercourse suspension" act[1] reached Liverpool on the 6h of June, by the brig "Tamaahmaah," which had but 22 days passage from New York: the "Venus" frigate had been previously appointed to bring out Mr Morier & he was to have sailed at about the same time with myself.

A few days before leaving England I received a letter of 30 May from Mr Hackley of Cadiz wherin he mentions that the Regency has removed from the "Isla" into that city: this measure, (taken doubtless in consequence of the occupation of "Matagorda" by the french) has an aspect very unfavorable to the affairs of the patriots:[2] Mr H also mentions that flour is becoming very scarce. I add nothing on these subjects hoping very soon to have the honor of paying my respects to you in person. Dear Sir with the Most respectful Attachment Your obdt & obliged St

GEORGE W ERVING

P. S. I met at Liverpool Mr Short, who has taken passage in the "Pacifick" which was to have sailed in about a week after my departure; Mr Short expecting to have a long passage gave into my charge a letter from Doctor Logan to yourself.[3] This I will transmit to you from Washington (where I expect to be in about four or five days from this time,) unless you shoud order otherwise.

GWE

RC (MHi: Erving Papers).

1. Macon's Bill No. 2.

2. In January 1810 the Supreme Junta of Spain, under increasing pressure from French invading forces, had moved from Seville to the Isla de León at the entrance to the port of

464

Cadiz. There the Junta members decided to hand over their responsibility for summoning the national *cortes* in 1810 to a regency, headed by the bishop of Orense. Despite the capture by the French of Fort Matagorda guarding the approaches to Cadiz on 23 Apr., the regency remained in the city and eventually organized a meeting of the *cortes* on 24 Sept. (Gabriel H. Lovett, *Napoleon and the Birth of Modern Spain* [2 vols.; New York, 1965], 1:357–70).

   3. Logan to JM, 6 May 1810.

From John Graham

DEAR SIR   DEPT OF STATE 6th Augt 1810.

I have the Honor to forward to you some English News Papers received at this office on Saturday. They were directed to the Secretary of State by Mr. Pinkney, and forwarded from New York by Mr Erwing. We received no Letter either from Mr Pinkney or Mr Erwing. It is stated however, in the News Papers that the latter is coming on from New York with Dispatches.

There are private Letters in Town from London to the 14th June. They don't mention any favorable change in our affairs there. With Sentiments of the Highest Respect I have the Honor to be Sir, Your Mo: Obt Sert

JOHN GRAHAM

RC (DLC). Docketed by JM.

§ **From John Bond.** *6 August 1810, Fort Constitution, New Hampshire.* Seeks a discharge from the U.S. Army for John Sandborn on the grounds that he is deranged and unfit to serve.

   RC (DNA: RG 107, LRUS, B-1810). 1 p. Readdressed to the Department of War by JM at Orange Court House, 17 Aug. 1810.

§ **From Richard Forrest.** *6 August 1810, Washington.* Proposes that he should go to Florida, posing as an ordinary tourist, seek information on the sympathies of the people, and prepare a secret report. Speaks of acquaintances already in Florida. "My plan would be, to hear and observe all that might be passing, & without expressing any opinion of my own." Also suggests a method of passing on his information to Captain Smith at Fort Hawkins in Georgia.

   Printed summary (Howard S. Mott Catalog No. 187 [Sheffield, Mass., 1968], item 106). According to the catalog, the letter is "2¼ pp., 4to" and docketed by JM.

§ **From Alexander Stephens.** *6 August 1810, Wilkes County, Georgia.* Inquires how and where he may obtain land bounties for his military services between 1755 and 1762 and also for his losses in the Revolution.

RC (DNA: RG 107, LRRS, S-181:5). 1 p. Docketed by a War Department clerk as received 27 Aug. 1810. JM referred the letter to the War Department, which informed Stephens that Congress had not yet passed legislation awarding land bounties for military service between 1755 and 1762 (John Smith to Stephens, 27 Aug. 1810 [DNA: RG 107, LSMA]).

From John Smith

SIR   WAR DEPARTMENT August 7th. 1810.

The Letter from Lieut. Colo. Sparks of which the enclosed is a Copy, came to hand by yesterday's Mail. The original I forward to the Secretary of War at Boston. I have the honor to be, with perfect Respect, Sir, Your obedient Servant

JNO. SMITH C C

[First Enclosure]

§ Richard Sparks to William Eustis. *12 July 1810, Fort Stoddert, Mississippi Territory.* Reports receiving on 25 June information from the Spanish governor at Mobile, Maximilian de St. Maxent, about plans of American settlers to attack that town. Believes the information to be correct and that hostilities against Pensacola can also be expected. Has discovered that the plans of the settlers include seizing the ammunition at Fort Stoddert in order "to disable the troops here from acting." Is convinced that the plot is "headed by the most popular characters, and . . . that it would be almost universally pleasing to the inhabitants of this Country." Discusses the grievances of the settlers against the Spanish authorities and reports that the Spanish have reinforced Mobile as well as sought allies among the Choctaw and Creek Indians. Includes a return of his troops at Fort Stoddert,[1] describes their weakened condition, and requests reinforcements to enable him to "overawe disaffection." Predicts that the settlers will attempt to implement their plans by 1 Oct. In a postscript mentions that the leader of the settlers, Joseph P. Kennedy, is the son-in-law of former Georgia senator Abraham Baldwin, brother-in-law of Joel Barlow. Also has assurances that St. Maxent has a letter from Kennedy to a citizen of Mobile containing proof of the plot.

RC and enclosures (DLC); letterbook copy (DNA: RG 107, LSP). RC docketed by JM. First enclosure (8 pp.) in a clerk's hand; docketed by JM; printed in Carter, *Territorial Papers, Mississippi*, 6:79–82. For second enclosure, see n. 1.

1. Sparks enclosed a return of troops for the month of June 1810 (2 pp.; in a clerk's hand).

From Elizabeth House Trist

⟨DR.⟩ SIR   PHILAD July [August] 7th — 10[1]

After acknowledging the receipt of your favor for which I am grateful
and to assure that beyond what is just and honorable to the public interest
I have neither expectation on or claim but if it wou'd not be improper to
ask the question I shou'd be glad to know upon what principle property
purchased by Mr Jones above a year previously, shou'd be liable for W
Browns debts Mr Jones left N Orleans previous to my departure from
that place, to obtain from his friends a loan to enable him to make a purchase and he wrote me soon after my arrival in Virginia that he had succeeded in obtaining the sum he wanted and had made proposals to William Brown to purchase half the Plantation and Negroes he then possess'd
and wrote me soon after that he had made the purchase and his family
removed there and that the management (as the collectors business kept
him in Town) was submitted to him, and I am well assured that the purchase was just and honorable nor do I believe Mr Jones wou'd have been
capable of any collusi⟨on or⟩ fraud for in every transaction I witness'd
relating to him I ever found him punctiliously correct generous and disinterested and I cant immagine that Mrs Jones can have forfited her claim
to the property of her husband tho Mr Grimes has obtain'd possession.
The enclosed papers I recd yesterday which she wish'd transmitted to you
I also send you an extract of Mrs. Jones's letter to me.

"Mr Grimes moved to the plantation the day after he turn'd me out, I
shall only observe that Notwithstanding he has in possession the Plantation and 34 Negroes and 220 acres of as fine cane as any in the Country I
fear much that the United States will be but little benefited by it; before
my trial took place a Lady observed to me Mrs Jones if you will allow me
to offer Mr Grimes 8000$. I will secure you your 31500$. No Madam he
has slandered my husbands character by doubting his honesty and I am
detirmined to submit the transaction to a Court of Justice. The same offer
has been made me since by another person but I rejected it, Judge Hall[2]
accused him of taking a *bribe* from *Shepherd* in a full Court and there is not
the least doubt, but he did, as I have given my self some trouble to asser-
tain it. It is the general opinion that when Government is made acquainted
with all the circumstances they will certainly reimburse me, I am intitled
to half of the last years crop, but my counsel informs me that Grimes
intimates it has been expended on the Plantation tho to my certain knowledge since my arrival the only articles purchased (except what I have expended and which I have not charged for) have been 50 barrels of corn
3 loads of hay, and two pair of Oxen I was obliged to purchase when I
was very much inconvenienced for Money as the Overseer assured me

unless I did it wou'd not be possible to put an acre of cane in the ground and Grimes wou'd not give the Money since he has purchased the estate the sheriff has paid me 200$ which I gave for them, as I declared that I wou'd take them with me if he did not.["]

I must trespass a little longer on your patience by observing that I am not insensible to the task assign'd Mr Grimes to a man of sensibility it must be a painful one but the complaint is against his illegal proceedings, tho his general conduct has been tyranical and unfeeling the sheriff had equally as unpleasant a part to perform and tho the family had no acquaintance with him his conduct was tender and humane tho strict in adherence to his duty. What asstonishes me is that any compromise shou'd be proposed by Mr Grimes as Mrs Jones's claim must be either just or unjust and the deci(s)ion of a court of justice has been in her favor. With my best respects to Mrs. Madison I am your much Obliged Humble Servt.

                                                        E. TRIST

RC and enclosures (DLC). Enclosures are (1) copy of a receipt dated 19 Apr. 1809 and signed by William Brown, acknowledging payment from P. L. Jones of $1,500 and a note for $3,000 for the estate transferred to Jones on 19 Oct. 1808; followed by a copy of a statement by William Brown, 17 Mar. 1809, binding himself to pay $8,090 for the children of Hore Browse Trist, deceased, to Philip L. Jones and his wife, Mary, guardian of the children (1 p.); (2) papers relating to the suit *U.S.* v. *Brown*, beginning on 29 May 1810 in the superior court at New Orleans (4 pp.).

    1. The date of 7 July on the RC is almost certainly erroneous. The August date is here assigned on the assumption that Elizabeth House Trist's letter to JM of 18 July 1810 was the opening letter in the correspondence relating to Mary Jones and that the letter Mrs. Trist acknowledged receiving from JM was the one he wrote on 25 July.
    2. Dominic A. Hall was judge of the superior court in Orleans Territory.

From John Graham

DEAR SIR   DEPT OF STATE 8th Augt 1810.

Yesterdays Mail brought on the Dispatches from Mr Pinkney which had been entrusted to Mr Erwing. They were forwar[d]ed by the latter from Phia. The inclosed[1] is a Copy of the last and only important Letter from Mr Pinkney.

From his other communications[2] it appeared, so well as I can recollect (from the very hasty perusal I gave them, before they were put up for the Bath Mail which closed yesterday), that orders would be sent to Admiral Saumarez[3] not to molest American vessels coming from Ports from which British vessels were not excluded and to suffer them to leave the Swedish Ports with the Cargoes they carried into them—that there was a partial relaxation of the Blockade of the Coast of Spain from Gigon &c. by which neutral vessels were enabled to bring off the productions of Spain liable, however, to the regulations of the Order in Council of April 1809—that that order was understood by the Board of Trade as replealing [*sic*] so much of the Novr order as rendered liable to condemnation such vessels as had certificates of Origin on board for their Cargoes. And finally that the usual Notice had been given to Mr Pinkney of the Blockade of Elsineur. This is the substance of five or six short Letters. With Sentiments of the most Sincere & Respectful attachment I have the Honor to be Sir, Your Most Obt Sert

JOHN GRAHAM

RC (DLC); enclosure (DLC: Rives Collection, Madison Papers). Both docketed by JM. Enclosure (4 pp.) in a clerk's hand; marked "(Copy.)" (see n. 1).

1. At a later time JM placed an asterisk here and wrote in the left margin, "*See Wm. Pinkney'[s] file." The enclosure is a copy of Pinkney to Robert Smith, 13 June 1810, where Pinkney reported that Lord Wellesley had not answered a letter concerning the British blockade of France prior to the Berlin decree. Pinkney was also waiting to hear from Wellesley regarding a settlement of the *Chesapeake* affair but warned that it was "impossible to prevail" on Smith's demand that Vice Admiral George Cranfield Berkeley should be "tried and punished."

2. This material was included in Pinkney's dispatch of 12 June 1810, which Graham forwarded to JM on 29 Aug. 1810.

3. Vice Admiral James Saumarez was commander of the Royal Navy squadron in the Baltic, 1808–13.

From William Lee

SIR,   SHIP ANN AT SEA Augt. 8. 1810

I beg leave to apologize to you for the state of the packet accompanying this. The boat in which I sent my baggage from St Jean de Luz to the Ship Ann was upset in crossing the bar of the harbour and all my papers, dispatches and clothes were nearly lost. I am happy to find that this packet & Genl. Armstrongs dispatch have suffered less than I expected.

Inclosed is a note of some things I have taken the liberty to ship in the Ann for your use. I shall forward them from the port we enter at. With great respect I have the honor to subscribe myself your devoted humble servant

WM LEE

RC (ViU). Addressed by Lee to JM at Washington and franked at "N. London Sep—11." Docketed by JM. Enclosures not found.

From John Smith

SIR,   WAR DEPTMT. Augt. 8th. 1810.

I have the honor of enclosing a Copy of Governor Harrison's Letter of the 25th. ultimo, and of stating that the original will be forwarded to the Secretary of War. I am, with perfect Respect, &c. &c. &c.

(signed.)   JNO. SMITH, C. C.

[Enclosure]

§ William Henry Harrison to William Eustis. *25 July 1810, Vincennes.* Reports that friendly Potawatomi chiefs are "forming a combination" of various tribes to disperse the Prophet and his "banditti" at Tippecanoe. Believes that some Indians have already agreed to leave Tippecanoe but the Prophet is not "intimidated" and "is as actively employed in poisoning the minds of the Indians as ever." Has recently conferred with two associates of the Prophet, who denied any intent to go to war but insisted on the right of the Indians to gather on the Wabash. "The encroachment of the Whites upon their lands, was still the burden of the Song." Is confident, however, that the Prophet's schemes "for forming a general confederacy against the United States, are for the present blasted." Describes the activities of the British Indian agent [Matthew Elliott], claiming that the agent wishes to influence "the most warlike of the Tribes, as a kind of barrier to Canada."

Refers to Jefferson's policy of controlling the Indians by building up strong settlements beyond the Ohio, thus so curtailing their hunting grounds "as to force them to change their mode of life & thereby to render them less warlike." Admits that both the Indians and the British understand this, hence their opposition to every treaty and "the bold stroke of collecting the remote Tribes upon the Wabash for the purpose of forming a confederacy." Advocates in response "holding the rod of correction" constantly over the Indians and believes his recent musterings of the militia have restrained them. But the alarm also caused settlers to flee; calls therefore for the construction of "one or two strong posts" on the Wabash to reassure settlers as well as to encourage the sales of public land.

Letterbook copy (DNA: RG 107, LSP); enclosure (DLC). Enclosure (6 pp.) in a clerk's hand; docketed by JM; printed in Esarey, *Messages and Letters of William Henry Harrison*, Indiana Historical Collections, 1:449–53.

From Samuel Smith

DEAR SIR,   BALTIMORE Augt. 8th. 1810

The Branch Bank has notified the Presidents of the Banks in this city, that on monday they had received orders from the Bank of the U. S. directing the Branch Bank to commence immediately the *lessening their*

Discounts and to call in *immediately* the money that may now be due, or hereafter become due from the different Banks.

The declared object is safety to themselves, and may be to create such an outcry & such difficulties to men in Commerce, or largely engaged in Manufactures as will tend to *compel* Congress to renew their Charter.[1] The drawing into the Vaults of the Bank of the U. S. specie to the amount of Ten Millions, may be attended with some inconvenience, but not at any time, *so much* as has been estimated—at this time *less* than for many years past. Trade *being circumscribed by the Belligerents*, leaves scarcely so much commerce for our pursuit, as will fully employ the actual capital of the Merchants, so that, men heretofore largely engaged in trade feel themselves now perfectly at ease; nor do I apprehend any danger to Commercial men from that amount of specie being locked up: but it may tend to lessen enterprize, *& thus injure the price of our Exports.*

To prevent this injury (to a greater amt. than the Capital of the Bank) is in the power of the Executive.

The Deposits belonging to the Treasury, now in the Bank cannot be less than four millions, and the payments will daily be making for Bonds that will become due, and which are deposited in the different Branch Banks of the U. S. The payment of those Bonds are a perpetual drain from the Vaults of the State Banks. From this drain it is in your power to releive, by directing the Secretary of the Treasury to draw (& that without delay) into some of the State Banks, the money collected or to be Collected by the U. S Bank; this will have a twofold operation: It will prevent the Bank of the U. S from accumulating more specie than the amt. of their Capital, and it will enable the State Banks (to which the Treasury transfers their funds) to discount for those persons, whose Discounts will be curtailed in the U. S. Banks under the late order.

I have been informed that Mr. Gallatin has on a former occasion transferred a part of the public money from the U. S Bank to the Manhattan Bank;[2] so that he has found it can be done without any great inconvenience.

Commerce has certainly been harrassed, but it is a fact that in this city the Merchts. have made money since the Embargo. I know only one exception.

Permit me to add that if this course should not be pursued, (or some other that will prevent the injury resulting from the collection of the Bonds made by the Bank of the U. S. and it's Branches,) there will be members of Congress who will attribute it to improper motives, and who will beleive that the Secretary of the treasury was thereby favoring the institution. We certainly had better have no such institution, if the consequence is, that it can awe the Government at it's pleasure. Excuse the frankness with which I write & beleive me to be with sincerity & truth Your friend & Servt.

S. SMITH

NB. A Ship just arrived left Bordeaux on the 8 June, the Sally (intended to Come from St. Sebastian for Genl. A.) had not arrived but was daily expected. A very intelligent Capt. whose Vessel & Cargo were seized & sold, Conjectures, that there is a well founded hope, that the property will all be restored, he forms this Conjecture from their being very particular in the sales, and from their Compelling him to attend & take an Acct. of the Sales of his Cargo—the Vessel is not yet up—there are on board he says Despatches for Govt. from Genl. A.

RC (DLC: Rives Collection, Madison Papers). In an unidentified hand with emendations, signature, and postscript in Smith's hand. Docketed by JM.

1. In April Congress had postponed a decision about rechartering the Bank of the United States until its next session. In the interim, enemies of the bank, of whom Smith was among the most prominent, leveled charges against it of concealed profits and mysterious operations. Smith had significant connections with state banking interests in Maryland and was to vote against recharter in 1811 (see John R. Smith to JM, 3 Feb. 1810, n. 2; Cassell, *Merchant Congressman in the Young Republic*, pp. 165–69; Hammond, *Banks and Politics in America*, pp. 211, 220; James O. Wettereau, "New Light on the First Bank of the United States," *Pa. Mag. Hist. and Biog.*, 61 [1937]: 268).

2. Smith was probably referring to Gallatin's decision to allow the Manhattan Company to remit government funds to London in 1805. The effect of this decision was to increase the deposits of the Manhattan Company at a time when it was in danger of suffering from a shortage of specie and the hostile activities of a rival bank, the Merchants Bank of New York (Hammond, *Banks and Politics in America*, pp. 159–60, 202–6).

From Thomas Jefferson

TH: J. TO J. M.   MONTO. Aug. 9. 10.

I have just time before closing the mail to send you the Memoir on the Batture.[1] It is long; but it takes a more particular view of the legal system of Orleans & the peculiar river on which it lies, than may have before presented itself. However you can readily skip over uninteresting heads. My visit to you depends on the getting a new threshing machine to work: which I expect will permit me to depart the last of this week or early in the next. Affectionate salutns.

RC (bound in an extra-illustrated volume of Esther Singleton, *The Story of the White House* [New York, 1907], in the collection of the White House, Washington, D.C.). For enclosure (63 pp.), see n. 1.

1. Jefferson enclosed his manuscript of "A Statement of the Usurpation of Edward Livingston on the Batture, or public Beach at New Orleans, and of the laws requiring his removal by the late Executive of the United States," dated 31 July 1810 at Monticello (DLC: Jefferson Papers [filed at 1807]). After the U.S. circuit court in the district of Virginia had dismissed Livingston's suit against Jefferson for want of jurisdiction, Jefferson published a revised version of the manuscript, with a preface, as *The Proceedings of the Government of the United States, in Maintaining the Public Right to the Beach of the Mississippi, Adjacent to New-Orleans, against the Intrusion of Edward Livingston* (New York, 1812; Shaw and Shoemaker 25742). For a more recent republication of the 1812 pamphlet, see Lipscomb and Bergh, *Writings of Jefferson*, 18:1–132.

§ From Charles Bryant. *9 August 1810, Durbians Creek, Greenville District, South Carolina*. Recounts his service in the Revolution and inquires how he can get a land bounty.

RC (DNA: RG 107, LRRS, B-181:5). 3 pp. Docketed by a War Department clerk as received 3 Sept. 1810. JM referred the letter to the War Department, which informed Bryant that a warrant for his land bounty would be issued to any person he authorized to receive it (John Smith to Bryant, 14 Sept. 1810 [DNA: RG 107, LSMA]).

¶ To Richard Forrest. Letter not found. *9 August 1810*. Acknowledged in Forrest to JM, 15 Aug. 1810. Comments on Forrest's offer to go to West Florida as an agent.

To William Eustis

DEAR SIR   MONTPELIER Augst. 10. 1810

I have just recd. from the War office a copy of the letter of July 12. from Lt. Colo. Sparkes,[1] the original of which addressed to you, had been forwarded. The present Mail allows me but a moment, to say that the request to have the garrison at Fort Stoddart reinforced, seems to be amply justified by the circumstances on which it is founded; at the same time that it accords with other arrangements relating to our South Western borders. You will best judge the source which ought to supply the requisite aid. I shall direct that a copy of Col. Sparke's letter be furnished to the Dept. of State, that the purport of it may be forwarded to Govr. Holmes with a view to put him on the alert, in the part accruing to him, in maintaining the authority of the laws. Sparkes ought to use all proper means for obtaining evidence to support any legal proceedings that may become proper, agst. guilty individuals. The letter alledged to be in possession of the Spanish Govr. is peculiarly an Object. Accept my respects & best wishes

JAMES MADISON

RC (MHi: Eustis Papers).

1. See John Smith to JM, 7 Aug. 1810, and enclosure.

To John Graham

Dear Sir   Montpelier Augst. 10. 1810

I have just recd. your favor of the 8th. with the copy of Mr. P.'s letter of June 13th. The same mail brings me a letter from Mr. Erving, in which he says he should be in Washington in a few days. Having not time to write to him, be so good as to tell him, that if it should be within the scope of his arrangements, not to be stationary, I shall be happy to find his movements take this direction. Whatever letters he may have for me may be forwarded by the mail.

I inclose a copy of an important letter to the Sey. of War, from the Commandt. at Fort Stoddart.[1] It merits the attention of the Dept. of State, as the basis of a communication to Govr. Holmes, within whose sphere the scene lies, and who will have a part to perform in maintaining the Authority of the laws. Please to return me, the copy after taking one from it; & to accept my friendly respects

James Madison

RC (DNA: RG 59, ML). Docketed by Graham.

1. Richard Sparks to Eustis, 12 July 1810 (enclosed in John Smith to JM, 7 Aug. 1810).

§ **From Bossange & Masson.** *10 August 1810, Paris.* Solicits JM's patronage of a translation of Homer's *Iliad*.

RC (DLC). 1 p. In French.

§ **From Paul Hamilton.** *Ca. 11 August 1810, Navy Department.* Transmits a statement of Navy Department appropriations up to 11 Aug. 1810 showing an aggregate balance of $1,245,712.75, "which will certainly be sufficient to carry us through the present year & to discharge all engagements." Because of repairs to vessels the Navy Department has in that account only $736.18. Recommends therefore transferring $100,000 from the funds for pay and subsistence and for provisions to the fund for repairs. Also recommends the transfer of $14,500 to cover deficits totaling $7,130 in the funds for medical supplies for the Navy and the Marines. May also need a transfer for the contingent fund. Encloses the form for JM's signature to authorize the transfers.

RC (DLC); letterbook copy and copies of enclosures (DNA: RG 45, LSP). RC 2 pp. In Goldsborough's hand, signed by Hamilton. RC and letterbook copy dated August 1810. Letterbook copy of enclosed authorization dated 20 Aug. 1810.

Notes on Jefferson's "Statement" on the Batture at New Orleans

[ca. 12 August 1810]

p. 16.   form of stating the consultation seems to imply a more elaborate inquiry into the law than was then made: better to give a summary of the grounds; & appeal to the full view of the argts. in support of the opinion given.[1]

Id.   too unqualified pre-eminence ascribed to Civil Law.[2]

17.   quer. the advantage of the note which seems rather erudite & curious, than strictly within the scope of the reasoning which is sufficiently voluminous of necessity.[3]

22.   Tho' true that a mere change of Govt. does not change laws, is it not probable, that by usage, or some other mode, the Spanish law had come into operation; since Thierry on the spot speaks so confidently?[4] This remark applicable to the enquiry into the state of the F. & Civil Law previously in force.

27.   comments on definition of Alluvion too strict.[5] They destroy the idea of Alln: altogether. Alluvion, when real & legal, is found not like plastering a Wall, but coating a floor.

30.   In the Etemologies, that of Platin, at least, far fetched.[6] It is more probably derived from Plat—flat.

35–36.   characteristic features distinguishing the cases of the lands back of the river & the batture seem to be 1: (the appendix to the argument supersedes the attempt here intended)[7]

37   et seq. Is not the point superfluously proved by so many quotations?[8]

49&c   trop recherchè peut être.[9]

51.   & seq: distinction between fedl & state—Ex. & Legis: auths. not observd. in the reasoning[10]

55.   conveys idea of spontaneous advice, & *concurrence* of the P.[11]

56.   Well to be sure that the local law or usage did not confer the Chancery power exercised by the Court in this case.[12] Moreau's Memoir must be important on this as on some other points depending on the law of usage & the Civil law.

The rationale[13] of the doctrine of Alluvion appears to be first, that the Claimant may lose as well as gain: secondly, that the space loses its fitness for common use, and takes a fitness for individual use: hence the doctrine does not apply to Towns where the gain would be disproporti[o]nate; and where the fitness of the space for public use, may be changed only, not lost.

The Batture would to Livingston be gain without possibility of loss; and retains its fitness for Pub: Use, as occasionally, a port, a Quay, and a quarry.

Ms (DLC: Jefferson Papers). In JM's hand. Dated 1807 in the *Index to the Thomas Jefferson Papers*. Conjectural date here assigned on the assumption that JM began making these notes after receiving the manuscript sent him by Jefferson on 9 Aug. and before Jefferson visited Montpelier on 13 Aug. (see Jefferson to JM, 9 Aug. 1810).

1. In his memoir on the batture, Jefferson described the circumstances leading to a cabinet meeting on 27 Nov. 1807 at which the attorney general advised him on the dispute between Edward Livingston and the city of New Orleans over the ownership of, and access to, the batture. Jefferson seems to have first written "On the facts before stated it became our duty to enquire, What was the law? And if not"; but he later deleted it and substituted: "We took of the whole case such views as the state of our information at that time presented. I shall now develope them in all the fulness of the facts then known, & of those which have since corroborated them" (cf. Lipscomb and Bergh, *Writings of Jefferson*, 18:30).

2. At this point in his manuscript Jefferson had embarked on a lengthy history of the French and Spanish law in Louisiana in order to answer his query about "what system of law" was to be applied to the case (ibid., 18:30–35). He placed a check mark in the margin of JM's notes to indicate that he had taken the point into consideration.

3. JM was evidently objecting to a note in which Jefferson sought to demonstrate that Roman law had served as a form of natural law to supplement French feudal law and therefore that elements of Roman law had been transplanted to Louisiana. Jefferson let the note stand (see ibid., 18:35).

4. Jefferson took exception to those sections of J. B. S. Thierry's pamphlet on the batture (see *PJM-PS*, 1:359 n. 1) where Thierry conceded that Spanish law in Louisiana had given alluvions to the riparian proprietor (see Lipscomb and Bergh, *Writings of Jefferson*, 18:49).

5. JM referred to Jefferson's efforts to adduce linguistic arguments in support of his claim that Roman law conferred alluvion rights on only rural, and not urban, proprietors of river banks (see ibid., 18:61–65).

6. To advance the argument that the Mississippi deposits claimed by Livingston were not covered by any laws relating to alluvion rights, Jefferson claimed that the land in question might be more properly considered as a beach—the area "which lies between the high & low water marks." Jefferson noted that the terms in New Orleans for such a beach were "*batture*, & sometimes *platin*," and he suggested that the latter may have derived, among other possibilities, from the Greek "percuture." In the margin opposite JM's remark, Jefferson indicated with a check mark that he had noted JM's point, and he may have added to his manuscript: "Perhaps however from *plat*, Fr. for flat" (see ibid., 18:71).

7. Here Jefferson surveyed some complex arguments comparing the Mississippi and the Nile rivers to see how far laws governing the bed and the banks of the latter might be applicable to the former. He finally settled for the simpler statement that the bed of a river indisputably belonged to the sovereign of a nation and that for as long as the bed was "oc-

cupied by the river, all laws, I believe, agree in giving it to the sovereign; not as his personal property, to become an object of revenue or of alienation, but to be kept open for the free use of all the individuals of the nation." JM seems to have been indicating his preference here for the latter argument (see ibid., 18:79–85, esp. 84–85).

8. For Jefferson's citation of a multiplicity of authorities demonstrating that the bed of the Mississippi belonged to the nation and that the public had navigation rights on the river, see ibid., 18:85–92.

9. After his demonstration that Livingston had no claim either to own or to develop the batture, Jefferson defended at great length the "natural right" of both men and governments to repossess property taken by force or fraud (ibid., 18:104–10).

10. Here Jefferson was asserting that there could be no restraint on a government exercising a "natural right" to repossess property and that the "US. cannot be sued" (ibid., 18:107–15).

11. In defending the decision of his administration to evict Livingston from the batture, Jefferson wrote that after weighing the evidence then available, "(the four heads of departments with the attorney general) were unanimously of Opinion, (and in the same opinion I entirely concurred) that we were authorized, & in duty bound, without delay to arrest the aggressions of mr. Livingston on the public rights." Noting JM's objection with a check mark in the margin, he deleted from his manuscript the phrases in angle brackets and wrote instead: "we were all unanimously of Opinion, that . . ." (see ibid., 18:116).

12. Livingston had obtained an injunction against his eviction from the batture in January 1808, but Jefferson argued that the injunction was not "authoritative," as it was a chancery process and "no Chancery jurisdiction has been given by any law to the Superior court of [Louisiana] territory" (see ibid., 18:117–18).

13. In the margin opposite JM's comment, Jefferson placed a check mark and wrote "pa. 28." to refer to the section of his manuscript where he had already discussed the point that "the equity on which the right of alluvion is founded is, that as the owner of the field is exposed to the danger of loss, he ought, as an equivalent, to have the chance of gain." Jefferson denied that the principle applied in Livingston's case (see ibid., 18:67).

¶ To John Graham. Letter not found. *12 August 1810.* Acknowledged in Graham to JM, 15 Aug. 1810. Forwards a letter from Mr. Balch [not found] and asks Graham to consult with Mr. Jones.

From John Graham

DEAR SIR   DEPT OF STATE 13th August 1810.

I had the Honor to receive your Letter of the 10th Inst. yesterday. Th[. . .] Mr Erwing was with us; but he went on to Alexandria in the afternoon, where he intended to take a Carriage for the purpose of going to Montpelier. He took with him the Letter he had for you, expecting to be at your House nearly as soon as the Mail which lea⟨v⟩es this today.

I return agreeably to your directions the Copy you sent me, of Colo Sparks[1] Letter to the Secy of War, having taken one from it for Govr

Holmes, which will be forwarded by the Mail today, with a Letter from myself[2] stating to him that the communication is made, as he will have a part to perform in maintaining the authority of the Laws in that Section of his Territory, where the Letter was written. I have marked my Letter "*confidential.*"

I have the Honor to inclose Despatches from Genl Armstrong,[3] which were received on Saturday and also a Letter from Mr Lee[4] recieved at the same time. We have taken *copies* for Mr. Smith which will be forwarded to him at Bath, by the Mail which goes tomorrow.

I have been obliged to write in great haste as the Mail is waiting for my Letter. With Sentiments of the Highest Respect I have the Honor to be, Sir Your Most Obt Sert

JOHN GRAHAM

RC (DLC). Torn by removal of seal. Docketed by JM. For enclosures, see nn. 1, 3, and 4.

1. JM placed an asterisk here at a later date and wrote in the margin "*See Sparkes filed." For the letter, see John Smith to JM, 7 Aug. 1810, and enclosure.

2. Graham later sent JM a copy of his 13 Aug. letter to David Holmes (Graham to JM, 3 Sept. 1810).

3. Graham forwarded a duplicate of Armstrong's dispatch of 5 May 1810 to Robert Smith (DNA: RG 59, DD, France) (29 pp.; docketed as received in August) reporting on the seizure of American vessels in Spain and covering copies of Armstrong's correspondence with Leonard Jarvis and Sylvanus Bourne.

4. Graham enclosed William Lee to Robert Smith, 4 June 1810 (DNA: RG 59, CD, Bordeaux) (7 pp.) reporting on the publication of the Rambouillet decree, the distress of American seamen, and the use of British and French licenses by American traders in Europe.

From William Pinkney

private

DEAR SIR   LONDON. August 13th. 1810.

I return you my sincere Thanks for your friendly Letter of the 23d. of May. Nothing could have been more acceptable than the Approbation which you are so good as to express of my Note to Ld. Wellesley on Jackson's Affair. I wish I had been more successful in my Endeavours to obtain an unexceptionable Answer to it. You need not be told that the actual Reply was, in its plan & Terms, wide of the Expectations which I had formed of it. It was unfortunately delayed until first Views & Feelings became weak of themselves. The Support which Jackson received in America was admirably calculated to produce other Views & Feelings; not only by its direct Influence on Ld. Wellesley & his Colleagues, but by the Influence which they could not but know it had on the British Nation

& the Parliament. The extravagant Conduct of France had the same pernicious Tendency; and the Appearances in Congress, with Reference to our future Attitude on the Subject of the Atrocious Wrongs inflicted upon us by France & England, could scarcely be without their Effect. It is not to be doubted that, with a strong Desire in the outset to act a very conciliatory part, the British Government was thus gradually prepared to introduce into the proceeding what would not otherwise have found a place in it, and to omit what it ought to have contained. The Subject appeared to it every Day in a new Light, shed upon it from France & the United States, and a corresponding Change naturally enough took place in the scarcely-remembered Estimates which had at first been made of the proper Mode of managing it. The Change in Lord Wellesley's Notions upon it, between our first Interview & the Date of his Answer to my Note, must have been considerable, if that Answer had, as doubtless it had, his Approbation. For, the Account of that Interview, as given in my private Letter to Mr. Smith of the 4th. of January, is so far from exaggerating Ld. Wellesley's Reception of what I said to him, that it is much below it. It is to be observed, however, that he had hardly read the Correspondence, and had evidently thought very little upon it. For which Reason, and because he spoke for himself only, and with less Care than he would perhaps have used if he had considered that he was speaking officially, I am glad that you declined to lay my private Letter before the Congress. The Publication of it, which must necessarily have followed, would have produced serious Embarrassment.

Do you not think that, in some Respects, Ld. Wellesley's Answer to my Note[1] has not been exactly appretiated in America? I confess to you that this is my Opinion. That the Paper is a very bad one is perfectly clear; but it is not so bad in Intention as it is in Reality, nor quite so bad in Reality as it is commonly supposed to be. It is the production of an indolent Man, making a great *Effort* to reconcile Things *almost* incongruous, and just shewing his Wish without executing it. Lord Wellesley wished to be extremely civil to the American Government; but he was at the same Time to be very stately—to manage Jackson's Situation—and to intimate Disapprobation of the Suspension of his Functions. He was stately, not so much from Design, as because he cannot be otherwise. In managing Jackson's Situation he must have gone beyond his original Intention, and certainly beyond any, of which I was aware before I received his Answer. If the Answer had been promptly written I have no Belief that he would have affected to praise Jackson's "Ability Zeal & Integrity," or that he wd. have said any thing about his Majesty's not having "marked his Conduct with any Expression of his Displeasure." He would have been content to forbear to censure him; and *that* I always took for granted he would do.

For Jackson personally Ld. Wellesley cares nothing. In his several Conferences with me he never vindicated him, and he certainly did not mean in his Letter to undertake his Defence. It is impossible that he should not have (*I am indeed sure that he has*) a mean opinion of that most clumsy and ill-conditioned Minister. His Idea always appeared to be that he was wrong in pressing at all the Topick which gave offence; but that he acted upon good Motives, and that his Government could not with Honour, or without Injury to the Diplomatic Service generally, *disgrace him*. This is explicitly stated in my private Letter of the 4th. of January to Mr Smith. There is a great Difference, undoubtedly, between that Idea, and the one upon which Ld. Wellesley appears finally to have acted. It must be admitted, however, that the Praise bestowed upon Jackson is very Meagre, and that it ascribes to him no Qualities in any Degree inconsistent with the Charge of gross Indecency & intolerable Petulance preferred against him in my Note. He might be honest, Zealous, able; and yet be indiscreet, ill-tempered, suspicious, arrogant, and ill-mannered. It is to be observed, too, that the Praise has no Reference whatever to the actual Case, and that, when the Answer speaks of the Offence imputed to Jackson by the American Government, it does not say that he gave no such Cause of Offence, but simply relies on his repeated Asseverations that he *did not mean to offend*.

If the Answer had been promptly written I am persuaded that another Feature, which now distinguishes it, would have been otherwise. It would not have contained any Complaint against the Course adopted by the American Government in putting an End to official Communication with Jackson. That Ld. Wellesley thought that Course objectionable from the first appears in my private Letter abovementioned to Mr. Smith. But he did not urge his Objections to it in such a Way at our first Interview, or afterwards, as to induce me to suppose that he would except to that Course in his written Answer. He said in the outset that he considered it a *Damnum* to the B. Government; and I knew that he was not disposed to acknowledge the Regularity of it. But I did not imagine that he would take any formal Notice of it. There was evidently no Necessity, if he did not approve the Course, to say any thing about it, and in our Conversations I always *assumed* that it was not only unnecessary but wholly inadmissible to mention it officially for any other purpose than that of approving it. After all, however, what he has said upon this Point (idle & illjudged as it is) is the mere Statement of the Opinion of the British Government that another Course would have been more in Rule than ours. It amounts to this, then, that we have Opinion against Opinion & Practice; and that our Practice has been acquiesced in.

As to that part of the Answer which speaks of a *Chargé d'Affaires*,[2] it must now be repented of here, especially by Lord Wellesley, if it was really intended as a Threat of future Inequality in the Diplomatic Establishments of the two Countries, or even to wear that Appearance. Ld. Wellesley's Letter to me of the 22d. ulto. abandons that Threat,[3] and makes it consequently much worse than nothing. His Explanations to me on that Head (*not official*) have lately been, that, when he wrote his Answer, he thought there was some person in America to whom Jackson could immediately have delivered Charge, and that, if he had not been under that Impression, he should not probably have spoken in his Answer of a *Chargé d'Affaires*, and should have sent out a Minister plenipotentiary in the first Instance. I know not what Stress ought to be laid upon these private & *ex post facto* Suggestions; but I am entirely convinced that there was no Thought of continuing a *Charge d'Affaires* at Washington for more than a short Time. Neither their Pride, nor their Interests, nor the Scantiness of their present diplomatic Patronage wd. permit it.

That Ld. Wellesley has long been looking out in *his dilatory Way* for a suitable Character (a Man of *Rank*) to send as Minister pleny. to the U. S. I have the best Reason to be assured. That the Appointment has not yet taken place is no proof at all that it has not been intended. Those who think they understand Ld. W. best, represent him as *disinclined to Business*—and it is certain that I have found him upon every Occasion given to Procrastination beyond all Example. The Business of the Chesapeake is a striking Instance. Nothing could be fairer than his various Conversations on that Case. He settles it with me verbally over & over again. He promises his written Overture in a few Days, and I hear no more of the Matter. There may be Cunning in all this, but it is not such Cunning as I shd. expect from Ld. Wellesley. In the affair of the Blockades it is evident that the Delay arises from the Cabinet, alarmed at every thing which touches the Subject of Blockades & that abominable Scheme of Monopoly called the Orders in Council. Yet it is an unquestionable Fact that they have suffered, and are suffering severely under the iniquitous Restrictions which they and France had imposed upon the Commerce of the World.

I mean to wait a little longer for Lord Wellesley's Reply to my Note of the 30th. of April.[4] If it is not soon received, I hope I shall not be thought indiscreet if I present a strong Remonstrance upon it, & if I take Occasion in it to advert to the Affair of the Chesapeake, & to expose what has occurred in that Affair between Ld. Wellesley & me.

I have a Letter from Genl. Armstrong, of the 24th. of last Month. He expects no Change in the Measures of the French Govt. with regard to the U. S. I cannot, however, refrain from hoping that we shall have no War with that Government. We have a sufficient Case for War against both France & England—an *equal* Case against both in point of Justice, even if we take into the Account the recent Violences of the former. But looking to *Expediency*, which shd. never be lost Sight of, I am not aware of any

Considerations, that shd. induce us in actual Circumstances to embark in a War with France. I have so often troubled you on this Topick that I will not venture to stir it again.

Before I conclude this Letter I beg your permission to mention a Subject in which I have a personal Interest. I am told, and, indeed, have partly seen; that I am assailed with great Acrimony & Perseverance in some of the American Newspapers. It is possible that encreasing Clamour, though it can give me no Concern, may make it convenient that I should be very soon recalled; and it certainly will not be worth while to make a point of keeping me here, for any Time however short, if many persons in America desire that it should be otherwise. I can scarcely be as useful to our Country as I ought to be under such Circumstances, and I have really no Wish to continue for any purpose looking to my own Advantage. If I consulted my personal Interest merely I should already have entreated your permission to return. The Disproportion between my unavoidable Expences & my Salary has ruined me in a pecuniary Sense. The Prime of my Life is passing away in barren Toil & Anxiety, and, while I am sacrificing myself and my Family in the public Service abroad, ill disposed or silly People are sacrificing my Reputation at Home. My affectionate Attachment to you need not be mentioned. If its Sincerity is not already manifest, Time only can make it so, & to that I appeal. But by seeking to remain in office under you, against the Opinion of those whose Remonstrances will at least be loud and troublesome, if they are not reasonable and just, I should show a Want of all Concern for your Character & Quiet. I do *not* seek it therefore. On the contrary I pray you most earnestly to recall me immediately (the *Manner* of it would I am sure be kind) if you find it in any Way expedient to do so. Believe me, I shall go back to my Profession with a cheerful Heart, and with a Recollection of your unvarying Kindness which nothing can ever impair. I should, indeed, look forward to Retirement from official Station with the deepest Sorrow, if I supposed that, in parting with me as a Minister, you were to part with me also as a Friend. But the Friend will remain—not for a Season only but always—and be assured that, though you will have many abler Friends, you can have none upon whose Truth & Zeal you may more confidently rely.

In a Word—I do not at this Moment request my Recall; but I shall receive it without Regret, if you, with better Means of judging than I can have, should think it advisable. That I should remain here much longer is hardly possible; but I flatter myself that in forbearing at present to ask your Consent to my Return I do not lose Sight of the public Good.

This is a very long Letter and full of Egotism—but it will have an indulgent Reader and will I know be excused.

RC (DLC: Rives Collection, Madison Papers); draft (NjP: Pinkney Papers). Complimentary close and signature clipped from RC. RC docketed by JM. Draft is heavily emended.

1. Pinkney was referring to Lord Wellesley's letter of 14 Mar. 1810, written in response to Pinkney's letter of 2 Jan. 1810 explaining JM's reasons for requesting the recall of Francis James Jackson (see *ASP, Foreign Relations*, 3 : 355–56).

2. See JM to Pinkney, 23 May 1810, n. 2.

3. On 22 July 1810, Wellesley, replying to a note from Pinkney of 7 July that had sought clarification about the intentions of the British government with respect to replacing Jackson, declared that it was his wish "immediately to recommend the appointment of an envoy extraordinary and minister plenipotentiary from the King to the United States." However, Jackson's replacement, Augustus John Foster, was not appointed until April 1811, by which time Pinkney himself had already decided to return to the U.S. (*ASP, Foreign Relations*, 3 : 363; Mayo, *Instructions to British Ministers*, p. 310).

4. On 30 Apr. 1810 Pinkney had inquired of Wellesley whether the British government, in order to expedite French repeal of the Berlin decree, would revoke those blockades of Europe imposed before the 1807 orders in council, particularly Fox's blockade of May 1806 (*ASP, Foreign Relations*, 3 : 357–58).

§ From James Leander Cathcart. *13 August 1810, Madeira.* Cathcart acknowledges JM's letters of 30 May and 15 and 26 June and informs him of the arrangements he has made for purchasing wine ordered by JM.

RC, duplicate, and enclosures (DLC). RC 2 pp.; docketed by JM. Duplicate (3 pp.; docketed by JM) includes 16 Aug. postscript mentioning enclosures: invoice for £249 (1 p.); and bill of lading (1 p.) for wine shipped on the *Mary Ann*.

To Albert Gallatin

DEAR SIR   MONTPELLIER Aug. 14. 1810

I understand that the measures taking by the Bank of the U. S. for provisionally winding up its affairs, are likely to bear hard on the other Banks, and that the evil will be increased, by the drain on the latter for paying the bonds, as they become due in the hands of the former. Would not some remedy be afforded by a distributive transfer, (which would also have a provisional reference to the fate of the B. of the U. S.) of the public money from its present vaults to those of ⟨the⟩ State Banks? In that case the sum locked up in the B. of the U. S. would be limited to its ten Millions; and the State Banks be, at the same time, aided in discounting for persons whose discounts are curtailed elsewhere. It is not difficult to foresee the impressions that will be made, if in addition to the general embarrassment resulting to the Monied interest, from the Bank operations, they should be chargeable with checking enterprize in purchasing

& exporting, the produce of the farmers & planters. How far was the aid given the Manhattan Bank a precedent for the course here suggested?[1]

The unsigned letter from N. Y. is inclosed, as well to have your assistance in ascertaining the writer, as your advice on the merits of the case.

I have recd your favor on the subject of my Nephew Macon; but have not yet recd. the final determination of his father, who is at present absent as well as his son.

Mr. Jefferson left me this morning, with a request that I wd. forward to you, a paper he has drawn up on the case of the Batture. It will go by the next mail.

As you have seen Irvine,[2] I presume you have gathered the amt. of P.s dispatches, and more too. It appears that on the 13th. of June, no answer had been given to the question whether a repeal of the primitive blockade[3] was objected to; nor any formal offer made, of reparation for the attack on the Chesapeak. It was inferred however the offer was intended. Mrs. M. sends her best regards to Mrs. Gallatin. Be pleased to add mine, & to be assured of my affectionate respects

                                                        JAMES MADISON

RC (NHi: Gallatin Papers). Enclosure not found.

1. See Samuel Smith to JM, 8 Aug. 1810, n. 2.
2. George W. Erving.
3. JM referred to Fox's blockade of May 1806 whereby Great Britain proclaimed the European coastline from Brest to the Elbe to be under blockade.

From Andrew Glassell

DEAR SIR,   TORTHORWALD[1] 14 Augt 1810.

Edward Sims, that I was mention to you as your Stuert; or overseer, has this year againe ingadged with Majr Jones. He is the only man I know our way that I Could with propriety recomend to you, I have not seen him but hearing from some person that he was ingadged, I wish for to let you know as soon as possable. If you had got Mr Simes you would been fixt. With much esteem I remaine your afft. freind.

                                                        ANDW GLASSELL

RC (DLC). Docketed by JM.

1. Torthorwald was the Madison County, Virginia, seat of Andrew Glassell, member of a Scottish merchant family based in Fredericksburg (*PJM*, 13:138 n. 3).

To Abigail Adams

Madam   Montpelier Aug: 15. 1810

I have received your letter of the 1st. instant. Altho' I have not learned that Mr. Adams has yet signified to the Department of State his wish to return from the Mission to St. Petersburg, it is sufficiently ascertained by your communication, as well as satisfactorily explained by the considerations suggested. I have accordingly desired the Secretary of State to let him understand that as it was not the purpose of the Executive to subject him to the personal sacrifices which he finds unavoidable, he will not, in retiring from them, impair the sentiments which led to his appointment.

Be pleased, Madam, to accept my acknowledgments for the gratifying expressions with which you favor me, and to be assured of my high esteem and my respectful consideration.

JAMES MADISON

RC, Tr (MHi: Adams Family Papers). Tr in Abigail Adams's hand, with her note: "These Letters were never communicated except to your Father & Brother."

To Thomas Jefferson

Dear Sir   Montpelier Aug. 15. 1810

I am offered the services of a Mr. Magee,[1] now living with Mr. Randolph, as an overseer. I have discountenanced his offer, partly from an ignorance of his character, but particularly from the uncertainty whether Mr. R. means to part with him. Will you be kind eno', by a line, merely to say 1st. whether it is decided that he is not to remain where he is, the only condition on which I wd. listen to a negociation. 2. whether his conduct as an overseer recommends him to attention.[2]

RC (DLC). Incomplete (see n. 2). Docketed by Jefferson, "recd Aug. 15."

1. William McGehee was probably one of the sons of the William McGehee from whom Jefferson had purchased nearly two hundred acres of land in Albemarle County, Virginia, in 1774. In August 1809 he had been engaged by Thomas Mann Randolph to manage Tufton, the property adjacent to Monticello that Jefferson intended to develop as his "main dependance" during his retirement (Edgar Woods, *Albemarle County in Virginia* [Charlottesville, Va., 1901], p. 259; "Agreement with William Macgehee," 8 Aug. 1809 [MHi: Jefferson Papers]; Jefferson to Martha Jefferson Randolph, 27 Feb. 1809, Betts and Bear, *Family Letters of Jefferson*, p. 386).

2. Paragraph ends here. Lower part of page has been clipped.

From Richard Forrest

DEAR & RESPECTED SIR, WASHINGTON Augt 15th. 1810
Having but this moment returned from Marlbro' where I went on Saturday even'g on a visit to my family, I have only time to offer my best thanks for your esteemed favor of the 9th inst, and to assure you that, I most cordially acquiesce in the plan which you recommend to be pursued in the case to which I refered in my letter of the 6th. inst.

I am happy to learn that the National Intelligencer gets regularly to hand, and will use my endeavor to render its future conveyance equally certain.

Docr. Tucker[1] was little or no better by the last accts. from him. I remain with the great respect &c Your Most obt Servt.

RD. FORREST

RC (ViU).

1. Thomas Tudor Tucker (1745–1828), a graduate of the medical school of the University of Edinburgh and a member of the House of Representatives from South Carolina, 1789–93, was treasurer of the U.S. (*PJM*, 5:273 n. 3).

From Albert Gallatin

DEAR SIR NEW YORK 15th August 1810
The instructions for the person to be sent to Buenos Ayres, having been filled with the name of Gelston instead of being left blank, and he having refused to go, they are now returned in order that you may direct other copies to be made and to be returned to me as early as possible, as I have found a gentleman who appears to me peculiarly fitted in every respect for the undertaking. It is Mr Poinsett[1] of South Carolina, with whose intellect, information, and standing you are already acquainted. He speaks French with perfect ease and is so far versed in Spanish that a few weeks practice will enable him to speak it fluently. To which may be added that his object being reputation and not money, there is no fear of his thinking of monopolies & private speculations instead of applying his whole time and faculties to the public objects. He has requested me to say that although his leisure and wish for useful public employment induce him cheerfully & gratefully to accept this confidential appointment, yet his studies & views had been more particularly directed to the army, specially in relation to its organisation and general staff; and that he hopes that, if you were favorably disposed towards him in that respect, his ab-

sence will not be prejudicial to any promotion in that line which any new arrangement may render practicable and for which you may think him fit.

There is not at present and it may be difficult to find an opportunity direct for Buenos Ayres. But there will be soon one for Rio Janeiro whence a passage may easily be had: and it may perhaps be advantageous that Mr Poinsett should go that way, as he would receive from Mr Sumpter general useful information both on the views of the Brazilian Court & family towards the Spanish Vice Royalty, and respecting the various parties and their designs at Buenos Ayres itself. Mr Sumpter might also give him some introductory letters which would facilitate his first steps. If this should strike you in the same manner it does me, Mr Poinsett should be furnished with a letter for Mr Sumpter (to whom he may by the bye carry answers to the last dispatches) & Mr Sumpter himself ought to have Mr Poinsett's cypher that they may correspond together. That cypher I do not send back to you with the instructions, but keep it to be delivered together with those which will be returned.

Perhaps on a view of these, you will find something to add either in writing or verbally. If to be done verbally, be pleased to communicate what you wish to be said. Considering the immediate land communication between Buenos Ayres and Peru, and the difficulty of obtaining agents perfectly qualified and willing to go; might not Mr Poinsett's commission be extended to the last? or some contingent instructions be given applicable to it? if in the course of his mission, he should think it necessary for the public service to go there or to do something in relation to it.

Should not also something be said respecting the views & pretensions of the Princess Regent and of her lately married daughter on the adjacent provinces?[2] I do not think it improbable that so far as relates to Buenos Ayres, the British being particularly obnoxious there will throw their weight in the Portuguese party: so that there may be four in all, Anglo-Portuguese, French, Spanish and Creole or for independence.

I told at once to Mr Poinsett that his reasonable expences would be paid; but he has no expectation that the allowance will be equal to what his actual expenses will amount to. An advance, however, must be made to him, which, I presume should amount to about fifteen hundred dollars. But I think that the promise to defray reasonable expences should be official & not merely verbal from me. If you think so, I wish that this might be inserted in the instructions. Respectfully Dear Sir, Your obedt. Servt.

ALBERT GALLATIN

The Gentleman's name is *Joel Roberts Poinsett*.

RC (DLC).

1. Joel Roberts Poinsett (1779–1851), the South Carolinian diplomat and statesman, had been introduced to JM by Thomas Sumter, Jr., in Washington in 1801, shortly before he traveled to Europe where he remained until 1804. He returned to Europe in 1806 but hastened back to the U.S. in 1809 in the expectation of performing military service in the event of war with Great Britain. JM and Gallatin were disposed to appoint Poinsett to office, but Secretary of War Eustis apparently was not, and Poinsett appears to have languished in Washington until Gallatin suggested him for the post in Buenos Aires (Thomas Sumter, Jr., to JM, 6 Aug. 1801 [DLC]; J. Fred Rippy, *Joel R. Poinsett, Versatile American* [Durham, N.C., 1935], pp. 31–32, 35–39).

2. The princess regent was Carlota Joaquina, sister of Ferdinand VII of Spain and wife of Dom João, prince regent of Portugal and later João VI. In May 1810 her daughter, Maria Teresa, had married Pedro Carlos, a nephew of Carlos IV of Spain. The marriage formed part of the schemes promoted by the Portuguese court from its exile in Rio de Janeiro after 1808 to permit Carlota Joaquina to rule Spanish America as regent for her imprisoned brother while also allowing the Portuguese crown to revive its claims to the province of Banda Oriental, which had been surrendered to the viceroyalty of La Plata in 1777. U.S. minister Sumter, who had presented credentials from JM to Carlota Joaquina on 24 June 1810, reported that it was the policy of the princess "to regain the River Plate" as the southern boundary of Brazil. It was not improbable, he added, that "the British gov. may be solicited to use their influence to obtain this" (Alan K. Manchester, *British Preeminence in Brazil: Its Rise and Decline* [Chapel Hill, N.C., 1933], pp. 118–30; Julián María Rubio, *La Infanta Carlota Joaquina y la Política de España en América [1808–1812]* [Madrid, 1920], pp. 18–19; Thomas Sumter, Jr., to Robert Smith, 23 July 1810 [DNA: RG 59, DD, Brazil]).

From John Graham

DEAR SIR   DEPT OF STATE 15th Augt 1810

I am much mortified that my Letter of the 13th Inst: and more particularly, that the Papers which were under cover with it did not go on by the Mail of that day. I had sent to the Post office to let them know that we were preparing Despatches for you and the Governor of the Mississippi Territory and to enquire when the Mail would close. I expected that they would of course detain the Mail if our Packets were not in time for it. It seems however, that they did not understand my Message as meaning more than an enquiry when the Mail would close and that they sent it off without waiting for us. Hence we were a few Minutes too late as I afterwards understood. I shall take care, however, that nothing of the sort shall happen in future.

As soon as I received your Letter of the 12th covering one from Mr Balch[1]—I made the enquiry it directed, of Mr Jones[2] and as he thought there could be no objection to liberating the Persons to whom Mr Balch's Letter referred, in the way you wished—I hastened to make known your wishes to the Marshal and I doubt not; but that they were immediately carried into effect. With Sentiments of the Most Respectful attachment I am Dear Sir Your Mo: Ob Sert

JOHN GRAHA⟨M⟩

RC (DLC). Docketed by JM.

1. No letter from Balch to JM has been found. Stephen Bloomer Balch (1747–1833), like his older brother Hezekiah Balch, with whom JM was also acquainted, was a graduate of the College of New Jersey at Princeton (class of 1774). He began a ministerial career in 1779 and spent most of his life as pastor of the Georgetown Presbyterian church (Richard A. Harrison, *Princetonians, 1769–1775: A Biographical Dictionary* [Princeton, N.J., 1980], pp. 359–62).

2. Walter Jones, Jr., was the U.S. attorney for the District of Columbia (Bryan, *History of the National Capital*, 1:584–85).

From Albert Gallatin

DEAR SIR   NEW YORK August 16th 1810

I forgot to mention in my letter of yesterday, that in addition to the letter designating the agent to Buenos Ayres as commercial agent of the U. States for that place, a passport in the usual form appears necessary. If this also designates him as commercial agent, the usual description of the person might be omitted. Will you have the goodness to give also directions to that effect.

You have seen the late Spanish decrees forbidding the admission into any of the colonies of any person not furnished with Spanish passports.[1] How far this decree will be respected in the colonies is uncertain: but it may create obstacles which would defeat the mission. As the exequatur of the Spanish Consul here, continues in force, and we acknowledge him as such, I do not perceive any objection to applying to him for one: but must it be done in Mr P.'s own name as a private individual? or is it best that the Consul should know that he is sent by Govt. as commercial agent? Respectfully

ALBERT GALLATIN

RC (DLC). Docketed by JM.

1. On 13 Aug. 1810 the Spanish consul in Philadelphia announced that the regency of Spain, in order to detect the activities of Bonapartist agents in the Americas, had decreed that "no Spaniard or foreigner of any nation or under any pretext whatever be permitted to land in any of the Spanish possessions . . . unless they are provided with proper passports from the public functionaries representing Ferdinand the 7th, at the places where they may embark, which passports shall minutely and correctly designate the persons to whom they are granted, and the object of their journey or voyage" (*National Intelligencer*, 20 Aug. 1810).

From Thomas Jefferson

DEAR SIR   MONTICELLO Aug. 16. 10.

Yours of yesterday was recieved last night. The McGehee who is the subject of it, is an overseer of mine at a place, which on account of it's importance to me, mr. Randolph takes care of. He employed McGehee, & solely superintends him. We consider him as extremely industrious, active, attentive, and skilful in the old practices, but prejudiced against any thing he is not used to. We have obliged him to adopt the level plough-ing, but he would get rid of it if he could. As far as we know or believe he is honest. So far good; but there are great set-offs, all proceeding from an unfortunate temper. To those under him he is harsh, severe, and tyranni-cal, to those above him, insubordinate, self-willed, capable of insolence if not personally afraid, dictatorial & unbending: with this he is the most discontented mortal under all circumstances I have ever known.[1] He has been overseer at three different places in our neighborhood, but not more than a year in either. Mr. Randolph had intended however to try him another year, and thought he had agreed with him the day before he went to you. Finding however that Mcgehee thinks otherwise, he feels himself at liberty to look out for another, and if he would suit you we would both wish you to take him, and should part with him without reluctance; and whether you take him or not, I think mr. Randolph, loosened from what he thought an engagement, will try to get another. He was to have for the present year £50. certain and more if his management was approved; and on the late negociation mr. R. had agreed to £125. for this & the next year. I called at mr. Lindsay's the day I left you, and enquired of him respecting McGehee as I knew he had been his overseer. He gave exactly the above character of him and added the fact that his insults were so intolerable that he wished to have got rid of him in the middle of the year, and offered him 200. D. instead of his share to go off. McGehee asked 250. which were refused. He was overseer for mrs Walker his neighbor, & carried a gun ordinarily for fear of an attack from the negroes. I have thus given you all the good & the bad I know of him that you may weigh & judge for yourself, which do freely as there is no attachment to him here. Always affectionly. yours

TH: JEFFERSON

RC (DLC); FC (DLC: Jefferson Papers).

1. Despite this unfavorable testimonial, McGehee seems to have remained in Jefferson's service until November 1811 (MHi: Thomas Jefferson Account Books, entries for 3 Jan., 8 May, and 17 Nov. 1811).

§ From Alexander Smyth.[1] *16 August 1810*. Encloses a letter stating some facts that the president should know. After reading the letter, JM is requested to seal and forward it.

RC and enclosure (DNA: RG 107, LRUS, S-1810). RC 1 p. Unsigned; undated. Enclosure (6 pp.) is Smyth to William Eustis, 16 Aug. 1810, Wythe, Virginia. In the letter, Smyth states the reasons for his refusal to serve under General Wilkinson and his reluctance to serve with General Hampton.

1. Alexander Smyth (1765–1830) was born in Ireland and raised in Virginia where he practiced law in Wythe County. He served several terms in both branches of the Virginia state legislature before Jefferson, in 1808, commissioned him as colonel of the Eighth Rifle Regiment. In July 1812 JM appointed him as inspector general of the army with the rank of brigadier general, and shortly thereafter Smyth took command of the American forces on the Niagara peninsula. His subsequent mishandling of the invasion of Canada provoked such a reaction against him that he was legislated out of the U.S. Army in March 1813 (Heitman, *Historical Register*, 1:905; *ASP, Military Affairs*, 1:490–510; *Senate Exec. Proceedings*, 2:281, 288; Frank Severance, ed., "The Case of Alexander Smyth," *Publications of the Buffalo Historical Society*, 18 [1914]: 224–41).

¶ To William Eustis. Letter not found. *16 August 1810*. Acknowledged in Eustis to JM, 26 Aug. 1810. Inquires about the authorship of a disrespectful note and forwards a letter from George Colbert.

¶ To John Graham. Letter not found. *16 August 1810*. Acknowledged in Graham to JM, 20 Aug. 1810. Requests a paper from the Paris files of the Department of State.

To Albert Gallatin

DEAR SIR   MONTPELIER Aug. 17. 1810

I now forward the paper on the Batture promised in my last. It appears by Mr. Pinkney's last letter that Brown[1] the fugitive was in London & had engaged his attention. As no proceeding, answerg our purpose, can be had agst. him, other than a suit for recovering the debt, will it not be proper to forward to Mr. P. whatever documents may sustain the action, particularly his official Bond; or an authenticated copy of it, if that be deemed adequate? Accept my esteem & best wishes

JAMES MADISON

RC (NHi: Gallatin Papers).

1. At the conclusion of his 13 June letter to Robert Smith (a copy of which was forwarded to JM by John Graham on 8 Aug.), Pinkney had mentioned that the defaulting New Orleans collector, William Brown, was in London and that he was endeavoring to have him arrested (DLC: Rives Collection, Madison Papers).

From Albert Gallatin

DEAR SIR   NEW YORK August 17. 1810

So far as can be judged from Grymes correspondence and official acts, he has done only what was necessary to save for the United States something from Brown's property. The Jones's Clar⟨k's⟩[1] and all the bar have as usual been as hostile as possible. It must be added that an intercepted letter from Brown to Jones, whom he thought still alive, informed him that he had at ⟨se⟩a destroyed his (Jones's) notes: so that we have reason to believe that, th⟨o⟩se notes having been given in payment for the plantation, it never was in fact paid for by Jones, & that the widow has recovered more than she was entitled to. I have however sent to the Comptroller the papers received through you, with a request that he would critically revise the whole transaction, & correct whatever might not appear perfectly equitable and necessary.

Mr Pease having resigned the office of *Surveyor of the public lands South of the State of Tenessee*, Mr Thomas Freeman[2] of the district of Columbia seems to have the fairest pretensions from the length & fidelity of his services, having been employed successively, under Mr Ellicot in laying out the city of Washington and running the Spanish boundary, & afterwards in Surveying most of the Indian boundaries, in an exploring expedition up the Red river, and lately in surveying Madison County on the Tenessee. He went last spring to Natchez on hearing of Mr Pease's resignation, and under an expectation which I did not discourage that he would be appointed Successor. As early appointment as practicable is desirable, as the business will in the mean while suffer some delay.

I also submit a recommendn. for the command of the New Orleans revenue cutter.

Excuse the bad paper which I am obliged to use. With attachment & respect Your obedt. Servt.

ALBERT GALLATIN

RC (DLC). Enclosure not found.

1. Gallatin referred to a New Orleans group in opposition to the administration of territorial governor William C. C. Claiborne, often known as "Clark, Livingston, & Com-

pany," which centered around Evan Jones and Daniel Clark (Hatfield, *William Claiborne*, pp. 157–59).

2. JM gave Thomas Freeman a provisional appointment and on 7 Jan. 1811 formally nominated him to be surveyor of lands south of Tennessee (JM to Gallatin, 22 Aug. 1810; *Senate Exec. Proceedings*, 2:159).

From Samuel Smith

SIR,   BALTIMORE 17 Augt. 1810
I do myself the honor to Enclose, an Extract of a letter just recieved from the Havannah.[1] I presume the Person is the same who dined with you last Winter and was introduced by Dr. Thornton to many Gentlemen. I have the honor [to] be sir, Your friend & Servt.

S. SMITH

RC and enclosure (DLC). Postmarked Baltimore, 16 Aug. Enclosure 1 p., in an unidentified hand (see n. 1).

1. Smith enclosed an extract from a 31 July 1810 letter by Vincent Gray, an American merchant who occasionally performed consular duties in Havana, reporting the execution of a Mexican, Manuel Rodríguez Alemán y Paña (or Peña), as a Bonapartist emissary. The credentials he bore from Joseph Bonaparte, Gray wrote, were "burnt under him, as he was suspended on the Gallows." Alemán had evidently confessed the names of many Bonapartist emissaries and agents in both North and South America, and Gray promised to forward a list of their names to the secretary of state. Although Gray regretted the death of "a young man of the first Talents & Respectability," he hoped that it would also "be the Cause of preventing that valuable Country Mexico, from being deluged in Blood." On the significance of Alemán's mission as an expression of Napoleon's policy toward Spanish America, see Robertson, *France and Latin-American Independence*, pp. 72–78, and Rydjord, *Foreign Interest in the Independence of New Spain*, pp. 304–5.

§ Bill of Exchange from James Leander Cathcart. *17 August 1810, Madeira.* The amount of £249 sterling ($1,106.67) is to be paid to James Latimer of Philadelphia.

RC (DLC). 1 p. Endorsed on verso by JM, "October 8. 1810 / Accepted."

From David Bailie Warden

SIR,   PARIS, 18 august, 1810.
General armstrong having informed me verbally of the appointment of Mr. Russell as *Charge d'affaire*, and having, at the same time intimated, that he is sooner, or later, to replace me as Consul, I feel myself obliged

to address you again on this subject, still cherishing the hope that you will be pleased to continue me in my present, or in some other Official situation at Paris. I am conscious of having performed my duties as public agent, and if any charge of improper conduct has been made against me, I shall be able to prove that it was prompted by falsehood and intrigue: for I have felt a species of enthusiasm, under the guidance of justice and probity, in being as useful as possible to every american who has asked my aid, or mediation; and this feeling has been increased by the consideration that I am but a Citizen, and not a native of the United States.

General Armstrong having several [times][1] informed me, that he had written to you in my favor, and described me as worthy of this trust, I flattered myself that I would be allowed to remain in my present Situation. In the defence of Prize-Causes, I have been, during two years, as I am at present, actively and zealously employed, and I have reason to believe, that the Americans generally who have known me at Paris, are pleased with my official, as well as private conduct. My views have not been directed to pecuniary purposes. Contrary to commercial usage, I have in no case asked, nor received a Commission, for any Prize-Cause committed to my care, or management; and I have advanced Monies for the prosecution of Claims, which, as a public Agent, I could not see adjudged without a defense. My numerous Memoirs, many of which are printed, afford a proof of this. The warmest wish of my heart is to have time and opportunity to give proofs of my attachment to the United States, and zeal for her Interests. With this view, I have written and published many memoirs since my arrival at Paris; and I have taken notes for communications relating to american Prize-Causes, and commercial subjects in relation to the united States, which, I hope, will be acceptable to you, and useful to the American Merchant. As a specimen of industry, and proof of my acquaintance with that species of information necessary to a person charged with the defence of Prize Causes, I have the honor to present you copies of my memoirs in the case of the *Ocean*, the *Whampoa*, *Governor Gore*, *Roboreus*[,] *James Cook*, *Perseverance* &c.[2] I am, Sir, with great respect—Your Most obedt and very humble Servt

DAVID BAILIE WARDEN

RC and triplicate (DLC); letterbook copy (MdHi: Warden Papers). RC docketed by JM. Minor variations between the copies have not been noted.

1. Warden omitted this word in the RC.
2. Warden evidently enclosed at least two publications. A translation from the French of his "Case of the *Ocean*" was printed in the *National Intelligencer* on 22 Nov. 1810, while five days earlier the same paper had published his *List of All the American Prize Cases Now Pending. before the Imperial Prize Court, at Paris*. That list included all the vessels named by Warden in his letter to JM at this date. Warden may also have included his *Mémoire pour les Capitaine et*

Propriétaires du bâtiment americain La Persévérance (Paris, n.d.). JM's copies of the last two works are in the Madison Collection, Rare Book Division, Library of Congress.

From Thomas Cooper

SIR   NORTHUMBERLAND PENNSYLVANIA August 19th. 1810

The liberty I am now about to take, I take on reflection; persuaded that if I am mistaken in my notions of propriety, you will attribute the present request to a good motive.

Since my arrival in this Country in 1793 the whole Science of Mineralogy in Europe has been new modelled. When my friend Mr Kirwan first published his elements of Mineralogy[1] in 1784, it was *the stock book*: it is now obsolete. The Germans and French have outstripp'd even the English, in this branch of Chemistry, and Mineralogy rests for the present on Werner and the Abbè Hauy.

In Philadelphia (elsewhere in the United States I cannot answer) about twenty well educated, well informed men, with all the necessary ardour, are pursuing the Study scientifically and practically, in a way that must ultimately tell very much to the advantage of the Country. The mineral riches of Pennsylvania in the course of a very few years will be explored & brought into action. I have felt with no common pleasure that it has taken me lately much labour to get up to the Knowledge of the day. But we all labour under great want of european information. Nothing of Werner's is translated into english but his External Characters of Fossils:[2] and the great work of the Abbe Hauy[3] to which every Mineralogist in Europe is consulting with anxious attention, is unknown to us except by Character. I have called it a great work not from its bulk for it is I believe confined to 2 or 3 8vo volumes, but for the new views it contains, and the condensed information of the modern day to be found in it, so far as I can collect from english Information. In illustration of this work, the Abbè has procured sets of Chrystals to be modelled and executed cheaply in Seve porcelain. But this dreadful war, cuts off all our European Sources of Knowledge, and we despair of getting classic books on the Subject from the Continent here. I think I could find time to translate it, *if I had a copy*.

I undertook a short time ago to compose and compile, a volume on the manufacturing processes dependant on Chemistry. I procured a friend to write to Genl Armstrong for a Copy of Loysel Sur l'Art de la Verrerie[4] some months ago but without effect. Latterly I found a Copy in Philada. at M. Godon's[5] the Mineralogical lecturer there; he lent it me; I translated it; meaning to incorporate all the facts in my proposed compilation. Since that, I find there is a later edition & still later works on the Subject. This is provoking. Formerly I knew any recent publication of the french press, now, I am in utter darkness.

Can you assist (not me, but) us, in this respect, by requesting Mr Armstrong or Mr Waddell to procure and send over two Copies of the late Mineralogical Work of the Abbè Hauy, together with half a dozen or a dozen sets of his porcelain illustrations of Chrystallography?

Also any other *late* publication of repute on the Subject (i e within five years) whether translated from the German or composed in France.

Also the last editions of Loysel sur l'Art de la Verrerie, together with any other late publication of repute on the Glass manufacture.

Also the publications of Brogniart (Director of the Seve establishment) on the Subject of fabricating & enamilling porcelain.[6]

Also the *last* edition of the elder & younger Berthollet sur la Teinture.[7]

I will transmit 100 Dollars cheerfully to your order for the purpose, or my friend Mr John Vaughan, Merchant of Philadelphia, and Secretary of our Philosophical society, will either do this for me, or pay instantly the amount on receiving advice of the books being forwarded.

I think I feel an honest and fair deference for your situation, your Character, and the claims upon your time; and yet I cannot persuade myself that you will be offended at my present request,[8] which I hope will not be deemed inconsistent with the sincere respect with which I remain Sir Your obliged friend and Servant

THOMAS COOPER

RC (DLC).

1. Richard Kirwan, *Elements of Mineralogy* (London, 1784).

2. Abraham Gottlob Werner, *Von den äusserlichen Kennzeichen der Fossilien* (Leipzig, 1774), translated by Thomas Weaver as *A Treatise on the External Characters of Fossils* (Dublin and London, 1805).

3. René Just Haüy was the author of several treatises, the best known of which was *Traité de minéralogie* (5 vols.; Paris, 1801).

4. Pierre Loysel, *Essai sur l'art de la verrerie* (Paris, 1800).

5. Silvain Godon was a French scientist who studied mineralogy in the eastern U.S. in the first decade of the nineteenth century. In 1808–9 he had published two sets of mineralogical "observations" relating to Boston and Maryland, and the following year he settled in Philadelphia where he gave a series of lectures on mineralogy to ten or twenty pupils (Charles Willson Peale to Stephen Elliott, 14 Feb. 1809, Lillian B. Miller et al., eds., *Selected Papers of Charles Willson Peale and His Family* [New Haven, 1988], 2:1182 n. 2).

6. Alexandre Brongniart, the son of a distinguished architect, was the author of several treatises on chemistry, including *Traité élémentaire de minéralogie, avec des applications aux arts* . . . (Paris, 1807), and he also held the position of director of the porcelain manufactory at Sèvres.

7. Claude Louis Berthollet, together with his son Amédée B. Berthollet, was the author

of several works on chemistry, bleaching, and dyeing, including *Eléments de l'art de la teinture* (Paris, 1791).

8. JM forwarded a copy of Cooper's letter to David Bailie Warden on 1 Sept. 1810.

From William Eustis

SIR,   BOSTON August 19. 1810.

I have had the honor to receive your Letter of the 10th instant. A copy of Colo. Spark's Letter has been forwarded to Genl. Hampton with general instructions to reinforce the post of Fort Stoddert (or Fort St. Stephens to which the garrison of F. Stoddert removes during the hot months) from such points as his judgment shall determine. The assemblage of the troops near the muscle shoals, for another purpose, will I think defeat the contemplated expedition: and it has been intimated to Genl. Hampton that they may be detached to the Tombigbee if circumstances urge it, leaving the object of their expedition to be effected thereafter by another detachment to be marched from the cantonment. I cannot bring myself to believe that the attempt will be made. Hampton & Cushing[1] are however informed & instructed: with one and only one condition, & that is not to move into a sickly station untill Autumn without the most unavoidable necessity. With perfect respect & regard I have the honor to be

W. EUSTIS

RC (DLC).

1. Thomas Cushing, formerly adjutant and inspector general of the army, 1802–7, was lieutenant colonel of the Second Infantry based at Washington Cantonment, Mississippi Territory (Heitman, *Historical Register*, 1:348).

From John Graham

DEAR SIR   DEPARTMENT OF STATE 20th Augt 1810

I had the Honor yesterday to receive your Letter of the 16th. and have this Morning been unsuccessfully employed in looking over Mr Bowdoin's, Genl Armstrong's, and Mr Skipwiths file, for the Paper a Copy of which you want.[1] I shall renew the search tomorrow. We have no Parisian file in the office and as neither Mr Brent[2] nor myself have any recollection of this Paper I have thought that you may possibly have seen it in the possession of the late President.

It does not appear from our Records that Mr Barnet has been particularly instructed to deliver the Papers he received from Mr Skipwith. From a Memo you once made[3] it appeared to be your wish that such instructions should be sent to him; but in the same Memo you referred the Secy of State to Mr Skipwith who was then expected here, application was accordingly made to him when he arrived, and he stated that he had directed Mr Barnet to send the *Books* which had been the object of contest to the Department of State.[4] Hence, I presume, no particular Instructions were sent from this office, as to *them*.

I inclose a Copy of a Letter just received from Genl Armstrong.[5] The original goes today to Mr Smith who is now I presume in Baltimore. There is a Letter from Mr Warden of the 12th June but it contains nothing new. With Sentiments of the Highest Respect I have the Honor to be, Sir Your Most Obt Sert

JOHN GRAHAM

RC and enclosure (DLC). Both docketed by JM. Enclosure (2 pp.) in a clerk's hand; marked "(Copy)" (see n. 5).

1. JM recently had received John Armstrong's letter of 6 May 1810 and evidently was seeking the document Armstrong referred to in the letter.

2. Daniel Brent was a clerk in the Department of State (*PJM-SS*, 1:350 n. 2).

3. Document not found.

4. The books referred to were the same consular registers Armstrong had been seeking from Isaac Cox Barnet after Skipwith had left France in September 1808. The minister believed that Skipwith had given them to Barnet, and in May 1809 he suspended Barnet from his consular duties after the latter refused to turn them over. Barnet protested that the suspension was illegal and further argued that Armstrong had no right to the registers as they were private rather than public documents. Barnet, moreover, told the secretary of state in June 1809 that he did not have the registers in his possession, though he did admit that he had "*true copies*" of some of Skipwith's letters and papers in his own personal records. If Skipwith did not bring the registers with him when he left France, Barnet must have forwarded them to the U.S. sometime after Skipwith's departure. The volumes were delivered to the State Department by Skipwith's wife, Evalina van der Clooster Skipwith, on 23 Aug. 1810, and JM subsequently directed that they should be returned to Paris (Barnet to Robert Smith, 24 June 1809 [DNA: RG 59, CD, Paris]; John Graham to JM, 24 Aug. 1810; Graham to Jonathan Russell, 5 Oct. 1810 [DNA: RG 59, IM]).

5. Graham enclosed a copy of Armstrong's dispatch of 24 May 1810 announcing the official publication of the Rambouillet decree and discussing seizures of American property in Holland and France by the French Council of Prizes. The original dispatch, marked "copy taken for the President" by Graham, covered an extract (8 pp.) from the register of the Imperial Customs Office in Cherbourg (DNA: RG 59, DD, France).

From Thomas Jefferson

DEAR SIR   MONTICELLO. Aug. 20. 10.

Mr. Wirt having suggested to me that he thought the explanations in my case of the Batture, respecting the Nile & Missisipi not sufficiently clear, and that the authority cited respecting the Nile might be urged against me, I have endeavored, by a Note,[1] to state their analogies more clearly. Being a shred of the argument I put into your hands I inclose it to you with a request, after perusal, to put it under cover to mr. Gallatin, the argument itself having, I presume, gone on. Mr. Irving will be with you tomorrow. I shall set out for Bedford the next day, to be absent probably about three weeks. You shall know when I return in the hope of having the pleasure of seeing you here. Affectionate salutations to mrs. Madison & yourself.

TH: JEFFERSON

RC (DLC); FC (DLC: Jefferson Papers).

1. Jefferson evidently enclosed four pages of notes (FC, DLC: Jefferson Papers; dated 1807 in the *Index to the Thomas Jefferson Papers*) on the similarities between the Mississippi and Nile rivers, which he later included in the 1812 publication of his pamphlet on the batture (see Lipscomb and Bergh, *Writings of Jefferson*, 18:81–83 n. 2, 84 n. 1).

From Albert Gallatin

DEAR SIR   NEW YORK 21st August 1810

I enclose a letter from Mr Duval on the subject of Brown's estate.[1] I cannot recollect whether his account &a. were sent to Mr. Pinkney, but will write to day to have it done. The report by the last arrival from England is that he has recovered a part of the money from Brown.

I received last night the Batture paper which I will return whenever I shall have read it. Is it intended as a brief for the lawyers or for publication?

It is extremely difficult to make at this moment any general alteration in the deposits of public money; for as we grow poorer, we are on the contrary obliged to concentrate what is left by drawing from the other Banks such as the Manhattan &a. And by the end of the year we will probably be reduced so low as to make the deposits of no importance to any Bank. I believe also that the lessening of discounts by the Bank of the U. States has not produced the effect you apprehend; as it is but trifling and is far exceeded by the new discounts made by the new Banks created since spring in New York, Baltimore &a.[2] But there is a general diminution of specie; and there may be partial inconveniencies to State Banks resulting from that source. If instead of a general observation, the place or places whence the complaint has arisen are made known to me, a temporary remedy may perhaps be administered. I have already been applied to by the Bank of Columbia,[3] where the evil arose from Davidson's[4] harshness and littleness, and have acted upon it. Mrs. G. presents her affectionate regards to Mrs. Madison. Respectfully & affectionately Your's

ALBERT GALLATIN

RC and enclosure (DLC). RC docketed by JM. Enclosure (see n. 1) is Gabriel Duvall to Gallatin, 15 Aug. 1810 (3 pp.), with a copy of Duvall to Philip Grymes, 14 July 1810 (2 pp.).

1. Duvall had instructed Grymes on 14 July to continue the proceedings against William Brown until the U.S. government could close the case against him. He was of the opinion that Grymes's actions against Brown could not be set aside—as Elizabeth House Trist and Mary Jones had wished—unless it was done by act of Congress (see Elizabeth House Trist to JM, 18 July 1810, Editorial Note).

2. Ten new commercial banks were chartered in 1810, one of them in New York and five in Maryland (J. Van Fenstermaker, *The Development of American Commercial Banking, 1782–1837* [Kent, Ohio, 1965], pp. 13, 136, 159).

3. The Bank of Columbia, located in Georgetown, had been chartered by the state of Maryland in 1793 and was used by the Treasury Department as both a depository and a medium for public payments (*ASP, Finance*, 2:516, 520–22).

4. James Davidson was cashier of the Washington branch of the Bank of the United States (Bryan, *History of the National Capital*, 1:432).

To Albert Gallatin

DEAR SIR   MONTPELIER Aug. 22. 1810

I have recd. your several letters of the 15, 16, & 17th. The appointment for the Revenue Cutter at N. O. is *approved* & so noted to the T. Dept. and a Commission for Freeman ordered to be made out without delay.

Poinsett promises, by his qualifications, every thing to be expected from a substitute for Gelston. I have sent the returned papers to the Dept. of State, that new ones may be forwarded to you. It was always my idea that the Country beyond the Andes should be joined to B. A: but it seems I failed to impart it. The document will now specify, both a port in Peru & Chili, as within the range of Mr. P. if visitable by him.[1] Should these come to you blank, you will fill them with Ports best combining commercial importance & proximity to the Seats of Govt. Your hints as to Sumpter & the Span⟨ish &⟩ Brasilian relations to S. Ama. have been attended to. Rio Jano. is in every view an eligible route for Mr. P. An advance of

$1500 is stated to the Dept. of State.* It may be well for you to suggest the best mode of making it from the Treasy. Secresy as far as possible is desireable. It will not do to apply for a Spanish passport, altho I fear the want of it may be a serious difficulty; unless Sumpter's letters of introduction, should answer an equivalent purpose. The Spanish Consul at Balt: on discovering that Lowry was going to Caraccas, entered a formal complaint on the ground that it was contrary to the Colonial system.[2] And to ask a passport, as for a private person, to cover a political one would not, of course, be allowable; if in these suspicious times, it were not probably unattainable.

I inclose, at the request of Mr. Jefferson, a note to a paragraph in his case of the Batture contained in my last; intended to make his argument more clear & apposite.[3]

The last dispatch from Armstrong is no later than May 24. It relates merely to the proceedings under the Rambouillet decree. Mr. Graham, mentions a letter from Warden of June 10. as unimportant. I have a private letter from A. of May 24.,[4] which contains the passage following: "The Imp: Decree of Mar. 23. sufficiently indicates its own cause—tho' from the personal explanations given to me, it wd. appear to have been less the result of the law itself than of its non-execution, which was construed & with some plausibility into a partiality for English Commerce. 'My wishes & interests (said the Emperor the other day) both lead to a free & friendly connection with the U. S. but I can not see with indifference on the part of this power, measures which expressly favor the trade of my enemy. Such is their non-intercourse law, wch. by its own provisions, however faithfully executed, wd. not be equal in its operation, but which so far from being faithfully executed, has been violated with impunity from its date to the present day, much to my prejudice, & greatly to the advantage of the Brit: commerce'—The error in this reasoning is in not going farther back for premises." He glances at some faint indications of jealousy between F. & Russia, and at an anticipated marriage between a Prince of Prussia, & a daughter of Lucien Bonaparte. In a preceding letter[5] he alludes to a like one between Ferdinand & the 2d. daughter of the Emp: Francis, with a view to its bearings on S. America, & warns us, that a Champ de Battaille, may then be found with the U. S.

I have a long letter from Judge Toulmin,[6] which authenticates the reality of a combination, headed by Caller & Kenady, for the purpose of occupying Mobille &c. The object is not denied, and impunity avowedly inferred, from the impossibility of finding a jury to convict. The party

---

* I can say nothing as to P's military views, more than that no particular decision is contemplated; Should his services be needed hereafter, the use now made of him, sufficiently denotes a disposition not to throw him out of sight.

engaged amounts, as given out, to abount [*sic*] 400. The conquest is to be offered to the U. S. Kenady is said to be on a visit to Georgia to consult the Senators of that State, whose advice is to be followed. It is not improbable therefore, as is intimated, that this movement is intended to cover a retreat from the project. The Commandant at Fort Stoddart has written for reinforcements; which are eligible, if practicable, in a general reference to that Quarter.

You will have seen the projected Constn: for W. Florida[7] & noted among other particulars, the power to the Temporary Govt. to *grant lands*. Should it become necessary, for the Ex. to exercise authority within those limits, before the meeting of Congs. I foresee many legal difficulties. What is to be done on the subject of the Custom House, in such an event? Be assured of my esteem & best wishes

JAMES MADISON

RC (NHi: Gallatin Papers).

1. On 27 Aug. 1810 Poinsett was instructed to "proceed without delay to Buenos Aires, and thence if convenient to Lima—in Peru or St. Iago—in Chile, or both" in order to "diffuse the impression that the United States cherish the sincerest good will toward the people of Spanish America." JM officially nominated Poinsett as consul general to all three Spanish provinces a year later, on 13 Nov. 1811 (Smith to Poinsett, 27 Aug. 1810 [PHi: Joel Roberts Poinsett Papers]; *Senate Exec. Proceedings*, 2:188).

2. See JM to Robert Smith, 26 July 1810, n. 3.

3. See Jefferson to JM, 20 Aug. 1810, and n. 1.

4. See Armstrong to JM, 25 May 1810.

5. JM referred to Armstrong's 5 May 1810 dispatch to Robert Smith, which had been forwarded to him on 13 Aug. by John Graham.

6. Harry Toulmin to JM, 28 July 1810.

7. On 17 Aug. 1810 the *National Intelligencer* published a constitution for West Florida, copies of which had been circulating in the region around Baton Rouge. This constitution, better described as a provisional code, had been drawn up by Edward Randolph and some other planters from the Feliciana district of West Florida before the meeting of the West Florida convention at St. Johns Plains on 25 July. It should not be confused with the constitution adopted by the province in October 1810 after the convention had declared its independence from Spain. The document, consisting of thirteen articles, established a governor, a secretary, and a council of state who were to carry on the government and to respect all existing laws and contracts until a convention could be convened to frame a new constitution (Arthur, *Story of the West Florida Rebellion*, pp. 45–47).

From John Graham

DEAR SIR   DEPT OF STATE 22d August 1810.

I had the Honor to write to you the day before yesterday to say that I had not been able to find the Paper transmitted from Paris previous to the

Departure of Mr Bowdoin from that Place, a Copy of which you directed to be sent to you. I have continued the search thro: the files of Mr Bowdoin, Genl Armstrong, Mr Skipwith & Mr Barnet; but have not been so fortunate as to find any traces of this Paper. In a Note[1] which Genl. A. adds in his own handwriting, to a Copy of a Projet offered by him in the year 1806 to the Spanish agent at Paris—it is stated that Mr Chew of New Orleans had told him (the General) that he, Clarke & Skipwith, had in Company, purchased from Morales, all the Country in West Florida, worth having, between the Mississippi and the Pearl River.

Yesterday just as we were leaving the office, Dispatches were recieved from Mr Pinkney dated late in June. They were brought to New York by Mr Short who sailed from Liverpool early in July. They do not contain any thing of importance, except that Mr Pinkney was of opinion that the British Government would very soon send out as Minister to this Country, a Man of Rank—and that he had recieved from Brown who run off from Orleans—Bills of Exchange to the amount of about £8000 Stg. and expected to get more. As it was not your Post day I sent the Despatches on to Mr Smith at Baltimore; as soon as they are returned I will forward them to you. I inclose two of the latest English Papers and one from Kentucky, shewing the result, as far as it was known, of the Congressional Elections in that State.[2] With Sentiments of the most Respectful attachment, I am Dear Sir Your Most Hbl Sert

JOHN GRAHAM

RC (DLC).

1. See Armstrong to JM, 10 Oct. 1806, covering copies of a treaty and a convention Armstrong had proposed to the Spanish agent, Eugenio Izquierdo de Ribera, as part of the unsuccessful American efforts to acquire West Florida by negotiation (DNA: RG 59, DD, France).

2. Graham may have enclosed a newspaper from Frankfort, Kentucky, with the results of the elections for the Twelfth Congress as far as they were known by 11 Aug. These revealed that William T. Barry, Henry Clay, Joseph Desha, Richard M. Johnson, and Samuel McKee had been elected, with the results still to come from two districts (*National Intelligencer*, 24 Aug. 1810).

§ From John B. Chandler. *22 August 1810, Tuckabatchee, Mississippi Territory*. Offers his services should JM wish to communicate with the Indians in the region.

RC (DNA: RG 107, LRRS, C-213:5). 1 p. Docketed by a War Department clerk as received 1 Oct. 1810.

From John Smith

Sir,   War Department, Augt. 23d. 1810.

I have the honor of enclosing a Copy of Governor Harrison's Letter addressed to the Department under date of the 1st. instant. A Copy has, also, been forwarded to the Secretary of War. I am, with perfect Respect, &c. &c. &c.

(signed.)   Jno. Smith, C. C.

[Enclosure]

§ William Henry Harrison to William Eustis. *1 August 1810, Vincennes*. Reports that Barron the interpreter has not yet returned from his mission to the Prophet and that he has received "very unpleasant" news of the Indians' having driven off settlers in the Jeffersonville district and destroyed their property. Has sent out a militia officer and an interpreter to confirm this news but suspects that the hostile Indians are "Kickapoos, Putawatamies and Shawanoes" sent by the Prophet "for the purpose of involving the Delawares in the quarrel with us." Fears that the settlers will be "so enraged . . . as to fall upon any Indians they may meet with." The alarm has extended as far south as Blue River, and people are "flying towards the Ohio from every direction," while near Vincennes several horses have been stolen and "the Indians manifest much more insolence than usual." Believes that "a display of force in this quarter, is at this time, more necessary than any where else, and may perhaps prevent a War."

Letterbook copy (DNA: RG 107, LSP); enclosure (DLC). Enclosure (3 pp.) in a clerk's hand; marked "(Copy)"; docketed by JM; printed in Esarey, *Messages and Letters of William Henry Harrison*, Indiana Historical Collections, 1:453–54.

To John Graham

Dear Sir   Augst. 24. 1810

Your favor of the 20th. has come duly to hand. I well recollect the rect. of the paper you were searching for, and can not but think that it is somewhere in the office. It would seem, that Barnet either had not recd. the order of Skipwith to deliver the Books, or had disobeyed it. The retention of them is so palpably improper, that it justifies the suspicions entertained of some improper view in it. Barnet, if I mistake not has been displaced. Would it be amiss for a positive instruction to be even now given on the subject, to be put into the hands of the Minister at Paris?

I inclose an interesting letter from Toulmin.[1] It will suggest to the Dept. an examination of the law forbidding such enterprizes; with a view to see how far authorities or instructions may be requisite for the use of force in suppressing them. Be so good as to return the letter.

Will you be so good also as to have the inclosed information from Docr. Logan, put under cover to Mr. Goldsborough member of Congs: whose address is as much unknown to me as to the writer. I ask the favor of your attention also to the letter for Genl. Fayette. It is from his agent Duplantier, & on a subject particularly interesting to him. Accept my sincere esteem & friendly wishes

JAMES MADISON

RC (DNA: RG 59, ML). Docketed by Graham.

1. Harry Toulmin to JM, 28 July 1810.

From John Graham

DEAR SIR   DEPT OF STATE 24th Augt 1810

The inclosed are Copies of Letters from Governor Holmes[1] and Mr Robinson[2] relative to the affairs of West Florida. The originals were sent to the Secretary of State.

We yesterday recieved from Mrs Skipwith two large Books entitled "Official Register" commencing in 1797 and ending in 1808. These are I presume the Books about which Genl Armstrong and Mr Barnet have written to this Dept. With the greatest Respect I have the Honor to be, Sir, Your Most Obt Sert

JOHN GRAHAM

RC (DLC). Enclosures (see nn. 1 and 2) were forwarded by JM in his letter to William Eustis, 30 Aug. 1810.

1. David Holmes to Robert Smith, 31 July 1810 (printed with its enclosure in Carter, *Territorial Papers, Orleans*, 9:889–91). Holmes reported on the deliberations of a convention of American settlers in West Florida at St. Johns Plains near Baton Rouge on 25 July 1810. He included a list of the members of the convention and an extract from a letter dated 26 July, which he had just received, declaring that although a majority of the convention members wished for West Florida to be incorporated into the U.S., they hesitated to apply for American protection out of fear that the Spanish authorities in Cuba would crush their revolt before the U.S. could respond. Holmes also mentioned rumors of plans by American settlers to attack Mobile but believed these had been abandoned.

2. Thomas B. Robertson to Robert Smith, 28 July 1810. Robertson discussed the political allegiances of the English and American settlers in West Florida. The former, Robertson believed, masked "their real wish for an union with England" behind "an affected zeal in favor of Ferdinand the 7th," while the latter aimed at "absolute independence . . . from every kind of European subordination." Robertson also included a letter addressed to him by

William Wykoff, Jr., dated 24 July 1810, reporting on the elections for delegates to the convention due to meet on 25 July and enclosing for Robertson a copy of the address of the electors of Baton Rouge to their delegates.

§ From John Armstrong. *24 August 1810, Paris.* Introduces "Mr. Jervas"[1] as "a man really attached to his country & to the administration which governs it."

RC (courtesy of an anonymous collector). 1 p. Docketed by JM.

1. Probably Leonard Jarvis, who arrived in Washington on 1 Nov. 1810 carrying dispatches from Armstrong (JM to Armstrong, 29 Oct. 1810, n. 1).

From Abner Cushing and Others

QUEBEC August 25th. 1810.

We, the undersigned Citizens of the United States, residing within the Province of Lower Canada, and in the State of New York; beg leave to represent to your Excellency, that the commercial intercourse between the United States and Lower Canada is rapidly increasing; and more security would be given to that intercourse, by the appointment of an Agent from the United States, for the protection of the rights and priviledges of our fellow Citizens trading to that Province. They trust that an institution of that kind, will be found both necessary and useful; as tending to promote Commerce, and prevent its diminution. They beg leave to state, that the appointment of an Agent, involves objects of a more important nature, than the mere protection of trade. That portion of our fellow Citizens, who navigate rafts down the river St Laurence; are frequently exposed to the inconvenience of Press Gangs, who, (though ultimately released when pressed into Service) for want of prompt and immediate interference, have been compelled to undergo many embarrassments and vexatious privations. The Security of our fellow Citizens whose contiguity of situation renders them dependant on the Province for the Sale of their Produce, forms a primary object in this request; it likewise involves principles of minor consideration, but of relative importance. Viewing it in this light, and considering that the appointment of an Agent; authorized to render every Service to his fellow Citizens, will be to promote their interest and prosperity, we feel confidant that your Excellency will afford every consideration to the Subject, which its importance demands.

We further beg leave to recommend for the above appointment, our fellow Citizen M M Noah[1]—the Bearer of this communication, who from his frequent intercourse with the Province, his Knowledge of the country,

its Commerce and resources, is considered competent to discharge the
duties attached to the station.

ABNER CUSHING—Quebec
[and twenty-six others]

RC (DNA: RG 59, LAR, 1809–17, filed under "Noah").

1. Mordecai M. Noah (1785–1851) was a prominent member of the Jewish communities
of Charleston and Philadelphia. After early employment as a Treasury Department messenger and in journalism, he sought a career in government service, only to be discouraged by
Secretary of State Robert Smith in his hopes for a position as commercial agent in Canada.
Later JM appointed him to consular positions in Riga (in 1811) and in Tunis (in 1813), and
Noah served in the latter until 1816, when he returned to the U.S. Noah then resumed his
career as a journalist and author, editing newspapers, including the N.Y. *National Advocate*,
and writing several plays. He also purchased Grand Island in the Niagara River in 1825 as
an unsuccessful first step in founding a Jewish homeland (Noah to Robert Smith, 7 Jan. 1811
[ibid.]; *Senate Exec. Proceedings*, 2:188, 190, 347; Jonathan D. Sarna, *Jacksonian Jew: The Two
Worlds of Mordecai Noah* [New York, 1981], pp. 8–10 and passim).

From Lafayette

MY DEAR SIR   PARIS 25h August 1810
    I Leave it With General Armstrong to inform You of the Happy Repeal
of the two Milan and Berlin decrees—a determination Which Gives me
Great pleasure and Great Hopes. I don't See How the British Cabinet
Can Avoid imitating the Example. That it Has Been Given By france
Greatly Adds to My Satisfaction.
    While I was Lamenting to find Nothing for me in the Government dis-
patches Brought By the *Flash* and the *Wasp*, those of the Later Vessel
Having Been Returned in England, I Have Received Your kind Letters of
the 18h and 19h May By Mr. david parish. He Will Be Here in the Course
of September and Bring Himself the patents Entrusted to His Care. I
most Heartily thank You for Your incessant and friendly Attention to My
Concerns.
    My Last Long Letters Sent Triplicate Will Have But too Much Con-
vinced You of the Necessity and Urgency there is for the Arrival of all the
documents particularly those Of the Lot Near the City Upon Which My
principal Hopes are founded—indeed the More We go on the Greater
difficulty is Announced to find European Monney Upon the Mortgage of
American Lands. M. La Bouchere Has, Since My Last, declared it Very
Explicitly. Yet My friend Mr. parker and Myself do still Hope Some thing
May Be done With Mr. parish.

Your letters that are not Under official Cover, or Brought By official Messengers Run Great Risk. I shall to day, My dear friend, write only a few lines to Acknowledge Your two favors, and the Arrival in Europe of the patents Entrusted to Mr. parish. I am Sure You Will Have Had the Goodness to Clear all difficulties Relative to the Remaining Locations, part of which May Be owing to the private Motives of other proprietors. I don't Write this time to Mr. duplantier as You Have Had lately long triplicates for Him.

My Heart is Most Affectionately Sensible of Your kindness to me. Receive the Expressions of the Attachment and Respect Which devote to You Your Grateful friend

LAFAYETTE

RC (PHi). Docketed by JM.

From John R. Bedford

SIR,   NASHVILLE August 26th 1810

Annexed hereto is the copy of another letter from Mr. William Barrow of West Florida. You will remark the frank expression of concern and solicitude and unpleasant suspense about their political situation. And I beleive he expresses genuinely the feelings, in common with his own, of all the most reputable people in West Florida. I inclosed you a copy of his first letter, dated 4th. June, which I presume you received. But I fear my communications upon this Subject may be deemed intrusive & too officious. The force of this impression was calculated at first, as well as now, to forbid my troubling you with any, communications, which may interrupt the more useful employment of Your time and attention. And this consideration will hereafter enforce my silence. But the possibility of doing good, and a sincere disposition to that, may perhaps have had an indiscreet influence in prompting me to intrude unnecessarily and uselessly. Also, I regret to have molested your attention, while in a more valuable & useful employment.

I have written Mr. Barrow very much at length—and attempted to excite a persuasion, which I sincerely believe, that they were absolved from all allegiance to the mother country—and of course have a natural right to assume the rights of self government—that their interests & the U. States were reciprocal & to a certain extent, inseperably linked—and therefore, Florida ought & must in time become a part of the U. States—and that the better to secure & facilitate this event, it might perhaps be better to constitute a seperate & independent government in West Florida & East, if she would co-operate, which I conceive might be maintained, untill it might be deemed proper & consistent with the policy of the American Government to protect or incorporate them with the U. States. Not knowing that the Executive had a right, or would assume the responsibility of giving any assurances, I suggested the propriety of continueing their present quiet Situation untill the sitting of Congress. That then their situation would become an interesting subject of consideration, relative to which, measures of decision might be adopted and promptly acted upon. I assured him of my sincere belief in the friendly dispositions & earnest solicitude of the American Government & people, for the people of Florida. And that although we conceived ourselves to be the lawful owners thereof, nevertheless the peaceful & neutral disposition of our Government will likely forbid us attempting[1] to acquire it by other, than peaceful means, untill they become hopeless or rather obstructive. With due Respect and sincere regard for your Character I am your Obt. Sert.

J. R. Bedford

[Enclosure]

[William Barrow to Bedford]

My Friend,   Bayou Sara August 5th. 1810

I rec[e]ived your letter of the 3d July and have perused it with every attention & satisfaction. I have now to inform you, that since I wrote to you, we have found people disposed to involve us in a civil war by declaring Independence and calling the U. States to aid, without knowing whether they would or not. As we find the people so much divided, we have been at a loss what to do—what plan to adopt. We found it was necessary to do something to appease the minds of the people & strengthen the government for our own Security. We had a meeting in all the District of Baton Rouge, and chose four members out of the District of New Feliciana, five from Baton Rouge, three from St Helena and two from the District of Tanchipaho. Among the number of Delegates, they have been weak enough to choose me. We have met and great harmony appears to prevail yet and I hope, will continue. We all are at great loss what plan is best to adopt. We find the people somewhat divided. Some for the U. States, some for Britain & many for F 7th. So that for the present, I think we had better adopt the Spanish Laws, making such Amendments, as we need. Put men in office, on whom we can rely—and distribute equal justice to all. I assure you, the minds of the people in this province are at this moment much confused. We lack information, as to what in justice we can ask of the U. States. It would be a very pleasing thing to us to know what aid they can or will give us. The people of character & standing here would not wish to act, so as to cast a stigma on themselves Or risk their best rights & interest. There is a report that Soldiers from Pensacola are coming, to enforce the ancient laws & order of things. I hope this will not be attempted. It might be attended with a bad consequence. The Delegates have been regularly appointed by the people—and I think they would support them & not suffer them to be exposed or injured. I hope the present plan, will quiet the minds of the people, so as to enable us to get such information, that we may perceive the best mode to pursue hereafter. I hope the U. States will feel themselves bound in justice, to declare to us what we ought to do. They have held out to us, that they have a claim to us. Now is the time to make it known to us. I hope they feel themselves a free & independent nation and will act accord⟨ingly⟩. My Friend, I do not wish my letters to you to be exposed to public view. I write ⟨to⟩ you as a friend to give me every inform⟨ation⟩ in your power. Believe me yr sincere friend & Hbl Servt.

WM. BARROW

RC and enclosure (DLC). Postmarked Nashville, 31 Aug. Enclosure in Bedford's hand.

1. Here Bedford wrote "Please turn to the 3d page," and he completed the letter on the second page of the enclosure.

From William Eustis

SIR,   PORTSMOUTH N. H. Aug. 26. 1810.

I have the honor to acknowlege your favor of the 16h. instt. From my knowlege of the hand writing & character of Mr Prince,[1] Marshal, I know it to be impossible that the disrespectful note is his. To-morrow I shall be in Boston when the fact will be ascertained without communicating to him the particulars which lead to the enquiry. He is communicative, and no chances ought to be afforded of gratification to the author of the imposition. Colbert's Letter[2] will be communicated to General Mason for enquiry into the conduct of the factor under his direction. It is customary to require at least the knowlege, & generally the opinion of the Agent for the tribe, previous to approving a visit from the chiefs. Colbert has had it in contemplation to visit the President for some time past: and has been expected. The present application is intended to cover his expences: and unless otherwise instructed I shall refer to the Agent before leave is granted. This day will determine whether the next delegation to Congress from this state is to be federal or republican: if the latter, principle & not exertion will give the victory (which I think doubtful).[3] My reception by the Essex Men is very different from that of the last season. The Letter respecting Pinckneys private communication, which was published by the friend to whom it was addressed, constitutes the unpardonable sin.[4] Many to this day believe there is no such letter, and I regret exceedingly that it cannot be made public. At the approaching session it is most devoutly to be wished that some decided ground may be taken: for the indecision which now lays at the door of Congress will creep upwards. With the highest respect & esteem

W. EUSTIS.

RC (DLC).

1. James Prince had been marshal for the district of Massachusetts since 1807 (*Senate Exec. Proceedings*, 2:56–59, 191).

2. Chickasaw Nation to JM, 17 July 1810.

3. In the New Hampshire elections for the Twelfth Congress the Federalists won all five seats in the House of Representatives (*National Intelligencer*, 14 Sept. 1810).

4. Eustis was referring to Pinkney's 4 Jan. 1810 letter to Robert Smith (see JM to the House of Representatives, 27 Mar. 1810, and n. 2).

From George Luckey

SIR   HARFORD COUNTY MAD. August 26. 1810

It is the privelige & the duty of every citizen of the United States to communicate With the officers of Government both legislative & executive respecting the public Welfare, & more especially for those Who Are much in public themselves & have a hearty & tender concern for their country. The presidency especially is a high, peculiarly important & responsible office & needs all possible assistance from every quarter to help & encourage in times of need.

Our chief magistrate has an ardu[o]us & difficult station at the present time & it is extremely difficult to know in what manner to proceed for the best. The extraordinary avar[i]ce of many has driven them to a course which has brought us to shame, danger, & loss every Way. Perhaps the experiment made by these gentlemen Will cure their temerity & unite them With the real friends to their country. It Would seem like infatuation to attempt fighting all the World. I have thought that the plan[1] proposed to the public last Winter Was Wise & most eligible; that is As soon as possible to have formed an Armed neutrality by sea of all European powers &c &c for defence against the tyrants of the Ocean & disturbers of the peace of the World. Such league in part was formed in the Years '77 & '78 with great eclat of Congress—Gen. Washington & the American Army. There can be no objection Against this now more than Was then,

& it terminated Well & much in our favour & we have more need now than ever of this. Those Against Whom We so long fought & who are now as inimical as ever engross our trade by compulsion & in their own way & at their own rates. The Quantum of price we receive from them is not half of what would be given by the Europian nations. I hope You enjoy good health. You have the best Wishes of all real Americans nay of all the citizens of the United States except a few in comparison who are selfish, unprincipled & care for no country; Against Whom Divivine [*sic*] providence ever has militated & we trust heaven Will ever oppose—believe me to be with high esteem ever yours

GEORGE LUCKEY

RC (DLC). Postmarked Baltimore, 6 Sept.

1. Luckey was probably referring to the schemes of armed neutrality advocated by William Duane, both in his correspondence with JM and in the columns of the Philadelphia *Aurora General Advertiser* (see Duane to JM, 1 Dec. 1809; *Aurora General Advertiser*, 14 Dec. 1809).

§ From William Jarvis. *26 August 1810, Lisbon.* Acknowledges the receipt of JM's two letters of 17 June. Is convinced of the great value of merino sheep for farming and for domestic manufacturing and has purchased two hundred sheep for his own use. Has also taken the opportunity to purchase more than a thousand sheep with the idea of serving his country by shipping them to the U.S. for sale there. His fears about the speculative risks for his private affairs were relieved by JM's letter and by news from Alexandria and New York of the high prices paid for the sheep in his earlier shipment. Discusses the purchase and shipping of merinos by British agents from Spanish and Portuguese ports. Encloses a bill of lading for two merino ewes for JM. Laments the high price of ordinary wine; old wine is not to be had in Lisbon.

RC and enclosure (DLC: Rives Collection, Madison Papers). RC 10 pp. Enclosed bill of lading (1 p.) endorsed by Jarvis on verso: "For the fulfillment of this Bill of Lading, such person as the President shall entrust, is to select two ewes, from the whole of my shipment by the Citizen, which J. H. Hooe Esqr. will please to permit."

¶ From Valentin de Foronda. Letter not found. *26 August 1810.* Calendared as a two-page letter in the lists probably made by Peter Force (DLC, series 7, container 2). Foronda had been chargé d'affaires ad interim for Spain in Philadelphia until September 1809.

From John Graham

Dear Sir   Dept of State 27th Augt 1810

I received this Morning the Letter you did me the Honor to write to me on the 24th Int. I shall attend to the instructions it contains some of them are already acted on. Freemans commission (for which Mr Pleasonton had a Blank[)] is sent to the Treasury—from whence, I presume it will go to him with his Instructions.

I inclose a Copy of a Letter received yesterday from Mr Shaler[1] and am with Sentiments of the Highest Respect Your Most Hble Sert

JOHN GRAHAM

RC (DLC). Docketed by JM.

1. Graham may have enclosed a copy, probably made by Richard Forrest, of William Shaler to Robert Smith, 12 Aug. 1810 (DNA: RG 59, Communications from Special Agents). Shaler had arrived in Havana on 1 Aug., but he failed to persuade the captain general, Don Salvador de Muro y Salazar, marqués de Someruelos, to grant him a passport for his journey to Veracruz. Much of the 12 Aug. letter was devoted to reporting conversations Shaler had held with an influential Cuban official and planter to the effect that Cubans believed it was unlikely that the rebels in Buenos Aires and Caracas could sustain an independence movement against Spain. It was the opinion of Shaler's informant that Cuba required a monarchy for stable government, and he included this among the reasons why American agents could not be received in Havana. Shaler added that his sources of information were in constant communication with the mainland (Mexico) and that he remained well placed to obtain news as well as to give effect to the wishes of the president.

From Elizabeth House Trist

Dr Sir   Mount Holly Augst 27—10

I hope you will pardon the trouble I occasion you, and indulge me so far as to let me know, if Mr Pinckney has communicated to the Goverment any thing respecting William Brown as the late account of his being taken at the Theatre at the suit of Mr Pinckney and of his giving up all the public Money is a circumstance I shou'd suppose wou'd be noticed by him if the fact is, as, represented in the news paper,[1] I am greatly interested in the event and most sincerely wish the news to be confirm'd as then there can be no possible plea against my Children having their property restor'd to them and by being rescued from beggery, My Grandsons may have a chance of obtaining a proper education which is an object that is nearest my heart of any thing in this World and knowing that they are endowed with a capacity to receive one, the Idea of their being deprived of the means of effecting it, has wounded me to the very soul, particularly as I find my self incompetent to doing any thing to aid their Mother for so desireable and important a design.

With Compliment to Mrs Madison Accept of Assurences of my best wishes for your mutual happiness

E. TRIST

RC (DLC).

1. Accounts of the arrest of William Brown in a theater in London and of his giving up "all his bills of exchange and other property" appeared in several newspapers, including the *National Intelligencer* on 22 Aug. 1810.

¶ From Richard Forrest. Letter not found. *27 August 1810*. Calendared as a one-page letter in the lists probably kept by Peter Force (DLC, series 7, container 2).

§ From William Montgomery.[1] *28 August 1810, Philadelphia*. Complains of the recent decisions of the Danish prize courts and urges JM to use naval vessels to protect American trade both in the Baltic and in East Asia. Approves of JM's policy of avoiding war but suggests the arming of merchant vessels in certain trades; however, "arming generally to protect lawfull trade might produce war very Soon." Considers the conduct of JM "wise so far" and hopes he will make the preservation of peace and the support of the Union his main objects. Advises JM not "to interfere with the colonies of Spain or any other power."

RC (DLC). 2 pp.

1. William Montgomery was a former Republican representative from Pennsylvania who had served with JM in the Third Congress, 1793–95.

To Samuel Smith

DEAR SIR   MONTPELIER Aug: 29. 1810

Your letter of the 8th. inst: came duly to hand & I have since been favored with that of the 17th.

It seems that in the decreasing amounts of the Treasury deposits, any distributive transfer of them to the State Banks, would not be convenient to the public, and must soon become unimportant to them. Nothing better therefore is practicable in that mode, than a temporary relief to particular Banks, particularly affected by the demands of the National Bank. Application has been made on this ground, in behalf of the Bank of Columbia, and equal attention would be due to any other applications.

The Spaniard who dined with me last winter, & was lately executed at the Havanna, was not the one introduced by Dr. Thornton. His particular title to my civilities, was a letter of strong recommendation, from Dr. Rush.[1] The other Spaniard, was never at my table.

If the French decree, releasing the Amn. property in the Warehouses of Holland, be authentic, may it not be the result of apprehended reprizals here?

Draft (DLC). Later docketed as being to Albert Gallatin and listed as a letter to Gallatin in the *Index to the James Madison Papers*. Recipient identified by comparison with Samuel Smith's letters to JM of 8 and 17 Aug. 1810.

1. Letter not found.

From John Graham

Dear Sir   Department of State 29th August 1810
I had the Honor by the last Mail to acknowledge the receipt of your Letter of the 24th. Inst. and to inform you that a Commission for Mr Freeman as Surveyor of the Public Lands South of Tennessee had been sent to the Treasury.

The Papers for Mr Poinset have been made out agreeably to your direction and sent to the Secy of State who is now at Baltimore for his Signature. Mr P. will get to Buenos-Ayres in good time, for I learn from an acquaintance of mine there, that a Revolution has taken place in that Country. I take the Liberty to send you the Printed Papers, which he sent me, and shall add to them his account of the Revolution[1] if I can get it from the Printer with whom I left it last Night.

Yesterday we received Despatches which came out, I beleive, with Mr Morier; tho we have got nothing from him which indicates that they were in his charge. I put them under cover to Mr Smith before I left the office, first having run over them to see if they contained any thing important which we could send you by this days Mail. The inclosed extract[2] is all that bears that character if indeed it does.

Mr Pinkneys former Despatches yesterday returned to the office from Mr Smith and I have now the Honor to forward them to you[3] with some of the News Papers received with Mr P.s last Despatches.

I return agreeably to your request Judge Toulmins Letter[4] & its inclosures and with them a Paper he sent me.[5] It appears that Govr Holmes had been apprised of the contemplated expedition against Mobile, I therefore thought it unnecessary to write to him on the subject a second time, as I did not feel myself authorised to give any particular instructions— least you should not have a Copy of the Laws with you I will take the

Liberty to observe that the Law of June 1794. makes it lawful for the President "or *any Person* he may have empowered for that purpose, to employ such part of the Land or Naval Forces of the UStates or of the Militia thereof as may be judged necessary for the purpose of preventing carrying on any (military) expedition or enterprise from the territories of the UStates against the Territories or Dominions of a Foreign Prince or State, with whom the UStates are at Peace.["] With Sentiments of the most Sincere & Respectful attachment I have the Honor to be, Sir, Your Most Obt Sert

JOHN GRAHAM

RC (DLC); first enclosure (DLC: Rives Collection, Madison Papers). First enclosure (2 pp.) in a clerk's hand; marked "(Copy.)"; docketed by Graham, "Recd 28th Augt."; marked by JM "to be returned to J. M." (see n. 2). For other enclosures, see nn. 3–5.

1. An "Extract of a letter from Buenos Ayres" appeared in the *National Intelligencer* on 31 Aug. 1810.

2. Graham enclosed an extract from William Pinkney's 6 July 1810 dispatch to Robert Smith, reporting on a conversation he had held that morning with Lord Wellesley on the state of Anglo-American relations. The two diplomats agreed that Pinkney should write a note on the subject, to which Wellesley promised to respond. Wellesley also undertook to write additional notes on the *Chesapeake* affair and the dispute over blockades. Pinkney was optimistic about the outcome and announced that John Philip Morier, who was carrying the dispatch to the U.S., would serve "for a short time, as *charges-des-affaires*" in Washington.

3. Pinkney to Robert Smith, 12 June 1810, with the enclosures: Pinkney to Wellesley, 5 June 1810, and Wellesley to Pinkney, 7 June 1810 (DNA: RG 59, DD, Great Britain). Graham had forwarded this material to Robert Smith on 7 Aug. (Graham to JM, 8 Aug. 1810).

4. Harry Toulmin to JM, 28 July 1810.

5. This was very probably Francisco Maximilian de St. Maxent to Richard Sparks, 25 June 1810, formally complaining about a society "in the neighbourhood of Fort Stoddert, named *Expedition of Mobile*," whose object was said to be to "take Mobile and to destroy all the houses of Commerce &c." Toulmin obtained copies of the document and evidently sent them to both John Graham and Mississippi territorial governor David Holmes. Toulmin had already mentioned this in his 28 July 1810 letter to JM, who had also received the same information from the enclosure in John Smith's letter to him of 7 Aug. 1810 (see Carter, *Territorial Papers, Mississippi*, 6:77, 79–82, 85).

To William Eustis

DEAR SIR   MONTPELIER Aug. 30. 1810

I have recd. your favor of the 19th. A long letter, now with the Dept. of State, from Judge Toulmin,[1] confirms the reality of a projected expedition from his neighborhood agst. Mobille; which he considered however as suspended, if not abandoned. The inclosed copies of letters from Govr.

Holmes, & Secretary Robinson,[2] will give you the latest information of what is passing on the other side of the Boundary. Will you turn your thoughts to the question, what steps are within the Executive Competency, in case the deliberations of the people of W. Florida should issue in an offer to place the territory under the Authority of the U. S.? I see that Mourier is arrived, & announced in the Newspapers as Chargé d'Affaires. The dispatches of which he is sd. to be the bearer from Mr. P. have not yet reached me. Accept my esteem & best wishes

JAMES MADISON

With the letter from Col. Smith, I send you the cover under which I recd it.[3]

RC and enclosures (PHi: Daniel Parker Papers). RC docketed by Eustis, "The President Aug 31. 1810. enclosing correspondence of Govr. Holmes &c. respecting Florida." For enclosures, see n. 2.

1. Harry Toulmin to JM, 28 July 1810.

2. JM forwarded to Eustis the clerks' copies that John Graham had sent to him on 24 Aug.: David Holmes to Robert Smith, 31 July 1810 (4 pp.; docketed by Graham as received 23 Aug.), enclosing two accounts (2 and 4 pp., respectively) of proceedings relating to the convention held at St. John's Plains on 25 July 1810; and Thomas B. Robertson to Robert Smith, 28 July 1810 (2 pp.; docketed by Graham as received 23 Aug.), enclosing William Wykoff, Jr., to Robertson, 24 July 1810 (2 pp.). For a discussion of the contents of these letters, see John Graham to JM, 24 Aug. 1810, nn. 1 and 2.

3. See Alexander Smyth to JM, 16 Aug. 1810.

¶ To John Graham. Letter not found. *30 August 1810*. Acknowledged in Graham to JM, 3 Sept. 1810. Asks Graham to examine the registers delivered to the State Department by Mrs. Skipwith to see whether they contain the papers JM had requested earlier. Also inquires about the delegation of executive powers under the law of June 1794.

§ Presidential Proclamation. *31 August 1810, Montpelier, Virginia*. Instructs customs collectors, under section 61 of "'An act to regulate the collection of duties on imports and tonnage,' passed 2d day of March, 1799," to establish the value of the ruble at 33⅓ cents in levying duties on imports from Russia and its dominions.

Printed circular (reproduced in *Papers of Gallatin* [microfilm ed.], reel 21). Printed with Treasury Department circular to collectors and naval officers, 3 Sept. 1810. Enclosed in Gabriel Duvall to Henry Dearborn, 3 Sept. 1810.

To David Bailie Warden

Sɪʀ   Mᴏɴᴛᴘᴇʟɪᴇʀ Sepr. 1. 1810

I have recd. from Judge Cooper of Pennsylva. a request, which I communicate in an entire copy of the letter containing it;[1] as this will best explain his object and at the same time impress you with the laudable views by which he is actuated. In the uncertainty whether Genl. A. wd. be found at Paris, I have thought it best to address the request immediately to you, & I ca⟨n not doubt⟩ that you will feel equally with myself a pleasure, in contributing to the patriotic as well as scientific gratification, of so respectable a fellow Citizen. I only add, that if in the difficulty of transfering funds, any use can be made of my responsibility, drafts for the amount requisite in the case, may be made on me. Accept my respects & good wishes

Draft (DLC).

1. Thomas Cooper to JM, 19 Aug. 1810.

From Benjamin Henry Latrobe

Sɪʀ,   Wᴀsʜɪɴɢᴛᴏɴ Septr. 1er. 1810

It is my duty to take up so much of your time, as is necessary to inform you of the progress of the public business under my charge.

By the arrangements made by Mr. Munroe, & the sale of useless materials, of which we have a very large stock on hand, I have been able to continue the work of the sculptors on the capitals of the Hall of Representatives, & when congress meet, there will be only two out of 24 Capitals which will not be in a state to require only the last hand of the Italian Sculptors.

I shall also be able to compleat the interior of the Senate Chamber. The great quantity of shelving & cases required for the Secretary's office is already finished & nearly put into place.

I expect to put Dr. Thornton into his new Patent-office in a fortnight. He will be better, more roomily, & more handsomely accomodated than any other public Officer. He is not a little pleased with what has been done. I have endeavored to give him no reason to complain, & have even sacrificed in some instances my judgement to his wishes, where it could be done without injury or expense to the public. In this building the expense of which will be within the estimate submitted to you (2.600$) I have no doubt but that the public will be satisfied with the expenditure of their money.

The fire proof at the Office of State is now going on & will be compleat by the beginning of Octr.

I regret exceedingly that circumstances which I cannot controul as well as the pressure of the business which is upon my shoulders at present, absolutely prevent my availing myself of the honor you offered to me of paying you a visit at Montpelier. That this is really the case, is a most serious disappointment to me. Your personal friends are so numerous & so much more capable of rendering that period of leisure if not of retirement, which the public business annually allows you agreeable, than I am, that your invitation flattered & obliged me, more than I can express; & should I never be able, when you may be resident at your country seat, to avail myself of it, I shall always bear this mark of your kindness in grateful remembrance.

As the uncertainty of public employment increases annually, I have thought it prudent to endeavor to get into some business independently of my profession, & am going to establish in connexion with a few of the most wealthy men in Baltimore a manufactory of cotton stuff of the success of which I have no doubt. I shall thus escape that calumny & abuse which it is very foolish to regard, but which it [is] not in human nature entirely to despise: and from which as neither You nor your immediate predecessor have escaped, no public man, even if his importance be as triffling as mine can expect to remain exempt. With the highest esteem & respect, I am very sincerely Your obedt. hble Servt.

B HENRY LATROBE

RC (DLC); letterbook copy (MdHi).

From George W. Erving

Private

DEAR SIR   PHILADELPHIA Septr 2. 1810

You have doubtless noticed lately in our gazettes, an informal paragraph[1] relative to the line of conduct which G. B. will probably observe, towards the spanish colonies in this delicate crisis of their affairs: that paragraph comes from Onis, & I had yesterday an opportunity of seeing a dispatch to him from his government which communicates a declaration formally made to it by the english government: It seems that this latter has given orders to its commanders &c to intercept all vessels bound to the spanish colonies which may have suspicious persons on board; & it declares in the strongest manner that it will oppose itself in every possible form to the independance of any of the colonies, as long as the fate of the mother country shall remain undecided: you will best judge how far this may be considered as squinting at us. It appears to me that G. B is now playing a deep speculating game with the poor spaniards: when I was at Seville she offered a loan of 200 millions of dollars; she was of course to have had a quid for this quo, & the supreme Junta, which always distrusted her, woud not acquiesce; now she offers 50 millions & they will be received, or are received; this fact may be relied on, I have it from Onis; it appears to me to be of very great importance; my surmise is that she will obtain her security not only for this loan, but for all her past & actual expences in the colonies; that they or a part of them stand mortgaged to her: this suggests an idea to me, which I hope that you will forgive me the liberty I am about to take in mentioning to you: taking it for granted that the English government cannot overlook the Floridas, but that on the contrary for many principal reasons, they will be disposed to make their first location there, it occurs to me that the U. S. shoud anticipate any movement of that sort, or any communication on the part of England of a guarantee &c—by a formal & bold declaration that in a certain state of things they will take posesion of the Floridas; in fine that they will never suffer them to be held by any European power other than that to which they now owe allegiance.

Onis beleives in the new project of the Emperor, & says boldly that Fernando will not be received under such auspices; in this I think that he is altogether wrong, Fernando will be received universally in old Spain; but then will begin a terrible work in the colonies in which England will of course be very active.

The Son of old Egalité[2] who as we see by the papers was so well received in Catalonia has arrived in Cadiz & has there also been received, with great acclamation; the English plan is to make him regent, & I collect from what Onis says that it will succeed. Captn Stewart (of our Navy) a very intelligent man who has just arrived from Cadiz, where he has passed six months, tells me also that the English influence is all powerful there: by Captn Stewarts account it woud seem that Cadiz is less than ever likely to fall, nor are provisions scarce there; but he says also that the french troops have great plenty, & that the harvests in the countries which they occupy are very abundant.

The Cortes are assembling at Cadiz, & as Onis thinks are at this time in activity: he allows that great disputes exist between the regency & the Junta of Cadiz; he makes light of the Junta, at the worst he looks to the Cortes as a remedy for every evil; he talks of these as the genuine constitutional representatives of the people, but at the same time tells me that the people of Madrid! (that is half a dozen individuals locked up in a garret) have sent a vocal.[3]

I have met with Mr Walsh or Welsh the pamphleteer,[4] he has just received a letter from Lord Landsdowne (Lord Henry Petty) which (proud
doubtless of his titled correspondent) he shewed at Onis's: His Lordship
asks *Mr W.* for information respecting the political state of affairs in
America observing that neither *they* (the opposition) nor the ministry,
know any thing about the matter. They surely know not any thing; will
they enhance their means of acquiring information, for information they
will not get, by these addresses to the prejudiced men of our country? and
will they regulate their policy by what such men may tell them? In political science the English are as tho they were just born into the world!

I beg to be most respectfully remembered to Mrs Madison Dear Sir
with the sincerest respect & attachment your very obliged & obt St

GEORGE W ERVING

RC (MHi: Erving Papers). Docketed by JM.

1. Erving referred to an extract from a letter, dated 29 June 1810, from a "Spanish gentleman of high respectability, to his friend in Philadelphia," first published in the Philadelphia *Freeman's Journal* and reprinted in the *National Intelligencer* on 3 Sept. 1810. The letter
advised that West Indian-based squadrons of the Royal Navy would search for French citizens on vessels bound for Spanish possessions on the assumption that their intent was to
subvert the loyalty of the Spanish colonies to Ferdinand VII. The letter also announced that
Great Britain would not acknowledge the independence movement at Caracas and promised
that the British government would maintain the integrity of Spain and its empire for as long
as Spain was not totally subjugated by France.

2. Accounts of the arrival in Catalonia and Cadiz of Louis-Philippe (later king of France,
1830–48), son of Louis-Philippe-Joseph, duc d'Orléans (Philippe-Egalité), appeared in Philadelphia in *Poulson's American Daily Advertiser*, 28 Aug. and 1 Sept. 1810.

3. Vocal: a member of a Roman Catholic body who has the right to vote in certain elections (*OED*).

4. See Pinkney to JM, 13 June 1810, n. 1.

§ From George Joy. *2 September 1810, Gothenburg.* Resumes the discussion of subjects raised in his last letter, in April, and considers the changes that have occurred
since then. Declares that the "enormous Duties" imposed by France will annul the
effects of the recent revocation of its decrees. Discusses the present state of the
trade in colonial goods in the Baltic and the prospects for the repeal of the British
orders in council. Believes that Great Britain is suffering from the effects of an
"obstructed Trade" in the Baltic; this situation might induce the British government to modify the orders in council, though not to abandon them completely and
cease to violate neutral rights. Apologizes for the length of his letter.

RC (DLC). 14 pp.

From John Graham

Dept of State 3d Sepr 1810

I received this Morning the Letter which you did me the Honor to write to me on the 30th Ult. and shall before next Mail look thro: the Registers left here by Mrs Skipwith for the purpose of ascertaining whether they contain any entries or Copies corresponding to the Papers you have asked for.

Our Records do not shew that any *delegated Power* has been given by the President under the Law of June 1794 thro: this Dept. It appears that his orders have gone thro: the War Dept. and that no particular form has been used there, for the purpose of calling out the Militia. The Instructions have generally been sent to the Governors of states or Territories; tho this has not uniformly been the case.

I send a Copy of my Letter to Govr Holmes[1] that you may know exactly what has been said to him, and also a Copy of a Letter from the War Dept to Govr Greenup,[2] to shew in what way they conveyed their instructions. With the Highest Respect I have the Honor to be Sir, Your Most Obt Sert.

JOHN GRAHAM

You will receive by this Mail Mr Pinkneys Letters by the British Frigate that brought out Mr Morier and also a communication this instant received from Mr Morier himself.[3]

RC and first enclosure (DLC). RC docketed by JM. For first enclosure, see n. 1. For other enclosures, see nn. 2 and 3.

1. Graham enclosed a press copy of his letter to David Holmes, 13 Aug. 1810 (1 p.; marked "Confidential"; printed in Carter, *Territorial Papers, Mississippi*, 6:99–100).

2. Graham was referring to a letter written by Secretary of War Henry Dearborn to Kentucky governor Christopher Greenup on 26 Nov. 1806, requesting the latter to be vigilant in detecting and preventing military expeditions setting out from American soil against the territories of powers at peace with the U.S. (DNA: RG 107, Misc. Letters Sent). The letter was one of a series of instructions sent to governors and army officers in the western states and territories, ordering them to obstruct Aaron Burr's anticipated enterprise against Spanish territory (see Lipscomb and Bergh, *Writings of Jefferson*, 1:463–64).

3. Graham probably enclosed three duplicate dispatches from William Pinkney (Pinkney to Robert Smith, 1 July and 6 July [two letters] 1810 [DNA: RG 59, DD, Great Britain]). The first reported that there had been no change in Lord Wellesley's attitude on a replacement for Francis James Jackson as Pinkney had conveyed it to the State Department in January 1810. The first of the dispatches of 6 July discussed John Armstrong's account of the secret overtures recently made by Napoleon to make peace with Great Britain, while the second letter of that date restated Pinkney's belief that Lord Wellesley eventually would satisfy American requests for a replacement for Francis James Jackson as well as for a settlement of the dispute over blockades and the *Chesapeake* affair. Graham also enclosed John

Philip Morier's 31 Aug. letter to Robert Smith, written from New York and announcing that he would present himself at Washington after the administration had assembled there (DNA: RG 59, NFL, Great Britain).

§ From William McIntosh. *3 September 1810, Vincennes.* Introduces himself as a former British army officer who settled in Vincennes in 1786 and who was territorial treasurer until he quarreled with William Henry Harrison over advancing Indiana to the second stage of territorial government. Relates his current dispute with Harrison over the 1809 Treaty of Fort Wayne, claiming that Harrison negotiated the agreement unfairly and that the Indians did not give their consent to it freely. States further that Harrison has misled the administration and that the published account of Harrison's dealings with Tecumseh,[1] which he encloses, is inaccurate. Advises that Tecumseh and other Indians will travel to Washington in the fall to lay before JM their complaints against Harrison. Declares Harrison to be corrupt and urges the administration to dismiss him and to withhold ratification of the 1809 treaty.

RC and enclosure (DNA: RG 107, LRRS, M-185:5). RC 4 pp. Docketed by a War Department clerk as received 17 Oct. 1810. Enclosure is a clipping from the Vincennes *Western Sun*, 25 Aug. 1810.

1. Tecumseh (1768–1813), born to a Creek mother and a Shawnee father, grew to maturity in western Kentucky and southern Indiana. He went to the Ohio country in the 1790s where he fought against U.S. forces in the campaigns that culminated in the Battle of Fallen Timbers in 1794. His role in the early stages of the Indian religious revival movement led by his brother, the Prophet, is unclear, but after 1806 he came increasingly into conflict with both American officials and many Indian chiefs as he attempted to discourage further land cessions to the U.S. In August 1810 Tecumseh had come to Vincennes to deliver his response to Harrison's suggestion that he and the Prophet visit JM in Washington (R. David Edmunds, *Tecumseh and the Quest for Indian Leadership* [Boston, 1984], pp. 19–42, 73–134).

To Thomas Cooper

DEAR SIR   MONTPELIER[1] Sepr. 4. 1810

I have recd. your favor of the 19th. Aug. and have transmitted the request it makes, to Mr. Warden, who will more certainly be found at Paris, than Genl. Armstrong, and who is perhaps, more in communication with those most capable of assisting his researches. I need not, I hope, assure you that I have felt a pleasure in contributing, in the way you have thought proper to make use of me, to an object which in affording you a personal gratification of the noblest kind, promises moreover advantage both to Science & to our Country. I[n] order to multiply the chances of providing for the expence that may be called for, I have authorized Mr.

Warden to make any use of my responsibility, that may lessen the present difficulty, of transferring funds from this Country to the Continent of Europe. Accept Sir my sincere esteem, and my friendly wishes.

JAMES MADISON

RC (owned by Mrs. D. Mercer Sherman, Albany, Ga., 1961); draft (DLC).

1. On the draft, JM wrote "Washington" instead of "Montpelier."

To Albert Gallatin

DEAR SIR   MONTPELIER Sepr. 5. 1810

I have recd. your favor of the 21st. Aug. I can not say precisely what use is to be made of the paper on the Batture, in its present form. If it be intended for publication, directly, as well as thro' a report of the arguments at the Bar, some alterations will be proper.

It appears that Brown, partly by the application of the Alien law, partly in consequence of his operations under a fictitious name, had fallen compleatly under the power of Pinkney, and had given up between 30 & 40,000 dollars, with a promise of somewhat more. The opinion of Counsel was, that no Civil action could be sustained, with no further evidence of debt, than the letter from Savage, our Agent at Jamaica, the only evidence then possessed by Mr. P.

The inclosed letter from Ronaldson, will strengthen the motives to caution, in facilitating the passage of French Emigrants.

Our farmers here never experienced such prosperity. They have reaped a double crop of Wheat, and get a double price; at the same time, that manufacturing for their own use, they will have little occasion, as indeed they seem to have little inclination, to lay it out in the usual purchases. They are very sore, nevertheless at the National humiliation stamped on the present state of things.

I hope Poinsett has recd. his outfit of documents, and will now find an easy access to his destination.

Mrs. M. presents her best regards to Mrs. Gallatin. Be pleased to add mine, & to accept assurances of my great esteem & friendly wishes.

JAMES MADISON

RC (NHi: Gallatin Papers). Enclosure not found.

To Harry Toulmin

Dear Sir   Montpelier Sepr. 5. 1810

Your favor of July 28. has been duly recd. The particulars which it communicates are of a nature to claim the attention of the Executive; & I thank you for yours in transmitting them. I am glad to find by subsequent information that the indications of a purpose to carry into effect the enterprize on Florida, had become less decisive. There can be no doubt of its unlawfulness, nor as to the duty of the Executive to employ force if necessary to arrest it, and to make examples of the Authors. These are the less to be excused, as there never was a time when private individuals should more distrust their competency to decide for the Nation, nor a case in which there was less ground to distrust the dispositions of the Govt. regulated as they must be by the limits of its authority, and by the actual state of our foreign relations. Be pleased to accept my sincere esteem & friendly wishes.

Draft (DLC).

To Elizabeth House Trist

Dr Madam   [ca. 5 September 1810]

Your letter of the 27th august has just come to hand that inclosing the papers from Mrs Jones having been previously recd.

It appears by Mr Pinkneys communication that W Brown, being compleatly in his power had given up between 30 and 40 thousand Dollars and there was some prospect of getting from him a further sum, which however was not likely to be very considerable. I sincerely wish not only on public account, but for the sake of those innocently Affected by his misfortune that the intire recoveries may satisfy the claims of the U. S. But this is the less to be hoped, as it is not easy to explain the elopement without supposing that pecuniary trespasses had been before committed, which could not long be conceald, and which will be brought to light by an examination of his accounts with the public.[1]

Tr (PPAmP). In the hand of Elizabeth House Trist; copied in her letter to Catharine Wistar Bache, 15 Sept. 1810.

1. Evidently dissatisfied with this reply, Elizabeth House Trist decided to call on JM in person as she returned to Virginia from a visit to friends in Philadelphia. She met with JM in Washington on or shortly after 18 Oct. 1810, and the following week she recorded the

meeting: "While I was out, the President and his Lady call'd to return my visit which it seems is a great mark of respect on his part, as he returns no visits. The morning after we returnd the visit and had the honor of an interview with the President. He took me by the hand but his manner appeard rather stiff. I got no information from him respecting William Brown. He had not seen him, nor had had any communication with either Mr Gallatin or Mr Duval on the subject but that he fancy'd that ⟨he?⟩ knew more than he had discoverd. When I spoke about Mary and the difficulties she had to encounter and read a part of her last letter he did not seem to feel much on the subject[,] excused Grimes or endeavour'd to do it, on the plea of his attention to the public interest. I observd that his conduct had been universally reprobated and that I presumed from the State of inebriety that he was prone to, he was led to do more than his duty exacted. He said Mr Grimes had lived in his Neighbourhoud and that he had never heard of his doing any thing improper except being a little wild. I told him that in Albemarle his character was considerd very exceptionable and that on my arrival I was asked how Mr Jefferson came to appoint such a man to that Office that he was both a Gamestar and a Drunkard, he seem'd, or effected surprise. However I found that I was not likely to get information from that quarter and I took my leave. Mrs Madison had left the room. He went to call her from the adjoining apartment but she was not there. Left compliments and retired as dignified as I cou'd. My Sister said he offerd me his hand but I did not observe the intended honor till I had pass'd him" (Elizabeth House Trist to Catharine Wistar Bache, 24 Oct. 1810 [PPAmP]; some periods supplied by the editors). The date of the meeting with JM has been assigned on the basis of Elizabeth House Trist's mentioning in the letter that William Brown (who was reported by the *National Intelligencer* as being in Washington under arrest on Wednesday, 10 Oct.) had left the city on "wednesday morning [17 Oct.] for Baltimore to take his Passage in the first Vessel for N Orleans."

From Albert Gallatin

DEAR SIR   NEW YORK 5th Septer. 1810

At Mr Astor's request I enclose a letter[1] which he read to me. I gave him no opinion on the contents. But he desired me to request that if it was not thought proper to give to the person he means to send a recommendatory letter for Mr Adams, the enclosed might be considered as private and not be sent to the Department of State.

I have not yet received the papers for Mr Poinsett; but there having been no opportunity for either Brasils or La Plata, the delay has not been injurious. Whenever they come, your observations will be duly attended to.

The sickness and death of Colo. Few's[2] only son have within the last week occupied all my time, and prevented my reading with the attention due to it Mr Jefferson's memoir on the batture. I suppose that my keeping it a week longer will produce no inconvenience, but beg, if you see him, that you will have the goodness to make this apology for the delay.

I understand that Mr Pinkney has recovered near ten thousand £ St. from Brown, but have not heard from him on the subject.

If we can get over the other difficulties respecting West Florida, the business of the custom house will offer none; the laws having been so worded as to include in the districts of Orleans & Mobile whatever we may claim & possess. This was the ground of offence to Yrujo.[3] The law also which authorizes the President to take possession of Louisiana will legally cover any other measures which policy may dictate in relation to that part of West Florida which lies between the Mississipi & the Perdido. But what ground ought generally to be taken consistent with justice, the rights and interests of the U. States, and the preservation of peace, is the difficult question.

Mrs. G. requests to be affectionately remembered to Mrs. Madison. With great respect Your obedt. Servt

ALBERT GALLATIN

RC (DLC). Docketed by JM.

1. Letter not found, but it was probably Astor to JM, 31 Aug. 1810, described as a four-page letter in the lists made by Peter Force (DLC, series 7, container 2). The contents almost certainly concerned the forthcoming visit to Russia of Adrian Benjamin Bentzon, John Jacob Astor's son-in-law, for business negotiations with the Russian American Company. Bentzon had been in Washington in July 1810 where he had sought and obtained the approval of the Russian diplomats Count Fedor Petrovich Pahlen and Andrei Dashkov for his plans. At that time Pahlen had introduced Bentzon to JM, and as JM's response suggests, Astor was now very likely seeking the president's sanction to make John Quincy Adams a party to negotiations in St. Petersburg between the Russian American Company and Astor's American Fur Company (Porter, *John Jacob Astor*, 1:192–96, 439–42; JM to Gallatin, 12 Sept. 1810, and n. 2).

2. William Few (1748–1828), formerly U.S. senator from Georgia, 1789–93, was married to Hannah Nicholson Gallatin's sister Catharine Nicholson Few. In 1799 he had moved to New York where he was active in city politics and business (Kline, *Papers of Burr*, 1:590).

3. Gallatin referred to the fourth and eleventh sections of the so-called Mobile Act of 24 Feb. 1804, providing for either the annexation to the Mississippi revenue district of "all the navigable waters . . . lying within the United States, which empty into the Gulf of Mexico, east of the river Mississippi" or the creation of a separate revenue district for the waters of "the bay and river Mobile . . . emptying into the Gulf of Mexico, east of the said river Mobile." The Spanish minister, Carlos Fernando Martínez de Yrujo, had protested strongly to JM in 1804 against this legislation's embodying American claims that the Louisiana Purchase had also included West Florida (*U.S. Statutes at Large*, 2:251–54; Cox, *The West Florida Controversy*, pp. 97–99).

From John Graham

DEAR SIR   DEPT OF STATE 5th Sepr 1810.

Agreeably to your request I have looked thro: the Registers sent here from Paris and do not find that they contain any thing in relation to the

Paper you want. They are a strange compound of Public & Private Papers—tho their general Character is I think decidedly official. I understood from Mr Skipwith when he was here, that he had directed them to be sent to the Dept of State 1st Because he did not consider them as strictly belonging to his office, the Law not having made it his Duty to keep such Books, & 2dly Because he was unwilling to place them under the controul of General armstrong as they contained Matter highly important to him as an Individual and directly connected with his dispute with the General.

You will have heared that Colo Whiting died the night before the last and Major Rogers[1] last night. As they lived in the same House and were both healthy Men their sudden deaths have not only cast a gloom thro our Society; but have given something like an alarm least a contagious should have gotten among us. I trust however, that this is not the case. With sentiments of the Most Sincere & Respectful attachment I am Dear Sir Your Most Ob Sert

JOHN GRAHAM

RC (DLC).

1. Hezekiah Rogers was a clerk in the Department of War (*National Intelligencer*, 7 Sept. 1810).

From Robert Smith

SIR,   WASHINGTON Sep 5. 1810.

I came from Balt to the office on Monday to attend for a few days to its general affairs and arrived just in time to receive & to forward to you Mr Moriers letter. I have in a letter to him acknowledged the receipt of it and have intimated to him that you would probably be at Washn in the course of the first week of the next month.

The papers, as prepared, in the case of the proposed return of our Minister at St. Petersburgh will go by this mail. Mr Adams, in taking this step, appears not to have sufficiently adverted to the surrounding obstacles. As he well knows the various opposing embarrassments under which the Mission to Russia was effected and also the harsh strictures to which it gave birth, he cannot but be sensible of the criticism to which the Executive will be exposed by permitting his return, and especially after so very short a term of service. Opposition will again and again illiberally repeat what it has before grossly asserted—namely—that the Mission was devised merely as a provision for certain favorites. Be this, however, as it may, Mr Adams ought, under the peculiar circumstances of the case, to have fortitude enough to endure any personal privations and mortifications rather than subject the executive to the painful animadversions, which will inevitably result from the permitting of his return. Would it not be well for you to admonish him in a private letter against this step? or rather ought we not to postpone acting in the case until we receive an Official Application from himself.

I propose to set out for Baltimore tomorrow. With great respect, sir Your Ob. servt

R SMITH

RC (DLC: Rives Collection, Madison Papers).

§ From Sylvanus Bourne. *5 September 1810, American Consulate, Amsterdam.* Requests that his commission as consul at Amsterdam be renewed to enable him to address the emperor of France. Adds in a postscript that U.S. minister John Armstrong will leave Paris on 20 Sept. for Bordeaux to depart for home.

RC (DNA: RG 59, LAR, 1809–17, filed under "Bourne"). 2 pp.

§ From the Settlers on Chickasaw Lands. *5 September 1810, "Ellk River, Sims'es settlement," Mississippi Territory.* Petitioners state that they settled in good faith on, and have good title to, land north of the Tennessee River sold by the Cherokee but now claimed by the Chickasaw. They argue that the Cherokee had a better claim to the land than the Chickasaw and deny that the latter have been done any injustice. They urge JM not to remove them from the land "mearly to gratify a heathan nation Who have . . . by estemation nearly 100000 acres of land to each man Of their nation and of no more use to government or society than to saunter about upon like so many wolves or bares." Petitioners believe that JM can with propriety allow them to remain "as tennants at will" until the Chickasaw sell their claim; and they remind JM that they are not "a set of dishoneste people who have fled from the lawes of their country." They point out the hardship they will suffer if required to remove, and they request JM to send them an answer as soon as possible.

RC (DNA: RG 107, LRUS, P-1810). 2 pp. Signed by William Sims and 449 others. Docketed by a War Department clerk as received 1 Oct. 1810. Printed in Carter, *Territorial Papers, Mississippi,* 6:106–13.

To William Eustis

DEAR SIR   MONTPELIER Sepr. 7. 1810

I have recd. your favor of the 26. That of the 19th. Ult. has been already acknowledged. Having written to Washington for the precedents in the case of calling out the Militia, & employing the regular force, to execute the Act of 1794. agst. unauthorized enterprizes on foreign nations, I have recd. a copy of Genl. Dearborns letter to Govr Greenup, now inclosed.[1] In your absence from the Office, it may not be disagreeable to see it; tho' it rather sanctions a dispensation with, than furnishes a ground of, any particular form, to be used in giving the requisite authorities to the State or territorial Govts. Govr. Holmes, I find has been apprized by the Dept. of State that he would have an Agency, in carrying the law into execution if necessary. But it is from the Secy. of War, that the regular power is to proceed. You will observe that the orders to the Military Commanders on the subject, must include a delegation of authority, according to the text of the law. This I presume is sufficiently done in your instructions to Genl. H. & Col. C.[2] I inclose for your perusal an interesting letter from Judge Toulmin.[3] One of later date from him to Mr. Graham, subtracts somewhat from the evidence it presents; but the details alone are worth knowing. The last letter from Mr Pinkney is of July 6. He was still kept under an expectation that satisfaction would be specialy tendered for the Chesapeake &c., and a hope that the Old blockades wd. be revoked in conformity to the French proposal. He was confident that a Minister Plenipo. wd. follow Morier, & assurances in writing be quickly given to that effect. He repeats that he wd. probably be a man of rank & talents, and the letter which is official, refers to his private letter of   [4] to Mr. Smith on that point. Should the letter go to Congs. it will satisfy the honest doubters as to the private letter; but it will be too late to controul the effect of their incredulity, on the current events. Will you be good eno' to do what may be proper in relation to the letter from Henry Burchsted?[5] Accept assurances of my great esteem & regard

JAMES MADISON

RC (MHi: Eustis Papers).

1. See John Graham to JM, 3 Sept. 1810, and n. 2.
2. Wade Hampton and Thomas Cushing.
3. Harry Toulmin to JM, 28 July 1810.
4. Left blank by JM. The official letter to which JM referred was Pinkney's 1 July 1810 dispatch to Robert Smith, where Pinkney repeated his claim, first made in his private letter of 4 Jan. 1810 to Robert Smith, that Lord Wellesley had always intended to send a new minister to the U.S. to replace Francis James Jackson. Administration critics had doubted the existence of Pinkney's 4 Jan. letter (see *ASP, Foreign Relations*, 3:360; JM to the House of Representatives, 27 Mar. 1810, and n. 2; Graham to JM, 3 Sept. 1810, n. 3).
5. Letter not found. Henry A. Burchsted was a cadet at the U.S. Military Academy. Evidently he was in some disciplinary difficulty, since he wrote to Eustis on 27 Nov. 1810 asking to be informed whether he had been "discharged entirely" from the army. According to Eustis's note on the verso, JM then ordered Burchsted to be restored to the service as of 1 Jan. 1811 (DNA: RG 107, LRRS, B-253:5).

From William Eustis

Dr Sir   Portsmouth N H Septr. 7. 1810.

Your ⟨last⟩ of the 30th of August with its enclosures was received the last evening. The movements of our own citizens as well as those of the Inhabitants of W. Florida I have observed with ⟨an interest?⟩ proportionate to the consequences which may ⟨result⟩ from them. But as it is impossible to ⟨divine?⟩ what course they might take, it is equally difficult to determine what part should be taken by Government. Should their deliberations issue in a proposal to place the territory under the authority of the U. S. on terms which shall be deemed ⟨admissible or⟩ justifiable, protection of some kind will ⟨necessarily be implied?⟩—protection under such circumstances ⟨implies force; how far?⟩, how near and to what extent must depend on ⟨events and?⟩ may not probably require to be determined before the ⟨next month⟩. In one of my Letters to Genl. Hampton,[1] stating to him the ⟨expediency⟩ of his providing to reinforce the post of Fort Stoddert, I ⟨intimated⟩ the expediency of his repairing to the encampment on the Mississippi as soon as his health would permit, adding that ⟨in case?⟩ of the occurrence of circumstances which should ⟨render it necessary to⟩ detach from his command in a southern or ⟨eastern direction⟩, his presence would be equally useful & desireable—⟨this circumstance?⟩ or perhaps the rumour of the ⟨order⟩ which he will give to reinforce Fort Stoddert has probably occasioned the report mentioned by Governor Holmes ⟨on the⟩ intended movement of the troops from the Miss: territory.

Coll. Smyths Letter contains information which I have been in possession of for some months past. His own situation & feelings have also been known to me. Active intelligent and of an ardent mind, perceiving his superiority in some respects over those who have commanded him, & being without command he is of course dissatisfied. In his case, after expressing a wish that he might be induced to remain with the troops, I ⟨observed?⟩ the general rule not to interfere between the commanding General & his subordinate officers. Hampton writes me that he has ordered Coll. S to take command of the troops on the ⟨Tennessee?⟩, Coll. ⟨Purdy⟩ having rendered himself unpopular by ⟨severity?⟩ with the people near Highwassee, which information is given confidentially.[2] How far this command will be acceptable to Coll. S ⟨remains to⟩ be seen.

My intimation to Genl H. that he ⟨should turn?⟩ his attention to the Miss. was in consequence of ⟨a suggestion⟩ from him of the usefulness which might be ⟨derived from⟩ a personal interview at the seat of Govt. However desireable such an interview might be I thought it more important that he should be with his command. The election in this state ⟨has terminated?⟩ federal because of the injudicious selection of candidates &

not for want of a real republican majority. Govr Langdon himself attributes it to the ⟨Admin.?⟩ & adds that if we do not manage things better he
must ⟨come?⟩ himself. The country ⟨prospers & yet no one appears satisfied?⟩. If you ask them to ⟨dress?⟩ up their ⟨main?⟩ *energy*, no two can agree
what uniform he shall wear, or which ⟨step?⟩ he shall march. Respectfully
& with great regard

W. Eust⟨is⟩

RC (DLC). Cover marked "confidential" by Eustis. RC badly blotted.

1. See Eustis to Wade Hampton, 22 Aug. 1810 (Carter, *Territorial Papers, Mississippi*,
6:101–2).
2. On 15 June Eustis had instructed Hampton to order Lieut. Col. Robert Purdy of the
Seventh U.S. Infantry to remove intruders from the Chickasaw and Cherokee lands in the
region bounded by the Elk and Tennessee rivers. Hampton assigned the task to Smyth after
reporting to Eustis that Purdy, although a valuable soldier, had unfortunately "gotten himself
involved in several disputes, and civil suits, with the citizens in the vicinity of Highwassee
garrison respecting the exercise of his military functions" (Eustis to Hampton, 15 June 1810,
ibid., 6:70–71; Hampton to Eustis, 22 Aug. 1810 [DNA: RG 107, LRRS, H-181:5]).

From John Smith

Sir,   War Department Septr. 7th. 1810.
   I have the honor of enclosing a transcript of Governor Harrison's Letter
of the 22d. Ult. & of the Papers therein mentioned. The originals have
been forwarded to the Secretary of War at Boston. I am with perfect respect, &c. &c. &c.

(signed.)   Jno. Smith, C. C.

[Enclosure]

§ William Henry Harrison to William Eustis. *22 August 1810, Vincennes*. Describes
his meetings between 12 and 21 Aug. with the brother of the Prophet, Tecumseh,
who is "the great man of the Party." Tecumseh's early speeches were "sufficiently
insolent & his pretensions arrogant," but Harrison encloses in full his speech of
20 Aug. as it was recorded by an interpreter who "speaks bad English, and is not
very remarkable for clearnes of intellect." Declares that Tecumseh admitted the
following facts: that he and the Prophet had always intended to form "a combination of all the Indian Tribes" to stop white settlement and to establish that Indian
"Lands should be considered common property and none sold without the consent
of all"; that they wished to put to death those chiefs who had signed the 1809
Treaty of Fort Wayne; and that in future warriors, and not village chiefs, should
manage Indian affairs. Tecumseh also denied any intention to go to war and
abused those who had so informed Harrison, especially Winnemac, as liars.
   Harrison's defense of U.S. policy toward the Indians was interrupted and con-

tradicted by Tecumseh with "the most violent gesticulations" and "in the most indecent manner." Guards were summoned to maintain order, and Harrison announced that he would "extinguish the Council Fire" and receive no further communications from Tecumseh. The interpreter later informed Harrison that Tecumseh wished for another interview to settle matters amicably and admitted that he had probably been misled about the extent of opposition among the whites to the purchase of Indian lands. Harrison assumes that "a Scotch Tory" [William McIntosh] and William Wells were the sources of Tecumseh's misinformation on this issue. Encloses a copy of a speech he originally sent to the Prophet [on 19 July], in which he promised to return lands to any tribe able to prove that it had a better claim to them than the treaty signatories at Fort Wayne in 1809. Tecumseh argued that the tribes he represented had never consented to the 1809 treaty, but Harrison denied that their consent was necessary. At the conclusion of the council, Harrison asked if the surveyor running the new boundary line would "receive any injury." Tecumseh replied that "the old Line must be the Boundary," from which Harrison concludes that the surveyor cannot safely proceed in his work.

Has promised Tecumseh to send his speech to the president and procure the president's answer. Requests a speech signed by either JM or Eustis to the effect that ceded lands will not be given up, in order to convince the Shawnee of the "falsehood" of their information. Repeats his long-held view that Indian war can best be avoided by "our shewing an ability to punish the first Aggressors," as the Indians will never forgo any opportunity to seek revenge for injuries "they think they have received from the Whites when it can be done with impunity." Admits to being uncertain about the extent of the Prophet's support but thinks it is decreasing, Tecumseh notwithstanding. Inquires about the best defense arrangements he can make with regulars, militia, and forts. In a postscript, requests arms for a local troop of volunteer dragoons.

Letterbook copy (DNA: RG 107, LSP); enclosures (DLC). Enclosures are clerks' copies of Harrison to Eustis, 22 Aug. 1810 (6 pp.; docketed by JM); "Tecamseh's Speech to Governor Harrison," 20–21 Aug. 1810 (9 pp.; docketed by JM); and "Governor Harrison's Speech to the Prophet," [19 July 1810] (2 pp.). Printed in Esarey, *Messages and Letters of William Henry Harrison*, Indiana Historical Collections, 1:447–48, 459–69.

§ From Joseph Ball[1] and Others. *7 September 1810, Philadelphia.* Petitioners believe that trade between the U.S. and Brazil is increasing and that the U.S. should therefore appoint a commercial agent at Rio de Janeiro. They recommend John Andrews of Philadelphia for the position.

RC (DNA: RG 59, LAR, 1809–17, filed under "Andrews"). 1 p. Signed by Ball and ten others. JM also received a letter on behalf of Andrews from John Mason, 14 Sept. 1810 (2 pp.), and a petition from Baltimore, signed by George Stiles and seventeen others, 20 Sept. 1810 (1 p.) (ibid.).

1. Joseph Ball (1748–1821) was a prominent Philadelphia merchant and one of the founders of the Insurance Company of North America in 1792. He had served as president of the company in 1798–99 (*Pa. Mag. Hist. and Biog.*, 6 [1882]: 76).

§ From George Joy. *8 September 1810, Gothenburg.* Recapitulates his activities in the region as well as the contents of the letters to which he has not yet received a reply. Reminds JM that the last letter he had from him was dated 16 Mar. 1809 [not found]. Discusses his dealings with Count von Bernstorff and the decisions of Danish prize courts. Is convinced that the Danish government is doing its best to protect neutral commerce. Mentions the vacillations of British naval commanders in their enforcement of the blockade of the sound; hopes to receive clarification on this subject from Pinkney. Laments the difficulty of obtaining for neutrals "a spark of Justice, but by the hard collision of flint & Steel."

RC (DLC). 12 pp. In a clerk's hand, corrected and signed by Joy.

From John Graham

Private
DEAR SIR   DEPT OF STATE 10th Sepr 1810
I have the Honor to send you inclosed the proceeds of your Check in my favor—in such notes as you requested[1] that is to say—
6 of 50 = 300.
10 – 20 = 200
10 – 10 = 100—600 in all.

The Eastern end of the City is represented to be sickly; but the West end and George Town are not at all so.

On Saturday we received from Mr Pinkney a Packet of News Papers; but no Letters. The News Papers you will find under Cover with this.

Something has already been said in the National Intelligencer about Mr Pinkneys supposed Speeches.[2] I have handed the News Papers you returned, to Mr. S H. Smith who will cause the correct version of Mr Pinkneys speech to be published—and add to it some Editorial Remarks—in which the Story of the *Diamonds* will be contradicted, as it is understood that even that is doing Mr. Pinkney some injury in the Public estimation.

I beg to be presented to Mrs Madison and to renew to you the assurances of my most Respect⟨ful⟩ attachment

JOHN GRAHAM

RC (DLC). Docketed by JM.

1. No letter from JM to Graham making such a request or enclosing a check has been found.

2. Throughout the summer of 1810 William Pinkney was frequently attacked in press accounts of his conduct as minister to Great Britain. Among the episodes receiving the most unfavorable notice were the award of a doctorate of civil laws to Pinkney from Oxford University, a version of an address to the Society for the Relief of Foreigners in London in which

Pinkney was alleged to have used the words "filial piety" to describe the proper relationship between Great Britain and the U.S., and a rumor that his wife had worn diamonds on the occasion of her last appearance at court. The *National Intelligencer*, on 7 Sept. 1810, had already denounced many of these stories as "flagrantly incorrect." It took up the matter again on 12 Sept. to print fuller versions of Pinkney's remarks in their proper context and to deny that his wife had worn diamonds at court.

From Thomas Jefferson

DEAR SIR   MONTICELLO Sep. 10. 10

I returned yesterday from Bedford, and according to my letter written just before my departure, I take the liberty of informing you of it in the hope of seeing mrs. Madison & yourself here. And I do it with the less delay as I shall ere long be obliged to return to that place. By a letter of Aug. 15. from Genl. Dearborn he said in a P. S. that he has just recieved information that Bidwell had fled on account of fraud committed by him in his office of county treasurer. These are mortifying & distressing incidents. Present my friendly respects to mrs. Madison and be assured of my constant affection

TH: JEFFERSON

RC (DLC); FC (DLC: Jefferson Papers).

§ From Elizabeth Carman. *10 September 1810, Shelbyville, Kentucky*. Petitions as a poor widow, nearly sixty years old, for the discharge from the army of her son, Joseph Carson, who as a minor enlisted in the Seventeenth Infantry. Her son has deserted to Ireland, but she promises to recall him if he receives a discharge. Encloses an affidavit attesting that her son enlisted as a minor.

RC and enclosure (DNA: RG 107, LRRS, C-214:5). RC 1 p. Docketed by a War Department clerk as received 1 Oct. 1810. Enclosure 1 p.

¶ From James Terrell. Letter not found. *10 September 1810, Elbert County, Georgia*. Listed in Registers of Letters Received by the Secretary of War (DNA: RG 107), which indicates that Terrell requested a pardon for his brother, William Terrell, a deserter from the U.S. Army who was "very penitent" and desired to return to duty. The entry in the register records that the letter was sent to the adjutant and inspector general on 16 Sept. with a pencil note from JM to the effect that the petition be granted.

§ From Thomas Worthington.[1] *11 September 1810, Chillicothe*. Reports that William Creighton will resign as U.S. attorney on 20 Sept. and in that event Worthington and several others will recommend Lewis Cass, the present U.S. marshal, as his successor. For the position vacated by Cass he recommends the appointment of Jessup N. Couch.

RC (DNA: RG 59, LAR, 1809–17, filed under "Couch"). 1 p. JM received similar letters on behalf of Cass and Couch from Jared Mansfield, 3 Sept. 1810 (1 p.), and Jeremiah Morrow, 5 Oct. 1810 (1 p.) (ibid.).

    1. Thomas Worthington served as a Republican U.S. senator from Ohio, 1810–14.

To Albert Gallatin

DEAR SIR   MONTPELIER Sepr. 12. 1810.

    I have recd. your favor of the 5th. inclosing one from Mr. Aster. Whatever personal confidence may be due to him, or public advantage promised by his projected arrangement with the Russian Fur Company, there is an obvious difficulty in furnishing the official patronage which he wishes; whether the arrangement be regarded as of a public or of a private character. In the former, it would require the solemnities of a Treaty; In the latter, it would be a perplexing precedent, and incur the charge of partiality: and in either, is forbidden by the proposed article depriving others[1] under the description of transient traders, of the common right of American Citizens.[2] Altho' the Russian Govt. or the Fur Company may make such a distinction, of themselves, it wd. be wrong for this Govt. to be a party to it: first because it would favor a monopoly, contrary to Constitutional principles, next because, in a general & political view, such distinctions from foreign sources, are justly regarded as an evil in themselves. The most that seems admissible wd. be an instruction to Mr. Adams, to promote the opening of the Russian Market *generally*, to the Articles which are now excluded, and which may be exported from the U.S. To such an instruction no objection occurs; and if it be thought advantageous may be given. In the mean time I shall not send Mr. Asters letter to the Dept. of State; nor take any step till I hear again from you. Mrs. M. sends her best regards to Mrs. Gallatin. Accept my best wishes

JAMES MADISON

    The sooner you send to Mr. J. the Batture paper, the better, as the use of it by his Counsel, is expedient; and I am not sure that the Session of the Court may not be near. I shall be at Monticello in a day or two, and will explain the delay as you desire.

RC (NHi: Gallatin Papers).

    1. JM altered this to read "other Citizens" but then apparently tried to erase "Citizens."
    2. Astor's plans for cooperation between the Russian American Company and his Ameri-

can Fur Company in the Pacific Northwest included an agreement that the latter would assist the former in excluding transient American traders from the region. The Russian company had complained that American transients had advanced their own interests by arming the local Indians who thus threatened both the security and the business of the Russian trading posts (Porter, *John Jacob Astor*, 1:195–96, 454–59).

To Robert Smith

DEAR SIR   MONTPELIER Sepr. 12. 1810

I have recd yours of the 5th. instant from Washington. The speedy return which it appears is wished by Mr. ⟨Adams⟩, is to be regretted; but if his anxiety be as great and the cause as powerful & unforeseen, as is stated, it is scarc[e]ly just to oppose his escape from ruin. I hope however that the extreme anxiety is rather that of the parent, than of Mr. ⟨A.⟩ himself; nor is it unprobable that it may be strengthened in her, by some collateral considerations not mentioned in her letter. It was my intention to accompany your ⟨official⟩ letter, with a private one to Mr. ⟨A.⟩ on the subject of his return, but postponed it, till the receipt of the papers which you forwarded, which I thought it probable, might include the expected application to which Mrs. ⟨Adams⟩ alludes. As this application has not yet arrived, and I have been & still am, much engaged otherwise, I shall wait for the next mail at least, before I return the papers with the intended addition of a private ⟨letter⟩[1] as you recommend.

I inclose a private letter from Mr. Erving, with the exception only of a paragraph, irrelative to the subject of it.[2] The information it gives is the more important, as it comes in so authentic a form. Be so good as to return it thro' the hands of Mr. H⟨amilton⟩, that its contents may be known to him. As Mr. E. was on his way to Boston thro' N. Y. I think it probable, that Mr. G⟨allatin⟩, & Mr. E⟨ustis⟩, may be made substantially acquainted with the matter, by conversations with him.

I have not yet fixed the time of my setting out for Washington. I expect it will be near about that anticipated in your answer to Mouriers communications. Accept my respects and good wishes

JAMES MADISON

RC (DNA: RG 59, LAR, 1809–17, filed under "Madison"). Words supplied in angle brackets have been partially erased.

1. The corner of the letter has been clipped where JM may have written the word supplied.

2. Erving to JM, 2 Sept. 1810. JM's remark suggests that he may have withheld the last paragraph of the letter, relating to Robert Walsh.

From Richard Forrest

DEAR SIR, WASHINGTON Sepr. 12. 1810

I have the pleasure to confirm the news of the arrival of the Blanchy from Algiers, which brought out a Horse for Doctr. Thornton, and 8 Sheep, 20 Bushls. of Wheat, a Basket of seeds and a Cask of Grape vine Cuttgs. for you. These very articles with the addition of several others including two Jack Asses, I not only requested Coln. Lear to send me; but I sent a Yellow man in the Brig with scarcely any other object, than the care of them on the passage. I also had a quantity of Plank sent out (supposing it to be scarce and high priced at Algiers) for the purpose of securing whatever might be sent. I had no idea of profit, but merely wished to avail myself of so good an opportunity of introducing into the Country, what I thought might prove of general utility. I stated to Coln. Lear, but more particularly to Mr. Baker (to whom I gave 170 dollars to purchas[e] the Jacks in Majorca, where I was told they were uncommonly large) that one of the Jacks and some of the Sheep were intended for you. I have recd no letter from Coln. Lear on this subject, the joint one to Mr Sterett[1] and myself, I have not yet seen, but I presume if it had contained any thing on this subject, Mr. S. would have informed me of it. The hasty letter which he wrote me yesterday, as well as *Mr Hoskyns,[2] both of which I enclose you, seem to confirm the idea that none of the things are for me, and unless Coln. Lear should have mentioned me as a part owner, I certainly shall have no just claim on any of the articles.

I hope your goodness will excuse the freedom I have taken to plague you on a subject of such a trivial nature. I must also apologise for the confused manner in which I have given the detail, it proceeds in a great degree from the state of my mind arising from the situation of my family. My youngest child has for the last ten days, been at the point of death, and can scar[c]ely at this moment be considered out of danger: My Son David, complained yesterday of a sick Stomach; was taken with a puking about Eleven oclock, and in the coarse of half an hour discharged from his Lungs at least two tablespoons full of blood. He is now rather better, and I hope will recover. I remain Dear Sir, with the highest respect Your very obt. Servt.

RICHD. FORREST

The Russian Consul

As this is the proper season for seeding wheat, had I not best send you that which came from Algiers by the first opportunity to Fredericksburg?

It is not to be understood that the Horse which came in the Brig forms any part of the articles I wrote for. Docr. Thornton wrote, not only for him; but I suspect for as many as could be procured. Two were to have come in this Vessel; but as the Ship Resource had arrived at Algiers from Constantinople, and would sail in a short time for Balto, it was concluded to sent [*sic*] one out in each Vessel.

RC (NN). Enclosures not found.

1. Probably Samuel Sterrett (1758–1833), a prominent Baltimore merchant and local civic leader (Papenfuse et al., *Biographical Dictionary of the Maryland Legislature*, 2:772–73).

2. John H. Hoskyns was a resident of Baltimore who evidently had written to JM on 9 Sept. 1810 (not found, but calendared as a two-page letter in the lists probably made by Peter Force [DLC, series 7, container 2]).

From John G. Jackson

Dr. Sir.   CLARKSBURG 13th. Septr. 1810

I thank you with great sincerity for your congratulations[1] on my union with Miss M.[2] Nothing is now wanting to complete my wishes but her introduction to my best friends beyond the mountains, & my restoration to health. The first is dependant upon the last, which has received so severe a shock by my late unfortunate fall that I shall be unable to travel to W-City this year: & hence the necessity of my resignation which is now decided on. You my dear friend have greatly overrated my services in supposing that the public is interested in them; my votes could only add one to the majority & that one could at any time be spared without public detriment. Still I will frankly declare that nothing but imperious necessity could induce me *now* to forego the pleasure of giving my feeble cooperation to those whose talents, virtues, & patriotism command the homage of every real friend to his Country. It would indeed afford me much gratification to spend the winter with Mrs. J near you in W City, if I even afterwards were compelled to retire: for it would afford me an early opportunity to present her to my dear Sisters, & to you my best of friends. Letters would in some degree compensate for the loss of that society, but it would be most unreasonable in me to ask an addition to your labors by becoming my correspondent. Sometimes nevertheless I am sure you will write me if you can spare ⟨a⟩ moment from business: On Sister D I shall draw more largely & hope she will honor my bills. Adieu my dear friend & believe me in sincerity & truth ever yours

J G JACKSON

RC (DLC). Docketed by JM.

1. Letter not found.

2. Jackson had married Mary Sophia Meigs, daughter of Return J. Meigs, Jr., of Ohio, on 19 July 1810 (Brown, *Voice of the New West*, pp. 95–100).

From John Smith

Sir,   War Department, Septr. 13th. 1810.
I have the honor of enclosing a Copy of a Letter from Governor Harrison under date of the 28th. ult. The original has been transmitted to the Secretary of War. I am, with perfect respect, &c. &c. &c.

(signed.)   Jno. Smith, C. C.

[Enclosure]

§ William Henry Harrison to William Eustis. *28 August 1810, Vincennes.* Discusses the role of the Wea Indians in his recent meetings with Tecumseh. Their principal chief had informed Harrison that he would tell the Shawnee at the council that they had no right to interfere with recent land sales on the Wabash, but on the day when he was to speak "he declined saying any thing." Attributes this conduct either to fear of the Shawnee or to the intrigues [of William McIntosh and William Wells] mentioned in his last letter, more probably the latter since the Wea chiefs have received a message from the Miami chiefs summoning them to a council at Mississineway.

Regrets that Indians are so easily "imposed upon" by the "villainous artifices" of "unprincipled & designing White men." A young Iaowa chief sent to Prophets-town to gain information reports that "the great [wampum] belt which had been sent round to all the Tribes for the purpose of uniting them had been returned"; that "a great number . . . had acceded to the Confederacy"; and that the belt has since been sent to British Indian agent Elliott, "who danced for joy upon seeing that so many Tribes had united against the United States." His informer also reports that many village chiefs have been divested of their authority and that affairs are now managed by warriors hostile to the U.S., but there is no immediate danger of war as it will take the Indians time to get ready.

Concludes by emphasizing his "respect and veneration" for the services rendered by Jefferson but feels that the former president made a "political error" in trying to foster peace among the Indian tribes on the frontier. The "mind of a Savage" cannot be happy unless stimulated by either the chase or by war. If an Indian "hunts in the Winter, he must go to War in the Summer"; thus, "the establishment of tranquility between the neighbouring Tribes will always be a sure indication of War against us."

Letterbook copy (DNA: RG 107, LSP); enclosure (DLC). Enclosure (3 pp.) in a clerk's hand; printed in Esarey, *Messages and Letters of William Henry Harrison*, Indiana Historical Collections, 1:470–72.

From Thomas Cooper

I feel myself much indebted to your kindness in sending for the books mentioned in my letter. I had omitted to mention a treatise on the manufacture of Glass by M. Bois D'Antic,[1] but Mr Warden in making general Enquiries, will not fail to have this work also suggested to him. In England there is not one treatise on the Subject, and the doors of every manufactory are closed upon a stranger, so that we are compelled to resort to the french press for information not else where to be had, altho' the processes of Great Britain may be superior in many branches of manufacture.

The exertions made here to establish manufactures and to render ourselves in some degree independant of Great Britain in this respect, will excite much attention, much jealousy, much hatred, and much fear, among the mercantile and manufacturing monopolists of that country, whose bigotry and rancour are fully adopted by the sciolists in political economy particularly among the literary lords, such as sheffield,[2] sidmouth[3] and I rather fear, Lauderdale,[4] who ought to know better. Be it so: oderint dum metuant;[5] at least so much we may say of the Ministry of that Country, who possess most impracticable understandings as to any matter of right in which this country is concerned. The middle class however, the literary gentlemen, and the writers by profession on statistics and political Œconomy in that country, are wise enough to adopt it as an axiom, that the surest way to wealth and prosperity for any country to pursue, is to promote the industry, knowledge, wealth, and prosperity of every other country also. The traders of England, in their individual capacity, well know that the richer their customers are, the more they will be able to buy; but the *people* of England do not, and the *ministry* will not know this.

I fear the prejudices among the common people of this Country founded on the Assessed Taxes under Mr Adams's administration, will form an unpleasant obstacle to an accurate return upon the Census now taking. In this County, the Germans in particular, were so averse to giving information, that Genl. Wilson[6] who is appointed by the Marshall to collect the facts in this County called upon me and requested I would explain the subject in some way to them, which I did (and as he tells me with very good effect) in the inclosed Letter,[7] which was translated & published in some of the other german counties at the same time.

The Plan adopted by Congress to make the present Census answer the purpose of a Statistical view of the United States occurred to me above two years ago, and a bookseller in Philadelphia, undertook to print a prospectus of a statistical periodical publication if I would draw up one for him. I send you a copy[8] of what I hastily put to paper then, because it notices two works that ought to be in the Congress Library viz The Agricultural Surveys of England,[9] & Buonaparte's work of the same nature in France.[10] I rejoice that in this Country, my proposal is now likely to be effectually superceded.

I have written to Mr John Vaughan of Philadelphia to assure you that he will see the expences paid of any package that may come for me from France, in such manner as you may direct. The best return I can make for your kindness is to promise that when the books do come, they shall be used so far as my health and leisure will permit, in propagating the knowledge they may contain. I remain with great respect sir Your obliged friend and Servant

THOMAS COOPER

RC and enclosure (DLC). For surviving enclosure, see n. 7.

1. Cooper was probably referring to Paul Bosc d'Antic (1726–1784), a French scientist and doctor, who published in 1761 a treatise *Sur les moyens les plus propres à porter la perfection et l'économie dans les verreries de France.*

2. John Baker Holroyd, first earl of Sheffield (1735–1821), was the most prominent defender of the British mercantilist system after American independence and the author of a number of pamphlets advocating commercial restrictions against the U.S., of which the most recent was *The Orders in Council and the American Embargo Beneficial to the Political and Commercial Interests of Great Britain* (London, 1809).

3. Henry Addington, Viscount Sidmouth (1757–1844), had been first lord of treasury and chancellor of the exchequer between 1801 and 1804. He was not known particularly as an author, although a number of his speeches on finance and other matters were published as pamphlets in the early nineteenth century.

4. James Maitland, eighth earl of Lauderdale (1759–1839), was in opposition to the Perceval ministry, but he had published in 1804 *An Inquiry into the Nature and Origin of Public Wealth, and into the Means and Causes of Its Increase* (Edinburgh), a tract which received a harsh notice in the liberal *Edinburgh Review*, 4 (1804): 343–77.

5. "Let them hate, so long as they fear," a fragment from the tragedy *Atreus* by Accius, was also, according to Suetonius, a maxim frequently quoted by Caligula (E. H. Warmington, ed., *Remains of Old Latin*, Loeb Classical Library [4 vols.; Cambridge, Mass., 1935–40], 2:382).

6. William Wilson of Chillisquaque (d. 1813) had served in the Revolutionary War and the Pennsylvania ratifying convention of 1787 (*Pa. Mag. Hist. and Biog.*, 11 [1887]: 272–73).

7. Cooper probably enclosed a copy of a letter to the citizens of Northumberland County that had appeared in the Northumberland, Pa., *Sunbury and Northumberland Gazette* on 31 July 1810. In it he justified the collection of census data on the grounds that the government needed to measure the resources of the nation in order to determine whether the U.S. could end its dependence on European nations, particularly France and Great Britain, and thus ground future policies on "ascertained facts, instead of uncertain conjecture." The clipping has been mistakenly attached to the verso of Cooper's 9 July letter to JM.

8. Enclosure not found.

9. Cooper was most likely referring to the *General View of Agriculture*, a series of regional surveys of British agriculture compiled and published after 1793 under the auspices of the Board of Agriculture (see J. D. Chambers and G. E. Mingay, *The Agricultural Revolution, 1750–1880* [London, 1966], p. 73).

10. Cooper was probably alluding to the annual departmental reports and cadastral surveys furnished by Napoleonic prefects, many of which were published after 1815 in "La Statistique agricole" series of the *Statistique de la France* (Maurice Agulhon, *Apogée et Crise de la Civilisation Paysanne, 1789–1914*, vol. 3 of *Histoire de la France rurale*, ed. Georges Duby and Armand Wallon [Paris, 1976], p. 52).

From William Eustis

SIR,   PORTSMOUTH N. H. Septr. 14. 1810

I am honored with your Letter of the 7th instant enclosing a communication from Judge Tolmin, as also a Letter from Cadet Burchsted, to which proper attention will be paid. The instructions to Genl. Hampton & Colo. Cushing, being predicated on a representation from Colo. Sparks the commanding officer at Fort Stoddert, expressive of his apprehension for the safety of the public stores at the post in consequence of an expected enterprize, amounted to no more than an order to reinforce the garrison as time & circumstances might require.

Respecting the military enterprise against W. Florida no instructions have been given by the war department. Judging from the evidence that such an enterprize would not be undertaken, I had thought that, in case it should be, the movement of the troops for the protection of Fort Stoddert, which would be hastened by the appearance of any operations on the part of the Insurgents, would have the same effect in checking, as if it had been ostensibly directed against them; that Govr. Holmes having the earliest information of their designs, & residing in the immediate vicinity of the encampment, would become informed of the order to Genl. Hampton, and by acting in concert with the commanding officer would under the authority of the order have it in his power to defeat any hostile operations which might be attempted. Still it may be proper that a special instruction to meet the case should be given to the Governor. With the highest respect I have the honor to be yr obedt servt

W EUSTIS

RC (DLC). Docketed by JM.

From Richard Forrest

DEAR & RESPECTED SIR,   CITY OF WASHINGTON Sepr. 14. 1810

The enclosed Bill was left with me a day or two ago by Mr. Whetcroft,[1] with a request that I would forward it to you.

Altho' I took no Copy of the hurried Note I wrote you by the last Mail, I have an impression, that I pushed the idea, of part of the articles brought by the Blanchy being for me, to an extent not fully warranted by circumstances, or by delicacy, neither of which, I would intentionally violate; as I have now every reason to believe that, the whole were exclusively intended for you; and that however strange it may appear, Coln. Lear has sent me nothing altho' I requested him to send me something of every thing that Algiers and the contiguous country could produce. I hope Sir, you will have the goodness to pardon the freedom I have taken; and that you will not consider me as having the smallest claim to any of the articles heretofore enumerated. With the highest respect, I have the honor to be Your Obt. Servt.

RICHD. FORREST

RC (ViU). Enclosure not found.

1. Henry Whetcroft was a notary public in Washington, where he attended St. John's Church, as did JM (*Records of the Columbia Historical Society*, 12 [1909]: 105, 114).

§ From George Joy. *14 September 1810, Gothenburg*. Has sent "copious Communications" to JM and to the secretary of state but vessels carrying them have been delayed by adverse winds. Requests JM to wait for the receipt of his letters before taking any measures or making any appointments relative to this region.

RC (DLC). 1 p.

From William Eustis

SIR,   PORTSMOUTH Septr. 16. 1810.
    I enclose for your amusement a copy of a Letter from J. Q. A. which may be destroyed after perusal. Accounts from the Baltic confirm his anticipation of Danish captures.[1] With perfect respect,

W. EUSTIS

Instructions to Govr. Holmes & the comdg. Officer, are also enclosed[2] if approved, they can be forwarded either to Washington M. T. or to the war office—in the former case the copies are desired at the office.

RC and enclosure (DLC). RC docketed by JM. For surviving enclosure, see n. 2.

1. Eustis evidently enclosed a copy of a letter (not found) he had received from John Quincy Adams, dated 10 May 1810, in which Adams discussed at length the reasons for Danish hostility to American traders in the Baltic (Ford, *Writings of John Quincy Adams*, 3:429–33).

2. Of the instructions and copies forwarded by Eustis, JM retained in his papers instructions (1 p.; in a clerk's hand; marked "Copy") addressed to "Comdg Officer." These instructions enclosed a transcript (not found) of the directions given to Governor Holmes "respecting a combination said to be forming for the purpose of carrying on a Military expedition against a neighbouring Colony." The "Comdg Officer" (either Col. Richard Sparks or Lt. Col. Thomas Cushing) was ordered to cooperate with the Mississippi governor in the event of his needing troops to apprehend "the persons concerned in And carrying on the said expedition; or who may be otherwise Acting in violation of the laws."

§ From George Joy. *16 September 1810, Gothenburg.* Has not yet had an answer from Saabye to the enclosure. Reports that he has been mortified by rumors "that Mr. Joy had no authority and could therefore be of no use" in protecting American ships in the Baltic. Discusses the methods of determining commissions paid by mercantile houses and the reasons for his preference of another Copenhagen firm over Saabye's. Stresses the importance of JM's appointing a competent consul at Gothenburg to support his efforts.

RC and enclosures, two copies (DLC). RC 17 pp. Enclosures are copies of Joy to Hans R. Saabye, 22 Aug. 1810 (8 pp.), and a covering letter from Joy to Saabye, 1 Sept. 1810 (2 pp.).

§ From "The Old Traveller." *16 September 1810, Harrisburg, Pennsylvania.* Refers to a letter [not found] he mailed to JM on 16 Dec. 1809 and a pamphlet sent on 31 May. Now encloses a copy of the Last Judgment and proclaims the end of the world in October 1810. Urges JM to publish the judgment in the *National Intelligencer.*

RC and enclosure (CSmH). RC 2 pp. Enclosure 8 pp.

From Albert Gallatin

DEAR SIR   NEW YORK 17th Septer. 1810

I have received the papers for Mr Poinsett and delivered them to him. We have found a vessel which will sail for Rio Janeiro in two or three weeks; it is the only one bound to Brasils & there is none for La Plata even if it was advisable to go directly there. Every circumstance corroborates the opinion that England will try to govern the Spanish colonies through a nominal Spanish regency, and will for that purpose keep up a war in some one corner of Spain, and oppose revolutionary movements in the colonies. I think also that she will attempt to take possession of Cuba where the Spanish regency may if necessary be removed. The English interest and prejudices against us arising from that source will therefore be the principal obstacles to our views in that quarter. These being merely commercial and both on that account & from political motives opposed to an undue British ascendancy, we may expect new sources of collision. Florida & Cuba are by far the most important objects & will require some immediate decision. In relation to the last might not Erving be sent to Havannah? which has an immediate connection with Florida, & may become a central point of communication both for Mexico and the Caracas coast?

I expect to set off this day week for Washington where I presume you intend to be about the beginning of October. With great respect Your obedt. Servt.

ALBERT GALLATIN

RC (DLC).

From Paul Hamilton

DEAR SIR   WASHINGTON Septr. 20th. 1810

I have the honor of forwarding to you the copy of Mr. Erving's letter which you directed Mr. Smith[1] to return to you, through me, after perusal. The information given by Mr. Erving in this paper, combined with what I have derived from other documents having reference to the transactions in the Floridas, tends very much to strengthen an opinion which I have held that, at no distant day, those countries would prove to be a source of occurrences very interesting to the United States. I think, Sir, that our Government will soon be called to the exercise of much circumspection and no little firmness. I anticipate an increase of your cares and responsibility, but I entertain not a doubt that the result will be an augmentation of public appropation [sic] of, and confidence in your measures. I might say much more on this subject but I will defer other remarks.

I have some matters which I might communicate to you, as bound to do on the score of duty, but as I think your retirement aught to be as much a season of relaxation as the substantial interests of the State will permit, and as they can be postponed without disadvantage I shall not, now, offer them to your consideration.

In your letter to Mr. Smith, which he sent with the enclosed, you speak of your return to this city but do not mention a day—permit me, therefore, to intreat that, unless you are imperiously called by public considerations you will not come here before the middle of next month: for, it is a truth that Washington is, at this moment, very sickly with fevers of a bilious type and of obstinate character. One of the physicians confessed to me yesterday that he had 14 cases in hand, 5 of which had arisen in the course of the day. The citizens, generally, oppose and controvert the idea of unhealthiness, but in doing so only manifest to one who is only a So-journer, but not the less an Observer, their partialities or prejudices. I am counting on the agitation which an equinoctial gale may produce, and if it is strong, we shall have a regenerated atmosphere and fever may cease, but the solid dependance is, in my judgment, on the commencement of cold weather—previously to which, if you come here (I do not mean actual frost) your change will be trying to you and Mrs. Madison. Excuse my freedom I pray you.

The deaths I have witnessed, and the knowledge of the general prevalence of fever have induced me to remain with my family. Had I gone abroad, I would have directed my course so as to avail myself of your hospitality, and next, to have commenced an acquaintance with Mr. Jefferson, in both which I had promised myself much happiness, but a due attention to my family and my own peace of mind have deprived me of this great promised gratification. At some other time I may be more fortunate.

I hope that you and Mrs. Madison enjoy health, of which and every other comfort, my family unite with me in wishing a long continuance to you both. Mrs. Hamilton and my children have, as yet, escaped fever but we are only on today relieved in our apprehensions as to our most useful servant who has been seriously attacked by it. Accept I pray you, Sir, the assurance that with the utmost regard and attachment I am yrs

PAUL HAMILTON

RC (DLC).

1. See JM to Robert Smith, 12 Sept. 1810, and n. 2.

From Lafayette

MY DEAR SIR   PARIS 20h 7ber 1810

Your Letters Sent By Mr. david parish are the Last I Have Received. He Has kept the patents to deliver them Himself at the end of this Month. Three Vessels Have Since Arrived With Government dispatches. They Contained Nothing for me So that I am without An Answer to my Long triplicates By the San Sebastian Ship, By Count palhen, and by Captain Fenwick. A Letter from this Last, Very Carefully Brought By Lieutenant Miller, Has Since, By a Mistake not Attributable to Him, Been forwarded to me Under a Bad direction. I now am in Quest of it.

While I most Affectionately thank You, My Excellent friend, for Your Constant Attention to My Concerns, I Beg You Will Have the Goodness to provide a line for me By Every Government packet You Are Sending.

The Means of Conveyance that Are not official Remain Exposed to dangers from all Quarters.

I Will not take Your time With political intelligence in a letter of which Gnl. Armstrong is the Bearer. The little I Might Have to Say Had Better Be directed to Him Untill He Sails. He Will inform You of Some Communications Between me and the New prince of Sweden[1] whom I ever Have Heard What I Could Wish Him to Be With Respect to America, and Who Now is desirous to Evince those Sentiments By Every Good office in His power. All diplomatic Measures to Sweden Will Be gladly Reciprocated. Your insisting Here on the freedom of Neutral trade in the North Will the More Help Him as His Situation With Respect to the powerful Ally is of Course Very dependant.

The Repeal of the Milan and Berlin decrees and Some posterior Communications Relative to indemnities Have Amended the State of things on this Side of the Channel. But the British Answer to Mr. pinkney Calls for the Nonintercourse which Has Been Announced. The Execution of that Engagement With Both Belligerent[s] is Eagerly Expected By the one Who Has Repealed His Acts. I Had flattered myself that Great Britain Would Have followed the Example.

Permit me to inclose a Note Relative to Chl Ternant Whose Services in the Continental army and Good dispositions as a french Minister are known to You. It Seems to me the testimony of Satisfaction may Be Considered as legally Given When officially promised and is not impeded By the Subsequent law. If You think So, my dear Sir, Will you please to take Up the forgotten Business.[2]

Of my own affairs I Can Say Nothing in Addition to What I Have So fully writen. It should only distress You Without Relieving me, as I know You are in no Need of further intrusions on Your time so do Whatever You Can to forward the Locations, titles, documents, and to proportionate them to a Situation which, with the Apologising Circumstances, is perfectly known to You. I Have informed You M. La Bouchere Has Expressed the Opinion Nothing Could now Be done in Europe on American lands. I Have Some Hopes of M. david parish.

Gnl. Armstrong Will tell You How Much tempted I Have Been to Go over With Him. But independant of the danger of Capture at Sea, it Has Been the Unanimous opinion of people Well Acquainted With Situations and tempers, that No form of passport or Verbal Engagement Could insure a Return.

I am Happy to think General Armstrong takes over with Him a Somewhat Better Result of His patriotic and Enlightened exertions than Could Have Been Carried Two months Ago, and I Hope this Government May Now keep the Good Road. An Additional Motive for Hope should I think

Be found in the interest to Encourage the total independance of the Spanish American States.

Be pleased to present My thankful Compliments to Mr. Smith, Mr. Gallatin, and to Remember me to all friends. I Would Have Been Very Happy in the Opportunity to offer My Respects to Mrs. Madison. Receive the Expressions of the Respectful affection Which forever devote to You Your Grateful friend

LAFAYETTE

RC (PHi). Cover marked by Lafayette, "favour'd by Gnl. Armstrong." Docketed by JM. Enclosure not found.

1. Jean-Baptiste Bernadotte had been elected crown prince of Sweden on 20 Aug. 1810.

2. Jean-Baptiste, chevalier de Ternant, formerly French minister to the U.S., 1791–93, had been awarded a claim of $9,754.68 in December 1793 in recognition of his services during the Revolutionary War. Since the law provided for payment of the principal in the U.S. and the interest in Paris, it is possible that Ternant, who did not return to France at the end of his diplomatic service, had still to receive part of his claim (Syrett and Cooke, *Papers of Hamilton*, 12:371–74, 15:535).

§ From James Cole Mountflorence. *20 September 1810, Paris*. Solicits appointment as consul at Paris and agent for prize cases. Provides a résumé of his career and public services.

RC, four copies (DNA: RG 59, LAR, 1809–17, filed under "Mountflorence"). 3 pp. Three copies in a clerk's hand; dated September 1810.

From John Graham

DEAR SIR   DEPT OF STATE 21st Sepr 1810.

I have the Honor to forward to you by this Mail a copy of a Letter received yesterday from Mr Robertson,[1] and also copies of a letter from[2] Mr Pinkney and its inclosures. The originals have all been sent to the Secretary of State. I retained for you the Quarterly Review and Cobbets Register, which came with Mr Pinkneys Letter. You will receive them by the Mail which takes this.

I was very happy to hear that the money you directed me to send you got safe to hand—and felt myself much flattered by your leaving open for my perusal Mr Erwings communication. The Secretary of State writes that he will be here on Monday with his Family and I hope that we shall soon have the pleasure of seeing Mrs Madison and yourself in the city. I apprehend however that there might be some risque as to Health, if you came here fro⟨m⟩ the Mountains, before the Equinoctial Gales and a good Frost had purified our atmosphere. With the most Sincere & Respectful attachment I have the Honor to be, Sir Your Most Hble Sert

JOHN GRAHAM

RC and first enclosure (DLC); second enclosure (DLC: Rives Collection, Madison Papers). RC docketed by JM, with his pencil notation, "To be left at Montpelier." For enclosures, see nn. 1 and 2.

1. Graham forwarded a copy (2 pp.) in his own hand of a letter from Thomas B. Robertson to Robert Smith, 26 Aug. 1810, which in turn had enclosed a copy of an address from the representatives of the people of Baton Rouge to Don Carlos Dehault Delassus. Graham added a note on his copy of Robertson's letter: "The President will see the address mentioned in this Letter, in the New[s]Paper which accompanies it" (not found). The address, dated 15 Aug. 1810, had first appeared in the Natchez *Weekly Chronicle* and was reprinted in the *National Intelligencer* on 24 Sept. 1810. It requested Delassus to redress a number of American grievances against Spanish rule in West Florida but more particularly insisted that he accept the work of the recent convention at St. Johns Plains in providing for the government of the region as well as permit the militia to arm "as a measure of necessary precaution." Robertson quoted from a letter accompanying the address to the effect that Delassus was unlikely to take any action without consulting "higher authority," that the English-born settlers in West Florida were the "cheif obstacle" to "measures leading to Independence," and that unless the president of the U.S. "shewed some disposition to countenance [measures leading to independence], a Messenger would be sent to England to propose an alliance with that Government" (see Carter, *Territorial Papers, Orleans,* 9:896–98).

2. JM placed an asterisk here at a later time and wrote in the margin "*See P. files." The enclosure was Graham's copy (3 pp.; docketed by JM) of Pinkney's 23 July 1810 dispatch to Robert Smith, reporting that Lord Wellesley was delaying the fulfillment of their agreement reached on 6 July (see Graham to JM, 29 Aug. 1810, n. 2). Graham also included clerks' copies of Pinkney's letter to Wellesley, 7 July 1810 (1 p.), requesting a statement of the latter's intentions about a replacement for Francis James Jackson, and Wellesley's "private" letter of reply, dated 22 July 1810 (1 p.), declaring that "it may be difficult" to enter into a discussion of Pinkney's request "in any official form."

From John Graham

DEPT OF STATE 21st Sepr. [1810] 3 Oclock

J Graham has the Honor to inform the President that a Letter has this Moment been received from Mr Pinkney dated 31st July—to say that the Bills in favor of Brown for £8,400 Stg had been paid. The Baring's have received the Money on account of the UStates. Mr P. gives no news of any kind.

Mr Maury writes under date 10th Augt that American Produce was very abundant at Liverpool and falling in price. Since the 14th of July no impressments had taken place at Liverpool.

RC (DLC). Docketed by JM.

From Elbridge Gerry

The death of Judge Cushing,[1] having produced a vacancy which must soon be filled, the general expectation in this quarter, I find is, that George Blake Esqr will be his successor. It is grounded, On the professional character of that Gentleman, which is supposed to be paramount to that of any person in this State, who can be a candidate for that office; On ten years practice in the federal Courts, as district attorney, by which he has a more thorough knowledge of the duties of the office, than any other practising lawyer in the State; And on the pointed opposition of the Anglo-federal party to him, resulting, as well from the strenuous & successful support which he has officially & uniformly given to the federal laws & administration, as from his firmness & decision on all great republican points & measures. These are the grounds of the public expectation, in regard to the promotion of Mr Blake; in addition to which, as your Excellency in making your decision, will be naturally desirous of all the information which can be obtained on the subject, I think it will be useful to add, That as a Statesman Mr Blake appears to me, on the one hand, bold, firm, & decisive, and on the other, candid, just, & liberal—always attentive to great, important, & essential points; but regardless of such as are trifling, & of little or no consequence . . .[2] We have in this State, several leading republican characters, of a contrary description; & the republican cause has heretofore suffered, & is now more in danger, from their strenuous & overzealous exertions in small affairs, than from the combined efforts of the federalists. These will probably be in favor of some of their own persuasion, but if the experiment should be made, I have no doubt of an unfortunate result, both in regard to the bench itself, & the republican character; for in these respects, Mr Blake's conduct will be most approved, by moderate men of both parties. I shall only add, that Mr Blake having lately married a very fine woman, is become a remarkable domestic character; well suited to the attentions, & studies of a Judge.[3]

I have now to touch on a point of a more delicate nature. James Trecothick Austin Esqr,[4] my son in law, is so high in the estimation of the public, of the bench, & of the bar, as to have had double the interest in recommendations to the office of Attorney General for this Common-Wealth, of all the other candidates for the office. And I do not hesitate, to declare to you, Sir, as I did to my Council, that my knowledge of his abilities, industry, & accomplishments, as a Scholar & as a Lawyer, Of his high public estimation & influence, as a firm & uniform republican Statesman, And of his pure, unspotted, & unimpeachable moral & social character, was such, as that I should certainly have nominated him to that office, as the most promising Candidate; had he stood in no personal relation to me. If then the office of district Attorney should be vacant, his appointment to it, would in my opinion, not only give generally to the public, but also to the federal executive, to the federal Judges & to the bar in general, the highest satisfaction. Mr Blake & he are united in their politicks, & his conduct in arguing causes, like Mr Blakes, has been entirely free from those political inuendoes & suggestions, which serve always to irritate parties, but never to promote a private cause, or public measures.

It is due to the delicacy of both Mr Blake & Mr Austin, to inform your Excellency, that I write this voluntarily, without their knowledge; and altho as it respects the latter, I have the natural propensity of a friend, yet I have no hesitation on the coolest reflection, to confirm what I have stated of both; convinced as I am, that more may be said in favor of each, with candor, truth, & Justice. I have the Honor to remain Sir, very sincerely, Your Excellency's friend, & with the highest esteem & respect Your obedt Servt

E GERRY.

RC (DLC). Cover marked "Confidential" by Gerry. Docketed by JM.

1. Associate Supreme Court Justice William Cushing died on 13 Sept. 1810.

2. Gerry's ellipsis points.

3. On 22 Sept. 1810 Henry Wheaton wrote to JM from Providence, also recommending George Blake for the Supreme Court vacancy (DNA: RG 59, LAR, 1809–17).

4. James Trecothick Austin had married Catherine Gerry in 1806 and had been appointed attorney for Suffolk County, Massachusetts, in 1807. JM did not give him an appointment until he nominated him as agent for the U.S. under article 4 of the Treaty of Ghent in April 1816 (*Senate Exec. Proceedings*, 3:42–43).

§ From Friedrich Wilhelm Heinrich Alexander von Humboldt. *23 September 1810, Paris.* Recalls JM's kindness during his visit to Washington in 1804 and makes him a gift of his geographical studies of Mexico.[1] The bearer of the letter, Mr. Warden, is greatly liked in Paris, and he has comforted Humboldt with the assurance that JM has not forgotten him.

RC (DLC). 3 pp. In French. For a translation, see Helmut de Terra, "Alexander Von Humboldt's Correspondence with Jefferson, Madison, and Gallatin," *Proceedings of the American Philosophical Society*, 103 (1959): 798.

1. Since Humboldt wrote a similar letter to Jefferson at this time offering him the fourth and fifth parts of his work on Mexico, it is likely that JM received the same sections of Humboldt's *Essai sur la Royaume de la Nouvelle-Espagne*. This work was published in installments in Paris between 1808 and 1813, and it formed part of Humboldt's magnum opus, *Voyage de Humboldt et Bonpland* (see Sowerby, *Catalogue of Jefferson's Library*, 4:290–92).

From John Vaughan

DEAR SIR   PHILAD: 24 Sep. 1810

Mr Thomas Cooper having communicated to me the active part taken by you to assist him, thro' Mr Warden, in procuring some publications from France, which May be made useful to this Country, has at the same time requested me to inform you, that I am ready at any time & in any mode which can be pointed out be ready to transmit the sum of 100$ for this Object—or to pay at sight, the Amount of the things when ascertained which he observes cannot exceed this Sum.

Mr Frederick Kinloch, son of Mr Francis Kinloch with whom you was acquainted—being on his way to Va. wished to have the opportunity of an introduction to you, as the much respected friend of his father. I took the liberty of giving him a line[1] & hope he was gratified by meeting with you. I remain D Sir Your friend &c

JN VAUGHAN

If adressed to my Care Philada
   Henry Galen N York
   Hugh Thompson Baltimore
The necessary attention will be paid at the Customhouse—Mr Warden in his letter Stating the *Cost*.

RC (DLC). Docketed by JM.

1. Letter not found.

§ From Anthony Charles Cazenove. *24 September 1810, Alexandria.* Informs JM of the arrival of the brig *Columbia* from Madeira with wine for JM and a draft to be paid to Messrs. Murdoch. Requests JM to accept and return the draft and to give him instructions for the delivery of the wine.

RC (DLC). 1 p. Docketed by JM.

§ From William W. Irwin and Ethan Allen Brown.[1] *24 September 1810, Marietta.* Recommends Thomas Scott, presently chief judge of the Ohio Supreme Court, to replace Lewis Cass as U.S. marshal in the event of Cass's being appointed to replace William Creighton as U.S. attorney.

RC (DNA: RG 59, LAR, 1809–17, filed under "Scott"). 2 pp.

1. William W. Irwin and Ethan Allen Brown were both judges of the Ohio Supreme Court. Scott later informed JM that he did not wish to be appointed U.S. marshal and recommended Jessup N. Couch instead (Scott to JM, 16 Oct. 1810 [ibid.]).

§ From Constant Taber and Others. *24 September 1810, Newport.* Recommends

Asher Robbins of Newport to fill Supreme Court vacancy created by the death of William Cushing.

RC (DNA: RG 59, LAR, 1809–17, filed under "Robbins"). 2 pp. Signed by Taber and four others.

From Paul Hamilton

DEAR SIR   CITY OF WASHINGTON September 25th. 1810
   I do myself the pleasure of enclosing to you a paper received this day from New York, the contents of which are very important, and as such, will speak for themselves.[1] I yield to my wishes when I believe that the information may be relied on, and venture to offer to you my congratulations on this dawn of returning justice on the part of the Belligerents of Europe towards us. If this paper states facts, and Britain follows the good example, our course will be plain and easy as to governmental affairs: while the tide of prosperity (considering the produce of the present year in our Country) will flow on individuals beyond any former example.
   The best wishes and most respectful salutations of my family, conjoint with my own, are offered to you and Mrs. Madison; and I beg you to believe that with the most friendly attachment and respectful devotion I am yrs

PAUL HAMILTON

RC (DLC). Enclosure not found, but see n. 1.

1. On 24 Sept. several New York newspapers published the news of the repeal of the Berlin and Milan decrees as announced in the letter of 5 Aug. from the duc de Cadore to John Armstrong. The full text of the letter appeared in the N.Y. *Columbian*, along with a report that Great Britain would shortly repeal the orders in council and appoint a new minister to Washington.

¶ To George W. Erving. Letter not found. *25 September 1810*. Acknowledged in Erving to JM, 20 Oct. 1810. Discusses Spanish-American affairs and the policies of Great Britain toward Spain's colonies.

From the Chiefs of the Northwestern Indians

COUNCIL FIRE AT BROWNSTOWN September the 26th. 1810.
TO OUR GREAT FATHER OF THE SEVENTEEN FIRES
   Open your ears and listen to your children.

FATHER.

We have lighted up our co[u]ncil fire at this place, and we are happy to inform you, that no smoke has arisen, to obstruct the light.

FATHER—

That you may know what we have done, we enclose copies of speechs, which we have sent, to our Shawonee Brethren, resideing near the Wabash, and to the several Nations we represent.[1]

FATHER—

Your Cheif Governor Hull has furnished us with tobacco to smoke and provisions to eat dureing our Councils. He has likewise attended at our own request with a number of your Cheifs, our Council, and afforded us all the assistance in his power.

FATHER—

We hope our young Brethren the Shawonees will give you no more trouble. We are all determined, that they shall not in future interfere with the concerns of the other Nations.

FATHER—

We salute you in friendship and assure you, it is our determination to live in peace with one another, and with all our white Brethren, as long as water runs, and the trees grow.

FATHER.

Our relation to you is such, that both duty and Interest dictate the propriety of liveing in friendship with you. We have a confidence in your goodness, and a firm beleif, you will do all in your power to improve our condition.

FATHER LISTEN—

The general Council fire for all the Nations north west of the River Ohio, has long been established at this place. Here it burns clear, we wish it may be continued here. Our elder Brethren the Wyondots have the immediate care of it. We all wish, and we hope, Father you wish for their accomodation. The seventeen fires have assigned to this nation five thousand Acres of land at this place and Maguago[2] a few miles above. Between the two Villages is a small bed of land, lying on Detroit River, on which our Wyondot Brethren have made improvements. We hope Father they will not be disturbed, but that the seventeen fires will grant to them this land, so as to join their villages, and as far back as will be necessary for their convenience, and one mile on Lake Erie west of River Huron. All the Nations Join in this request, and hope the seventeen fires will listen and grant it.

FATHER.

We now in the presence of Governor Hull, whom you have appointed to superintend our affairs, and under the direction of the great Spirit, with pure and white hearts, renew all the treaties of friendship which the sev-

their accomodation – The seventeen fires have assigned
to this nation five thousand Acres of land at this place
place and Maguago a few miles above – Between the
two Villages is a small bed of land, lying on Detroit
River, on which our Wyondot Brethren have made
improvements – we hope Father they will not be
disturbed, but that the seventeen fires will grant to
them this land, so as to join their villages, and as far
back as will be necessary for their convenience, and
one mile on Lake Erie west of River Huron.
All the Nations join in this request, and hope the seventeen fires will listen and grant it. –

    Father. –

        We now in the presence of Governor
Hull, whom you have appointed to superintend our
affairs, and under the direction of the great Spirit, with
pure and white hearts, renew all the treaties of friendship
which the several Nations, we represent have entered into
with the Seventeen Fires, and on the part of the Seventeen
fires your Commissioner has promised, and renewed the
Obligations of protection, stipulated in those treaties – we
take you by the hand, and pledge to you the friendship
of all our Nations. –   In testimony whereof, we have
signed these presents in behalf of our respective Nations.

               miera. or Walk-in-the-water.

        The Crane – … Two Chiefs of the
             Wyondots – – – – – – – –

Signatures on letter to JM from chiefs of the Northwestern Indians, 26 Sept. 1810 (DNA: RG 107, LRRS, H-214:5). Diamond-shaped pieces of paper were applied at some later time to cover drops of sealing wax next to each signature.

eral Nations, we represent have entered into with the Seventeen Fires, and on the part of the Seventeen fires your Commissioner has promised and renewed the Obligations of protection, stipulated in those treaties. We take you by the hand, and pledge to you the friendship of all our Nations. In testimony whereof, we have signed these presents in behalf of our respective Nations.

Miera. or Walk-in-the-water.

The Crane—First Cheifs of the Wyandots

Shawnoese

GEORGE BLUEJACKET. wrote his own name.

Logan.

In behalf of the Six Nations.

Red Jacket

Young King

Tuequidhah

Tontowgona, or the dog, an Ottawa Cheif

Machonee, or little Bear a Chippewa Cheif

Nawast, an Ottawa Cheif—

Tisquawan or Mc.Carty, an Ottawa Cheif—

Ninnematiques or little Thunder a Chippewa Chief.

All lo-hawta ⎫
              ⎬ Munsee Chiefs
Hindrich   ⎭

Mushshelman paw a Delaware Cheif

Signed in presence of the subscribing Witnesses.
JACOB VISGER
DANIEL CURTIS
SAMUEL SANDERS
W KNAGGS

RC and enclosures (DNA: RG 107, LRRS, H-214:5). For pictographic signatures of Indian chiefs, see illustration. For enclosures, see n. 1.

1. The enclosures, "To Our Brethren of the Several Nations We Represent" (3 pp.) and "To Our Younger Brethren the Shawanese" (3 pp.), were included in William Hull to Eustis,

4 Oct. 1810 (ibid.), which described the proceedings of "a very general council of the northern Indians" held at Brownstown, Michigan Territory, on 24 Sept. 1810.

2. Maguago was a Wyandot village situated opposite Grosse Island in the Detroit River,
between Brownstown and River Rouge (Cappon et al., *Atlas of Early American History*, p. 21).

From John Graham

DEPT OF STATE 26th Sepr 1810.

J Graham has the Honor, by direction of the Secretary of State, to forward to the President the inclosed Letter from General Armstrong and to
inform him that it is the same which he lately sent to this Department
unopened.[1]

RC (DLC).

1. Graham probably forwarded the original of Armstrong's 5 May 1810 dispatch to
Robert Smith (DNA: RG 59, DD, France). A duplicate had reached Washington in August
and had already been sent to JM (see Graham to JM, 13 Aug. 1810, and n. 3).

From Lafayette

MY DEAR SIR   PARIS 26h September 1810
    I Have Had Lately the pleasure to Write By Gnl. Armstrong, But Can-
not let the Homer depart Without Repeating a tender of My Grateful
friendship. My Last did inform You that I Had Received Your kind Letters 18h and 19h May, But that No Answer to My Long triplicate By the
John Adams Had Come to Hand. I Have Since Got the Nine patents
delivered By Mr. parish Himself. The Homer Brought Me a Very oblig-
ing Letter from Captain fenwick, intrusted to Mr. Miller, July 25h. He
Gives me the Louisiana intelligence in His power. He Has a High Opin-
ion of the Unimproved Land at pointe Coupee, from 15 to 30 dollars an
Acre. The Canal Carondelet Business Goes Very Slowly Which I Lament
Both on public Account and for My own Concerns So Much depending
Upon it. But Nothing is Said of the Location Near the City, its Extent,
Situation, present and future Value. Those particulars I Mention to Let
You know the Actual State of My information. I am Sure, My dear friend,
that, Had You Received Mr. duplantier's Answer to Your Letter and
Mine, the Homer Would Have Brought me a Letter from You in the Gov-
ernment dispatches.
    I Have Had only one Conversation With Mr. david parish, the only

Man in Europe who is Likely to take or Manage an Arrangement on My American Lands. I found Him Very friendly disposed, But Not knowing How, Untill the titles and documents are Completed, We Can frame a plan to be Submitted to Your Approbation. I would Be Very Sorry to over Rate the Value of the Lands But think it Will Be proper that the Estimation Comes Up to present Reality and Approaching prospects. We Shall together See My Excellent friend Mr. parker. I fear the Speedy departure of Mr. Miller will not permit me Any longer to Avail Myself of that Opportunity.

You Will find in the public dispatches as Much intelligence as I Might Give. The Verbal one By General Armstrong Cannot fail to Be More Extensive and particular. The Repeal of the decrees of Milan And Berlin, the last letter of M. de Cadore and the Verbal Explanation Given to it are, I am Happy to See, So Many Steps on the Good Road. I Had Expected Great Britain Would follow the Example. But Unless Subsequent Communications to Mr. pinckney are Very different from the Answer Confidentially imparted to me I dont See there Any Sign of a disposition More Yielding than that Which Had Been thought deserving the Nonintercourse Measures.

General Armstrong Will tell You How it Has Been thought We Might Avail ourselves of the Election of a prince Royal of Sweden Whom, Some Years Ago, when He Was on the point to Embark for America, I Had taken Much pleasure to introduce to You.[1] His Respect and Attachment for the United States Have at all times of our friendly intercourse Been Expressed to me. He Cannot But Be a planet in the System of His Omnipotent Ally. But I much depend on His personal dispositions.

It Would Be Very kind to me, My dear Sir, to inform our Excellent and Now Retired friend Jefferson of the Opportunities to let me Hear from Him. All My letters to Monticelo are Unanswered. I Happily Know that He is well. With the Most Affectionate Respect I am Your old Grateful friend

LAFAYETTE

Mr. Russel Will Have the Goodness to put this Letter in His dispatches, through Him, in the Same Way, I Beg You to write.

RC (PHi). Docketed by JM.

1. Lafayette to JM, 31 Mar. 1803 (NjP: Crane Collection).

From Caesar A. Rodney

My Dear Sir,   WILMINGTON Sept 26. 1810.

The enclosed letter, from Captain R. C. Dale was received the day before yesterday.[1] The resignation he speaks of, if I recollect, was put into the hands of some officer of the U. S. army, & when I spoke to the Secretary at war, had not reached the office. His answer was that it should be accepted *when received*. Mr. Dale has been selected as the Democratic candidate for congress, & with a prospect I hope of success.[2] Should this county give 2.800 votes my confidence will be considerable in the result of the state election, as the two Federal counties are divided in some degree; & I should not be surprized if the Republicans succeeded in Kent. Our State election would have been secure, had they not healed the great division in Sussex, by taking up my relation Daniel Rodney as their candidate for Governor.[3] This situation he has been long desirous to obtain, and would have deserted his old friends with a numerous force, had they not gratified his wishes, which I flattered myself they would not have done. The methodists will finally revolutionise this state. Religion alone is equal to the task of thorough reform.

After a severe & long attack of bilious fever in the early part of summer, a person is generally an invalid until frost. With respect to myself, it has been unfortunately the case this season. And in a very infirm state of health I have been afflicted with the loss of my eldest & my favourite son in his fourteenth year. From these scenes of personal calamity I turn my eyes to the more charming prospects of public prosperity which the late news presents. France has at len[g]th yielded to the dictates of justice & interest combined. May England soon follow in her wake. Yours Truly & Affectionately

C. A. RODNEY

RC (DLC). Docketed by JM. For enclosure, see n. 1.

1. In a letter of 22 Sept. 1810 addressed to JM, Dale complained that he had not received "a final & official discharge" from the U.S. Army after resigning his commission from the camp at Terre aux Boeufs. He requested JM to notify him that his resignation was accepted to take effect on 30 Sept. 1810. At the end of the letter JM wrote: "Capt. Dale has been informed, that the rec[e]ipt & acceptance of his resignation will be noted in the War office, as of the date requested" (DNA: RG 107, LRRS, D-75:5; docketed by a War Department clerk as received 4 Oct. 1810).

2. Dale lost the election for the Delaware seat in the House of Representatives to Federalist Henry M. Ridgely by seventeen votes (*National Intelligencer*, 10 Oct. 1810).

3. Republican Joseph Haslet defeated Daniel Rodney by seventy-one votes in the Delaware gubernatorial election (ibid.).

¶ From Robert Smith. Letter not found. *26 September 1810*. Described as a two-page letter in the lists probably made by Peter Force (DLC, series 7, container 2). Also referred to in Smith to JM, 28 Sept. 1810. Concerns the drafting of a proclamation to be issued upon the revocation of the French decrees. Smith probably enclosed as well a letter (not found) from William Harris Crawford of 27 July 1810 (Crawford to Smith, 2 Oct. 1810 [DNA: RG 59, DL]).

From Caesar A. Rodney

My Dear Sir,   Wilmington Sept. 27. 1810.
The enclosed were received by the mail of this day. They contain very ample testimony of Col. Munroe's principles & qualifications. If the fact stated by Mr. Clay, be correct, of which I have not the least doubt, it would furnish a sufficient excuse for selecting a character from Kentucky.[1]
The late Governor Sullivan would have been a suitable person to have succeeded judge Cushing. So is the late Governor Lincoln if his health will admit of it, tho' I have understood he is likely to loose his eye sight. He is a sound lawyer, & what is more an upright honest man. I fear Bidwell has injured himself too much to be thought of. Yours Truly & Affecy.

C. A. Rodney

RC (DLC). For enclosures, see n. 1.

1. Henry Clay had written to Rodney on 15 Sept. 1810 to recommend John Monroe, a judge of the Kentucky Superior Court, for an anticipated vacancy in the office of U.S. attorney in Ohio. Clay admitted that Monroe's Kentucky residence might be an obstacle to his appointment, but he believed Monroe would move to Ohio in the event of his receiving the position. Rodney may have also forwarded a similar letter, dated 15 Sept. 1810, from Thomas Todd on Monroe's behalf (DNA: RG 59, LAR, 1809–17, filed under "Monroe").

From Robert Smith

Sir,   Sep. 28. 1810.
In my last letter I took the liberty of intimating to you that I would by the next Mail forward for your consideration a sketch of a proclamation to be issued upon the revocation of the Fr. Decrees. This was my first idea, formed, indeed, without having considered the subject and under the impression that the same Course would be pursued as was taken in the case of Erskine's arrangement. Upon looking at the act of Congress I find that the proclamation cannot be issued before the 1st. November. Indepen-

dently of other considerations there is this Objection that the restrictions imposed by the Act would cease from the *date* of the proclamation in relation to France while the restrictions imposed by the Fr. decrees in relation to us would not cease until the 1st. November. This, however, is not a desirable Construction as the term of three months allowed to G. Britain to revoke their orders is to be computed from the *date* of the Proclamation.

The result of the Maryld. Elections will be entirely to our satisfaction.[1] Respectfy. Yours

R Smith

RC (DLC: Rives Collection, Madison Papers).

1. Elections for the Maryland state legislature and for the state's congressional delegation were held on 1 Oct. 1810. The Republicans increased their majority in the House of Delegates and won six of the nine seats for the House of Representatives (*National Intelligencer*, 3, 5, and 8 Oct. 1810; Parsons et al., *United States Congressional Districts*, pp. 92–95).

§ From Moses Hoyt. *28 September 1810, New York*. Begs JM's assistance in obtaining his release from imprisonment for debt.

RC (DLC). 2 pp. Docketed by JM.

From John G. Jackson

Sir.   Clarksburg 29th. September 1810

Some of the leading Republicans of Ohio have joined in recommending to you Samuel Herrick Esq of Zanesville to fill the vacancy occasioned by the resignation of Mr. Creighton District Attorney of Ohio.[1] I am personally acquainted with that Gentleman and ask permission to join my opinion with theirs that he is a man of worth & talents & *unquestionable* political principles: And it will afford me pleasure to learn that he has met with your approbation & confidence.

I know Mr. Cass the Marshall[2] who is also recommended to you, & believe that his conversion to republicanism has been too recent & his conduct since too equivocal to be sincere. When I heard of his appointment as Marshall it surprised me, because he has indulged in the most indecent abuse of Mr. Jefferson viz that "he deserved to be hung" &c & has even since he held the office behaved worse than suspiciously. If Mr. Herrick is not appointed I hope the choice will fall on some person beside the other Candidate, for I can assure you that his success will be disgusting to many who have always been firm & ask nothing for themselves or friends so that they may claim the reputation if [*sic*] disinterestedness. To such men the appointment of a federal Gentleman who has been moderate, tho firm will be more acceptable—And knowing this I have thought it incompatible with the friendship I feel for you & your Administration to conceal or withhold these truths.

When I began to write you I intended this letter should be filed as is usual (I believe) in such cases. But although I can substantiate its assertions I do not wish to be placed in a situation to require it—& because I think you know me too well to believe I have a sinister motive to gratify, I presume to request that my letter may be considered as confidential. Your Mo. Obt Servt

J G JACKSON

RC (DLC). Docketed by JM.

1. JM received two testimonials from Zanesville, Ohio, on Herrick's behalf. He nominated Herrick to the position of U.S. attorney for Ohio on 18 Dec. 1810, and the Senate confirmed the nomination the next day (George Jackson and four others to JM, 24 Sept. 1810, John Hamm and nineteen others to JM, 21 Nov. 1810 [DNA: RG 59, LAR, 1809–17, filed under "Herrick"]; *Senate Exec. Proceedings*, 2:157).

2. Jefferson had appointed Lewis Cass as marshal for Ohio in 1807. JM reappointed him for a further four years on 25 Jan. 1811 (*Senate Exec. Proceedings*, 2:54, 163, 164).

§ From Mathew Arnold Hœvel.[1] *29 September 1810, Santiago de Chile.* Informs JM that the people of Chile met in convention on 18 Sept. to take measures to defend the country against threats from abroad and to correct the abuses of the previous regime. They have established a provisional board of government until a congress can meet, and the board is considering opening Chile's ports to neutral commerce. Hitherto American vessels have been mistaken for English and have been seized on that account. Recommends appointing a commercial agent and minister to deal with Chile and offers his services as the only American citizen in the country. Has resided in Chile for five years, is familiar with all parts of the country, and in America he is known to the Livingston family of New York.

RC, three copies (DLC; DNA: RG 59, ML; and DNA: RG 59, LAR, 1809–17, filed under "Havel"); Tr (PHi: Poinsett Papers). RC 3 pp.

1. Mathew Arnold Hœvel, a native of Sweden, was a naturalized American citizen who had first come to Chile in a vessel owned by J. R. Livingston. He was instrumental in establishing a newspaper, the *Aurora*, in Santiago, and on 1 May 1811 Secretary of State James Monroe forwarded a copy of his letter to JM to Joel Roberts Poinsett with the suggestion that Poinsett consider employing Hœvel if appropriate. In 1812 Hœvel received a vice-consular appointment from Poinsett as part of the latter's efforts to persuade José Miguel Carrera and other Chilean leaders to declare their province independent of Spain (Monroe to Poinsett, 1 May 1811 [PHi: Poinsett Papers]; Henry Clay Evans, *Chile and Its Relations with the United States* [Durham, N.C., 1927], pp. 17–18).

¶ From Oliveira & Sons. Letter not found. *29 September 1810.* Mentioned in Oliveira & Sons to JM, 26 Oct. 1810. Informs JM of the arrival of Madeira wine from Lisbon.

To Caesar A. Rodney

DEAR SIR   MONTPELLIER Sepr. 30. 1810

I am just favored with yours of the 26th. & sincerely sympathize with you, in the loss you have sustained.

The new scene opened by the revocation of the F. Decrees, will I hope, terminate in a removal of the embarrassments which have been as afflicting as they have been unexampled. It promises us, at least an extrication from the dilemma, of a mortifying peace, or a war with both the great belligerents. The precise course which G. B. will take, remains to be seen. Whatever the immediate one may be, it is probable that we shall ultimately be at issue with her, on her fictitious blockades.

No official communication of the French Act has yet come to hand; and its precise shape can not be inferred from what has appeared, should the letter to Genl. Armstrong be authentic as it probably is, and accurate in its translation, which it probably may not be. In every view important questions will occur as to the construction of the Act of Congs. & the French revocations, in their mutual bearings on each other. It is an occasion therefore on which your legal counsels will be so particularly desireable, that I flatter myself the restoration of your health will enable you to join us at Washington in time to afford us that advantage. I propose to set out thither on wednesday morning, & expect to be there on Saturday.[1] By that time the other heads of Depts. will probably be all there. The official communications from Genl. A. may of course be hourly looked for; and something also from Mr. P. which may be interesting. Should it be impracticable for you to get to Washington, I must ask the favor of you, as the next best assistance, to consider, & let us have your ideas, on the several points which are likely to come into question, in deliberating on the course to be taken by the Executive, and on the form of a proclamation best adapted to the case.

Will you be so good as to have the inclosed delivered to Capt: Dale.[2] Accept my sincere respects & best wishes

JAMES MADISON

RC (DLC: Thomas and Caesar A. Rodney Papers). Cover dated Orange Court House, 2 Oct. 1810.

1. JM arrived in Washington on Saturday evening, 6 Oct. 1810 (*National Intelligencer*, 8 Oct. 1810).

2. Enclosure not found, but see Rodney to JM, 26 Sept. 1810, n. 1.

From Christopher Ellery

SIR,   PROVIDENCE, R. I. September 30. 1810.

When, the last winter, the late Mr. Cushing, then one of the justices of the supreme court, U. S. left this town on his way to the seat of government, intending there to give in his resignation, I had the honor of writing to you,[1] and of inviting your attention towards the state of Rhode Island; naming from among her citizens a successor. The old gentleman proved too infirm to reach Washington, but his bones having lately been deposited with those of his fathers, and a vacancy thus produced, it has occurred to the minds of many persons here, that, very possibly, in selecting a Judge to fill the place, the President might be inclined to distinguish this state by the appointment, provided that a suitable character should be found in her corps of lawyers for a station so exalted. The claim for distinction as a state is, of course, on the score of favor; to expect which the ground, perhaps, is the failure heretofore in calculations of this sort, and the consequent greater probability of success at the present or on some future occasion: but supposing that a disposition to yeild somewhat to the real or imaginary merits of Rhode Island has an existence in the breast of the President, where is the man worthy of his approbation and the honor of filling the vacant seat in the supreme court? As an answer to this question none better could be offered than the letter of Col. Wheaton, Smith, Coles & myself, addressed to the President a few days since,[2] upon the subject of this letter. It is true that other men might recommend other persons, but it is as true that no names could be of equal weight with those who know men and motives as existing here. However, there are among us, persons, high too in office, who may, if they have not already, propose such characters as David Howel, Esquire; in relation to which it is only necessary to observe, that it is contemplated to forward a remonstrance that shall exhibit him in proper light.[3] Thus far, Sir, I have written without regard to the fact that Mr. Granger will be presented by his friends for the vacant seat on the bench of the supreme court; and that, if preferred, he will reside in the circuit, possibly in this state. Until yesterday no intimation of this came to our ears. It is suggested, also, that an approbation of Mr. Granger, signified from this quarter, might have the tendency to further his advancement. Mr. Granger has for many years stood well with us, but what, now, can we, with propriety, attempt in aid of him. For myself, I am peculiarly and unpleasantly situated. Mr. Robbins is my brother-in-law & friend. My debts of friendship to Mr. Granger can never be paid. Their talents entitle either of them to the elevation where their friends would be happy to place them. The names which, in my estimation, must most weigh, are proffered for Mr. Robbins; yet my intimate acquaintance with these gentlemen enables me to say, that the appointment of Mr. Granger would be agreeable to them and to the people of this state generally; but this is not said to prejudice the appointment of Mr. Robbins.

Obtrusive I must appear to be, but duty & friendship propel; and while acting in obedience to their injunctions my errors cannot be unpardonable: nor am I, how great soever my infirmities, wanting in the most perfect respect for you, Sir; of which I beg leave to offer assurances, and of the devotion with which I am Yr. Mt. Ob. servant

CHRIST. ELLERY

RC (DNA: RG 59, LAR, 1809–17, filed under "Robbins").

1. Ellery to JM, 21 Dec. 1809.

2. Seth Wheaton, Henry Smith, Thomas Coles, and Ellery had signed a letter (in Ellery's hand) to JM on 26 Sept. recommending Asher Robbins for the vacancy on the Supreme Court (DNA: RG 59, LAR, 1809–17). Sometime in September 1810 JM also received a letter signed by Benjamin B. Mumford and six others on behalf of Robbins (ibid.).

3. See Henry Smith and others to JM, 1 Oct. 1810.

¶ To Robert Smith. Letter not found. *Ca. 30 September 1810*. Mentioned in Robert Smith to William Harris Crawford, 2 Oct. 1810 (DNA: RG 59, DL), where Smith informed Crawford that his letter of 27 July (not found) had been sent to the president, who was "perfectly satisfied with the arrangement made by you in the execution of the delicate trust which we took the liberty of committing to your management."

From Henry Smith and Others

SIR,   PROVIDENCE 1rst October 1810.

We are sensible that this intrusion upon your high public cares demands an apology: but trust that it will be found in our sincere zeal for the honour and success of your Administration, and in the importance of the occasion which suggests this Address.

There will probably be several candidates for the office of Judge of the Supreme Court, for the eastern Circuit, vacated by the decease of the late Mr. Cushing. Among others, it has been suggested that David Howell,[1]

District Attorney for this District, aspires to that important station. Although we are not aware that he has received the recommendations of any of the friends of the Administration in this quarter, yet we should be doing violence to our own feelings were we to omit respectfully to tender our advice against his appointment, which we are most firmly convinced would neither promote the credit nor serve the interests of the Government.

If political fidelity & consistency be considered as qualifications for promotion to the honours & emoluments of office, this gentleman's pretentions are light indeed. He has at no period of his public life been remarkable for his political virtue; & the latter part of his career has deprived him of what little merit the public voice allotted him in this respect. He was recommended to the office he now holds by a reputation for talents, of which he has given very unequal proofs, and especially because he was the only gentleman of the bar in this State, who at that time even *proffessed* an attachment to the Administration of your illustrious predecessor— but he pertinaciously supported all the anti-republican measures of Mr. Adam's administration, until Mr. Jefferson was elected; & even since this great change of men & measures, he has alternately supported the friends and foes of the Government in this State, according to the dictates of his caprice, or imaginary views of interest.

In the execution of the official duties incumbent upon him as the District Attorney he has manifested gross incapacity, & been guilty of great misconduct. In support of this allegation we beg leave to refer you to the Treasury department where the evidences of his misconduct & neglect of duty are multiplied & abundant.[2] We do not deem it necessary to state any particular fact, because the fullest information on the subject is already in the hands of the Secretary of the Treasury, who, we have no doubt will entirely confirm the statement we have made. But though it would be superfluous for us to designate any particular instance of this gentleman's official misfeasance, yet we cannot refrain from calling the notice of the President to the surreptitious and highly improper manner in which he procured the appointment of Mr. Ebenezer Knight Dexter, his son in law, to the office of Marshal of this District;[3] an appointment which we are confident would never have been made had the near relationship of the parties been known to the executive. Mr. Dexter was recommended entirely without the knowledge, and contrary to the wishes of nearly all the influential friends of the Administration in this State; but we are at no loss to determine what share Mr. Howell partook in his recommendation.

To conclude, Sir; we are confident that the elevation of Mr. Howell to the high station in question would be so far from gratifying the friends of the Government, or the public generally in this quarter, that it would afford them much more satisfaction to see him removed from the office he now occupies.

We beg you, Sir, to be assured that nothing but the most imperious and pressing sense of duty would have compelled us to this painful disclosure of the real pretensions of a man, over whose imperfections we would willingly have drawn the viel [*sic*] of charity. Our confidence that the purity of the motives which dictate it will be duly appreciated by your candour, is the consolation upon which we rely in support of the step we have taken. We have the honour to be with sentiments of respect your fellow citizens

HENRY SMITH

[and four others]

RC (DNA: RG 59, LAR, 1809–17, filed under "Howell"). In the hand of Seth Wheaton and signed by Smith, Thomas Coles, Christopher Ellery, and Levin and Seth Wheaton.

1. David Howell (1747–1824), born in New Jersey and graduated from Princeton in 1766, had several careers in law, politics, and education. He taught at Rhode Island College (later Brown University), sat in the Continental Congress, 1782–85, and since 1801 had been serving as U.S. district attorney for Rhode Island. In November 1812 JM nominated him to be judge of the district court of Rhode Island (McLachlan, *Princetonians, 1748–1768*, pp. 562–67; *Senate Exec. Proceedings*, 2:303).

2. Thomas Coles was collector at Providence, Rhode Island, and Christopher Ellery's uncle, William, held the same post at Newport. Their correspondence with the Treasury Department frequently included accounts of their dealings with Howell in his capacity as district attorney. Christopher Ellery himself was later to complain that Howell had used improper influence to secure the election of his son, Jeremiah B. Howell, to the U.S. Senate in 1810 at the expense of Henry Smith (see Christopher Ellery to Gallatin, 20 Nov. 1810, reproduced in *Papers of Gallatin* [microfilm ed.], reel 21).

3. JM had appointed Dexter to this position on 17 Apr. 1810. He reappointed him to the post in 1814 (*Senate Exec. Proceedings*, 2:146, 513).

§ From Daniel Eccleston. *1 October 1810, Lancaster*. Acknowledges JM's letter of 18 July 1810 and states that he shares his opinions about General Washington.

RC (DLC). 1 p.

§ From Richard Brent. *2 October 1810, Fauquier Court House, Virginia*. Had intended to visit JM at Montpelier during the summer but was twice prevented from doing so by "some untoward circumstance." Has received a letter from Thomas Jones, son of Walter Jones, who resides in the Mississippi Territory and who wishes to be considered for territorial secretary in the event that the office becomes vacant. Admits Jones has at times been accused of "dissipation" but believes he has entirely gotten over the failing.

RC (DNA: RG 59, LAR, 1809–17, filed under "Jones"). 2 pp. Brent misdated the letter "Sepr the 2d. 1810." Cover dated "Fauqr Ch 2d Octr."

¶ To Richard Forrest. Letter not found. *Ca. 2 October 1810.* Mentioned in Forrest to JM, 6 Oct. 1810. Gives instructions for the purchase of merino sheep.

From William Pinkney

private

DEAR SIR   LONDON. 3. Octr. 1810

I thought it possible that the Hornet would touch at Cowes—although I gave no order to that Effect. But I did not expect that Mr. Spence wd. come up to Town, or that the Brig wd. be detained a Moment.

My Despatches were sent to Mr Auldjo[1]—to be delivered with the least possible Delay to Mr Spence on Board in Case Circumstances should render it proper for the Brig to call. Mr Spence, however, left the Brig before she reached Cowes and thus has come unnecessarily (though with the best Intentions) to London.

I feel particularly anxious that Captain Hunt's Conduct on this occasion & that of Mr Spence should not be disapproved—for though I gave no precise order that the Brig shd. come to Cowes I certainly wished it if it should happen to suit—& Captn. Hunt knew that I wished it—& has I am sure acted upon that Wish & with a sincere View to the Good of the public Service.[2] I have heard nothing further of the Appointment of a Minister pleny. to the U.S. Nothing further of the Case of the Chesapeake! Ld Wellesley is a surprizing Man!

As I think it important to send Mr Spence off immediately I will only add the assurances of my Respect & Attachment

WM PINKNEY

RC (DLC: Rives Collection, Madison Papers). Docketed by JM.

1. Thomas Auldjo had been U.S. consul at Cowes since 1790.
2. Pinkney's concern that he had delayed the *Hornet* probably resulted from his belief that the vessel was bearing news from France about the repeal of the Berlin and Milan decrees (see Brant, *Madison*, 5:220).

From Elbridge Gerry

DEAR SIR,   CAMBRIDGE 4th Octr 1810

On the 22d of Sepr last, I had the honor of addressing you a letter, on the subject of a candidate to supply the vacancy, caused by the death of Judge Cushing; & also of one for the office of district attorney, if that should be vacant by the promotion of the present incumbent. Being then in haste, I had omitted to mention, that my Son in law, by the appointment of Governor Sullivan, had filled the office of Attorney for the Common Wealth about two years, within the County of Suffolk, which includes Boston; at the end of which period, the office, under Governor Gores administration was abolished: & that during this time, he commenced & finished, upwards of four hundred indictments, in his office of Attorney for the State. I also omitted to enclose a letter addressed to me by Judge Dawes, formerly one of our supreme Judges, an office which he resigned for that which he now fills. The Judge is a high federalist, & knowing or presuming that a republican would be nominated to fill the office of attorney general, made vacant by the absconding of Mr Bidwell, he volunteered in behalf of my son Austin, & wrote the letter enclosed. I have the Honor to remain with every sentiment of the highest esteem & respect Your Excellency's obedt Sert

E GERRY

RC and enclosure (DNA: RG 59, LAR, 1809–17). RC misfiled under "Rustin, James T." Enclosure (1 p.; filed under "Austin, James T.") is Thomas Dawes to Gerry, 30 Aug. 1810.

§ From William Rogers.[1] *4 October 1810, Philadelphia.* Introduces the Reverend Dr. Thomas Baldwin, currently chaplain to the Massachusetts House of Representatives.[2] Baldwin wishes an interview with JM, and Rogers has "taken the liberty from my personal knowledge of the President & the general Satisfaction which his administration affords, to recommend Dr. & Miss Baldwin to your and Mrs. Madison's affectionate attention."

RC (DLC). 2 pp. Docketed by JM.

1. William Rogers (1751–1824) was born in Newport, Rhode Island, but moved to Philadelphia where, in 1772, he was ordained as a Baptist minister. He served as a chaplain for the Continental army during the American Revolution, and in 1789 he was appointed professor of oratory and English at the College and Academy of Philadelphia. He also held the same position at the University of Pennsylvania, 1792–1812 (William B. Sprague, *Annals of the American Pulpit* [1857–69; 9 vols.; New York, 1969 reprint], 6:145–47).

2. Thomas Baldwin (1753–1826) was born in Connecticut and in the 1780s had served as an itinerant Baptist preacher throughout New Hampshire and Vermont. In 1790 he accepted a call to the ministry of the Second Baptist Church in Boston where he became one of the most prominent and prolific Baptist leaders in New England. He was the author of more than forty tracts and sermons as well as being the editor of the *Massachusetts Baptist Missionary Magazine*. In 1810 he published his most important theological work, *A Series of Letters. In Which the Distinguishing Sentiments of the Baptists Are Explained and Vindicated*, in defense of the practice of adult immersion (ibid., 6:208–13).

From Benjamin Henry Latrobe

Sir,   Washington Octr. 5h. 1810

I have been unfortunate in the construction of the fireproof. Depending on the old Walls, which ought to have been amply sufficient to carry the light Vault I placed upon them, had they been tolerably well built, I lowered the center. Finding that the arch settled I examined the Walls, & perceived that they were ⟨much⟩[1] cracked; but it appearing that the cracks were not new, being very black, the center was further lowered. The arch continuing however to settle I ordered it, during a few days visit which I paid in Virginia, to be taken down. The Walls continued to open as long as it stood, & tho' the Arch itself was perfectly firm, prudence demanded that it should be removed. In this state the place remains. I hasten to state to you the facts, lest they should come to you misrepresented, or exagerated. On Monday I will wait upon you, after your first engagements shall be over. With high respect I am Your obedt &c

                                        B H Latrobe.

RC (DLC); letterbook copy (MdHi). RC damaged by tear.

1. Word supplied from letterbook copy.

§ From Gideon Gardner. *5 October 1810, Nantucket.* Urges the appointment of Gideon Granger to the Supreme Court.

RC (DNA: RG 59, LAR, 1809–17, filed under "Granger"). 1 p. Gideon Gardner was a Republican representative from Massachusetts in the Eleventh Congress.

§ From David Gelston. *5 October 1810, New York.* Encloses a copy of a bill from London for the expenses—"£2.13.2 Sterlg is $11.01"—for a pipe of brandy. Will remit the amount.

RC (DLC). Docketed by JM. Enclosure not found.

From Richard Forrest

Dear Sir,   Baltimore. Saturday Even'g [6 October 1810]

On the rect. of your respected favor, I prevailed on Mr. Eno to go to Alexa. and examine the Merino Sheep addressed to Mr. Hoe. Mr. H was not at home, nor expected 'till the sale,[1] which would have been too late for those Advertised by Mr. Barry;[2] and having a little business of my own here, I concluded it would be best to come on and bring Mr. Eno with me to take both chances; I therefore attended the sale in the hope of accomplishing your object; and purchased two Ewes at 145 dollars each, which tho' small, are young and healthy—the one two, and the other a year old. I then desisted because many were very old, and they often classed the old and young together, which interfered with your instructions. I consulted Mr. Patterson as to the quality of the wool, who thinks it equal to any he ever saw. The Ew[e]s went off from 115 to 170 dollars. The Rams from 150 to 315 dolls. I have seen Genl. Smith's,[3] which appear to be of the same breed; but from having come in a small schooner, where they were much crouded, they do not look so generally healthy. Upwards of five hundred people attended the sale, most of whom were from a distance. The last sale at Alexandria, was far below this, owing, it is said, to a secret combination amongt the purchasers, who agreed not to oppose each other; but it is believed, that Measures will be taken to prevent a similar practice at the next. I nevertheless think they will go off much lower than these have done. I have therefore despatched Mr. Eno to Washington that he may receive your instructions on the subject. I have not communicated to any one that I was purchasing for you, nor has it been suspected.

I shall not leave this place till Monday Even'g, therefore if you have any commands, and will send them on by the Mail, I shall get them by one Oclock on that day. I only contemplate going a few miles the first afternoon.

You may rest assured Sir, that I have done the best I possibly could to comply with your wishes, and nothing but the hope of purchasing on better terms at Alexa, has prevented me from going to the extent of your Order.

I pray you to excuse haste, and to believe me with the highest respect, Your Most Obt. Servt.

RICHD. FORREST

RC (ViU). Docketed "1810," probably by JM at a later time. Date assigned on the basis of internal evidence (see nn. 1 and 2).

1. On 18 Sept. Hooe had advertised a sale of 14 rams and 42 ewes from Spain, to be held at Broomlawn near Alexandria on 8 Oct. (*Alexandria Daily Gazette*, 18 Sept. 1810).

2. On 1 Oct. Robert Barry announced in Baltimore the sale of 140 ewes and 60 rams to be held at the property Canton on Saturday, 6 Oct. (*National Intelligencer*, 1 Oct. 1810).

3. A sale of 35 rams and 170 ewes at Samuel Smith's property of Montebello was due to take place on 8 Oct. (Baltimore *American & Commercial Daily Advertiser*, 17 Sept. 1810).

§ From Levi Lincoln. *6 October 1810, Worcester*. Reminds JM that he had earlier recommended the former attorney general of Massachusetts [Barnabas Bidwell] for the seat on the Supreme Court held by Judge Cushing. "Thanks now to an overruling Providence . . . that arrangement did not take place." Stresses the "importance to this part of the Union" of filling the vacancy recently created by the death of Cushing with "an enlightened, decided, & devoted republican" and therefore recommends Gideon Granger. Believes Granger is "ranked high" by "both descriptions of political characters" in Massachusetts, and in instances when he practiced before the court of Hampshire County, "he so acquitted himself & such was his display of ingenuity & Learning, as to extort from our Supreme Judges although of opposite politics, his eulogium in the face of the County."

RC (DNA: RG 59, LAR, 1809–17, filed under "Granger"). 2 pp. In a clerk's hand, signed by Lincoln. Enclosed in Lincoln to Granger, 6 Oct. 1810 (ibid.).

§ From George Joy. *7 October 1810, Gothenburg.* Reports that his letter of 16 Sept. to JM had not left the port when he received the enclosed letter from Saabye. Finds Saabye's reply personally satisfactory and is convinced that Saabye is a man of integrity; but is still at a loss how to proceed. Suspects that there is an effort to "conceal from our Countrymen the Object of my residence in these cold Regions." Notes that a common ground for the seizure of American vessels is their possession of a certificate from Gérard in Boston, which the Danes (on the basis of a report in the *Moniteur*) consider to be false. They assume therefore that all American papers are fabricated in England. Joy will continue his efforts to obtain the restoration of property thus condemned. Mentions in a postscript that he intends to leave for Copenhagen on 9 Oct.

RC and enclosure, two copies (DLC). RC 5 pp. Enclosure (2 pp.) is a copy of Hans R. Saabye to Joy, 11 Sept. 1810, discussing the reasons why American vessels from Gothenburg have not been allowed to depart from Copenhagen.

§ From George Joy. *8 October 1810, Gothenburg.* Continues "the thread of my discourse of yesterday." Stresses the importance of JM's appointing good men to office in the region and hopes to recommend, as he promised, a good man for the consulship at Gothenburg. Is going to Copenhagen and regrets not being able to accomplish his purposes here. Believes that Sweden, having elected a French prince to its throne, will not be able to escape from the Continental System. Mentions Danish affairs and thinks that Denmark will be subjected to new French duties. Digresses at length about his financial difficulties and argues the merits of formal and informal diplomatic representation in the region. Tends to favor informal representation but would not be averse to acting in an official capacity should JM so decide. Promises to continue the discussion.

RC, two copies (DLC). 17 pp.

§ From Orchard Cook. *9 October 1810, Wiscasset.* Urges appointment of Gideon Granger to the Supreme Court. Also informs JM that because of ill health he will not seek reelection to Congress. Peleg Tallman of Bath has been nominated by local Republicans for the Twelfth Congress.

RC (DNA: RG 59, LAR, 1809–17, filed under "Granger"). 2 pp. Orchard Cook was a Republican representative from Massachusetts in the Ninth through Eleventh Congresses (1805–11).

§ From George de Passau.[1] *10 October 1810, Pointe Coupee.* Provides an account of his efforts to become a cotton planter near Baton Rouge after 1803. Owing to his political views, he was forced to abandon his plantation and immigrate to the Orleans Territory. Purchased lands in Pointe Coupee Parish in 1808 and made extensive improvements on them after receiving assurances from Armand Duplantier that his claims would not conflict with those made for Lafayette in the same area. Has since learned the deputy surveyor has instructions to survey for Lafayette lands he has developed. Has made no remonstrance to Duplantier, but at current staple prices he cannot afford to relocate his plantation. Appeals to the "exalted character & refined sentiments" of JM and Lafayette to allow him to remain on his land; suggests alterations to the survey for this purpose. Encloses letter and affidavits to support his case.

RC, duplicate, triplicate, and enclosures (DNA: RG 59, ML). RC 4 pp.; addressed to JM "as Agent for the Marquis de la Fayette." Enclosures are John Dutton to de Passau, 15 Sept. 1810 (1 p.), and two copies of affidavits by George Mather (1 p.) and Philip Hickey (1 p.). One copy of the affidavits is certified by Fulwar Skipwith, 3 Oct. 1810, the other copy by William C. C. Claiborne, 10 Mar. 1811.

1. George de Passau was extensively involved in the insurgent activities against Spanish authority in West Florida in the fall of 1810, as were his associates Philip Hickey and George Mather (see Cox, *The West Florida Controversy,* pp. 158, 349–51, 380, 398).

From James Maury

DEAR SIR.   LIVERPOOL 11th. October 1810

I am much obliged to you for your consignment of Tobacco ℔ Adeline, of which I am just advised by Mr Stone,[1] with orders for insurance. It is done at 3 Guineas ℔ Cent, so as to cover £20 ℔ Hhd. This market now is so much overdone with Tobacco as to contain nearly double the quantity I ever knew. It is greatly lowered in value & of dull sale. Whenever the Vessell arrive & the cargo be landed & sampled, I will have the honour to write to you farther on the subject.

The Newspapers of the day state an American Sloop of War, with General Armstrong on board, having put into Falmouth on her way home from France. I rather believe the information, although, as yet, I have no better authority for it than newspapers. With perfect respect I have the honour to be, Dear Sir, Your obliged Friend & Servant

JAMES MAURY

RC (DLC). In a clerk's hand, signed by Maury. Marked "Duplicate." Docketed by JM.

1. William S. Stone was a Fredericksburg, Virginia, merchant who often handled sales and purchases for JM and his family (JM to James Madison, Sr., 9 June 1798, *PJM*, 17:148 n. 2).

From Gideon Granger

SIR   October 12th 1810

Emboldened by having devoted the best portion of my life to the Service of my Country, by being the only Attorney and Solicitor in New England, who practised at the Supreme Courts of New Hampshire, and Massachusetts, by the solicitations and profferred support of a number of the most distinguished Republicans in the Eastern Circuit, and by a firm conviction that my appointment would be, at least as satisfactory to the people of that Circuit as that of any other man in the Nation; I take the liberty to remark, that it would give me great pleasure to receive the Office vacated by the death of the late Judge Cushing; as it would enable me to retire to the Country where I was born and educated; which, notwithstanding party struggles, has ever by marks of affection and confidence softened my afflictions. I cannot hope for the Office, unless you shall be convinced that the appointment will be satisfactory generally to the Republicans of the Circuit, of which fact I have no doubt.

I enclose a Letter, lately received, from Gove[r]nor Langdon of New Hampshire; also the letter of the District Attorney of Massachusetts. I am informed that the leading Republicans of Rhode Island have expressed to you the satisfaction which the Republicans of that State would feel in my appointment; and our friend General Dearborn has expressed to me the gratification he should feel at such an event, and his belief that my appointment would be of more solid use, and advantage than the appointment of any other Man.

In no other instance have I ever allowed myself to express a wish for any Office, nor have I ventured on this Step, which to you may appear indelicate, without the deepest reflection and firmest belief, that it was due to my Family, and would meet the approbation of the great body of the people of New England.

Allow me, Sir, to suggest that I would not be considered as entering into competition with my friend Mr. Lincoln, who I understand, and from people directly from his neighbourhood, labours under that affliction, which will forever deprive his Country of his talents.

Sir, if another should be deemed more worthy, it will only furnish evidence, that my self love has blinded my understanding. With great esteem and respect I have the honor to be, Sir, your most obedient servant.

GIDN: GRANGER

RC and enclosures (DNA: RG 59, LAR, 1809–17, filed under "Granger"). RC in a clerk's hand, signed by Granger. Enclosures are George Blake to Granger, 25 Sept. 1810 (2 pp.), and John Langdon to Granger, 5 Oct. 1810 (3 pp.). A note on a separate sheet, dated 12 Oct. 1810, reads: "G. Granger presents his Compliments to Mr. Madison & encloses two Letters from Mr Lincoln which were received since sealing the enclosed" (see Lincoln to JM, 6 Oct. 1810, and n.).

§ From John Drayton. *12 October 1810, Charleston*. Transmits a model designed by Jonathan Lucas, Jr., for "Mounting Cannon on a New Construction." Encloses a letter from Lucas explaining its construction. Acknowledges receipt of JM's letter of 12 Sept. 1810 [not found].

RC (DLC); enclosure (DNA: RG 107, LRRS, L-115:5). RC 2 pp. Docketed by JM. Enclosure is Jonathan Lucas, Jr., to John Drayton, 11 Oct. 1810 (2 pp.; docketed by a War Department clerk as received 19 Nov. 1810).

§ From Gabriel Richard. *12 October 1810, Detroit*. Reports that [territorial secretary] Reuben Attwater recently demanded $205 in rent for the year 1809 for the farm that supports the Indian school at Spring Hill. Attwater also stated his intention to collect a proportional amount for the first ten months of 1810. Complains that the charging of rent violates the oral agreement he made with the U.S. government when he was in Washington in January 1809. After trying in vain for two years to finalize this agreement he suggested that the farm be sold at public auction, where it was purchased by [territorial judge] James Witherell for $5,000. Since Richard could not afford that sum he is now required to move at great expense. Requests that the War Department be consulted for its minutes of the meeting in January 1809 or that former president Jefferson be asked for a statement. If the U.S. government still wishes to charge rent he asks that the improvements made to the farm be considered as an equivalent. Otherwise, he can only pay the rent by selling "the best part of our apparatus as Spinning wheels, looms, Electrical Machine &c. which shall prove exceedingly fatal and hurtfull to so valuable an Institution."

Resuming the text of the letter on 28 Jan. 1811, Richard announces that he has rented "pro tempore" a farm between Spring Hill and Detroit but he would prefer to return to the former location if the government would purchase it from Witherell. Cannot purchase the property himself, unless on long terms at no interest, though he could offer some tracts of land in exchange. Asks that the accounts for paying a carpenter be approved and begs JM to extend "your benevolent hand near the walls of the Edifice I have erected under your patronage."

RC (DNA: RG 107, LRRS, R-147:5). 4 pp. Misfiled at 12 Dec. 1810; docketed by a War Department clerk as received 17 July 1811. Printed in Carter, *Territorial Papers, Michigan*, 10:334–36.

§ From Jedediah K. Smith. *12 October 1810, Amherst, New Hampshire.* Recommends Gideon Granger for the vacancy on the Supreme Court.

RC (DNA: RG 59, LAR, 1809–17, filed under "Granger"). 2 pp. Jedediah Kilburn Smith had been a representative from New Hampshire in the Tenth Congress.

§ From John Stark. *12 October 1810, Derryfield.* Requests a position for his son-in-law, Benjamin Franklin Stickney. Expresses pleasure at the "brightening prospect in our foreign relations" and believes that if Congress will support JM "in decisive measures, we may yet be preserved in honourable peace."

RC (DLC). 2 pp. Docketed by JM.

§ From Joshua Wingate, Sr. *12 October 1810, Boston.* Believes Levi Lincoln would decline a nomination to the Supreme Court; therefore recommends Gideon Granger.

RC (DNA: RG 59, LAR, 1809–17, filed under "Granger"). 2 pp.

From James H. Hooe

Sir,   Alexa. Oct 13. 1810.

I have receieved [*sic*] another parcel of Sheep from Mr Jarvis of Lisbon, and he writes me that you are to select two Ewes from the whole parcell. As I saw a Letter from Mr Jarvis to your Excy.,[1] I did suppose you wou'd have sent 'ere now for these Sheep, and as I am desirous of making some dispositions of them,[2] I have to request that you'll send down for yours as soon as convenient. I have the honor to be sir Your Obt Servt

J H. Hooe

RC (DLC).

1. Hooe was possibly referring to William Jarvis to JM, 26 Aug. 1810.
2. On the same day that he wrote this letter to JM, Hooe placed an advertisement in the *Alexandria Daily Gazette*, announcing that he had recently received a consignment of merino sheep from Jarvis by the ship *Citizen* and would be selling them at auction on 3 Nov. 1810.

§ From Phinehas Wheeler. *13 October 1810, Caldwell, Washington County, New York.* Requests JM at the next session of Congress to redress the grievances of Revolutionary War veterans. Recalls General Washington's promise to the effect that all men who were discharged before receiving their pay would have an "honorable Setlement" within a year. Concedes there was a settlement but denies that being paid in certificates circulating at fifty cents on the dollar was honorable. Doubts the government would now pay its officials and soldiers in such a manner and experiences "disagreable fealings" when he hears veterans praised in Congress as heroes and patriots. Declares that he served in Capt. Benjamin Hayward's company of the Sixth Massachusetts Regiment and claims he was told to consider himself as being on furlough between 10 June 1783 and the ratification of the treaty of peace. Wants his pay for this period.

RC (DLC). 4 pp.

From Robert Smith

SIR,   Sunday Morning [14 October 1810]
    Would it not be well to annex to the despatch to Mr Pinkney that part of the first letter of Mr King which relates to Blockades marked with a pencil // // ?[1]

R SMITH

P. S. Owing to a very severe cold I will not be able to accompany to your house Mr Jarvis. But I will send him.

RS

RC (DLC: Rives Collection, Madison Papers); enclosure (DNA: RG 59, DD, Great Britain). Date of RC assigned on the basis of internal evidence (see n. 1). Enclosure (18 pp.) is Rufus King to Timothy Pickering, 15 July 1799 (see n. 1).

1. Robert Smith's 19 Oct. 1810 letter to William Pinkney (DNA: RG 59, IM) instructed the American minister to press for the repeal of the orders in council and any other "system of paper blockades" devised by Great Britain as a substitute. To underline the point that both Federalist and Republican administrations had rejected such "paper blockades," the letter included extracts from the first (no. 43) of Rufus King's two 15 July 1799 dispatches to Secretary of State Pickering, in which the former had tried to persuade the British government to accept the view that there could be "no effective blockade" without "a competent force stationed and present at or near the entrance of the blockaded port." The section marked in pencil by Robert Smith is on pages 2–3 of the triplicate of the dispatch; it was later published in *ASP, Foreign Relations*, 3:370.

¶ To Oliveira & Sons. Letter not found. *14 October 1810*. Acknowledged in Oliveira & Sons to JM, 25 Oct. 1810, and mentioned in Oliveira & Sons to JM, 26 Oct. 1810. Places an order for some Madeira wine and gives directions for it to be shipped to William Stone in Fredericksburg.

To James H. Hooe

Ocr. 15. 1810

Mr. Eno, the Bearer being authorized to select and receive the two Ewes allotted for J. Madison, by Mr. Jarvis, Mr. Hooe will please to furnish him with the oppy. He will pay also the freight & other charges.

JAMES MADISON

RC (NN: Lee Kohns Memorial Collection). Docketed by Hooe.

To Caesar A. Rodney

Monday Oct. 15th [1810]

J. Madison requests a consultation with the Heads of Departments tomorrow at 12 Oclock.

RC (PSC). In the hand of Edward Coles. The cover bears the following notes, later crossed out, in Rodney's hand: "Take home— / the no. of ⟨Banks?⟩ / Rep— / Marriott's forms / Letters— / J. G. Jackson / T. Jefferson / Dale ⟨Letters?⟩ / Mr. ⟨Dawson?⟩ / W. Eustis / ⟨J. W. Smith?⟩." There are also some calculations relating to wine purchases.

From Thomas Jefferson

DEAR SIR   MONTICELLO Oct. 15. 10.

Tho late, I congratulate you on the revocation of the French decrees, & Congress still more; for without something new from the belligerents, I know not what ground they could have taken for their next move. Britain will revoke her orders of council, but continue their effect by new paper blockades, doing in detail what the orders did in the lump. The exclusive right to the sea by conquest is the principle she has acted on in petto, tho' she dared not yet avow it. This was to depend on the events of the war. I rejoice however that one power has got out of our way, & left us a clear field with the other.

Another circumstance of congratulation is the death of Cushing. The Nation ten years ago declared it's will for a change in the principles of the administration of their affairs. They then changed the two branches depending on their will, and have steadily maintained the reformation in those branches. The third, not dependent on them, has so long bid defiance to their will, erecting themselves into a political body to correct what they deem the errors of the nation. The death of Cushing gives an opportunity of closing the reformation by a successor of unquestionable republican principles. Our friend Lincoln has of course presented himself to your recollection. I know you think lightly of him as a lawyer; and I do not consider him as a correct common lawyer: yet as much so as any one which ever came, or ever can come from one of the Eastern states. Their system of Jurisprudence, made up from the Jewish law, a little dash of Common law, & a great mass of original notions of their own, is a thing sui generis, and one educated in that system can never so far eradicate early impressions as to imbibe thoroughly the principles of another system. It is so in the case of other systems, of which Ld. Mansfield is a splendid example. Lincoln's firm republicanism, and known integrity, will give compleat confidence to the public in the long desired reformation of their judiciary. Were he out of the way, I should think Granger prominent for the place. His abilities are greater, I have entire confidence in his integrity, tho' I am sensible that J. R.[1] has been able to lessen the confidence of many in him. But that I believe he would soon reconcile to him, if placed in a situation to shew himself to the public, as he is, and not as an enemy has represented him. As the choice must be of a New Englander, to exercise his functions for New England men, I confess I know of none but these two characters. Morton is really a republican, but inferior to both the others in every point of view. Blake calls himself republican, but never was one at heart. His treachery to us under the embargo should put him by for ever. Story & Bacon are exactly the men who deserted us on that measure & carried off the majority. The former is unquestionably a tory, & both are too young. I say nothing of professing federalists. Granger & Morton have both been interested in Yazooism. The former however has long been clear of it. I have said thus much because I know you must wish to learn the sentiments of others, to hear all, and then do what on the whole you percieve to be best. Does mr. Lee go back to Bordeaux? If he does I have not a wish to the contrary. If he does not, permit me to place my friend & kinsman G. J.[2] on the list of Candidates. No appointment can fall on an honester man, and his talents, tho' not of the first order, are fully adequate to the station. His judgment is very sound, & his prudence consummate. Ever affectionately yours

TH: JEFFERSON

RC (DLC: Rives Collection, Madison Papers); FC (DLC: Jefferson Papers).

1. In 1804–5 John Randolph had led the opposition in Congress to the efforts of the New England Mississippi Land Company to obtain federal compensation for the Yazoo land sales set aside by the Georgia legislature in 1795. Randolph, in particular, had accused Postmaster General Gideon Granger of trying to "buy and sell corruption in the gross" in Congress. All of the other potential candidates for the Supreme Court vacancy discussed by Jeffer-

son—Perez Morton, George Blake, Joseph Story, and Ezekiel Bacon—had either been members of, or lobbyists for, the New England Mississippi Land Company (Magrath, *Yazoo*, pp. 37–49).

2. Jefferson referred to his cousin George Jefferson, whom JM nominated as consul at Lisbon on 1 Mar. 1811 (*Senate Exec. Proceedings*, 2:173).

To John Quincy Adams

private

DEAR SIR   WASHINGTON Octr. 16. 1810

Previous to my return to this City, I recd. a letter[1] from Mrs. Adams, your highly respectable Mother, communicating your anxiety to leave a situation rendered insupportable by the ruinous expences found to be inseparable from it; & taking for granted that you had written or would write to the Secy. of State to the same effect. The answer[2] to her was, that as it was not the intention of the Executive to expose you to unreasonable sacrifices, it could not withold a permission to retire from them, and that you would be so informed from the Department of State. You will accordingly receive a letter[3] of leave, and a blank Commission, providing for the care of our Affairs, till a successor may be appointed. As no communication of your wishes, however, has yet been recd. from yourself, I can not but hope, that the peculiar urgency, manifested in the letter of Mrs. Adams, was rather hers, than yours; or that you have found the means, of reconciling yourself to a continuance in Your Station. Besides that confidence in the value of your services which led to the call upon them, there are considerations which you will readily appreciate, bearing agst. a sudden return, from a short Mission, the occasion for which has been made the subject of so much lucubration. Among them, is the difficulty of shielding the step against unfavorable conjectures as to its cause, in the mind of the Emperor; and the evil might become the greater, from the possibility, of a protracted intermission, if not entire discontinuance, of a representation of the U. S. at St Petersburg, corresponding with the grade of the Russian Minister here. It will for this reason, be particularly expedient, in case you should make immediate use of the documents Sent you, to spare no pains, in guarding agst. a misconstruction of your departure, and in preparing the Russian Govt for a delay in filling the vacancy; which may be unavoidable notwithstanding the purpose of preventing it. As far as assurances of unabated friendship here, can be of aid to you, they may be given with every emphasis, which the sincerity of these sentiments can warrant.

I will add that whilst I do not disguise my wish that the continuance of your valuable services, may be found not inconsistent with your other & undeniable duties; I can not, on the other hand wish that the latter should be sacrificed, beyond a reasonable measure; & within that measure, I am entirely persuaded that your patriotism will cheerfully make the sacrifice. Accept my sincere respects & friendly wishes

JAMES MADISON

RC (MHi: Adams Family Papers); FC (DLC). RC docketed by Adams, "7. February 1811. recd: / 8. Do: Ansd." FC in a clerk's hand, possibly that of Edward Coles; docketed by JM.

1. Abigail Adams to JM, 1 Aug. 1810.
2. JM to Abigail Adams, 15 Aug. 1810.
3. Robert Smith to John Quincy Adams, 15 Oct. 1810 (DNA: RG 59, IM).

From James H. Hooe

SIR,   ALEXANDRIA 14th [16?][1] Oct 1810

I delivered to Mr. Eno the two Ewes allotted to you by Mr Jarvis, which he selected out of the whole Flock recd. by the Ship Citizen. I have this day delivered to him the two other Ewes which he selected out of the same Flock, next after yours. The Freight of your two Ewes is Six Dollars each, and I estimate your propo: of the expences attending them since they were landed, at one dollar.

You will therefore be pleased to remit me at your convenience, *Four hundred and Thirteen Dollars*, for the two extra Ewes, and the expences on your own pair.

With regard to the Lamb, of which your Excelly. has made mention,[2] I scarcely know what to say. I certainly never meant to urge any further pretention to it, nor shoud I have shewn my Letter from Mr Jarvis to Mr Deblois, but for my justification in having laid claim to a pair of Lambs when Mr Daugherty made choice of the Ewes intended for yourself & Mr Jefferson.

However, I am at all events, very willing, & desirous, that you shou'd consult your own Inclination althogether [*sic*], with regard to this Sheep, either by transferring to me, this particular Lamb, another Merino Sheep, or the value of one. Whatever you may be pleased to do about it, will be perfectly agreable to me. I have the honor to be with due Consideration & Respect Sir Yr Mt Obt St

J H: HOOE

RC (DLC). Docketed by JM.

1. Hooe evidently misdated this letter. Date assigned here on the basis that Hooe could not have written the letter before Eno arrived in Alexandria with JM's 15 Oct. letter authorizing him to take delivery of the sheep (see JM to Hooe, 15 Oct. 1810).

2. Hooe was probably referring to the unresolved dispute over the ownership of a merino lamb born after the arrival of an earlier consignment of sheep from Portugal (see JM to Jefferson, 8 June 1810).

From James Taylor

MY DEAR SIR   BELLE VUE KY October 16th. 1810

I have taken the liberty of inclosing to you a letter to my friend Mrs. M and one to Mr. Coles. I hope this will find your self and Mrs. M in the enjoyment of perfect health. It leaves my family and our friends generally in the enjoyment of that blessing.

I am sure you are pleased at the event of our election, The result in Lyons district will shew that when ever a man deviates from Correct principles in our state he loses the confidence of the people.[1] I think Geo M Bibb[2] will be our next Senator in Congress. I have not seen my brother as yet but I do not think he will Offer. I am much pleased at the prospect of an accommodation with France & England and sincerely hope that some permanent adjustment may take place. The ensuing session will in my opinion be a very important one and I sincerely hope there will be more harmony at the next session than there was at the last. With great respect & Esteem I am Dr. sir Your friend & Servt

JAMES TAYLOR

RC (DLC).

1. Matthew Lyon's increasing dissatisfaction with administration foreign policy led to accusations from other Kentucky Republicans that he was a "tory" and a "British partisan." In the elections for the Twelfth Congress he was defeated by Anthony New (Aleine Austin, *Matthew Lyon: "New Man" of the Democratic Revolution, 1749–1822* [Philadelphia and London, 1981], pp. 147–48).

2. George M. Bibb (1776–1859) represented Kentucky in the U.S. Senate from November 1811 until his resignation on 23 Aug. 1814.

§ From Charles Turner, Jr. *16 October 1810, Scituate, Massachusetts.* Recommends the appointment of Gideon Granger to the Supreme Court.

RC (DNA: RG 59, LAR, 1809–17, filed under "Granger"). 1 p. Charles Turner, Jr., served as a Republican representative from Massachusetts in the Eleventh and Twelfth Congresses.

¶ To James H. Hooe. Letter not found. *17 October 1810.* Acknowledged in Hooe to JM, 19 Oct. 1810. Offers to purchase the merino lamb claimed by Hooe.

To Thomas Jefferson

DEAR SIR   WASHINGTON Ocr. 19. 1810

I have recd. your favor of the 15th. All we know of the step taken by France towards a reconciliation with us, is thro' the English papers sent by Mr. Pinkney, who had not himself recd. any information on the subject from Genl. A. nor held any conversation with the B. Ministry on it, at the date of his last letters. We hope from the step, the advantage at least of having but one contest on our hands at a time. If G. B. repeals her orders, without discontinuing her Mock-blockades, we shall be at issue with her on ground strong in law, in the opinion of the world, and even in her own concessions.[1] And I do not believe that Congs. will be disposed, or permitted by the Nation, to a tame submission; the less so as it would be not only perfidious to the other belligerent, but irreconciliable with an honorable neutrality. The Crisis in W. Florida, as you will see, has come home to our feelings and our interests.[2] It presents at the same time serious questions, as to the Authority of the Executive, and the adequacy of the existing laws, of the U. S. for territorial administration. And the near approach of Congs. might subject any intermediate interposition of the Ex. to the charge of being premature & disrespectful, if not of being illegal. Still, there is great weight in the considerations, that the Country to the Perdido, being our own, may be fairly, taken possession of, if it can be done without violence, above all if there be danger of its passing into the hands of a third & dangerous party. The successful party at Baton Rouge have not yet made any communication or invitation to this Govt. They certainly will call in, either our Aid or that of G. B, whose conduct at the Caraccas[3] gives notice of her propensity to fish in troubled waters. From present appearances, our occupancy of W. F. would be resented by Spain, by England, & by France, and bring on, not a triangular, but quadrangular contest. The Vacancy in the Judiciary, is not without a puzzle in supplying it. Lincoln, obviously, is the first presented to our choice; but I believe he will be inflexible in declining it. Granger is *working hard* for it. His talents are as you state, a strong recommendation; but it is unfortunate, that the only legal evidence of them known to the public, displays his Yazooism; and on this as well as some other accts the more particularly offensive to the Southern half of the Nation. His bodily infirmity, with its effect on his mental stability is an unfavorable circumstance also.[4] On the other hand, it may be difficult to find a successor free from objections, of equal force. Neither Morton, nor Bacon, nor Story have yet been brought forward. And I believe Blake will not be a candidate. I have never lost sight of Mr. Jefferson of Richmond. Lee I presume returns to Bourdeaux. Jarvis is making a visit to the U. S. but apparently with an intention to return to Lisbon.[5] All the other consulships worthy of him are held by persons who manifest no disposition to part with their births. My overseer G. Gooch is just setting out with the Algerine Rams. Two of them, I have directed him to forward to Monticello; I beg you to accept whichever of them you may prefer; and let Capt: Isaac Coles have the other. Of the 8 sent from Algiers, one was slaughtered on the passage, and a Wether substituted. Another was not of the large tail family: but a very large handsome sheep with 4 horns. His fleece is heavy, but like the others coarse. I send him to Virga. with the others, tho' at a loss what to have done with him there. Two of the large tails I have disposed of here, one of them to Claiborne, for the benefit of the Orleans meat Market. I send home also, by this oppy. six Merino Ewes, two of them recd. from Jarvis, & the rest purchased here out of his late shipments. I have purchased also, the Ewe lamb, which had been destined for Hooe of Alexanda. Finding that the arrangements necessary for the original pair, would provide for a small flock, I have been tempted to make this addition to them; as a fund of pure Merino blood, worth attending to. The Ewes will stand me in abt. $175 a piece. Accept my affectionate respects

JAMES MADISON

RC (DLC). Docketed by Jefferson, "recd. Oct. 21."

1. Shortly after JM returned to Washington, the *National Intelligencer*, on 15 Oct. 1810, editorialized on this theme, predicting that "questions may hereafter arise, between the American and British governments, on the subject of blockades." The newspaper then reprinted admiralty orders of 5 Jan. 1804 withdrawing the Royal Navy blockade of Guadeloupe and Martinique *"unless in respect to particular ports which may be ACTUALLY INVESTED, and then not to capture vessels bound to such ports unless they shall previously have been warned not to enter them."* The editorial concluded that this British position embraced "the principles cordially admitted by the United States, beyond which they have never advanced any pretensions, and contrary to which, it is hoped, Great Britain will set up no new rule."

2. In a postscript to its 19 Oct. edition the *National Intelligencer* printed a report that an armed force, acting in the name of the West Florida convention, had attacked the Spanish fort at Baton Rouge on the night of 22–23 Sept. 1810 and seized its commander, Don Carlos Dehault Delassus. Two days earlier, on 17 Oct., the new editor of the *National Intelligencer*, Joseph Gales, Jr., had called on JM and mentioned during the course of conversation the possibility of American involvement in West Florida. According to the diary Gales kept at the time, JM responded that "he imagined measures had been adopted which would prevent our being involved by the ardor of our citizens." As to the independence of the Floridas, the president continued, "if Bonaparte was sincere in the declarations he was said to have made, he would not object to it: if he was opposed to their independence, policy should induce him to leave them alone, for his interference would immediately throw them into the arms of

Britain. He thought the British party, together with the refugees from justice, deserters from the United States Army, and land-jobbers, would constitute a majority who would be unwilling that West Florida should come under the jurisdiction of the United States" ("Recollections of the Civil History of the War of 1812," *Historical Magazine*, 3d ser., 3 [1874–75]: 157).

3. On 15 Oct. the *National Intelligencer* had printed a decree issued by the junta at Caracas on 3 Sept. 1810 reducing by one-quarter for British subjects the duties charged on foreign exports and imports made through Venezuelan customhouses. The decree mentioned that these terms had been negotiated for the British by Colonel Robertson. The editorial comment observed that while Great Britain supported the authority of Ferdinand VII and the Supreme Junta in Europe, it was not above undermining legitimist principles for commercial advantage in Spain's American colonies. In his conversation with Gales two days later JM remarked that "the steps taken by the British, in South America, were the strangest he had seen lately; for this Colonel Robertson would not dare to act as he had done, unless authorized by the British Ministry." The president further stated that while it was "a politic course of the independent party, to give this eclat to the British commercial favors" and thus "strengthen their party," it would also cause the "adherents of old Spain" to look upon the British "with a very jealous eye." In response to Gales's opinion that the Spanish colonies would be unable to sustain a republican system and would, like France, "recur to a despotic Government," JM said "it was very probable; but still they would have their choice of the form of government, and, so far, be independent" (ibid.).

4. Gideon Granger had long suffered from depression and other health problems, which on one occasion he described as "severe shocks on the brains and bowels" (Arthur S. Hamlin, *Gideon Granger* [Canandaigua, N.Y., 1982], pp. 13–14, 34).

5. William Jarvis was still in Lisbon at the time, but JM had probably heard of a report from New York two days earlier that Jarvis was about to depart for the U.S. He arrived in Boston in late November (*National Intelligencer*, 22 Oct. 1810; Jarvis to Robert Smith, 30 Nov. 1810 [DNA: RG 59, CD, Lisbon]).

From James H. Hooe

SIR   ALEXA. Octr 19. 1810.

I recd. in due time the Letter you did me the honor to write me on the 17th., and have to observe in reply, that I shall be perfectly satisfied with such Sum as you may please to remit me for the Lamb.

But as you have referred the decision of this point to me, I cannot but express *the opinion*, that a Lamb of the present Season is worth the average price of the Flock I have just sold. A number of that Flock were sickly, and were infected with a dangerous disease which had killed several, and by Which the purchaser calculated on losing others, in-so-much that he sold three Sheep to Mr Threlkeld[1] for 100 dolls. I obtained for the whole Flock, (upwards of 80 Sheep)—250$ for the Rams & 150$ for the Ewes. Independant of their Health, the greater number were old, & Yet the purchaser has been understood to have gotten a good bargain.

If then, the Lamb is worth the average price of the Flock I sold, you will be pleased to remit me 150$, but shoud you think otherwise, I shall be satisfied with $100. I have the honor to be with due Consideration & Respect Sir, yr Obt Servt

                                                                    J H: Hooe

One of my Ewes yeaned a Ewe Lamb on the 3d. of June last, which Lamb I now have. Several who have seen this Lamb, & are considered good Judges, think it worth more than any Ewe I have. This is decidedly my opinion, for it is in perfect health, very large of its age, and very fine-wooled.

RC (DLC). Docketed by JM.

1. John Threlkeld was a resident and sometime mayor of Georgetown (Bryan, *History of the National Capital*, 1:275 n. 2).

To Levi Lincoln

Dear Sir   Washington Ocr. 20. 1810
    I have recd. your favor on the subject of a successor to Judge Cushing.[1] I feel all the importance of filling the vacancy, with a character particularly acceptable to the Northern portion of our Country, and as generally so as possible to the whole of it. With these views, I had turned my thoughts & hopes to ⟨the⟩ addition of your Learning, principles, and weight, to a Department which has so much influence on the course and success of our political system. I cannot allow myself to despond of this solid advantage to the public. I am not unaware of the infirmity which is said to afflict your eyes: But these are not the organs most employed in the functions of a Judge; & I would willingly trust that the malady which did not unfit you for your late high & important Station, may not be such as to induce a refusal of services which your patriotism, will, I am sure be disposed, to yield.[2] If your mind should have taken an adverse turn on this subject, I pray that you will give it a serious reconsideration; under an assurance that besides the general sentiment which would be gratified by a favorable decision, there is nothing which many of your particular friends have more at heart, as important to the public welfare. As there are obvious reasons for postponing the appointment, till the meeting of the Senate, you will have time to allow due weight to the considerations on which this appeal is founded; and it will afford me peculiar pleasure to learn that it has found you not inflexible to its object. Accept Dear Sir assurances of my high esteem & friendly respects

                                                                    James Madison

RC (MHi). Docketed by Lincoln.

1. Lincoln to JM, 6 Oct. 1810.
2. Lincoln declined JM's offer (Lincoln to JM, 27 Nov. 1810 [DLC]).

From George W. Erving

DEAR SIR   AMBOY Oct: 20t 1810
I had the pleasure to receive in Boston your letter of Septr 25, acknowledging rect of that which I took the liberty of addressing to you from
Philadelphia: the views of the english government as to the matter therein
referred to stand now confessed in the most unequivocal form; & the *har-
diesse* of its policy in relation to the spanish colonies generally, seems rather
to surpass all that we have before witnessed of a similar character; it woud
appear by a late decree of the government at Carraccas (dated Sep. 3d)
that independance of the mother country is to be encouraged, in places
where it can be converted into a commercial dependance on G. B.!!¹ Combining this however with some late articles of intelligence from Europe, I
am persuaded that the cause of the peninsula is despaired of, & that the
contest there, will be continued only 'till the means are fully prepared of
carrying into execution the contemplated operations elsewhere: it may be
that this abandonement is motived by a beleif that the Emperor will restore Ferdinand, a measure which I have long thought to be most politick,
& even necessary; whatever the patriotick spaniards here may say to the
contrary, the terms of such restoration will not defeat its object. As to
Portugal, the sudden fall of Almeida & Badajos seems to have decided the
fate of the english army; & Lord Wellington will be too fortunate if he can
reach his ships.²
    I am now from Boston in my way to Washington, where I hope to pay
my respects to you very early in the Ensuing month. Dear Sir with the
truest respect & attachment Your very obliged & obt St
                                            GEORGE W ERVING

RC (MHi: Erving Papers). Docketed by JM.

1. See JM to Jefferson, 19 Oct. 1810, n. 3.
2. Erving referred to reports reaching New York by 17 Oct. that French forces had taken
Almeida on 25 Aug. and had also occupied Badajoz. The information with respect to Badajoz
proved to be incorrect, but the reports assumed that the duke of Wellington would have to
withdraw from Portugal (*National Intelligencer*, 5, 19, 22 Oct. 1810).

§ From George Joy. *Ca. 20 October 1810, Copenhagen.* Reports that he arrived in
Copenhagen on 11 Oct. and that he has had discussions and correspondence with

the French minister and Danish cabinet officials on the subjects already mentioned in his letters of 7 Oct. and 8 Sept. The French minister asked him what he thought of the extension of the Continental System. Privately the minister admitted the absurdity of condemning American vessels on grounds that their papers are British fabrications, but he was instructed by his court to maintain that the certificates of origin justify the seizures. Has had discussions with Count Rosencrantz over the date when French confiscatory orders should apply in Danish ports. After some initial disagreement, it has been arranged so that these orders will only apply to vessels that arrived after 22 Sept. Speculates that this will either be accepted silently or be protested by France. Hopes for the former but would not be surprised at the latter. Wishes to hear from JM.

RC (DLC). 7 pp. Dated "Octr. 1810" and marked "(Dupl:)." Docketed by JM. Dated ca. 11 Oct. 1810 in *Index to the James Madison Papers*. Date here assigned on the basis of internal evidence.

From Samuel Smith

SIR,   BALTIMORE 22 Octr. 1810

The Note of Mr. P——y is pointedly Specific as to its Object[1]—it required only a plain & Simple Answer—what reply did he recieve? An *Jesuitical* One, that may be made to mean *anything* or *nothing*. His Lordship referrs to a former promise made by his Govt. which (least we Should understand as it was generally understood at the time) he goes on to explain, "He repeats it, *and assures you that whenever the repeal of the French Orders Shall have actually taken effect, <u>and the Commerce of neutral nations Shall have been restored to the Condition in which it Stood previously to the promulgation of those Orders</u>,* his Majesty will &c &c &c.["] The Simple question that presents itself, to Enable us to understand the Equivocal language used by his Ld. Ship, is, *Will the Revocation of the Fr. decrees place the Commerce of Neutrals in the Condition in which it existed prior to the Berlin Decree?* If it will, then the Orders of Council are repealed, if it will not, then his Ld. Ships Note is a declaration that the British System will be continued, and an Argument given to the British partizans, to Shew that the former promise only bound G. B to a repeal in Case Trade was made perfectly free, and that their Manufactures & Colonial produce were (as was then the Case) freely admitted into the Continent. I recollect that prior to those Decrees, Goods were shipped direct from London in Am: Ships to the Isle of France, and that British E. India Goods were shipped from the U. S. to every part of Europe even to France, and that the Commerce of England to almost all Europe was open & free, either in their own or Am: ships. Can that be again the Case when the French Decrees are revoked? If it will not, then the Orders of Council & Blockading System will remain in full force with *additional Activity*. That Such a free & open trade will not be countenanced on the Continent must be Evident, the plain language of the British Note appears to me & to all with whom I have conversed to be—Unless France permits the introduction of British Produce & Manufactures to those Countries which admitted them prior to the Berlin Decree, no trade Shall be carried on by the U. S. to the Ports now Called in a State of Blockade. Had the Intention been fair, Wellesly's Answer would have been Specifically to the plain question put by Mr. P——y. No Merchant here will Act under the Note. So that our Commerce must remain Shut up (as at present) from a trade to the ports declared to be in a State of Blockade, Viz Holland, France, Spain (possessed by France) Italy & the Adriatic Sea.

Is it not to be apprehended, that if we are lulled into Security by this Evasive Note that the Emperor will Consider that we are trifling with our promise and will revoke his Repeal and hold the Sequestered property.

Those Ideas having presented themselves to my Mind, I have taken the liberty to offer them to your Consideration and am sir, With Respect Your Obedt. servt.

S. Smith

RC (DLC: Rives Collection, Madison Papers). Docketed by JM.

1. Smith had evidently read either in the 20 Oct. extra edition of the *National Intelligencer* or in the edition of 22 Oct. a copy of Pinkney's 25 Aug. 1810 note to Lord Wellesley informing the British government of the repeal of the Berlin and Milan decrees and stating his assumption that the revocation of the orders in council of 1807 and 1809 as well as "all other orders dependent upon, analogous to, or in execution of them, will follow of course." The newspaper had also published an undated duplicate copy of Wellesley's reply of 31 Aug. 1810 containing the British foreign secretary's response, quoted here by Smith.

From William Madison

Dr Brother   23d Octr 1810

The money left in my hands to pay for the Waggon is exhausted by the purchase of two horses as you requested: it therefore becomes necessary that a further supply should be furnished by the next mail. I sent to Rockingham & engaged a Waggon which will be sent for next Monday. The cost, including some expence, will be $120.

I saw young Mr Blaky[1] yesterday at Orange Court. He expressed much disappointment at not meetg with Gooch according to promise—he says that Gooch has so frequently deceived him, that he is now instructed to resort to coercive steps. I prevailed on him to postpone doing so 'till I wrote you. I had not as much money or I would certainly have settled the claim.

I think it is to be regreted that your pecuniary matters are not managed by some friend residing near your farms. Tell my Sister that the Chapaux & Plume did not accompany her Note. Yrs Affectly

WM MADISON

Alfred I expect will be with you by the time you get this. Be so good as to hand him the inclosed. I shall expect to hear from him by next mail.

RC (NjP). Docketed by JM.

1. Either Reuben or William Blakey, sons of John Blakey and Sarah Cowherd Blakey of Orange County, Virginia (*VMHB*, 28 [1920]: 152, 263).

§ From Robert Taylor. *23 October 1810*. Believes that the U.S. marshal for Virginia is in poor health and "not likely long to survive." As the practice of law is "daily growing less profitable and more irksome" Taylor seeks the position, provided JM sees "no impropriety in the appointment." Has also been asked to recommend John W. Green of Fredericksburg for the same position, and he assures JM that Green would be a satisfactory appointment.

RC (DNA: RG 59, LAR, 1809–17, filed under "Taylor"). 2 pp.

Hobohoilthle to John Roger Nelson Luckett

CHAT,TOOK,CHU,FAU,LEE IN THE CREEK AGENCY 24th. Octr. 1810
. . . I am now speaking to the President you have appointed an officer to act in your business[1] I am not vexed but I am speaking plain, I am the President of this nation of people and so I give an Answer to it. I call myself Muscogee A nation of people, I am so, I wish to be friendly I am a native master of this country and I wish to be good neighbours, you are too gready after my land, I am Speaking of my rights I have got sense yet I have not lost my senses, he that made us is above us looking on us, he made the ground for us, and before we have agreed on the matter you are eager after it. I am Speaking before it goes too far. If your officer should go on there may be some mad crazy people who would do mischief, and before this mischief is thrown upon us, I wish to prevent it if I could. When I find things are going wrong, I must prevent it, before it comes on us, by preventing it makes strong the chain of friendship. I am Speaking on this subject in this way, if any bodys wants a masters property he must ask the owner if he is willing, and if the owner says no, I love it, we cant force him to doing a thing against his will. Now I am speaking our friends

and brothers have a great King President of the United States. My wish is not to be cutting our paths in our Country. I am a poor nation of people, I wish my Warriors women & families to walk on the Country as little as they have got. You have taken all the lands in the Country and what little lands we have got we wish we may possess it and not be kept in uneasiness. Now I am Speaking to the great King the President, you have asked me for a path, and I have agreed to lend you my path, the one I lent you, the Nation lent you, and you use it and I am Contented, and we are Contented that you should use the path, that your people use. If you are Contented with that post road you use now, as it is. But the Upper path which you wish will bring in Mischief and I should be sorry blood should be spilt on acct. of a path. There is a great many of our people in that country who may bring on some mischief upon us, and I dont wish that should be done. Most of our people near it have not much sense, and without knowing it right might do mischief. I am in distress a poor people, you must not force it upon us, we are the masters of it, wish there may [be] no harm, then you let us be in peace and contented. On account of the water course called Coosau river you asked me and I told you I could not agree to lend it, this river we use the water of, families are settled on it on both sides, the country is settled and filled up. That same river Coosau, you asked me to pass up and down for the purpose of trade, when I was at Cowetuh, I saw your letter asking me then, and I said the nation is not agreed to it.[2] I thought you know that before this time; when a man has any property, and says no, it is all I shall ask I never forces it. I am speaking as a nation, when you ask me I say no, I am born upon it, I walk on it, I love it, I use it. I wish we may not mix together at once, when the red and white skin mix passing thro the Country, there might be some not agreeable. It is my wish the family of red people may settle by themselves on their own lands, they suit by themselves, its natural to them, as their bodies. I am Speaking as I wish for my country and nation. When I am asked I say no I love my property. When I say no, you thought I was small that you were big and able and you would kick me down, my warriors say as you are Strong, you would take advantage of our weakness force us and kick us down, th⟨en⟩ they tell me to speak I beg you to consider upon us. . . .

his
Hoboheilthle ⊔ Micco
mark
Speaker for the nation

Extract from RC (DNA: RG 107, LRRS, H-229: 5). Certified as a true copy by Christian Limbaugh, assistant agent for Indian affairs. Enclosed in Benjamin Hawkins to William Eustis, 5 Nov. 1810 (ibid.). Docketed by a War Department clerk as received 29 Nov. 1810.

1. On 23 June 1810 the secretary of war had instructed Lt. Col. Richard Sparks at Fort Stoddert to organize parties to explore and report on the land and river routes between Mobile and east Tennessee. The people of the Creek townships, alarmed by the presence of men carrying compasses and measuring chains and assuming that they were land hunters, met in council at Chattuckchufaula on 24 Oct. to demand an end to their activities. Hobohoilthle was particularly incensed at the exploration of the Coosa River by a party under Lieutenant Luckett, and after stating his case in the council he requested Hawkins to obtain a response from the president before the Creek townships held their national council in the following spring (Eustis to the commanding officer at Fort Stoddert, 23 June 1810 [DNA: RG 107, LSMA]; Hawkins to Capt. Edmund Pendleton Gaines, 25 Oct. 1810, and Hawkins to Eustis, 25 Oct. 1810 [DNA: RG 107, LRRS]; Southerland and Brown, *The Federal Road*, pp. 34–36).

2. At a council held at Cowetah at the end of May 1810, Hobohoilthle and other Creek chiefs rejected a request conveyed by Timothy Barnard and Christian Limbaugh to grant Americans permission to navigate the Coosa River. Their reasons included resentment at previous encroachments on Creek lands by settlers and livestock as well as the fear that increased traffic on the river would spread the use of whiskey among the Creek people (Timothy Barnard to Hawkins, 1 June 1810, enclosed in Hawkins to Eustis, 30 June 1810 [DNA: RG 107, LRRS]).

§ From Oliveira & Sons. *25 October 1810, Norfolk.* The firm has received JM's letter of 14 Oct. and has shipped one hogshead of old Madeira wine to Fredericksburg. Requests JM to pay the charges, amounting to $192.25, with a draft from the Washington branch of the Bank of the United States.

RC and enclosure (DLC). RC 2 pp.; docketed by JM. Enclosure (1 p.) is a receipt from John Cooper, 24 Oct. 1810, for the wine he is to deliver to Fredericksburg.

¶ From Luis de Onís. Letter not found. *25 October 1810.* Described as a one-page letter in the lists probably made by Peter Force (DLC, series 7, container 2). On 9 Oct. 1810 Onís had written to Robert Smith proposing that he be allowed to carry on a private correspondence with both Smith and JM to supplement consular communications as a means for maintaining Spain's relations with the U.S. (DNA: RG 59, NFL, Spain).

§ From Oliveira & Sons. *26 October 1810, Norfolk.* After their 29 Sept. letter to JM the firm had several orders for the Madeira wine they recently imported, but they declined selling any before hearing from JM. The hogshead ordered in JM's letter of 14 Oct. was sent to Fredericksburg yesterday, and they regret they are able at present to send only "the two remaining qrCasks; and another, in which we will put the balance of a hogshead fined, for the use of some freinds." The three casks will be addressed to the collector at Alexandria. Also offer JM some "L P. dry Lisbon wine" which "is of such quality, as we can recommend for table use."

RC (DLC). 2 pp. Docketed by JM.

Presidential Proclamation

[27 October 1810]

By the President of the United States of America.
A Proclamation.

WHEREAS the Territory South of the Mississippi Territory and East-ward of the river Mississippi, and extending to the River Perdido, of which possession was not delivered to the United States in pursuance of the Treaty concluded at Paris on the 30th April 1803, has at all times, as is well known, been considered and claimed by them, as being within the Colony of Louisiana conveyed by the said Treaty, in the same extent that it had in the hands of Spain, and that it had when France originally possessed it.

And whereas the acquiescence of the United States in the temporary continuance of the said Territory under the Spanish Authority was not the result of any distrust of their title, as has been particularly evinced by the general tenor of their laws, and by the distinction made in the application of those laws between that Territory and foreign Countries; but was occasioned by their conciliatory views, and by a confidence in the justice of their cause; and in the Success of candid discussion and amicable negotiation with a just and friendly power:

And whereas a satisfactory adjustment, too long delayed, without the fault of the United States, has for some time been entirely[1] suspended by events over which they had no controul, and whereas a crisis has at length arrived subversive of the order of things under the Spanish Authorities[2] whereby a failure of the United States to take the said Territory into its possession may lead to events ultimately contravening the views of both parties, whilst in the mean time the tranquility and security of our adjoining territories are endangered, and new facilities given to violations of our Revenue and Commercial laws, and of those prohibiting the introduction of Slaves:

Considering moreover that under these peculiar and imperative circumstances, a forbearance on the part of the United States to occupy the Territory in question, and thereby guard against the confusions and contingences which threaten it, might be construed into a dereliction of their title, or an insensibility to the importance of the stake: considering that in the hands of the United States it will not cease to be a subject of fair and friendly negotiation and adjustment: considering finally that the Acts of Congress tho' contemplating a present possession by a foreign authority, have contemplated also an eventual possession of the said Territory by the United States, and are accordingly so framed as in that case to extend in their operation, to the same: Now be it known That I JAMES MADISON,

President of the United States of America, in pursuance of these weighty and urgent considerations, have deemed it right and requisite, that[3] possession should be taken of the said Territory, in the name and behalf of the United States. William C. C. Claiborne Governor of the Orleans Territory of which the said territory is to be taken as part, will accordingly proceed to execute the same; and to exercise over the said Territory the Authorities and functions legally appertaining to his office.[4] And the good people inhabiting the same, are invited and enjoined to pay due respect to him in that character, to be obedient to the laws; to maintain order; to cherish harmony; and in every manner to conduct themselves as peaceable Citizens; under full assurance, that they will be protected in the enjoyment of their liberty, property and religion.

IN TESTIMONY Whereof, I have caused the seal of the United States to be hereunto affixed and signed the same with my hand. Done at the City of Washington the Twenty seventh day of October A. D 1810, and in the thirty fifth year of the Independence of the said United States.

JAMES MADISON

By the President

R SMITH

Secretary of State

Ms (DNA: RG 11, Presidential Proclamations); FC (DNA: RG 46, TP, Florida); draft (owned by the Karpeles Manuscript Library, Santa Barbara, Calif., 1990). Ms in a clerk's hand, signed by JM and Smith. Draft, originally dated 26 Oct. 1810, in a clerk's hand, corrected by JM, and docketed by William Pinkney. This copy, with the date altered to 27 Oct., was later sent as an enclosure in Robert Smith to Pinkney, 2 Nov. 1810. The proclamation was enclosed in JM to Congress, 5 Dec. 1810; it was printed in the *National Intelligencer*, 6 Dec. 1810, and appeared in many newspapers soon thereafter.

1. JM inserted this word in pencil in the draft of the proclamation.
2. The draft included here the phrase, later deleted, "and substituting in lieu thereof a self created independent Government."
3. The word "a" was deleted here from the draft.
4. Claiborne was directed to implement the proclamation with the proviso that "should . . . any particular place however small remain in possession of a Spanish force, you will not proceed to employ force against it but you will make immediate report thereof" (Smith to Claiborne, 27 Oct. 1810 [DNA: RG 59, DL]). According to Robert Smith, JM "annexed, with his *own pen*" this qualification to Claiborne's orders. The secretary of state later declared that the idea of the American occupying forces "suddenly halting at the first appearance of a Spanish bayonet, or of their being restrained from taking possession to the full extent of what Mr. Madison himself considered *our legitimate claim*, was, to my mind, so humiliating, that I really could not disguise my opinion of the restriction under the mask of official reverence" (*National Intelligencer*, 2 July 1811).

§ From Barzillai Gannett.[1] *27 October 1810, Gardiner, Maine.* Encloses a petition from several "respectable" gentlemen to remind JM that in February 1809 some state legislators from Maine had petitioned for the removal of Silas Lee as U.S. attorney and for his replacement by Nathan West, Jr. President Jefferson responded that since he had appointed Lee himself the matter was best left to his successor. West has reputation and experience and is "warmly attached to the government," while Lee, in addition to holding the office of probate judge in Lincoln County, was also recently appointed to the court of common pleas by Governor Gore. Petitioners regard Lee's last appointment as superseding his federal appointment, which is also incompatible with his state offices. Gannett endorses the petition and states that there is a general desire for Lee's removal on the grounds of his being unfriendly to the administration and system of government.

RC and enclosure (DNA: RG 59, LAR, 1809–17, filed under "West"). RC 2 pp. Enclosure (3 pp.) signed by Thomas Fillebrown and twelve others and dated 12 Sept. 1810.

1. Barzillai Gannett served as a Republican representative from Massachusetts in the Eleventh Congress. He was reelected to the Twelfth Congress but resigned without taking his seat.

To John Armstrong

private

DEAR SIR   WASHINGTON Oct. 29. 1810

Your two favors of the 6th. & 25 of May were both recd. tho' at a late day. Of the latter a duplicate has also come to hand.

The Consular Register of Paris, has, I find been transmitted to the Dept. of State instead of remaining in the Office there. It has been examined with a view to that part of your letter which supposed it to contain a Deposition meant to implicate your name in a certain land speculation. It does not appear that any such deposition, or any other record, having that tendency, either makes a part of the Register, or was transmitted along with it. Nor do the files of the Office of State contain any correspondence on the subject. Were the fact otherwise, and the correspondence such as you were led to believe, there wd. as your recollection will suggest, be a difficulty in fulfilling your wish to have a copy of it; it being contrary to the rule of Office, established here & every where, to give copies of *confidential* communications without the assent of the party making them. The rule is certainly a hard one, as it may hoard up injurious calumnies, to find their way to the public, after the falsification has become impossible. On the other hand, a disregard of such a rule, might shut the door agst. information of critical importance, which would not be given, but under a pledge of secresy. Perhaps a refusal to receive any information on such terms, would be the soundest, as it would be the noblest policy. The experiment however has never been made. But if Govts. shrink from such an innovation, they ought at least, from time to time, to select from their Archives, & commit to the flames, every deposit no longer of public use, & of a nature to injure private reputation.

Having indulged in these remarks, I proceed to add that altho' no communication on the subject of a land speculation has been made by Mr. Bowdoin to the Dept. of State, or is now deposited there, I have learnt from Mr. Jefferson, that such a communication was made to him whilst he was in Office at Washington. It appears however, that there is not in the letter of Mr. Bowdoin a single expression implicating you in any land speculation whatever; that the contents of the Deposition made it proper that it should be transmitted to this Govt; and that in the Deposition itself there is nothing that merits your attention. I need not say that no evidence of that sort, whatever might have been its particular complexion, would have been permitted either by Mr. Jefferson or myself, to withdraw a particle from the perfect confidence felt by both in your honor & integrity.

You will learn from the Dept. of State that altho' no direct authentication of the repeal of the F. decrees has been recd. from you,[1] a proclamation issues on the ground furnished by your correspondence with Mr. Pinkney. It is to be hoped that France will do what she is understood to be pledged for, & in a manner that will produce no jealousy or embarrassment here. We hope in particular that the sequestred property will have been restored; without which the Ex. may be charged wth. violating their own instruction to you on that point.[2] Whether that instruction was not itself a departure from the law, & must not have been set aside in case the repeal of the decrees had arrived, with a knowledge that F. had made no satisfactory provision as to sequestrations, are questions which it wd. be well to have no occasion to decide. The course which G. B. will take, is left by Wellesley's pledge, a matter of conjecture. It is not improbable that the Orders in C. will be revoked & the sham blockades be so managed if possible, as to irritate France agst. our non-resistance, without irritating this Country to the resisting point. It seems on the whole that we shall be at issue with G. B. on the ground of such blockades, and it is for us, a strong ground.

You will see also the step that has been produced by the posture of things in W. Florida. If France is wise she will neither dislike it herself, nor promote resentment of it in any other quarter. She ought in fact, if guided by prudence & good information, to patronize at once, a general separation of S. America from Old Spain. This event is already decided, and the sole question with F. is whether it is to take place under her auspices, or those of G. B. The latter, whether with or without the privity of the expiring Authority at Cadiz, is taking her measures with reference to that event; and in the mean time, is extorting commercial privileges as the recompence of her interposition. In this particular her avarice is defeating her interest. For it not only invites F. to outbid her; but throws in seeds of discord, which will take effect, the moment peace or safety is felt by the party of whom the advantage is taken. The contrary policy of the old F. Govt. in its commercial Treaty with the U. S. at the epoch of their Independence,[3] was founded in a far better knowledge of human nature, and of the permanent interest of its Nation. It merits the consideration of France also, that in proportion as she discourages, in any way, a free intercourse of the U. S. with their revolutionary neighbors, she favors the exclusive commerce of her rival with them; as she has hitherto favor'd it with Europe, by her decrees agst. our intercourse with it. As she seems to be recovering from the one folly, it may be hoped she will not fall into the other.

The ship sent on this occasion will afford you & your family good accomodations, if you should be decided agst. prolonging your important services at Paris, and a Winter passage should not be an insuperable objection. Accept dear Sir assurances of my Great esteem and most friendly wishes

JAMES MADISON

RC (owned by Mrs. Richard Aldrich, Rokeby Collection, Barrytown on Hudson, N.Y., 1961); FC (DLC). FC in the hand of Edward Coles; docketed by JM.

1. JM had not yet received either Armstrong's personal letter of 5 Aug. 1810 or his dispatch to Robert Smith of the same date conveying the offer to repeal the Berlin and Milan decrees. The bearer of these letters, Leonard Jarvis, did not arrive in New York until 31 Oct., but he was apparently able to reach Washington by the end of the next day (N.Y. *Commercial Advertiser*, 31 Oct. 1810; *National Intelligencer*, 2 Nov. 1810).

2. In a postscript to his 5 Aug. dispatch, added on 7 Aug., Armstrong requested Smith to inform JM that "what remains of his wishes (to be fulfilled here) shall be accomplished before my departure from france, if it be possible." In another postscript Armstrong added that he would also obtain "a specific revocation of the decree of the 23d of March last, but it ought to be known to you, that this decree has had no operation since my *unofficial* communication of the Law of the first of May" (DNA: RG 59, DD, France).

3. Presumably JM referred to articles 2 through 5 of the 1778 Treaty of Amity and Commerce whereby France and the U.S. granted each other the status of most favored nation (Hunter Miller, ed., *Treaties and Other International Acts of the United States of America, 1776–1813* [8 vols.; Washington, 1931–48], 2:5–7).

To Benjamin Rush

Dear Sir   Washington Ocr. 29. 1810

The Bearer, Alfred Madison, a son of my brother, labours under a complaint,[1] which being thought to require the best advice, has produced a resort to yours. You will best understand the nature of it from his own explanations, and your examination of it. His friends take the greater interest in his case, as he join⟨s⟩ to a capacity, beyond the ordinary rate in the opinion of his tutors, very amiable dispositions. Knowing the mutual friendship subsisting between yourself, and Dr. Physic, I shall drop a line to the latter also,[2] requesting his communication with you; and the rather, as his case is attended with symptoms, of a watery collection, which in a similar one of a brother, was thought to require a surgical operation. His youth, and distance from his home, will ensure, from Your benevolence the kindness of every sort which he may need. Accept Dear Sir assurances of my affectionate esteem.

James Madison

RC (NHyF). Docketed by Rush.

1. On 27 Oct. Dolley Madison had informed Anna Cutts that "Alfred Madison is also here, & in a deep decline. He will sail for the West Indias, I believe soon" (owned by Mrs. George B. Cutts, Wellesley, Mass., 1982).

2. Letter not found.

From Isaac A. Coles

Dr. Sir,   Green Mountain[1] Oct: 29th. 1810.

The Broad tail Ram which you have been good enough to send me is particularly Acceptable, as I have been for some time seeking to cross a part of my flock with this breed. My Neighbor, Mr. Cocke of Bremo,[2] has by this mixture the very best Lamb and mutton I ever saw, and that too from pastures where the Common Sheep is not at all remarkable. The Moment I hear of his arrival at Monticello, I will send for him, & as I have taken my own Ram from the flock, there will still no doubt, be some gleanings left for him.

The next year I mean to give him a small flock, on a detached farm, where I propose to rear the half bloods for the Table alone.

The Sheep Mania is beginning to rage in this part of the Country with considerable violence; and as it was said by Salmagundy of some old Lady, that she had died of a Frenchman[3]—so it is reported that old Colo. Fountain has Actually died of a *Sheep*.[4] Should it rage many years I should not be surprized to see half the Country Converted into Sheep walks.

The good news from abroad has gladdened the hearts of our farmers and planters, who are looking forward to excellent markets—the corn crop is better than it was imagined to be, & no sales as yet, have been effected in this part of the country at more than $2.50.—the Tobacco crop is of good quality tho' small; & the Wheat ⟨binding⟩ is going on, tho' more than the half yet remains to be done.

The fall having been uncommonly dry, our Pippins have not rotted as usual, so that they were never better. I have been induced by this circumstance to order some Barrels to be put up for Mrs. Madison, which I shall take the liberty of sending round to Washington in the course of the next month. I pray you to Accept for her, as well as for yourself, assurances of my warm and respectful Attachment.

I. A. COLES.

RC (ICHi). Docketed by JM.

1. Green Mountain, where the Coles family plantation, Enniscorthy, was located, is fifteen miles south of Charlottesville, Virginia.

2. John Hartwell Cocke (1780–1866) of Bremo resided on his Fluvanna County, Virginia, estates for some years after 1808. He was noted for his lifelong devotion to moral reform and agricultural improvement, and in 1810 he contracted "a small Touch of the Merino Mania" with his purchase of three ewes and a ram (see Martin Boyd Coyner, Jr., "John Hartwell Cocke of Bremo: Agriculture and Slavery in the Ante-Bellum South" [Ph.D. diss.; 2 vols.; ViU, 1961], 1:26–27, 251–56).

3. Coles was probably referring to Washington Irving's ninth "Salmagundi" essay, which described the death of Charity Cockloft of a "whim-wham," contracted from "the pangs of unsatisfied curiosity" about the wardrobe of "a little meagre, weazel-faced frenchman, of the most forlorn, diminutive and pitiful proportions" (Bruce Granger and Martha Hartzog, eds., *Letters of Jonathan Oldstyle, Gent., & Salmagundi; or, The Whim-whams and Opinions of Launcelot Langstaff, Esq., & Others* [Boston, 1977], pp. 164, 167–68).

4. Col. William Fontaine of Hanover County, Virginia, died on 5 Oct. 1810 (*Marriages and Deaths from Richmond, Virginia, Newspapers, 1780–1820* [Richmond, 1983], p. 54).

From Benjamin Rush

DEAR SIR,   PHILADELPHIA Octobr 29th. 1810

I have the honor to send you herewith the 4th report of the directors of the African institution in London and an adjudication of an appeal connected with the African trade, both of which appear to contain matter highly interesting to the National honor of the United States.[1]

Can nothing be done to wipe away the Stain that has been brought upon our moral and national character by the infamous practices alluded to in the report?[2] Health, respect and friendship! from Dear Sir yours sincerely

BENJN: RUSH

RC (DLC). Enclosures not found, but see n. 1.

1. The African Institution had been formed in London in 1807, partly to bring philanthropy to Africa and, more importantly, to monitor the suppression of the slave trade, which Great Britain and the U.S. had abolished in 1807 and 1808, respectively. Its fourth *Report*, read at the annual meeting in London in March 1810, had deplored continued American participation in the slave trade under the fraudulent use of foreign flags and papers. The adjudication Rush mentioned was the case of the *Amedie*, decided by the lords commissioners of appeals on 17 Mar. 1810. Sir William Grant upheld the sentence of a vice-admiralty court in Tortola that had condemned the *Amedie* for violating the orders in council of November 1807 as well as for engaging in an illegal trade in slaves between Africa and Cuba. Grant affirmed the sentence on the latter grounds, ruling that as "there is no right established to carry on this trade, no claim to restitution of this property can be admitted" (Lyman H. Butterfield, ed., *Letters of Benjamin Rush* [2 vols.; Princeton, N.J., 1951], 2:1072; David Eltis, *Economic Growth and the Ending of the Transatlantic Slave Trade* [Oxford, 1987], pp. 104–8; J. B. Moore, ed., *Digest of International Law* [2 vols.; Washington, 1910], 2:914–15).

2. The administration was already familiar with the *Amedie* case, having received the details, accompanied by a note from James Stephen, in a dispatch from William Pinkney dated 23 Mar. 1810. In response, Robert Smith declared JM had "learned with pleasure" that Great Britain shared his "anxiety" to suppress the slave trade, and he directed Pinkney "to facilitate, as far as the respect essentially due to national prerogative will permit, rather than embarrass the means of attaining the common object." In his annual message delivered on 5 Dec. 1810 JM also urged Congress to suppress both the abuse of the American flag and American involvement in the slave trade (Pinkney to Smith, 23 Mar. 1810 [DNA: RG 59, DD, Great Britain]; Smith to Pinkney, 16 June 1810 [DNA: RG 59, IM]; Madison, *Writings* [Hunt ed.], 8:127–28).

§ From Elijah Boardman and Robert Fairchild. *29 October 1810, Stratford, Connecticut*. Recommends Gideon Granger for the vacancy on the Supreme Court.

RC (DNA: RG 59, LAR, 1809–17, filed under "Granger"). 1 p. Elijah Boardman was a Connecticut Republican who later served in the U.S. Senate, 1821–23.

§ From Barzillai Gannett. *29 October 1810, Gardiner, Maine*. Recommends Gideon Granger for the vacancy on the Supreme Court.

RC (DNA: RG 59, LAR, 1809–17, filed under "Granger"). 1 p.

¶ To Oliveira & Sons. Letter not found. *29 October 1810*. Acknowledged in Oliveira & Sons to JM, 3 Nov. 1810 (DLC). Encloses a bank draft for $192.25 in payment for Madeira wine.

¶ To Robert Patton. Letter not found. *29 October 1810*. Acknowledged in Patton to JM, 8 Nov. 1810 (DLC). Inquires about the purchase of a gray horse to replace one of a pair that has died.

To William Pinkney

private

DEAR SIR   WASHINGTON Ocr. 30. 1810

Your letter of Aug. 13. was duly recd. Its observations on the letter & conduct of Ld. Wellesley, are an interesting comment on both. The light in which the letter[1] was seen by many in this Country, was doubtless such as gave to its features an exaggerated deformity. But it was the natural effect of its contrast to the general expectation founded on the tenor of your private letter to Mr Smith, and on the circumstances, which in the case of Jackson, seemed to preclude the least delay in repairing the insults committed by him. It is true also that the letter, when viewed in its most favorable light, is an unworthy attempt, to spare a false pride on one side, at the expence of just feelings on the other, & is in every respect infinitely below the elevation of character assumed by the B. Govt. & even of that ascribed to Ld. W. It betrays the consciousness of a debt, with a wish to discharge it in false coin. Had the letter been of earlier date, & accompanied by the prompt appt. of a successor to J. its aspect would have been much softened. But every thing was rendered as offensive as possible by evasions & delays, which admit no explanation without supposing a double game, by which they were to cheat us into a reliance on fair promises, whilst they were playing into the hands of partizans here, who were turning the delays into a triumph over their own Govt. This consideration had its weight in the decision last communicated, with respect to your continuance at London, or return to the U. S.[2]

The personal sensibilities which your letter expresses are far greater than I can have merited, by manifestations of esteem & confidence which it would have been unjust to withold. As a proof of your partiality, they ought not on that account, to excite less of a return. As little ought your readiness to retire from your station, from the honorable motives which govern you, to be viewed in any other light, than as a proof of the value which attaches itself to your qualifications and services. It is not to be denied that a good deal of dissatisfaction has issued thro' the press, agst. some of your intercourse with the B. Govt. But this could have the less influence on the Ex.[3] mind, as the dissatisfaction, where not the mere indulgence of habitual censure, is evidently the result of an honest misconstruction of some things, and an ignorance of others, neither of which can be lasting. I have little doubt that if your sentiments & conduct, could be seen thro' media not before the public a very different note would have been heard; and as little, that the exhibitions, likely to grow out of the questions & discussions in which you are at present engaged, will more than restore the ground taken from you.

The sole question, on which your return depends, therefore, is whether the conduct of the Govt. where you are, may not render your longer stay incompatible with the honor of the U. S. The last letter of the Secy. of State has so placed the subject, for your determination; in which the fullest confidence is felt. Waving other depending subjects, not of recent date, a review of the course pursued in relation to Jackson & a successor, excites a mixture of indignation & contempt, which ought not to be more lightly expressed, than by your *immediately* substituting a Secretary of Legn. for the grade you hold; unless the step be absolutely forbidden, by the weighty consideration, which has been stated to you; and which coincides with the sound policy, to which you allude, of putting an adversary compleatly in the wrong. The prevailing opinion here is that this has already been abundantly done.

Besides the public irritation produced by the persevering insolence of J. in his long stay,[4] & his conduct during it; there has been a constant heart burning on the subject of the Chesapeak, and a deep & settled indignation on the score of impressments, which can never be extinguished without a liberal atonement for the former, and a systematic amendment of the latter.

You have been already informed[5] that a Proclamn. would issue giving effect to the late act of Congs. on the ground of the D. de. C.s letter to Genl. A.[6] which states an *actual* Repeal of the F. Decrees. The letter of W. to you,[7] is a promise only, & that in a very questionable shape; the more so as G. B. is known to have founded her retaliating pretensions on the *unprecedented mode* of warfare agst: her, evidently meaning the exclusion of her trade from the Continent. Even the Blockade of May 1806. rests on the same foundation. These considerations, with the obnoxious exercise, of her sham-blockades, in the moment of our call for their repeal, backed by the example of France, discourage the hope, that she contemplates a re-conciliation with us. I sincerely wish your next communications may furnish evidence of a more favorable disposition.

It will not escape your notice, and is not undeserving that of the B. Govt. that the non-intercourse, as now to be revived, will have the effect of giving a monopoly of our exportations to G. B. to our own vessels, in *exclusion* of hers; whereas, in its old form, G. B. obtained a substantial monopoly for hers thro' the entrepots of N. Scotia, E. Florida &c. She cannot therefore deprive our vessels, which may now carry our exports

directly to G. B. of this monopoly, without refusing the exports altogether, or forcing them into difficult & expensive circuits, with the prospect of a counteracting interposition of Congress, shd. the latter experiment be resorted to. Nothing wd. be necessary to defeat this experiment
but to prohibit, as was heretofore contemplated—the export of our productions to the neighboring ports belonging to G. B. or her friends.

The Course adopted here towards West Florida, will be made known
by the Secy. of State.[8] The occupancy of the Territory as far as the Perdido, was called for by the crisis there, and is understood to be within the
authy. of the Executive. E. Florida also is of great importance to the U. S.
and it is not probable that Congs. will let it pass into any new hands. It is
to be hoped G. B. will not entangle herself with us, by seizing it, either
with or without the privity of her Allies in Cadiz. The position of Cuba
gives the U. S. so deep an interest in the destiny even of that Island, that
altho they might be an inactive they could not be a satisfied spectator, at
its falling under any European Govt. which might make a fulcrum of that
position, agst. the commerce or security of the U. S. With respect to
Spanish America, generally, you will find, that G. B. is engaged in the
most eager, and if without the concurrence of the Spanish Authy at Cadiz,
the most reproachful grasp of political influence and commercial preferences. In turning a provident attention to the new world, as she loses
ground in the old, her wisdom is to be commended, if regulated by justice
& good faith; nor is her pursuit of commercial preferences, if not seconded
by insidious & slanderous means agst. our competition, as are said to be
employed, to be tested by any other standard, than her own interest.
A sound judgment of this, does not seem to have been consulted in the
specimen given in the Treaty at Carraccas,[9] by which a preference in trade
over all other Nations, is extorted from the temporary fears & necessities
of the Revolutionary Spaniards. The policy of the French Govt. at the
epoch of our Independence, in renouncing every stipulation agst. the
equal privileges of all other nations in our trade, was dictated by a much
better knowledge of human Nature, and of the stable interest of France.

The Elections for the next Congs. are nearly over. The result is another
warning agst. a reliance on the strength of a B. party, if the B. Govt. be
still under a delusion on that subject. Should F. effectually adhere to the
ground of a just & conciliary policy, & G. B. bring the U. S. to issue on
her paper Blockades; so strong is this ground in right & opinion here, &
even in the commitment of all the great leaders of her party here, that
G. B. will scarce have an advocate left.

Draft (DLC: Rives Collection, Madison Papers).

1. See Pinkney to JM, 13 Aug. 1810, and n. 1.
2. Robert Smith had written to Pinkney on 19 Oct. 1810: "On the receipt of this letter

therefore, should the appointment of a Plenipotentiary successor [to Jackson] not have been made and communicated to you, you will let your purp⟨ose⟩ be known of returning to the United States, unless indeed, the British Government should have unequivocally manifested a disp⟨o⟩sition to revoke their orders in Council conformably to the act of Congress of May last, and our affairs with them should have accordingly taken so favorable a turn as to justify in your judgment a further suspension of it" (DNA: RG 59, IM).

3. At a later time JM interlined the remainder of "Executive" here.

4. After leaving Washington in November 1809, Francis James Jackson had removed to Philadelphia and New York, from where he made tours of western New York and Canada. He finally departed for Great Britain on 16 Sept. 1810 (Jackson to George Jackson, 19 Oct. 1810, in Jackson, *The Bath Archives*, 1 : 175).

5. In Pinkney's instructions of 19 Oct., Robert Smith had informed him that "if the proceedings of the French Government, when officially received, should correspond with the printed letter of the Duke of Cadore, enclosed in your despatch, you will let the British Government understand that on the first day of November the President will issue his proclamation conformably to the act of Congress, and that the non-intercourse law will consequently be revived against Great Britain" (DNA: RG 59, IM).

6. At a later time JM interlined "Duke de Cadore's" and "Armstrong" above the text.

7. Wellesley to Pinkney, 31 Aug. 1810 (see Samuel Smith to JM, 22 Oct. 1810, and n. 1).

8. See Robert Smith to Pinkney, 2 Nov. 1810, enclosing a copy of the presidential proclamation of 27 Oct., and Robert Smith's explanatory letter to John Armstrong, 2 Nov. 1810 (DNA: RG 59, IM). For the copy of the proclamation received by Pinkney, see Presidential Proclamation, 27 Oct. 1810, and n.

9. See JM to Jefferson, 19 Oct. 1810, and n. 3.

§ From Nahum Parker. *30 October 1810, Fitzwilliam, New Hampshire.* Recommends Gideon Granger for the vacancy on the Supreme Court.

RC (DNA: RG 59, LAR, 1809–17, filed under "Granger"). 1 p. Parker represented New Hampshire in the U.S. Senate, 1807–10.

§ From William Plumer. *30 October 1810, Epping, New Hampshire.* Recommends Gideon Granger for the vacancy on the Supreme Court.

RC (DNA: RG 59, LAR, 1809–17, filed under "Granger"); FC (DLC: William Plumer Papers). RC 1 p. William Plumer (1759–1850) had been a Federalist senator from New Hampshire, 1802–7. He later served as a Republican governor of New Hampshire, 1812–13 and 1816–19.

From Harry Toulmin

DEAR SIR　　　　　　　　　　　FORT STODDERT 31st. Octr. 1810.

I have just been honoured with your favour of Septr. 5th. which has been so long on the road in consequence of its going round by way of Natchez.

I am gratified to find that my communication to you was acceptable, and still more so to be able to repeat my assurances that the expedition is at an end.

One of the leading partizans[1] takes to himself the merit of having induced the government to make some overtures which he learnt, in the Creek nation, had been made to the Spanish authorities; and has at the same time seen fit to denounce me as a Spanish pensioner, on account of the opposition which I made to the projected enterprize. But few I trust, however, will be disposed to give credit to either, tho' I am sensible at the same time, that not a device will be left unemployed, to injure me to the utmost.

Our situation here has become very interesting not only on account of the dispositions manifested among ourselves, but on account of the movements among our neighbours: and I have from time to time in letters to Genl. Wilkinson & to Mr Graham, made mention of any thing which I deemed important.

A crisis seems to be fast approaching with the province of West Florida. The utmost panic has seized the people of Mobile on the rumour of a convention army of 1600s men being on its way from Baton-rouge, and certain intelligence, as they thought had brought them to this side of Pearl river. Scouts are kept out by the government, and the people have been packing up their valuables, which some, I am told have actually removed to places of supposed safety. Some of the French below the line have applied to me in much distress to know whether it will be illegal for them to bring their families up, and there are several accordingly who have sought an asylum within the American limits.

Their minds however, I hope will soon be at ease, as they will learn that an armed force coming against them has no existence but in the fears of their rulers.

Col. Ruben Kemper, who has been introduced to me by an old friend in the inclosure No. 1.[2] as well as (through a friend here) by an American officer living near the Mississippi, comes as an agent from the Baton-rouge convention, with offers of good will & friendship to the people in this part of the province, where it is evident that there are none at present ingaged to act in concert with the settlements in the west.

There was a Major White[3] joined with him in the mission who it is said was held in esteem among the Spaniards, but sickness on the road occasioned his return, and Coll. K. will not deem it prudent to venture below the American boundary. He will have an opportunity, however, of communicating, through the french settlers who reside near the line, the pacific views of the convention, and their desire ultimately to unite themselves to the American government. It is indeed supposed by well informed people that even the Spanish officers at Mobile would give up the country to the U. S. without any resistance.

I have seen the address of the convention to the people of Mobile:[4] it is altogether temperate & friendly: but I have no idea that they will be able to form any open party among the people, or to obtain possession of the country by pacific means, unless arrangements can be made to secure in the first instance a good understanding with the Spanish officers. Tho' many may wish a change; no man will stand forward as an advocate for it. Even the french are generally peacable, domestic men, who have no idea of encouraging civil commotion.

I venture to inclose the extract No. 2. but you will observe from the conclusion, that I dare not give the name:[5] nor should I deem it proper to send the extract itself to any person but yourself, as the writer, having considerable property under different governments, might feel himself aggrieved, whatever may be the result of the present crisis.

I am the more pleased with it, as I did expect that British predilections would have rendered him blind to any advantages which might be enjoyed under the American government. Be pleased to accept assurances of the very high and sincere respect, with which I have the honour to be, dear Sir, your faithful & obedt sert.

HARRY TOULMIN.

RC and enclosures (DLC). RC docketed by JM. Enclosure no. 1 (2 pp., docketed by JM) is Jonathan Longstreth to Toulmin, 14 Oct. 1810. Enclosure no. 2 (2 pp.; in Toulmin's hand) is an "Extract from a letter dated 28th. Octr."

1. Probably Joseph Pulaski Kennedy.

2. Reuben Kemper had been recently entrusted by the convention at Baton Rouge with the task of organizing an expedition to seize the Spanish post at Mobile. He arrived at Fort Stoddert on 24 Oct. 1810 and was introduced to Toulmin by the commander, Lt. Col. Richard Sparks. The letter he carried from Jonathan Longstreth to Toulmin was a defense of the conduct of the convention at Baton Rouge, first in seizing the Spanish post there and subsequently in declaring West Florida independent of Spanish rule (John H. Johnson to Kemper, 11 Oct. 1810, Padgett, "Official Records of the West Florida Revolution and Republic," *La. Historical Quarterly*, 21 [1938]: 747–48; Cox, *The West Florida Controversy*, pp. 457–58).

3. Joseph White had been commissioned by the convention at Baton Rouge to assist Kemper in the enterprise against Mobile (Cox, *The West Florida Controversy*, p. 421).

4. On 10 Oct. 1810 the convention at Baton Rouge had issued an address to the people of Mobile and Pensacola, announcing the appointment of Kemper and White as its commissioners to request that the people in those Spanish possessions either authorize the convention to act on their behalf or send deputies of their own to Baton Rouge (ibid.).

5. The writer of the extract acquitted the U.S. government of involvement in the disturbances in West Florida and stated his aversion to any change in the status of the province. He doubted, however, that West Florida could sustain its independence, and he preferred therefore to see the region come under the control of the U.S. His letter, the writer stressed to Toulmin, was for "*yourself alone*. Should the sentiments contained in it be divulged as mine; they would probably subject me to the charge of disaffection or treason with both parties, and you know what I have at stake." Toulmin's description of his correspondent as a

man of "British predilections" with "considerable property under different governments" suggests that it was either James or John Innerarity, the two leading Scottish-born clerks of the trading firm Panton, Leslie, and Co.

To Lafayette

My dear Sir   Washington Novr. 1. 1810

I have recd. yours of the 25. Augst: I am glad that you were so near being put in possession of your Patents sent by Mr. Parish. I learn from Mr. Duplantier, that he has made two additional locations, for which I hope ere long to be able to obtain & forward the patents. The residue will be located, if possible near N. Orleans. But I dare not authorize a reliance on the prospect. Besides the uncertainty of finding unincumbered land, it may become necessary, in order to effectuate a location there under the circumstances of the case, to resort to the interposition of Congs; and you know the delicate nature of such a resort, especially considering the intrinsic value of the grant already secured, and the exaggerated use that wd. be made of it, by opponents. I can only say therefore that I shall continue to do the best for you possible; and that I most anxiously wish that you may be able to turn what has been done by Mr. Duplantier, to your effectual aid. I understand that his locations have been judiciously made; and may be expected to rise fast & far above their present market price, which is itself a solid basis for a pecuniary operation, with those who annex no other condition to friendly arrangements.

You will find that the revocation of the French decrees, has been followed by the proclamation, provided for, by the Act of Congs. I hope the spirit which dictated this measure to the F. Cabinet, will produce other fruits, of a similar tendency to renew confidence & good will between the two Countries. Accept My dear Sir of my great esteem & affectionate salutations

James Madison

RC (NIC: Dean Collection).

From John Wayles Eppes

Dear Sir,   Cumberland Near Ca-Ira Nov. 1. 1810

My absence from chesterfield prevented my receiving your letter[1] until a few days since.

When the papers relating to the proceedings of the convention were put into my hands for the purpose of being copied[2] Mr. Jefferson was very particular in his charge. I understood from him perfectly that it was a trust entirely confidential. The particular and confidential manner in which he entrusted them to me prevented my making the smallest extract from any part of them—and so careful was I of preserving sacred a document the importance of which to posterity I could not but feel, that I never suffered the papers to mix either with my own or any others entrusted to my care. They were kept in a Trunk in which whenever I ceased writing they were replaced and each original as copied was returned with the copy to Mr. Jefferson.

I remember among the papers one headed "plan of a constitution by Colo: Hamilton"—it was on smaller paper than your copy and fastened with a pin to one of the leaves of the original. Whether it was in your handwriting or Colo: Hamiltons I do not remember—I remember its features & that after copying it I fastened it again with the same pin. I still think that by turning carefully over the original you will find the paper fastened with a pin to one of the sheets.

I have but few papers remaining of those I possessed in Philadelphia. As you requested it I have carefully gone through them. I was certain however prior to the search that it was utterly impossible from the precautions I took in consequence of Mr. Jeffersons charge that any paper belonging to your Manuscript could be mixed with mine. For years after the copy was taken so far did I consider the whole transaction on my part confidential that I did not even consider myself at liberty to mention that a copy of the debates of the convention existed. It was not until within a few years since when I found the fact known to others through yourself and Mr. Jefferson that I thought it unnecessary to impose on myself the same rigid silence. I should as a member of the community deeply deplore the loss of the paper as it contains proof clear as holy writ that the idol of the Federal party was not a Monarchist in Theory merely, but the open zealous and unreserved advocate for the adoption of the monarchical system in this Country. Your evidence however of the fact will be sufficient with posterity; and that you will find among the originals a paper headed in the way I mention containing his plan of Government as Suggested to you I have no doubt.

I received a few days since from Nelson Patterson[3] the enclosed letter. He was many years an inhabitant of this county and much respected. The young man he mentions is an only son. I cannot suppose from the manner in which the young man was brought up (entirely in a domestic circle) that he can have embarked in any scheme hostile to the Government of Spain. If on perusing his letter you think the case worthy the attention of the Government you will confer a favour on a worthy and affectionate parent by causing application in his behalf to be made through the proper officers of our Government. With my respects and friendly wishes to Mrs. Madison & yourself I am yours &ca

JNO: W: EPPES

RC (DLC). Docketed by JM. Enclosure not found.

1. JM's letter to Eppes has not been found, but it was evidently on the same subject and probably written at approximately the same time as JM to Jefferson, 17 July 1810.

2. On Eppes's making copies in 1791 of JM's notes on the debates in the Federal Convention of 1787, see *PJM*, 10:7–8.

3. Possibly Nelson Patterson (or Patteson) (1762–1824), a resident of Chesterfield County, Virginia, who at some time seems to have moved to Tennessee. His son may have been George W. Patterson, who resided near Baton Rouge in West Florida and who later signed a petition requesting Congress to incorporate the region into the Mississippi Territory (*VMHB*, 5 [1897–98]: 334–35; *ASP, Miscellaneous*, 2:155).

From Paul Hamilton

SIR,   NAVY DEPARTMENT 1st. Novr 1810

The enclosed paper marked A will inform you of the state of the Navy appropriations up to the 31st ult.

From this paper you will perceive, sir, that of the appropriation for "Repairs of Vessels," there is on hand the sum of $10,500:21; but the demands upon that appropriation at this time exceed 20,000$—so that altho' there is a nominal balance of $10,500, we are that sum deficient in the means of discharging existing demands.

Of the appropriation for "Contingent Expences" there is on hand a nominal balance of $15:16; but the demands upon that appropriation at this time exceed 6000$—so that there is a real deficit of 6000$.

The appropriation for "Quarter Master's Department" has inadvertently been overdrawn to the amount of $172:18.

Hence, sir, these three appropriations appear to me to require the aid of transfers—which other appropriations will however admit.

To cover existing deficits, & to provide funds for the discharge of other engagements under these heads of appropriation which may arise in the course of the current year, I recommend the transfer, of Sixty thousand dollars to the appropriation for Repairs—of thirty thousand dollars to the appropriation for Contingent Expences—& of two thousand five hundred dollars to the appropriation for quarter Master's Department; & should you approve these transfers, I request your signature to the enclosed paper.[1] I have the honor to be, with great respect, Sir, yr: mo: Obt. servt.

PAUL HAMILTON

RC and enclosure A (DLC); letterbook copy and copy of second enclosure (DNA: RG 45, LSP). RC in Goldsborough's hand, signed by Hamilton. Docketed by JM. Enclosure A (1 p.) is "Statement of Navy Appropriations October 31st 1810." Letterbook copy of enclosed authorization is dated 7 Nov. 1810.

1. JM alluded to the transfers briefly in his annual message of 5 Dec. 1810. On 17 Dec. 1810 Hamilton submitted to Congress a more detailed report (not found) on the transfers (*Annals of Congress*, 11th Cong., 3d sess., 414).

Presidential Proclamation

[2 November 1810]

BY THE
PRESIDENT OF THE UNITED STATES,
A PROCLAMATION.

WHEREAS by the fourth section of the act of Congress, passed on the first day of May, 1810, entitled "An act concerning the commercial intercourse between the United States and Great Britain and France and their dependencies and for other purposes," it is provided "that in case either Great Britain or France shall, before the third day of March next, so revoke or modify her edicts as that they shall cease to violate the neutral commerce of the United States, which fact the President of the United States shall declare by[1] proclamation, and if the other nation shall not within three months thereafter so revoke or modify her edicts in like manner, then the third, fourth, fifth, sixth, seventh, eighth, ninth, tenth and eighteenth sections of the act, entitled 'An act to interdict the commercial intercourse between the United States and Great Britain and France and their dependencies, and for other purposes,' shall, from and after the expiration of three months from the date of the proclamation aforesaid, be revived and have full force and effect, so far as relates to the dominions, colonies and dependencies, and to the articles the growth, produce or manufacture of the dominions, colonies and dependencies of the nation thus refusing or neglecting to revoke or modify her edicts in the manner aforesaid. And the restrictions imposed by this act shall, from the date of such proclamation, cease and be discontinued in relation to the nation revoking or modifying her decrees in the manner aforesaid:"

And whereas it has been officially made known to this government that the[2] edicts of France violating the neutral commerce of the United States have been so revoked as to cease to have effect, on the first of the present month: Now, therefore, I, JAMES MADISON, President of the United States, do hereby proclaim that the said edicts of France have been so revoked as that they ceased[3] on the said first day of the present month to violate the neutral commerce of the United States; and that, from the date of these presents, all the restrictions imposed by the aforesaid act shall cease and be discontinued in relation to France and her dependencies.

IN testimony whereof, I have caused the seal of the United States to be hereunto affixed, and signed the same with my hand at the city of Washington, this second day of November, in the year of our Lord one thousand eight hundred and ten, and of the independence of the United States the thirty-fifth.

JAMES MADISON.

By the President,
R. SMITH, *Secretary of State.*

Printed circular (DNA: RG 233, President's Messages, 11th Cong., 3d sess.); draft (DLC). Printed with Treasury Department circular to customs collectors, 2 Nov. 1810. Enclosed in JM's message to Congress, 14 Jan. 1811. Draft in the hand of Caesar A. Rodney, amended and docketed by JM.

1. In Rodney's draft the remainder of this paragraph reads: "proclamation,' then, the restrictions imposed by the said act, 'shall cease & be discontinued in relation to the nation so revoking or modifying her decrees.'"

2. Here Rodney's draft reads: "French decrees of Berlin & Milan were revoked, & that they would cease to have effect on the first instant." JM altered it to: ". . . were so revoked, as that . . ." and wrote "the present" after "the first instant."

3. Rodney's draft from this point reads: "to have effect on the first instant, & that from the date of these presents . . ." Someone, probably JM, interlined "to violate &c" above "effect."

Index

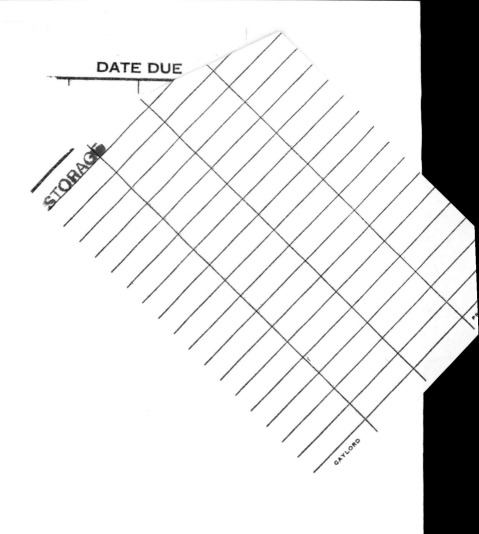